T0189413

Lecture Notes in Computer Science 12893

More information about this subseries at http://www.springer.com/series/7407

Igor Farkaš · Paolo Masulli ·
Sebastian Otte · Stefan Wermter (Eds.)

Artificial Neural Networks and Machine Learning – ICANN 2021

30th International Conference on Artificial Neural Networks
Bratislava, Slovakia, September 14–17, 2021
Proceedings, Part III

Springer

Editors
Igor Farkaš 🆔
Comenius University in Bratislava
Bratislava, Slovakia

Paolo Masulli 🆔
iMotions A/S
Copenhagen, Denmark

Sebastian Otte 🆔
University of Tübingen
Tübingen, Baden-Württemberg, Germany

Stefan Wermter 🆔
Universität Hamburg
Hamburg, Germany

ISSN 0302-9743   ISSN 1611-3349 (electronic)
Lecture Notes in Computer Science
ISBN 978-3-030-86364-7   ISBN 978-3-030-86365-4 (eBook)
https://doi.org/10.1007/978-3-030-86365-4

LNCS Sublibrary: SL1 – Theoretical Computer Science and General Issues

This Springer imprint is published by the registered company Springer Nature Switzerland AG
The registered company address is: Gewerbestrasse 11, 6330 Cham, Switzerland

Preface

Research on artificial neural networks has progressed over decades, in recent years being fueled especially by deep learning that has proven, albeit data-greedy, efficient in solving various, mostly supervised, tasks. Applications of artificial neural networks, especially related to artificial intelligence, affect our lives, providing new horizons. Examples range from autonomous car driving, virtual assistants, and decision support systems to healthcare data analytics, financial forecasting, and smart devices in our homes, just to name a few. These developments, however, also provide challenges, which were not imaginable previously, e.g., verification of raw data, explaining the contents of neural networks, and adversarial machine learning.

The International Conference on Artificial Neural Networks (ICANN) is the annual flagship conference of the European Neural Network Society (ENNS). Last year, due to the COVID-19 pandemic, we decided not to hold the conference but to prepare the ICANN proceedings in written form. This year, due to the still unresolved pandemic, the Organizing Committee, together with the Executive Committee of ENNS decided to organize ICANN 2021 online, since we felt the urge to allow research presentations and live discussions, following the now available alternatives of online conference organization. So for the first time, ENNS and the Organizing Committee prepared ICANN as an online event with all its challenges and sometimes unforeseeable events!

Following a long-standing successful collaboration, the proceedings of ICANN are published as volumes within the Lecture Notes in Computer Science Springer series. The response to this year's call for papers resulted, unexpectedly, in a record number of 557 article submissions (a 46% rise compared to previous year), of which almost all were full papers. The paper selection and review process that followed was decided during the online meeting of the Bratislava organizing team and the ENNS Executive Committee. The 40 Program Committee (PC) members agreed to check the submissions for the formal requirements and 64 papers were excluded from the subsequent reviews. The majority of the PC members have doctoral degrees (80%) and 75% of them are also professors. We also took advantage of filled-in online questionnaires providing the reviewers' areas of expertise. The reviewers were assigned one to four papers, and the papers with undecided scores also received reports from PC members which helped in making a final decision.

In total, 265 articles were accepted for the proceedings and the authors were requested to submit final versions. The acceptance rate was hence about 47% when calculated from all initial submissions. A list of PC members and reviewers who agreed to publish their names is included in the proceedings. With these procedures we tried to keep the quality of the proceedings high while still having a critical mass of contributions reflecting the progress of the field. Overall we hope that these proceedings will contribute to the dissemination of new results by the neural network community during these challenging times and we hope that we can have a physical ICANN in 2022.

Finally, we very much thank the Program Committee and the reviewers for their invaluable work.

September 2021

Igor Farkaš
Paolo Masulli
Sebastian Otte
Stefan Wermter

Organization

Organizing Committee

Cabessa Jérémie	Université Paris 2 Panthéon-Assas, France
Kerzel Matthias	University of Hamburg, Germany
Lintas Alessandra	University of Lausanne, Switzerland
Malinovská Kristína	Comenius University in Bratislava, Slovakia
Masulli Paolo	iMotions A/S, Copenhagen, Denmark
Otte Sebastian	University of Tübingen, Germany
Wedeman Roseli	Universidade do Estado do Rio de Janeiro, Brazil

Program Committee Chairs

Igor Farkaš	Comenius University in Bratislava, Slovakia
Paolo Masulli	iMotions A/S, Denmark
Sebastian Otte	University of Tübingen, Germany
Stefan Wermter	University of Hamburg, Germany

Program Committee

Andrejková Gabriela	Pavol Jozef Šafárik University in Košice, Slovakia
Atencia Miguel	Universidad de Malaga, Spain
Bodapati Jyostna Devi	Indian Institute of Technology, Madras, India
Bougie Nicolas	Sokendai/National Institute of Informatics, Japan
Boža Vladimír	Comenius University in Bratislava, Slovakia
Cabessa Jérémie	Université Paris 2 Panthéon-Assas, France
Di Nuovo Alessandro	Sheffield Hallam University, UK
Duch Włodzisław	Nicolaus Copernicus University, Poland
Eppe Manfred	Universität Hamburg, Germany
Fang Yuchun	Shanghai University, China
Garcke Jochen	Universität Bonn, Germany
Gregor Michal	University of Žilina, Slovakia
Guckert Michael	Technische Hochschule Mittelhessen, Germany
Guillén Alberto	University of Granada, Spain
Heinrich Stefan	University of Tokyo, Japan
Hinaut Xavier	Inria, France
Humaidan Dania	University of Tübingen, Germany
Jolivet Renaud	University of Geneva, Switzerland
Koprinkova-Hristova Petia	Bulgarian Academy of Sciences, Bulgaria
Lintas Alessandra	University of Lausanne, Switzerland
Lü Shuai	Jilin University, China
Micheli Alessio	Università di Pisa, Italy

Oravec Miloš	Slovak University of Technology in Bratislava, Slovakia
Otte Sebastian	University of Tübingen, Germany
Peltonen Jaakko	Tampere University, Finland
Piuri Vincenzo	University of Milan, Italy
Pons Rivero Antonio Javier	Universitat Politècnica de Catalunya, Barcelona, Spain
Schmidt Jochen	TH Rosenheim, Germany
Schockaert Cedric	Paul Wurth S.A., Luxembourg
Schwenker Friedhelm	University of Ulm, Germany
Takáč Martin	Comenius University in Bratislava, Slovakia
Tartaglione Enzo	Università degli Studi di Torino, Italy
Tetko Igor	Helmholtz Zentrum München, Germany
Triesch Jochen	Frankfurt Institute for Advanced Studies, Germany
Vavrečka Michal	Czech Technical University in Prague, Czech Republic
Verma Sagar	CentraleSupélec, Université Paris-Saclay, France
Vigário Ricardo	Nova School of Science and Technology, Portugal
Wedemann Roseli	Universidade do Estado do Rio de Janeiro, Brazil
Wennekers Thomas	Plymouth University, UK

Reviewers

Abawi Fares	University of Hamburg, Germany
Aganian Dustin	Technical University Ilmenau, Germany
Ahrens Kyra	University of Hamburg, Germany
Alexandre Frederic	Inria Bordeaux, France
Alexandre Luís	University of Beira Interior, Portugal
Ali Hazrat	Umeå University, Sweden
Alkhamaiseh Koloud	Western Michigan University, USA
Amaba Takafumi	Fukuoka University, Japan
Ambita Ara Abigail	University of the Philippines Diliman, Philippines
Ameur Hanen	University of Sfax, Tunisia
Amigo Galán Glauco A.	Baylor University, USA
An Shuqi	Chongqing University, China
Aouiti Chaouki	Université de Carthage, Tunisia
Arany Adam	Katholieke Universiteit Leuven, Belgium
Arnold Joshua	University of Queensland, Australia
Artelt André	Bielefeld University, Germany
Auge Daniel	Technical University of Munich, Germany
Bac Le Hoai	University of Science, Vietnam
Bacaicoa-Barber Daniel	University Carlos III of Madrid, Spain
Bai Xinyi	National University of Defense Technology, China
Banka Asif	Islamic University of Science & Technology, India
Basalla Marcus	University of Liechtenstein, Liechtenstein
Basterrech Sebastian	Technical University of Ostrava, Czech Republic
Bauckhage Christian	Fraunhofer IAIS, Germany
Bayer Markus	Technical University of Darmstadt, Germany

Bečková Iveta	Comenius University in Bratislava, Slovakia
Benalcázar Marco	Escuela Politécnica Nacional, Ecuador
Bennis Achraf	Institut de Recherche en Informatique de Toulouse, France
Berlemont Samuel	Orange Labs, Grenoble, France
Bermeitinger Bernhard	Universität St. Gallen, Switzerland
Bhoi Suman	National University of Singapore, Singapore
Biesner David	Fraunhofer IAIS, Germany
Bilbrey Jenna	Pacific Northwest National Lab, USA
Blasingame Zander	Clarkson University, USA
Bochkarev Vladimir	Kazan Federal University, Russia
Bohte Sander	Universiteit van Amsterdam, The Netherlands
Bouchachia Abdelhamid	Bournemouth University, UK
Bourguin Grégory	Université du Littoral Côte d'Opale, France
Breckon Toby	Durham University, UK
Buhl Fred	University of Florida, USA
Butz Martin V.	University of Tübingen, Germany
Caillon Paul	Université de Lorraine, Nancy, France
Camacho Hugo C. E.	Universidad Autónoma de Tamaulipas, Mexico
Camurri Antonio	Università di Genova, Italy
Cao Hexin	OneConnect Financial Technology, China
Cao Tianyang	Peking University, China
Cao Zhijie	Shanghai Jiao Tong University, China
Carneiro Hugo	Universität Hamburg, Germany
Chadha Gavneet Singh	South Westphalia University of Applied Sciences, Germany
Chakraborty Saikat	C. V. Raman Global University, India
Chang Hao-Yuan	University of California, Los Angeles, USA
Chang Haodong	University of Technology Sydney, Australia
Chen Cheng	Tsinghua University, China
Chen Haopeng	Shanghai Jiao Tong University, China
Chen Junliang	Shenzhen University, China
Chen Tianyu	Northwest Normal University, China
Chen Wenjie	Communication University of China, China
Cheng Zhanglin	Chinese Academy of Sciences, China
Chenu Alexandre	Sorbonne Université, France
Choi Heeyoul	Handong Global University, South Korea
Christa Sharon	RV Institute of Technology and Management, India
Cîtea Ingrid	Bitdefender Central, Romania
Colliri Tiago	Universidade de São Paulo, Brazil
Cong Cong	Chinese Academy of Sciences, China
Coroiu Adriana Mihaela	Babes-Bolyai University, Romania
Cortez Paulo	University of Minho, Portugal
Cuayáhuitl Heriberto	University of Lincoln, UK
Cui Xiaohui	Wuhan University, China
Cutsuridis Vassilis	University of Lincoln, UK

Cvejoski Kostadin	Fraunhofer IAIS, Germany
D'Souza Meenakshi	International Institute of Information Technology, Bangalore, India
Dai Feifei	Chinese Academy of Sciences, China
Dai Peilun	Boston University, USA
Dai Ruiqi	INSA Lyon, France
Dang Kai	Nankai University, China
Dang Xuan	Tsinghua University, China
Dash Tirtharaj	Birla Institute of Technology and Science, Pilani, India
Davalas Charalampos	Harokopio University of Athens, Greece
De Brouwer Edward	Katholieke Universiteit Leuven, Belgium
Deng Minghua	Peking University, China
Devamane Shridhar	KLE Institute of Technology, Hubballi, India
Di Caterina Gaetano	University of Strathclyde, UK
Di Sarli Daniele	Università di Pisa, Italy
Ding Juncheng	University of North Texas, USA
Ding Zhaoyun	National University of Defense Technology, China
Dold Dominik	Siemens, Munich, Germany
Dong Zihao	Jinan University, China
Du Songlin	Southeast University, China
Edwards Joshua	University of North Carolina Wilmington, USA
Eguchi Shu	Fukuoka University, Japan
Eisenbach Markus	Ilmenau University of Technology, Germany
Erlhagen Wolfram	University of Minho, Portugal
Fang Tiyu	University of Jinan, China
Feldager Cilie	Technical University of Denmark, Denmark
Ferianc Martin	University College London, UK
Ferreira Flora	University of Minho, Portugal
Fevens Thomas	Concordia University, Canada
Friedjungová Magda	Czech Technical University in Prague, Czech Republic
Fu Xianghua	Shenzhen University, China
Fuhl Wolfgang	Universität Tübingen, Germany
Gamage Vihanga	Technological University Dublin, Ireland
Ganguly Udayan	Indian Institute of Technology, Bombay, India
Gao Ruijun	Tianjin University, China
Gao Yapeng	University of Tübingen, Germany
Gao Yue	Beijing University of Posts and Telecommunications, China
Gao Zikai	National University of Defense Technology, China
Gault Richard	Queen's University Belfast, UK
Ge Liang	Chongqing University, China
Geissler Dominik	Relayr GmbH, Munich, Germany
Gepperth Alexander	ENSTA ParisTech, France
Gerum Christoph	University of Tübingen, Germany
Giancaterino Claudio G.	Catholic University of Milan, Italy
Giese Martin	University Clinic Tübingen, Germany

Gikunda Patrick	Dedan Kimathi University of Technology, Kenya
Goel Anmol	Guru Gobind Singh Indraprastha University, India
Göpfert Christina	Bielefeld University, Germany
Göpfert Jan Philip	Bielefeld University, Germany
Goyal Nidhi	Indraprastha Institute of Information Technology, India
Grangetto Marco	Università di Torino, Italy
Grüning Philipp	University of Lübeck, Germany
Gu Xiaoyan	Chinese Academy of Sciences, Beijing, China
Guo Hongcun	China Three Gorges University, China
Guo Ling	Northwest University, China
Guo Qing	Nanyang Technological University, Singapore
Guo Song	Xi'an University of Architecture and Technology, China
Gupta Sohan	Global Institute of Technology, Jaipur, India
Hakenes Simon	Ruhr-Universität Bochum, Germany
Han Fuchang	Central South University, China
Han Yi	University of Melbourne, Australia
Hansen Lars Kai	Technical University of Denmark, Denmark
Haque Ayaan	Saratoga High School, USA
Hassen Alan Kai	Leiden University, The Netherlands
Hauberg Søren	Technical University of Denmark, Denmark
He Tieke	Nanjing University, China
He Wei	Nanyang Technological University, Singapore
He Ziwen	Chinese Academy of Sciences, China
Heese Raoul	Fraunhofer ITWM, Germany
Herman Pawel	KTH Royal Institute of Technology, Sweden
Holas Juraj	Comenius University in Bratislava, Slovakia
Horio Yoshihiko	Tohoku University, Japan
Hou Hongxu	Inner Mongolia University, China
Hu Ming-Fei	China University of Petroleum, China
Hu Ting	Hasso Plattner Institute, Germany
Hu Wenxin	East China Normal University, China
Hu Yanqing	Sichuan University, China
Huang Chenglong	National University of Defense Technology, China
Huang Chengqiang	Huawei Technology, Ltd., China
Huang Jun	Chinese Academy of Sciences, Shanghai, China
Huang Ruoran	Chinese Academy of Sciences, China
Huang Wuliang	Chinese Academy of Sciences, Beijing, China
Huang Zhongzhan	Tsinghua University, China
Iannella Nicolangelo	University of Oslo, Norway
Ienco Dino	INRAE, France
Illium Steffen	Ludwig-Maximilians-Universität München, Germany
Iyer Naresh	GE Research, USA
Jalalvand Azarakhsh	Ghent University, Belgium
Japa Sai Sharath	Southern Illinois University, USA
Javaid Muhammad Usama	Eura Nova, Belgium

Jia Qiaomei	Northwest University, China
Jia Xiaoning	Inner Mongolia University, China
Jin Peiquan	University of Science and Technology of China, China
Jirak Doreen	Istituto Italiano di Tecnologia, Italy
Jodelet Quentin	Tokyo Institute of Technology, Japan
Kai Tang	Toshiba, China
Karam Ralph	Université Franche-Comté, France
Karlbauer Matthias	University of Tübingen, Germany
Kaufhold Marc-André	Technical University of Darmstadt, Germany
Kerzel Matthias	University of Hamburg, Germany
Keurulainen Antti	Bitville Oy, Finland
Kitamura Takuya	National Institute of Technology, Japan
Kocur Viktor	Comenius University in Bratislava, Slovakia
Koike Atsushi	National Institute of Technology, Japan
Kotropoulos Constantine	Aristotle University of Thessaloniki, Greece
Kovalenko Alexander	Czech Technical University, Czech Republic
Krzyzak Adam	Concordia University, Canada
Kurikawa Tomoki	Kansai Medical University, Japan
Kurpiewski Evan	University of North Carolina Wilmington, USA
Kurt Mehmet Necip	Columbia University, USA
Kushwaha Sumit	Kamla Nehru Institute of Technology, India
Lai Zhiping	Fudan University, China
Lang Jana	Hertie Institute for Clinical Brain Research, Germany
Le Hieu	Boston University, USA
Le Ngoc	Hanoi University of Science and Technology, Vietnam
Le Thanh	University of Science, Hochiminh City, Vietnam
Lee Jinho	Yonsei University, South Korea
Lefebvre Grégoire	Orange Labs, France
Lehmann Daniel	University of Greifswald, Germany
Lei Fang	University of Lincoln, UK
Léonardon Mathieu	IMT Atlantique, France
Lewandowski Arnaud	Université du Littoral Côte d'Opale, Calais, France
Li Caiyuan	Shanghai Jiao Tong University, China
Li Chuang	Xi'an Jiaotong University, China
Li Ming-Fan	Ping An Life Insurance of China, Ltd., China
Li Qing	The Hong Kong Polytechnic University, China
Li Tao	Peking University, China
Li Xinyi	Southwest University, China
Li Xiumei	Hangzhou Normal University, China
Li Yanqi	University of Jinan, China
Li Yuan	Defence Innovation Institute, China
Li Zhixin	Guangxi Normal University, China
Lian Yahong	Dalian University of Technology, China
Liang Nie	Southwest University of Science and Technology, China
Liang Qi	Chinese Academy of Sciences, Beijing, China

Liang Senwei	Purdue University, USA
Liang Yuxin	Northwest University, China
Lim Nengli	Singapore University of Technology and Design, Singapore
Liu Gongshen	Shanghai Jiao Tong University, China
Liu Haolin	Chinese Academy of Sciences, China
Liu Jian-Wei	China University of Petroleum, China
Liu Juan	Wuhan University, China
Liu Junxiu	Guangxi Normal University, China
Liu Qi	Chongqing University, China
Liu Shuang	Huazhong University of Science and Technology, China
Liu Shuting	University of Shanghai for Science and Technology, China
Liu Weifeng	China University of Petroleum, China
Liu Yan	University of Shanghai for Science and Technology, China
Liu Yang	Fudan University, China
Liu Yi-Ling	Imperial College London, UK
Liu Zhu	University of Electronic Science and Technology of China, China
Long Zi	Shenzhen Technology University, China
Lopes Vasco	Universidade da Beira Interior, Portugal
Lu Siwei	Guangdong University of Technology, China
Lu Weizeng	Shenzhen University, China
Lukyanova Olga	Russian Academy of Sciences, Russia
Luo Lei	Kansas State University, USA
Luo Xiao	Peking University, China
Luo Yihao	Huazhong University of Science and Technology, China
Ma Chao	Wuhan University, China
Ma Zeyu	Harbin Institute of Technology, China
Malialis Kleanthis	University of Cyprus, Cyprus
Manoonpong Poramate	Vidyasirimedhi Institute of Science and Technology, Thailand
Martinez Rego David	Data Spartan Ltd., UK
Matsumura Tadayuki	Hitachi, Ltd., Tokyo, Japan
Mekki Asma	Université de Sfax, Tunisia
Merkel Cory	Rochester Institute of Technology, USA
Mirus Florian	Intel Labs, Germany
Mizuno Hideyuki	Suwa University of Science, Japan
Moh Teng-Sheng	San Jose State University, USA
Mohammed Elmahdi K.	Kasdi Merbah university, Algeria
Monshi Maram	University of Sydney, Australia
Moreno Felipe	Universidad Católica San Pablo, Peru
Morra Lia	Politecnico di Torino, Italy

Morzy Mikołaj	Poznań University of Technology, Poland
Mouček Roman	University of West Bohemia, Czech Republic
Moukafih Youness	International University of Rabat, Morocco
Mouysset Sandrine	University of Toulouse, France
Müller Robert	Ludwig-Maximilians-Universität München, Germany
Mutschler Maximus	University of Tübingen, Germany
Najari Naji	Orange Labs, France
Nanda Abhilasha	Vellore Institute of Technology, India
Nguyen Thi Nguyet Que	Technological University Dublin, Ireland
Nikitin Oleg	Russian Academy of Sciences, Russia
Njah Hasna	University of Sfax, Tunisia
Nyabuga Douglas	Donghua University, China
Obafemi-Ajayi Tayo	Missouri State University, USA
Ojha Varun	University of Reading, UK
Oldenhof Martijn	Katholieke Universiteit Leuven, Belgium
Oneto Luca	Università di Genova, Italy
Oota Subba Reddy	Inria, Bordeaux, France
Oprea Mihaela	Petroleum-Gas University of Ploiesti, Romania
Osorio John	Barcelona Supercomputing Center, Spain
Ouni Achref	Institut Pascal UCA, France
Pan Yongping	Sun Yat-sen University, China
Park Hyeyoung	Kyungpook National University, South Korea
Pateux Stéphane	Orange Labs, France
Pecháč Matej	Comenius University in Bratislava, Slovakia
Pecyna Leszek	University of Liverpool, UK
Peng Xuyang	China University of Petroleum, China
Pham Viet	Toshiba, Japan
Pietroń Marcin	AGH University of Science and Technology, Poland
Pócoš Štefan	Comenius University in Bratislava, Slovakia
Posocco Nicolas	Eura Nova, Belgium
Prasojo Radityo Eko	Universitas Indonesia, Indonesia
Preuss Mike	Universiteit Leiden, The Netherlands
Qiao Peng	National University of Defense Technology, China
Qiu Shoumeng	Shanghai Institute of Microsystem and Information Technology, China
Quan Hongyan	East China Normal University, China
Rafiee Laya	Concordia University, Canada
Rangarajan Anand	University of Florida, USA
Ravichandran Naresh Balaji	KTH Royal Institute of Technology, Sweden
Renzulli Riccardo	University of Turin, Italy
Richter Mats	Universität Osnabrück, Germany
Robine Jan	Heinrich Heine University Düsseldorf, Germany
Rocha Gil	University of Porto, Portugal
Rodriguez-Sanchez Antonio	Universität Innsbruck, Austria
Rosipal Roman	Slovak Academy of Sciences, Slovakia

Rusiecki Andrzej	Wroclaw University of Science and Technology, Poland
Salomon Michel	Université Bourgogne Franche-Comté, France
Sarishvili Alex	Fraunhofer ITWM, Germany
Sasi Swapna	Birla Institute of Technology and Science, India
Sataer Yikemaiti	Southeast University, China
Schaaf Nina	Fraunhofer IPA, Germany
Schak Monika	University of Applied Sciences, Fulda, Germany
Schilling Malte	Bielefeld University, Germany
Schmid Kyrill	Ludwig-Maximilians-Universität München, Germany
Schneider Johannes	University of Liechtenstein, Liechtenstein
Schwab Malgorzata	University of Colorado at Denver, USA
Sedlmeier Andreas	Ludwig-Maximilians-Universität München, Germany
Sendera Marcin	Jagiellonian University, Poland
Shahriyar Rifat	Bangladesh University of Engineering and Technology, Bangladesh
Shang Cheng	Fudan University, China
Shao Jie	University of Electronic Science and Technology of China, China
Shao Yang	Hitachi Ltd., Japan
Shehu Amarda	George Mason University, USA
Shen Linlin	Shenzhen University, China
Shenfield Alex	Sheffield Hallam University, UK
Shi Ying	Chongqing University, China
Shrestha Roman	Intelligent Voice Ltd., UK
Sifa Rafet	Fraunhofer IAIS, Germany
Sinha Aman	CNRS and University of Lorraine, France
Soltani Zarrin Pouya	Institute for High Performance Microelectronics, Germany
Song Xiaozhuang	Southern University of Science and Technology, China
Song Yuheng	Shanghai Jiao Tong University, China
Song Ziyue	Shanghai Jiao Tong University, China
Sowinski-Mydlarz Viktor	London Metropolitan University, UK
Steiner Peter	Technische Universität Dresden, Germany
Stettler Michael	University of Tübingen, Germany
Stoean Ruxandra	University of Craiova, Romania
Su Di	Beijing Institute of Technology, China
Suarez Oscar J.	Instituto Politécnico Nacional, México
Sublime Jérémie	Institut supérieur d'électronique de Paris, France
Sudharsan Bharath	National University of Ireland, Galway, Ireland
Sugawara Toshiharu	Waseda University, Japan
Sui Yongduo	University of Science and Technology of China, China
Sui Zhentao	Soochow University, China
Swiderska-Chadaj Zaneta	Warsaw University of Technology, Poland
Szandała Tomasz	Wroclaw University of Science and Technology, Poland

Šejnová Gabriela	Czech Technical University in Prague, Czech Republic
Tang Chenwei	Sichuan University, China
Tang Jialiang	Southwest University of Science and Technology, China
Taubert Nick	University Clinic Tübingen, Germany
Tek Faik Boray	Isik University, Turkey
Tessier Hugo	Stellantis, France
Tian Zhihong	Guangzhou University, China
Tianze Zhou	Beijing Institute of Technology, China
Tihon Simon	Eura Nova, Belgium
Tingwen Liu	Chinese Academy of Sciences, China
Tong Hao	Southern University of Science and Technology, China
Torres-Moreno Juan-Manuel	Université d'Avignon, France
Towobola Oluyemisi Folake	Obafemi Awolowo University, Nigeria
Trinh Anh Duong	Technological University Dublin, Ireland
Tuna Matúš	Comenius University in Bratislava, Slovakia
Uelwer Tobias	Heinrich Heine University Düsseldorf, Germany
Van Rullen Rufin	CNRS, Toulouse, France
Varlamis Iraklis	Harokopio University of Athens, Greece
Vašata Daniel	Czech Technical University in Prague, Czech Republic
Vásconez Juan	Escuela Politécnica Nacional, Ecuador
Vatai Emil	RIKEN, Japan
Viéville Thierry	Inria, Antibes, France
Wagner Stefan	Heinrich Heine University Düsseldorf, Germany
Wan Kejia	Defence Innovation Institute, China
Wang Huiling	Tampere University, Finland
Wang Jiaan	Soochow University, China
Wang Jinling	Ulster University, UK
Wang Junli	Tongji University, China
Wang Qian	Durham University, UK
Wang Xing	Ningxia University, China
Wang Yongguang	Beihang University, China
Wang Ziming	Shanghai Jiao Tong University, China
Wanigasekara Chathura	University of Auckland, New Zealand
Watson Patrick	Minerva KGI, USA
Wei Baole	Chinese Academy of Sciences, China
Wei Feng	York University, Canada
Wenninger Marc	Rosenheim Technical University of Applied Sciences, Germany
Wieczorek Tadeusz	Silesian University of Technology, Poland
Wiles Janet	University of Queensland, Australia
Windheuser Christoph	ThoughtWorks Inc., Germany
Wolter Moritz	Rheinische Friedrich-Wilhelms-Universität Bonn, Germany

Wu Ancheng	Pingan Insurance, China
Wu Dayan	Chinese Academy of Sciences, China
Wu Jingzheng	Chinese Academy of Sciences, China
Wu Nier	Inner Mongolia University, China
Wu Song	Southwest University, China
Xie Yuanlun	University of Electronic Science and Technology of China, China
Xu Dongsheng	National University of Defense Technology, China
Xu Jianhua	Nanjing Normal University, China
Xu Peng	Technical University of Munich, Germany
Yaguchi Takaharu	Kobe University, Japan
Yamamoto Hideaki	Tohoku University, Japan
Yang Gang	Renmin University of China, China
Yang Haizhao	Purdue University, USA
Yang Jing	Guangxi Normal University, China
Yang Jing	Hefei University of Technology, China
Yang Liu	Tianjin University, China
Yang Sidi	Concordia University, Canada
Yang Sun	Soochow University, China
Yang Wanli	Harbin Institute of Technology, China
Yang XiaoChen	Tianjin University of Technology, China
Yang Xuan	Shenzhen University, China
Yang Zhao	Leiden University, The Netherlands
Yang Zhengfeng	East China Normal University, China
Yang Zhiguang	Chinese Academy of Sciences, China
Yao Zhenjie	Chinese Academy of Sciences, China
Ye Kai	Wuhan University, China
Yin Bojian	Centrum Wiskunde & Informatica, The Netherlands
Yu James	Southern University of Science and Technology, China
Yu Wenxin	Southwest University of Science and Technology, China
Yu Yipeng	Tencent, China
Yu Yue	BNU-HKBU United International College, China
Yuan Limengzi	Tianjin University, China
Yuchen Ge	Hefei University of Technology, China
Yuhang Guo	Peking University, China
Yury Tsoy	Solidware, South Korea
Zeng Jia	Jilin University, China
Zeng Jiayuan	University of Shanghai for Science and Technology, China
Zhang Dongyang	University of Electronic Science and Technology of China, China
Zhang Jiacheng	Beijing University of Posts and Telecommunications, China
Zhang Jie	Nanjing University, China
Zhang Kai	Chinese Academy of Sciences, China

Zhang Kaifeng	Independent Researcher, China
Zhang Kun	Chinese Academy of Sciences, China
Zhang Luning	China University of Petroleum, China
Zhang Panpan	Chinese Academy of Sciences, China
Zhang Peng	Chinese Academy of Sciences, China
Zhang Wenbin	Carnegie Mellon University, USA
Zhang Xiang	National University of Defense Technology, China
Zhang Xuewen	Southwest University of Science and Technology, China
Zhang Yicheng	University of Lincoln, UK
Zhang Yingjie	Hunan University, China
Zhang Yunchen	University of Electronic Science and Technology of China, China
Zhang Zhiqiang	Southwest University of Science and Technology, China
Zhao Liang	University of São Paulo, Brazil
Zhao Liang	Dalian University of Technology, China
Zhao Qingchao	Harbin Engineering University, China
Zhao Ying	University of Shanghai for Science and Technology, China
Zhao Yuekai	National University of Defense Technology, China
Zheng Yuchen	Kyushu University, Japan
Zhong Junpei	Plymouth University, UK
Zhou Shiyang	Defense Innovation Institute, China
Zhou Xiaomao	Harbin Engineering University, China
Zhou Yucan	Chinese Academy of Sciences, China
Zhu Haijiang	Beijing University of Chemical Technology, China
Zhu Mengting	National University of Defense Technology, China
Zhu Shaolin	Zhengzhou University of Light Industry, China
Zhu Shuying	The University of Hong Kong, China
Zugarini Andrea	University of Florence, Italy

Contents – Part III

Graph Neural Networks II

Hierarchical and Ensemble Models

Human Pose Estimation

Image Processing

Image Segmentation

Knowledge Distillation

Medical Image Processing

Generative Neural Networks

Binding and Perspective Taking as Inference in a Generative Neural Network Model

Mahdi Sadeghi[1]([✉]) [iD], Fabian Schrodt[1,2] [iD], Sebastian Otte[1] [iD],
and Martin V. Butz[1] [iD]

[1] Neuro-Cognitive Modeling Group, University of Tübingen,
Sand 14, 72076 Tübingen, Germany
{mahdi.sadeghi,sebastian.otte,martin.butz}@uni-tuebingen.de
[2] Quantum Gaming GmbH, Sand 14, 72076 Tübingen, Germany
fabian@q-gaming.com

Abstract. The ability to flexibly bind features into coherent wholes from different perspectives is a hallmark of cognition and intelligence. This binding problem is not only relevant for vision but also for general intelligence, sensorimotor integration, event processing, and language. Various artificial neural network models have tackled this problem. Here we focus on a generative encoder-decoder model, which adapts its perspective and binds features by means of retrospective inference. We first train the model to learn sufficiently accurate generative models of dynamic biological, or other harmonic, motion patterns. We then scramble the input and vary the perspective onto it. To properly route the input and adapt the internal perspective onto a known frame of reference, we propagate the prediction error (i) back onto a binding matrix, that is, hidden neural states that determine feature binding, and (ii) further back onto perspective taking neurons, which rotate and translate the input features. Evaluations show that the resulting gradient-based inference process solves the perspective taking and binding problems in the considered motion domains, essentially yielding a Gestalt perception mechanism. Ablation studies show that redundant motion features and population encodings are highly useful.

Keywords: Social cognition · Generative recurrent neural networks · Feature binding · Perspective taking · Gestalt perception

1 Introduction

Social cognition depends on our ability to understand the actions of others. The simulation theory of social cognition [3,10] suggests that visual and other sensory dynamics are mapped onto the own sensorimotor system. The mirror neuron system has been proposed to play a fundamental role in this respect. It

MB is part of the Machine Learning Cluster of Excellence, EXC number 2064/1 - Project number 390727645.

I. Farkaš et al. (Eds.): ICANN 2021, LNCS 12893, pp. 3–14, 2021.
https://doi.org/10.1007/978-3-030-86365-4_1

appears to project and interpret visual information about others with the help of ones own motor repertoire [11]. Cook et al. [8] argue that the involved mirror neurons can develop via associative learning, but the perspective taking and binding problems remain challenging. The *perspective taking problem* addresses the challenge that visual information about others comes in a different frame of reference than information of the own body. Modeling work suggests that our brain is able to project our own perspective into the other person by some form of spatial transformation [15,22]. The challenge is to transform an observed action into a canonical perspective, thus priming corresponding motor simulations [9]. The *binding problem* [7,26] requires the integration of individual visual features, such as motion patterns, color, texture, or edges, into a complete Gestalt [16] recognized as an entity, such as another person's body. With respect to biological motion recognition, a related problem is the *correspondence problem* [18], asking the question how motor codes are brought in correspondence with visual motion patterns. Accordingly, action understanding and imitation appears to be facilitated by establishing correspondences between the own body schema and the one of an observed person [13]. To selectively bind observed features, top-down expectations appear to interact with bottom-up saliency cues in an Bayesian-like manner [4,16]. The details of the involved processes, however, remain elusive.

Here we propose a generative, autoencoder-based neural network model, which solves the perspective taking and binding problems concurrently by means of retrospective, prediction error-minimizing inference. The encoder part of the model is endowed with a transition vector and a rotation matrix for perspective taking and a binding matrix for flexibly integrating input features into one Gestalt percept. The parameters of these three modules are tuned online by means of retrospective, gradient based latent state inference [6]. As a result, the model mimics approximate top-down inference, attempting to integrate all bottom-up visual cues into a Gestalt from a canonical perspective. The model is first trained on a canonical perspective of an ordered set of motion features, simulating self-grounded Gestalt perception [11]. Next, perspective taking and feature binding are evaluated by projecting the reconstruction error back onto the perspective and binding parameters, which can be viewed as specialized parametric bias neurons [24,25]. Our evaluations show that it is highly useful (i) to split the motion feature information into relative position, motion direction, and motion magnitudes and (ii) to use population encodings of the individual features. We evaluate the model's abilities on a 2D, two joint pendulum and on 3D cyclic dynamical motion patterns of a walking person.

2   Proposed Model

The proposed model is a modified version of the model published in the PhD thesis of Fabian Schrodt [20]. It learns a generative, autoencoder-based model of motion patterns, which it employs to bind visual features and to perform spatial perspective taking. Here, each visual feature corresponds to a location, which is represented by a Cartesian coordinate relative to a global frame of reference, which encodes origin and orientation.

2.1   Sub-modal Population Encoding

Each Cartesian input coordinate is segregated into three distinct sub-modalities: relative position, motion direction, and motion magnitude. While the relative position of a visual feature depends on the choice of origin and the orientation of the coordinate frame, motion direction depends only on the orientation but not on the origin, and motion magnitude is completely independent of perspective. As a result, given a visual input coordinate and its velocity, three types of submodal information are derived each transformed via a rotation matrix R and a translation bias b, which determine orientation and origin. At each point in time t, the following transformations are applied:

$$P_i(t) = R(t) \cdot X_i(t) + b(t), \tag{1}$$

determining the relative position $P_i(t)$ of the input feature $X_i(t)$;

$$m_i(t) = \|R(t) \cdot V_i(t)\|, \tag{2}$$

where $V_t = X_t - X_{t-1}$ is the velocity and $m_i(t)$ denotes the motion magnitude;

$$d_i(t) = \frac{R(t) \cdot V_i(t)}{m_i(t)}, \tag{3}$$

calculating the relative motion direction $d_i(t)$. Figure 1 shows a sketch of the proposed model as a connectivity graph, including the processing pipeline for a single three dimensional visual feature. Upon extracting relevant submodal information and projecting them onto a particular visual frame of reference, we encode each submodality separately by one population of topological neurons with Gaussian tuning curves. The individual neuron centers in each submodal population are evenly distributed in the anticipated range of the stimulus in accordance to its dimension, range, and configuration of the perceived submodal stimuli. Such encodings can be closely related to encodings found in the visual cortex and beyond [19]. However, to assess the effectiveness of population coding, we also evaluate the model's performance on the raw submodal information. Activity of α-th neuron associated with the i-th visually observed feature in a population that encodes the position p is computed by:

$$\dot{P}_{\alpha,i}(t) = (r^p)^{D^p} \cdot N\left(P_i(t); c_\alpha^p, \Sigma^p\right) \tag{4}$$

Where each neuron has a specific center c_α^p and a response variance Σ^p. Also, the density of the multivariate Gaussian distribution at l with mean μ and a D^p-dimensional diagonal covariance matrix Σ is $N(l; \mu, \Sigma)$. The factor $(r^p)^{D^p}$ scales the neural activities, dependent on the relative distance r^p between neighboring neurons. The relative distance r^p is also used to determine the diagonal variance entries: $\sigma^p = \zeta^p \cdot (r^p)^2$, where $\zeta^p \in (0, 1]$ denotes the breadth of the cell tunings. Similarly, topological neurons' activation's for direction and magnitude sub-modalities are computed by:

$$\dot{d}_{\alpha,i}(t) = (r^d)^{D^d} \cdot N\left(d_i(t); c_\alpha^d, \Sigma^d\right), \tag{5}$$

$$\dot{m}_{\alpha,i}(t) = (r^m)^{D^m} \cdot N\left(m_i(t); c_\alpha^m, \Sigma^m\right), \tag{6}$$

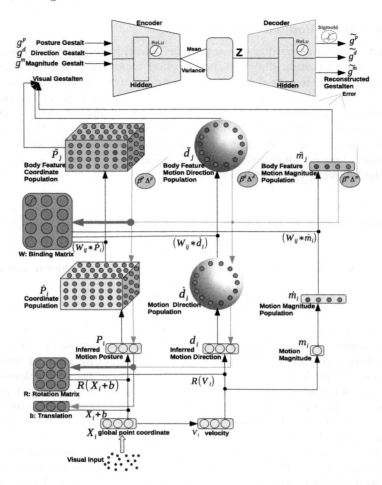

Fig. 1. Our neural network model first translates and rotates the input features, encoding them into redundant posture, motion direction, and magnitude-respective population codes. A neural gating matrix routes the features to autoencoder inputs. Variational autoencoders compress posture, motion direction, and magnitude. The reconstruction loss is used to adapt the parameters of the gating and rotation matrices and the translation vector via retrospective inference.

Posture neurons ($D^p = 3$; 2 for pendulum) are evenly distributed in a specific range on a grid. Direction neurons are evenly scattered on the surface of a unit sphere ($D^d = 3$; 2 for pendulum), while neurons that encode the motion magnitude of the observed feature are distributed linearly ($D^m = 1$). According to the motion capture data and the applied skeleton, posture, direction, and magnitude populations configured to contain 64, 32, and 4 neurons, respectively (For 2D pendulum we distributed 16 posture neurons on a rectangle area around the stimuli, 8 direction neurons on a unique circle and 4 magnitude neurons).

2.2   Gestalt Perception and Feature Binding

The binding problem [26] arises when we select separate visual features and integrate them in a correct order. We approach this problem by selectively routing respective feature patterns matching them with expected Gestalt dynamics. The routing procedure (i.e. selecting relevant observed features $i \in \{1...N\}$ and assigning them to the correct neural processing pathways or bodily features $j \in \{1...M\}$) is addressed by an adaptive gated connectivity matrix:

$$\ddot{p}_j(t) = \sum_{i=1}^{N} w_{ij}(t)\ddot{p}_i(t) \qquad \ddot{d}_j(t) = \sum_{i=1}^{N} w_{ij}(t)\ddot{d}_i(t) \qquad \ddot{m}_j(t) = \sum_{i=1}^{N} w_{ij}(t)\ddot{m}_i(t)$$

$$(7) \qquad\qquad\qquad (8) \qquad\qquad\qquad (9)$$

Population-encoded activations of the i-th unassigned or observed feature for position, direction, and magnitude are denoted by $\ddot{p}_j$, $\ddot{d}_j$, and $\ddot{m}_j$, respectively. Their relative j-th assigned or bodily feature are represented by $\ddot{p}_j$, $\ddot{d}_j$ and $\ddot{m}_j$. $w_{ij} = (1 + e^{-w_{ij}^b})^{-1} \in (0,1)$ indicates the corresponding assignment strength, while the adaptive parametric bias neuron activity is denoted by w_{ij}^b. Each set of submodal bodily feature populations is joined into a Gestalt vector g^x:

$$g^p(t) = (\ddot{p}_1(t), \ddot{p}_2(t), ..., \ddot{p}_M(t)), \tag{10}$$

$$g^d(t) = (\ddot{d}_1(t), \ddot{d}_2(t), ..., \ddot{d}_M(t)), \tag{11}$$

$$g^m(t) = (\ddot{m}_1(t), \ddot{m}_2(t), ..., \ddot{m}_M(t)), \tag{12}$$

yielding Gestalt vectors for the posture, motion direction, and magnitude submodalities, respectively. For each submodal Gestalt $x \in \{p, d, m\}$, one variational autoencoder [17] was employed in order to learn predictive Gestalt encodings. The bottom-up submodal Gestalt vectors g^x are thus passed through the autoencoder, generating reconstructions of the Gestalt perceptions. Consequently, a sufficiently trained autoencoder always infers the closest known stimulus pattern in accordance with its self-perceptual experience, even when it observes actions with unknown features and perspectives. After model learning, the difference between the Gestalt input to the autoencoder and the regenerated Gestalt output is to be minimized by adapting the parametric bias neurons' activities of the binding matrix and the perspective taking modules. We denote the respective squared losses by $\mathcal{L}_p$, $\mathcal{L}_d$, and $\mathcal{L}_m$, respectively. We scale the loss signals by respective factors β^p, β^d, and β^m to balance the error signal influences. The actual adaptation of the parametric bias neurons' activities $w_{ij}^b(t)$ is computed by typical gradient descent with momentum:

$$\Delta w_{ij}^b(t) = -\eta^f \frac{\partial \mathcal{L}(t)}{\partial w_{ij}^b(t)} + \gamma^f (w_{ij}^b(t-1) - w_{ij}^b(t-2)), \tag{13}$$

where γ^f denotes the momentum, η^f the learning rate; for the feature binding adaptation process, and the loss signal $\mathcal{L}(t)$ equals to:

$$\mathcal{L}(t) = \beta^p \mathcal{L}_p(t) + \beta^d \mathcal{L}_d(t) + \beta^m \mathcal{L}_m(t) \tag{14}$$

During training, the assignment biases w_{ij}^b are fixed to 1000 for all $i = j$ (leading to $w_{ii} \approx 1$) and to -1000 for all $i \neq j$ (leading to $w_{ij} \approx 0$), because the assignment is fixed during self-observations. During testing, all assignment biases are initialized at -5 (leading to an initial subtle mixture of all possible assignments) and are adapted over time by means of Eq. 13.

2.3 Perspective Taking

Perspective taking can be considered as a mental transformation procedure that aligns the observer's perspective with a self-centered perspective. The employed mechanism is based on [23] and aims at co-adapting both the bottom-up input routing, manifested in translation- and rotation-based perspective taking and binding, and the top-down autoencoder-based reconstructions.

Translation encodes the center of the imagined frame of reference. It is encoded by 0-initialized bias neurons b_a, which, again, are adapted by gradient descent with momentum to minimize the top-down loss signal $\mathcal{L}(t)$:

$$\Delta b_a(t) = -\eta^b \frac{\partial \mathcal{L}(t)}{\partial^t b_a(t)} + \gamma^b(b_a(t-1) - b_a(t-2)) \qquad (15)$$

where $a \in \{x, y, z\}$ denotes the affected axis, γ^b the momentum term, and η^b the adaptation rate. Note that motion direction and magnitude are invariant to translations. As a result, the adaptation is determined by the posture-respective weighted error signals $\beta^p \Delta_{1...M}^p$ only (cf. also Fig. 1).

Rotation is performed via a neural 3×3 matrix R, which is driven by three Euler angles α_x, α_y, and α_z, each of which represents a rotation around a specific Cartesian axis. $R = R_x(\alpha_x(t))R_y(\alpha_y(t))R_z(\alpha_z(t))$ is the corresponding connectivity structure. Similar to translation, rotation is represented by zero-initialized bias neurons, which can be adapted online by gradient descent. The adaptation over time follows the rule:

$$\Delta \alpha_a(t) = -\eta^r \frac{\mathcal{L}(t)}{\partial^r \alpha_a(t)} + \gamma^r(\alpha_a(t-1) - \alpha_a(t-2)), \qquad (16)$$

where $a \in \{x, y, z\}$, γ^r specifies the momentum, and η^r the adaptation rate. Magnitude is not considered for rotation adaptation as it is invariant to rotation.

3 Experimental Results

We evaluate our model on a simple two-joint pendulum task as well as on more challenging 3D bodily motion capture data. For the 3D walking task, we use the CMU motion capture database [1], where every tracking marker provided a 3D bodily position, which was then mapped onto a skeleton file, which specifies limb connectivity and lengths. Here we focus on continuous, cyclic actions of three different participants. Specifically, we use 7 cycles with 1,000 frames of Subject 35 for training and 7 cycles with 1,000 frames of Subject 5 and Subject 6 for testing.

Table 1. Used parameters for training the variational autoencoder

Experiment	Learning rate pos	Learning rate dir	Learning rate mag	Opt.	Hidden size	Latent size	ζ^p	ζ^d	ζ^m
Motion (pop. coding)	$1 \cdot 10^{-3}$	$8 \cdot 10^{-4}$	$5 \cdot 10^{-4}$	Adam	45	25	0.85	0.85	0.95
Motion (raw data)	$1 \cdot 10^{-3}$	$2 \cdot 10^{-5}$	$8 \cdot 10^{-4}$	Adam	25	10	–	–	–
Pendulum	$1 \cdot 10^{-2}$	$1 \cdot 10^{-2}$	$1 \cdot 10^{-3}$	Adam	45	25	0.85	0.85	0.95

As another generic case we trained the model with generated two joint pendulum data, which we adapted from mathplotlib's animation example. The pendulum consists of two joints with 0.8 and 0.6 m length, and 1.25 and 1 kg mass, respectively. The data used for training and testing encode the pendulum swinging back and forth seven times with completely loose lower limb. Thus, 7 cycles with 1,000 frames for training and the same amount of data (different cycles) for testing. If not stated differently, all results reported below show averages (and standard deviations) over ten independently trained networks.

3.1   VAE Prediction Error

During training the model has full access to visual information and visual stimuli are perceived from an egocentric point of view (perspective taking and feature binding adaptations are disabled). The aim is to analyze the compression quality of the autoencoder. We used the PyTorch library of Python. The chosen network parameters are specified in Table 1. Grid search was used to determine good parameter settings. To evaluate the influence of population coding on the model, we also trained another VAE model without the population encoding, feeding the raw Cartesian data into the VAE. In both cases, the model was able to significantly improve its reconstruction error over time, as can be clearly seen in Fig. 2 (right). Albeit the different error measures without and with population encoding cannot be directly compared, it is well-noticeable that learning takes place in both cases. Moreover, the relative improvement particularly of posture and motion direction Gestalt reconstruction error is much stronger in the case of population encoding (note the different ranges of the y-axes).

3.2   Adaptation of Feature Binding

While the results above show that the VAE does learn good encodings, the critical question in this work was whether the resulting signal is useful to accomplish feature binding and perspective taking, which we evaluate separately. To focus on feature binding, we disabled perspective taking. Neural feature binding bias activities w_{ij}^b were reset to -5 for each test trial, resulting in assignment strengths of $w_{ij} \approx 0.0067$ effectively distributing all feature value information uniformly over the VAE inputs. Please note that by initialising all elements of binding matrix with the same value the model loses its knowledge about the correct assignment and therefore there is no need for shuffling the observed features orders for evaluation purposes. The hyperparameters used during the feature binding experiments are shown in Table 2.

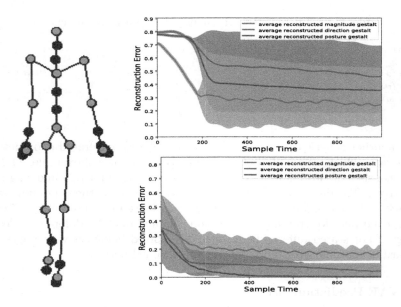

Fig. 2. Left: Motion capture skeleton data indicating the 15 chosen visual inputs; **Right**: Visual spatial reconstruction error (i.e. Binary Cross-Entropy Loss) of posture, direction, and magnitude Gestalt perceptions; **Right-up**: trained when using no population coding; **Right-down**: trained using population coding

Table 2. Hyperparameters used for feature binding

Experiment 1	Experiment 2	Experiment 3	Experiment 4
No Pop Code	With Pop Code	With Pop Code	2D Pendulum
$\beta^{pos} = 5$	$\beta^{pos} = 6$	$\beta^{pos} = 8$	$\beta^{pos} = 1$
$\beta^{dir} = 1$	$\beta^{dir} = 0$	$\beta^{dir} = 2$	$\beta^{dir} = 8$
$\beta^{mag} = 0.125$	$\beta^{mag} = 0$	$\beta^{mag} = 0.125$	$\beta^{mag} = 2$
$\eta^f = 1$	$\eta^f = 1$	$\eta^f = 1$	$\eta^f = 0.1$
$\gamma^f = 0.9$	$\gamma^f = 0.9$	$\gamma^f = 0.9$	$\gamma^f = 0.9$

We use Feature Binding Error (FBE) as the sum of Euclidean distances between the correct assignment and the model's inferred assignment to investigate the binding progress; $FBE(t) = \sum_{j=1}^{M} \sqrt{(w_{jj}(t) - 1)^2 + \sum_{i=1, i \neq j}^{N} w_{ii}(t)^2}$. Figure 3 shows that the feature binding error decreases in all encoding cases. Moreover, it shows the resulting binding matrix (confusion matrix) values after 1000 steps of feature binding adaptation. Clearly, the applied population encoding is highly useful to decrease the FBE, which corresponds to the diagonal. However, other feature binding constellations can be found equally well. Without population encoding, the binding matrix does not fully converge. For example, the hip joint is confused with the femur, and even severe confusions

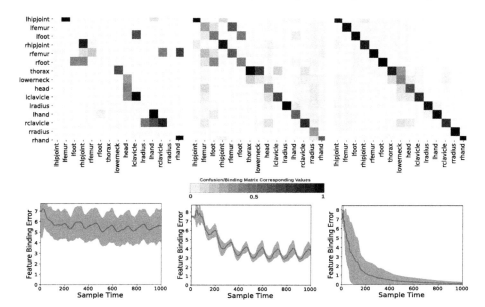

Fig. 3. Feature binding adaptations in experiments 1 to 3 (cf. Table 2), where columns correspond to the respective experiments. **First Row** shows the resulting confusion matrices (input feature columns mapped onto respective body feature rows). **Second Row** depicts the corresponding feature binding error dynamics.

can be observed, such as the left foot with the left clavicle. With population encoding, the FBE drops significantly lower. When only providing the posture encoding, left-right and neighboring limb confusions remain even with population encoding. Only when complete motion information is added in population encoded form, hardly any confusions remain, indicating full Gestalt perception. It may be noted that the probability to guess the correct assignment by chance is virtually impossible (225 choose 15 yields a value of $9.1 \cdot 10^{22}$ possibilities). To verify the generality of our results, we also evaluated binding performance on the pendulum data. Figure 4 confirms that binding also works robustly for the two joint pendulum data. Even if some latent activity of Joint 2 is added to Joint 1, this disruption seems to be minor, also indicating robust Gestalt perception.

3.3   Adaptation of Perspective Taking

Focusing on perspective taking[1] next, we fix the binding matrix to the correct diagonal binding values and evaluate the development of spatial translation and orientation. Thus, we confront the fully trained models with trials of the test set, fix the binding matrix, and evaluate the development of spatial translation and orientation parametric biases. Each trial's observed data

---

[1] A video of the Binding and Perspective Taking adaptation processes is accessible here: https://uni-tuebingen.de/de/206397.

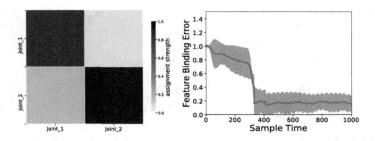

Fig. 4. Adapting the feature binding on two jointed pendulum

is transformed by a translation vector followed by a constant rotation matrix, before feeding it into the model. Accordingly, the model perceives the data from an unknown perspective and should transfer it to it's known perspective or self-perceptual experience. In order to monitor the transformation progress, we define orientation difference (OD) and translation difference (TD) measures to be $OD(t) = \frac{180}{2\Pi} Acos(\frac{tr(A^{model}(t)A^{data}(t))-1}{2})$ in $°$, where A^{model} is the dynamic, currently inferred rotation matrix and A^{data} is a constant rotation matrix applied to all visual inputs before testing; $TD(t) = \left\| b^{data}(t) - b^{model}(t) \right\|$ in cm, where b^{model} is the currently inferred translation of the model and b^{data} is the constant offset applied to data. Employed model parameters are shown in Table 3. Figure 5 (left) shows the dynamic inference progression of the rotation matrix values, when the input data was rotated by randomly assigned α_x, α_y and α_z for one of the trained networks (results were qualitatively equivalent for the other trained networks). Figure 5 (right) shows the corresponding translation bias inference for the same network. As can be seen for both translation and rotation, the stronger the perspective is disturbed, the longer it takes to infer the correct perspective.

Table 3. Hyperparameters used for perspective taking

Parameter	η^r	γ^r	η^b	γ^b	β^{pos}	β^{dir}	β^{mag}
Value	1.10^{-2}	9.10^{-1}	8.10^{-2}	9.10^{-1}	8	3	0

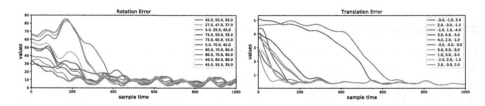

Fig. 5. Left: Rotation adaptation where the initial input data rotations over each axis are shown in the legend. **Right:** Translation adaptation where the initial translation biases given to the test set are shown in the legend.

4 Summary and Conclusion

We have introduced a generative neural network architecture, which tackles the perspective taking and binding challenges. Transformer networks [14], attention-based architectures [27], and object representation learning models [12] can be considered closely related to our approach. In contrast to related approaches, our system applies retrospective inference, tuning parametric bias neurons [24,25]. In this case, these neurons are dedicated to establish feature bindings and adapt the internal perspective onto the observed features. Starting from a canonical perspective on a biological motion pattern, we have shown that perspective taking and binding work highly reliable, particularly when complementary spatio-temporal feature patterns are available and encoded with population codes. We believe that this is the case because complementary motion encodings embed accordingly complementary inference information. Meanwhile, the population encodings enable the concurrent testing of different Gestalt hypotheses by dynamically adapting multimodal bottom-up and top-down probability densities. Interestingly, the resulting ability can be related to embodied social cognition, mirror neurons, perspective taking, and Gestalt perception.

We currently extend the model with an LSTM-based temporal encoder-decoder architecture [2], in order to reap additional information from the temporal dynamics retrospectively [6,20,21] as well as to be able to distinguish multiple Gestalt patterns. Overall, we hope that our technique will be useful also in other domains, where information needs to be flexibly bound together and associated to other data on the fly, striving for overall consistency. In particular, we hope to tackle related problems in cognitive science, such as the inference of event-predictive and compositional structures [5,7].

References

1. Motion capture database (2018). http://mocap.cs.cmu.edu
2. Bahdanau, D., Cho, K., Bengio, Y.: Neural machine translation by jointly learning to align and translate. In: International Conference on Learning Representations (2015)
3. Barsalou, L.W.: Perceptual symbol systems. Behav. Brain Sci. **22**, 577–600 (1999)
4. Buschman, T.J., Miller, E.K.: Top-down versus bottom-up control of attention in the prefrontal and posterior parietal cortices. Science **315**(5820), 1860–1862 (2007)
5. Butz, M.V.: Towards a unified sub-symbolic computational theory of cognition. Front. Psychol. **7**, 925 (2016)
6. Butz, M.V., Bilkey, D., Humaidan, D., Knott, A., Otte, S.: Learning, planning, and control in a monolithic neural event inference architecture. Neural Netw. **117**, 135–144 (2019)
7. Butz, M.V., Kutter, E.F.: How the Mind Comes Into Being: Introducing Cognitive Science from a Functional and Computational Perspective. Oxford University Press, Oxford (2017)
8. Cook, R., Bird, G., Catmur, C., Press, C., Heyes, C.: Mirror neurons: from origin to function. Behav. Brain Sci. **37**, 177–192 (2014)

9. Edwards, M.G., Humphreys, G.W., Castiello, U.: Motor facilitation following action observation: a behavioural study in prehensile action. Brain Cogn. **53**(3), 495–502 (2003)
10. Gallese, V., Goldman, A.: Mirror neurons and the simulation theory of mind-reading. Trends Cogn. Sci. **2**(12), 493–501 (1998)
11. Gallese, V., Keysers, C., Rizzolatti, G.: A unifying view of the basis of social cognition. Trends Cogn. Sci. **8**(9), 396–403 (2004)
12. Greff, K., et al.: Multi-object representation learning with iterative variational inference. In: International Conference on Machine Learning, pp. 2424–2433. PMLR (2019)
13. Jackson, P.L., Meltzoff, A.N., Decety, J.: Neural circuits involved in imitation and perspective-taking. Neuroimage **31**(1), 429–439 (2006)
14. Jaderberg, M., Simonyan, K., Zisserman, A., Kavukcuoglu, K.: Spatial transformer networks. Adv. Neural. Inf. Process. Syst. **28**, 2017–2025 (2015)
15. Johnson, M., Demiris, Y.: Perceptual perspective taking and action recognition. Int. J. Adv. Rob. Syst. **2**(4), 301–309 (2005)
16. Jäkel, F., Singh, M., Wichmann, F.A., Herzog, M.H.: An overview of quantitative approaches in gestalt perception. Vis. Res. **126**, 3–8 (2016)
17. Kingma, D.P., Welling, M.: Auto-encoding variational bayes. arXiv:1312.6114 (2013)
18. Nehaniv, C.L., Dautenhahn, K., et al.: The correspondence problem. Imitation Animals Artifacts **41** (2002)
19. Pouget, A., Dayan, P., Zemel, R.: Information processing with population codes. Nat. Rev. Neurosci. **1**(2), 125–132 (2000)
20. Schrodt, F.: Neurocomputational principles of action understanding. Ph.D. thesis, University of Tübingen (2018)
21. Schrodt, F., Butz, M.V.: Just imagine! learning to emulate and infer actions with a stochastic generative architecture. Front. Robot. AI **3**, 5 (2016)
22. Schrodt, F., Layher, G., Neumann, H., Butz, M.V.: Modeling perspective-taking upon observation of 3D biological motion. In: 4th International Conference on Development and Learning and on Epigenetic Robotics, pp. 305–310. IEEE (2014)
23. Schrodt, F., Layher, G., Neumann, H., Butz, M.V.: Embodied learning of a generative neural model for biological motion perception and inference. Front. Comput. Neurosci. **9**, 79 (2015)
24. Sugita, Y., Tani, J., Butz, M.V.: Simultaneously emerging braitenberg codes and compositionality. Adapt. Behav. **19**, 295–316 (2011)
25. Tani, J.: Exploring Robotic Minds. Oxford University Press, Oxford (2017)
26. Treisman, A.: Feature binding, attention and object perception. Philos. Trans. R. Soc. Lond. Ser. B: Biol. Sci. **353**(1373), 1295–1306 (1998)
27. Vaswani, A., et al.: Attention is all you need. In: Advances in Neural Information Processing Systems 30, pp. 5998–6008 (2017)

Advances in Password Recovery Using Generative Deep Learning Techniques

David Biesner[1,2,3], Kostadin Cvejoski[1,3(✉)], Bogdan Georgiev[1,3],
Rafet Sifa[1,2,3], and Erik Krupicka[4]

[1] Fraunhofer IAIS, Sankt Augustin, Germany
Kostadin.cvejoski@iais.fraunhofer.de
[2] University of Bonn, Bonn, Germany
[3] Competence Center for Machine Learning Rhine-Ruhr (ML2R),
Dortmund, Germany
[4] Federal Criminal Police Office, Wiesbaden, Germany

Abstract. Password guessing approaches via deep learning have recently been investigated with significant breakthroughs in their ability to generate novel, realistic password candidates. In the present work we study a broad collection of deep learning and probabilistic based models in the light of password guessing: *attention-based deep neural networks, autoencoding mechanisms* and *generative adversarial networks*. We provide novel generative deep-learning models in terms of variational autoencoders exhibiting state-of-art sampling performance, yielding additional latent-space features such as interpolations and targeted sampling. Lastly, we perform a thorough empirical analysis in a unified controlled framework over well-known datasets (RockYou, LinkedIn, MySpace, Youku, Zomato, Pwnd). Our results not only identify the most promising schemes driven by deep neural networks, but also illustrate the strengths of each approach in terms of generation variability and sample uniqueness.

1 Introduction and Motivation

Most authentication methods commonly used today rely on users setting custom passwords to access their accounts and devices. Password-based authentications are popular due to their ease of use, ease of implementation and the established familiarity of users and developers with the method [10]. However studies show that users tend to set their individual passwords predictably, favoring short strings, names, birth dates and reusing passwords across sites [16,17]. Since chosen passwords exhibit certain patterns and structure, it begs the question whether it is possible to simulate these patterns and generate passwords that a human user realistically might have chosen.

Password guessing is an active field of study, until recently dominated by statistical analysis of password leaks and construction of corresponding generation algorithms (see Sect. 2). These methods rely on expert knowledge and analysis

---

D. Biesner and K. Cvejoski—Equal contribution.

© Springer Nature Switzerland AG 2021
I. Farkaš et al. (Eds.): ICANN 2021, LNCS 12893, pp. 15–27, 2021.
https://doi.org/10.1007/978-3-030-86365-4_2

of various password leaks from multiple sources to generate rules and algorithms for efficient exploitation of learned patterns.

On the other hand, in recent years major advances in machine-driven text generation have been made, notably by novel deep-learning based architectures and efficient training strategies for large amounts of training text data. These methods are purely data driven, meaning they learn only from the structure of the input training text, without any external knowledge on the domain or structure of the data. Major advancements in the field have been fueled by the development of new architectures and mechanisms, advanced representation capabilities and training procedures.

In this paper we will continue the exploration of data driven deep-learning text generation methods for the task of password-guessing. While some applications to password guessing already show promising results, most frameworks still can not reach or surpass state-of-the-art password generation algorithms. Ideally, one would attempt to design more efficient password-guessing models aided by neural networks and cutting-edge practices. Our findings and contributions can be summarized as follows: (1) we provide extensive unified analysis of previous as well as novel password guessing models based on deep learning and probabilistic techniques; (2) our collection of architectures based on deep learning exhibits varying performance, with the top-performing models being able to reach sophisticated password generation algorithms in the password recovery task; (3) We show that attention-driven text generation methods (Transformers) can be applied to password guessing with little additional adjustments; (4) we additionally analyse the effect of model pre-training on general language data for the password generation task against training on pure password data; (5) our novel variational autoencoder (VAE) approach allows more flexible latent representations and outperforms previous autoencoding methods based on Wasserstein training [26]; (6) the VAE provides a state-of-art password matching performance as well as further sampling possibilities (conditional and targeted sampling). However, the password latent space geometry is quite sensitive to training and regularization yielding promising grounds for future investigations in terms of conditional sampling.

2   Related Work

Password generation has a long history outside of deep-learning architectures. There are tools available for purely rule-based approaches (Hashcat [1] and John-TheRipper [4]), which generate password candidates either by brute-force or dictionary attacks, in which a dictionary of words or previously known passwords is augmented by a set of rules, either hand-written or machine generated [2].

Machine-learning based approaches to password guessing may come in their most simple form as regular n-gram Markov Models [27] or more sophisticated approaches like *probabilistic context free grammar* (PCFG) [31], which analyses likely structures in a password training set and applies various generation algorithms based on these observations.

Neural network based password generation has become an active field of study in the recent years. Ranging from relatively simple recurrent neural net

(RNN) architectures [25] to recent seminal works applying state-of-the-art text generation methods to password generation: Generative adversarial networks (GANs) [20, 26], Wasserstein Autoencoders [26], and bidirectional RNNs trained with the aid of pre-trained Transformer models [24].

Our work extends this palette of deep learning architectures with the Variational Autoencoder [23] and Transformer-based language models [28]. We additionally offer an extensive, unified and controlled comparison between the both various deep-learning based methods and more established methods mentioned above. This analysis yields a stable benchmark for the introduction of novel models.

3   Models

GAN. A central idea of adversarial methods is the construction of generative models by game-theoretic means: a "generator" neural network produces data samples, whereas a "discriminator" neural network simultaneously attempts to discern between the real and artificially produced (by the generator) samples. The training of such a system consists in optimizing the performance of both the generator and discriminator (usually, via types of suitably chosen gradient descents and additional regularization). An important tool that smooths out gradients and makes the model more robust is the Wasserstein distance, which provides means to efficiently compute discrepancies between two given distributions. We refer to [14, 18, 19] for further background.

Concerning password guessing and generation our starting point is the well-known PassGAN model proposed in [20]. The PassGAN defines a discriminator and generator in terms of residual networks [32] - these are assembled from the so-called residual blocks (e.g. a stack of convolutional neural networks followed by a batch-normalization [21]).

Deep Latent Variable Models. The *Variational Auto Encoder* (VAE) [23] is a framework for efficient optimization of *deep latent variable models* (DLVM). It comprises of two main components: *encoder* and *decoder*. The encoder is a stochastic function $\phi : \mathbf{X} \to \mathbf{Z}$ that maps the input space (passwords) $\mathbf{X}$ to the latent space $\mathbf{Z}$. The decoder is deterministic function that maps a code from the latent space to the input space $\theta : \mathbf{Z} \to \mathbf{X}$. The model is trained by maximizing the evidence lower bound (ELBO)

$$\mathcal{L}(\theta, \phi, \mathbf{x}^{(i)}) = -D_{KL}(q_\phi(\mathbf{z}|\mathbf{x}^{(i)})||p_\theta(\mathbf{z})) + \mathbb{E}_{q_\phi(\mathbf{z}|\mathbf{x}^{(i)})} \left[\log p_\theta(\mathbf{x}^{(i)}|\mathbf{z})\right]. \quad (1)$$

The model learns to reconstruct the password $\mathbf{x}$ given to the input by first, mapping the password to a distribution of latent codes $q_\phi(\mathbf{z}|\mathbf{x})$, then sampling from the posterior distribution and passing the latent code $\mathbf{z}$ to the decoder $p_\theta(\mathbf{x}^{(i)}|\mathbf{z})$. During training a strong prior $p_\theta(\mathbf{z})$ is imposed on the learned latent code distribution. Usually in the VAE framework the prior is set to be centered isotropic Gaussian distribution $p_\theta(\mathbf{z}) = \mathcal{N}(\mathbf{z}; \mathbf{0}, \mathbf{I})$, which enables us to later easily sample from the prior and generate new passwords.

The latent space learned by the encoder imposes a geometric connections among latent points that have some semantic similarity in the data space. As a result *similar* points in the data space have latent representation that are close to each other. The notation of *similarity* depends on the modeled data, in the case of password generation it may be based on the structure of the password, like a common substring.

Transformers. In recent years the transformer, originally applied to machine translation in [30], has become increasingly popular, with transformer-based architectures setting new benchmarks in text generation, machine translation and many other natural language processing tasks.

Transformers rely almost solely on self-attention to process an input text, which considers all pairs of words in the sentence instead of the linear sequence of words. While RNNs may lose the memory of words in the beginning of a sentence rather quickly, transformers are able to capture long-term dependencies between words in a sentence and between sentences.

The self-attention mechanism evaluates attention for each word pair by multiplying their entries in the query, key and value matrices $Q, K \in \mathbb{R}^{n, d_k}$ and $V \in \mathbb{R}^{n, d_v}$ (d_k dimensionality of the query and key, d_v of the value vectors respectively) as $\textbf{Attention}(Q, K, V) = \textbf{softmax}\left(\frac{QK^T}{\sqrt{d_k}}\right) V$, where the output of the softmax operation provides for each word a probability distribution over all other words in the sequence, which is then used to weight the word values to produce the attention output.

In our work we apply the GPT2 [28] architecture to the password modeling task. GPT2 is a transformer-based language model, trained on the causal language modeling objective, meaning given an incomplete sentence it will try to predict the next upcoming word. A tokenized input sentence is therefore read by a transformer block which outputs a probability distribution p_θ over the vocabulary. For a corpus of tokens $\mathcal{U} = (u_1, \ldots, u_N)$ and a context window $k \in \mathbb{N}$ the loss is then given as $\mathcal{L}(\mathcal{U}) = \sum_{i=1}^{N} p_\theta(u_i | u_{i-1}, \ldots, u_{i-k})$.

To generate text, given a text prompt (e.g. "Hello my") the model will start generating text that continues the sentence ("name is GPT2!"). We provide details on the model and training in Sect. 4.2.

4   Results

4.1   Data

There are several datasets of passwords publicly available. These lists contain passwords that were at some point in time leaked to the public from certain websites. Leaks contain in rare cases plaintext passwords (e.g. the RockYou leak), but more commonly only password hashes that are then recovered using password guessing methods. Password datasets contain either passwords from a single leak or are aggregated from several leaked sources. We apply the same preprocessing to all datasets: Removing duplicates, removing passwords <4 and >12 characters and removing passwords containing characters other than letters, numbers and punctuation .!?* \$_#&/+.

The specific password datasets we employ for training or evaluation are: 'rockyou' (13.0M passwords, [7]); 'Have I Been Pwnd V1'/'pwnd' (274.8M, [3]), 'linkedin' (60.1M, [5]), 'myspace' (53k, [6]), 'yahoo' (430k, [11]), 'youku' (48M, [12]), 'seclist' (969k, [8]), 'skullsecurity' (6.2M, [9]), 'zomato' (6.3M, [13]). All counts after preprocessing. Note that all datasets are sets of unique passwords. Since the main task is not accurate learning of the training data distribution but generation of new passwords we hypothesize that training on unique passwords improves the guessing performance. Benchmarks on the VAE-model have shown a slight improvement over training on the original non-unique password leak.

For training we employ splits of the rockyou (80%, 10.4M training/20%, 2.6M testing) and pwnd (80%, 219.8M training/20%, 54.9M testing).

4.2 Experimental Setup

GAN-Based Models. In our setup, we essentially utilize the PassGAN as a standard benchmark - this is well motivated by previous substantial studies of GAN-based models [20,26]. The generator/discriminator are defined as residual neural networks consisting of 6 standard residual blocks followed by a linear projection/softmax function, respectively. Each of the standard residual blocks consists of 2 convolutional layers (with kernel-size 3, stride 1, no dilation) followed by a batch-normalization layer. The generator's latent space (i.e. the input space) is set to 256 inspired by [20].

The PassGAN training is based on state-of-art practices such as Wasserstein GAN and gradient clipping (cf. [14]), as well as gradient penalty regularization (cf. [19]). We used a batch-size of 256, a gradient-penalty-hyperparameter $\lambda = 10$ and 10 discriminator iterations per generator step. The preferred gradient descent was based on ADAM [22] with an initial learning rate $\eta = 10^{-4}$ and momentum parameters $\beta_1 = 0.5, \beta_2 = 0.9$; a fixed-interval annealing with an iteration step of 10^6 was also used.

Note that [26] report improvements of the GAN-architecture and training for password generation by adding additive noise to the input, replacing the residual blocks with deeper residual bottleneck blocks and applying batch normalization to the generator. We compare to the results reported in their paper in Sect. 4.4, Table 2.

Variational Autoencoders. For both the encoder and the decoder we use a CNN with fixed kernel size of 3. The depth and the dilation of the convolution is gradually increase from [1, 2, 4], [1, 2, 4, 8], [1, 2, 4, 8, 16] to [1, 2, 4, 8, 16, 32]. We use cross-validation to pick the best hyper-parameters for the model. The number of channels for the CNN block is 512, the latent dimension of the model $\mathbf{z}$ is chosen from [64, 128, 256]. We use the ADAM [22] with learning rate $\eta = 10^{-4}$ and momentum $\beta_1 = 0.5$, $\beta_2 = 0.9$. The batch size is chosen to be 128 and we also use early stopping. Following [15], we use KL cost annealing strategy.

Table 1. Most common generated passwords per model, separated by training dataset.

Model	'rockyou'	'pwnd'	Model	'rockyou'	'pwnd'	Model	'rockyou'	'pwnd'	Model	'rockyou'
	leslie	MARIA		love	2010		ilove	1234		123456
	yankee	hilton		mrs.	love		love	2010		12345
	kirsty	SEXY		baby	1234		baby	love		123456789
	jeremy	4678		sexy	2000		iluv	2000		1234567
VAE	claudia	NATA	GPT2S	girl	2009	GPT2F	sexy	2009	PassGAN	12345678
	gangsta	ALEX		angel	2008		pink	2008		angela
	violet	JOSE		1992	12345		memyself	12345		angels
	andrei	BABY		1993	2011		caoimhe	2011		angel1
	jennifer	MAMA		1994	2007		cintaku	2007		buster
	natalie	ANGEL		2007	1992		jess	1987		128456

GPT2-Based Models. The original openly available GPT2 model is trained on a large corpus of internet text. Training data is provided simply as a sequence of raw, unlabeled text that is fed into the model. For training on passwords, one can therefore take a dataset of passwords and construct training data by concatenating shuffled passwords into continuous text. In our report we train two GPT2-based models:

(i) We finetune (i.e. continue the training of) the pre-trained model with our password dataset. We expect that the original training gives the model some background on how language is generally structured as well as a vocabulary of common words. Finetuning on passwords should then give the model an understanding of the structures and the vocabulary of passwords and force it to generate passwords when prompted. We call this model GPT2-Finetuned or GPT2F;

(ii) The other model only uses the architecture of GPT2 and trains a randomly initialized model from scratch. A concern using a pre-trained and finetuned model is whether the model resorts back to generating regular English text when faced with certain prompts, this problem will not appear with a model trained from scratch since all the text it has ever known are passwords. We call this model GPT2-Scratch or GPT2S.

We train the model using an openly available implementation of GPT2,[1] with the default *gpt2*[2] model as pre-trained base and default hyperparameters. The model is therefore a 12 layer, 12 attention-head model with latent dimension 768, maximum sequence length of 1024 and a vocabulary size of 50257. GPT2 applies byte-pair encoding trained on general English text to tokenize text [29].

4.3   Analysis of Generated Passwords

In Table 1 we compare the most common passwords generated by our models along with the most commonly generated passwords by the comparison methods.

---

[1] https://huggingface.co/transformers/model_doc/gpt2.html.
[2] https://huggingface.co/transformers/pretrained_models.html.

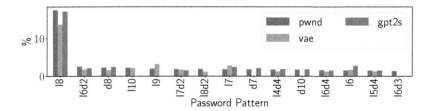

Fig. 1. Statistics on password structure for 'pwnd' dataset and passwords generated by models trained on 'pwnd'.

We observe that each model and training dataset generates a unique set of password candidates.

While the GPT2-based models trained on 'pwnd' commonly generate year numbers and short sequences of digits, the equivalent models trained on 'rockyou' produce strings that generally look more like real words that one might commonly find as a password or password substring. The VAE model focuses for both training datasets on names, with the 'rockyou' model generating lowercase names and the 'pwnd' model prefering all-caps strings. Finally, for the PassGAN model implemented on the 'rockyou' training data. we observe a combination of simple number strings containing some variation of **12345** and character strings based on the substring **angel**. In general the most common passwords seem similar to each other, with less variance as observed for the other models when trained on 'rockyou'.

Additionally, to estimate whether our trained model follow the distribution of the empirical dataset (the training set), we introduce *PCFG-like* statistics [31] – password **password!23** is split into pure segments as **L8S1D2** where **L** is alpha character, **S** is special symbol character and **D** is a digit.

The most common password structure for the 'pwnd' dataset is l8 (see Fig. 1) with almost 20% of the whole dataset. The GPT2S model successfully matches the number of passwords with structure l8. For the rest of the password structures the GPT2S and the VAE model perform roughly the same and approximately match the underlying empirical distribution.

4.4   Password Guessing Performance

To evaluate the power of our password generation methods we match generated passwords to a predefined test set. As mentioned in Sect. 4.1, given a dataset of passwords we split into train and test (80%/20%) and use the train set to train the deep learning text generation model. Once the model is trained we generate a fixed number of passwords (in our experiments up to 10^9). We are interested in the number (both total and as ratio) of generated passwords that appear in the test set.

Table 2 presents all the deep models trained on the 'rockyou' or 'pwnd' dataset and evaluating on the full 'linkedin', 'myspace', 'yahoo', 'seclist',

Table 2. Evaluate the model password-matching performance on all datasets with 10^9 generated passwords. (*) Models trained on the 'rockyou' dataset; (**) Models trained on 'pwnd' dataset. Evaluation is done on the full size of the dataset except for the 'rockyou' and 'pwnd' where the models are evaluated only on the test set (20% of the full size). Pasquini [26] trained PassGAN on a different 80/20 'rockyou' split and report 23.3%.

Model	rockyou	linkedin	pwnd	myspace	yahoo	seclist	skullsec	youku	zomato
VAE*	44.9%	**21.8%**	15.4%	62.5%	47.3%	57.4%	32.1%	13.8%	20.3%
PassGAN*	15.9%	6.8%	4.7%	24.6%	19.0%	30.7%	13.6%	5.1%	8.3%
GPT2F*	**45.1%**	20.3%	14.7%	**65.8%**	**47.6%**	55.3%	31.1%	11.8%	18.6%
GPT2S*	41.7%	18.7%	13.9%	61.1%	45.0%	53.6%	31.0%	13.4%	17.8%
VAE**	26.7%	13.5%	14.6%	44.7%	33.1%	46.2%	24.8%	9.7%	16.5%
GPT2F**	36.4%	19.9%	22.1%	57.1%	42.4%	56.5%	34.8%	14.4%	24.3%
GPT2S**	37.6%	20.7%	**22.7%**	58.3%	43.7%	**58.0%**	**36.0%**	**14.5%**	**25.3%**

'skullsecurity', 'youku' and 'zomato' dataset. In the case of 'rockyou' and 'pwnd' only the test set is used for evaluation.

First, focusing on the 'rockyou' trained models in Table 2 we see that the PassGAN benchmark is significantly outperformed by VAE and transformer-based models (up to almost three times on e.g. 'rockyou' and 'linkedin' datasets). The improved GAN-architecture and training from [26] reports a 23.3% recovery performance for a model trained on rockyou evaluated on rockyou. This is a clear improvement over the PassGAN benchmark from [20] but still does not reach the latent variable or transformer architectures. On one hand, this demonstrates how effective model selection may lead to substantial matching improvements; on the other hand, one might speculate that the direct application of GAN-based methods is sub-optimal when one works with password datasets with richer latent structure.

Interestingly, although having a very different structure, the VAE performs very similarly to the proposed GPT-models, thus suggesting that perhaps some internal password dataset features (e.g. complexity/margins/topology) are crucially guiding the performance of both approaches.

A similar analysis of the 'pwnd' trained models in Table 2 can be brought forward, where the overall model performance is reduced in comparison to the 'rockyou' trained models. Here, in contrast, the transformers seem to have a clear advantage over the autoencoding method.

These observations illustrate the effect of the training dataset's generalization ability - the 'rockyou' training appears much richer than the 'pwnd' one and, curiously, renders VAE almost equivalent in performance to the attention-driven solutions.

4.5   Comparison to Established Methods

In order to compare our models to the established methods mentioned in Sect. 2, we evaluate on a third dataset. We use our training split of 'rockyou' (80%, 10.4M passwords) to generate new passwords using various established methods and evaluate on a subset of the 'linkedin' dataset (originally 60.7M passwords). Additionally to the preprocessing mentioned in Sect. 4.1 we remove all entries that also appear in our 'rockyou' training split. We are left with a test set of 47.3M passwords.

Table 3. Results of our evaluation on the 'linkedin' dataset (47.3M passwords). All our models were trained on 'rockyou' and generated 10^9 passwords, all models above generated 10^9 passwords or the maximum number of possible combinations from the 'rockyou' training split. (*) Numbers taken from [20] for comparison, trained and evaluated on different data splits.

Model	Unique Passwords	Matches
3-gram Markov Model	4.35×10^8	4.27×10^6
Hashcat – best64	6.66×10^8	7.26×10^6
Hashcat – gen2	8.49×10^8	2.55×10^6
PCFG v4.1	9.71×10^8	12.52×10^6
PRINCE v0.22	9.99×10^8	1.65×10^6
FLA*	7.4×10^8	8.29×10^6
PassGAN (ours)	2.95×10^8	3.2×10^6
GPT2S	4.54×10^8	8.85×10^6
GPT2F	4.57×10^8	9.60×10^6
VAE	5.99×10^8	10.3×10^6

For comparison, we train PCFG[3] on a non-unique version of the training split, i.e. passwords appear multiple times in the frequency of the original leak, and generate 10^9 passwords. We use Hashcat to apply two rulesets to the training split of unique passwords. Ruleset *best64* contains 64 rules and generates 6.9×10^8 passwords in total. Ruleset *generated2*[4] contains 65k rules and generates an exceedingly large number of password candidates, of which we sample 10^9 passwords. Both lists are the result of large-scale quantitative evaluations of the effect of various hand-written and machine generated rules on multiple wordlists, password datasets and target hashes. We additionally train a simple 3-gram Markov Model[5] on the unique training split and generate 10^9 passwords. Finally we use the PRINCE algorithm[6] to construct 10^9 passwords of length 4 to 12 from the 'rockyou' training set.

---

[3] https://github.com/lakiw/pcfg_cracker.
[4] https://github.com/hashcat/hashcat/tree/master/rules/generated2.rule.
[5] https://github.com/brannondorsey/markov-passwords.
[6] https://github.com/hashcat/princeprocessor.

Additionally we compare to the FLA [25] experiments done in [20]. Note that the model is trained on a 'rockyou' split of 9.9M passwords, evaluated on 'linkedin' test set of 40.6M passwords, both only containing passwords ≤ 10 characters.

For our models, we train on the 'rockyou' training split, generate 10^9 passwords each and count the matches in the 'linkedin' test data. Table 3 shows the results. We first observe that all trained models recover a significant amount of passwords from the 'linkedin' test data. Ranging from 3.2 (PassGAN) to 10.3M (VAE) there is large variance in the performance of the individual models. For these models we additionally observe a correlation between number of unique generated passwords and number of matches.

Both implementations of VAE and GPT2 respectively achieve very high matching results, with the character-based VAE representing the top-performer with 10.3M matches. Only the probabilistic PCFG algorithm can surpass this model by another 20%. The VAE and GPT2 models additionally score higher than all other comparison methods.

4.6   Operations in Latent Space

The learned latent space by the encoder imposes geometric connections among latent points that have some semantic similarity in the data space. This means that similar points in data space have latent representation that are close to each other. This property can be used also for password generation. Let us assume that we have the password `veronica2296` and we want to generate variants of this passwords. To this end we encode the password `veronica2296` into its latent representation z_t. We parametrize the posterior using the z_t as mean ($\mu = z_t$), sample latent codes from that region, $z_i \sim \mathcal{N}(\mu, \sigma \mathbf{I})$ with $\sigma = 0.001$, and then generate passwords by passing the latent codes to the decoder. The results from this task are presented in Table 4. One can see that most of the passwords generated from this region contain the word `veronica` in combination with different number or variants of the name `veronica` (e.g. `veronico`) and a number. This shows that our models have learned semantically meaningful latent space given the training set.

Table 4. Latent space models allow for conditioning generation on prior information. **Left:** Samples with latent representation close to the latent representation of `veronica2296`. **Right:** Conditional generation of passwords. We condition the generation on `***love***`.

veronica2286	veronica296			
veronica22U6	veronic22259	9alolove71u	nublove85/9	miblovenv11
verogama2296	veronica2269	licloverrs9	siclove00me	riglover2k
veroga_a2986	veronic2205	hicloven3ke	failoveye4	n2ulovemswo
verosgaj2!98	vertinac2219	lyaloveji8	gemloveso1	irolovesor
veronica2229	veroicata22U	ltelovejr*	vatlover10	mejlovey4u
veroneza2269	veron_ma2295	cetlovesder	biolove121	inudlove12

Having latent representation for each password allows us to also do conditional generation. Let `***love***` be a template password, where `*` is a placeholder for any character defined in the vocabulary. We can condition our model to generate passwords that contain the word 'love' in the middle, with three random characters as prefix and suffix by encoding `***love***` (representing the `*` by an `UNK` character) and sampling from the region in latent space. In Table 4 we present some conditionally generated samples. For a further thorough analysis of conditional password sampling in terms of EM-based algorithms we refer to [26].

5   Conclusion and Future Work

The present work illustrates various deep learning password generation techniques. Conducting a thorough unified analysis we discuss password-matching capabilities, variability and quality of sampling and robustness in training. On one hand, we bridge and extend previously established methods based on attention schemes and GANs; on the other hand, we provide a promising novel approach based on Variational Autoencoders that allows for efficient latent space modeling and further sampling mechanisms. Lastly, we hope our work will facilitate and provide benchmark lines for further deep learning and ML practitioners interested in the field of password guessing.

In terms of further investigation, the application of deep learning techniques to password generation poses further intriguing questions on the interplay between classical probabilistic methods and neural networks, where one would ultimately hope to construct more efficient and reliable domain-inspired password representation schemes - e.g. based on carefully crafted fragmentations.

Acknowledgement. This project was funded by the Federal Ministry of Education and Research (BMBF), FZK: 16KIS0818. The authors of this work were supported by the Competence Center for Machine Learning Rhine Ruhr (ML2R) which is funded by the Federal Ministry of Education and Research of Germany (grant nos. 01—S18038B, 01—S18038C). We gratefully acknowledge this support.

References

1. Hashcat - advanced password recovery. https://hashcat.net/hashcat/. Accessed 07 Dec 2020
2. Hashcat raking generated2.rule. https://github.com/evilmog/evilmog/wiki/Hashcat-Raking---generated2.rule. Accessed 07 Dec 2020
3. Have i been pwnd v1. https://hashes.org/leaks.php?id=70. Accessed 07 Dec 2020
4. John the ripper password cracker. https://www.openwall.com/john/. Accessed 07 Dec 2020
5. Linkedin leak. https://hashes.org/leaks.php?id=68. Accessed 07 Dec 2020
6. Myspace leak. https://weakpass.com/wordlist/22. Accessed 07 Dec 2020
7. Rockyou leak. https://weakpass.com/wordlist/90. Accessed 07 Dec 2020
8. Seclist compilation. https://weakpass.com/wordlist/50. Accessed 07 Dec 2020

9. Skullsecurity compilation. https://weakpass.com/wordlist/671. Accessed 07 Dec 2020
10. Troy hunt: Here's why [insert thing here] is not a password killer. https://www.troyhunt.com/heres-why-insert-thing-here-is-not-a-password-killer/. Accessed 07 Dec 2020
11. Yahoo leak. https://weakpass.com/wordlist/44. Accessed 07 Dec 2020
12. Youku leak. https://hashes.org/leaks.php?id=508. Accessed 07 Dec 2020
13. Zomato leak. https://hashes.org/leaks.php?id=587. Accessed 07 Dec 2020
14. Arjovsky, M., Chintala, S., Bottou, L.: Wasserstein generative adversarial networks. In: 34th International Conference on Machine Learning, ICML 2017 (2017)
15. Bowman, S.R., Vilnis, L., Vinyals, O., Dai, A.M., Jozefowicz, R., Bengio, S.: Generating sentences from a continuous space. arXiv preprint arXiv:1511.06349 (2015)
16. Chanda, K.: Password security: an analysis of password strengths and vulnerabilities. Int. J. Comput. Netw. Inf. Secur. **8**, 23–30 (2016)
17. Dell'Amico, M., Michiardi, P., Roudier, Y.: Password strength: an empirical analysis, pp. 1–9 (2010)
18. Goodfellow, I.J., et al.: Generative adversarial nets. In: Advances in Neural Information Processing Systems (2014)
19. Gulrajani, I., Ahmed, F., Arjovsky, M., Dumoulin, V., Courville, A.: Improved training of wasserstein GANs. In: Advances in Neural Information Processing Systems (2017)
20. Hitaj, B., Gasti, P., Ateniese, G., Perez-Cruz, F.: PassGAN: a deep learning approach for password guessing. In: Deng, R.H., Gauthier-Umaña, V., Ochoa, M., Yung, M. (eds.) ACNS 2019. LNCS, vol. 11464, pp. 217–237. Springer, Cham (2019). https://doi.org/10.1007/978-3-030-21568-2_11
21. Ioffe, S., Szegedy, C.: Batch normalization: accelerating deep network training by reducing internal covariate shift. In: 32nd International Conference on Machine Learning, ICML 2015 (2015)
22. Kingma, D.P., Ba, J.: Adam: a method for stochastic optimization. arXiv preprint arXiv:1412.6980 (2014)
23. Kingma, D.P., Welling, M.: Auto-encoding variational bayes. arXiv preprint arXiv:1312.6114 (2013)
24. Li, H., Chen, M., Yan, S., Jia, C., Li, Z.: Password guessing via neural language modeling. In: Chen, X., Huang, X., Zhang, J. (eds.) ML4CS 2019. LNCS, vol. 11806, pp. 78–93. Springer, Cham (2019). https://doi.org/10.1007/978-3-030-30619-9_7
25. Melicher, W., et al.: Fast, lean, and accurate: modeling password guessability using neural networks. In: 25th USENIX Security Symposium (USENIX Security 2016), Austin, TX, pp. 175–191. USENIX Association, August 2016
26. Pasquini, D., Gangwal, A., Ateniese, G., Bernaschi, M., Conti, M.: Improving password guessing via representation learning. In: 42nd IEEE Symposium on Security and Privacy (Oakland) (2021)
27. Rabiner, L., Juang, B.: An introduction to hidden Markov models. IEEE ASSP Mag. **3**(1), 4–16 (1986)
28. Radford, A., Wu, J., Child, R., Luan, D., Amodei, D., Sutskever, I.: Gpt2. Open AI (2019)
29. Sennrich, R., Haddow, B., Birch, A.: Neural machine translation of rare words with subword units. arXiv preprint arXiv:1508.07909 (2015)
30. Vaswani, A., et al.: Attention is all you need. In: Advances in Neural Information Processing Systems (2017)

31. Weir, M., Aggarwal, S., de Medeiros, B., Glodek, B.: Password cracking using probabilistic context-free grammars, pp. 391–405 (2009)
32. Zagoruyko, S., Komodakis, N.: Wide residual networks. In: British Machine Vision Conference 2016, BMVC 2016 (2016)

Dilated Residual Aggregation Network for Text-Guided Image Manipulation

Siwei Lu[1], Di Luo[1], Zhenguo Yang[1(✉)], Tianyong Hao[2], Qing Li[3], and Wenyin Liu[1,4(✉)]

[1] Guangdong University of Techonology, Guangzhou, China
{yzg,liuwy}@gdut.edu.cn
[2] South China Normal University, Guangzhou, China
[3] The Hong Kong Polytechnic University, Hong Kong, China
qing-prof.li@polyu.edu.hk
[4] Cyberspace Security Research Center, Peng Cheng Laboratory, Shenzhen, China

Abstract. Text-guided image manipulation aims to modify the visual attributes of images according to textual descriptions. Existing works either mismatch between generated images and textual descriptions or may pollute the text-irrelevant image regions. In this paper, we propose a dilated residual aggregation network (denoted as DRA) for text-guided image manipulation, which exploits a long-distance residual with dilated convolutions (RD) to aggregate the encoded visual content and style features and the textual features of the guiding descriptions. In particular, the dilated convolutions increase the receptive field without sacrificing spatial resolutions of intermediate features, benefiting to reconstructing the texture details matching with the textual descriptions. Furthermore, we propose an attention-guided injection module (AIM) to inject textual semantics into feature maps of DRA without polluting the text-irrelevant image regions by combining triplet attention mechanism and central biasing instance normalization. Quantitative and qualitative experiments conducted on the CUB-200-2011 and Oxford-102 datasets demonstrate the superior performance of the proposed DRA.

Keywords: Text-guided image manipulation · Long-distance residual · Attention-guide injection

1 Introduction

Text-guided image manipulation [1,2] aims to modify certain aspects of an image to meet users' preferences. On one hand, textual descriptions provide complementary semantics to the visual images from viewpoint of natural language. On the other hand, textual descriptions as nature carriers for humans to express their expectations benefit to the user-friendly interactions with machines.

In the context of text-guided image manipulation, generative adversarial networks (GANs) [3] are widely adopted. For instance, Dong et al. [1] proposed a GANs-based architecture to modify images according to given textual descriptions. Nam et al. [2] introduced a text-adaptive discriminator to provide word-level

© Springer Nature Switzerland AG 2021
I. Farkaš et al. (Eds.): ICANN 2021, LNCS 12893, pp. 28–40, 2021.
https://doi.org/10.1007/978-3-030-86365-4_3

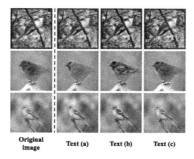

Original   Text (a)   Text (b)   Text (c)
image

Fig. 1. Illustration of DRA with different text as guidance for image manipulation. **Text (a):** "This small yellow bird has gray wings and a black bill." **Text (b):** "This small bird has a blue crown and white belly." **Text (c):** "A small brown bird with a brown crown has a white belly". (Color figure online)

feedback for the generator. However, the aforementioned methods fail to effectively integrate image and textual semantics through the traditional latent code injection (LCI) strategy [6], which directly concatenates image features with textual features, thus the results do not match with the text descriptions. For fine-grained manipulation, Yu et al. [5] proposed a unified framework (DMIT) to disentangle images into latent representations and used central biasing instance normalization (CBIN) [6] to inject textual semantics into image disentangled features. However, the generator of DMIT inevitably loses some information of the intermediate features by simply stacking a bunch of residual blocks, which makes it difficult to reconstruct the texture details matching with the given text. In addition, DMIT may pollute text-irrelevant regions of the image, as the textual information may not be injected into the critical areas of the image accurately.

To reconstruct the texture details, quite a few works focus on retaining intermediate information in the residual networks. For instance, Zhang et al. [7] proposed a residual dense network, which integrated intermediate features via dense connections in an individual residual block. Liu et al. [8] proposed a residual feature aggregation network (RFANet) for image super-resolution, which grouped several residual blocks and directly sent the features of the local residual blocks to the final block with the intermediate features. In the context of text-guided image manipulation, RFANet cannot fully integrate the semantics of images and textual descriptions, which forces the model to generate some texture details inconsistent with the textual descriptions, even pollutes the text-irrelevant image regions. In terms of injecting the textual features, attention mechanism (e.g., SENet [9] and non-local block [10]) can be used. However, these methods fail to capture the cross-dimension dependencies between different dimensions (e.g., channel dimension, height dimension, and width dimension) of the images, which affects the performance of the model.

In this paper, we design a dilated residual aggregation network (DRA) to modify the visual attributes of images according to various textual descriptions, as illustrated in Fig. 1. Given the visual content and style features extracted from images and textual features from descriptions, DRA adopts a long-distance residual with dilated convolutions (RD) to aggregate the features, which avoids losing intermediate information during network propagations. Particularly, the dilated convolutions increase the receptive field to obtain high-level semantic information while keeping the spatial resolutions of the feature maps. Meantime, DRA introduces an attention-guided injection module (AIM) to focus on the critical areas corresponding to textual descriptions by using triplet attention mechanism [11], benefiting to injection of textual information into image feature maps, which keeps the text-irrelevant regions free from being polluted.

The contributions of this paper are summarized as follows:

- We design a dilated residual aggregation network (DRA) to integrate multi-modal (text and image) semantics for text-guided image manipulation.
- We propose a long-distance residual with dilated convolutions (RD), which aggregates local informative residual features to capture visual and textual semantics for reconstructing the texture details matching with the textual descriptions.
- We devise an attention-guide injection module (AIM) to inject textual semantics into the corresponding feature maps without polluting the text-irrelevant image regions.

The rest of the paper is organized as follows. Section 2 reviews the related works. Section 3 introduces the details of the proposed DRA. Experiments and discussions are conducted in Sect. 4, followed by conclusions in Sect. 5.

2   Related Work

Text-guided image manipulation has attracted much attention, which provides users with a user-friendly tool to modify an image given textual descriptions. Dong et al. [1] proposed an encoder-decoder architecture based on text-to-image method to synthesize manipulated images according to textual descriptions. Sugimoto et al. [4] proposed to model the foreground and background distributions with two different discriminators. Nam et al. [2] proposed a text-adaptive discriminator which provided specific word-level training feedback to the generator. However, the aforementioned methods directly concatenate the image features with textual features by latent code injection (LCI) strategy [6], resulting in unsatisfactory modification on the text-required image attributes. Recently, Li et al. [18,19] proposed multi-stage networks with a novel text-image combination module and a word-level discriminator, which was limited on the efficiency. In addition, inspired by disentangled representation learning, Yu et al. [5] proposed to learn the disentangled features of images and used style-based injection strategy (e.g., AdaIN [13] and CBIN [6]) to inject the textual information into the disentangled features for fine-grained text-guided image manipulation, which unavoidably neglected some information of the intermediate features for reconstructing the texture details and may pollute the text-irrelevant regions of the original images.

3   Methodology

3.1   Overview of DRA

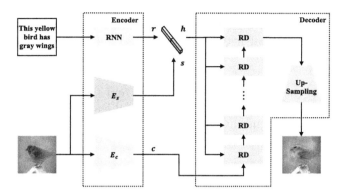

Fig. 2. Overview of the proposed DRA.

In the context of image generation, high-resolution intermediate feature maps are favorable for reconstructing texture details while large receptive field benefits to capturing high-level semantic information. To this end, we propose dilated residual aggregation network (DRA), which adopts an encoder-decoder architecture to modify images according to textual descriptions. As shown in Fig. 2, the encoder extracts the textual features, content features, and style features from textual descriptions and images, respectively. In terms of the decoder, it stacks a certain number of long-distance residuals with dilated convolutions (RD) to integrate the encoded features, which exploits attention-guided injection module (AIM) to inject textual semantics. The details of the encoder and decoder are specified subsequently.

3.2   Encoder of DRA

Given the raw images $\mathcal{X} = \{x_1, x_2, \cdots, x_{n-1}, x_n\}$, where $x_n \in \mathbb{R}^{H \times W \times 3}$ and textual descriptions $\mathcal{T} = \{t_1, t_2, \cdots, t_{k-1}, t_k\}$, the encoder of DRA extracts disentangled visual features corresponding to content and style as well as textual features, respectively. Furthermore, the visual style features are concatenated with the textual features, which will be sent to the decoder of DRA in addition to the visual content features.

(1) **Visual content features.** We build a content encoder E_c by exploiting convolutional down-sampling layers and residual blocks [12,13] to extract visual content features. For a given image $x_i \in \mathcal{X}$, the content encoder E_c extracts visual content features c as follows,

$$c = E_c(x_i) \tag{1}$$

(2) **Visual style features.** In terms of the visual style features s, we build a style encoder E_s by using a fully convolutional network with global pooling [13], which is defined as follows,

$$s = E_s(x_i) \tag{2}$$

(3) **Textual features.** We feed textual description into a pretrained bidirectional recurrent neural network (B-RNN) to obtain textual features r as follows,

$$r = R(t) \tag{3}$$

where $R(\cdot)$ is the pretrained RNN network and $t \in \mathcal{T}$ is the input textual description. Given the style features s, textual features r, we obtain hybrid features h by concatenating them jointly. Furthermore, the hybrid features and content features will be sent to the decoder of DRA, which is specified subsequently.

3.3 Decoder of DRA

Given the hybrid features h and visual content features c obtained by the encoder, we exploit a decoder to modify the visual attributes of image (e.g., texture, and color) according to textual descriptions as follows,

$$x_m = G(c, h) = G(c, s, r) \tag{4}$$

where G is the decoder of DRA and x_m is the output modified image.

In particular, the low-level features may be forgotten during encoding with the networks go deeper, which suffers from gradient vanishing as well. As a result, researchers [14,16] usually stack a number of residual blocks to pass the low-level features from the former network layers to the latter ones in order to alleviate gradient vanishing. On one hand, the information underlying the intermediate layers may be forgotten, leading to unrealistic texture during image reconstruction. On the other hand, the existing works usually adopt conventional convolutions, which suffer from either limited receptive field or low-resolution feature maps. As shown in Fig. 3, DRA exploits long-distance residuals with dilated convolutions (RD) to keep intermediate features by long-distance residuals and obtain high-resolution feature maps with high-level semantics by dilated convolutions. Furthermore, DRA uses an attention-guide injection module (AIM) to inject textual semantics into feature maps of DRA without polluting the text-irrelevant image regions.

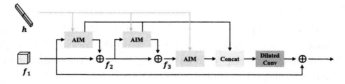

Fig. 3. Details of the long-distance residual with dilated convolutions (RD).

(1) **Long-distance residual with dilated convolutions (RD).** To keep intermediate information in the residual networks, we design a long-distance residual with dilated convolutions (RD) as shown in Fig. 3. RD groups three attention-guided injection modules (AIM, whose details are shown in Fig. 4) through long-distance residual connections, in which the output features of the first two AIMs are directly connected with the output of the subsequent AIM. Furthermore, we adopt a dilated convolution with dilation rate d to fuse the aggregated features before the element-wise addition with the input features. The output of the RD can be represented as follows,

$$RD\left(f_1, h\right) = DConv\left(A_3\left(f_3, h\right) \| A_2\left(f_2, h\right) \| A_1\left(f_1, h\right)\right) + f_1 \qquad (5)$$

where $f_n = \{f_1, f_2, f_3\}$ denote latent feature maps in RD, h denotes hybrid features, $DConv(\cdot)$ is dilated convolution, $A_n(\cdot)$ denotes the output of the n-th AIM, '$\|$' is concatenation operation. The feature map of the second layer in RD is defined as follows,

$$f_2 = A_1\left(f_1, h\right) + f_1 \qquad (6)$$

The feature map of the third layer in RD is defined as follows,

$$f_3 = A_2\left(f_2, h\right) + f_2 \qquad (7)$$

Instead of stacking residual blocks, the residual aggregation architecture in RD aggregates local residual features for retaining intermediate information. In addition, dilated convolution in RD increases the receptive field without changing the spatial resolutions of the feature maps. Furthermore, a number of RDs that are equipped with dilated convolutions in different dilation rates d (e.g., $d = 1, 2, 4, 2, 1$, respectively) can be cascaded in the DRA, aiming to capture multi-scale semantic information from the aggregated features, which benefits to the reconstruction of texture details corresponding to textual descriptions.

(2) **Attention-guide injection module (AIM).** In order to inject text information into images, we propose an attention-guide injection module (AIM), as shown in Fig. 4, which consists of two branches. One branch contains convolutional layer, central biasing instance normalization layer, ReLU, convolutional layer, central biasing instance normalization layer, dropout layer,

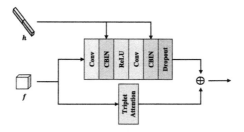

Fig. 4. Details of the attention-guided injection module (AIM).

etc. The other branch is a triplet attention block [11] to capture important features, focusing on the critical image areas corresponding to textual descriptions. The output of AIM can be represented as follows,

$$A(f,h) = Inject\,(f,h) + Triplet\,(f) \tag{8}$$

where $f \in \mathbb{R}^{C \times H \times W}$ is the input tensor, h is the hybrid features concatenated by visual style features and textual features, $Inject(\cdot)$ denotes the output of the upper branch, and $Triplet(\cdot)$ denotes the output of the triplet attention block.

In particular, the triplet attention block is defined as a lightweight three-branch module. Compared with other attention mechanism [9,17], the triplet attention mechanism requires few learnable parameters and can calculate the cross-dimension dependencies between the channel dimension (C), height dimension (H), and width dimension (W) of image features, which captures richer critical information for guiding the injection of textual information into the image feature maps.

3.4 Objective Function of DRA

DRA aims to disentangle latent content and style features and make image manipulation simultaneously. More specifically, given the input image $x_i \in \mathcal{X}$ and textual description $t \in \mathcal{T}$, the loss terms of DRA are specified as follows.

(1) **Disentangling latent features.** The loss for feature disentangling $\mathcal{L}_{cVAE}$ [5] consists of a few terms as follows,

$$\mathcal{L}_{cVAE} = \lambda_{rec}\mathcal{L}_{rec} + \lambda_{KL}\mathcal{L}_{KL} + \mathcal{L}_{D_c} \tag{9}$$

where $\mathcal{L}_{rec}$ denotes the image reconstruction loss, $\mathcal{L}_{KL}$ denotes KL-divergence loss using the prior Gaussian distribution $\mathcal{N}(0, I)$ to constrain the style feature space, and $\mathcal{L}_{D_c}$ denotes the conditional adversarial loss in content feature space [5], which encourages E_c obtaining the text-irrelevant content c.

(2) **Image manipulation.** The loss term $\mathcal{L}_{Mani}$ is defined as follows,

$$\mathcal{L}_{Mani} = \lambda_{rec}\mathcal{L}_{re.g.} + \mathcal{L}_{D_x} \tag{10}$$

where $\mathcal{L}_{reg}$ denotes latent regression loss [13] that enforces cycle consistency to the content and the style features, and $\mathcal{L}_{D_x}$ denotes the conditional adversary loss in pixel space [5]. $\mathcal{L}_{D_x}$ matches the distributions of manipulation images and real images, discriminates the mismatched pair of the real image x_i and textual description t_m, and encourages the generator to generate images that correspond to t_m, which is defined as follows,

$$\mathcal{L}_{D_x} = \mathbb{E}_{x_i \sim \mathcal{X}}\left[\,log\,(D_x\,(x_i, R\,(t_i))) + \mathbb{E}_{t_m \sim (\mathcal{T} - \{t_i\})}\left[\tfrac{1}{2}\,log\,(1 - D_x\,(x_i, R\,(t_m)))\right.\right.$$
$$\left.\left. + \mathbb{E}_{s_m \sim \mathcal{N}}\left[\tfrac{1}{2}\,log\,(1 - D_x\,(G\,(E_c\,(x_i), s_m, R\,(t_m)), R\,(t_m)))\right]\right]\right] \tag{11}$$

where D_x denotes the discriminator used in pixel space, s_m is the style feature sampled from Gaussian distribution and t_m is the target textual description.

In summary, the overall objective function of DRA is defined as follows,

$$\min_{G,E_c,E_s} \max_{D_c,D_x} \mathcal{L}_{cVAE} + \mathcal{L}_{Mani} \tag{12}$$

4 Experiments

4.1 Datasets

(1) **CUB-200-2011** contains 200 bird species with 11,788 images, and each bird has 10 textual descriptions. For preprocessing, we crop all images by using annotated bounding boxes of the birds and resize them to 128×128.

(2) **Oxford-102** contains 8,189 images of 102 flower species, and each image has 10 corresponding text descriptions. We scale the initial images to 143×143 and crop the images in size of 128×128 around the center.

For quantitative evaluations, Fréchet inception distance (FID), Peak Signal-to-Noise Ratio (PSNR), and Structural Similarity (SSIM) are adopted. For qualitative evaluations, Amazon Mechanical Turk (AMT) is used.

4.2 Baselines

(1) **SISGAN** [1] takes the original image and textual description of the target image as input to generate manipulated image.

(2) **PDGAN** [4] proposes two discriminators which guide the generator to generate the foreground and background of the manipulated image.

(3) **TAGAN** [2] provides word-level feedback for the generator by introducing a text-adaptive discriminator.

(4) **DMIT** [5] is a unified image-to-image translation model that takes the original image and target attribute vector as input. The target attribute vector is extracted from the input of textual description by a RNN network.

(5) **MMFL** [15] is a text-guided image inpainting model that takes the corrupted image and textual description as input.

4.3 Implementation Details

We train DRA by using Adam optimizer with a learning rate of 0.0001 and exponential decay rates $(\beta_1, \beta_2) = (0.5, 0.999)$, respectively. The batch size is set as 8 for both datasets, and the hyper-parameters of the loss functions are set as $\lambda_{rec} = 10$, $\lambda_{KL} = 0.01$, and $\lambda_{reg} = 1$, respectively.

4.4 Results

(1) **Quantitative comparisons.** Table 1 summarizes the quantitative performance of baselines and DRA on the two datasets, from which we have some observations. 1) DMIT and DRA tend to obtain better performance than

Table 1. Quantitative comparisons of the approaches. $^-$ indicates lower is better and $^+$ indicates higher is better.

	CUB-200-2011			Oxford-102		
	FID$^-$	SSIM$^+$	PSNR$^+$	FID$^-$	SSIM$^+$	PSNR$^+$
SISGAN	67.24	0.193	11.27	112.5	0.043	7.42
PDGAN	34.49	0.736	19.01	90.83	0.065	7.99
TAGAN	32.93	0.886	22.34	46.07	0.575	20.64
MMFL	29.69	0.811	19.84	37.37	0.817	20.16
DMIT	14.53	0.846	25.23	34.41	0.796	25.33
DRA	**13.38**	**0.903**	**28.48**	**33.13**	0.823	**26.08**

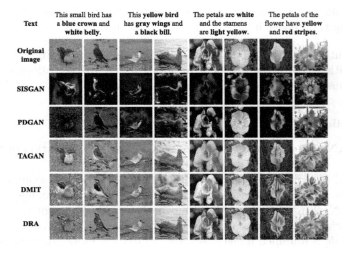

Fig. 5. Qualitative comparisons on the CUB-200-2011 and Oxford-102 datasets.

the methods that concatenate image features with textual features directly, e.g., SISGAN, PDGAN, TAGAN, and MMFL. The reason is that DMIT and DRA inject textual semantics into disentangled style and content visual features, which allows the models to perform fine-grained manipulation. 2) Compared with DMIT, the proposed DRA achieves better FID values and higher PSNR and SSIM scores, benefiting from that RD aggregates a large amount of intermediate information to reconstruct image texture details, and AIM injects the textual semantics into corresponding areas of images.

(2) **Qualitative comparisons.** Intuitively, some visual examples generated by the approaches are shown in Fig. 5, from which we have some observations. 1) SISGAN and PDGAN fail to generate images that match with the textual descriptions and may destroy text-irrelevant image regions. The reason is that directly concatenating image features with textual features through LCI strategy cannot effectively combine the visual information and

textual semantics. 2) TAGAN can roughly modify images according to textual descriptions due to the injection of word-level semantics, while the quality of the manipulated images is unsatisfactory. 3) DMIT generates modified images matching with the textual descriptions well, while the images may lose some texture details and the text-irrelevant regions have been polluted, resulting in unrealistic and unnatural images. 4) Overall, DRA can generate realistic images with clear texture details matching with the textual descriptions quite well without polluting the text-irrelevant image regions.

Table 2. Ranking scores of AMT results.

	Semantic consistency	Background consistency
SISGAN	4.058	4.061
PDGAN	3.613	3.618
TAGAN	3.365	3.367
DMIT	2.137	2.289
DRA	**1.835**	**1.678**

(3) **Qualitative comparisons with AMT.** We randomly selected 100 manipulated images of the approaches in CUB-200-2011 dataset, and recruit 20 volunteers to rank them according to text-image semantics consistency, and background consistency with the original images. The ranking scores are summarized in Table 2, from which we can observe that the proposed DRA outperforms the baselines, achieving the best ranking scores on both aspects. The experimental results manifest that DRA generates manipulated images matching with the given textual descriptions without polluting text-irrelevant regions of images.

4.5   Ablation Studies

The proposed DRA contains two main components, including a long-distance residual with dilated convolutions (RD) and an attention-guided injection module (AIM). In order to verify their effectiveness, we evaluate the performance of the variations of DRA as shown in Table 3, including DRA without RD (DRA_RD), DRA without triplet attention mechanism (DRA_AIM). From the table, we have some observations. 1) DRA with RD and AIM benefits to improving FID metric, which indicates that the modified images are more realistic and natural. 2) DRA without AIM may obtain higher PSNR and SSIM scores, while text-related content of the images may not be modified or the text-irrelevant regions may be polluted, as shown in the visual examples in Fig. 6. Furthermore, we can observe that the images generated by DRA_RD in Fig. 6 may lose some realistic texture details.

4.6　Failure Examples

Figure 7 shows some failure examples of DRA, from which we can observe that the modified birds are quite consistent with textual descriptions. However, the color of fingers has been changed as well, which is not expected. The reason may be that the shape of the fingers and bird are quite similar with unclear boundaries, which may distract the model.

Table 3. Performance of the variations of DRA on both datasets.

	CUB-200-2011			Oxford-102		
	FID$^-$	SSIM$^+$	PSNR$^+$	FID$^-$	SSIM$^+$	PSNR$^+$
DRA_RD	13.97	0.883	27.67	34.77	0.770	24.18
DRA_AIM	14.39	**0.923**	**28.98**	35.48	**0.825**	**26.24**
DRA	**13.38**	0.903	28.48	**33.13**	0.823	26.08

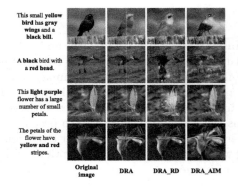

Fig. 6. Visual examples of the variations of DRA on both datasets.

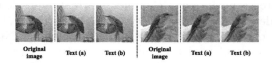

Fig. 7. Failure examples of DRA. **Text (a):** "This particular bird with a red head and breast and features grey wings." **Text (b):** "This small yellow bird has gray wings and a black bill." (Color figure online)

5   Conclusions

We present a dilated residual aggregation network (DRA) for text-guided image manipulation, which reconstructs image texture details matching with textual descriptions by long-distance residual with dilated convolution (RD) while protecting the text-irrelevant regions of images from pollution by attention-guided injection module (AIM). Quantitative and qualitative experiments conducted on two public datasets manifest the superior performance of DRA in terms of both the effectiveness in semantic consistency to the textual guidance and retention of text-irrelevant information.

Acknowledgment. This work is supported by the National Natural Science Foundation of China (No. 62076073, No. 61902077), the Guangdong Basic and Applied Basic Research Foundation (No. 2020A1515010616), Science and Technology Program of Guangzhou (No. 202102020524, No. 202007040005), the Guangdong Innovative Research Team Program (No. 2014ZT05G157), the Key-Area Research and Development Program of Guangdong Province (2019B010136001), and the Science and Technology Planning Project of Guangdong Province (LZC0023), and Hong Kong RGC CRF Project C1031-18G.

References

1. Dong, H., Yu, S., Wu, C., Guo, Y.: Semantic image synthesis via adversarial learning. In: Proceedings of the IEEE International Conference on Computer Vision (2017)
2. Nam, S., Kim, Y., Kim, S. J.: Text-adaptive generative adversarial networks: manipulating images with natural language. arXiv preprint arXiv:1810.11919(2018)
3. Goodfellow, I.J., et al.: Generative adversarial networks. arXiv preprint arXiv:1406.2661 (2014)
4. Vo, D.M., Sugimoto, A.: Paired-D GAN for semantic image synthesis. In: Jawahar, C.V., Li, H., Mori, G., Schindler, K. (eds.) ACCV 2018. LNCS, vol. 11364, pp. 468–484. Springer, Cham (2019). https://doi.org/10.1007/978-3-030-20870-7_29
5. Yu, X., Chen, Y., Li, T., Liu, S., Li, G.: Multi-mapping image-to-image translation via learning disentanglement. arXiv preprint arXiv:1909.07877 (2019)
6. Yu, X., Ying, Z., Li, T., Liu, S., Li, G.: Multi-mapping image-to-image translation with central biasing normalization. arXiv preprint arXiv:1806.10050 (2018)
7. Zhang, Y., Tian, Y.: Residual dense network for image super-resolution. In: Proceedings of the IEEE Conference on Computer Vision and Pattern Recognition (2018)
8. Liu, J., Zhang, W., Tang, Y., Tang, J., Wu, G.: Residual feature aggregation network for image super-resolution. In: Proceedings of the IEEE/CVF Conference on Computer Vision and Pattern Recognition (2020)
9. Hu, J., Shen, L., Sun, G.: Squeeze-and-excitation networks. In: Proceedings of the IEEE Conference on Computer Vision and Pattern Recognition (2018)
10. Wang, X., Girshick, R., Gupta, A., He, K.: Non-local neural networks. In: Proceedings of the IEEE Conference on Computer Vision and Pattern Recognition (2018)

11. Misra, D., Nalamada, T., Arasanipalai, A.U., Hou, Q.: Rotate to attend: convolutional triplet attention module. In: Proceedings of the IEEE/CVF Winter Conference on Applications of Computer Vision (2021)
12. Huang, X., Liu, M.Y., Belongie, S.: Multimodal unsupervised image-to-image translation. In: Proceedings of the European Conference on Computer Vision (2018)
13. Anokhin, I., Solovev, P., Korzhenkov, D., Kharlamov, A., Khakhulin, T.: High-resolution daytime translation without domain labels. In: Proceedings of the IEEE/CVF Conference on Computer Vision and Pattern Recognition (2020)
14. Lee, H.Y., Tseng, H.Y., Huang, J.B., Singh, M., Yang, M.H.: Diverse image-to-image translation via disentangled representations. In: Proceedings of the European Conference on Computer Vision (2018)
15. Lin, Q., Yan, B., Li, J., Tan, W.: MMFL: multimodal fusion learning for text-guided image inpainting. In: ACM MM (2020)
16. Chen, S., Huang, K., Xiong, D., Li, B., Claesen, L.: Fine-grained channel pruning for deep residual neural networks. In: Farkaš, I., Masulli, P., Wermter, S. (eds.) ICANN 2020. LNCS, vol. 12397, pp. 3–14. Springer, Cham (2020). https://doi.org/10.1007/978-3-030-61616-8_1
17. Zhang, H., Goodfellow, I., Metaxas, D., Odena, A.: Self-attention generative adversarial networks. In: International Conference on Machine Learning (2019)
18. Li, B., Qi, X.: Manigan: text-guided image manipulation. In: Proceedings of the IEEE/CVF Conference on Computer Vision and Pattern Recognition (2020)
19. Li, B., Qi, X.: Lightweight Generative Adversarial Networks for Text-Guided Image Manipulation. arXiv preprint arXiv:2010.12136 (2020)

Denoising AutoEncoder Based Delete and Generate Approach for Text Style Transfer

Ting Hu[✉], Haojin Yang, and Christoph Meinel

Hasso Plattner Institute, University of Potsdam, Potsdam, Germany
{ting.hu,haojin.yang,meinel}@hpi.de

Abstract. Text style transfer task is transferring sentences to other styles while preserving the semantics as much as possible. In this work, we study a two-step text style transfer method on non-parallel datasets. In the first step, the style-relevant words are detected and deleted from the sentences in the source style corpus. In the second step, the remaining style-devoid contents are fed into a Natural Language Generation model to produce sentences in the target style. The model consists of a style encoder and a pre-trained DenoisingAutoEncoder. The former extracts style features of each style corpus and the latter reconstructs source sentences during training and generates sentences in the target style during inference from given contents. We conduct experiments on two text sentiment transfer datasets and comprehensive comparisons with other relevant methods in terms of several evaluation aspects. Evaluation results show that our method outperforms others in terms of sentence fluency and achieves a decent tradeoff between content preservation and style transfer intensity. The superior performance on the Caption dataset illustrates our method's potential advantage on occasions of limited data.

Keywords: Text style transfer · Denoising autoencoder · Natural Language Generation

1 Introduction

Text style transfer is a vibrant research area that attracts sustained attention [4,5,9,24]. The task is to transfer given sentences into other styles, meanwhile, preserve the semantics as far as possible [2]. The styles refer to pre-defined categories of texts such as sentiment [7], formality [16], and gender [13]. Text style transfer approaches have been integrated into many practical applications [3]. The most relevant example is widely used writing tools [3], where text style transfer methods enable users to switch their writings among different styles while preserving the contents. Though many algorithms have been explored on parallel text style transfer task, the lack of parallel data leads to more recent research on the non-parallel task setting, where only corpora in different styles are available.

The predominant approaches manage to either disentangle the style features and semantic information in the latent representations of texts or exteriorly disentangle style-relevant words and style-devoid contents [7,11,19]. In general, the

© Springer Nature Switzerland AG 2021
I. Farkaš et al. (Eds.): ICANN 2021, LNCS 12893, pp. 41–52, 2021.
https://doi.org/10.1007/978-3-030-86365-4_4

texts' latent representations are obtained by models like AutoEncoder (AE) [18] and Variational AutoEncoder (VAE) [8]. The disentanglement can be achieved by applying strategies such as adversarial training [20]. However, the latent space's non-smoothness may lead to influent sentences, and the introduction of adversarial training poses a rise in the training instability. In terms of exterior style and contents disentanglement, [7] firstly proposes the three-step text style transfer process, where the style related n-grams are deleted from the sentence, the corresponding n-grams in the target style are then retrieved, and the content remaining in the sentence and retrieved n-grams are combined to generate transfer results. Obviously, the critical factors that impact the transfer performance are how to define the style relevant n-grams, how to retrieve the target-style n-grams, and the generative model's rewriting capability.

Our work follows the idea of [7] while skipping the retrieval step, considering its inflexibility and possible failures. For the first step, we detect and delete style related words or phrases in each source sentence, i.e., style makers, and keep the rest of the sentence, i.e., content. For the second step, we feed the content into a generative model that directly produces a target-style sentence. We think the model's generation capability is important under the circumstance, while the exploration of varied language models in current works [5,19] is insufficient. For instance, [7] employs a Recurrent Neural Network (RNN) as the generative model, [19] uses the pre-trained language model GPT [15], and [5] bases their work on the Transformer [21] architecture. We further regard mapping content texts into intact sentences as a denoising process. The large pre-trained Denoising AutoEncoder (DAE) BART [6] with robust denoising and reasoning capability is therefore employed in our application scenario.

The remaining of the paper is organized as follows. In Sect. 2, we introduce various approaches related to text style transfer. In Sect. 3, we describe our method and the model architecture. In Sect. 4, we describe our experiments and analyze the results. Lastly, we draw the conclusion in Sect. 5. We summarize our contributions as follows.

- We propose a pre-trained Denoising AutoEncoder based framework for the delete and generate approach on the text style transfer task.
- We conduct experiments on Yelp and Caption datasets [7] and detailed comparisons with other variants of three-step text style transfer methods.
- Experiments demonstrate that our approach achieves decent and stable performance on two datasets on different evaluation aspects. The good performance on the Caption dataset indicates its underlying advantage over others in applications where only a small amounts of data are available.

2   Related Work

Text style transfer tasks can be categorized as parallel, non-parallel, and label-free. In parallel data setting, pairs of sentences with different styles are provided. The seq-to-seq model and its variants [16] are commonly used in this task. Since parallel text pairs could be difficult to collect, many methods [5,7,24] focus on the non-parallel setting, where only the source and the target style corpus are available. Some recent works [4,9,17] explore label-free approaches that further get rid of any training style labels and manipulate sentences into arbitrary styles during inference. In this work, we study the non-parallel text style transfer task.

There are three primary methods for text style transfer with non-parallel data: representation disentanglement, back-translation, and sentence editing. Representation disentanglement approaches generally follow the process of encoding, manipulating, and decoding [2]. AE [18], VAE [8], and Generative Adversarial Network [25] have been used to encode the input texts into representations and decode the manipulated representations into target style texts. The manipulation procedure is based on representation disentanglement, where the style information and style-devoid semantic information are disentangled by applying an additional style classifier [9], or adversarial learning [20].

Back-translation is commonly used in machine translation. When it comes to text style transfer, one route is iterative back-translation [24], consisting of two steps: (1) Initialize two specific style transfer models and produce pseudo-parallel corpora. (2) Iteratively update transfer models and produce better pseudo-parallel data. [14] applies online back-translation, where the latent codes devoid of style information are obtained through back-translation, and multiple decoders are then employed to produce texts in different styles.

Our approach belongs to the sentence editing category, firstly proposed by [7]. Unlike representation disentanglement, this type of method directly disentangles style words and content words at the sentence level. The sentence editing process is: (1) Delete the source style markers in each sentence, and obtain the remaining content. (2) Retrieve the counterpart style markers in the target style corpus. (3) Combine the content and the retrieved target markers and generate a fluent transferred sentence.

For the first step, there are multiple ways to detect the markers. [7] defines the salience of an n-gram with respect to the source style to be its relative frequency in the source corpus versus the target corpus. The n-grams of which the salience are higher than a specified threshold are declared as the style markers. [11] calculates the ratio of mean Term Frequency-Inverse Document Frequency (TF-IDF) between two style corpus for each n-gram and regards the normalized ratio as the salience. [19] trains a BERT classifier using the training corpora and considers words with attention weights larger than average as the markers. [22] employs the frequency-ratio method to predict the markers, supplemented by the attention weights method.

The second step is to retrieve each content-only source sentence's closest neighbor in the content-only target corpus. Then the deleted markers in the retrieved content-only target sentence are the corresponding target-style markers. In order to search for the nearest neighbor, sentence embeddings are generally used to evaluate the similarities between the content-only sentences, such as TF-IDF, Glove Embeddings, and Universal Sentence Encoder.

For the generation step, [7] feeds the content and retrieved target markers into an RNN to produce transferred outputs. [19] further feeds them into a pre-trained language model GPT [15] to generate fluent sentences. Considering markers retrieval may fail if the target corpus does not have sentences similar to that in the source corpus, some works circumvent the retrieval step and train a generative model that directly maps the input contents into sentences in a specific style. [19] concatenates the source style label, the content, and the original complete sentence as the input of GPT and fine-tune it to reconstruct the original sentence. During inference, the model produces the transferred sentence given the target style label concatenated with the content. [5] employs the Transformer [21] architecture, where the encoder's input is the content tokens, and the decoder's input is the original sentences prepended with the style labels. The model is trained to minimize the reconstruction loss and the style loss measured by a pre-trained classifier.

3   Approach

The Non-parallel text style transfer setting is as follows. Source style corpus and target style corpus C_s and C_t are given. Here, we consider negative and positive sentiments as two styles. The sentiment transfer model is supposed to transfer each sentence in C_s to the target sentiment implied in C_t and vice versa. Transferred texts are considered to preserve the semantics of the source sentence and accord with the target style. We divide the text style transfer process into deleting and generating procedures described below.

3.1   Delete

We need to at first detect the markers in both style corpora. Since we are focusing on semantic text transfer in this work, the assumption is that different sentiments can be captured by the most frequent N-grams. As [7] described, the salience of an n-gram u with respect to the source style is defined by its relative frequency in the source corpus C_s, that is,

$$s(u, C_s) = \frac{count(u, C_s) + \lambda}{count(u, C_s) + count(u, C_t) + \lambda} \qquad (1)$$

where $count(u, C_s)$ is the number of times that u appears in C_s, $count(u, C_t)$ is the number of times that u appears in C_t, and λ is a smoothing parameter. The n-grams of which the salience scores are above a pre-defined threshold are then regarded as markers. The selection of the threshold is obviously of importance. A lower threshold leads to more markers and fewer contents, which provides a broader space for exploring transfer intensity. A higher threshold eventually results in a stronger content constraint and limited transfer intensity. In effect, this is the tradeoff between content preservation and transfer intensity that many text style transfer models go through.

We also attempted to employ the method of [19] to detect markers, where a BERT classifier pre-trained by two corpora is used to measure words' salience according to their attention weights. However, the detection results are inferior

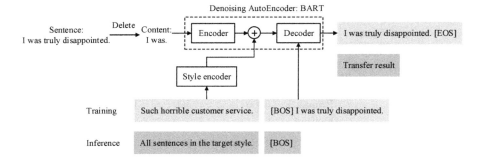

Fig. 1. The two-step text style transfer process. The words in red are deleted markers. The style encoder has the same architecture as the encoder and is initialized by its parameters. Token [BOS] and [EOS] stand for the beginning and the end of a sentence, respectively. When training, a random source-style sentence is fed into the style encoder, and the decoder is trained to reconstruct the original sentence. When inference, all target-style sentences are fed into the style encoder to obtain the mean style vector, based on which the decoder auto-regressively generates the transferred sentence.

to this simple statistical method. The possible reason could be the indirect and unclear relationship between the words' style representation capabilities and their attention weights.

3.2 Generate

For this step, the pre-trained Denoising AutoEncoder BART [6] is used as our basic framework. BART consists of a bidirectional encoder like BERT and a uni-directional decoder like GPT. BART is pre-trained to reconstruct input sentences corrupted by shuffling, tokens deletion, and spans of texts masking. Our basic idea is to regard the marker deleting procedure as the noise that BART is pre-trained to overcome. Hence, the encoder's inputs are the style devoid contents obtained from the deleting step, and the decoder's inputs are the corresponding intact sentences. The encoder-decoder architecture is fine-tuned to reconstruct the original sentences.

However, we need two separate style transfer models for each style under this setting, making style transfer inflexible. Inspired by [4,17], we keep the single BART architecture and employ an additional style encoder to extract style information from sentences in the same style as the original intact sentences. The style encoder has the same architecture as the encoder of BART and is initialized by its parameters. We conduct a max-pooling operation on the final output hidden states of the style encoder to obtain the style vector. Then the style vector is added to the content encoder's top hidden states which are used as the initial hidden states of the decoder.

The complete process framework is illustrated in Fig. 1. During training, the decoder combines the style features extracted by the style encoder and the

Table 1. Dataset statistics.

Dataset	Sentiment	Training set	Dev set	Test set
Yelp	Positive	270k	2000	500
	Negative	180k	2000	500
Caption	Humorous	6000	300	0
	Romantic	6000	300	0
	Factual	0	0	300

content information extracted by the content encoder and reconstructs original sentences. For inference, we only alter the style encoder's input to be a random target style sentence, and the decoder is expected to generate sentences in the target style. In practical implementation, we find that the randomly chosen sentence may lead to weak transfer intensity, considering the dataset is noisy, and sentences have varied style intensity. Consequently, we use the trained style encoder to obtain all style vectors from the source style corpus and the target style corpus, respectively, and take the mean vector on each corpus as the representative style vector, which is then used by the decoder to produce transferred results. The potential benefits of our training strategy are: i) the additional style encoder has seen sentences in both styles and learns to extract the most salient features regarding two styles; ii) even sentences in the same style could have variations in style and semantics, the decoder learns to discard disturbing information and make better use of useful information and becomes more robust.

Our method is different from [17], where only a small set of most representative sentences are selected and contribute to two mean style vectors. The deviation of them is considered as the basic transfer direction, with a hyperparameter β involved in the instance-wise transfer direction determination. In contrast, our model has seen sentences in both styles during training. The style encoder learns to extract the most salient features regarding two styles, and the deviation operation is not a must.

4   Experiments

4.1   Datasets

We conduct experiments on two sentiment style transfer datasets provided by [7]: Yelp and Caption. Yelp dataset contains business reviews on Yelp, and each review is labeled as positive or negative sentiment. The Caption is originally a parallel dataset, where caption pairs in the training set are labeled as romantic and humorous, respectively. Only factual captions are provided in the test set, and the style transfer model is supposed to transfer them into romantic and humorous sentiment. In our implementation, we treat Caption as a non-parallel dataset. The statistics of these datasets are displayed in Table 1, the same as [7]. All models included in our comparison are evaluated on the same test set.

4.2   Models for Comparisons

We compare with three conventional methods related to adversarial learning, including CrossAligned (CA) [18], StyleEmbedding (SE)[1], and MultiDecoder (MD) [1], and method BackTranslation (BT) [14]. Other approaches related to the three-step text style transfer process are the focus of our comparison. DelOnly and DelAndRet are from [7], where the former directly produces the output from the content and the target style with an RNN, and the latter generates the output from the content and retrieved target style markers with an RNN. [19] proposes Generative Style Transformer (GST): B-GST generates the output given the content and the target style, blind to specific markers, and G-GST produces the output given the content and retrieved target style markers. [5] proposes the Stable Style Transformer (SST), which produces outputs from the contents and the style classifier's feedback based on the encoder-decoder framework.

4.3   Evaluation Metrics

Following [2,5,12], we mainly evaluate style transfer results from four perspectives: content preservation, style transfer intensity, fluency, and the similarity to human references.

We employ self-BLEU (s-BLEU) and masked Word Mover Distance (mWMD) [12] to measure content preservation. S-BLEU is the BLEU score between the original sentences and the transferred candidates. To compute mWMD, we mask the style-related words in both the candidates and the references and calculate the minimum distance between the word embeddings of them. A smaller mWMD indicates better content preservation capability.

Accuracy (Acc) and Earth Mover's Distance (EMD) [12] are used to measure the style transfer intensity. We train a BERT classifier using given training data to predict the transferred sentences' style conformity. However, the accuracy provided by the binary classifier could not reveal transfer sentences falling in between two styles. The EMD between the style distributions of the source style corpus and the transfer outputs could better reflect the nuanced style difference. A larger EMD indicates a stronger transfer intensity.

Considering models usually experience the tradeoff between the aspects of content preservation and transfer intensity, we take the Geometric mean Score(GScore) of the aforementioned four metrics: s-BLEU, 1/mWMD, Acc, and EMD, to evaluate the tradeoff capability of different models. We take the inverse of mWMD to make the GScore decrease monotonically with respect to the worse performance.

In terms of fluency, we use general-PPL (g-PPL) and data-PPL (d-PPL) [5] to perform evaluation. G-PPL is obtained by using a pre-trained GPT-2 model and measures how transferred sentences are fluent in terms of massive natural texts used to pre-train GPT-2. D-PPL is obtained by fine-tuning a pre-trained GPT model on training data and measures how transferred results fit the data distribution of specific style corpora. We then take the GScore of them and use it as the indicator of transferred sentences' fluency.

Since human written references are provided in these datasets, we evaluate the transfer outputs' similarity to human references by BERTScore [23]. Unlike BLEU, which measures the n-gram overlapping between the references and the candidates, BERTScore measures the semantic similarity between them and is demonstrated to have better correlation to human judgments.

4.4   Experiment Details

For marker detecting, n-grams that span up to 4 words are considered as potential style markers, and the smoothing parameter is set to 1. Following the setting of [7], the thresholds of defining style markers are 15 and 5 for Yelp and Caption, accordingly. We use the Pytorch implementation of Transformer by Huggingface[1] for experiments. Our framework's components are built from the base-size BART, consisting of a six-layer encoder and a six-layer decoder with a hidden size of 768. The maximum input sequence length is 60. The framework is fine-tuned up to 10 epochs using cross entropy loss, with a batch size of 32 and a learning rate of 1e-5. The model performs best on the dev set is saved and used for inference on the test set. During inference, we merely conduct greedy search without any results selection module. For evaluation metrics, we use the tool provided at the link[2] to compute mWMD and EMD. Other metrics are from the link[3].

4.5   Result Analysis

The evaluation results on Yelp dataset are listed in Table 2. H:DRG [7] and H:DualRL [10] are taken as references. It is worth noting that two human references do not achieve the best performance in content preservation and style transfer intensity metrics. For instance, Human:DualRL obtains an accuracy of 77% and a self-BLEU score of 37.79, far behind other neural network methods. The possible reasons are that human's definitions of different sentiments are varied, and humans are better at creative sentence rewriting. On the other hand, this reveals the limitation of current widely used evaluation metrics. Automatic evaluation metrics that correlate better to human judgments are to be studied.

As we can see, B-GST [19] attains the best tradeoff between content preservation and style transfer intensity and the highest semantic similarity to human references. Even though GST methods surpass ours, we achieve decent results in the above aspects and the lowest PPL compared with other variants of three-step approaches, demonstrating the transfer results of our methods are more fluent and fit to training texts distribution. We attribute this to the denoising and generation capability of the pre-trained Denoising AutoEncoder we use, considering SST employs the encoder-decoder architecture as well while inferior to ours.

---

[1] https://github.com/huggingface/transformers.

[2] https://github.com/SenZHANG-GitHub/graph-text-style-transfer.

[3] https://github.com/rungjoo/Stable-Style-Transformer.

Table 2. Automatic evaluation results on Yelp dataset. The best result among methods based on the delete-retrieve-generate approach on each evaluation metric is shown in bold. *GScore* is the Geometric mean of the evaluation results on specific aspects. *Sem* is the semantic similarity between the transfer results and the references.

Model	Content and Style					Fluency			Sem↑
	s-BLEU↑	mWMD↓	Acc↑	EMD↑	GScore↑	d-PPL↓	g-PPL↓	GScore↓	
H:DRG [7]	26.97	0.503	72.8	0.726	7.30	121.2	153.5	136.4	95.83
H:DualRL [10]	37.79	0.388	77.0	0.766	8.71	178.6	196.2	187.2	95.83
CA [18]	17.02	0.512	74.8	0.713	6.49	69.1	319.1	148.5	88.12
SE [1]	71.80	0.880	8.9	0.412	4.16	121.7	379.8	215.0	90.56
MD [1]	40.81	0.580	46.4	0.634	6.75	201.6	642.1	359.8	88.35
BT [14]	0.67	0.757	96.2	0.912	2.97	148.8	67.4	100.1	87.36
DelOnly [7]	33.94	0.454	84.8	0.830	8.52	171.7	279.6	359.8	89.28
DelAndRet [7]	34.48	0.461	**87.7**	**0.855**	8.65	137.0	343.8	219.1	89.39
B-GST [19]	43.45	**0.237**	86.1	0.832	**10.71**	165.6	**184.0**	174.6	**91.78**
G-GST [19]	43.94	0.246	77.2	0.740	10.05	441.4	274.3	348.0	91.15
SST [5]	**49.09**	0.277	70.4	0.661	9.53	197.8	295.9	241.9	90.65
Ours	45.87	0.342	87.2	0.843	9.96	**132.5**	224.7	**172.5**	90.26

According to the results on Caption dataset in Table 3, our approach achieves the best performance regarding the content and style tradeoff and fluency. In our method, the auxiliary style encoder sees sentences in both sentiments and is trained to extract these two sentiments' representative features, which are then fed into the decoder for reconstruction. Under the circumstance of limited data, more salient features are extracted in our approach and results in a stronger transfer intensity and a lower PPL score. In addition, method DelAndRet attains a remarkably high accuracy of 94.7%. Intuitively, the reason is that target style markers are easily and accurately retrieved in parallel sentence pairs, which further leads to the strong transfer intensity.

Two groups of transferred sentences from other three-step relevant methods are displayed in Table 4, where markers are shown in bold. For the first group, method DelAndRet apparently fails to convert the source sentence into the target style, and SST produces a contradictory sentence with both *good* and *wrong* involved. In the second group, the results from DeleteOnly and G-GST are influent with repeated word *love*, and others manage to indicate the romantic sentiment through word *lover* or *loving*. These exactly demonstrate how style transfer methods perform diversely on different instances, making the applications of automatic evaluation metrics on the corpus level indispensable. The overall transfer results of our methods are shared at the link[4].

In conclusion, these variants of the three-step text style transfer method have different strengths and weaknesses. GST methods consistently attain the highest semantic similarity to human references, though human references do not

---

[4] https://drive.google.com/drive/folders/1H5Jg7psMRpGMWbBXnk5E1WMhq1zvJ gIy?usp=sharing.

Table 3. Automatic evaluation results on Caption dataset. The best result among methods based on the delete-retrieve-generate approach on each evaluation metric is shown in bold. *GScore* is the Geometric mean of the evaluation results on specific aspects. *Sem* is the semantic similarity between the transfer results and the references.

Model	Content and Style					Fluency			Sem↑
	s-BLEU↑	mWMD↓	Acc↑	EMD↑	GScore↑	d-PPL↓	g-PPL↓	GScore↓	
Human [7]	16.38	0.345	74.5	0.223	4.06	145.2	144.7	144.9	100.0
CA [18]	0.76	0.485	78.0	0.263	2.38	11.4	75.9	29.4	88.45
SE [1]	30.79	0.226	53.5	0.029	3.81	122.9	404.7	223.0	88.70
MD [1]	22.72	0.247	68.3	0.134	5.39	60.9	239.3	120.7	88.67
DelOnly [7]	39.88	**0.216**	77.3	0.176	7.08	464.3	345.1	400.3	89.38
DelAndRet [7]	33.32	0.243	**94.7**	0.135	6.47	559.9	160.1	299.4	89.51
B-GST [19]	**64.71**	0.345	59.1	0.223	7.05	126.1	140.3	133.0	**90.70**
G-GST [19]	51.43	0.243	57.3	0.135	6.36	1300.5	133.7	417.0	86.40
Ours	45.22	0.247	63.8	**0.228**	**7.18**	**88.2**	**126.9**	**105.8**	90.09

Table 4. Transfer results from different methods on two datasets. For Yelp dataset, the tokens in bold are style makers. Since the given sentence is factual in the test set of Caption, there is no style markers to be deleted in the source.

Yelp: negative → positive	
Source	We sit down and we got some really **slow** and **lazy** service
DelOnly	We sit down and we got some **great** and **quick** service
DelAndRet	We got very nice place to sit down and we got some service
B-GST	We sit and we got some really **good** and **friendly** service
G-GST	We sit and we got some really **amazing** food and **great** service
SST	We sit and we got some really **good** and **wrong** customer service
Ours	We sit down and we got some really **nice** and **fast** service
Caption: factual → romantic	
Source	A brown dog runs with a toy in its mouth
DelOnly	**People in love carrying** a brown dog runs with a toy in its mouth
DelAndRet	A brown dog runs with a toy in its mouth **to meet its lover**
B-GST	A brown dog runs with a toy in it's mouth, **towards his lover**
G-GST	**People in love carrying** a brown dog runs with a toy in its mouth
Ours	A brown dog runs with a toy in its mouth **towards his loving master**

achieve the best performance on these automatic evaluation metrics. DelOnly and DelAndRet perform stably on two datasets while their content preservation capability and style transfer intensity are limited. Ours surpasses the counterpart SST and achieves the best sentence fluency and a decent content and style trade-off. Moreover, our method is advantageous in the case of limited data regarding its good performance on the Caption dataset.

5   Conclusion

We have studied a two-stage exterior style and content disentanglement method for text style transfer. In the first stage, the style markers are detected and deleted from the sentences. In the second stage, the style-irrelevant contents are fed into a generative model to produce sentences in the target style. The model we propose consists of a content encoder, a decoder, and a style encoder. The former two components are directly built from the pre-trained Denoising AutoEncoder BART, and the latter has the same architecture as the content encoder while functioning differently. We conduct experiments on two text sentiment transfer datasets and carry out comprehensive evaluations on the variants of three-step transfer approaches. We hope these can promote a better understanding of the strengths and weaknesses of diverse methods. Moreover, our method's transfer results achieve decent performance regarding content preservation, transfer intensity, and semantics and stand out in terms of sentence fluency. For future work, the study of other marker detecting methods is desirable, considering the current commonly used methods are limited and the detecting results have a significant impact on the following generating step.

References

1. Fu, Z., Tan, X., Peng, N., Zhao, D., Yan, R.: Style transfer in text: exploration and evaluation. In: Proceedings of the AAAI Conference on Artificial Intelligence, vol. 32 (2018)
2. Jin, D., Jin, Z., Hu, Z., Vechtomova, O., Mihalcea, R.: Deep learning for text style transfer: a survey. arXiv preprint arXiv:2011.00416 (2020)
3. Klahold, A., Fathi, M.: Word processing as writing support. In: Klahold, A., Fathi, M., et al. (eds.) Computer Aided Writing, pp. 21–29. Springer, Cham (2020). https://doi.org/10.1007/978-3-030-27439-9_4
4. Lample, G., Subramanian, S., Smith, E., Denoyer, L., Ranzato, M., Boureau, Y.L.: Multiple-attribute text rewriting. In: International Conference on Learning Representations (2018)
5. Lee, J.: Stable style transformer: delete and generate approach with encoder-decoder for text style transfer. In: Proceedings of the 13th International Conference on Natural Language Generation, pp. 195–204 (2020)
6. Lewis, M., et al.: BART: denoising sequence-to-sequence pre-training for natural language generation, translation, and comprehension. arXiv preprint arXiv:1910.13461 (2019)
7. Li, J., Jia, R., He, H., Liang, P.: Delete, retrieve, generate: a simple approach to sentiment and style transfer. In: 2018 Conference of the North American Chapter of the Association for Computational Linguistics: Human Language Technologies, NAACL HLT 2018, pp. 1865–1874. Association for Computational Linguistics (ACL) (2018)
8. Liao, Y., Bing, L., Li, P., Shi, S., Lam, W., Zhang, T.: Quase: sequence editing under quantifiable guidance. In: Proceedings of the 2018 Conference on Empirical Methods in Natural Language Processing, pp. 3855–3864 (2018)

9. Liu, D., Fu, J., Zhang, Y., Pal, C., Lv, J.: Revision in continuous space: unsupervised text style transfer without adversarial learning. In: Proceedings of the AAAI Conference on Artificial Intelligence, vol. 34, pp. 8376–8383 (2020)

10. Luo, F., et al.: A dual reinforcement learning framework for unsupervised text style transfer. arXiv preprint arXiv:1905.10060 (2019)

11. Madaan, A., et al.: Politeness transfer: a tag and generate approach. arXiv preprint arXiv:2004.14257 (2020)

12. Mir, R., Felbo, B., Obradovich, N., Rahwan, I.: Evaluating style transfer for text. arXiv preprint arXiv:1904.02295 (2019)

13. Prabhumoye, S., Chandu, K.R., Salakhutdinov, R., Black, A.W.: "My way of telling a story": persona based grounded story generation. arXiv preprint arXiv:1906.06401 (2019)

14. Prabhumoye, S., Tsvetkov, Y., Salakhutdinov, R., Black, A.W.: Style transfer through back-translation. In: Proceedings of the 56th Annual Meeting of the Association for Computational Linguistics (Volume 1: Long Papers), pp. 866–876 (2018)

15. Radford, A., Narasimhan, K., Salimans, T., Sutskever, I.: Improving language understanding by generative pre-training (2018). https://s3-us-west-2.amazonaws.com/openai-assets/research-covers/language-unsupervised/language_understanding_paper.pdf

16. Rao, S., Tetreault, J.: Dear sir or madam, may i introduce the GYAFC dataset: corpus, benchmarks and metrics for formality style transfer. arXiv preprint arXiv:1803.06535 (2018)

17. Riley, P., Constant, N., Guo, M., Kumar, G., Uthus, D., Parekh, Z.: TextSETTR: label-free text style extraction and tunable targeted restyling. arXiv preprint arXiv:2010.03802 (2020)

18. Shen, T., Lei, T., Barzilay, R., Jaakkola, T.: Style transfer from non-parallel text by cross-alignment. arXiv preprint arXiv:1705.09655 (2017)

19. Sudhakar, A., Upadhyay, B., Maheswaran, A.: Transforming delete, retrieve, generate approach for controlled text style transfer. In: Proceedings of the 2019 Conference on Empirical Methods in Natural Language Processing and the 9th International Joint Conference on Natural Language Processing (EMNLP-IJCNLP), pp. 3260–3270 (2019)

20. Tian, Y., Hu, Z., Yu, Z.: Structured content preservation for unsupervised text style transfer. arXiv preprint arXiv:1810.06526 (2018)

21. Vaswani, A., et al.: Attention is all you need. arXiv preprint arXiv:1706.03762 (2017)

22. Wu, X., Zhang, T., Zang, L., Han, J., Hu, S.: "Mask and infill": applying masked language model to sentiment transfer. arXiv preprint arXiv:1908.08039 (2019)

23. Zhang, T., Kishore, V., Wu, F., Weinberger, K.Q., Artzi, Y.: BERTScore: evaluating text generation with BERT. arXiv preprint arXiv:1904.09675 (2019)

24. Zhang, Z., et al.: Style transfer as unsupervised machine translation. arXiv preprint arXiv:1808.07894 (2018)

25. Zhao, J., Kim, Y., Zhang, K., Rush, A., LeCun, Y.: Adversarially regularized autoencoders. In: International Conference on Machine Learning, pp. 5902–5911. PMLR (2018)

GUIS2Code: A Computer Vision Tool to Generate Code Automatically from Graphical User Interface Sketches

Zhen Feng, Jiaqi Fang, Bo Cai$^{(\boxtimes)}$, and Yingtao Zhang

Key Laboratory of Aerospace Information Security and Trusted Computing,
Ministry of Education, School of Cyber Science and Engineering, Wuhan University,
Wuhan, China
{zhenfeng,fangjiaqi,caib,zhangyingtao}@whu.edu.cn

Abstract. It is a typical task for front-end developers to repetitively transform the graphical user interface model provided by the designer into code. Automatically converting the design draft provided by the designer into code can simplify the task of the front-end engineer and avoid a lot of simple and repetitive work. In this paper, we propose *GUIS2Code* using deep neural network, which is trained on the datasets of the design drafts to detect the UI elements of the input sketches and generate corresponding codes through the UI parser. Our method can generate code for three different platforms (i.e., iOS, Android, and Web). Our experimental results illustrates that *GUIS2Code* achieves an average GUI-component classification accuracy of 95.04% and generates code that can restore the target sketches more accurately while exhibiting reasonable code structure.

Keywords: Graphical user interface · Deep learning · Code generation

1 Introduction

Nowadays, almost all applications are user-oriented with a graphical user interface (GUI), relying on a simple user interface (UI) and intuitive user experience to attract customers [9]. The process of front-end developers implementing the UI based on the graphic user interface design sketches created by the designer is very time-consuming, which will reduce the time they use to implement the actual functions and logic of the software they build [12]. In addition, when the software to be built needs to run on multiple platforms, it will bring a lot of repetitive work. Therefore, the automated conversion of UI design drafts to executable code will greatly improve the efficiency of developers.

Using deep learning to automatically generate code from UI design sketches is a relatively new research field. The key issue is how the machine understands the design sketches and extracts logical information from it, which can be regarded as a computer vision problem. There are some methods that use CNN to extract the visual features of the entire image, such as pix2code [1], HGui2Code [14], etc.,

© Springer Nature Switzerland AG 2021
I. Farkaš et al. (Eds.): ICANN 2021, LNCS 12893, pp. 53–65, 2021.
https://doi.org/10.1007/978-3-030-86365-4_5

which have achieved good results, but they all rely on domain-specific languages (DSL) and are less flexible. The object detection method of real images has always been a key research area of computer vision. Part of our task can be regarded as a object detection task in a specific scene, but it is unknown whether the general object detection approach is suitable for the design drafts we deal with. So, we explored various object detection models, and studied whether their structures and methods are useful for our research.

Finally, in this paper, we proposed *GUIS2Code*, a tool for automatic GUI code generation based on object detection, which can generate corresponding codes only by taking screenshots of UI design drafts as input. We divide the whole task into two steps, the first step is to use object detection methods to classify UI elements into various types (such as buttons, pictures, etc.) and represent them as specific objects; the second step is to generate code for different platforms through the UI parser.

The contribution of work is summarized as follows:

- We develop a deep learning based generative tool: *GUIS2Code* for overcoming the barrier for translating UI images to code.
- Other methods such as pix2code train the entire design draft, but our approach trains each element, so it has higher UI detection accuracy than them and also does not require DSL. Our generative tool combines object detection and text recognition method for learning a crowd-scale knowledge of UI images and component position information from a large number of mobile apps or rendered websites.
- We show our model's robust visual understanding and code generation capability through experiments. Compared with other methods, our model has better performance in terms of accuracy and visual understanding.

2   Related Work

2.1   Object Detection and Text Recognition

The first step of this task actually similar to the object detection problem of computer vision. Object detection can generally be divided into two categories. The first category is a two-stages recognition method represented by Fast R-CNN [6]. The first stage of this structure focuses on proposal extraction, and the second stage performs classification and precise coordinate regression on the extracted proposals. The accuracy of the two-stages structure is higher, but because the second stage needs to classify each proposal separately, the speed is compromised. The second type of structure is a one-stage structure represented by YOLO [15] and SSD [11]. They abandon the process of extracting the proposal and complete the recognition with only one stage. Although the speed is faster, the accuracy rate is far behind two-stages structure. In this paper, we studied various models and whether their structures and methods are useful for our task.

The text recognition process based on deep learning mainly includes text region detection and text sequence recognition. There are already many mature text recognition networks such as CRNN [16], RARE [17], ESIR [20], etc. In our task, the text is in the component, so the text region detection step can be omitted, and the result of the object detection network can be directly used as the input of the text recognition network. And the recognition network we need does not require a complex structure, so DenseNet [8] is used as a text recognition network in our model to recognize the text of each component.

2.2   GUI Code Generation

A lot of work has achieved good results in the field of automatically generating code for UI design drafts. The method REMAUI developed by Nguyen et al. [13] uses computer vision and optical character recognition (OCR) technology to identify user interface elements and further infer Appropriate user interface hierarchy and export it as source code that can be compiled and executed. The pix2code [1] proposed by Beltramell is a deep learning model that can convert UI screenshots into codes for the Web, Android and iOS platforms. Sketch2Code [9] proposed by Jain and other Microsoft researchers consists of a convolutional neural network, which takes a hand-drawn sketch image on a pure white surface and creates an Object representation of the UI, which is read by the UI parser to generate code for the target platform. Moran et al. proposed REDRAW [12], which achieves precise GUI prototyping through the three tasks of detection, classification, and assembly. Chen et al. [3] designed a neural converter. Given an input UI image, CNN extracts a set of different image features through a series of convolution and pooling operations. Then, the RNN encoder and RNN decoder generate a GUI framework form the spatial layout information of these image features. Pang et al. [14] first proposed a model called HGui2Code, which will enable the GUI function of visual attention and the semantic features that support DSL attention Integrated. In addition, they proposed SGui2Code, a novel model that uses the ON-LSTM network to generate syntactically correct DSL codes. The approach proposed by Chen et al. [4] combines the old-fashioned computer vision methods for non-textelement region detection, and deep learning models for region classification and GUI text detection.

3   Approach Description

3.1   Overall Architecture

As mentioned in Sect. 1, we divide the entire task into two steps. The first step includes object detection and text recognition technology, and the second step is the code parser. Modern object detector is usually composed of several parts, a backbone which is pre-trained on ImageNet, as well as the neck that makes better use of the features extracted by the backbone part and a head which is used to predict classes and bounding boxes of objects [2]. We tested the performance of the current mainstream object detection algorithms on our datasets, and finally we chose YOLOv3 as the head of our model. Inspired by YOLOv4 [2], We made a suitable simplification of YOLOv4 for our dataset as the object detection part of *GUIS2Code*, and our backbone chooses CSPDarkNet65 [18]. For the text recognition module, we choose DenseNet [8] as the recognition network. Next, we developed a Code parser to generate code for our model. The architecture of *GUIS2Code* is shown in Fig. 1, we use CSPDarkNet for feature extraction, and then add the SPP [7] module to increase the receptive field, separates out the most important context features. And we use PANet [10] as the method of parameter aggregation from different backbone levels for different detector levels.

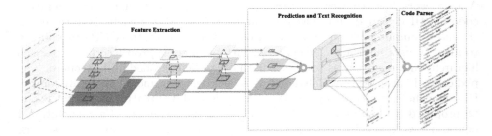

Fig. 1. Overall architecture of our model

3.2   UI Component Detection

For the first sub-problem, to understand the context of the elements present in the image, we have employed a deep neural network based object detection by mapping the input image with a set of classes and generating bounding boxes for the regions where they are present in the image. This mapping allows the training to be done independently of any language or platform restriction. As shown in Fig. 1, given the input UI image, our model extracts the category and location information of the UI element through a series of operations.

The backbone network of *GUIS2Code* is CSPDarknet65, which is based on the Yolov4 backbone network CSPDarknet53 and draws on the experience of Gao et al. [5] to generate the backbone structure, which contains 5 CSPNet modules and two types of modifications to improve the performance of CSPDarknet53, as shown in Fig. 2.

The full name of CSPNet [18] is Cross Stage Paritial Network, which mainly solves the problem of large amount of calculation in reasoning from the perspective of network structure design. The feature map of the base layer is divided into two parts, one of which is directly connected to the end of the stage, and the other part will pass through the res block, as shown in Fig. 3(a), thereby reducing repeated gradient information and computational bottlenecks while ensuring accuracy.

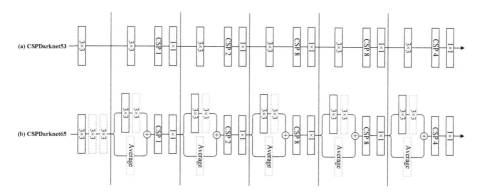

Fig. 2. Illustration of backbone networks. Each rectangle includes Conv, BN and Mish. CSP N, N in {1, 2, 8, 4}, denoted as the residual block repeated N times with CSP structure, as shown in the Fig. 3(a). (a) CSPDarknet53: original structure proposed in [2]. (b) CSPDarknet65: additional residual block (blue block) and substituted downsampling residual block (green block). (Color figure online)

Additional Root Block. In [22], extensive experiments have shown that performance can be improved by using a stack of 3×3 convolution filters. A useful but straightforward scheme is increasing one 3×3 convolution to three 3×3 convolutions. Through a large amount of input, the Root-Stage with three 3×3 convolutions can exploit more local information from the image, so as to extract powerful features for UI component detection. Therefore, an additional block is added at the root stage and is shown as a green block in Fig. 2(b).

Average Pooling Block. The size of the convolution kernel in front of the CSPNet module is 3×3, and the step size is 2, so it can play the role of downsampling. In order to strengthen the gradient propagation in the network, we replace this downsampling layer with Average Pooling block, which is shown as blue blocks in Fig. 2(b). In the projection shortcut path of such block, a 2×2 average pooling layer with a stride of 2 and the 1×1 convolution layer is added to replace downsampling layer, and the stride of 1×1 convolution is set to 1. In comparison with the original downsampling block in CSPDarknet, the improved structure can avoid information loss in projection shortcuts.

We added the SPP block to CSPDarknet65. We improve SPP module to the concatenation of max-pooling outputs with kernel size $k \times k$, where $k = \{1, 5, 9, 13\}$, and stride equals to 1, as shown in Fig. 3(b). Under this design, a relatively large $k \times k$ maxpooling effectively increase the receptive field of backbone feature. We tested the performance of SPP in our datasets in the experiment. Compared with no spp, our model has improved AP after adding SPP, while the computational cost is very small. Then we add PANet [10] to FPN as a parameter aggregation method from different backbone levels for different detector levels. We have added a bottom-up feature pyramid behind the FPN layer, which contains two PAN structures. In this combination of operations, the

FPN layer conveys strong semantic features from the top to the bottom, while the feature pyramid conveys strong positioning features from the bottom to the top. They work together to aggregate different detection layers from different backbone layers. This structure is shown in Fig. 3(c).

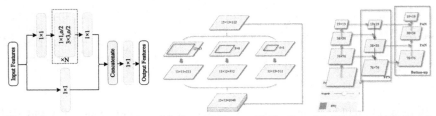

(a) Darknet structure using CSP.   (b) Spatial Pyramid Pooling Block   (c) FPN and PANet in our model

Fig. 3. Architecture details

Then, for bounding box regression, we use CIoU loss algorithms [21]. About evaluation metric for bounding box regression, Intersection over Union (IoU) is defined as

$$IoU = \frac{|A \bigcap B|}{|A \bigcup B|} \tag{1}$$

where $B = (x^{gt}, y^{gt}, w^{gt}, h^{gt})$ is the ground-truth bounding box, and $A = (x, y, w, h)$ is the predicted box [19]. The CIoU loss is proposed by imposing the consistency of aspect ratio, then, the CIoU loss function can be defined as

$$\mathcal{L}_{CIoU} = 1 - IoU + \frac{\rho^2(\mathbf{a}, \mathbf{b})}{c^2} + \frac{v}{(1 - IoU) + v}v \tag{2}$$

where $\mathbf{a}$ and $\mathbf{b}$ denote the central points of A and B, $\rho(\cdot)$ is the Euclidean distance, and c is the diagonal length of the smallest enclosing box covering the two boxes. v measures the consistency of aspect ratio:

$$v = \frac{4}{\pi^2}\left(arctan\frac{w^{gt}}{h^{gt}} - arctan\frac{w}{h}\right)^2. \tag{3}$$

In this way, overlapping area factors have higher priority in regression, especially for non-overlapping cases [21].

Finally, we choose CSPDarknet65 backbone network which reduces the amount of calculation while ensuring accuracy, SPP additional module which can improved accuracy and the computational cost is very small, PANet path-aggregation neck with strong positioning features, and YOLOv3 (anchor based) head as the architecture of our model. Through the combination of these approaches, the object detection module of *GUIS2Code* achieved higher accuracy on our UI design draft dataset when compared with other models.

3.3   Text Recognition

At the same time, we considered the text problem of components such as label and text. General text recognition has two parts, text region detection and text recognition. In our method, the result of object detection and recognition can be directly used as the text region to be recognized, so we only used the text recognition network.

DenseNet [8] can achieve good performance in text recognition, so we add trained DenseNet as a text recognition network to our model. In our approach, we label the text area in the GUI element corresponding to the text, use DenseNet-169 as the feature extraction network to extract the features of the text, and train it, and finally get the GUI text detection network.

3.4   Code Parser

The generated token sequence from network mentioned earlier can then be compiled with traditional compilation methods to the desired target language. The code parser is the final step, which converts the UI components in the UI representation object into code that can be executed on the target platform. The generated file is an XML or HTML document containing the UI components which can be run easily. In our experiment, the generated iOS and Android are UIs in the XML format while Web is web-based UIs implemented in HTML/CSS. The algorithm of code parser is shown in Algorithm 1. For space reasons, we have omitted some details.

4   Experimental Results and Analysis

4.1   Dataset and Experiment Setup

The screenshots of the UI interface in our datasets use pictures from the pix2code [1] datasets. The types and numbers of UI interfaces included in this dataset are shown in Fig. 4(a). At the same time, we manually annotated the UI components in each UI interface screenshot, and the dataset annotation format is shown in the Fig. 4(b). Our experimental standards are based on MS COCO, various IoU thresholds are used for more comprehensive calculation. The metric to evaluate detection performance is the mean Average Precision (mAP). The proposed networks are based on the Tensorflow framework. The results in figure are generated on a NVIDIA Tesla V100 16GB GPU with cuDNN (CUDA Deep Neural Network Library) acceleration. The processor used is In-tel(R) Xeon(R) E5-2640 and CentOS 7.5 operating system.

4.2   The Ablation Study and Evaluate

We have verified tricks we have introduced above, the ablation experiments are designed to verify the effects of the network modifications. The results of the ablation experiment are shown in the Table 1. The performance of CSPDarknet53 is

---

Algorithm 1: Algorithm of code parser.

Input: Bounding box and text pairs $P(B, T)$ of the network output; UI map $M(Class, Code)$;
Output: Generated xml or html file F;
1: Sort P according to position information
2: **Initialize** $parent = Node('start', None), current\_parent = parent$
3: **for** $p(b, t) \in P(B, T)$ **do**
4:      $token = p.b.class$
5:      **if** $M.find(token)! = -1$ **then**
6:          $element = Node(token, p.t)$
7:          $current\_parent.children.append(element)$
8:          $current\_parent = current\_parent.children$
9:      **end if**
10: **end for**
11: $F =$RENDER$(parent.children, M)$
12: **return** F
13: **function** RENDER$(parent, mapping)$
14:      **Initialize** $content = NULL$
15:      **for** $BFS(parent)$ **do**
16:          $content+ =$REPLACE$(child, mapping)$
17:      **end for**
18:      New a file F
19:      $F.write(content)$
20:      **return** F
21: **end function**

81.9%. The second and third rows of Table 1 show that the modifications of the Additional Root block and the Average Pooling blocks improve the performance to 83.1% and 84.4%, respectively. Moreover, with both modifications mentioned above, CSPDarknet65 can achieve 85.3%.

Table 1. Ablation experiment

Backbone	AP (%)	AP$_{50}$ (%)	AP$_{75}$ (%)	Delta (AP)
CSPDarknet53	81.9	99.6	96.9	0
CSPDarknet63 (Average Pooling)	83.1	99.6	98.0	1.2
CSPDarknet55 (Root block)	84.4	99.7	98.3	2.5
CSPDarknet65	**85.3**	**99.7**	**98.6**	**3.4**

The final performance of the UI object detection model reached 85.3% in mAP and 98.6% in AP$_{75}$. Figure 5 show samples consisting of input GUIs (i.e. ground truth), output GUIs, and generated code (part of the code is omitted). These output GUI screenshots are obtained by sampling code with a trained *GUIS2Code* model, the outputs is then compiled to the appropriate target language producing UI code that can be rendered and captured as an image.

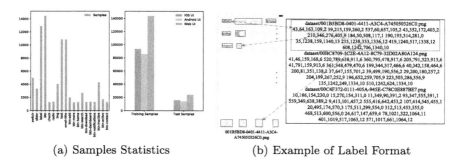

(a) Samples Statistics   (b) Example of Label Format

Fig. 4. Dataset details

4.3 Comparison with Other Approaches

In order to compare with pix2code, we used the code provided by the author of the paper on GitHub and the dataset provided to reproduce the model of pix2code, and compared with our model. We also compared with other models, the comparison experiment results are shown in Table 2. Our model is more accurate than all other models. The evaluation indicator is the accuracy rate of the generated code, which is defined as the ratio of the number of samples with accurate classification to the total number of samples.

Table 2. Comparison with other approaches.

Approaches	Accuracy (%)			
	iOS	Android	Web	Total
Pix2code [1]	77.27	77.66	77.65	77.53
HGui2Code [14]	80.80	81.13	90.40	84.11
AGui2Code [14]	94.00	65.76	64.80	74.85
SGui2Code [14]	77.20	77.71	90.00	81.64
ABHD [23]	81.00	81.35	88.50	83.62
GUIS2Code (Ours)	**95.16**	**94.60**	**95.37**	**95.04**

(a) Android, left to right: Groundtruth, Generated, Code

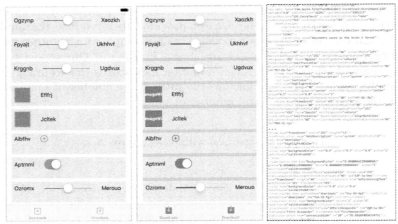

(b) iOS, left to right: Groundtruth, Generated, Code

(c) Web, top to bottom: Groundtruth, Generated, Code

Fig. 5. Examples of output from *GUIS2Code*.

5   Conclusion

In this paper, we propose an approach based on deep neural network, which uses screenshots of UI design drafts as input to transform and generate corresponding codes in different languages. Our method uses object detection technology, which can improve the recognition rate of UI components. At the same time, we consider the text problem on the component and restore it through text recognition technology. It has succeeded in three different platforms (i.e., iOS, Android and web) Generate code. Through evaluation, our method achieves an accuracy of 95.04%, and the generated code can restore the target model with maximum accuracy. Our dataset comes from pix2code, but it is manually generated by the author, which is different from the actual running application or web page. In fact, we can crawl website screenshots and associated HTML code datasets or Android and iOS. And now there are a large number of web pages and Android and iOS GUIs available on the Internet. Therefore, theoretically, we can obtain almost unlimited training data, thereby enhancing the capabilities of our model, and even generating code from the GUI completely automatically.

References

1. Beltramelli, T.: Pix2Code: generating code from a graphical user interface screenshot. In: Proceedings of the ACM SIGCHI Symposium on Engineering Interactive Computing Systems, pp. 3:1–3:6. ACM (2018). https://doi.org/10.1145/3220134.3220135
2. Bochkovskiy, A., Wang, C.Y., Liao, H.Y.M.: YOLOv4: optimal speed and accuracy of object detection. arXiv e-prints arXiv:2004.10934, April 2020
3. Chen, C., Su, T., Meng, G., Xing, Z., Liu, Y.: From UI design image to GUI skeleton: a neural machine translator to bootstrap mobile GUI implementation. In: Proceedings of the 40th International Conference on Software Engineering, pp. 665–676. ACM (2018). https://doi.org/10.1145/3180155.3180240
4. Chen, J., et al.: Object detection for graphical user interface: old fashioned or deep learning or a combination? In: ESEC/FSE 2020: 28th ACM Joint European Software Engineering Conference and Symposium on the Foundations of Software Engineering, pp. 1202–1214. ACM (2020). https://doi.org/10.1145/3368089.3409691
5. Gao, F., Yang, C., Ge, Y., Lu, S., Shao, Q.: Dense receptive field network: a backbone network for object detection. In: Tetko, I.V., Kůrková, V., Karpov, P., Theis, F. (eds.) ICANN 2019. LNCS, vol. 11729, pp. 105–118. Springer, Cham (2019). https://doi.org/10.1007/978-3-030-30508-6_9
6. Girshick, R.B.: Fast R-CNN. In: IEEE International Conference on Computer Vision, Santiago, Chile, pp. 1440–1448. IEEE Computer Society (2015). https://doi.org/10.1109/ICCV.2015.169
7. He, K., Zhang, X., Ren, S., Sun, J.: Spatial pyramid pooling in deep convolutional networks for visual recognition. In: Fleet, D., Pajdla, T., Schiele, B., Tuytelaars, T. (eds.) ECCV 2014. LNCS, vol. 8691, pp. 346–361. Springer, Cham (2014). https://doi.org/10.1007/978-3-319-10578-9_23
8. Huang, G., Liu, Z., van der Maaten, L., Weinberger, K.Q.: Densely connected convolutional networks. In: IEEE Conference on Computer Vision and Pattern Recognition, pp. 2261–2269. IEEE Computer Society (2017). https://doi.org/10.1109/CVPR.2017.243

9. Jain, V., Agrawal, P., Banga, S., Kapoor, R., Gulyani, S.: Sketch2Code: transformation of sketches to UI in real-time using deep neural network. arXiv e-prints arXiv:1910.08930, October 2019

10. Liu, S., Qi, L., Qin, H., Shi, J., Jia, J.: Path aggregation network for instance segmentation. In: IEEE Conference on Computer Vision and Pattern Recognition, pp. 8759–8768. IEEE Computer Society (2018). https://doi.org/10.1109/CVPR.2018.00913

11. Liu, W., et al.: SSD: single shot multibox detector. In: Leibe, B., Matas, J., Sebe, N., Welling, M. (eds.) ECCV 2016. LNCS, vol. 9905, pp. 21–37. Springer, Cham (2016). https://doi.org/10.1007/978-3-319-46448-0_2

12. Moran, K., Bernal-Cárdenas, C., Curcio, M., Bonett, R., Poshyvanyk, D.: Machine learning-based prototyping of graphical user interfaces for mobile apps. IEEE Trans. Softw. Eng. **46**(2), 196–221 (2020). https://doi.org/10.1109/TSE.2018.2844788

13. Nguyen, T.A., Csallner, C.: Reverse engineering mobile application user interfaces with REMAUI (T). In: 30th IEEE/ACM International Conference on Automated Software Engineering, pp. 248–259. IEEE Computer Society (2015). https://doi.org/10.1109/ASE.2015.32

14. Pang, X.W., Zhou, Y., Li, P., Lin, W., Wu, W., Wang, J.Z.: A novel syntax-aware automatic graphics code generation with attention-based deep neural network. J. Netw. Comput. Appl. **161**, 102636 (2020). https://doi.org/10.1016/j.jnca.2020.102636

15. Redmon, J., Divvala, S.K., Girshick, R.B., Farhadi, A.: You only look once: unified, real-time object detection. In: IEEE Conference on Computer Vision and Pattern Recognition, pp. 779–788. IEEE Computer Society (2016). https://doi.org/10.1109/CVPR.2016.91

16. Shi, B., Bai, X., Yao, C.: An end-to-end trainable neural network for image-based sequence recognition and its application to scene text recognition. IEEE Trans. Pattern Anal. Mach. Intell. **39**(11), 2298–2304 (2017). https://doi.org/10.1109/TPAMI.2016.2646371

17. Shi, B., Wang, X., Lyu, P., Yao, C., Bai, X.: Robust scene text recognition with automatic rectification. In: IEEE Conference on Computer Vision and Pattern Recognition, pp. 4168–4176. IEEE Computer Society (2016). https://doi.org/10.1109/CVPR.2016.452

18. Wang, C., Liao, H.M., Wu, Y., Chen, P., Hsieh, J., Yeh, I.: CSPNet: a new backbone that can enhance learning capability of CNN. In: IEEE/CVF Conference on Computer Vision and Pattern Recognition, CVPR Workshops 2020, pp. 1571–1580. IEEE (2020). https://doi.org/10.1109/CVPRW50498.2020.00203

19. Yu, J., Jiang, Y., Wang, Z., Cao, Z., Huang, T.: UnitBox: an advanced object detection network. In: Proceedings of the 24th ACM International Conference on Multimedia, pp. 516–520. Association for Computing Machinery, New York (2016). https://doi.org/10.1145/2964284.2967274

20. Zhan, F., Lu, S.: ESIR: end-to-end scene text recognition via iterative image rectification. In: IEEE Conference on Computer Vision and Pattern Recognition, pp. 2059–2068. Computer Vision Foundation/IEEE (2019). https://doi.org/10.1109/CVPR.2019.00216

21. Zheng, Z., Wang, P., Liu, W., Li, J., Ye, R., Ren, D.: Distance-IoU loss: faster and better learning for bounding box regression. In: The Thirty-Fourth AAAI Conference on Artificial Intelligence, pp. 12993–13000. AAAI Press (2020). https://doi.org/10.1609/aaai.v34i07.6999

22. Zhu, R., et al.: ScratchDet: training single-shot object detectors from scratch. arXiv e-prints arXiv:1810.08425, October 2018
23. Zhu, Z., Xue, Z., Yuan, Z.: Automatic graphics program generation using attention-based hierarchical decoder. In: Jawahar, C.V., Li, H., Mori, G., Schindler, K. (eds.) ACCV 2018. LNCS, vol. 11366, pp. 181–196. Springer, Cham (2019). https://doi.org/10.1007/978-3-030-20876-9_12

Generating Math Word Problems from Equations with Topic Consistency Maintaining and Commonsense Enforcement

Tianyang Cao[1,2], Shuang Zeng[1,2], Songge Zhao[1], Mairgup Mansur[3], and Baobao Chang[1,2(✉)]

[1] Key Laboratory of Computational Linguistics, Peking University, MOE, Beijing, China
{ctymy,zengs,zhaosongge}@pku.edu.cn
[2] School of Software and Microelectronics, Peking University, Beijing, China
chbb@pku.edu.cn
[3] Sogou Technology Inc., Beijing, China
maerhufu@sogou-inc.com

Abstract. Data-to-text generation task aims at generating text from structured data. In this work, we focus on a relatively new and challenging equation-to-text generation task – generating math word problems from equations and propose a novel equation-to-problem text generation model. Our model first utilizes a template-aware equation encoder and a Variational AutoEncoder (VAE) model to bridge the gap between abstract math tokens and text. We then introduce a topic selector and a topic controller to prevent topic drifting problems. To avoid the commonsense violation issues, we design a pre-training stage together with a commonsense enforcement mechanism. We construct a dataset to evaluate our model through both automatic metrics and human evaluation. Experiments show that our model significantly outperforms baseline models. Further analysis shows our model is effective in tackling topic drifting and commonsense violation problems.

Keywords: Math word problem generation · Topic controlling · Commonsense enforcement

1 Introduction

Text generation, aiming to automatically generate fluent, readable and faithful natural language text from different types of input, has become an increasingly popular topic in NLP community.

Many recent text generation approaches [3,6,7,10,13,14] focus on data-to-text generation task, which generates textual output from structured data such as tables of records or knowledge graphs (KGs). However in this paper, we focus on a relatively new type of data-to-text generation task: generating math word

© Springer Nature Switzerland AG 2021
I. Farkaš et al. (Eds.): ICANN 2021, LNCS 12893, pp. 66–79, 2021.
https://doi.org/10.1007/978-3-030-86365-4_6

| Equations: $y = 3 * x$; $y - 20 = 100$
Problem: The teacher said if you multiply my age by *3*, then subtract *20*, the result is *100*. *How old is the teacher*? |
| Equations: $1 - 1/4 - 2/5 = x$
Problem: If *1/4* of a pie is eaten and later *2/5*, *what is the remaining fraction*? |

Fig. 1. Two examples selected from the MWP generation dataset.

| Bad Case 1:
The adult hat is \$50 for sale. How much of each kind should be used to make a mixture that is 70% protein … |
| Bad Case 2:
The hypotenuse of a square is 7.9 meters long, … |
| Bad Case 3:
What is the dimensions of the original number, … |

Fig. 2. Three bad cases generated by baseline (Seq2Seq) model.

problems (MWP) from equations [15], which seems has not been fully studied by NLP community. Successful math word problems generation has the potential to automate the writing of mathematics questions. Thus it can alleviate the burden of school teachers and further help improve the teaching efficiency (Fig. 1).

Our target is to design a model to generate math problem text from the given equations and the generated math problem could be solved by the equations. Different from the traditional text generation task, there are three major challenges in effective MWP generation from equations:

(1) Encoding math equations is much more difficult than encoding plain text, tables or KGs. A math equation consists of different type of tokens, such as number, variable and operator. They express different meanings and are very abstract for generating text. So a model should use different methods to encode them and need to bridge the gap between the abstract math tokens and natural language text.
(2) Recent language modeling advancements indeed make generated text more fluent, but still lacking of coherence, especially in the aspect of topic drifting, has always been a non-trivial problem that traditional text generation models usually suffer from [4]. And we find this problem is even worse in MWP generation since target math word problems in MWP dataset covers a broad variety of topics. Figure 2 shows three bad cases generated by a Seq2Seq model. The first case reveals the topic drifting problem where the topic of the first generated sentence is the *price of goods* but the topic of the second sentence is changed to *substance mixture*. So how to maintain the topic consistency in generated text to avoid topic drifting is very challenging.
(3) The task requires generated problem text to be in line with the commonsense which is very hard for existing architecture. As shown in the last two cases in Fig. 2, we cannot say "hypotenuse of a square" or "dimension of a number", because they aren't in accordance with the commonsense. So we should design an effective architecture to avoid commonsense violation problem.

To tackle these challenges, we propose a novel architecture for generating MWP from equations. First, to effectively encode different kinds of math tokens in the given equations, we propose a template-aware equation encoder that considers both template information and equation information. We further utilize a problem-aware Variational AutoEncoder (VAE) with a Kullback-Leibler distance loss to bridge the gap between abstract math tokens and problem text. Then we propose a topic selection mechanism that selects a fixed topic for each generated text and a topic controlling mechanism that controls the topic at every decoding step to avoid topic drifting problem. To cope with the possible commonsense violation issue of generated text, we design a pre-training stage as well as a commonsense enforcement module to encourage our model to generate math problem text that is in line with the commonsense.

Our contributions can be summarized as follows:

- We propose an effective way of encoding different math tokens and a problem-aware VAE to bridge the gap between abstract math tokens and generated text.
- We utilize a topic selection and a topic controlling mechanism, so topic consistency of generated math problem text could be maintained.
- We design a pre-training stage and a commonsense enforcement module to alleviate commonsense violation.

In order to verify the effectiveness of our model, we construct a dataset by obtaining math word problems and their corresponding equations from *Yahoo!*[1]. Experimental results on this dataset show our model significantly outperforms previous models. Further analysis and human evaluation show our model is effective in tackling the three challenges mentioned before, especially the topic drifting and commonsense violation problems.

2   Task Definition

The input of MWP generation task is a set of equations $\{E_1, E_2, ..., E_{|E|}\}$, each equation can be denoted as a sequence of math tokens: $E_k = x_1 x_2 ... x_{|E_k|}$, where $|E_k|$ is the length of k-th equation measured by the number of math tokens. Each math token belongs to one of the following three types: math operator (e.g., $+, -, *, \div, =, ...$), number (e.g., $0.2, 1, 30, ...$), variable (e.g., $x, y, z, ...$). The output of the task is the MWP text: $\boldsymbol{y} = y_1 y_2 ... y_L$, which could be solved by the input equations. L is the length of problem text. Our model aims to estimate the following conditional probability depending on equations and previously generated words $\boldsymbol{y}_{<t}$:

$$P(\boldsymbol{y}|\boldsymbol{x}) = \prod_{t=1}^{L} P(y_t|\boldsymbol{y}_{<t}, E_1, E_2, ...) \tag{1}$$

The difficulty of the input equations in this task is not beyond middle school level, only involving algebra operation in elementary mathematics: "$+, -, *, /, \wedge, ...$".

---

[1] https://github.com/caotianyang/math2textcs1.

3   Model

The overall architecture of our model is shown in Fig. 3. We start with a variational encoder-decoder model as our base model which consists of a template-aware equation encoder and a math word problem generation decoder. Since the math tokens in the original input equation are very abstract and lack enough context information for generating text, we introduce a problem-aware Variational AutoEncoder to encourage the equation encoder to produce text-sensitive representation that is more suitable for decoding problem text.

To tackle the problem of topic drifting, we introduce a topic selector with a topic controller. The topic selector chooses a specific topic based on the latent representation of equations. The dynamic topic memory is used to control the decoding process to favor the topic-consistent text. To alleviate the commonsense violation, we introduce a pre-training step to produce commonsense embedding for words and use a commonsense enforcement module to aggregate commonsense information which will influence the following choice at each step of decoding.

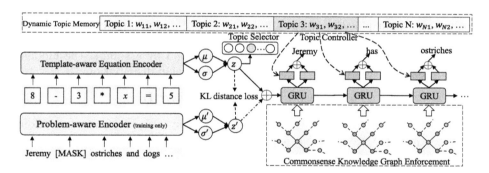

Fig. 3. The overview of our proposed model. We omit the pretraining step for simplicity. In our variational autoencoder enhanced model, the problem encoder serves as prior network and the equation encoder serves as posterior network. Topic type predicted by the hidden equation representation z is used to select the corresponding row in topic memory. Next, the MWP decoder resorts to both the dynamic topic memory and the Commonsense KG reasoning to generate MWP text.

3.1   Variational Encoder-Decoder Module

As we mentioned before, we choose the variational encoder-decoder model as the basic model to generate the MWP text from equations. The backbone of our model consists of a template-aware equation encoder and a problem text decoder.

Template-Aware Equation Encoder: The input to our model is a sequence of math tokens $x_1 x_2 ... x_n$, our input encoder encodes each token to one fixed hidden vector. Math equations encoding is different from encoding other natural languages, we should distinguish numbers, variables and operations to assign them different encoding.

We exploit BiGRU as the basic module, it consumes token embedding of the equation sequences and the hidden states are computed by: $\overleftarrow{\boldsymbol{h}}_i = GRU(emb(x_i), \overleftarrow{\boldsymbol{h}}_{i-1})$, $\overrightarrow{\boldsymbol{h}}_i = GRU(emb(x_i), \overrightarrow{\boldsymbol{h}}_{i-1})$. $emb(x_i) = \boldsymbol{E}_{token}(x_i) + \boldsymbol{E}_{type}(x_i)$ is the sum of corresponding token embedding and type embedding. Combining forward and backward state yields $\boldsymbol{h}_i = \overleftarrow{\boldsymbol{h}}_i + \overrightarrow{\boldsymbol{h}}_i$.

To improve the generalization capacity of the equation encoder, we further incorporate a soft gate controlled by equation template. The equation template is constructed by replacing all numbers in the equation to a fixed mask [M]. We separately feed the original sequence and the template sequence into two different GRUs, then encoded hidden states are denoted as $\{\boldsymbol{h}_{a,1}, \boldsymbol{h}_{a,2}, ..., \boldsymbol{h}_{a,n}\}$ and $\{\boldsymbol{h}_{b,1}, \boldsymbol{h}_{b,2}, ..., \boldsymbol{h}_{b,n}\}$, respectively. Here we utilize Gated Linear Unit (GLU) [5] to compute final encoded hidden state:

$$\boldsymbol{h}_k = MLP_1(\boldsymbol{h}_{a,k}) \odot \sigma(MLP_2(\boldsymbol{h}_{b,k})) \ 1 \leq k \leq n \qquad (2)$$

where $\sigma(\cdot)$ is a sigmoid function and $MLP(\cdot)$ is a linear layer. $\odot$ indicates element-wise multiplication. $\boldsymbol{h}_{b,k}$ can be understood as a weight matrix to select salient information in $\boldsymbol{h}_{a,k}$. We perform linear transformation to $\boldsymbol{h}_n$ and approximate mean and variance of z's posterior distribution by assuming the hidden equation representation z follows multivariate Gaussian distribution.

$$[\boldsymbol{\mu}, \boldsymbol{\sigma}] = MLP(\boldsymbol{h}_n) \ z|\boldsymbol{x} \sim \mathcal{N}(\boldsymbol{\mu}, \boldsymbol{\sigma}^2 \mathbf{I}) \qquad (3)$$

$\mathbf{I}$ is an identity matrix and z can then be sampled by using reparameterization trick: $\boldsymbol{z} = \boldsymbol{\mu} + \boldsymbol{r} \odot \boldsymbol{\sigma}$, where $\boldsymbol{r}$ is a standard Gaussian distribution variable.

Problem Decoder: For generating problem text, we use GRU based decoder. We first initialize the decoder state by $\boldsymbol{s}_0 = MLP([\boldsymbol{h}_n; \boldsymbol{z}; \boldsymbol{h}_n \odot \boldsymbol{z}])$. We denote the hidden state of the decoder at tth step as $\boldsymbol{s}_t$ and context vector obtained by attentions over the input equation as $\boldsymbol{c}_t$. Assume the decoder generates word w_{t-1} in step $t-1$, decoding process can be formulated by:

$$\boldsymbol{s}'_t = f(\boldsymbol{s}_t) \ \ \boldsymbol{s}_t = GRU(\boldsymbol{s}_{t-1}, g(\boldsymbol{e}_{w_{t-1}})) \qquad (4)$$

$$p_D(y_t|y_{<t}, \boldsymbol{x}, z, \hat{p}; \theta_D) = softmax(\boldsymbol{W}^o tanh(\boldsymbol{W}^{vs} [\boldsymbol{s}'_t; \boldsymbol{c}_t])) \qquad (5)$$

where $\boldsymbol{W}^{vs} \in \mathbb{R}^{d \times d}$, $\boldsymbol{W}^o \in \mathbb{R}^{d \times |V|}$. $|V|$, $\hat{p}$ and d is the vocabulary size, topic category and embedding size, respectively. $f(\cdot)$ and $g(\cdot)$ is designed for leveraging topic restriction and commonsense restriction, respectively, which will be explained later. We further adopt copy mechanism [11] to copy numbers from equations.

3.2   Enhancing Equation Encoder by Variational Autoencoder

Hidden equation representation $\boldsymbol{z}$ derived by (3) fails to capture interaction between equations and MWP text. We thus introduce a problem-aware VAE to further restrict z into similar vector space of MWP text to obtain problem text aware representation. In this paper, the VAE is comprised of the problem encoder and the problem decoder. As the problem text is known when training, posterior distribution of z generated by the equation encoder is conditioned on prior distribution generated by the problem encoder.

The problem encoder summarizes the MWP text to a vector q and works as a prior network. It takes the corrupted version of problem text y as input to guarantee robustness when testing, i.e., we randomly mask and delete some words in the original MWP text. We implement the problem encoder module based on convolutional neural network (CNN) with F different convolutional kernels to extract multi-scale features:

$$h_k^q = MaxPool(f_{conv}([\boldsymbol{y}_i; \boldsymbol{y}_{i+1}; ...; \boldsymbol{y}_{i+l_k-1}])) \tag{6}$$
$$q = tanh(\boldsymbol{W}^q [\boldsymbol{h}_1^q; \boldsymbol{h}_2^q; ...; \boldsymbol{h}_F^q]) \tag{7}$$

where $\boldsymbol{W}^k \in \mathbb{R}^{dl_k}$ is the kth convolutional kernel and parameter matrix $\boldsymbol{W}^q \in \mathbb{R}^{Fd \times d}$. Similar to (3), we perform linear transformation to q and obtain mean and variance of z's prior distribution: $[\boldsymbol{\mu}', \boldsymbol{\sigma}'] = MLP(q)$ $z'|\boldsymbol{y} \sim \mathcal{N}(\boldsymbol{\mu}', \boldsymbol{\sigma}'^2 \mathbf{I})$.

We denote the problem decoder parameterized by θ_D as $p_D(\boldsymbol{y}|\boldsymbol{x}, z, \hat{p}; \theta_D)$, during training, z is obtained by prior network. We aim to minimize Kullback-Leibler distance (KL loss) between prior distribution and posterior distribution. Loss function of our Variational Encoder-Decoder framework can then be computed by combining KL loss and generator decoding loss:

$$\mathcal{L}_{VAE} = -KL(p(z|\boldsymbol{y})||p(z|\boldsymbol{x}))$$
$$+ \mathbb{E}_{z \sim \mathcal{N}(\boldsymbol{\mu}', \boldsymbol{\sigma}'^2 \mathbf{I})} p_D(\boldsymbol{y}|\boldsymbol{x}, z, \hat{p}; \theta_D) \tag{8}$$

Besides, we use KL cost annealing to avoid KL-vanishing phenomenon [2]. During inference, z is approximated by posterior network.

3.3   Topic Selection and Controlling

Generally speaking, given an input equation, for example, $0.5 * x + 0.3 * y = 10$, our model should first select a certain type of topic and then incorporate related topic words under this type into the problem decoder.

Topic Selection: To leverage topic background to the hidden equation representation z, we apply an unsupervised document topic model– Latent Dirichlet Allocation (LDA) [1] to assign a topic type for each math problem text. We treat each math question as a document, each document is associated with a topic distribution over all topics, meanwhile each topic contains several words with the highest probability in this topic. We then estimate the problem topic type through z:

$$\hat{p} = \arg\max softmax(\boldsymbol{W}_z \boldsymbol{z} + \boldsymbol{b}_z) \tag{9}$$

Topic Controling: Topic controling renders our generator to interact with topic word distribution. With the help of LDA, a topic memory $C \in \mathbb{R}^{|P| \times K \times d}$ is constructed for storing pretrained embedding of topic keywords, where $|P|$ is the total topic number. K means each row of $\boldsymbol{C}$ contains information of top-K words of one topic and d is the vector dimension. With the most probably topic type $\hat{p}$ predicted in (9), the concatenation of $\boldsymbol{s}_t$ and $\boldsymbol{c}_t$ is used as a query to the $\hat{p}$th row of topic memory and update $\boldsymbol{s}_t$ with the weighted sum of topic embedding in $\boldsymbol{C}$:

$$score(t,j) = \frac{\exp([\boldsymbol{s}_t; \boldsymbol{c}_t] \boldsymbol{W}^t \boldsymbol{C}_{\hat{p},j})}{\sum_{j=1}^{K} \exp([\boldsymbol{s}_t; \boldsymbol{c}_t] \boldsymbol{W}^t \boldsymbol{C}_{\hat{p},j})} \quad 1 \le j \le K \tag{10}$$

and $f(\boldsymbol{s}_t)$ in (4) is realized by:

$$f(\boldsymbol{s}_t) = \boldsymbol{s}_t + \boldsymbol{V} \sum_{j=1}^{K} score(t,j) \boldsymbol{C}_{\hat{p},j} \tag{11}$$

where $\boldsymbol{W}^t \in \mathbb{R}^{2d \times d}$ and $\boldsymbol{V} \in \mathbb{R}^{d \times d}$ serves for linear projection. Futhermore, memory contexts are initialized by the pretrained word representation, but during the generating process, it should be dynamicly updated with the produced sequence to keep recording new information, thus the topic memory can provide better guidance for the generator. We achieve this goal by computing a weight vector with a gated mechanism to weight in what degree the topic memory should be updated, then we obtain candidate state based on $\boldsymbol{s}_t'$ and $\boldsymbol{C}_{\hat{p},j}$, where $\boldsymbol{W}^u, \boldsymbol{W}^c \in \mathbb{R}^{d \times d}$:

$$\boldsymbol{u} = \sigma(\boldsymbol{W}^u [\boldsymbol{s}_t'; \boldsymbol{C}_{\hat{p},j}]) \tag{12}$$

$$\tilde{\boldsymbol{C}}_{\hat{p},j} = tanh(\boldsymbol{W}^c [\boldsymbol{s}_t'; \boldsymbol{C}_{\hat{p},j}]) \tag{13}$$

$$\boldsymbol{C}_{\hat{p},j} = \boldsymbol{u} \otimes \tilde{\boldsymbol{C}}_{\hat{p},j} + (1 - \boldsymbol{u}) \otimes \boldsymbol{C}_{\hat{p},j} \tag{14}$$

3.4   Commonsense Enforcement

We argue it's beneficial to make our network leverage context-related concepts. We thus implement commonsense enforcement in two aspects: word knowledge pretraining and commonsense aware generator.

Word Embedding Pretraining For Commonsense Enforcement: We directly enrich information of our generator by pretraining word-level representation in an external commonesense KB. Note that word embedding pretraining is an off line step and is based on Graph Attention Network (GAT) [12]. For detail, see the Appendix.

Commonsense Aware Generator: In decoding phase, we merge neighbour nodes information in commonsense KB of generated words in the previous step to inject commonsense knowledge into our generator. For example, if "original cost" has been generated, we hope next sequence is "of the stock", other than "of the volume", for stock has the property "cost". Assume the decoder generates word w_{t-1} in step $t-1$, we extract a sub-graph within two-hop paths starting

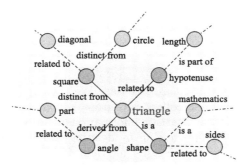

Fig. 4. Illustration of searching adjacent nodes. For word "triangle", first-order neighbors in knowledge graph are colored in blue while second-order neighbors are colored in orange. (Color figure online)

from w_{t-1} by Breadth First Search (BFS), as is shown in Fig. 4. Let e_{ij} denote the path representation from node i to node j if i and j are directly connected:

$$e_{ij} = \phi(W^g [e_i; e_j]) \tag{15}$$

where $W^g \in \mathbb{R}^{2d \times d}$. If i and j are connected via intermediate node k, we aggregate the shortest path representation from i to j to obtain e_{ij}:

$$e_{ij} = \alpha\phi(W^g [e_i; e_j]) + (1 - \alpha)\sigma(e_{ik} \otimes (U e_{kj})) \tag{16}$$

where $U \in \mathbb{R}^{d \times d}$, $\phi(\cdot)$ is a nonlinear function, in this paper we use $tanh(\cdot)$. $\sigma(\cdot)$ is Sigmoid function. $\alpha \in [0, 1]$ is a scalar to control the contribution of direct and indirect information. Denote first order neighbour set and second order neighbour set of w_{t-1} as $\mathcal{N}_1(w_{t-1})$ and $\mathcal{N}_2(w_{t-1})$, respectively. We use an attention mechanism to tend to all possible paths, i.e., we calculate the aggregate summary of $e_{w_{t-1},j}$ when j goes through $\mathcal{N}_1(w_{t-1}) \cup \mathcal{N}_2(w_{t-1})$:

$$\beta_{t-1,j} \propto \exp(e_{w_{t-1}} W^b e_{w_{t-1},j}) \tag{17}$$

$$g_{t-1} = \sum_{j \in \mathcal{N}_1(w_{t-1}) \cup \mathcal{N}_2(w_{t-1})} \beta_{t-1,j} e_{w_{t-1},j} \tag{18}$$

Followed by (18), to better reflect the effect of concept knowledge to word choice, we combine $e_{w_{t-1}}$ with g_{t-1} to realize $g(e_{w_{t-1}})$ in (4):

$$g(e_{w_{t-1}}) = GRU(e_{w_{t-1}}, H g_{t-1}) \tag{19}$$

3.5 Training Objective

We aggregate 1): VAE loss mentioned in (8) 2) auxiliary topic prediction loss $\mathcal{L}_{topic} = \mathbb{E}_{z \sim \mathcal{N}(\mu', \sigma'^2 I)} p(\hat{p}|z, x)$ to obtain total loss:

$$\mathcal{L}_{total} = \mathcal{L}_{VAE} + \mu \mathcal{L}_{topic} \tag{20}$$

where μ is a hyperparameter.

4   Experiments

4.1   Datasets

Dolphin-18K [16] is the largest MWP dataset with various types of MWP text, while only a part of it (3154) are released. We then reuse the python script provided by [16] to crawl and collect data from Yahoo, which extends Dolphin-18K to 9643 samples in total. Statistic information of our data is listed in Table 3. We conduct some data preprocessing by deleting those equation-problem text pairs whose problem text length is longer than 45 tokens, besides, we replace those words appearing less than 2 times to ⟨UNK⟩.

4.2   Motivation of Creating New Dataset

MWP solving datasets currently used include Alg514 [18], Dolphin1878 [19], DRAW-1K [20], Dolphin18K [16]. Table 3 gives the statistic of these datasets. Alg514, Dolphin1878, DRAW-1K are all public available, while neural generation models for generative tasks are usually data-hungry thus equation-MWP pairs in those datasets are insufficient. Though Dolphin18K is a large scale dataset, only a part of it (3154) are released. Moreover, existing datasets only include a certain type of MWP text, e.g., MWP text for linear equations, which restricts their practical application. We then reuse the python script provided by [16] and acquire 14943 equation-MWP text pairs in total from Yahoo !. Generally, the public available datasets can be treated as the subset of our dataset. Next, we conduct data preprocess as follows, which is beneficial to train the generation model:

- We normalize the equations by replacing all the equation variables in each sample to $x, y, z, ...$ in order, e.g., $u + v + r = 100, u - r = 10$ is replaced to $x + y + z = 100, \ x - z = 10$.
- We manually correct the wrong spelling words in MWP text (Table 1).

Table 1. Statistics of several existing MWP solving datasets. Avg EL, Avg Ops refer to average equation length and average numbers of operators in equations, respectively. * indicates only 3154 equation-MWP pairs of Dolphin18K are available.

Dataset	Size	Problem type	Avg EL	Avg Ops
Alg514	514	Algebra, linear	9.67	5.69
Dolphin1878	1878	Number word problems	8.18	4.97
DRAW-1K	1000	Algebra, linear, one-variable	9.99	5.85
Dolphin18K	18460*	Algebra, linear, multi-variable	9.19	4.96
Our Dataset	14943	Algebra, linear/nonlinear, multi-variable	16.64	6.41

4.3 Model Settings

The batch size for training is 32. We employ ConceptNet5[2] to construct KB, it has 34 types of relationship in total. 2 layer graph attention network is implemented for word knowledge pretraining step. The embedding size and all hidden state size of GRU are set to 256. In problem encoder three different convolutional kernels are used and their kernel sizes are 2,3,4, respectively. To be fair, we use 1-layer GRU for both our model and baseline. For LDA we divide all samples into 9 topic types and their amount and representative words are reported in Table 2. Each problem is associated with a topic distribution over 9 topics. The topic with the highest probability is adopted as the golden category. Meanwhile each topic contains several words and we choose top 30 words to construct topic memory for each topic. μ in (20) is set to 0.5. Weight coefficient in (16) is set to $\alpha = 0.7$. We use Adam optimizer [17] to train our model, the learning rate is set to 0.0005.

Table 2. Topic classes statistics and representative words sampled from each topic

Topic type	Train	Representative words
1	810	Do, people, divided, men, mean...
2	758	Length, width, rectangle, area, inches...
3	1573	Probability, quarter, dimes, coins, marbles...
4	557	Sum, difference, larger, smaller, less...
5	1087	Solution, gallon, mixture, grams, water...
6	633	Interest, year, invested, dollars, rate...
7	663	Angles, degrees, percent, digit, increased...
8	879	Sold, ticket, prices, children, adult...
9	754	Speed, minutes, travels, took, plane...

4.4 Automatic Evaluation

We report automatic evaluation in five aspects: BLEU (up to bigrams) [9], ROUGE-L [8], Dist-1, Dist-2, which indicates the proportion of different unigrams (bigrams) in all unigrams (bigrams), Number recall, which is used to measure how many numbers in problem text are correctly copied. Results are reported in Table 4. In Table 4 we also present results of ablation study. We can observe 1) our model yields higher performance in all metrics compared with baselines, especially in Dist-1 and Dist-2, which proves our model can generate more diversity math word problems. We consider this is because baseline models have no guidance in topic words and knowledge, thus they tend to generate the simplest question type like "one number is twice the second number...".

---

[2] https://github.com/commonsense/conceptnet5.

2) taking out topic control or commonsense enhancement will both decrease evaluation scores, which verifies their effectiveness. For example, removing commonsense enhancement declines BLEU score by 24.4%, while removing VAE & topic memory declines BLEU score by 35.5%.

We also separately compare MAGENT with our model including the same keywords as an extra input in Table 5, which demonstrates our model can still achieve performance gain with the same input.

Table 3. Statistic of datasets.

	Train	Dev	Test
Size	7714	964	965
Equation Length (average)	16.69	16.23	16.63
Problem Length (average)	28.90	29.64	28.74
Tokens	7445	3065	2875

Table 4. Automatic results in test dataset with BLEU, ROUGE-L (ROU), Dist-1 (D1), Dist-2 (D2) and Number Recall (NR). TP, TM and V denote the equation template, topic memory and VAE, respectively. CE includes both the pretraining step and the commonsense enforcement for the decoder.

Model	BLEU	ROU	D1 (%)	D2 (%)	NR (%)
Seq2seq	0.0259	0.2025	14.56	34.99	47.60
SeqGAN	0.0262	0.1922	12.96	30.02	44.00
DeepGCN	0.0304	0.2094	16.81	45.17	49.21
Transformer	0.0277	0.2036	16.69	37.57	50.89
Our model	**0.0433**	**0.2415**	**20.84**	53.81	55.14
w/o TP	0.0385	0.2377	18.88	**57.41**	**55.84**
w/o CE	0.0327	0.2273	18.75	51.19	54.42
w/o TM	0.0345	0.2256	20.00	55.00	54.31
w/o V & TM	0.0280	0.2141	18.79	50.05	53.82

Table 5. Comparison between our model with keywords (KW) and MAGNET in automatic results

Model	BLEU	ROU	D1 (%)	D2 (%)	NR (%)
MAGNET	0.0976	0.3793	**21.72**	57.22	42.62
Our model (KW)	**0.1152**	**0.4006**	18.81	**58.85**	**51.50**

4.5   Human Evaluation

Automatic metrics such as BLEU and ROUGE only focus on n-gram similarity, but fail to measure true generation quality (i.e., if topic drifting occurs). We invite three human annotators to judge generation quality in four aspects. 1) **Fluency (Flu)**: it mainly judges whether the problem text is fluent, i.e., whether the generated problem text has some grammar errors. 2) **Coherence (Coh)**: it weights if the problem text is coherent in text-level; 3) **Solvability-1 (S1)**: as our target is a math word problem, we should pay attention to whether the problem text can be solved, i.e., in what percentage we can set up the same (or equivalent) equations and solve them according to the generated problem text; 4) **Solvability-2 (S2)** is a more relaxed criterion compared with Solvability-1, it only requires the text produced is a valid math problem and could be solved regardless what equations could be set. We randomly select 50 generated MWP texts and score them in five grades. The scores are projected to 1–5, where higher score implies better performance (for solvability we use percentage). We report the average scores in Table 6.

Table 6 (*upper*) confirms our proposed model receives significant higher score in coherence and solvability, we assume this is because our model restricts the problem text into a certain topic and provides related words for reference.

In Table 6 (*bottom*) we report comparison between our model with keywords and MAGNET. Human scores reflect that our method achieves 12% relative improvement over MAGNET in Solvability-1. Especially, with keywords fed into the model, the problem of topic drifting is no longer notable for both our model and MAGNET.

Table 6. Human evaluation results: comparison between the proposed model and baseline models.

	Flu	Coh	S1 (%)	S2 (%)
Our model	**4.03**	**4.02**	**35**	**55**
Seq2seq	3.78	3.48	23	34
SeqGAN	3.75	3.28	20	40
DeepGCN	3.61	3.55	29	52
Transformer	3.80	3.53	20	45
MAGNET	4.00	4.33	44	**76**
Our model (KW)	**4.27**	**4.60**	**56**	74

4.6   Case Study

Table 7 shows some math word problems generated by different models. It's easy to show problem text generated by Seq2seq suffers from lack of coherence, e.g., in the above case, the baseline result talks about different topics in the same sentence. As a comparison, our generator discusses the same topic and generates words around this topic. What's more, the topic of problem text generated by our proposed model is highly consistent with reference answer, which verifies the effectiveness of the proposed model.

We can also observe commonsense violation appears in baseline results, for example, "chemist has a perimeter" and "geometric is 4 more than" are obviously illogical. Relatively speaking, MWP text generated by our model, is more in line with commonsense, such as "the hypotenuse of a right triangle". These results reflect that our model can benefit from both the topic consistency maintaining and commonsense enforcement mechanism.

Table 7. Three examples of math word problems generated by different models. Transformer is abbreviate to Trans. Topic words in the left column indicate the overlap between selected topic words and the generated MWP text, which is also highlighted in the right column. CG reflects the reasoning procedure adopted by the decoder.

Equation: $equ : 4 * (x - y) = 800 \ equ : 2 * (x + y) = 800$ **Reference:** An airplane travels 800 miles against the wind in 4 hrs and makes the return trip with the same wind in 2 hrs . Find the speed of the wind. **Topic Words:** travels, miles, speed **CG:** travel $\xrightarrow{RelatedTo}$ trip travel $\xrightarrow{RelatedTo}$ take	**Ours:** A plane travels 800 miles in 4 hours . the return trip against the same wind took 4.5 hours. Find the speed of the current wind. **Seq2seq:** A chemist has a perimeter of 80 cm, the area of the rectangle is 800 m. what is the length of the rectangle. **SeqGAN:** The perimeter of a rectangle is 800 inches. Find the length. **DeepGCN:** A man has 800 more than four times as old as his son . If the current is 800 m. Find the speed of the plane. **Trans:** The sum of two numbers is 800. The sum of their squares is 25% . Find the numbers.
Equation: $equ : 0.1 * x + 0.05 * y = 1.95 \ equ : y = x + 3$ **Reference:** Ken has $ 1.95 in nickels and dimes . There are 3 more nickels than dimes. How many of each does he have? **Topic Words:** nickels, dims, ticket **CG:** nickel $\xrightarrow{IsA}$ coin $\xrightarrow{RelatedTo}$ dime	**Ours:** Arnold has some nickels and dimes . If he made a number of $ 3 .50 . If she had 3 more nickels than dimes. Find the amount of each ticket . **Seq2seq:** A total of 1.95 seats is in the ratio of 10%. If the total area of the coins is 1.95. Find **SeqGAN:** A carpet is 3 times as many more than the other. The total value is 3. **DeepGCN:** Dan invested $ 1.95 . part a t 10% annual interest. the total value of the cost of a 10% salt solution is added to **Trans:** A computer has a mixture of $ 3 . 000 and a mixture contains 5% profit of 5% . How much does each have.
Equation: $equ : 0.1 * x + 0.05 * y = 1.95 \ equ : y = x + 3$ **Reference:** A car radiator contains 10 liters of 30% antifreeze solution. How many liters will have to be replaced with the pure antifreeze if the resulting solution is to be 50% antifreeze? **Topic Words:** acid, solution **CG:** acid $\xrightarrow{IsA}$ liquid $\xrightarrow{RelatedTo}$ solution	**Ours:** How many liters of a 30% acid solution must be added to 10 liters of 20% solution on the mixture to make l0 litters of a 50% solution. **Seq2seq:** A raditor contains 50% nitric acid. If we take the same place to be 10. What is the total number of water. **SeqGAN:** A boat travels 10 miles per hour. How much would a 20% acid solution to be worth in 100 account **DeepGCN:** A <UNK> radiator is $ 10 . 00 a t a certain number. and the rest a t the same time . **Trans:** A car traveled in a car point is going a t a constant speed. If the car going a car point in the car . about 0 mph . how many miles apart.

5   Conclusion

We propose a novel model and a dataset for generating MWP from equations. Our model can effectively encode different types of math tokens in equations and reduce the gap between abstract math tokens and generated natural language text. It is also very useful in tackling the topic drifting and commonsense violation problems. Experiments on our dataset show our model significantly outperforms baseline models.

References

1. Blei, D.M., Ng, A.Y., Jordan, M.I.: Latent Dirichlet allocation. J. Mach. Learn. Res. (2003)
2. Bowman, S.R., Vilnis, L., Vinyals, O., Dai, A.M., Jozefowicz, R., Bengio, S.: Generating sentences from a continuous space. In: SIGNLL. ACL (2016)
3. Chen, S., Wang, J., Feng, X., Jiang, F., Qin, B., Lin, C.Y.: Enhancing neural data-to-text generation models with external background knowledge. In: EMNLP-IJCNLP. Association for Computational Linguistics (2019)
4. Cui, L., Wu, Y., Liu, S., Zhang, Y., Zhou, M.: Mutual: a dataset for multi-turn dialogue reasoning (2020)
5. Dauphin, Y.N., Fan, A., Auli, M., Grangier, D.: Language modeling with gated convolutional networks. arXiv, Computation and Language (2016)
6. Gong, L., Crego, J., Senellart, J.: Enhanced transformer model for data-to-text generation. In: Proceedings of the 3rd Workshop on Neural Generation and Translation. Association for Computational Linguistics (2019)
7. Gyawali, B., Gardent, C.: Surface realisation from knowledge-bases. In: ACL. The Association for Computer Linguistics (2014)
8. Lin, C.: Rouge: a package for automatic evaluation of summaries, pp. 74–81 (2004)
9. Papineni, K., Roukos, S., Ward, T., Zhu, W.: Bleu: a method for automatic evaluation of machine translation. In: ACL. ACL (2002)
10. Puduppully, R., Dong, L., Lapata, M.: Data-to-text generation with content selection and planning. In: AAAI. AAAI Press (2019)
11. See, A., Liu, P.J., Manning, C.D.: Get to the point: summarization with pointer-generator networks. In: SIGNLL. Association for Computational Linguistics (2017)
12. Velickovic, P., Cucurull, G., Casanova, A., Romero, A., Lio, P., Bengio, Y.: Graph attention networks. arXiv, Machine Learning (2017)
13. Wiseman, S., Shieber, S.M., Rush, A.M.: Challenges in data-to-document generation. In: EMNLP. Association for Computational Linguistics (2017)
14. Zhao, C., Walker, M., Chaturvedi, S.: Bridging the structural gap between coding and decoding for data-to-text generation. In: ACL. Association for Computational Linguistics (2020)
15. Zhou, Q., Huang, D.: Towards generating math word problems from equations and topics. In: INLG. Association for Computational Linguistics (2019)
16. Huang, D., Shi, S., Lin, C.-Y., Yin, J., Ma, W.-Y.: How well do computers solve math word problems? Large-scale dataset construction and evaluation. In: ACL. Association for Computational Linguistics (2016)
17. Kingma, D.P., Ba, J.: Adam: a method for stochastic optimization. arXiv, Learning (2014)
18. Kushman, N., Artzi, Y., Zettlemoyer, L., Barzilay, R.: Learning to automatically solve algebra word problems. In: ACL, pp. 271–281. Association for Computational Linguistics (2014)
19. Shi, S., Wang, Y., Lin, C.-Y., Liu, X., Rui, Y.: Automatically solving number word problems by semantic parsing and reasoning. In: EMNLP. Association for Computational Linguistics (2015)
20. Upadhyay, S., Chang, M.-W.: Annotating derivations: a new evaluation strategy and dataset for algebra word problems. In: EACL. Association for Computational Linguistics, April 2017

Generative Properties of Universal Bidirectional Activation-Based Learning

Kristína Malinovská[(✉)] and Igor Farkaš

Faculty of Mathematics, Physics and Informatics, Comenius University in Bratislava,
Bratislava, Slovakia
{malinovska,farkas}@fmph.uniba.sk
http://cogsci.fmph.uniba.sk/cnc/

Abstract. UBAL is a novel bidirectional neural network model with bio-inspired learning. It enhances contrastive Hebbian learning rule with an internal echo mechanism enabling self-supervised learning. UBAL approaches any problem as a bidirectional heteroassociation, which gives rise to emergent properties, such as generation of patterns while trained for classification. We briefly discuss and illustrate these properties using the MNIST dataset and conclude that with a slight trade-off in accuracy we can achieve feasible image generation without explicitly setting up the objective to do so.

Keywords: Biologically inspired learning · Bidirectional connectivity · Generative networks

1 Towards More Brain-Like Learning

Well-known error-backpropagation (BP) algorithm is traditionally argued to lack biological plausibility [2,7]. Learning in the brain is based on local interactions between presynaptic and postsynaptic neurons. The brain makes a great use of bidirectional flow of information in order to classify and reconstruct patterns [7], but the activation never propagates back via the same synaptic weights. Our Universal Bidirectional Activation-based Learning (UBAL) model [6] is mainly inspired by the canonical recirculation algorithm proposed by Hinton [3] conceiving the autoencoder, and by the Generalized Recirculation which is an adaptation of Contrastive Hebbian Learning (CHL) [7].

UBAL shares the features with other models of this new wave of biologically inspired neural models. Random synaptic weights are proposed to avoid back-propagating via the same neural pathway in the Feedback Alignment model [5]. The Equilibrium propagation [9] as well as the whole family of Target propagation models [8] make use of the target clamping which is essential in contrastive learning.[1]

---

[1] The target (ground truth) is directly inserted (clamped) into the output layer of a model as a neural activation which can be propagated backwards in the network. Instead of using error derivatives, the weights are adapted based on local differences between forward (estimated) and backward (clamped) activation variables.

© Springer Nature Switzerland AG 2021
I. Farkaš et al. (Eds.): ICANN 2021, LNCS 12893, pp. 80–83, 2021.
https://doi.org/10.1007/978-3-030-86365-4_7

2   UBAL Model

UBAL is a heteroencoder model that maintains separate weight matrices for two different activation propagation directions between the visible layers. In the context of classification the propagation of input activation would be called the prediction in the forward direction and propagation of the clamped targets would be called the prediction in the backward direction. Inspired by [3] we also propagate the network's immediate prediction in the opposite direction which we call the *echo*.

Since the same learning rule applies for any two consecutive bidirectionally connected layers, hidden or visible, we define the model here for just two connected layers p and q and their synaptic weights W_{pq} for the forward direction and M_{qp} for the backward direction (Fig. 1). As listed in Table 1, the activation of propagation is expressed as the product of the presynaptic activation and the bias and the synaptic weight with the activation function f applied. The biases are added in both directions and labeled b or d. Their synaptic connections are already assumed in the weight matrices.

The resulting activation variables are combined using the hyperparameters β and γ defined for each direction of activation propagation (F and B) into learning rule terms (Table 2). The learning rule in Eq. 1 and 2 is formed by these intermediate terms with the aim to emphasize its relationship to the contrastive Hebbian learning.

$$\Delta W_{pq} = \lambda\, t_p^{\mathrm{B}}(t_q^{\mathrm{F}} - e_q^{\mathrm{F}}) \tag{1}$$

$$\Delta M_{qp} = \lambda\, t_q^{\mathrm{F}}(t_p^{\mathrm{B}} - e_p^{\mathrm{B}}) \tag{2}$$

Table 1. Activation propagation.

Activation phase	Note	Computation
Forward prediction	q^{FP}	$f(W_{pq}p^{\mathrm{FP}} + b_p)$
Forward echo	p^{FE}	$f(M_{qp}q^{\mathrm{FP}} + d_q)$
Backward prediction	p^{BP}	$f(M_{qp}q^{\mathrm{BP}} + d_q)$
Backward echo	q^{BE}	$f(W_{pq}p^{\mathrm{BP}} + b_p)$

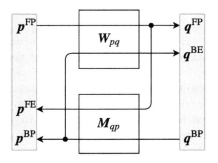

Fig. 1. UBAL connectivity of two connected layers p and q.

Table 2. Learning rule terms.

Learning rule term	Note	Computation
Forward target	t_q^{F}	$\beta_q^{\mathrm{F}}q^{\mathrm{FP}} + (1 - \beta_q^{\mathrm{F}})q^{\mathrm{BP}}$
Forward estimate	e_q^{F}	$\gamma_q^{\mathrm{F}}q^{\mathrm{FP}} + (1 - \gamma_q^{\mathrm{F}})q^{\mathrm{BE}}$
Backward target	t_p^{B}	$\beta_p^{\mathrm{B}}p^{\mathrm{BP}} + (1 - \beta_p^{\mathrm{B}})p^{\mathrm{FP}}$
Backward estimate	e_p^{B}	$\gamma_p^{\mathrm{B}}p^{\mathrm{BP}} + (1 - \gamma_p^{\mathrm{B}})p^{\mathrm{FE}}$

The hyperparameters β mediate the clamping and trade-off the predicted and the clamped activation contributing to the weight change. The hyperparameters

γ trade-off the prediction and the echo activation variables. The values of βs and γs differ across the tasks that the network has to learn and are under continuous examination. Our general observation so far is that, setting all γs to 0.5 works well for associative tasks (encode-retrieve) and values around 0.0 and 1.0 enable UBAL to master classification.

3   Classification and Generative Properties

With the hyperparameter setups in Table 3 (input–hidden–output) and large-enough hidden layer (1500 neurons), the performance of UBAL in the MNIST [4] benchmark is comparable to the related models. UBAL can reaches up to 96% accuracy on the testing set, without any kind of image augmentation or any supplementary regularization techniques. We use a 3-layer network with standard sigmoidal units (softmax for output layer) and Gaussian weight initialization $\mathcal{N}(0.0, 0.5)$ and learning rate 0.05. MNIST digit targets are encoded as one-hot vectors and images are normalized to $(0, 1)$.

Table 3. Two setups of UBAL hyper-parameters for MNIST.

	Setup A	Setup B
β^{F}	0.0–1.0–0.0	1.0–1.0–0.9
γ^{F}	1.0–1.0	1.0–1.0
γ^{B}	1.0–1.0	0.9–1.0
β^{B}	1.0–0.0–1.0	0.0–0.0–0.1

Fig. 2. Example of projected digit 3 with Setup A (left) and Setup B (right).

Hence UBAL is a heteroencoder, apart from classifying the digits, it also naturally makes projections of those digits in its input layer, which could be understood as the network's imagination as shown in Fig. 3. Our preliminary results suggest that these images differ among network initializations and they are different from the computed averages of all images in the dataset. Decreasing the hidden layer β^{F} from 1.0 to a smaller value (0.995–0.999999) yields slight decrease in accuracy, but more variable and graded images with soft edges.

A natural step in exploration of generative properties is to introduce noise into the network. Currently, we are adding small Gaussian noise to the labels. Our experiments show that the generalization ability of UBAL is not much impeded by a very low-variance noise, yet it yields more diverse backward projections in case the noise is added to the targets when gathering the backward projections. The ability of UBAL to generate patterns in the backward direction while trained for the classification task is mostly influenced by the β and γ hyperparameter setup. There are setups that do work well in terms of classification accuracy, but do not allow generation of legible numbers (Fig. 2). We will

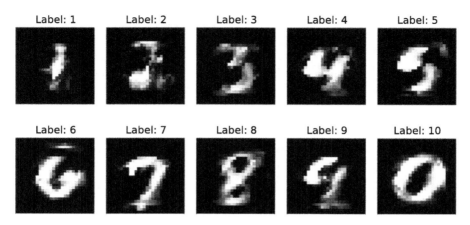

Fig. 3. MNIST digits generated by UBAL.

further explore the properties of the projected images and how they are classified by a UBAL and by other models. This relates to explainable AI, where there is a prospect of using UBAL for generating noise for adversarial examples [1]. In this line we plan to investigate the robustness of UBAL against adversarial attacks.

Acknowledgments. This research was supported by KEGA grant no. 042UK-4/2019.

References

1. Goodfellow, I.J., Shlens, J., Szegedy, C.: Explaining and harnessing adversarial examples. arXiv preprint arXiv:1412.6572 (2014)
2. Grossberg, S.: Competitive learning: from interactive activation to adaptive resonance. Cogn. Sci. **11**(1), 23–63 (1987)
3. Hinton, G.E., McClelland, J.L.: Learning representations by recirculation. In: Neural Information Processing Systems, pp. 358–366 (1988)
4. LeCun, Y., Bottou, L., Bengio, Y., Haffner, P.: Gradient-based learning applied to document recognition. Proc. IEEE **86**(11), 2278–2324 (1998)
5. Lillicrap, T.P., Cownden, D., Tweed, D.B., Akerman, C.J.: Random synaptic feedback weights support error backpropagation for deep learning. Nat. Commun. **7**, 13276 (2016)
6. Malinovská, K., Malinovskỳ, L., Krsek, P., Kraus, S., Farkaš, I.: UBAL: a Universal Bidirectional Activation-based Learning Rule for Neural Networks. In: Proceedings of the 2019 2nd International Conference on Computational Intelligence and Intelligent Systems, pp. 57–62 (2019)
7. O'Reilly, R.C., Munakata, Y., Frank, M., Hazy, T., et al.: Computational Cognitive Neuroscience. PediaPress, Mainz (2012)
8. Ororbia, A.G., Mali, A.: Biologically motivated algorithms for propagating local target representations. arXiv preprint arXiv:1805.11703 (2018)
9. Scellier, B., Bengio, Y.: Equilibrium propagation: bridging the gap between energy-based models and backpropagation. Front. Comput. Neurosci. **11**, 24 (2017)

Graph Neural Networks I

Joint Graph Contextualized Network for Sequential Recommendation

Ruoran Huang[1,2], Chuanqi Han[1,2], and Li Cui[1(✉)]

[1] Institute of Computing Technology, Chinese Academy of Sciences, Beijing, China
{huangruoran,hanchuanqi18b,lcui}@ict.ac.cn
[2] University of Chinese Academy of Sciences, Beijing, China

Abstract. Sequential recommendation aims to suggest items to users based on sequential dependencies. Graph neural networks (GNNs) are recently proposed to capture transitions of items by treating session sequences as graph-structured data. However, existing graph construction approaches mainly focus on the directional dependency of items and ignore benefits of feature aggregation from undirectional relationship. In this paper, we innovatively propose a joint graph contextualized network (JGCN) for sequential recommendation, which constructs both the directed graphs and undirected graphs to jointly capture current interests and global preferences. Specifically, we introduce gate graph neural networks and model the combined embedding of weighted position and node information from directed graphs for capturing current interests. Besides, to learn global preferences, we propose a graph collaborative attention network with correlation-based similarity of items from undirected graphs. Finally, a feed-forward layer with the residual connection is applied to synthetically obtain accurate transitions of items. Extensive experiments conducted on three datasets show that JGCN outperforms state-of-the-art methods.

Keywords: Sequential recommendation · Graph neural networks · Graph attention networks · Weighted position embedding · Correlation-based similarity

1 Introduction

Sequential recommender system (SRS) has become an emerging direction in recommendation domain, e.g., music, ecommerce and social media, which aims to predict the next item based on the sequence session of the user's historical behaviors. The key challenges of SRS are the uncertainty of the user's behaviors and limited interacted information, making it difficult to precisely predict the user's next action [1]. Early works based on Markov Chains (MC) assume that the next action is based on the previous ones [2]. Under such a strong assumption, an independent combination of the past interactions would confine the

---

Supported by the National Natural Science Foundation of China (NSFC) under Grant No. 61672498.

I. Farkaš et al. (Eds.): ICANN 2021, LNCS 12893, pp. 87–100, 2021.
https://doi.org/10.1007/978-3-030-86365-4_8

prediction accuracy. With tremendous achievements in deep neural networks, Hidasi et al. [3] attempt to highlight the importance of leveraging recurrent neural networks (RNN) to model temporal shifts of user behaviors. Distinct from that, Caser abandons conventional RNN structures and introduce convolutional neural networks (CNN) to distill local dependent information [4], which treats the item embedding matrix as an "image" by sliding over the rows. Some researchers to date have tended to focus on attention mechanism, which employ memory networks [5] and attentive structures [6] to selectively retain information from user-item interactions to predict the future items. Recently, graph-based structures have received considerable attention in SRS by effectively extracting complex relationships and interdependency among items [7]. SR-GNN [8] is a typical work to learn graph contextualized representations by aggregating local dependencies over adjacent items, and the core idea of SR-GNN is to consider the deep transitions between items by constructing directed graphs from historical session sequences. Similarly, Xu et al. [9] propose GC-SAN by combining gated graph neural network (GGNN) [10] and the self-attention layer to learn long-range dependencies. Despite achieving significant results, existing works still have some inevitable limitations. RNN-based models suffer from interference of noise and irrelevant interactions in chronological order. For attention-based and CNN-based models, they do not adequately consider dynamic representations of item sequences and have limited power of learning long-term behaviors. Current graph-based solutions e.g., SR-GNN and GC-SAN only consider single-way transitions between consecutive items from directed graphs with a weak integration of temporal interests and intrinsic preferences, which ignore partially critical information from undirectional data.

Towards this end, we propose a joint graph contextualized network (JGCN) for sequential recommendation. The major structure of JGCN is illustrated in Fig. 1. We first construct directed and undirected graphs from all session sequences. Specifically, we adopt the combined embedding of weighted position and node information, then we feed them into gate graph neural networks to learn the current interest of users. Besides, we propose a graph collaborative attention network by improving graph attention network with the correlation-based similarity among items, extracting global and inherent preferences. Finally, we combine the current interest with global preference together by using a pointwise feed forward layer to compute the probability of selecting on next item.

Our main contributions are summarized as follows: 1) We propose a joint graph contextualized network to synthetically capture current interests and global preferences of users by modeling graph-structured sessions from directed and undirected graphs. 2) We design a weight-position mechanism to encode position embeddings of gate graph neural networks. 3) We enhance graph attention networks by introducing correlation-based similarity among overall items in feature aggregation phase. 4) Extensive experiments conducted on three real-world datasets show that JGCN evidently outperforms the state-of-the-art methods.

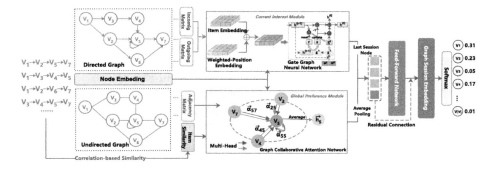

Fig. 1. The overall structure of the proposed JGCN model.

2   Methods

Preliminaries. Formally, let $\mathcal{V} = \{v_1, v_2, \ldots, v_{|\mathcal{V}|}\}$ indicate existing all unique items. For one anonymous session, user actions are represented by a list $\mathcal{S} = [s_1, s_2, \ldots, s_{L'}]$ in chronological order, where $s_t \in \mathcal{S}$ $(1 \leq t < L')$ denotes an interacted item of the user u within the session $\mathcal{S}$. Considering an item may appear more than once, we record the last occurrence of each item in session $\mathcal{S}$ at the position encoding since the behaviors close to the current moment often make greater impact on the next user action, then the actual session length can be marked as L. We define $\hat{y}_i$ as a probability value of item i that will occur in the next event (e.g., clicking, viewing or purchasing), then our model generates a ranking list over all candidate items $\hat{\mathbf{y}} = [\hat{y}_1, \hat{y}_2, \ldots, \hat{y}_{|\mathcal{V}|}]$. Conceptually, SRS typically makes more than one recommendation for the user and we select the top-N items from $\hat{\mathbf{y}}$ for sequential recommendations.

2.1   Graph Construction and Embedding

Constructing Session Graphs. For a session $\mathcal{S}$, we exploit the meaningful interactions between users and items from the perspective of graph structure. We regard each item s_i as a node and (s_{i-1}, s_i) can be seen as the edge which means a user interacts with interacted item s_i after s_{i-1} in session $\mathcal{S}$. Thus, a session graph is represented as $\mathcal{G}_s = (\mathcal{V}_s, \mathcal{E}_s)$, where $\mathcal{V}_s$ denotes the set of nodes and $\mathcal{E}_s$ is the set of edges. Distinct from previous works on graph-structured data, which mainly focus on directional dependences while ignoring potential undirectional correlations between nodes, we propose to simultaneously construct directed and undirected graphs from one session $\mathcal{S}$ to jointly learn temporal interests and inherent preferences of users on graphs. More concretely, each session sequence is modeled as a directed graph $\overrightarrow{\mathcal{G}_s} = \langle \mathcal{V}_s, \mathcal{E}_s \rangle$ and undirected graph $\overline{\mathcal{G}_s} = (\mathcal{V}_s, \mathcal{E}_s)$, where $\langle, \rangle$ means the directional relationship and $(,)$ denote the undirectional relationship. We define $\mathbf{M}^I, \mathbf{M}^O \in \mathbb{R}^{L \times L}$ of directed graph $\overrightarrow{\mathcal{G}_s}$ as weighted connections of incoming and outgoing edges in the session graph, respectively. Since several items may appear in the sequence repeatedly, each edge is assigned to a normalized weight, which is calculated as the occurrence of the edge divided by the outdegree of that edge's start node (or indegree of that edge's end node). For undirected graph $\overline{\mathcal{G}_s}$, let $\mathbf{M}^A$ be the adjacency matrix of graph $\overline{\mathcal{G}_s}$, where $\mathbf{M}^A$ is a $\mathbb{R}^{L \times L}$ matrix with $\mathbf{M}^A_{(i-1,i)} = 1$ if $\mathcal{E}_{(s_{i-1},s_i)} \in \mathcal{E}_s$ and $\mathbf{M}^A_{(i-1,i)} = 0$ if $\mathcal{E}_{(s_{i-1},s_i)} \notin \mathcal{E}_s$. The construction process is illustrated in Fig. 2.

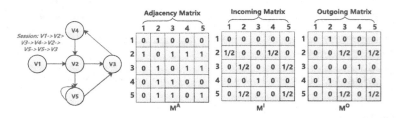

Fig. 2. An example of directed and undirected graph structures from one session sequence.

Node Embedding. In order to obtain node information representation, each item $v_i \in \mathcal{V}$ is embedded into an unique embedding space and converted into the learnable vector $\mathrm{h}_i^e \in \mathbb{R}^d$, where i is the unique index of the item set and d is the dimension of vector h_i^e.

2.2   Current Interest Module

Weighted-Position Embedding. Traditional approaches only consider the coarse-grained contextual message from sequence data, resulting in the loss of fine-grained position information. Remarkably, the length of sessions are usually variable and the tail items in the session sequences will be assigned to smaller weights if we employ the zero position operation. To tackle these issues, we propose a weighted-position mechanism to encode these position embeddings. To be exact, for item v_i in session $\mathcal{S}$, $\mathrm{h}_i^p \in \mathbb{R}^d$ denote position embedding vector at position p. Considering the importance of different positions of the session sequence, we put the position-aware weight on each position embedding by multiplying reciprocal of the relative location, which could be formulated as follows:

$$\mathbf{h}_i = \mathrm{h}_i^e + \frac{p}{L}\mathrm{h}_i^p, \text{ where } 1 \leq p \leq L, \tag{1}$$

Learning Dynamic Session Graphs. For each node s_i of directed graph $\overrightarrow{\mathcal{G}_s}$, we connect incoming and outgoing matrices $\mathbf{M}^I, \mathbf{M}^O$ to jointly capture the local features of the session sequence. The feed-forward propagation process among neighboring nodes at time t is formalized as:

$$\mathbf{g}_i^t = Concat[\mathbf{M}_i^I([\mathbf{h}_1^{t-1}, \ldots, \mathbf{h}_L^{t-1}]\mathbf{W}_{in} + \mathbf{b}_{in}),$$
$$\mathbf{M}_i^O([\mathbf{h}_1^{t-1}, \ldots, \mathbf{h}_L^{t-1}]\mathbf{W}_{out} + \mathbf{b}_{out})], \qquad (2)$$

where $[\mathbf{h}_1^{t-1}, \ldots, \mathbf{h}_L^{t-1}]$ denotes the input sequence represented by node vectors in session $\mathcal{S}$. $\mathbf{M}_i^I, \mathbf{M}_i^O \in \mathbb{R}^{1 \times L}$ denote i-th row of matrices $\mathbf{M}^I, \mathbf{M}^O \in \mathbb{R}^{L \times L}$, respectively. $\mathbf{W}_{in}, \mathbf{W}_{out} \in \mathbb{R}^{d \times d}$ are the projection matrices and $\mathbf{b}_{in}, \mathbf{b}_{out} \in \mathbb{R}^d$ represent bias vectors. In this way, $\mathbf{g}_i^t$ can be seen as an aggregation factor which retrieves the neighbouring contextual message for each node s_i at timestamp t.

Node Vector Updating. Thereafter, we put this graph-structured vector $\mathbf{g}_i^t$ and the previous state $\mathbf{h}_i^{t-1}$ into the gated graph neural networks [10] (gated GNN) to automatically learn abundant node connection information of each session graph:

$$\mathbf{z}_i^t = \sigma\left(\mathbf{W}_z \mathbf{g}_i^t + \mathbf{U}_z \mathbf{h}_i^{t-1}\right), \qquad (3)$$

$$\mathbf{r}_i^t = \sigma\left(\mathbf{W}_r \mathbf{g}_i^t + \mathbf{U}_r \mathbf{h}_i^{t-1}\right), \qquad (4)$$

$$\tilde{\mathbf{h}}_i^t = tanh\left(\mathbf{W}_o \mathbf{g}_i^t + \mathbf{U}_o\left(\mathbf{r}_i^t \odot \mathbf{h}_i^{t-1}\right)\right), \qquad (5)$$

$$\mathbf{h}_i^t = \left(1 - \mathbf{z}_i^t\right) \odot \mathbf{h}_i^{t-1} + \mathbf{z}_i^t \odot \tilde{\mathbf{h}}_i^t, \qquad (6)$$

where $\mathbf{W}_z, \mathbf{W}_r, \mathbf{W}_o \in \mathbb{R}^{2d \times d}$, $\mathbf{U}_z, \mathbf{U}_r, \mathbf{U}_o \in \mathbb{R}^{d \times d}$ are learnable weight matrices. $\mathbf{z}_i$ and $\mathbf{r}_i$ denote update and reset gates, which decide whether existing computed state to be preserved and discarded, respectively. $\odot$ indicates the Hadamard product operator and σ is the logistic sigmoid function. $\mathbf{h}_i^t \in \mathbb{R}^d$ is the embedded vector of node s_i at timestamp t. Through gated GNN, we obtain the vector representation of nodes $\mathbf{H_s} = [\mathbf{h}_1^t, \mathbf{h}_2^t, \ldots, \mathbf{h}_L^t]$, which support the current and temporal interest representation of users by aggregating the neighbors of items over the short period GNN.

2.3   Global Preference Module

Correlation-Based Similarity. Although the attention mechanism show its advantages in extracting adjacent information without considering the chronological order of session graph nodes, it still ignores the similarity effect of overall items that go beyond the neighbor nodes, failing to acquire comprehensively global preferences of users. To tackle this issue, we introduce the item similarity [11] to specify different weights for each neighborhood node according to the holistic items. Since there exist two typical types of data, i.e., explicit feedback (browsing, clicking or purchasing) and implicit feedback (rating or grading), we perform two correlation-based strategies on these two data types. Let users who both rated item p and item q be denoted by the set U, then the correlation similarity is given by:

$$\xi_{s,pq}^{(Implicit)} = \frac{|N(p) \cap N(q)|}{\sqrt{|N(p)||N(q)|}}, \qquad (7)$$

$$\xi_{s,pq}^{(Explicit)} = \frac{\sum_{u \in U}(R_{u,p} - \bar{R}_p)(R_{u,q} - \bar{R}_q)}{\sqrt{\sum_{u \in U}(R_{u,p} - \bar{R}_p)^2}\sqrt{\sum_{u \in U}(R_{u,q} - \bar{R}_q)^2}}, \qquad (8)$$

where $|N(p)|$, $|N(q)|$ denote the number of users preferring item p, q, respectively, and $\cap$ means that users who both like items of p and q. $R_{u,p}$ denotes the rating of user u on item p, $\bar{R}_q$ is the average rating of item q among all items. Instead of learning global dependency message from the limited/fixed length of the conventional deep learning approaches, we capture the global collaborative information by calculating relevant dependency among all items without considering the interaction distance or windows size.

Graph Collaborative Attention Network. Graph attention networks (GAT) [12] can allow nodes of the graph to attend over their neighborhood features instead of depending on the specific network structure, thus it is well suited to capture inherent and long-term preferences. By intergrating the correlation-based similarity of overall items, the global preferences can be comprehensively acquired as follows:

$$e_{pq} = \mathbf{a}(\mathbf{W}_d h_p^e, \mathbf{W}_d h_q^e), \tag{9}$$

where $\mathbf{a}$ is a general feed-forward neural network, $\mathbf{W}_d \in \mathbb{R}^d$ is a transition matrix. After that, the normalized importance α_{pq} between two connected nodes is computed in the following way:

$$\alpha_{pq} = \text{softmax}_q(e_{pq}) = \frac{\exp(\xi_{s,pq} \cdot e_{pq})}{\sum_{w \in \mathcal{N}_p} \exp(\xi_{s,pw} \cdot e_{pw})}, \tag{10}$$

where $\mathcal{N}_p$ represents the immediate neighbors of node p. Mathematically, coefficient α_{pq} can be reformulated as:

$$\alpha_{pq} = \frac{\exp\left(\psi\left(\mathbf{M}_{pq}^A \cdot \mathbf{a}^\mathsf{T}\left[\mathbf{W}_d h_p^e \| \mathbf{W}_d h_q^e\right] \xi_{s,pq}\right)\right)}{\sum_{w \in \mathcal{N}_p} \exp\left(\psi\left(\mathbf{M}_{pw}^A \cdot \mathbf{a}^\mathsf{T}\left[\mathbf{W}_d h_p^e \| \mathbf{W}_d h_w^e\right] \xi_{s,pw}\right)\right)}, \tag{11}$$

where $\mathbf{M}_{pq}^A \in \mathbf{M}^A$ is the edge weight of the adjacency matrix between p and q. ψ is the activation function *LeakyReLU*. $\mathbf{a}^\mathsf{T}$ denotes a feed-forward neural network of the attention function parameterized by weight vector $\mathbb{R}^{2d}$, while $\|$ indicates the concatenation operation of tensors. Intuitively, $\mathbf{a}^\mathsf{T}\left[\mathbf{W}_d h_p^e \| \mathbf{W}_d h_q^e\right]$ is a linear combination of h_p^e and node h_q^e, which can be expressed as an aggregate relationship of distance between p and q. Subsequently, to serve as the final output for graph nodes, the normalized attention coefficient α_{pq} is used to compute a linear combination of the features:

$$h_p = \sigma\Big(\sum_{q \in \mathcal{N}_p} \alpha_{pq} \mathbf{W}_d h_q^e\Big), \tag{12}$$

where h_p is the learned hidden representation, which can be regarded as the semantic information of global and inherent preferences of the user.

Multi-head Mechanism. To benefit from the attention operation stably, we also employ a *multi-head mechanism* into our model:

$$h_p =_{\text{avg}} \|_{k=1}^K \mathbf{GAT}(\mathbf{h}^e, \xi_{s,pq})^{(k)}$$

$$= \sigma\left(\frac{1}{K}\sum_{k=1}^K \sum_{q \in \mathcal{N}_p} \boldsymbol{\alpha}_{pq}^{(k)} \mathbf{W}_d^{(k)} \mathbf{h}_q^e\right), \tag{13}$$

where K is the number of heads and $\boldsymbol{\alpha}_{pq}^{(k)}$ is the attention coefficient computed by the k-th attention mechanism. In this way, the multi-head output of node s_i can be represented as $\boldsymbol{h}_i \in \mathbb{R}^d$. Successively, we put these nodes of the output together in session $\mathcal{S}$ to form $\mathbf{H} = [\boldsymbol{h}_1, \boldsymbol{h}_2, \ldots, \boldsymbol{h}_L]$.

2.4 Prediction Layer and Model Training

Through the above two core modules, we achieve the short-term representation $\mathbf{H}_s$ and long-term representation $\mathbf{H}$. To better predict the user's next actions, we combine the short-term interest with the long-term preference to synthetically obtain the session graph embeddings. For a session $\mathbf{H}_s = [\mathbf{h}_1^t, \mathbf{h}_2^t, \ldots, \mathbf{h}_L^t]$, we take the last dimension as the current interest of users, i.e., $\mathbf{S}_c = \mathbf{h}_L^t$, while the global preference is computed by the average pooling of $\mathbf{H}$, i.e., $\mathbf{S}_g = \frac{1}{L}\sum_{i=1}^L \boldsymbol{h}_i$. Let γ be a weight factor with the default value of 0.5, which controls the trade-off between the current interest module and the global preference module. Then we weight them together via:

$$\mathbf{S}_f = \gamma\mathbf{S}_c + (1-\gamma)\mathbf{S}_g. \tag{14}$$

Feed-Forward Network. To boost the non-linear transformation of our model, we perform a two layer perceptron network by adding residual connection and GELU activation function, which could be formulated as:

$$\mathbf{S}_h = \text{GELU}(\mathbf{S}_f\mathbf{W}_1 + b_1)\mathbf{W}_2 + b_2 + \mathbf{S}_f, \tag{15}$$

where $\mathbf{W}_1, \mathbf{W}_2 \in \mathbb{R}^{d \times d}$ are projection matrices and $b_1, b_2 \in \mathbb{R}^d$ are bias vectors.

Finally, we predict the next selection for each candidate item $v_i \in \mathcal{V}$ by multiplying its original session embedding $\mathbf{h}_i^e$ as follows:

$$\hat{y}_i = \frac{\exp(\mathbf{S}_h^{\mathsf{T}}\mathbf{h}_i^e)}{\sum_{j=1}^{|\mathcal{V}|}\exp(\mathbf{S}_h^{\mathsf{T}}\mathbf{h}_j^e)}, \tag{16}$$

where $\hat{y}_i$ denotes the recommendation probability of item v_i to be the next item. For each session graph $\mathcal{S}$, the loss function is defined as the cross-entropy:

$$\mathcal{L} = -\sum_{i=1}^m \mathbf{y}_i log(\hat{\mathbf{y}}_i) + (1 - \mathbf{y}_i)log(1 - \hat{\mathbf{y}}_i) + \beta\|\Theta\|_2^2. \tag{17}$$

Here, $\mathbf{y}$ indicates the one-hot encoding vector of the ground truth item. β controls the regularization strength and Θ represents the set of all learnable parameters.

Datasets. We conduct experiments on three real-world datasets: MovieTweet-ings[1], Diginetica[2] and LastFM.[3] Analogously, we follow [8,9] to filter out sessions of length 1 and items which appear less than 5 times on three datasets. We also convert ratings whose values are beyond the half of total ratings to implicit feed-back records and sort out the sequence order on timestamps, where data of the last time period as the testing set. For clarity, the historical sequence of datasets are randomly split into training(70%), validation (5%), and testing (25%) sets. For session $\mathcal{S}=[s_1, s_2, \ldots, s_L]$, we generate a series of sequences and correspond-ing labels $\{s_1, [s_2]\}$, $\{s_1, s_2, [s_3]\}$, $\ldots$, $\{[s_1, \ldots, s_{L-1}], s_L\}$. Statistics of datasets are listed in Table 1.

3   Experimental Setup

Table 1. Statistics of datasets

Dataset	#Sessions	#Items	#Interactions	Avg. Len
LastFM	38,821	9,742	100,836	8.46
Diginetica	780,312	43,097	982,961	5.42
MovieTweetings	13,504	36,383	888,452	12.81

Metrics. We use HR@N (Hit Ratio), MRR@N (Mean Reciprocal Rank), and NDCG@N (Normalized Discounted Cumulative Gain) to evaluate all baselines, where N is the truncation value which is set to 5 and 20. Specifically, HR@N measures the proportion with the correct recommended items in the top-N posi-tion of the ranking. MRR@N is the average of reciprocal ranks of the desired item while the reciprocal rank is set to 0 when the rank exceeds N. NDCG evaluates scores by computing relative position in ranking list.

Baselines. 1) MostPop is a fundamental baseline by ranking the items based on popularity. 2) BPR-MF [13] optimizes a pairwise ranking objective function with implicit user feedback data. 3) Item-KNN [11] obtains recommendations accord-ing to the previously interacted items based on the cosine similarity. 4) FPMC [2] integrates matrix factorization and first-order Markov Chains. 5) GRU4Rec [3] is a RNN-based model by resorting to item-to-item recommendations. 6) Caser [4] treats the item embedding matrix as an "image" and performs 2D convo-lution on it. 7) SASRec [6] introduces a self-attention mechanism to identify which items are relevant. 8) STAMP [5] extracts the current interest from the last interaction. 9) SR-GNN [8] captures transitions of items and incorporates directed graphs to represent session sequences. 10) GC-SAN [9] combines GNN and the self-attention network to make the sequential recommendation.

[1] https://github.com/sidooms/MovieTweetings.
[2] https://competitions.codalab.org/competitions/11161#learn_the_details.
[3] https://grouplens.org/datasets/movielens/latest.

Parameters. Empirically, we set the dimension of embedding vectors $d = 64$ for all datasets, and the embeddings are initialized using a Gaussian distribution with a mean of 0 and a standard deviation of 0.1. The learning rate is selected ranging from 0.001 to 0.01, while the other hyperparameters are searched by a empirical search based on the validation set. We use the mini-batch Adam optimizer to optimize parameters and set the batch size to 128. To prevent overfitting, we employ L_2 penalty as well as the early stop strategy and stop the training if there is no progress in 15 consecutive epochs.

4   Results and Analysis

Comparisons of Performance. The experimental results w.r.t. three metrics over all datasets are illustrated in Table 2 and we have following observations:

1) We observe that our proposed JGCN achieves state-of-the-art performance and gains improvements on average against the strongest baseline of approximately 9.69%, 9.01%, 8.30% w.r.t. HR, MRR and NDCG, respectively, which demonstrates the overall effectiveness of JGCN. 2) The performance of Most-Pop is the most poor and it indicates that making recommendations only based on recurring repetitive items is often impractical. Limited by relatively shallow structures, traditional algorithms such as BPR-MF, Item-KNN and FPMC, still have not achieved satisfactory results. In contrast, depending on deep neural networks, GRU4Rec, Caser and SASRec, achieve the promising performances in top-N sequential recommendation. GRU4Rec is inferior to Caser on LastFM and Diginetica and have a stronger ability on MovieTweetings, which indicates that RNN- and CNN-based structures are affected by characteristics of different datasets. SASRec outperforms GRU4Rec and Caser with automatic selection capability of attention mechanism. 3) The recent graph-based models, e.g., SR-GNN and GC-SNN, strengthen the performance of node vectors from neighborhoods' features by treating each session as a directed graph, acquiring the favorable performances than other baselines. Compared with them, JGCN explicitly integrates the short- and long-term preferences from both directed and undirected graphs, enhancing the transitions of items information from neighborhoods' information. Moreover, proposed techniques of weight-position and graph collaborative networks further improve the representation of sessions sequences.

Table 2. Performance comparison w.r.t. three metrics on all datasets. The best result is in boldface and Impro. denotes improvements of JGCN relative to the best baseline.

LastFM

Metrics	HR@5	HR@20	MRR@5	MRR@20	NDCG@5	NDCG@20
MostPop	0.0163	0.0352	0.0053	0.0063	0.0109	0.0161
BPR-MF	0.1012	0.1625	0.0349	0.0547	0.0776	0.0966
Item-KNN	0.1765	0.2843	0.0501	0.0762	0.1131	0.1345
FPMC	0.1875	0.3077	0.0614	0.0896	0.1325	0.1548
GRU4Rec	0.2759	0.3316	0.0918	0.1018	0.1772	0.1955
Caser	0.2815	0.3482	0.0983	0.1052	0.1815	0.1983
SASRec	0.3015	0.3691	0.1273	0.1354	0.2019	0.2134
STAMP	0.3176	0.3725	0.1354	0.1469	0.2218	0.2367
SR-GNN	0.3416	0.3814	0.1583	0.1687	0.2533	0.2652
GC-SAN	0.3386	0.3756	0.1422	0.1596	0.2430	0.2507
JGCN	**0.3761**	**0.4146**	**0.1709**	**0.1823**	**0.2791**	**0.2842**
Impro.	10.01%	8.70%	7.95%	8.06%	10.18%	7.16%

Diginetica

Metrics	HR@5	HR@20	MRR@5	MRR@20	NDCG@5	NDCG@20
MostPop	0.0028	0.0064	0.0016	0.0029	0.0023	0.0038
BPR-MF	0.0959	0.1534	0.0698	0.0723	0.0714	0.0945
Item-KNN	0.2013	0.2447	0.0982	0.1179	0.1513	0.1702
FPMC	0.1955	0.2418	0.0958	0.1218	0.1469	0.1673
GRU4Rec	0.2839	0.3115	0.1124	0.1356	0.1648	0.1892
Caser	0.2897	0.3142	0.1135	0.1382	0.1685	0.1913
SASRec	0.3151	0.3318	0.1205	0.1433	0.1807	0.2016
STAMP	0.3215	0.3569	0.1418	0.1517	0.2233	0.2529
SR-GNN	0.3612	0.3925	0.1613	0.1701	0.2598	0.2694
GC-SAN	0.3723	0.4015	0.1658	0.1774	0.2701	0.2830
JGCN	**0.4115**	**0.4527**	**0.1861**	**0.1932**	**0.2988**	**0.3067**
Impro.	10.52%	12.75%	12.24%	8.90%	10.62%	8.37%

MovieTweetings

Metrics	HR@5	HR@20	MRR@5	MRR@20	NDCG@5	NDCG@20
MostPop	0.0076	0.0158	0.0021	0.0026	0.0045	0.0067
BPR-MF	0.0615	0.1123	0.0354	0.0455	0.0491	0.0637
Item-KNN	0.0894	0.1563	0.0577	0.0612	0.0639	0.0895
FPMC	0.1123	0.1897	0.0695	0.0731	0.0842	0.1094
GRU4Rec	0.1650	0.2417	0.0897	0.0941	0.1233	0.1436
Caser	0.1599	0.2352	0.0851	0.0913	0.1189	0.1403
SASRec	0.1712	0.2581	0.0955	0.1052	0.1369	0.1674
STAMP	0.1923	0.2876	0.0995	0.1121	0.1436	0.1752
SR-GNN	0.2011	0.3122	0.1134	0.1369	0.1672	0.1853
GC-SAN	0.2038	0.3136	0.1140	0.1389	0.1721	0.1933
JGCN	**0.2263**	**0.3298**	**0.1274**	**0.1461**	**0.1900**	**0.1993**
Impro.	11.04%	5.16%	11.75%	5.18%	10.40%	3.10%

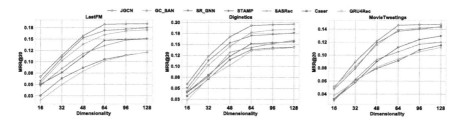

Fig. 3. MRR@20 (y-axis) vs. the number of embedding sizes (x-axis) on three datasets.

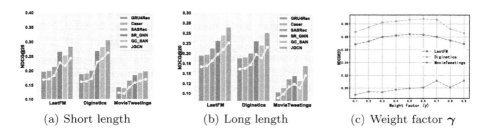

(a) Short length   (b) Long length   (c) Weight factor γ

Fig. 4. (a) and (b) show the performance of different methods with different session lengths evaluated in terms of NDCG@20. (c) depicts the impact of weight factor γ.

Impact of Embedding Size d. In Fig. 3, we investigate the effectiveness of the embedding size d ranging from 16 to 128 on three datasets. We notice that proposed JGCN outperforms other baselines with variable dimensions and shows the stable fluctuation range. Clearly, we find that the performance of all methods gradually grow with continuously increasing learning parameters. Although the rising trend of our method tends to flatten than some methods when d becomes large, the results of JGCN still consistently advances all existing methods in different dimensions.

Impact of Sequence Length. We study the performance about sequence length by partitioning sessions of datasets into two groups, where the length of sessions has more than 5 times belong to "Long", while each session is less than or equal to 5 means "Short". Figure 4(a) and 4(b) display the results. Notably, our proposed JGCN is superior to other baselines over three datasets with two session lengths, verifying the robustness and generalization of JGCN in different scenarios. We also observe that GC-SAN and SR-GNN change greatly in both groups, and they achieve great performance on the short group, but they drop sharply with the session length increasing. This discrepancy could be attributed that existing GNN models have shortcomings in capturing long sequences.

Trade-off of Weight Factor γ. Weight factor γ is defined to control the contribution of current interests and global performances. Intuitively, the lower value of γ means the less importance of current interest module and vice versa.

Observing from Fig. 4(b), the curves of LastFM and Diginetica obtain the best scores when γ are approximately 0.5 and 0.6, indicating that both two modules of current interests and global preferences can contribute to the results in sequential recommendation. On MovieTweetings, the performance improves 12.05% than it begins. This is reasonable since the average sequences of MovieTweetings is longer than LastFM and Diginetica, with the increasing weight of global preferences, the model are easier to capture the long dependence.

Ablation Analysis. To verify the contribution of proposed schemes i.e., weighted position embedding mechanism, correlation-based similarity, short- and long-term components, we develop several variants and cover comparative experiments to prove the effectiveness: 1) CGCN (Current-interest GCN) is a variant of JGCN which discards global preference module. 2) CGCN/w is a derivant of CGCN and removes the weight-position mechanism. 3) GGCN (Global-preference GCN) is a version abandoning the current interest module and adds position embedding to supply order information. 4) GGCN/s is a derivant of GGCN without considering correlation-based similarity of items.

Table 3. Impact of different variants on all datasets. The second best approach in each column is underlined.

Dataset	Diginetica			MovieTweetings		
Metrics	HR@5	MRR@5	NDCG@5	HR@5	MRR@5	NDCG@5
CGCN	<u>0.3892</u>	<u>0.1741</u>	<u>0.2791</u>	0.2089	0.1165	0.1749
CGCN/w	0.3617	0.1605	0.2576	0.2022	0.1142	0.1705
GGCN	0.3811	0.1705	0.2742	<u>0.2143</u>	<u>0.1182</u>	<u>0.1798</u>
GGCN/s	0.3594	0.1588	0.2521	0.2062	0.1155	0.1731
JGCN	**0.4115**	**0.1861**	**0.2988**	**0.2263**	**0.1274**	**0.1900**

Table 3 reports the results of different variants on two datasets and following findings have been made: 1) The performance of CGCN exceeds GGCN on Diginetica dataset, while CGCN is inferior to GGCN on MovieTweetings. Since the average length of Diginetica is short than MovieTweetings, and we argue that it may contain the more users' short-term interests, making CGCN more efficient in capturing sequence features. 2) The derivants of CGCN/w and GGCN/s are worse than CGCN and GGCN respectively, which supports that the proposed weight-position mechanism and correlation-based similarity scheme indeed promote the node expression of graph embeddings. 3) Even the single modules, i.e., CGCN and GGCN, still perform better than competitive approaches such as SR-GNN and GC-SAN, providing empirical evidence for the effectiveness of two core modules from session graphs. 4) Compared with above variants, JGCN has made a significant improvement and justifies the importance of combining both current interest drifts and global inherent preferences from session graphs.

5 Conclusion

In this paper, we propose a joint graph contextualized network (JGCN) based on graph neural networks for sequential recommendation. Specifically, we construct directed and undirected graphs from each session sequence. Then, we introduce gate graph neural networks by modeling directed graphs to generate latent vectors containing temporal and current interests, while we propose a graph collaborative attention network by enhancing graph attention networks with the correlation-based similarity from overall nodes to learn inherent and global preferences. Besides, we design a weight-position mechanism to supply time-series information on the session graph. Comprehensive experiments on three datasets demonstrate that JGCN outperforms state-of-the-art methods.

References

1. Wang, S., Hu, L., Cao, L., Orgun, M.: Sequential recommender systems: challenges, progress and prospects. In: Proceedings of International Joint Conferences on Artificial Intelligence (2019)
2. Rendle, S., Freudenthaler, C., Schmidt-Thieme, L.: Factorizing personalized Markov chains for next-basket recommendation. In: Proceedings of the 19th International Conference on World Wide Web, pp. 811–820 (2010)
3. Hidasi, B., Karatzoglou, A., Baltrunas, L., Tikk, D.: Session-based recommendations with recurrent neural networks. In: Proceedings of the International Conference on Learning Representations (2016)
4. Tang, J., Wang, K.: Personalized top-n sequential recommendation via convolutional sequence embedding. In: Proceedings of the Eleventh ACM International Conference on Web Search and Data Mining, pp. 565–573 (2018)
5. Liu, Q., Zeng, Y., Mokhosi, R., Zhang, H.: STAMP: short-term attention/memory priority model for session-based recommendation. In: Proceedings of the 24th ACM SIGKDD International Conference on Knowledge Discovery & Data Mining, pp. 1831–1839 (2018)
6. Kang, W.C., McAuley, J.: Self-attentive sequential recommendation. In: IEEE International Conference on Data Mining (ICDM), pp. 197–206. IEEE (2018)
7. Wu, Z., Pan, S., Chen, F., Long, G., Zhang, C., Philip, S.Y.: A comprehensive survey on graph neural networks. IEEE Trans. Neural Netw. Learn. Syst. (TNNLS) **32**, 1–21 (2020)
8. Wu, S., Tang, Y., Zhu, Y., Wang, L., Xie, X., Tan, T.: Session-based recommendation with graph neural networks. In: Proceedings of the AAAI Conference on Artificial Intelligence, vol. 33, no. 1, pp. 346–353. AAAI (2019)
9. Xu, C., et al.: Graph contextualized self-attention network for session-based recommendation. In: International Joint Conferences on Artificial Intelligence, vol. 19, pp. 3940–3946 (2019)
10. Li, Y., Tarlow, D., Brockschmidt, M., Zemel, R.: Gated graph sequence neural networks. In: Proceedings of 4th International Conference on Learning Representations (2016)
11. Sarwar, B., Karypis, G., Konstan, J., Riedl, J.: Item-based collaborative filtering recommendation algorithms. In: Proceedings of the 10th international conference on World Wide Web, pp. 285–295 (2001)

12. Veličković, P., Cucurull, G., Casanova, A., Romero, A., Liò, P., Bengio, Y.: Graph attention networks. In: Proceedings of International Conference on Learning Representations (2018)
13. Rendle, S., Freudenthaler, C., Gantner, Z., Schmidt-Thieme, L.: BPR: Bayesian personalized ranking from implicit feedback. In: Proceedings of the Conference on Uncertainty in Artificial Intelligence (2009)

Relevance-Aware Q-matrix Calibration for Knowledge Tracing

Wentao Wang[1], Huifang Ma[1,2(✉)], Yan Zhao[1], Zhixin Li[2], and Xiangchun He[3]

[1] College of Computer Science and Engineering, Northwest Normal University,
Lanzhou 730070, Gansu, China
`mahuifang@yeah.net`
[2] Guangxi Key Lab of Multi-source Information Mining and Security, Guangxi
Normal University, Guilin 541004, Guangxi, China
[3] School of Educational Technology, Northwest Normal University,
Lanzhou 730070, Gansu, China

Abstract. Knowledge tracing (KT) lies at the core of intelligent education, which aims to diagnose students' changing knowledge level over time based on their historical performance. Most of the existing KT models either ignore the significance of Q-matrix associated exercises with knowledge concepts (KCs) or fail to eliminate the subjective tendency of experts within the Q-matrix, thus it is insufficient for capturing complex interaction between students and exercises. In this paper, we propose a novel **R**elevance-**A**ware **Q**-matrix **C**alibration method for knowledge tracing (**RAQC**), which incorporates the calibrated Q-matrix into Long Short-Term Memory (LSTM) network to model the complex students' learning process, for getting both accurate and interpretable diagnosis results. Specifically, we first leverage the message passing mechanism in Graph Convolution Network (GCN) to fully exploit the high-order connectivity between exercises and KCs for obtaining a potential KC list. Then, we propose a Q-matrix calibration method by using relevance scores between exercises and KCs to mitigate the problem of subjective bias existed in human-labeled Q-matrix. After that, the embedding of each exercise aggregated the calibrated Q-matrix with the corresponding response log is fed into the LSTM to tracing students' knowledge states (KS). Extensive experimental results on two real-world datasets show the effectiveness of the proposed method.

Keywords: Knowledge tracing · Calibrated Q-matrix · High-order connectivity · Graph convolution network

1 Introduction

Nowadays, computer-assisted learning (CAL) has been a critical part of intelligent education for improving students' learning ability [7,10]. Knowledge tracing (KT) lies at the core of CAL, with the goal of estimating how much they master on every single knowledge concept. Figure 1 presents a toy example KT task, generally, students usually first select some items from a set of exercises (e.g., e_1,

© Springer Nature Switzerland AG 2021
I. Farkaš et al. (Eds.): ICANN 2021, LNCS 12893, pp. 101–112, 2021.
https://doi.org/10.1007/978-3-030-86365-4_9

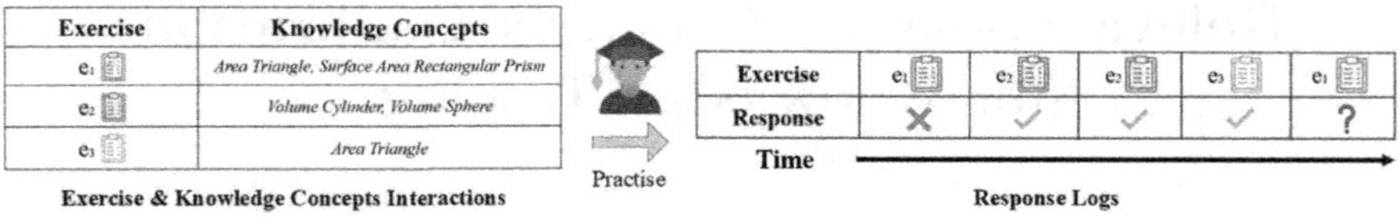

Fig. 1. A showcase of KT task for a student on mathematical exercises. The student chooses some exercises from different knowledge points for practice and leave the response logs. Now the student is going to answer exercise e_3.

e_2, e_3) to practice and leave their response logs (e.g., right or wrong). Then, the purpose of KT is to infer their latent knowledge states on each KC through their past attempts on exercises. In effect, these latent knowledge states of students are necessary as they are the basis of further services, such as target knowledge training [6] and personalized exercise recommendation [12].

Many efforts have been dedicated to KT task, which broadly fall into two classes: the methods abstaining Q-matrix and the ones based on Q-matrix, where the basic Q-matrix is binary, with 1's for association representing that which KC is covered by an exercise, and similarly, 0's for non-association [4]. In terms of the former, such as Deep Knowledge Tracing (DKT) [9] and Dynamic Key-Value Memory Network (DKVMN) [13], they simply abandon the Q-matrix since the KCs can be automatically discovered within those methods. As for the latter, these methods usually leverage the Q-matrix to represent exercises like Content-Based linear approach using Contextualized Q-matrix (CBCQ) and LSTM-Based contextual KT approach using Contextualized Q-matrix (LSTMCQ) [3]. Although both of them take Q-matrix into consideration during the process of tracing students' KS and update Q-matrix by injecting contexts of learning into it, in essence, they fail to explore relationships between exercises and KCs and are not able to eliminate subjective tendency in Q-matrix.

As the matter of fact, it is of great necessity to utilize Q-matrix for diagnosing and tracing KS of students, since Q-matrix is the source of information about KCs [12]. Thereby, in this work, we primarily pay attention to tackling the following two challenges: How to exploit the semantic information in Q-matrix as fully as possible in an effective manner to improve the performance of KT model? How do we eliminate the subjective tendency in Q-matrix to a great degree?

To conquer these challenges, in this paper, we keep abreast of the ongoing developments of knowledge tracing techniques [3,9,13] and pertinent cognitive models [5,12], and propose the RAQC method. Concretely, we first attempt to exploit the high-order connectivity between exercises and KCs within an exercise-KC interaction graph (i.e. Q-matrix) via message passing mechanism in GCN to obtain a list of potential KCs of each exercise. Then, a relation-aware Q-matrix calibration approach is designed by using relevance scores between exercises and KCs to alleviate the problem of subjective bias existed in human-labeled Q-matrix. Furthermore, the embedding of each exercise represented by the calibrated Q-matrix along with historical student interactions is sent as input to the LSTM to track students' knowledge proficiency on each KC. Finally, extensive experimental studies on two real-world benchmark datasets show that the proposed framework enables to trace and diagnosis actual KS of students effectively. Meanwhile, the practicability of this method is also verified by two fundamental diagnostic tasks involved in score prediction and diagnosis result visualization. In summary, our contributions are three folds:

1. A novel Relation-Aware Q-matrix Calibration method for Knowledge Tracing (RAQC) based on GCN is developed. To the best of our knowledge, this is the first attempt to explore the inherent information embodied in Q-matrix by GCN and use it to refine and calibrate the raw Q-matrix;
2. A Q-matrix calibration method via a pairwise partial order with relevance scores between exercises and KCs is presented. In particular, the pairwise partial order is complete enough to cover the importance of different KCs;
3. Extensive experimental results on two real-world datasets show that our method enables to track the knowledge proficiency of students effectively and have impressive practicability on two educational diagnostic tasks.

2   Related Work

We review the existing approaches that work on KT and Q-matrix estimation, which most pertain to our method. Then we summarize these methods and briefly reveal the differences from our method.

KT task indirectly evaluates the students' knowledge proficiency of concepts on the basis of their response data. Recently many KT models based on deep learning show that there is a leap in score prediction performance of students. DKT is the first attempt to model students' complex learning process using neural network [9]. Moreover, DKVMN [13] introduces a Memory Augmented Neural Network (MANN) and is more interpretable than DKT to solve KT task using two matrices, key and value, which learn the correlation between exercises and the latent KCs and students' KS, respectively. Since all these deep learning models enable to automatically discover underlying concepts of exercises, Q-matrix annotated by human experts is abandoned. Another line of research includes methods via leveraging the rows of Q-matrix to represent exercises like CBCQ and LSTMCQ [3]. Both of them tackle the KT problem depending on the contexts of learning, such as the difficulty of exercises, factors related to teaching, and connections with other KCs, etc., which are integrated into Q-matrix.

Considering the subjective tendency of Q-matrix labeled by domain experts and possible misspecifications in Q-matrix, several Q-matrix estimation approaches have been developed to solve these problems [11]. Basically, these approaches can be divided into two broad strands of works. One is the Q-matrix estimation method based on cognitive diagnosis model, and the other is depending on extra information (e.g. text information). In effect, for the first kind of the Q-matrix estimation methods, they have been heavily studied in the area of educational measurement for many years and most of them have critically positive impact on calibrating Q-matrix. The G-DINA Discrimination Index (GDI) method is proposed in [4], which can be used in conjunction with the G-DINA model. As an extension of GDI method, the stepwise method [8] devised to validate Q-matrix for the sequential G-DINA model is based on GDI and Wald statistic. In literature [11], three approaches are developed on the basis of the likelihood ratio test to estimate Q-matrix with a partial known Q-matrix and response data, which can be used with a wide variety of CDMs. On the other hand, recently, another kind of Q-matrix estimation methods based on extra information has been proposed and yielded great success. Specifically, in Neural Cognitive Diagnosis (NeuralCD) [12] framework, a novel Q-matrix estimation method utilized a pre-trained Convolutional Neural Network (CNN) to predict KCs related to the text information of exercises is incorporated into the NeuralCD framework. Defining a partial order, this method connects the KCs estimated by CNN with those annotated by experts.

Unlike the aforementioned methods, although our approach leverages Q-matrix estimation methods to calibrate the raw Q-matrix and solves KT problem, we further distill the high-order connectivity between exercises and KCs and use it to eliminate the subjective tendency in Q-matrix for calibration without heavily relying on certain cognitive diagnosis models.

3   Preliminaries

In this section, we introduce some preliminary knowledge about knowledge tracking, including necessary definitions and notations used in this paper then present an overview for our solution.

Let $S = \{s_1, s_2, \cdots, s_N\}$, $E = \{e_1, e_2, \cdots, e_M\}$ and $Kn = \{k_1, k_2, \cdots, k_K\}$, where N is the number of students, M is the number of exercises, and K is the number of knowledge concepts at a learning system, respectively. A student selects some exercises from E for practice, and his/her response logs $X = \{x_1, x_2, \cdots, x_T\}$ are characterized by a set of tuple $x_t = (e_t, r_t)$, where $e_t \in E$ denotes the exercise attempted, $r_t \in \{0, 1\}$ denotes the correctness of the corresponding answer which is leaved by a student at timestep t. Besides, for explainable diagnosis of students' KS, a manually-labeled Q-matrix $\mathbf{Q} \in \mathbb{R}^{M \times K}$ which is a binary knowledge matrix is also required. If a KC k is involved in an exercise j, then $Q_{jk} = 1$; $Q_{jk} = 0$ otherwise. Without loss of generality, the research problem can be formulated as follows:

Definition (Knowledge Tracing): Given students' response logs R and the corresponding Q-matrix $\mathbf{Q}$, our goal is twofold: (1) predicting the knowledge proficiency on K KCs and response scores on next candidate exercise of each student at timestamp $T+1$; (2) tracing the dynamics of KS of each student and estimating the level of how he/she masters on KCs from time 1 to T.

Here we present an overview of the RAQC approach for KT, consisting of four major steps: constructing interaction graph, exploiting potential KC list, modeling response logs and calibrating Q-matrix and tracking knowledge proficiency, respectively. The first step is devised to transform a raw Q-matrix into an exercise-KC interaction graph. Additionally, in the next step, the exercise embeddings and the KC embeddings are obtained from the interaction graph by using message passing mechanism based on GCN model and the high-order connectivity is exploited, as such, the potential KC list can be attained. Then, towards more realistic modeling, the response logs are required to be modeled as the student-exercise interaction sequences and the calibrated Q-matrix can be estimated by the RAQC method in the third step. Finally, with the help of the calibrated Q-matrix and the student-exercise interaction sequences, our method has the mechanism to track the change of students' KS during their learning process and enables to predict their performance scores on exercise e_{t+1} in the last step.

4   Method

In this section, we first introduce the Q-matrix-based Knowledge Tracing (QKT) model, which is both a baseline and a premise of the RAQC method. Next, based on the QKT model, a Relation-Aware Q-matrix Calibration approach on the basis of a partial order is designed to eliminate the subjective tendency existed in Q-matrix. Last, we integrate the QKT model with the RAQC method to conquer those problems defined in Sect. 3.

4.1   QKT

Following existing works [2,3], where relevant KCs are used for representing exercises, we develop a method called QKT which describes exercises by replacing all exercises' one-hot representation vectors with KC-based representation vectors. One reason for this shift of interest is that more explainable results of KS of students are what we exactly expect for.

Students' response logs $X = \{x_1, x_2, \cdots, x_T\}$ are formulated as a set of tuple $x_t = (e_t, r_t)$. Herein, at timestep t, each row of Q-matrix as the raw exercise embedding $\mathbf{q}_t$ is a vector of a certain exercise in relation to one or more KCs:

$$\mathbf{q}_t = \mathbf{e}_t^T \times \mathbf{Q} \qquad (1)$$

where $\mathbf{e}_t$ indicates the one-hot representation vector of an exercise and the length of $\mathbf{e}_t$ is M.

To model such semantic rich and less dimensional exercise representations than DKT, we also take students' response logs into account, where the $\mathbf{x}_t = [\mathbf{q}_t, r_t]$ is fed into the LSTM model and each of these vectors has a length of $K+1$. The output of LSTM is a predicted vector of probabilities of getting each KC correct (i.e. the mastery level on each of KCs), denoted by $\hat{\mathbf{y}}_t$, and its length is equal to the number of KC. After the probability of getting each KC correctly has been computed, the corresponding exercise vector in the Q-matrix can be leveraged to compute the predicted value $\hat{p}_t$. As the output layer adopts a sigmoid activation function on top of the linear transformation, the value of each element in $\hat{\mathbf{y}}_t$ is independent of the others:

$$\hat{p}_t = \hat{\mathbf{y}}_t^T \times \mathbf{q}_{t+1} \tag{2}$$

The loss function of QKT is the cross entropy between the output $\hat{p}_t$ and the true label r_{t+1}:

$$loss_{QKT} = -\frac{1}{T} \sum_{t=0}^{T-1} [r_{t+1} \log(\hat{p}_t) + (1 - r_{t+1}) \log(1 - \hat{p}_t)] \tag{3}$$

After training, the value of $\hat{\mathbf{y}}_t$ is the diagnosis result, which denotes the student's knowledge proficiency on each KC at timestep t.

4.2 RAQC

Inspired by high-order connectivity, we pre-train a GCN model [1] to obtain the embeddings of all vertices in the exercise-KC interaction graph for predicting relevance scores between the input exercise and KCs, where the human-labeled Q-matrix is utilized as label for training. GCN has the advantage of extracting semantic signals from the exercise-KC interaction graph, thus it is able to capture potential KCs for the input exercise. Specifically, first, following mainstream GCN models, we describe an exercise e_i (a knowledge concept k_j) with an embedding vector $\mathbf{e}_{e_i} \in \mathbb{R}^d$ ($\mathbf{e}_{k_j} \in \mathbb{R}^d$), where d denotes the embedding size. Then, the pre-trained network takes the embedding vector $\mathbf{e}_{e_i} \in \mathbb{R}^d$ and the embeddings of all KCs as input, and output the relevance score set RS_i of those KCs related to e_i:

$$RS_i = \left\{ rs_{e_i,k_j} \right\}_{j=1}^K \tag{4}$$

where $rs_{e_i,k_j} = sigmoid(\mathbf{e}_{e_i}^T \cdot \mathbf{e}_{k_j})$. After descending sort all relevance scores in RS_i, we define $V_i^n = \{V_{ij_1}, V_{ij_2}, \cdots, V_{ij_n}\}$ as the set of top-n KCs of exercise e_i according to RS_i. Thus we develop a method to calibrate Q-matrix by combining V_i^n with Q-matrix: RAQC.

In view of an idea that KCs annotated by domain experts have higher confidence than those predicted by the pre-trained model, we consider that KCs labeled by Q-matrix are more relevant to e_i than concepts in $\{k_j | k_j \in V_i^n \wedge Q_{ij} = 0\}$. To this end, we propose a partial order with relevance score, that is:

$$
\begin{aligned}
&\underbrace{a_{expert\ \&\ model\ \&\ (rs_{e_i,k_g} > rs_{e_i,k_h})}^{(g)} >_i^+ a_{expert\ \&\ model\ \&\ (rs_{e_i,k_g} > rs_{e_i,k_h})}^{(h)}}_{a_{expert\ \&\ model}} >_i^+ \\
&b_{expert\ \&\ \overline{model}} >_i^+ \\
&\underbrace{c_{expert\ \&\ model\ \&\ (rs_{e_i,k_p} > rs_{e_i,k_q})}^{(p)} >_i^+ c_{expert\ \&\ model\ \&\ (rs_{e_i,k_p} > rs_{e_i,k_q})}^{(q)}}_{c_{\overline{expert}\ \&\ model}} >_i^+ \\
&d_{\overline{expert}\ \&\ \overline{model}}
\end{aligned} \tag{5}
$$

where a, b, c, and d are the elements of KC set Kn. Here $a_{expert\,\&\,model}$ denotes the KC a which is both annotated by expert and can also be found in V_i^n, while $b_{expert\,\&\,\overline{model}}$ implies that KC b is labeled by domain expert in Q-matrix but does not exist in V_i^n. Analogous to the KC a and the KC b, the meanings of $c_{\overline{expert}\,\&\,model}$ and $d_{\overline{expert}\,\&\,\overline{model}}$ can be interpreted in a similar way. Along this line, we are able to draw a conclusion that 'a is more important than b in e_i'. Notably, in the KCs $a_{expert\,\&\,model}$, the KC $a^{(g)}_{expert\,\&\,model}$ is more significant than $a^{(h)}_{expert\,\&\,model}$ in e_i due to $rs_{e_i,k_g} > rs_{e_i,k_h}$ even if both of them are annotated by expert and are obtained by model. Thereby, according to Eq. (5), we define the partial order relationship set as:

$$D = \left\{ (i, k_r, k_s) | k_r >_i^+ k_s, i = 1, 2, ..., M \right\} \tag{6}$$

Then, following traditional Bayesian treatment, we hypothesize $\hat{\mathbf{Q}} \in \mathbb{R}^{M \times K}$ follows a zero mean Gaussian prior with standard deviation σ of each dimension. In order to assign higher confidence to Q-matrix labels, we define $p(a >_i^+ b | \hat{\mathbf{Q}}_i)$ with a pairwise logistic-like function:

$$p(a >_i^+ b | \hat{\mathbf{Q}}_i) = \frac{1}{1 + e^{-\lambda(\hat{Q}_{ia} - \hat{Q}_{ib})}} \tag{7}$$

The hyperparameter λ controls the discrimination of relevance values between labeled and unlabeled KCs. Consequently, the log posterior probability on $\hat{\mathbf{Q}}$ is finally formulated as:

$$
\begin{aligned}
\ln p(\hat{\mathbf{Q}} | D) &= \ln \prod_{(i, k_r, k_s) \in D} p(k_r >_i^+ k_s | \hat{\mathbf{Q}}_i) p(\hat{\mathbf{Q}}_i) \\
&= \sum_{(i, k_r, k_s) \in D} \ln p(k_r >_i^+ k_s | \hat{\mathbf{Q}}_i) + \sum_{i=1}^{M} p(\hat{\mathbf{Q}}_i) \\
&= \sum_{i=1}^{M} \sum_{k_r=1}^{K} \sum_{k_s=1}^{K} I(k_r >_i^+ k_s) \ln \frac{1}{1 + e^{-\lambda(\hat{Q}_{ik_r} - \hat{Q}_{ik_s})}} + C - \sum_{i=1}^{M} \sum_{j=1}^{K} \frac{\hat{Q}_{ij}^2}{2\sigma^2}
\end{aligned}
\tag{8}
$$

where C is a constant which can be ignored during optimization and $I(\cdot)$ is an indicator that equals to 1 if the condition '$\cdot$' is satisfied. Ultimately, the calibrated Q-matrix $\hat{\mathbf{Q}}$ is estimated by RAQC approach with completely covering partial order relationships between all KCs based on relevance score set RS.

4.3 RAQC for Knowledge Tracing

Before using $\hat{\mathbf{Q}}$ to improve QKT, we need to restrict its elements to the range [0, 1], and let the elements of KCs which are unlabeled or are not predicted in top-n KC list be 0. Therefore, $sigmoid(\hat{\mathbf{Q}}) \circ \mathbf{M}$ is leveraged to be the substitution of Q-matrix in QKT, where $\mathbf{M} \in \{0, 1\}^{M \times K}$ is a mask matrix, and $M_{ij} = 1$ if $j \in V_i^n$ or $Q_{ij} = 1$; $M_{ij} = 0$ otherwise. To track knowledge proficiency of students and calibrate Q-matrix simultaneously, we combine all the loss functions to form a joint optimization framework, namely, we solve:

$$\min L = \min[-\ln p(\hat{\mathbf{Q}}|D) + \sum_{i=1}^{N} loss_i^{QKT}] \qquad (9)$$

5   Experiments

In this section, we conduct extensive experiments to evaluate the performance of our proposed RAQC method. Specifically, we describe the datasets and introduce the experimental setup and we also demonstrate the effectiveness of our framework on two educational tasks including score prediction and diagnosis result visualization. The details of the experiments will be discussed below.

5.1   Datasets

Two real-world datasets are used for our experiments. One is $ASSISTment09$, an open dataset collected by the $ASSISTments$ online tutoring systems, which is widely leveraged by researchers for purposes such as KT and student modeling. We choose the public corrected version which mitigates the duplicated data problem proposed by previous research [12]. The other dataset is $Intellilence18$ supplied by Oneoftops Ltd., a company offering teaching and learning resources to middle and high school teachers and students, which provides language learning and practicing services to young language learners [3].

We filter out students with less than 30 and 15 response logs for $Intellilence18$ and $ASSISTment09$ respectively to guarantee that each student has enough data for diagnosis.

5.2   Experimental Setup

We set hyperparameters $\lambda = 0.1$ (Eq. (7)) and $\sigma = 1$ (Eq. (8)). For n in top-n KCs filtering, the value we utilize can make the predicting GCN model reach 0.85 recall. Thereby, in our experiment, $n = 20$. We implement the initialization of the parameters depending on $Xavier$, which fill the weights with random values sampled from $\mathcal{N}(0, std^2)$, where $std = \sqrt{2/(n_{in} + n_{out})}$, n_{in} is the number of neurons feeding into the weights, n_{out} is the number of neurons which the results are sent to.

To evaluate the performance of our RAQC method, we compare them with previous approaches. The details of them are as follows:

1. DKT: DKT is an implementation using a LSTM which leverages a series of one-hot representations of exercise and trains a unified network for predicting students' next interaction on certain exercise [9].

2. *DKVMN*: DKVMN uses a key-value memory network to store the KCs' underlying concept representations and states [13].
3. *LSTMCQ*: LSTMCQ is implemented by an RNN with LSTM cells. The architecture of it is similar to that of DKT, but the one-hot input vectors are replaced with the contextualized representation [3].
4. *QKT*: This is an extension to the DKT model, which directly uses KCs pertaining to exercise in conjunction with students' response log as the input of DKT and predicts students' response for each question.

We perform 80%/20% train/test split of each student's historical interactions and all the models are evaluated with 5-fold cross validation.

5.3 Experimental Results on Two Tasks

In this subsection, we compare the performance of all the baselines with RAQC on two educational tasks to demonstrate the effectiveness and the interpretation of this method.

Student Score Prediction. The first educational task is to predict student performances on exercises in the future, where we assess the predictive performance of our models. With trained RAQC method, we use it to predict whether or not a student can correctly answer a certain exercise at time $T + 1$. In this experiment, we select all the baselines aforementioned in Sect. 5.2 for comparison. Moreover, we select evaluation metrics from both classification perspective and regression perspective, including the Area Under the Curve of the ROC (AUC, the higher the better) and the Root Mean Square Error (RMSE, the lower the better).

Table 1. Comparison of methods: AUC for classification and RMSE for regression.

Model	*ASSISTment09*		*Intellilence18*	
	AUC	RMSE	AUC	RMSE
DKT	0.7479	0.426	0.6874	0.3285
DKVMN	0.7534	0.4156	0.6931	0.3214
LSTMCQ	0.7703	0.3975	0.7131	0.3047
QKT	**0.7551**	**0.4138**	**0.6974**	**0.3208**
RAQC	**0.8122**	**0.3517**	**0.7632**	**0.2704**

Table 1 presents the holistic results of all models for predicting scores of students. To be specific, there are several observations from the figure: First, the methods adopting Q-matrix (i.e., LSTMCQ, QKT and RAQC) outperform almost the ones without Q-matrix. This demonstrates that it is effective to take

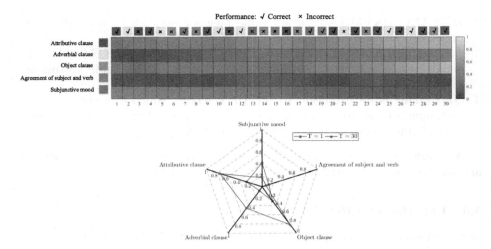

Fig. 2. An instance of the knowledge mastery level tracking of a certain student on five concepts during his 30 exercising steps, which is painted in the top heatmap. Left side presents all concepts, which are labeled in different colours. Top line indicates his performance on the 30 exercises. Bottom radar figure exhibits his knowledge mastery levels on five KCs after practicing from $T = 1$ to $T = 30$.

association between exercises and KCs with Q-matrix into modeling for prediction. However, there is an exception in Table 1, where DKVMN performs comparably with QKT. This has two possible implications: (1) the utility of MANN in DKVMN helps to offset the insufficiency of a non-linear model using embarrassingly simple one-hot exercise representation without taking Q-matrix into consideration [13]; (2) as the QKT results do not support the former statement, it is more probable that the deficiency in the QKT is caused by the subjective bias in Q-matrix. This can be further validated in Table 1. There, the improvement in the AUC from QKT to RAQC is 0.0571, whereas it is only 0.0072 from DKT to QKT in ASSISTment09. The improvement brought about by eliminating subjective bias in Q-matrix is 7.9 times as much as that brought about by simply using KC as exercise representation. In effect, RAQC shows better performance than QKT in general, by, on average, 0.0615 in AUC and 0.0563 in RMSE. Both are directly significant improvements. This is the strongest evidence of effectiveness caused by Q-matrix calibration. Second, among those methods using Q-matrix, the method with Q-matrix calibration consistently outperform the ones without (i.e., LSTMCQ, QKT), which indicates the effectiveness of the strategies proposed in Sect. 4.2 and the rationality of exploiting the high-order connectivity between exercise and KCs. In summary, all these evidences demonstrate the effectiveness and rationality of our proposed method.

Diagnosis Result Visualization. As mentioned before, our proposed RAQC method performs well on tracing the knowledge proficiency of a specific student in an explainable manner on the basis of the student's proficiency vectors $\hat{\mathbf{y}}$ at different timestamps.

Figure 2 provides a case study of visualizing the diagnosis results of a student on five knowledge concepts in Intellilence18 (we only show five KCs for better illustration). From the figure, he continuously makes progress on Attributive Clause from $T = 1$ (0.28) to $T = 30$ (0.76), since he practices the increasing number (e.g., 1, 3, 4, et al.) of exercises related to Attributive Clause during this period. However, his mastery levels on Subjunctive Mood declines gradually following the heatmap and the radar figure (from 0.42 to 0.16). We notice that he only attempts very few relevant exercises (i.e., 7, 13, 18) at each time, and thus he may forget the Subjunctive Mood knowledge. These observations imply that he needs a timely review on Subjunctive Mood. Based on the diagnostic result visualization, our method has the ability to provide more personalized training services for him in practice.

6 Conclusion

In this paper, we provided a focused study on dynamically diagnosing the knowledge proficiency of students. We designed a Relevance-Aware Q-matrix Calibration (RAQC) method for KT task. Specifically, we first attempted to exploit the high-order connectivity between exercises and KCs to obtain potential KCs of each exercise by using graph convolution network. Then, a pairwise Bayesian Q-matrix calibration approach was devised to refine and calibrate the raw Q-matrix to eliminate the subjective tendency of the Q-matrix defined by subject matter experts. After that, the embedding of each exercise aggregated the calibrated Q-matrix with historical student interactions was fed into the LSTM network to tracking students' knowledge states. The results of extensive experiments conducted on two real-world benchmark datasets confirmed that our method could trace the knowledge proficiency of students effectively and we demonstrated the practicability of this method depending on applying it on two fundamental diagnostic tasks, including score prediction and diagnosis result visualization.

Acknowledgments. This work is supported by the National Natural Science Foundation of China (61762078, 61363058, 61966004, 62167007), Research Fund of Guangxi Key Lab of Multi-source Information Mining and Security (MIMS18-08), Northwest Normal University Young Teachers Research Capacity Promotion Plan (NWNU-LKQN2019-2), Northwest Normal University Postgraduate Research Funding Project (2020-KYZZ001151), and Research Fund of Guangxi Key Laboratory of Trusted Software (kx202003).

References

1. He, X., Deng, K., Wang, X., Li, Y., Zhang, Y.D., Wang, M.: LightGCN: simplifying and powering graph convolution network for recommendation. In: Proceedings of the 43rd International ACM SIGIR Conference on Research and Development in Information Retrieval, pp. 639–648 (2020)
2. Huo, Y., Wong, D., Ni, L., Chao, L., Zhang, J.: HeTROPY: explainable learning diagnostics via heterogeneous maximum-entropy and multi-spatial knowledge representation. Knowl.-Based Syst. **207**, 106389 (2020)
3. Huo, Y., Wong, D., Ni, L., Chao, L., Zhang, J.: Knowledge modeling via contextualized representations for LSTM-based personalized exercise recommendation. Inf. Sci. **523**, 266–278 (2020)
4. Jimmy, D.L.T., Chiu, C.Y.: A general method of empirical Q-matrix validation. Psychometrika **81**(2), 253–273 (2016)
5. Jimmy, D.L.T.: DINA model and parameter estimation: a didactic. J. Nutr. Educ. Behav. Stat. **523**, 266–278 (2009)
6. Liu, Q., et al.: EKT: exercise-aware knowledge tracing for student performance prediction. IEEE Trans. Knowl. Data Eng. **33**(1), 100–115 (2021)
7. Liu, Y., Yang, Y., Chen, X., Shen, J., Zhang, H., Yu, Y.: Improving knowledge tracing via pre-training question embeddings. In: Proceedings of the 29th International Joint Conference on Artificial Intelligence, pp. 1577–1583. Morgan Kaufmann (2020)
8. Ma, W., Jimmy, D.L.T.: GDINA: an R package for cognitive diagnosis modeling. J. Stat. Softw. **93**(14), 1–26 (2020)
9. Piech, C., et al.: Deep knowledge tracing. In: Proceedings of the 28th International Conference on Neural Information Processing Systems, pp. 505–513 (2015)
10. Wang, C., et al.: Temporal cross-effects in knowledge tracing. In: Proceedings of the 14th ACM International Conference on Web Search and Data Mining, pp. 517–525. ACM (2021)
11. Wang, D., Cai, Y., Tu, D.: Q-matrix estimation methods for cognitive diagnosis models: based on partial known Q-matrix. Multivar. Behav. Res. **2020**, 1–13 (2020)
12. Wang, F., et al.: Neural cognitive diagnosis for intelligent education systems. In: Proceedings of the 34th AAAI Conference on Artificial Intelligence, pp. 6153–6161. AAAI (2020)
13. Zhang, J., Shi, X., King, I., Yeung, D.Y.: Dynamic key-value memory networks for knowledge tracing. In: Proceedings of the 26th International Conference on World Wide Web, pp. 765–774 (2017)

LGACN: A Light Graph Adaptive Convolution Network for Collaborative Filtering

Weiguang Jiang[1], Su Wang[2(✉)], Jun Zheng[2], and Wenxin Hu[2]

[1] School of Computer Science and Technology, East China Normal University, Shanghai 200062, China
[2] School of Data Science and Engineering, East China Normal University, Shanghai 200062, China
swang@cc.ecnu.edu.cn

Abstract. To relieve information flood on the web, recommender system has been widely used to retrieve personalized information. In recommender system, Graph Convolutional Network (GCN) has become a new frontier technology of collaborative filtering. However, existing methods usually assume that neighbor nodes have only positive effects on the target node. A few methods analyze the design of traditional GCNs and eliminate some invalid operations. However, they have not considered the possible negative effects of neighbors to adapt collaborative filtering. Thus, we argue that it is crucial to take the positive and negative effects of neighbors into consideration for collaborative filtering.

In this paper, we aim to alter the neighbor aggregation method and layer combination mechanism of GCN to make it more applicable for recommendation. Inspired by LightGCN, we propose a new model named LGACN (Light Graph Adaptive Convolution Network), including the most important component in GCN - neighborhood aggregation and layer combination - for collaborative filtering and alter them to fit recommendations. Specifically, LGACN learns user and item embeddings by propagating their positive and negative information on the user-item interaction graph by an adaptive attention-based method and uses the self-attention mechanism to combine the embeddings learned at each layer as the final embedding. Such a neat model is not only easy to implement but also interpretable, outperforming strong recommender baselines. Our model achieves about 15% relative improvement on Amazon-book and 5% relative improvement on Yelp2018 compared with Light-GCN.

Keywords: Collaborative filtering · Recommendation · Graph Convolution Network

1 Introduction

With the rapid development of the Internet, information is flooded on the Internet. People are overwhelmed by the information flood, making it difficult to find

© Springer Nature Switzerland AG 2021
I. Farkaš et al. (Eds.): ICANN 2021, LNCS 12893, pp. 113–126, 2021.
https://doi.org/10.1007/978-3-030-86365-4_10

what they want. To mitigate the effects of information overload, recommender systems are proposed and widely deployed in all aspects to meet users' interests [23,24].

Collaborative filtering(CF) [1] is a traditional recommendation technique that maps the single ID of users(items) to their latent features(a.k.a. embeddings). Due to the rapid development of neural networks, Neural Attention History Similarity(NAIS) [7] uses the attention mechanism to distinguish items of users' historical behaviors that are more important for future prediction, and it has been proved that the model is more effective than the traditional item-based CF [15]. In essence, NAIS utilizes users' single-hop neighbor information to improve embeddings. To deepen the uses of users' high-hop neighbor information, graph neural networks (GNNs) [5,9] has been applied to learn the user-item interaction graph structure. Graph Convolution Network(GCN) is a kind of Graph Neural Network, applying convolution operation to extent traditional data(such as images) to graph data. Inspired by GCN, Neural Graph Collaborative Filtering (NGCF) [18] is proposed and achieves significant improvement for CF. It follows the same operations to refine embeddings. Recently, He et al. [6] proposes LightGCN, which largely simplifies the GCN structure by including only the most central components for recommendation: neighborhood aggregation and layer combination. However, it does not consider the possible negative effects of neighbor nodes and the importance of different layers when combined.

In general, GCNs learn nodes' representations by aggregating neighbors' information, which can be treated as a specific application from a low-pass filter [20] to retain the commonality of node features. Recently, some studies [13,21] show that the signals' smoothness, i.e., low-frequency signal called positive information in our paper, is the key to achieving good performance. However, it is well known that the low-frequency filter will make node feature representation more indistinguishable because of over-smoothing which easily occurs with the increase of the number of network layers and the number of iterations in the training process in GCNs. So, the question is that whether the positive information is the only important information that should be considered in the user-item interaction graph from collaborative filtering. On the other hand, traditional layer combination mechanism usually ignores the different importance of different levels of users' neighbors. For example, inactive users may need more information from higher-order neighbors compared to active users.

To solve the problems above, we design a new attention-based light graph adaptive convolutional network called LGACN to learn the weights of positive information and negative information in different neighbors and combine different layers' feature information adaptively. Inspired by FAGCN [2], we design an embeddings propagation mechanism to allocate different neighbors with different weights. Theoretically, this mechanism is a generalization of symmetric sqrt normalization–an important design of most existing GCNs, which can alleviate the possible noise. At layer combination operation, we design an attention-based personalized weight allocation module. In this way, users and items with different activity levels will combine neighborhoods of different depths with different importance adaptively.

To summarize, this work makes the following main contributions:

- We design an adaptive embedding propagation mechanism, a generalization of symmetric sqrt normalization, to aggregate different neighbors in collaborative filtering to alleviate over-smoothness.
- We design a personalized weight allocation module, allowing different users and items to aggregate different depths of neighbors adaptively, bringing explainability for recommendation.
- We propose LGACN, which utilizes the adaptive embedding propagation mechanism and attention-based adaptive layer combination method, to alleviate the noise problem in neighbor aggregation and allow users to assign different weights to different layers adaptively. It brings the effective improvement of performance and improves the interpretability of recommendations.

The rest of the paper is organized as follows: we first introduce the related works methods to collaborative filtering and graph convolutional network. In Sect. 3, we describe the details of our proposed model LGACN. Experiments and discussions are conducted in Sect. 4. Finally, we conclude with a summary of our main contributions.

2   Related Work

2.1   Collaborative Filtering

CF models' basic idea is to project users and items into embeddings and learn the embedding representation by refactoring historical user-item interactions. Matrix factorization-a typical early CF model decomposes user-item interactions into user and item latent feature matrix, in which each row corresponds to the embedding of the user(item) [11]. Later, Neural Networks are deployed in collaborative filtering. NCF [8], a popular neural recommender model, maps users and items to latent vector and learns the embeddings of users and items by enhancing the interaction modeling with neural networks.

Due to the difficulty to solve the cold start problem in traditional CF, another kind of CF method attempts to enhance users' feature representations by leveraging their historical interaction items. For example, SVD++ [10] takes users' historical interaction items into account and uses the weighted average of the historical item ID embeddings as the target user's embedding. However, not all interactions are equally important to users, and different historical interaction items have different degrees of importance to users. Inspired by the attention mechanism [16], ACF [3] considers user-item interaction as a bipartite graph and uses an attention mechanism to learn embedding parameters of users and items. Essentially, the performance improvement of ACF is attributed to effective learning of the feature of one-hop neighbors.

2.2   Graph Convolution Network

The core idea of GCN is learning a function $f(\cdot)$ to aggregate node v_i 's features $\boldsymbol{x}_i$ and its neighbors' features $\boldsymbol{x}_j$ $(j \in N(v_i))$ to generate its new representation. In recommender system, another related study is using the user-item interaction graph structure. ItemRank [4] is a typical model which attempts to broadcast users' preferences for movies across a relational graph made up of movies. It encourages connected nodes having similar features. Recently, GNNs shine a light on building high-hop neighbors graph structure. Early GNNs aim at spectral GNN and defines the convolution kernel on the spectral domain. Later, GraphSage [5] and GCN [9] re-define graph convolution in the spatial domain, whose basic idea is aggregating neighbors' attributes information to learn the target node's embedding.

Due to the studies of graph convolution, NGCF [18], PinSage [22] and Light-GCN [6] adapt GCNs to the interaction graph of users and items. NGCF explicitly models the high-order connectivity between users and items to improve the embeddings. Inspired by [20], LightGCN simplifies the design of GCN to make it lighter and more suitable for recommendation. LightGCN retains the symmetric normalized terms in NGCF to aggregate the neighbors of users and items for collaborative filtering.

According to the latest research, the low-frequency signal of node characteristics utilized by the existing GNN is not the only information we need [19]. Bo et al. [2] think that the low-pass filter in GNNs mainly retains the commonality of node features, leading to the similarity of connected nodes. For collaborative filtering, most GCNs prefer to attach a positive effect to the target node's all neighbors [17], which can be seen as the application of a low-frequency filter. However, we believe that the neighbors of the target node do not always play a positive role in learning the feature representation of the target node. Noise from neighbors will reduce the effect of node feature learning and even bring negative effects.

3   Methodology

In this section, we describe the proposed LGACN model, the architecture of which is illustrated in Fig. 1. Four components are in the framework: (1) an embedding layer that offers and randomly initializes embeddings of users and items; (2) an adaptive embedding propagation layer to learn the embeddings by aggregating high-order neighborhood information; (3) an attention-based layer combination layer to personalize the different layers' weights of users and items; and (4) a prediction layer that combines the improved embeddings from different propagation layers and outputs the ranking score for recommendation generation.

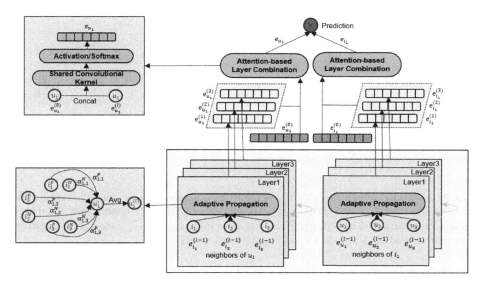

Fig. 1. An illustration of LGACN model architecture.

3.1   Embedding Layer

We describe a user u (an item i) with an embedding vector $\mathbf{e}_u \in \mathbb{R}^d$ $\left(\mathbf{e}_i \in \mathbb{R}^d\right)$, where d denotes the embedding size. An embedding look-up table can be built to describe the parameter matrix of users and items as follows:

$$E = [\mathbf{e}_{u_1}, \cdots, \mathbf{e}_{u_M}, \mathbf{e}_{i_1}, \cdots, \mathbf{e}_{i_N}] \tag{1}$$

where $\mathbf{e}_u$ and $\mathbf{e}_i$ are the embeddings of users and items, M and N represent the size of users and items. We use the Xavier initialization method to initialize embeddings of users and items randomly to make information flow better in the user-item interaction network. In LGACN, embeddings will be refined by propagating them on the interaction graph structure.

3.2   Adaptive Embedding Propagation Layers

We first compare the aggregation process of existing GNNs (e.g. LightGCN) and LGACN in Fig. 2. The left shows that LightGCN aggregates the collaborative signals from their neighbors and only considers the magnitude of neighbors' degrees to give them different positive weights. The right is LGACN that uses two feature representations to aggregate positive and negative information from the same neighbor node respectively. In FAGCN, node signals are divided into low-frequency signals and high-frequency signals, and both are helpful for learning node representations. Inspired by FAGCN, we design a positive-information filter F_P and a negative-information filter F_N to separate the positive and negative information from the node features. Considering user-item interaction graph as

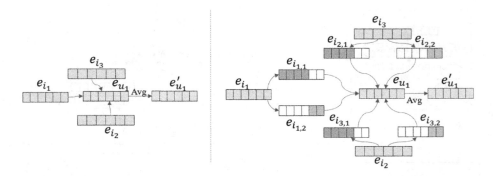

Fig. 2. Left: The aggregating method of LightGCN, and each node is equally important to the target node. Right: The aggregation process of LGACN, and each neighbor node is deconstructed into positive and negative information ($\mathbf{e}_{i_*,1}$ stands for positive information and $\mathbf{e}_{i_*,2}$ stands for the negative information).

an undirected graph $G = (V, E)$ with adjacency matrix $A \in \mathbb{R}^{N \times N}$, where V is a set of nodes with $|V| = N$ and E is a set of edges. We define the positive-information filter F_P and negative-information filter F_N as follows:

$$F_P = D^{-1/2}AD^{1/2} \qquad (2)$$

$$F_N = -D^{-1/2}AD^{1/2} \qquad (3)$$

where $\mathrm{D} \in \mathbb{R}^{N \times N}$ is a diagonal degree matrix with $D_{ii} = \sum_j A_{ij}$.

When we use F_P and F_N to replace the graph convolution operation (a.k.a. propagation rule in LightGCN [6]), the graph convolution operation is defined as follows:

$$\tilde{\mathbf{e}}_i = \left(\alpha_{ij}^P F_p + \alpha_{ij}^N F_N\right) E = \sum_{j \in N_i} \frac{\alpha_{ij}^P - \alpha_{ij}^N}{\sqrt{|N_i|}\sqrt{|N_j|}} \mathbf{e}_j \qquad (4)$$

where $\tilde{\mathbf{e}}_i$ is the aggregated representation of node i. α_{ij}^P and α_{ij}^N denote the proportions of positive information and negative information to node i. $N_i(N_j)$ denotes the neighbor set of node $i(j)$. $|N_i|$ and $|N_j|$ denote the number of neighbors of node i and node j. For the reasonableness of parameter setting and the simplicity of convolution operation formula, we set $\alpha_{ij}^P + \alpha_{ij}^N = 1$ and $\alpha_{ij} = \alpha_{ij}^P - \alpha_{ij}^N$. To learn the coefficients α_{ij}, we consider the features of both the node itself and its neighbors. Therefore, we design a shared gating mechanism to learn the coefficients:

$$\alpha_{ij} = \tanh\left(f^T \left[\mathbf{e}_i \| \mathbf{e}_j\right]\right) \qquad (5)$$

where f^T denotes the shared convolutional kernel and $\|$ denotes the concatenation operation. $tanh$ is an activation function to limit the value of α_{ij} in $[-1,1]$ naturally. Compared with LightGCN, our graph convolution operation can be written as follows:

$$\mathbf{e}_u^{(k+1)} = \sum_{u \in N_u} \frac{\alpha_{ui}}{\sqrt{|N_u|}\sqrt{|N_i|}} \mathbf{e}_i^{(k)} \tag{6}$$

$$\mathbf{e}_i^{(k+1)} = \sum_{i \in N_i} \frac{\alpha_{iu}}{\sqrt{|N_i|}\sqrt{|N_u|}} \mathbf{e}_u^{(k)} \tag{7}$$

where $\mathbf{e}_u^k$ and $\mathbf{e}_i^k$ denote the k-th layer embeddings of users and items. We can think of $\mathbf{e}_u^k$ and $\mathbf{e}_i^k$ from two perspectives. One is that they represent the ratio of positive and negative information in neighbors. Another is that they are the weights of neighbors in aggregation.

3.3   Attention-Based Layer Combination and Model Prediction

After we obtain the embeddings at each layer, we can combine them to form the final representation of a user(an item). In LightGCN, the layer combination mechanism is expressed by the following formula:

$$\mathbf{e}_u = \sum_{k=0}^{K} \frac{1}{K+1} \mathbf{e}_u^{(k)} \tag{8}$$

$$\mathbf{e}_i = \sum_{k=0}^{K} \frac{1}{K+1} \mathbf{e}_i^{(k)} \tag{9}$$

where k denotes the number of combination layers. However, we think that the embedding weights of each layer should be treated as a hyperparameter to be tuned for better performance. In general, compared with active users, inactive users need more information from higher orders. To personalize the layer combination weights from different users(items), we design an adaptive layer combination module based on the self-attention mechanism as follows:

$$\mathbf{e}_u = \sum_{k=0}^{K} \beta_u^{(k)} \mathbf{e}_u^{(k)} \tag{10}$$

$$\mathbf{e}_i = \sum_{k=0}^{K} \beta_i^{(k)} \mathbf{e}_i^{(k)} \tag{11}$$

where $\beta^{(k)}$ denotes the importance of k-th layer representation. We define the $\beta_u^{(k)}$ as follows:

$$\beta_k = \text{Softmax}\left(\text{Relu}\left(g^T\left[\mathbf{e}^{(0)}\|\mathbf{e}^{(k)}\right]\right)\right) \tag{12}$$

where g^T can be seen as a shared convolution kernel, and $Relu(\cdot)$ is the activation function to limit the weights in $[0, 1]$ to avoid the problem of gradient disappearance and sparsity. Finally, we use the softmax function to guarantee the sum of each layer's weight is 1.

We use the inner product of user and item final embeddings as model prediction as follows:

$$\hat{y}_{ui} = \mathbf{e}_u^T \mathbf{e}_i \tag{13}$$

which is applied as the ranking score to generate recommendation.

4   Experiments

In this section, we evaluate our proposed model by performing experiments on two open real-world datasets. According to the experimental results, we aim to answer the following research questions:

- RQ1: How does LGACN perform as compared with state-of-the-art CF methods?
- RQ2: How does LGACN perform compared with state-of-the-art GCN-based methods LightGCN?
- RQ3: How does the value of the L2 regularization coefficient affect LGACN?
- RQ4: How do adaptive embedding propagation and attention-based layer combination affect the performance of LGACN?

4.1   Datasets and Evaluation Metrics

To keep the comparison fair and reduce the experiment workload, we use the same experimented datasets which NGCF and LightGCN use except Gowalla. Table 1 shows the statistics of datasets. The datasets are described as follows:

Table 1. Statistics of the experimented datasets.

Dataset	User #	Item #	Interaction #	Density
Amazon-Book	52,643	91,599	2,984,108	0.00062
Yelp2018	31,688	38,048	1,561,406	0.00130

- **Amazon-Book:** Amazon-review dataset is widely used for product recommendation. We select Amazon-book from the collection as experimented datasets. To ensure data quality, we use the 10-core setting to ensure that each user and item have at least 10 interactions.
- **Yelp2018:** Yelp is the largest review site in the United States. This dataset comes from the 2018 edition of the Yelp challenge. In Yelp2018, local businesses such as restaurants and bars are viewed as the items. We use the same 10-core setting like LightGCN does to ensure data quality.

In Table 1, we made statistic on the number of users, items and interactions between users and items in Amazon-Book and Yelp2018. And we calculated the density(the radio between the number of observed interactions to the theoretical maximum number of interactions) of each dataset. The numbers of users, items, and interactions of Amazon-Book are all larger than that of Yelp2018. However, Yelp2018's density is 0.00130, roughly double that of Amazon-book. It indicates that we are more likely to get better performance on Yelp2018 than on Amazon-Book. For each dataset, we use the same training set and test set which LightGCN uses. Due to the Yelp2018 and Amazon-book being quite the same as the LightGCN paper [6] used, we directly use the results in the LightGCN paper.

Recall@20 and ndcg@20 are used as evaluation metrics, which are widely-used evaluation protocols in recommender system. For each user in the test set, all the items that the user has not interacted with are considered as negative items. LGACN will output the user's preference scores over all the items, excluded the positive ones used in the training set.

4.2   Compared Methods

Our proposed model LGACN is mainly compared with LightGCN. LightGCN has shown better performance than several existing methods, including GCN-based methods(e.g. PinSage, GC-MC and NGCF), neural network-based models(e.g. NeuMF and CMN) and traditional factorization-based models(e.g. MF and Hop-Rec). In addition to LightGCN, we further compare with Mult-VAE, GRMF and NGCF, which are compared in LightGCN paper. The four compared models are described as follows:

– **Mult-VAE** [12]: This is a variable value method for implicit feedback data for collaborative filtering, allowing us to go beyond linear factor models with limited modeling capabilities. It is a generative model with polynomial likelihood and uses Bayesian inference for parameter estimation.
– **GRMF** [14]: This model adds the graph Laplacian regularizer to smooth matrix factorization. We replace the rating prediction loss with BPR loss for fair comparison. GRMF-norm uses the normalization in graph Laplacian, and other hyper-parameter settings are the same as LGACN.
– **NGCF** [18]: By leveraging high-order connectivities in the user-item integration graph, this model incorporates collaborative signal into the embedding function of model-based CF. NGCF follows the standard GCN, which includes the nonlinear activation function and feature transformation.
– **LightGCN** [6]: This model only consists of two most central components for collaborative filtering - light graph convolution and layer combination, discarding feature transformation and nonlinear activation which are two standard designs in traditional GCNs.

4.3   Parameter Settings

We initialize the embedding parameters with the Xavier method and optimize LGACN with Adam. Like LightGCN and NGCF, we use the default learning rate of 0.001 and the regularization coefficient λ of 0.0001. The mini-batch size is set to 2048. We test the number of layers in the range of 1 to 4. The validation strategies and early stopping are the same as LightGCN.

Table 2. Overall performance comparison.

Dataset	Amazon-Book		Yelp2018	
Method	Recall	ndcg	Recall	ndcg
Mult-VAE	0.0407	0.0315	0.0584	0.0450
GRMF	0.0354	0.0270	0.0571	0.0462
GRMF-norm	0.0352	0.0269	0.0561	0.0454
NGCF	0.0344	0.0263	0.0579	0.0477
LightGCN	0.0411	0.0315	0.0649	0.0530
LGACN (ours)	**0.0472**	**0.0365**	**0.0671**	**0.0562**

4.4 Performance Comparison(RQ1)

Table 2 reports the performance comparison results. We obtain the following observations:

- Our proposed method performs the best performance on the two datasets, especially in Amazon-Book. Compared with LightGCN, LGACN obtains 15% relative improvement on Amazon-book and 5% relative improvement on Yelp2018 on average.
- LGACN and LightGCN shows better performance than NGCF. It means that nonlinear activation and feature transformation from traditional GCN have no positive effects on collaborative filtering. By removing nonlinear activation and feature transformation from traditional GCN, LGACN achieves better performance and reduces the model size.
- Except for LGACN and LightGCN, Mult-VAE exhibits the strongest performance than other baseline methods. GRMF and NGCF are comparable in performance. But GRMF-norm shows no benefits on both datasets.

4.5 Performance Comparison with LightGCN(RQ2)

We conduct detailed comparative experiments with LightGCN at different layers(1 to 4) in Table 3. We compute the percentage of relative improvement compared with LightGCN on recall and ndcg metric. To further reveal the advantage of our proposed model, we draw the training loss recall and testing recall compared with the results shows in the LightGCN paper on Amazon-Book. The observations are as follows:

- In most cases, LGACN is significantly improved than LightGCN, especially on Amazon-Book. For example, the highest recall and ndcg in our paper is 14.84% and 15.87% higher than LightGCN. In LightGCN paper, the variant of LightGCN, which only uses the final layer embeddings as the final representation, also obtains better performance than LightGCN. It means that LGACN is a generalization of LightGCN and has strong robustness.

– LGACN performs better than LightGCN on Yelp2018. However, LGACN is less effective than LightGCN in 1 layer. We think that the adaptive embedding propagation mechanism does not work and degenerate into the same neighborhood aggregation mode as LightGCN uses. However, as the number of layers increases, its advantage becomes apparent and shows the improvement of performance.

Table 3. Overall performance comparison.

Dataset		Amazon-Book		Yelp2018	
Layer #	Method	Recall	ndcg	Recall	ndcg
1 layer	LightGCN	0.0384	0.0298	0.0631	0.0515
	LGACN	0.0440 (+14.58%)	0.0339 (+13.76%)	0.0622 (−1.43%)	0.0513 (−0.39%)
2 layers	LightGCN	0.0411	0.0315	0.0622	0.0504
	LGACN	**0.0472 (+14.84%)**	**0.0365 (+15.87%)**	0.0652 (+4.82%)	0.0539 (+6.82%)
3 layers	LightGCN	0.041	0.0318	0.0639	0.0525
	LGACN	0.0459 (+11.95%)	0.0353 (+11.01%)	0.0665 (+4.07%)	0.0549 (+4.57%))
4 layers	LightGCN	0.0406	0.0313	0.0649	0.0530
	LGACN	0.0452 (+11.33%)	0.0346 (+10.54%)	**0.0671 (+3.39%)**	**0.0562 (+6.04%)**

4.6 Hyper-parameter Studies and Ablation Experiments (RQ3 and RQ4)

Hyper-parameter Studies. In LGACN, the most important hyper-parameter is the L_2 regularization coefficient λ. Here we explore the performance change of LGACN with the change of L_2 regularization coefficient λ.

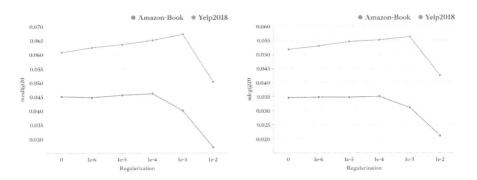

Fig. 3. Performance of 3-layer LGACN w.r.t. different regularization coefficient λ on Amazon-Book and Yelp2018

As shown in Fig. 3, LGACN shows less sensitivity to the change of λ. LGACN is less prone to over-fitting similar to LightGCN but achieving better performance. The possible reason is that LGACN generalizes neighborhood aggregation and layer combination which exist in LightGCN. The optimal value of λ for Amazon-Book and Yelp2018 is $1e^{(-4)}$ and $1e^{(-3)}$.

Table 4. Performance of LGACN and its two variant

Dataset	Amazon-Book		Yelp2018	
Method	Recall	ndcg	Recall	ndcg
LGACN-e	0.0452	0.0343	0.0663	0.0550
LGACN-l	0.0461	0.0356	0.0658	0.0544
LGACN	**0.0472**	**0.0365**	**0.0671**	**0.0562**

Ablation Experiments. To verify the effectiveness of adaptive embedding propagation and attention-based layer combination, we conduct ablation experiments. The results can be found in Table 4. As shown in Table 4, LGACN-e, replacing the adaptive embedding propagation method in LGACN with the traditional one in LightGCN, shows the degradation of performance. It means that our adaptive neighbor aggregation can effectively filter the noise from neighbors. On the other hand, LGACN-l, removing attention-based layer combination from LGACN and using fixed layer combination weights, shows performance degradation compared with LGACN. It means that attention-based layer combination can adaptively allocate the appropriate layer weights for users and items. LGACN-e and LGACN-l all perform better than other baseline methods on the two datasets. It also proves the effectiveness of our proposed adaptive neighbor aggregation mechanism and attention-based layer combination method.

5 Conclusion

In this work, we propose LGACN, which drops the redundant components of GCNs and adds adaptive neighborhood aggregation and layer combination mechanisms. In neighborhood aggregation, we divide neighbor information into positive information and negative information to adjust the embedding weights of the neighbor to the target node adaptively. In layer combination, we use an attention-based layer combination mechanism to offer personalized layer combination weights, aiming to provide adaptive smoothing for different users and items. From another perspective, LGACN can be seen as a generalization of LightGCN on neighborhood aggregation and layer combination and achieves better performance.

Acknowledgments. We thank all viewers who provided thoughtful and constructive comments on this paper. This work is funded by the Fundamental Research Funds for the Central Universities. East China Normal University, Shanghai 200062, China. The experiment is completed with the support of ECNU Multifunctional Platform for Innovation (001).

References

1. Blei, D.M., Ng, A.Y., Jordan, M.I.: Latent Dirichlet allocation. J. Mach. Learn. Res. **3**, 993–1022 (2003)

2. Bo, D., Wang, X., Shi, C., Shen, H.: Beyond low-frequency information in graph convolutional networks. arXiv preprint arXiv:2101.00797 (2021)
3. Chen, J., Zhang, H., He, X., Nie, L., Liu, W., Chua, T.S.: Attentive collaborative filtering: multimedia recommendation with item-and component-level attention. In: Proceedings of the 40th International ACM SIGIR Conference on Research and Development in Information Retrieval, pp. 335–344 (2017)
4. Gori, M., Pucci, A., Roma, V., Siena, I.: ItemRank: a random-walk based scoring algorithm for recommender engines. In: IJCAI, vol. 7, pp. 2766–2771 (2007)
5. Hamilton, W.L., Ying, R., Leskovec, J.: Inductive representation learning on large graphs. arXiv preprint arXiv:1706.02216 (2017)
6. He, X., Deng, K., Wang, X., Li, Y., Zhang, Y., Wang, M.: LightGCN: simplifying and powering graph convolution network for recommendation. In: Proceedings of the 43rd International ACM SIGIR Conference on Research and Development in Information Retrieval, pp. 639–648 (2020)
7. He, X., He, Z., Song, J., Liu, Z., Jiang, Y.G., Chua, T.S.: NAIS: neural attentive item similarity model for recommendation. IEEE Trans. Knowl. Data Eng. 30(12), 2354–2366 (2018)
8. He, X., Liao, L., Zhang, H., Nie, L., Hu, X., Chua, T.S.: Neural collaborative filtering. In: Proceedings of the 26th International Conference on World Wide Web, pp. 173–182 (2017)
9. Kipf, T.N., Welling, M.: Semi-supervised classification with graph convolutional networks. arXiv preprint arXiv:1609.02907 (2016)
10. Koren, Y.: Factorization meets the neighborhood: a multifaceted collaborative filtering model. In: Proceedings of the 14th ACM SIGKDD International Conference on Knowledge Discovery and Data Mining, pp. 426–434 (2008)
11. Koren, Y., Bell, R., Volinsky, C.: Matrix factorization techniques for recommender systems. Computer 42(8), 30–37 (2009)
12. Liang, D., Krishnan, R.G., Hoffman, M.D., Jebara, T.: Variational autoencoders for collaborative filtering. In: Proceedings of the 2018 World Wide Web Conference, pp. 689–698 (2018)
13. Nt, H., Maehara, T.: Revisiting graph neural networks: all we have is low-pass filters. arXiv preprint arXiv:1905.09550 (2019)
14. Rao, N., Yu, H.F., Ravikumar, P., Dhillon, I.S.: Collaborative filtering with graph information: consistency and scalable methods. In: NIPS, vol. 2, p. 7. Citeseer (2015)
15. Sarwar, B., Karypis, G., Konstan, J., Riedl, J.: Item-based collaborative filtering recommendation algorithms. In: Proceedings of the 10th International Conference on World Wide Web, pp. 285–295 (2001)
16. Vaswani, A., et al.: Attention is all you need. arXiv preprint arXiv:1706.03762 (2017)
17. Veličković, P., Cucurull, G., Casanova, A., Romero, A., Lio, P., Bengio, Y.: Graph attention networks. arXiv preprint arXiv:1710.10903 (2017)
18. Wang, X., He, X., Wang, M., Feng, F., Chua, T.S.: Neural graph collaborative filtering. In: Proceedings of the 42nd International ACM SIGIR Conference on Research and Development in Information Retrieval, pp. 165–174 (2019)
19. Wang, X., Zhu, M., Bo, D., Cui, P., Shi, C., Pei, J.: AM-GCN: adaptive multi-channel graph convolutional networks. In: Proceedings of the 26th ACM SIGKDD International Conference on Knowledge Discovery & Data Mining, pp. 1243–1253 (2020)

20. Wu, F., Souza, A., Zhang, T., Fifty, C., Yu, T., Weinberger, K.: Simplifying graph convolutional networks. In: International Conference on Machine Learning, pp. 6861–6871. PMLR (2019)
21. Xu, B., Shen, H., Cao, Q., Cen, K., Cheng, X.: Graph convolutional networks using heat kernel for semi-supervised learning. arXiv preprint arXiv:2007.16002 (2020)
22. Ying, R., He, R., Chen, K., Eksombatchai, P., Hamilton, W.L., Leskovec, J.: Graph convolutional neural networks for web-scale recommender systems. In: Proceedings of the 24th ACM SIGKDD International Conference on Knowledge Discovery & Data Mining, pp. 974–983 (2018)
23. Yuan, F., Karatzoglou, A., Arapakis, I., Jose, J.M., He, X.: A simple convolutional generative network for next item recommendation. In: Proceedings of the Twelfth ACM International Conference on Web Search and Data Mining, pp. 582–590 (2019)
24. Zhou, D., Dai, S.M., Tong, Q.: COVID-19: a recommendation to examine the effect of hydroxychloroquine in preventing infection and progression. J. Antimicrob. Chemother. **75**(7), 1667–1670 (2020)

HawkEye: Cross-Platform Malware Detection with Representation Learning on Graphs

Peng Xu[1]([✉]), Youyi Zhang[2], Claudia Eckert[1], and Apostolis Zarras[3]

[1] Technical University of Munich, Munich, Germany
peng@sec.in.tum.de
[2] Tongji University, Shanghai, China
[3] Delft University of Technology, Delft, Netherlands

Abstract. Malicious software, widely known as malware, is one of the biggest threats to our interconnected society. Cybercriminals can utilize malware to carry out their nefarious tasks. To address this issue, analysts have developed systems that can prevent malware from successfully infecting a machine. Unfortunately, these systems come with two significant limitations. First, they frequently target one specific platform/architecture, and thus, they cannot be ubiquitous. Second, code obfuscation techniques used by malware authors can negatively influence their performance. In this paper, we design and implement HawkEye, a control-flow-graph-based cross-platform malware detection system, to tackle the problems mentioned above. In more detail, HawkEye utilizes a graph neural network to convert the control flow graphs of executable to vectors with the trainable instruction embedding and then uses a machine-learning-based classifier to create a malware detection system. We evaluate HawkEye by testing real samples on different platforms and operating systems, including Linux (x86, x64, and ARM-32), Windows (x86 and x64), and Android. The results outperform most of the existing works with an accuracy of 96.82% on Linux, 93.39% on Windows, and 99.6% on Android. To the best of our knowledge, HawkEye is the first approach to consider graph neural networks in the malware detection field, utilizing natural language processing.

1 Introduction

With the development of 5G and IoT networks, as well as autonomous driving, Linux-based devices are becoming ubiquitous around the world. Meanwhile, the malicious software targeting these systems increasingly attracts the attention of both academia and industry, especially for Linux-based IoT devices and cloud servers. Historically, the security community concentrates on detecting and analyzing malware samples that primarily target Windows-based systems. However, this has changed as embedded systems and cloud servers rely on various architectures and operating systems. Unfortunately, most of the existing malware detection systems target a single platform and cannot recognize the cross-platforms'

I. Farkaš et al. (Eds.): ICANN 2021, LNCS 12893, pp. 127–138, 2021.
https://doi.org/10.1007/978-3-030-86365-4_11

malware. Take modern ICT environments as an example; it is common to find a mixture of different operating systems on servers (e.g., Linux) and workstations (e.g., Windows). Without anti-malware products for all the different operating systems, malware can easily infiltrate an organization's premice [12]. As a matter of fact, more and more malware is targeting cross-platforms [5]. Additionally, the native libraries of Android apps, including the malicious native code, are cross-platform (i.e., x86, ARMv7, ARMv8).

There are currently numerous malicious code detection methods using machine learning to characterize and discover the malicious behavior patterns of malware. Although these methods serve the target platforms with an extra security layer, nearly all of them suffer cross-platform issues because they leverage specific features to target a distinct type of malware. For example, the permission-based Android malware detection system cannot detect malicious Windows PE examples. For instance, the Windows Richer Header [14] feature cannot detect Linux ELF malware and Android's DEX files.

To address cross-platform issues in general, Control Flow Graphs (CFG) based method is a solution in the right direction because all programs have CFGs, which makes this approach platform-independent. However, the existing CFG-based methods [4,16] have two inevitable drawbacks. On the one hand, these approaches are far from scalable because of the expensive graph matching computation and sub-graph isomorphism. These techniques conduct pairwise graph matching for malware search, the complexity of which makes them unusable in large-scale datasets. On the other hand, the fixed graph pattern [4,16] is hard to adapt to different code because of too many manually fixed features.

In this paper, we design and implement HawkEye, a cross-platform malware detection framework to tackle these problems. HawkEye is based on a hybrid Control Flow Graph and Graph Neural Networks and is inspired by Natural Language Processing. HawkEye includes three primary components: (i) a graph generator, which extracts both static and dynamic control flow graphs from executable files; (ii) a graph-neural-network-based graph embedding method responsible for converting the whole attributed graph to a unique vector; (iii) a machine-learning classification system able to classify malware samples. Overall, this framework not only can be used by various platforms but also outperforms numerous malware detection solutions.

In summary, we make the following main contributions:

- We develop a cross-platform malware detection framework, which can detect not only Windows-based malware but also Linux and Android malware. HawkEye currently supports Intel, ARM, and MIPS architectures.
- We implement a representation-learning-based feature engineering-based on graph neural networks capable of identifying malware samples. To the best of our knowledge, HawkEye is the first approach to leverage graph neural networks (GNN) for cross-platform malware detection with the help of trainable features and transform learning.[1]

---

[1] Although Devign [17] uses GNN in the cybersecurity field, it only targets the C source code of famous CVE.

- We introduce instruction, basic-block, and graph embedding to assist out feature engineering and convert the program code to vectors,
- We evaluate `HawkEye` with real-world applications and various metrics. For Windows and Android malware detection, the results outperform most of the existing works. For Linux, we also retrieve significant results.

2   Related Work

MalConv [10] models the execution sequences of disassembled malicious binaries. It implements a neural network that consists of convolutional and feedforward neural constructs. That architecture embodies a hierarchical feature extraction approach that combines the convolution of n-grams of instructions with plain vectorization of features derived from the *Portable Executable* (PE) files' headers.

Ember [3] presents an open dataset for training static PE malware machine learning models. It extracts eight groups of raw features that include parsed features, format-agnostic histograms, and counts of strings. Those features include features extracting from the header file, imported functions table, exported functions table, raw byte histogram, and string information.

Adagio [4] implements a kernel-hashing-based malware detection system on the function call graph. It is based on the efficient embeddings of function call graphs with an explicit feature map inspired by a linear-time graph kernel. In an evaluation with real malware samples purely based on structural features, Adagio outperforms several related approaches. MAGIN [16], on the other hand, takes the manually fixed 11 features from the attributed CFG, which is the same with Gemini [15].

3   Motivation

3.1   Cross-Platform Malware Detection

On the one hand, the reason why we need cross-platform malware detection is primarily stimulated by the increasing native library-based Android malware. Furthermore, those native libraries are not only targeting the ARM32/ARM64 CPUs but also Intel X86/X64 CPUs. So far, most Android malware detection works are only concentrating on Android byte-code (DEX files), especially for the static code analysis based malware detection. Although few works consider the native library-based malware, no work so far takes care of the malicious code introducing by various version native libraries (i.e., for Intel and ARM platforms).

On the other hand, although it seems unimaginable to design a malware detection system targeting not only to Windows platform but also Linux and macOS, there are more and more examples illustrating that the same malicious code or vulnerability affects not only Windows but also Linux Users [5]. Even in cases with similar methods to detect malware on different platforms, it is nearly impossible to adopt one approach directly from one platform to another due

Table 1. Comparison with previous works

	Approaches	Description
CFG	Gemini [15], MAGIN [16]	*ACFG + Manually indicated features*
	Adagio [4]	*CFG + Manual one-hot embedding features*
Byte sequences	MalConv [10]	*Convolutional + trainable embedding*
	Ember [3]	*Gradient boosted decision tree + LightGBM*
CFG + NLP	Pektaş et al. [9]	*Malware Detection + call graph + graph embedding*
	HawkEye	*Cross-platforms + Representation learning on graph*

to some differences. For example, the API-based malware detection systems [9] are tightly associated with the underlying operating system. It means that Windows, Linux, Android, and macOS operating systems have significantly different underlying support for those detection systems.

Therefore, a malware detection system for various operating systems is a new topic in the cybersecurity field. To detect malware for cross-platform CFGs are considered a fundamental feature since they are platform-independent and thus are proper to represent a program behavior [4,16].

3.2   Representation Learning Based Feature Engineering

To generate the node attribute in the control flow graph, we take representation learning into consideration. Representation learning, which can automatically learn features from raw data, has increasingly attracted researchers' and engineers' focus. Compared to those manually indicated attributed control flow graph (ACFG) methods, like Xu et al. [15], Adagio [4], and Yan et al. [16], HawkEye can extract ACFG automatically without preparing manual features and avoiding the challenge of manual indicated methods (how to pick up the useful features is a challenge) because of the representation learning. For example, to represent the vertex of ACFG, Xu et al. [15] manually indicated six block-level attributes (numbers of calls, instructions, arithmetic instruction and transform instruction, string constants, and number of constants) and two inter-block attributes (numbers of offspring and betweenness). Additionally, HawkEye borrows ideas from natural language processing (NLP) to assist feature engineering. HawkEye uses the word2vec to convert instructions to vectors. Although MalConv [10] and Ember [3] also take benefits from NLP and leverage the n-gram method to extract features, n-gram also loses the bag-to-word information.

In brief, HawkEye introduces representation learning as the fundamental technique to represent code, which is different compared to [4,15,16], and use the control flow graph as fundamental to organize the program, which is different with those target-specific methods [9,10]. Additionally, it utilizes NLP to convert the byte sequences (instruction and basic block) to vectors, used to replace the manually indicated features [4,15,16]. The differences between HawkEye and the current works are summarized in Table 1.

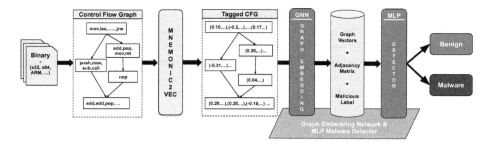

Fig. 1. System architecture

4   System Design

4.1   Architecture

We formalize our cross-platform malware detection system as a binary classification problem. We define the graph sets, which represents the structural information of the executable files (malware and benign), as our input, like $G^D(V^D, E^D)$, where V^D presents the set of graph's nodes, and E^D presents the edges among those nodes and D presents the number of the graph. For each graph g_i, it is encoded as $g_i(V, X, A)$, where $A \in \{0, 1\}^{m*m}$ is the adjacency matrix and m is the number of the graph's node, $m = |V|$. $X \in R^{m*d}$ presents a d-dimensional real-valued vector $x_j \in R^d$.

$$loss = \min \sum_{i=1}^{n} \lambda(f(g_i(V, X, A)) + \delta w(f)) - y_i \qquad (1)$$

where $i \in n$ and $n = |D|$. The goal of HawkEye is to learn a mapping from G^D to Y^D, $f : G \rightarrow Y$ to predict whether an executable file is malicious or not. The prediction function f can be learned by minimizing the loss function in Eq. 1, where g is the graph embedding and f is the MLP-classifier. In our work, we also add one $w(*)$ function to adjust the stability (reduces the influence of the difference from graph size) of HawkEye, and δ is a coefficient to scale the function w. Figure 1 illustrates HawkEye's architecture. The executable binary is the framework's input, and the prediction label (malware or benign) is the output. In summary, it includes three primary modules:graph generator, Feature embedding and MLP-based classifier as our malware detector.

4.2   Graph Generator

Based on the Angr framework (including angr-utils and bingraphvis) [11], we build our own *CFG Generator* to extract flow graphs from the executable binaries. The extracted graphs from cross-platform binaries include the static and dynamic CFG as well as the fCG (function call graph). For the static CFG, HawkEye constructs a directed graph $G = (N, E)$ with the basic block addresses and assembly code inside of basic blocks, where N represents all the nodes of the graph, including the node name and content (assembly instructions), and E represents the set of edges of the graph. The dynamic CFG and the fCG can be considered as a reduced graph of the static CFG. The dynamic CFG only concludes the basic blocks covered by symbolic execution. The fCG, on the other hand, collects the assembly code at the function level.

4.3   Feature Embedding

This component aims to generate a finite-dimensional nonlinear vector for each instruction in basic blocks. We divide this task into three modules: (i) mnemonic (opcode) embedding, (ii) block embedding, and (iii) CFG embedding.

Mnemonic Embedding. All the assembly instructions usually come with the following form: *label:[mnemonics][operands][comment]*. The label is an identifier that is a position marker for instructions and data. The instruction mnemonic is a brief word that marks an instruction, such as *mov*, *add*, and *sub*. The operands represent the value of instruction control and transfer. We only consider the mnemonic part because those mnemonics are linked to behaviors; the operands are the corresponding behaviors objects. As the final operands usually depend on the immediate number, register, and memory, we cannot use them as a feature because of their inherent variability. Therefore, we concentrate on analyzing the sequence of mnemonics. We show the difference between mnemonic and instruction embedding in the evaluation. There exist numerous methods to convert the sequence mnemonics into a vector sequence. In this work, we adjust the skip-gram sampling model of *word2vec* [6] to reduce word to the opcode of instruction to implement the mnemonic embedding.

Block Embedding. The embedding of a basic block is derived from all the instructions contained in the embedded block. The method for producing block embedding is *normalization*. Then, the normalization method is represented as: $x_{normalization} = \frac{x - Min}{Max - Min}$, where Max and Min are the maximal and minimal values among all embedding vectors in the basic block. The first element of vectors is picked up to get the maximal and minimal values. The list of block embedding vectors is forwarded to our adapted graph embedding network and malware detector for training.

Graph Embedding. To calculate the graph embedding from embedding vectors of the generated tagged CFG, we combine the graph structure characteristics and the node features with a settable iteration size (one Hyperparameter of GNN). For the graph embedding, in our case, the vertices (nodes) of a graph are functions, and the edges are connections among those functions. Those vertices (nodes) contain a set of opcodes inside them. The function embedding constructs each node's feature. In essence, we apply the graph embedding network based on *structure2vec* to convert the vectors of one graph to a unique vector. This neural network mainly considers two aspects of information: the instruction sequence in the node and the connection between the basic blocks. Our GNN combines

Table 2. The number of samples in different datasets

Platforms	Training		Validation		Testing		Total	
	Malware	Benign	Malware	Benign	Malware	Benign	Malware	Benign
Windows-x86	17,910	19,043	5,970	6,347	5,970	6,346	29,850	31,736
Android	15,331	15,000	5,111	5,000	5,111	5,000	25,553	25,000
Linux-x86	5,501	5,693	1,834	1,898	1834	1,897	9,169	9,488
Linux-x64	319	923	106	307	106	307	533	1,539
Linux-ARM32	434	446	144	148	144	148	724	744

these two kinds of information to generate our graph embedding vectors through deep neural structures. The realization of graph embedding generation is the execution of a graph neural network with unsupervised feature learning. So far, HawkEye can transform the input data into a group of graph embedding vectors containing feature information.

4.4 MLP-Based Malware Classifier

In this step, we establish a machine learning model that distinguishes malware from benign executables following the generated graph embedding vectors. The trained model with the best accuracy is stored as the final malware detection model. We use a multi-layer perceptron (MLP) for classification tasks. More specifically, we use one input layer, two hidden layers with 32 units, and one output layer in our MLP. We take the hinge loss as our loss function, which determines the difference between raw output prediction value $<P = MLP(X)>$ and real value $<R = Y\_label>$.

5 Evaluation

5.1 Dataset and Experimental Setup

Dataset Preparation. We collected our malware samples from VirusShare [1] and AndroZoo [2]. For benign samples, we collected ELF binary samples from libraries and executable files from Ubuntu 18.04-x64, Ubuntu {14.04, 16.04, 18.04}-x86 on Intel, and Raspbian 32-bit on ARM. For Windows-x86, we collected the benign binary samples from Windows XP, 7, 8, and 10. For Android samples, we collected all the samples from AndroZoo and used VirusTotal [13] API to label malicious samples classified as malware by more than five frameworks in VirusTotal. The samples in the training dataset account for 60% of the total binaries, while the samples in the validation dataset account for 20%. Finally, the samples in the testing dataset account for 20% of the total binaries. The detailed statistics are shown in Table 2.

Learning Setup. In our implementation, for the graph embedding network, we selected minibatch as 1, which is analogous to an online learning model. The

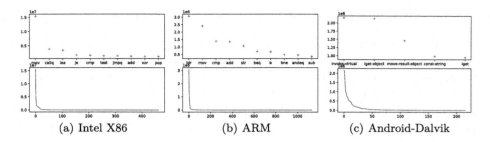

Fig. 2. Power-law distribution for Intel, ARM and Dalivk opcodes.

reason behind our choice is that the input data contains the adjacency matrix, which consumes a significant amount of memory, especially some APKs have more than 90,000 nodes (basic blocks of control flow graph). The classifier takes an input feature size of 32. The supervised classifier takes a loss value among the mean absolute error, sigmoid cross-entropy, and hinge loss to compare the rate of convergence using the ADAM [7] optimization algorithm with a 0.04 learning rate over 10 to 25 epochs. To avoid over-fitting, we use the model parameters at the minimum validation loss as the final learned weighted matrix θ. We execute the learning process for diverse situations on a Tensorflow computation framework on a server equipped with AMD EPYC Processor (64 cores) and 128 GB DDR4 memory RAM.

5.2 Power Law and Opcode Embedding

Before moving to our evaluation tasks, we use power-law distribution to prove the reasonability of using natural language processing techniques in our work. Figure 2 presents the opcode distribution for various platforms with the above datasets. Figure 2(a) shows the opcode distribution for Intel X86/X64 (we consider 32-bit and 64-bit opcode together since 96% of them are overlapped). In total, we have 463 opcodes; the 10 largest usage opcodes are illustrated. Figure 2(b) shows the ARM's opcode and its distribution. We have 1,131 ARM-opcode in total; the top 10 opcodes are shown. Meanwhile, Fig. 2(c) shows Dalvik's opcode distribution, which has 216 opcodes; the top 5 opcodes are presented. All of them follow the power-law distribution, which means borrowing word embedding techniques from natural language processing to do opcode embedding is reasonable.

5.3 Evaluation Tasks

After determining the experimental setup, we evaluate HawkEye's performance on the following tasks: malware detection performance, CFG generation, and training efficiency.

We tested our model's accuracy using the standard *Area Under Curve - Receiver Operating Characteristic* (AUC-ROC) curve. We utilize four metrics:

Table 3. Performance comparison with other approaches

Model	Accuracy (%)	Precision (%)	Recall (%)	F1 (%)	AUC: (%)
WIN-Ge	93.39	94.79	**97.74**	**96.24**	94.61
WIN-MalConv [10]	90.77	**98.88**	34.34	50.97	82.43
WIN-Ember [3]	**98.23**	97.47	89.72	93.43	**96.67**
WIN-MAGIC [16]	82.46	86.63	82.46	81.96	84.78
ANDROID-Ge	**99.85**	**99.74**	**99.74**	**99.74**	**99.57**
ANDROID-Adagio [4]	95.00	91.07	94.0	95.32	91.07

precision, recall, F1, and FPR, often used to describe a binary classification model's testing accuracy.

As Fig. 3 and Table 3 reveal, we compared our results with other works on Windows-32 and Android platforms. The reason for this choice is as follows. For Windows-32 and Android samples, there are efficiently labeled malware samples. In addition, there are enough related works to compare the performance of our framework. However, to detect malware on Linux platforms, such as Linux-32, Linux-64, and Linux-ARM32, we cannot find any comparable works to support our achievement.

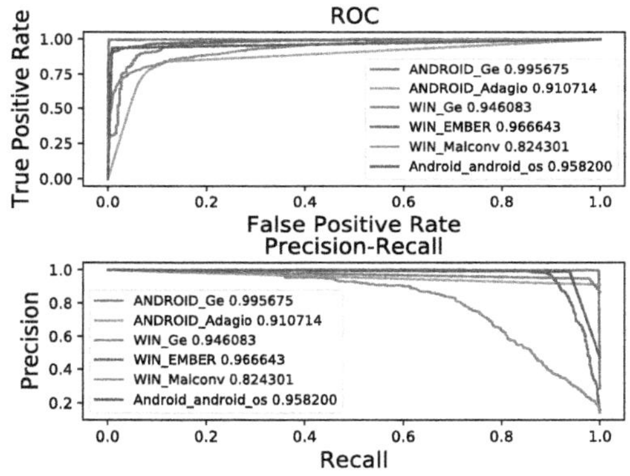

As Table 3 shows, on the Windows-x86 platform, for accuracy and precision, Ember [3] gets a better result than our graph embedding (GE) approach. However, for recall and F1-score, Ember does not work better. MAGIC gets the worst results among all of our experiments. When compared with MalConv [10], `HawkEye` outperforms its results. Similar to the Windows-x86 platform, we compare our performance on the Android platform with Adagio [4], which is a one-hot embedding-based malware detection with CFG. Our GE-based approach outperforms Adagio's results. In conclusion, our `HawkEye` outperforms other related works in nearly all metrics, especially on the recall and F1-function.

Fig. 3. ROC and precision-recall on Windows-x86 and Android

5.4 Hyper-parameters Selection

Different Number of Epochs. To evaluate our module's convergence feature, we set a different number of epochs, between 10 and 25, in order to test the differences in the performance. The validation is processed every five epochs to

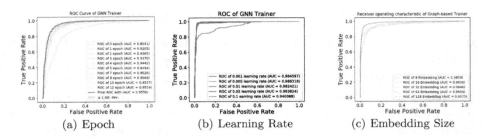

(a) Epoch   (b) Learning Rate   (c) Embedding Size

Fig. 4. ROC results with different iteration

select the best-weighted matrix. As Fig. 4(a) depicts, the accuracy rises, and the loss decreases shapely in the first three epochs in an ordinary situation. After 12 epochs, the ROC value will be maintained at a certain level and only slightly float up and down. In essence, we get the best ROC results after 12 epochs. We then save the model parameters for future restoration in the test process. In conclusion, our model can have convergence quickly and achieve the best performance after about 15 epochs. In this experiment, the other hyper-parameters are fixed as the learning rates equal 12, the iteration size equals 2, and the embedding size is 32.

Different Learning Rates. The learning rate is a configurable hyper-parameter used in the training of neural networks. It is referred to as the step size that the weights are updated during training. The various value of learning rate affects the performance significantly. In this section, the influence of learning rates is studied. HawkEye evaluates the various learning rates with values: {0.001, 0.005, 0.01, 0.05, 0.1}. In this experiment, the other hyper-parameters are fixed as epoch equals 12, the iteration size equals 2, and the embedding size is 32. Figure 4(b) illustrates the outcomes. In detail, the AUCs of HawkEye achieve more than 98% for learning rate of {0.001, 0.005, 0.01, 0.05}, and when learning rate equals to 0.005, HawkEye gets the best of AUC with 98.83%. Only for the 0.1 learning rate, the AUC drops to 94%, which is due to the big step size of weight updating.

Different Embedding Sizes. From Fig. 4(c), we can conclude that the embedding size in a specific range does not impact the performance significantly. The ROC curves are similar to each other, with an embedding size from 8 to 32. Considering the embedding size is positive relative to the training time and evaluation time, we decided to use 8 as embedding size for the trade-off between performance and efficiency. It is worth mentioning that if we select a bigger embedding size (e.g., 64) compared to a small input feature size (e.g., 32), the performance will decrease sharply because the features get dilute.

5.5 Detection on Obfuscated Samples

Table 4. Detection rate of obfuscated APK

	ClassEnc.	StrEnc.	Refl.	Triv.	Triv.-Str.	Triv.-Ref.-Str.	Triv.-Ref.-Str.-Class.
PRAGuard[a]	38.0	64.0	96	90.0	50.0	44.0	32.0
Drebin	99.12	98.99	86.58	98.32	98.99	99.32	96.98
Our framework	99.33	98.99	86.58	98.32	98.99	99.32	96.98

[a]PRAGuard's median

Here, we present our experimental results for the detection of obfuscated samples. We only take obfuscated Android samples as our input and compare our work with PRAGuard [8]. The obfuscated methods include class encryption, string encryption, reflection, and various combinations. For other platform samples, our work can be extended easily. PRAGuard mentions the influence of obfuscated applications on Android malware detection. It presents seven types of obfuscation techniques and influenced performance. We evaluate our

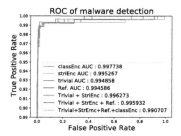

Fig. 5. ROC of obfuscated APK

framework on the PRAGuard dataset. The ROC is illustrated in Fig. 5. We compare the detection rate with PRAGuard in Table 4. From the extracted results, we identify that obfuscation does not influence our framework.

6 Conclusion

In this paper, we investigate a new methodology that detects malware on cross-platform architectures. We design and implement three separate tools: (*i*) a CFG generator, (*ii*) a feature embedding (includes opcode embedding and graph embedding) networks, and (*iii*) an MLP neural network malware detector. The combination of the above tools allowed us to build `HawkEye`, a combined detector. `HawkEye` solves the classification accuracy by training itself via diverse inner maximization methods, different embedding maps, and a specific type of CFG. The experiments validate that `HawkEye` can fast and accurately classify malware. Overall, it proves that the control flow graph and the graph neural networks can be successfully applied in malware detection.

Acknowledgments. This project has received funding from the European Union's Horizon 2020 research and innovation programme under grant agreements No 883275 (HEIR) and No. 833115 (PREVISION).

References

1. VirusShare.com. https://virusshare.com/. Accessed 5 July 2019
2. Allix, K., Bissyandé, T.F., Klein, J., Le Traon, Y.: AndroZoo: collecting millions of android apps for the research community. In: IEEE/ACM Working Conference on Mining Software Repositories (MSR) (2016)
3. Anderson, H.S., Roth, P.: EMBER: an open dataset for training static PE malware machine learning models. ArXiv e-prints (2018)
4. Gascon, H., Yamaguchi, F., Arp, D., Rieck, K.: Structural detection of android malware using embedded call graphs. In: ACM Workshop on Artificial Intelligence and Security (2013)
5. Germain, J.M.: New security hole puts windows and Linux users at risk. https://www.technewsworld.com/story/86778.html (2020)
6. Goldberg, Y., Levy, O.: Word2vec explained: deriving Mikolov et al.'s negative-sampling word-embedding method. arXiv preprint arXiv:1402.3722 (2014)
7. Kingma, D.P., Ba, J.: Adam: a method for stochastic optimization. arXiv preprint arXiv:1412.6980 (2014)
8. Maiorca, D., Ariu, D., Corona, I., Aresu, M., Giacinto, G.: Stealth attacks: an extended insight into the obfuscation effects on android malware. Comput. Secur. **51**, 16–31 (2015)
9. Pektaş, A., Acarman, T.: Deep learning for effective android malware detection using API call graph embeddings. Soft Comput. **24**(2), 1027–1043 (2020)
10. Raff, E., Barker, J., Sylvester, J., Brandon, R., Catanzaro, B., Nicholas, C.K.: Malware detection by eating a whole exe. In: AAAI Workshop on Artificial Intelligence for Cyber Security (2018)
11. Shoshitaishvili, Y., Wang, R., Hauser, C., Kruegel, C., Vigna, G.: Firmalice - automatic detection of authentication bypass vulnerabilities in binary firmware. In: Network & Distributed System Security Symposium (NDSS) (2015)
12. Stange, S.: Detecting malware across operating systems. Netw. Secur. **2015**(6), 11–14 (2015)
13. Total, V.: Virustotal-free online virus, malware and url scanner. Online: https://www.virustotal.com/en (2012)
14. Webster, G.D., et al.: Finding the needle: a study of the PE32 rich header and respective malware triage. In: International Conference on Detection of Intrusions and Malware & Vulnerability Assessment (DIMVA) (2017)
15. Xu, X., Liu, C., Feng, Q., Yin, H., Song, L., Song, D.: Neural network-based graph embedding for cross-platform binary code similarity detection. In: ACM SIGSAC Conference on Computer and Communications Security (CCS) (2017)
16. Yan, J., Yan, G., Jin, D.: Classifying malware represented as control flow graphs using deep graph convolutional neural network. In: Annual IEEE/IFIP International Conference on Dependable Systems and Networks (DSN) (2019)
17. Zhou, Y., Liu, S., Siow, J., Du, X., Liu, Y.: Devign: effective vulnerability identification by learning comprehensive program semantics via graph neural networks. In: Advances in Neural Information Processing Systems (2019)

An Empirical Study of the Expressiveness of Graph Kernels and Graph Neural Networks

Giannis Nikolentzos[1,2]([⊠]), George Panagopoulos[1], and Michalis Vazirgiannis[1,2]

[1] École Polytechnique, Palaiseau, France
[2] Athens University of Economics and Business, Athens, Greece
{nikolentzos,mvazirg}@lix.polytechnique.fr,
george.panagopoulos@polytechnique.edu

Abstract. Graph neural networks and graph kernels have achieved great success in solving machine learning problems on graphs. Recently, there has been considerable interest in determining the expressive power mainly of graph neural networks and of graph kernels, to a lesser extent. Most studies have focused on the ability of these approaches to distinguish non-isomorphic graphs or to identify specific graph properties. However, there is often a need for algorithms whose produced graph representations can accurately capture similarity/distance of graphs. This paper studies the expressive power of graph neural networks and graph kernels from an empirical perspective. Specifically, we compare the graph representations and similarities produced by these algorithms against those generated by a well-accepted, but intractable graph similarity function. We also investigate the impact of node attributes on the performance of the different models and kernels. Our results reveal interesting findings. For instance, we find that theoretically more powerful models do not necessarily yield higher-quality representations, while graph kernels are shown to be very competitive with graph neural networks.

Keywords: Expressive power · Graph neural networks · Graph kernels

1 Introduction

In recent years, graph-structured data has experienced an enormous growth in many domains, ranging from chemo- and bio-informatics to social network analysis. Several problems of increasing interest require applying machine learning techniques to graph-structured data. Examples of such problems include predicting the quantum mechanical properties of molecules [13] and modeling physical systems [2]. In the past years, the problem of machine learning on graphs has been governed by two major families of approaches, namely graph kernels (GKs) [26] and graph neural networks (GNNs) [35].

Recently, much research has focused on measuring the expressive power of GNNs [1,5,6,19,22–24,36]. On the other hand, in the case of GKs, there was a limited number of similar studies [17]. This is mainly due to the fact that the

© Springer Nature Switzerland AG 2021
I. Farkaš et al. (Eds.): ICANN 2021, LNCS 12893, pp. 139–150, 2021.
https://doi.org/10.1007/978-3-030-86365-4_12

landscape of GKs is much more diverse than that of GNNs. Indeed, although numerous GNN variants have been recently proposed, most of them share the same basic idea, and can be reformulated into a single common framework, so-called message passing neural networks [13]. These models employ a message passing procedure to aggregate local information of vertices and are closely related to the Weisfeiler-Lehman test of graph isomorphism, a powerful heuristic which can successfully test isomorphism for a broad class of graphs.

When dealing with learning problems on graphs, a practitioner needs to choose one GNN or one GK for her particular application. The practitioner is then faced with the following question: Does this GNN variant or GK capture graph similarity better than others? Unfortunately, this question is far from being answered. Most of the above studies investigate the power of GNNs in terms of distinguishing between non-isomorphic graphs or in terms of how well they can approximate combinatorial problems. However, in graph classification/regression problems, we are not that much interested in testing whether two (sub)graphs are isomorphic to each other, but mainly in classifying graphs or in predicting real values associated with these graphs. In such tasks, it has been observed that stronger GNNs do not necessarily outperform weaker GNNs. Therefore, it seems that the design of GNNs is driven by theoretical considerations which are not realistic in practical settings. Ideally, we would like to learn representations which accurately capture the similarities or distances between graphs.

A practitioner can then choose an algorithm based on its empirical performance. Indeed, GNNs and GKs are usually evaluated on standard datasets derived from bio-/chemo-informatics and from social media [21]. However, several concerns have been raised recently with regards to the reliability of those datasets, mainly due to their small size and to inherent isomorphism bias problems [15]. More importantly, it has been observed that the adopted experimental settings are in many cases ambiguous or not reproducible [8]. The experimental setup is not standardized across different works, and there are often many issues related to hyperparameter tuning and to how model selection and model assessment are performed. These issues easily generate doubts and confusion among practitioners that need a fully transparent and reproducible experimental setting.

Present Work. In this paper, we empirically evaluate the expressive power of GNNs and GKs. Specifically, we build a dataset that contains instances of different families of graphs. Then, we compare the graph representations and similarities produced by GNNs and GKs against those generated by an intractable graph similarity function which we consider to be an oracle function that outputs the true similarity between graphs. We perform a large number of experiments where we compare several different kernels, architectures, and pooling functions. Secondly, we study the impact of node attributes on the performance of the different models and kernels. We show that annotating the nodes with their degree and/or triangle participation can be beneficial in terms of performance in the case of GNNs, while it is not very useful in the case of GKs. Finally, we investigate which pairs of graphs (from our dataset) lead GNNs and GKs to the highest error in the estimated similarity. Surprisingly, we find that several GNNs and GKs assign identical or similar representations to very dissimilar graphs.

2   Related Work

Over the past years, the expressiveness of GKs was assessed almost exclusively from experimental studies. Therefore, still, there is no theoretical justification on why certain GKs perform better than others. From the early days of the field, it was clear though that the mapping induced by kernels that are computable in polynomial time is not injective [12]. Recently, a framework was developed to measure the expressiveness of GKs based on ideas from property testing [17]. It was shown that some well-established GKs such as the shortest path kernel, the graphlet kernel, and the Weisfeiler-Lehman subtree kernel cannot identify basic graph properties such as planarity or bipartitness.

With a few exceptions [28], until recently, there has been little attempt to understand the expressive power of GNNs. Several recent studies have investigated the connections between GNNs and different variants of the Weisfeiler-Lehman (WL) test of isomorphism. For instance, it was shown that standard GNNs do not have more power in terms of distinguishing between non-isomorphic graphs than the WL algorithm [22,36]. Morris *et al.* proposed in [22] a family of GNNs which rely on a message passing scheme between subgraphs of cardinality k, and which have exactly the same power in terms of distinguishing non-isomorphic graphs as the set-based variant of the k-WL algorithm. In a similar spirit, Maron *et al.* introduced in [19] k-order graph networks which are at least as powerful as the folklore variant of the k-WL graph isomorphism test in terms of distinguishing non-isomorphic graphs. These models were also shown to be universal [20], but require using high order tensors and therefore are not practical. Chen *et al.* showed in [5] that the two main approaches for studying the expressive power of GNNs, namely graph isomorphism testing and invariant function approximation, are equivalent to each other. Furthermore, the authors propose a GNN that is more powerful than 2-WL. Based on a connection between the WL algorithm and first order logic, Barceló *et al.* characterized in [1] the expressive power of GNNs in terms of classical logical languages. The impact of random features on the expressive power of GNNs is considered in [27]. Nikolentzos *et al.* showed in [24] that standard GNNs cannot identify fundamental graph properties such as triangle-freeness and connectivity, and they proposed a model that can identify these properties. Other studies take into account all possible node permutations and produce universal graph representations [6,23]. The emerging problems become intractable once the number of nodes is large and they propose approximation schemes to make the computation feasible. Some recent works have studied the generalization properties of GNNs [11,29,34].

3   Comparing Graphs to Each Other

Formally, for any two graphs $G_1 = (V_1, E_1)$ and $G_2 = (V_2, E_2)$ on n vertices with respective $n \times n$ adjacency matrices $\mathbf{A}_1$ and $\mathbf{A}_2$, we define a function $f : \mathcal{G} \times \mathcal{G} \to \mathbb{R}$ where $\mathcal{G}$ is the space of graphs which quantifies the similarity of G_1 and G_2. Note that in the literature, this problem is often referred to as *graph comparison*.

In this paper, we consider a graph comparison function which is not computable in polynomial time. The function can be expressed as a maximization problem, and is defined as follows:

$$f(G_1, G_2) = \max_{\mathbf{P} \in \Pi} \frac{\sum_{i=1}^{n} \sum_{j=1}^{n} \left[\mathbf{A}_1 \odot \mathbf{P} \mathbf{A}_2 \mathbf{P}^{\top} \right]_{ij}}{||\mathbf{A}_1||_F \, ||\mathbf{A}_2||_F} \tag{1}$$

where Π denotes the set of $n \times n$ permutation matrices, $\odot$ denotes the element-wise product, and $|| \cdot ||_F$ is the Froebenius matrix norm. For clarity of presentation we assume n to be fixed (i.e., both graphs consist of n vertices). In order to apply the function to graphs of different cardinality, one can append zero rows and columns to the adjacency matrix of the smaller graph to make its number of rows and columns equal to n. Therefore, the problem of graph comparison can be reformulated as the problem of maximizing the above function over the set of permutation matrices. A permutation matrix $\mathbf{P}$ gives rise to a bijection $\pi : V_1 \rightarrow V_2$. The function defined above seeks for a bijection such that the number of common edges $|\{(u, v) \in E_1 : \big(\pi(u), \pi(v)\big) \in E_2\}|$ is maximized. Then, the number of common edges is normalized such that it takes values between 0 and 1. Solving the above optimization problem for large graphs is clearly intractable since there are $n!$ permutation matrices of size n. In this paper, we investigate how different graph comparison/representation learning approaches approximate the above-defined function from an empirical standpoint.

4   Empirical Evaluation

4.1   Dataset

Since the function defined in (1) is intractable for large graphs, we generated graphs consisting of at most 9 vertices. Furthermore, each graph is connected and contains at least 1 edge. We generated 191 pairwise non-isomorphic graphs. The dataset consists of different types of synthetic graphs. These include simple structures such as cycle graphs, path graphs, grid graphs, complete graphs and star graphs, but also randomly-generated graphs such as Erdős-Rényi graphs, Barabási-Albert graphs and Watts-Strogatz graphs. Table 1 shows statistics of the synthetic dataset that we used in our experiments. Figure 1 illustrates the distribution of the similarities of the generated graphs as computed by the proposed measure. There are $191*192/2 = 18,336$ pairs of graphs in total (including pairs consisting of a graph and itself). Interestingly, most of the similarities take values between 0.5 and 0.8.

4.2   Selected Approaches

Suitable GKs and GNNs were selected according to the following criteria: (1) publicly available implementations, (2) strong architectural differences, (3) popularity, and (4) peer reviewed. We next present the GKs and GNNs that were

Table 1. Summary of the synthetic dataset that we used in our experiments.

Synthetic dataset	
Max # vertices	9
Min # vertices	2
Average # vertices	7.29
Max # edges	36
Min # edges	1
Average # edges	11.34
# graphs	191

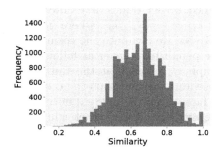

Fig. 1. Distribution of similarities between the synthetically generated graphs.

included into our evaluation. For a detailed description of each kernel and each GNN, we refer the reader to their respective papers.

We selected the following 6 GKs: (1) random walk kernel (RW) [12], (2) shortest path kernel (SP) [4], (3) graphlet kernel (GR) [31], (4) Weisfeiler-Lehman subtree kernel (WL) [30], (5) pyramid match kernel (PM) [25], and (6) Graph-Hopper kernel [9]. Note that GR can only operate on unlabeled graphs. The rest of the kernels can handle graphs with discrete node labels, while GraphHopper is the only kernel that can deal with continuous multi-dimensional node features.

We also selected the following GNNs: (1) GCN [16], (2) GAT [33], (3) 1-GNN [22], (4) GG-NN [18], (5) GraphSAGE [14], (6) GIN [36], (7) ChebNet [7], (8) ARMA [3], (9) 1-2-GNN [22], (10) k-hop GNN [24], and (11) Provably Powerful GNN [19]. To produce graph representations, we use 3 pooling functions, namely the sum aggregator, the mean aggregator and the max aggregator.

4.3 Baselines

We utilize some simple baselines whose purpose is to understand the extent to which GKs and GNNs can indeed learn representations that capture graph similarity. The first baseline is a function that randomly computes the similarity of two graphs by sampling a number from $[0,1]$ with uniform probability. The second baseline is a constant function (output equal to 1). Using such simple baselines as a reference is crucial since they can provide feedback on the effectiveness of GKs and GNNs in the considered task. If the performance of a GNN or a GK is close to that of one of the baselines, that would mean that the GNN/GK fails to encode accurately graph representations and similarities.

4.4 Experimental Settings

Normalization. As discussed above, the function defined in (1) gives an output in the range $[0,1]$. The similarity of two graphs G_1 and G_2 is equal to 1 if and only if G_1 and G_2 are isomorphic to each other. We normalize the obtained kernel values as follows such that they also take values in the range $[0, 1]$: $k_{ij} = k_{ij}/\sqrt{k_{ii}}\sqrt{k_{jj}}$. where k_{ij} is the kernel between graphs G_i and G_j. For the GNNs, we compute the cosine similarity between the graph representations of the penultimate layer as follows: $\mathbf{z}_i^\top \mathbf{z}_j/\|\mathbf{z}_i\| \|\mathbf{z}_j\|$ where $\mathbf{z}_i$ is the representation of graph G_i. Note that the ReLU function has already been applied to these representations, and thus the cosine similarity also takes values between 0 and 1. In fact, the two employed normalization schemes (i.e., for kernels and GNNs) are equivalent since a kernel value corresponds to an inner product between the representations of two graphs in some Hilbert space.

Evaluation Metrics. To assess how well the different approaches approximate the similarity function defined in (1), we employed two evaluation metrics: the Pearson correlation coefficient and the mean squared error (MSE). The Pearson correlation coefficient measures the linear relationship between two variables. It takes values between -1 and 1, while a value of 1 denotes total positive linear correlation. In our setting, a high value of correlation would mean that the approach under consideration captures the relationships between the similarities (e.g., whether the similarity of a pair of graphs is greater or lower than that of another pair). The second measure, MSE, is equal to the average squared difference between the estimated values and the actual values. A very small value of MSE denotes that the derived similarities are very close to those produced by the function defined in (1). A credible graph representation learning/similarity approach would yield both a high correlation and a small MSE. Note that the correlation between the output of a constant function and the output of (1) is not defined since the values produced by the constant function have a variance equal to zero.

Hyperparameters. For RW, we set λ to 0.01. For GR, we count all the graphlets of size 3. For the WL kernel, we choose the number of iterations from $\{1, 2, \ldots, 6\}$. For PM, the dimensionality of the embeddings d and the number of levels L are set equal to 6 and 4, respectively. For the GraphHopper kernel, a linear kernel is used on the continuous-valued attributes.

For the GNNs, we use 2 neighborhood aggregation layers. For GraphSAGE, we use the mean function to aggregate the neighbors of a node. For ChebNet, we use polynomials of order 2, and for ARMA, we set the number of stacks K to 2 and the depth T also to 2. The hidden-dimension size of the neighborhood aggregation layers is set equal to 64. We apply the ReLU activation function to the output of each neighborhood aggregation layer. As mentioned above, we use 3 common readout functions: sum, mean and max. The output of the readout function is passed on to a fully-connected layer with 32 hidden units followed by ReLU nonlinearity. The output of the ReLU function corresponds to the representation of the input graph (i.e., each graph is represented by a 32-dimensional vector). For Provably Powerful GNN, we use a network suffix that consists of an invariant readout function followed by 2 fully connected layers. To train all neural networks, we use the Adam optimizer with learning rate 0.001. We set the batch size to 32 and the number of epochs to 100. We store the model that achieved the best validation accuracy into disk. At the end of training, the model is retrieved from the disk, and we use it to generate graph representations.

Protocol. For deterministic approaches, we compute the graph similarities once and report the emerging correlation and MSE. For the remaining approaches (e.g., GNNs, since their parameters are randomly initialized), we repeat the experiment 10 times and report the average correlation, the average MSE and the corresponding standard deviations.

Implementations. For the GKs, we used the implementations contained in the GraKeL library [32]. For 1-2 GNN, k-hop GNN, and Provably Powerful GNN, we use the implementations provided by the authors. The remaining GNNs were implemented with the Pytorch Geometric library [10].

4.5   Results

No Features. In the first set of experiments, we do not use any pre-computed features, and therefore, the emerging representations/similarities rely solely on the representational capabilities of the different approaches. Note that all GNNs except Provably Powerful GNN and most GKs require the nodes to be annotated with either continuous attributes or discrete labels. Therefore, for these approaches, we annotate each node with a single feature (i.e., the discrete label 1 or the real value 1.0).

For GNNs, we consider two alternatives: (1) we randomly initialize the parameters of the models and we perform a feedforward pass to generate the graph representations or (2) we randomly initialize the parameters of the models, we train the models on some independent dataset and then we perform the feedforward pass to generate the representations. GKs are, in a sense, unsupervised, and cannot be trained on any dataset. The obtained results for the two aforementioned cases are illustrated in Fig. 2. Note that in the second case, the models were trained on the IMDB-BINARY graph classification dataset.

In terms of correlation, 1-GNN and GIN are the best-performing approaches followed by GG-NN and one variant of Chebnet. The 6 GKs along with 2-hop GNN and Provably Powerful GNN perform slightly worse than the above models. In terms of MSE, the GKs outperform in general the GNNs. Notably, some GKs such as WL and PM achieve very low values of MSE. On the other hand, most GNNs fail to outperform the random baseline. Specifically, the only models that outperform this baseline are 1-GNN, 2-hop GNN, GG-NN with sum pooling, Chebnet with sum pooling and Provably Powerful GNN with max pooling. With regards to the three pooling functions, the sum operator seems to outperform the others. Furthermore, it is important to mention that more powerful architectures (e.g., 1-2-GNN, 2-hop GNN, Provably Powerful GNN) do not necessarily lead to higher correlation and lower MSE than standard, less expressive GNNs. We next investigate how the performance of the GNNs changes when the models are first trained on the IMDB-BINARY dataset. The results are shown in Fig. 2 (Bottom). We observe that there is a decrease in correlation, and no GNN achieves higher correlation than the ones achieved by the WL and PM kernels anymore. On the other hand, the MSE of most GNNs also decreases. For instance, most GNNs now yield lower MSEs than the random baseline. However, still, GCN, GAT and GraphSAGE fail to outperform this baseline.

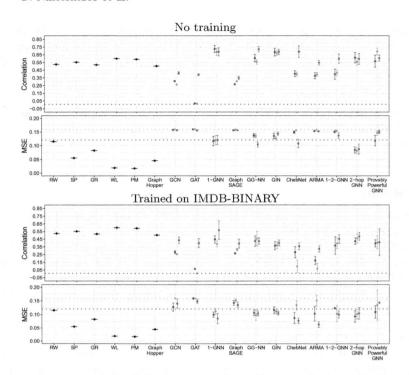

Fig. 2. Performance of the different approaches without node features. The GNNs were either not trained (Top) or trained on the IMDB-BINARY dataset (Bottom). For GNNs, the different colors indicate the three pooling functions: sum (•), mean (•), and max (•). The horizontal lines correspond to the two baselines (random, constant) (Color figure online).

The Effect of Node Features. In GNN literature, it is common practice to use local features (e.g., degree) as node attributes. In previous studies, it has been reported that using node degrees as input features leads to an increase in performance on almost all graph classification datasets [8]. We next investigate what is the impact of such features on the learned graph representations. Specifically, each node is annotated with a 2-dimensional vector where the two elements correspond to its degree and to the number of triangles in which it participates. Note that the GR kernel cannot handle node labels/attributes, and hence, it is excluded from the evaluation. Furthermore, all the other GKs except Graph-Hopper can only handle discrete node labels, and thus we map each unique pair of features (i.e., degree and triangle participation) to a natural number.

Figure 3 illustrates the obtained results for the case of randomly initialized GNNs and GNNs trained on IMDB-BINARY. We observe that GraphHopper, the only kernel that can naturally handle multi-dimensional continuous node features, takes advantage of the node degree and triangle participation information since it exhibits a very high correlation and a small MSE. On the other hand, the quality of the representations learned by the remaining GKs seems to be lower

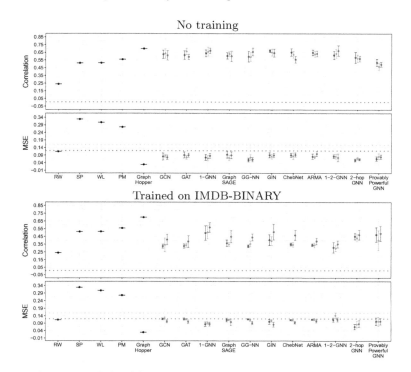

Fig. 3. Performance of the different approaches with node features. The GNNs were either not trained (Top) or trained on the IMDB-BINARY dataset (Bottom). For GNNs, the different colors indicate the three pooling functions: sum (•), mean (○), and max (•). The horizontal lines correspond to the two baselines (random, constant) (Color figure online).

when these features are taken into account. The addition of the features leads to slight decrease in correlation, and also to a large increase in MSE. This suggests that for GKs that are not designed to operate on graphs with continuous node attributes, using these features may result into a decrease in performance. In the case of randomly initialized GNNs, we observe an increase in the correlation between most models and the considered graph similarity function. 1-2-GNN, 1-GNN and GG-NN achieve the highest levels of correlation, while 2-hop GNN, GG-NN and Provably Powerful GNN are the best-performing models in terms of MSE. Again, more complicated models do not necessarily outperform simpler models. When trained on IMDB-BINARY, the correlation between the models and (1) decreases. At the same time, the models yield slightly higher MSEs.

Which Pairs are Hard? We next find for each approach the similarity that deviates most from the one computed using (1). These pairs of graphs can be thought of as the most challenging for a model or kernel. For each approach, we find the pair of graphs which maximizes the absolute difference between the similarity computed using (1) and the one produced by the model/kernel. Note that for GNNs, we focus on the worst-case scenario independent of the pooling

148   G. Nikolentzos et al.

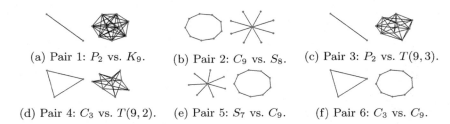

(a) Pair 1: P_2 vs. K_9.   (b) Pair 2: C_9 vs. S_8.   (c) Pair 3: P_2 vs. $T(9,3)$.

(d) Pair 4: C_3 vs. $T(9,2)$.   (e) Pair 5: S_7 vs. C_9.   (f) Pair 6: C_3 vs. C_9.

Fig. 4. Examples of challenging pairs of graphs for certain GNNs/GKs.

function. The different pairs of graphs are illustrated in Fig. 4. Surprisingly, a lot of methods fail to accurately estimate the similarity of structurally very dissimilar graphs. For instance, GCN, GAT, GraphSAGE, ARMA, Chebnet, SP and GraphHopper all found the first two graphs (the path graph P_2 and the complete graph on 9 vertices) to be identical to each other (i.e., similarities equal to 1), while the output of (1) is 0.166. In the case of the two GKs, this is because the implicit vector representation of one graph is a positive scalar multiple of the representation of the other. With regards to the GNNs, note that the above models use the mean function to aggregate the representations of their neighborhoods. When such neighborhood aggregation approaches are followed by mean or max pooling functions, they produce identical representations for the P_2 and K_9 graphs. Another pair of graphs which turns out to be challenging for several approaches is the one consisting of the cycle graph with 9 vertices and the star graph S_8. The output of (1) for this pair is equal to 0.235, while the similarities produced by all the following approaches are greater than 0.900: GIN, 1-GNN, GG-NN, 2-hop GNN and RW. The next four pairs of graphs correspond to the worst-case scenarios for Provably Powerful GNN, 1-2-GNN, PM and WL, respectively. The similarity between the path graph P_2 and the Turán graph $T(9,3)$ (i.e., 3rd pair) is 0.192 according to (1), while the representations generated by Provably Powerful GNN yielded a similarity equal to 0.955. Likewise, the output of (1) is 0.258 for the 4th pair of graphs, while 1-2-GNN produced a value equal to 0.922. The star graph S_7 along with the cycle graph with 9 vertices (i.e., 5th pair) led PM to the worst similarity estimation. While (1) gave a similarity of 0.251, the normalized kernel value was equal to 0.773. The last pair of graphs, the cycle graph with 3 vertices and the cycle graph with 9 vertices, turns out to be the hardest for the WL kernel. While the value of (1) is 0.384, the normalized kernel value is equal to 1. Again, this is due to the fact that the representation of one graph is a positive scalar multiple of the representation of the other.

5   Conclusion

In this paper, we studied the expressive power of GNNs and GKs from an empirical standpoint. The produced representations and similarities were compared against those generated by an intractable graph similarity function. The results showed that theoretically more powerful GNNs do not necessarily yield higher-quality representations, while GKs were found to be competitive with GNNs.

References

1. Barceló, P., Kostylev, E.V., Monet, M., Pérez, J., Reutter, J., Silva, J.P.: The logical expressiveness of graph neural networks. In: International Conference on Learning Representations (2020)
2. Battaglia, P., Pascanu, R., Lai, M., Rezende, D.J., et al.: Interaction networks for learning about objects, relations and physics. In: Advances in Neural Information Processing Systems, pp. 4502–4510 (2016)
3. Bianchi, F.M., Grattarola, D., Alippi, C., Livi, L.: Graph neural networks with convolutional ARMA filters. arXiv preprint arXiv:1901.01343 (2019)
4. Borgwardt, K.M., Kriegel, H.P.: Shortest-path kernels on graphs. In: Proceedings of the 5th IEEE International Conference on Data Mining, pp. 74–81 (2005)
5. Chen, Z., Villar, S., Chen, L., Bruna, J.: On the equivalence between graph isomorphism testing and function approximation with GNNs. In: Advances in Neural Information Processing Systems, pp. 15894–15902 (2019)
6. Dasoulas, G., Santos, L.D., Scaman, K., Virmaux, A.: Coloring graph neural networks for node disambiguation. In: Proceedings of the 29th International Joint Conference on Artificial Intelligence, pp. 2126–2132 (2020)
7. Defferrard, M., Bresson, X., Vandergheynst, P.: Convolutional neural networks on graphs with fast localized spectral filtering. In: Advances in Neural Information Processing Systems, pp. 3844–3852 (2016)
8. Errica, F., Podda, M., Bacciu, D., Micheli, A.: A fair comparison of graph neural networks for graph classification. In: 8th International Conference on Learning Representations (2020)
9. Feragen, A., Kasenburg, N., Petersen, J., de Bruijne, M., Borgwardt, K.: Scalable kernels for graphs with continuous attributes. In: Advances in Neural Information Processing Systems, pp. 216–224 (2013)
10. Fey, M., Lenssen, J.E.: Fast graph representation learning with PyTorch geometric. arXiv preprint arXiv:1903.02428 (2019)
11. Garg, V.K., Jegelka, S., Jaakkola, T.: Generalization and representational limits of graph neural networks. In: Proceedings of the 37th International Conference on Machine Learning (2020)
12. Gärtner, T., Flach, P., Wrobel, S.: On graph kernels: hardness results and efficient alternatives. In: Schölkopf, B., Warmuth, M.K. (eds.) COLT-Kernel 2003. LNCS (LNAI), vol. 2777, pp. 129–143. Springer, Heidelberg (2003). https://doi.org/10.1007/978-3-540-45167-9_11
13. Gilmer, J., Schoenholz, S.S., Riley, P.F., Vinyals, O., Dahl, G.E.: Neural message passing for quantum chemistry. In: Proceedings of the 34th International Conference on Machine Learning, pp. 1263–1272 (2017)
14. Hamilton, W.L., Ying, R., Leskovec, J.: Inductive representation learning on large graphs. arXiv preprint arXiv:1706.02216 (2017)
15. Ivanov, S., Sviridov, S., Burnaev, E.: Understanding isomorphism bias in graph data sets. arXiv preprint arXiv:1910.12091 (2019)
16. Kipf, T.N., Welling, M.: Semi-supervised classification with graph convolutional networks. arXiv preprint arXiv:1609.02907 (2016)
17. Kriege, N.M., Morris, C., Rey, A., Sohler, C.: A property testing framework for the theoretical expressivity of graph kernels. In: In Proceeding of the 27th International Joint Conference on Artificial Intelligence, pp. 2348–2354 (2018)
18. Li, Y., Tarlow, D., Brockschmidt, M., Zemel, R.: Gated graph sequence neural networks. arXiv preprint arXiv:1511.05493 (2015)

19. Maron, H., Ben-Hamu, H., Serviansky, H., Lipman, Y.: Provably powerful graph networks. In: Advances in Neural Information Processing Systems, pp. 2156–2167 (2019)
20. Maron, H., Fetaya, E., Segol, N., Lipman, Y.: On the universality of invariant networks. In: Proceedings of the 36th International Conference on Machine Learning, pp. 4363–4371 (2019)
21. Morris, C., Kriege, N.M., Bause, F., Kersting, K., Mutzel, P., Neumann, M.: TUDataset: a collection of benchmark datasets for learning with graphs. arXiv preprint arXiv:2007.08663 (2020)
22. Morris, C., et al.: Weisfeiler and leman go neural: higher-order graph neural networks. In: Proceedings of the AAAI Conference on Artificial Intelligence, pp. 4602–4609 (2019)
23. Murphy, R., Srinivasan, B., Rao, V., Ribeiro, B.: Relational pooling for graph representations. In: Proceedings of 36th the International Conference on Machine Learning, pp. 4663–4673 (2019)
24. Nikolentzos, G., Dasoulas, G., Vazirgiannis, M.: k-hop graph neural networks. Neural Netw. **130**, 195–205 (2020)
25. Nikolentzos, G., Meladianos, P., Vazirgiannis, M.: Matching node embeddings for graph similarity. In: Proceedings of the 31st AAAI Conference on Artificial Intelligence, pp. 2429–2435 (2017)
26. Nikolentzos, G., Siglidis, G., Vazirgiannis, M.: Graph kernels: a survey. arXiv preprint arXiv:1904.12218 (2019)
27. Sato, R., Yamada, M., Kashima, H.: Random features strengthen graph neural networks. arXiv preprint arXiv:2002.03155 (2020)
28. Scarselli, F., Gori, M., Tsoi, A.C., Hagenbuchner, M., Monfardini, G.: Computational capabilities of graph neural networks. IEEE Trans. Neural Netw. **20**(1), 81–102 (2008)
29. Scarselli, F., Tsoi, A.C., Hagenbuchner, M.: The Vapnik-Chervonenkis dimension of graph and recursive neural networks. Neural Netw. **108**, 248–259 (2018)
30. Shervashidze, N., Schweitzer, P., Van Leeuwen, E.J., Mehlhorn, K., Borgwardt, K.M.: Weisfeiler-Lehman graph kernels. J. Mach. Learn. Res. **12**(9) (2011)
31. Shervashidze, N., Vishwanathan, S., Petri, T., Mehlhorn, K., Borgwardt, K.: Efficient graphlet kernels for large graph comparison. In: Proceedings of the 12th International Conference on Artificial Intelligence and Statistics, pp. 488–495 (2009)
32. Siglidis, G., Nikolentzos, G., Limnios, S., Giatsidis, C., Skianis, K., Vazirgiannis, M.: GraKeL: a graph kernel library in python. J. Mach. Learn. Res. **21**(54), 1–5 (2020)
33. Veličković, P., Cucurull, G., Casanova, A., Romero, A., Lio, P., Bengio, Y.: Graph attention networks. arXiv preprint arXiv:1710.10903 (2017)
34. Verma, S., Zhang, Z.L.: Stability and generalization of graph convolutional neural networks. In: Proceedings of the 25th ACM SIGKDD International Conference on Knowledge Discovery & Data Mining, pp. 1539–1548 (2019)
35. Wu, Z., Pan, S., Chen, F., Long, G., Zhang, C., Philip, S.Y.: A comprehensive survey on graph neural networks. IEEE Trans. Neural Netw. Learn. Syst. **32**(1), 4–24 (2020)
36. Xu, K., Hu, W., Leskovec, J., Jegelka, S.: How powerful are graph neural networks? In: International Conference on Learning Representations (2019)

Multi-resolution Graph Neural Networks for PDE Approximation

Wenzhuo Liu[1,2]([✉]), Mouadh Yagoubi[1], and Marc Schoenauer[2]

[1] IRT SystemX, Orsay, France
{wenzhuo.liu,mouadh.yagoubi}@irt-systemx.fr
[2] INRIA TAU, LISN CNRS and U. Paris-Saclay, ORsay, France

Abstract. Deep Learning algorithms have recently received a growing interest to learn from examples of existing solutions and some accurate approximations of the solution of complex physical problems, in particular relying on Graph Neural Networks applied on a mesh of the domain at hand. On the other hand, state-of-the-art deep approaches of image processing use different resolutions to better handle the different scales of the images, thanks to pooling and up-scaling operations. But no such operators can be easily defined for Graph Convolutional Neural Networks (GCNN). This paper defines such operators based on meshes of different granularities. Multi-resolution GCNNs can then be defined. We propose the MGMI approach, as well as an architecture based on the famed U-Net. These approaches are experimentally validated on a diffusion problem, compared with projected CNN approach and the experiments witness their efficiency, as well as their generalization capabilities.

Keywords: Graph Neural Networks · PDEs · Multi-resolution GNNs

1 Introduction

Numerical simulation techniques are widely used to predict the behavior of complex systems in the real world. Partial differential equations (PDEs) are typically used to model the physical problem, and their solutions are approximated by numerical techniques such as the finite element (FEM) and finite volume (FVM) methods. Such typical approaches discretize the domain into *meshes* and compute the approximated values of the quantities of interest on each node of the mesh. These approaches can predict the physical behavior of the systems accurately, however, at a high computational cost for complex systems.

In recent years, there has been a rapid rise in the use of machine learning algorithms to solve problems from different domains where the conventional mathematical models are hard to build or expensive to compute. Deep neural networks have become the most popular approach due to the ability to solve complex tasks such as computer vision and natural language processing, outperforming existing algorithms when large-scale data are available. The great success of deep learning has naturally encouraged researchers to investigate its

ⓒ Springer Nature Switzerland AG 2021
I. Farkaš et al. (Eds.): ICANN 2021, LNCS 12893, pp. 151–163, 2021.
https://doi.org/10.1007/978-3-030-86365-4_13

use of learning numerical solutions of PDEs for the purpose of reducing simulation time. Indeed, with the wide applications of numerical simulations, a high volume of data has been accumulated. Many scientists have proposed data-driven methods, making full use of such data [3,5,11,19]. The first approaches [5,19] applied convolutional neural networks(CNNs) to construct deep learning models, due to their tremendous successes for image analysis, thanks to their capacity to capture spatial features. However, when it comes to PDEs simulations, complex geometries and the construction of unstructured meshes are inevitable. In such cases, data generated from numerical simulations is not similar to an image with regular pixels. A visible solution is to embed the complex domain into a regular rectangle domain and use interpolation, so that CNNs can be applied directly. However, in the real world, physical problems have complex geometric domains, and such *CNN approach* can lead to a significant interpolation error, in particular on the boundary of an actual domain. Furthermore, such an approach can hardly take into account the necessary mesh refinements that are frequently needed for a good approximation of the solution of the PDE at hand.

Graph Neural Networks (GNNs) are ML methods that handle data that live on graphs. Convolutional GNNs aim at reproducing the locality properties of CNNs, but one drawback is the lack of a recognized approach to down-sampling (aka pooling) and up-sampling that allow GNNs to extract local features.

In such context, the overall goal of the present work is to learn from examples a model for the numerical solution of a PDE using GNNs and to preserve locality, such that solving the same PDE with different source or on different domains can be done at a much lower computational cost than with the classical numerical approaches (e.g., FEM) while giving a good approximation of the solution. To this end, the contributions of this work are twofold. First, we propose generic up- and down-sampling procedures for Convolutional GNNs taking advantage of meshes of different granularities; from thereon, inspired by the multi-grid methods in the numerical field [6], we introduce two such architectures for GNNs in the context of PDE simulations: the Multi-Grid U-Net (MG-UNet), based on the famous U-Net [17] proposed for image segmentation, and the novel Multi-Grid Multi-Input (MGMI). Second, we validate experimentally these multi-grid approaches against the *CNN approaches* (based on projections on a regular grid).

The paper is organized as follows: Sect. 2 briefly surveys the state-of-the-art in terms of Machine Learning approaches to PDE solving, as well as the use of GNNs in such context. Section 3 introduces, based on a hierarchy of meshes on the domain of the PDE, the multi-grid architectures MGMI and MG-UNet. Section 4 describes the experiments (solving a nonlinear diffusion equation on different types of domains), while Sect. 5 discusses the results that validate the proposed approach in the case of irregular domains.

2   Related Works

2.1   Machine Learning for PDEs

Using machine learning algorithms to solve PDEs has received special attention in the last few years. Current numerical solutions on PDEs are inefficient for problems with high dimensions or on complex geometry. A major difficulty for such problems is meshing. On the one hand, forming a mesh is costly for complex geometric problems; on the other hand, it becomes infeasible in high dimensional space. Some scientists proposed mesh-free methods based on unsupervised learning to avoid mesh construction. These algorithms train a deep neural network to approximate PDE solution by satisfying the differential operator, initial conditions and boundary conditions for a specific PDE. By entering a variable x_0, the network will predict the value $u(x_0)$. [4] used fully connected layers to approximate the solution on complex geometry. [16,18] discussed the possibility to solve high dimensional problems by neural networks. The authors of [18] proved that the neural network converges to the PDE as the number of hidden units increases. However, the proposed algorithms has been applied on only one physical problem, and every slightly change on the PDE may require to re-investigate the proposed architecture.

Other approaches are based on data-driven methods. Similar to our work, the model learned from mesh data simulated by numerical solvers (e.g.: FEM, FVM) predicts solutions for unseen inputs. [19] construct a convolutional model to approximate electromagnetic problems by solving Poisson's equation on a squared domain. Training data is generated by finite differential solver, making it in Euclidean space, which ensures the feasibility of applying CNN layers. A U-Net model is proposed by [5] to solve Reynolds Averaged Navier-Stokes (RANS) flow problems on airfoil shapes. The generated data on the unstructured mesh is first projected on structured grids as images before training. Comparing with traditional methods, the CNN models can reduce computational time. Since these models apply CNN layers on structured grids, they are less adaptable for problems with complex domains, which we will discuss in this paper.

In recent years, many attempts have been made to construct a deep learning model that can be applied directly on mesh data instead of projection into structured grids. [11] discussed fluid flow fields problems on different irregular geometries. It considers CFD data as a set of points (called point clouds) and applies the PointNet [14] architecture specially designed for such data type. [3] combines graph neural networks with traditional CFD solver (run on a coarse mesh) to accelerate fluid flow prediction on a much finer mesh. Although this combination allows improving prediction on new situations from the same family with the studied problems (i.e., without any change in the geometry), the generalization to new problems with different geometries/meshes is not confirmed. Unlike these methods, that apply GNNs directly on a fin mesh, we proposed a hierarchical structure aiming at extracting both global and local features from mesh data.

2.2   Graph Neural Networks

An increasing number of studies have focused on data from non-Euclidean space such as graphs, meshes, and manifolds where CNN is no longer suited. The graph neural networks (GNNs) generalize deep learning models on non-Euclidean space. Inspired by the great success of CNN on images, there are plenty of studies searching for a method to define convolutional operators on non-Euclidean data.

The first spectral-based convolution operator is proposed by [7]. It defines the operator on graph Laplacian spectrum space. After graph Fourier transformation, the convolution can be defined as the multiplier on Fourier space which enables the construction of a graphical convolutional layer. Since then, several works [9,12] improved spectral-based graph networks. In the meantime, some scientists attempt to construct the convolution on the spatial space. These approaches, such as [2,20], aggregate the feature information from its neighbors. The MoNet layer [13], used in this paper, is also a spatial based method where edge features are trained to decide aggregation weights.

There are several kinds of research made to solve problems with a set of points(point clouds). The PointNet [14] is the first neural network for point clouds. The basic idea is that each point feature is encoded and then aggregated to a global vector by a symmetric function. PointNet++ [15] improved the PointNet by introducing hierarchical structures to capture local features.

3   Multi-grid Graph Neural Networks

3.1   Graph Convolutional Neural Networks

Rationale. The Finite Element Method (FEM) is based on a variational formulation of the PDE and an approximation space for the solution described by basis vectors attached to the mesh at hand (e.g., a given basis vector is 1 at a given node, and 0 on all other nodes). Applying the variational formulation to each basis vector, in turn, gives a system of equations whose unknowns are the coordinates of the solution $(x_1, \ldots, x_N)$ on the chosen basis, and in which the equation for unknown x_i only involves neighbors x_j of node i in the mesh. If the PDE is linear (e.g., the linear Poisson equation), this system is a linear system that is usually solved numerically using some iterative methods due to its size. For instance, the Jacobi iterative method computes a sequence of vectors that ultimately converges to the solution of the linear system, by

$$x_i^{k+1} = \frac{1}{A_{ii}}(b_i - \sum_j A_{ij}x_j^k)$$

If the PDE is not linear, the system to be solved to compute $(x_1, \ldots, x_N)$ is nonlinear, and it is usually approximated by a sequence of linear systems that are solved sequentially. The whole process can be considered as using Jacobi iterative method multiple times with different A_{ij} and b_i. And this is exactly what Graph Convolutional Neural Networks like MoNet [13] do.

The MoNet Architecture. Consider a weighted graph $G = (N, E, \mathcal{V}, \mathcal{E})$, where N is the number of nodes, E the set of edges, $\mathcal{V} \in \mathbb{R}^{N \times F}$ are the node features (to each of the N nodes, an F-dimensional feature vector is attached), and $\mathcal{E} \in \mathbb{R}^{E \times D}$ the edge features (D-dimensional vectors). Let $x_i \in \mathbb{R}^F$ be the feature vector of node i, and $e_{ij} \in \mathbb{R}^D$ be the feature of the edge $i \to j$ defining the set of neighbours $N(i)$ of node i. The basic idea of MoNet is to define a trainable function w that computes an edge weight w_{ij} from the edge feature e_{ij}. MoNet then defines the convolutional operator on node i as:

$$\mathbf{x}'_i = \frac{1}{|\mathcal{N}(i)|} \sum_{j \in \mathcal{N}(i)} \frac{1}{K} \sum_{k=1}^{K} \mathbf{w}_k(\mathbf{e}_{ij}) \odot \mathbf{\Theta}_k \mathbf{x}_j$$

where $\mathbf{x_j} \in \mathbb{R}^N$ represents the feature on node j, $\mathbf{K}$ is the user-defined kernel size, $\mathbf{\Theta_k} \in \mathbb{R}^{M \times N}$ stands for the trainable matrix applying a linear transformation on the input data, $\odot$ is the element-wise product, and $w_k, k = 1, \ldots, K$ are trainable edge weights. Following [13], we chose Gaussian kernels defined as:

$$w_k(e_{ij}) = exp(-\frac{1}{2}(e_{ij} - \mu_k)^T \Sigma_k^{-1}(e_{ij} - \mu_k))$$

Both μ_k and Σ_k are trainable variables representing the mean vector and covariance matrix of the Gaussian kernel.

MoNets for PDEs: Node and Edge Features. Given a PDE defined on some domain Ω (see Sect. 4) and a mesh of its domain of definition, this work is concerned with training a MoNet-like Neural Network to approximate the numerical solution of the PDE on the mesh.

A first node feature is the right-hand side of the PDE, defined on domain Ω, that will be represented by its values on the nodes. Another node feature g is used to describe whether the node is on the boundary ($g = 1$) or not ($g = 0$).

Finally, the 2-dimensional edge features are defined as $e_{ij} = p_j - p_i$, where p_k is the coordinates of node k. This ensures the translation-invariance of the approach.

3.2 Multi-grid Approaches

Many variants of multi-grid algorithms have been proposed in the context of numerical simulations (see, e.g., Chap. 3 in [6]): the main idea is to compute approximate solutions to the problem at hand on meshes of different resolution. The steps on coarse meshes are fast and help to unveil global features of the solution, while fine meshes refine the solutions, removing unwanted spatial oscillations. In order to extend this notion to the GNN framework, we assume in the following having a hierarchy of meshes $\mathcal{M}_i$ of the same domain, of increasing complexity (# nodes).

As a matter of fact, the idea of multi-grid has already been used in the neural network framework, in the context of image analysis and is based on pooling and upsampling layers that merge or expand rectangle patches of the image. Among well-known examples are the Autoencoders, and the famed U-Net architecture [17] which adds to the reduction/reconstruction structure some "horizontal" connection between downstream and upstream layers of the same dimension.

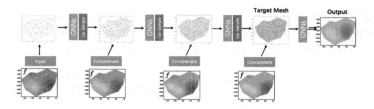

Fig. 1. The MGMI architecture: Coarse-to-fine meshes are linked with up-sampling operators, and the right-hand side is input to the NN at all different resolutions.

However, when it comes to Graph Neural Networks, no obvious down-sampling (pooling) and up-sampling operators exist. Some operators have been proposed in the context of graph or node classification on graphs [10], but they inevitably destroy the graph structure and lose node connections. Moreover, to the best of our knowledge, no explicit pooling operators for graphs with edge features have yet been proposed. The situation here is different, thanks to the hierarchy of meshes of increasing complexity over the same 2D-domain. It easily defines operators that transform the features from one mesh to the next, up- or downward.

Sampling Operators. The sampling operators from mesh $\mathcal{M}_1$ to mesh $\mathcal{M}_2$ use the k-nearest interpolation proposed in PointNet++ [15]. Let y be a node from $\mathcal{M}_1$, and assume its k nearest neighbors on $\mathcal{M}_2$ are $(x_1, \ldots, x_k)$. The interpolated feature for y is defined from those of the x_i's as:

$$\mathbf{f}(\mathbf{y}) = \frac{\sum_{i=1}^{k} w(x_i)\mathbf{f}(x_i)}{\sum_{i=1}^{k} w(x_i)}, \text{ where } w(x_i) = \frac{1}{||y - x_i||_2}$$

Based on these operators, it is straightforward to define multi-grid architectures in the context of PDE simulation.

The Multi-grid U-Net Architecture. First, we propose a simple adaptation of the U-Net architecture proposed in [17], where each block is a MoNet block (Sect. 3.1), followed by one sampling operator as described above. The "horizontal" connections that characterize U-Net are added, the input f is provided to the first layer, and the solution u of the PDE is the output of the last layer (details in Sect. 5).

The Multi-grid Multi-input Architecture. Figure 1 displays the proposed architecture (MGMI). Here, only upsampling operators are used: the model starts from the coarsest mesh, and the input is the projection of f on this mesh. After a GNN block, an upsampling operator adapts the output to the next mesh, and a projection of f on the current mesh concatenated with the previous output is again fed to the next GNN block. The process repeats until reaching the finest mesh (4 different levels will be used throughout this paper). This should allow the features of different granularities to be discovered gradually, from global to local features.

This architecture takes advantage of the hierarchy of meshes from the input perspective, feeding the different dimensions with ad hoc samples of the input f as well. Note that a similar strategy with the U-Net architecture did not make any significant difference.

4   Experimental Conditions

The Partial Differential Equation. The case study in this paper is a numerical simulation of the following nonlinear Poisson equation with constant Dirichlet boundary condition, an elliptic PDE defined on some domain $\Omega \in \mathbb{R}^2$:

$$-\nabla((1 - u(x) + u(x)^2) \cdot \nabla u(x)) = f(x) \ \ in \ \Omega \ with \ u(x)|_{\partial\Omega} = 1$$

The goal is to compute a numerical approximation of $u(x)$, solution of problem (1), for any continuous function $f(x)$ defined Ω. Note that any boundary condition can be handled by the proposed approach (not shown here).

The Finite Element Library. There are numerous FEM packages that can solve problem (4): *FEniCS* [1] was used throughout this work. *FEniCS* includes a mesh generator that generates a mesh from a user-defined criterion and discretization of the boundary of Ω, balancing the mesh so that all triangles are as close as possible from the equilateral (to make a long story short). Hence, the coarseness of the mesh can be roughly controlled by the user, allowing them to reach a target number of nodes approximately.

The Input Functions. The source terms f of Eq. (4) are randomly generated as a linear combination of eight isotropic Gaussian functions sharing the same standard deviation, resulting in 25 control parameters: the coordinates of the means of the Gaussian functions, their weights in the linear combination and the standard deviation. They are chosen uniformly in domain-dependent intervals.

Ground Truth and Loss Function. *FEniCS* also includes a FEM solver that computes an approximated solution of the target PDE based on the decomposition of the solution on a basis defined from a given mesh [8]. In all cases, the solution provided by *FEniCS* on the finest mesh will be considered as the ground truth. The loss function is defined by the **Mean Absolute Error** (MAE) between the network output and this ground truth. Note, however, that we will report the **Relative MAE(%)** in Sect. 5, to allow a meaningful comparison between the different experiments.

Algorithms. Our ultimate goal is to validate the proposed multi-grid approaches that use Graph NNs, MG-UNet and MGMI, i.e., to investigate the accuracy of their results when predicting the solution of some unknown test case w.r.t the ground truth given by *FEniCS*. The baseline algorithm here, called

Direct, is a simple MoNet-like GNN that works only on the finest mesh and directly predicts the solution from the input. But another goal is to compare the mesh-based GNN approach with the straightforward CNN-based more common approach. Hence each of the three algorithms described above will be transposed in the CNN framework, i.e., applied to a structured mesh and using the standard up- and down-sampling operators of deep image processing. In this framework, the Direct algorithm is simply a plain CNN. In case the mesh is not on regular grid, the data from the unstructured mesh is interpolated on the structured mesh where the CNN model is applied, and the data is projected back on the unstructured mesh, giving the approximate solution we are looking for.

Neural Networks Topology. The multi-grid architectures (Fig. 1) alternate Graph Convolutional blocks with up- or down-sampling operators. Each block is defined by 3 hyper-parameters: the number of layers, the kernel size, and the number of channels. The Direct architecture only contains GCNN blocks with the same parameters; the number of blocks is adjusted so that the order of magnitude of the number of weights is similar to the Multi-Grid ones. For the CNN architecture, the number of CNN layers is similarly adjusted.

After some preliminary experiments, the number of nearest neighbors in all sampling operators was set to 6; The kernel size was set to 5 (see 3.1) for Graph-based architectures; And the filter of CNN models is set to 3×3. Other hyper-parameters were adjusted using the validation set[1].

Implementation is done in PyTorch using the PyTorch-Geometric for the MoNet layers and the Adam optimizer, with batch size 100, with an exponentially decaying learning rate and early stopping condition, based on the loss on the validation set.

Domains. Three different types of 2D domains will be considered: First, a simple square domain that should favor the CNN approach; then a 'donut-like' domain to somehow penalize the CNN approach. In both cases, the domain and the meshes will be fixed; only the right-hand side f of the PDE will be subject to learning. Finally, the last experiment will also learn the domain itself: all samples will have different domain shapes and different function f.

Methodology and Result Presentation. For each type of domain, a training set of 42 000 examples is generated. A 12-folds cross-validation is used to assess the robustness of the approach, and we report the averages and standard deviations of the relative MAE errors on the 12 hold-out test sets (labeled "Val"). For CNN algorithms, we also report the relative MAE errors computed on the grid mesh (before projecting back onto the unstructured mesh), labeled "CNN Error". Furthermore, as some of these 40000 samples have been used for hyper-parameter tuning, we also report the errors on test sets that have never

---

[1] Due to space limitation, all details cannot be included here. An INRIA Technical Report will soon be available with details and many more experimental results.

Table 1. Relative MAE (%) results on Squared domain (see text for row details)

Models	Graph			CNN		
	MGMI	MG-UNet	Direct	MGMI	U-Net	Direct
GPU cost(s)	63.98	61.58	138.12	23.58	23.61	44.72
Val	0.61 ± 0.08	**0.40 ± 0.04**	4.00 ± 0.31	0.93 ± 0.01	1.00 ± 0.03	1.07 ± 0.05
CNN error	\	\	\	0.25 ± 0.02	0.40 ± 0.05	0.53 ± 0.04
Test	0.61 ± 0.08	**0.40 ± 0.04**	4.02 ± 0.30	0.93 ± 0.01	1.01 ± 0.03	1.08 ± 0.05
OoD 1	1.46 ± 0.13	**0.71 ± 0.07**	6.76 ± 0.35	1.09 ± 0.01	1.31 ± 0.11	1.76 ± 0.07
OoD 2	1.50 ± 0.31	**1.21 ± 0.31**	4.46 ± 0.44	1.83 ± 0.92	2.73 ± 0.52	1.63 ± 0.19

been used during the tuning phase (row "Test"). Finally, in order to check the generalization capabilities of all models, we compute some out-of-distribution errors (i.e., errors on test cases that do not belong to the same distribution as the training samples), labeled "OoD". All reported error values are expressed in percentage terms. We also report the GPU cost of training one epoch (inference CPU costs are discussed in Sect. 5.3). Another interesting quantity is the average *interpolation error*, that is computed by projecting on the regular grid a solution u defined on the unstructured mesh, and projecting it back onto the unstructured mesh. For each training set, we compute its relative MAE *interpolation error* to better compare graph and CNN models.

Statistical Significance. For all pair-wise comparisons between test errors, we performed a Wilcoxon signed-rank statistical test with 95% confidence on the results of the 12 models obtained through the 12-fold procedure. As most differences are statistically significant, and because of space limitation, we will only signal the non-statistically significant differences.

5 Experimental Results

5.1 Fixed Domains

A first experiment deals with examples in the same **square domain** $\Omega = [0,1] \times [0,1]$, that is meshed in 31×31 squares, or into unstructured meshes with respectively 961, 249, 70, 23 nodes. In this case, the boundary, in particular, is exactly discretized by both the structured (regular grid) and unstructured mesh. The average interpolation error is $0.91\% \pm 0.25$.

Table 1 shows the results of all algorithms. Multi-Grid models outperform Direct models, especially in the context of Graph NNs. Furthermore, in the Graph context, the training time of the Direct model is also larger. Hence we will not consider these Direct models any further in this work.

Graph-based models clearly outperforms CNN-based ones. However, CNN models have an excellent performance on the regular grid, and the discrepancy is only due to the interpolation error. Final remark for the square domain: whereas

MG-UNet slightly outperform MGMI in the graph-based approaches, the reverse is true for the CNN-based approaches.

Another fixed domain was also experimented with, some **donut** shape, for which the boundary is ill-represented on the regular grid. As could be expected, the performances of CNN-based approaches are much worse than on the square domain, while those of the graph-based ones remain very similar.

Out-of-Distribution Generalization. All source terms up to now had been drawn using the same distribution (see Sect. 5). The out-of-distribution generalisation is assessed by two test datasets. "OoD 1" in Table 1 uses a larger standard deviation (in $\mathbb{U}(40, 50)$ instead of $\mathbb{U}(10, 40)$), while "OoD 2" uses larger weights ($\mathbb{U}(20, 35)$ instead of $\mathbb{U}(-20, 20)$). The results are very good compared to the "Test" ones . And MG-UNet slightly, but significantly, outperforms MGMI.

5.2 Variable Domains

This case aims at checking the ability of different models to also generalize w.r.t. the domain itself, as well as the right-hand side f. Each training sample is defined on a different polygonal domain (and hence a different mesh), also involving a different f. Domains are defined by n vertices lying at a normally-distributed distance (with mean 1 and tunable variance) from the origin $(0, 0)$, at

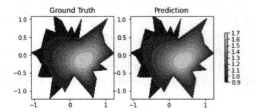

Fig. 2. Comparison between ground truth and prediction from MGMI.

angular $\frac{2\pi}{n} \pm \epsilon$ for some uniformly distributed ϵ ($n = 30$ here). This process ensures that all domains have similar areas – see on Fig. 2 a sample domain, and the solutions of FEM (left) and MGMI (right). As before, 4 different meshes are created for each domain, with the largest mesh size in $[1000, 1200]$ (average in the dataset: 1037). The regular meshes are defined on the $[-2, 2]^2$ square with 73×73 discretization, and the average number of grid points inside the polygon domains is 1023. The average interpolation error is $1.63\% \pm 0.57$.

The top part of Table 3 shows the overall errors are greater than that in the previous test cases – which was to be expected. However, graph models largely outperform CNN models on unfixed meshes. Also, MGMI is slightly but significantly better than MG-UNet on these problems with very different graph structures.

Out-of-Distribution Generalization. Two out-of-distribution experiments are presented here. 5000 examples are generated in each case, with random domains and source terms f.

Mesh Complexity. The first experiment (second set of rows in Table 3) investigates the influence of the number of nodes of the meshes. In the training set, the finest meshes had from 1 000 to 1 200 nodes. Two test sets were generated, with #nodes in [1200, 1600] and [1600, 2000] respectively. All performances nicely degrade when departing from the training distribution. And the graph-based approaches still perform much better than the CNN ones, with a slight but significant advantage to MGMI over MG-UNet.

Domain Shape. Whereas the training set was made of polygons with 30 vertices, this second OoD experiment concerned shapes made respectively with 5, 10, and 20 vertices, keeping the number of mesh nodes approximately the same. The bottom set of rows of Table 3 gives the results. Here again, the graph-based approaches outperform the CNN ones, and MGMI slightly outperforms MG-UNet (though not significantly in the case of 5 and 10 vertices). However, more severely than expected, the performance degrades when going from 30 vertices (Test) down to 5 vertices: the learned models seem more sensitive to the shape of the meshes than to their complexity. Further experiments (not shown for space reasons) used a variable number of vertices during training. The training accuracy remained good with a relative error of 2.37% ± 0.34, while the test on 20, 10 and 5 vertices were greatly improved (to 2.20, 2.44 and 2.94% respectively). But of course, these test sets are not Out-of-Distribution anymore.

5.3   Computational Costs

We use a batch size 100 to solve 5 000 unknown PDEs on the different domain types, and compare the forward computational cost of the graph-based approaches on a single GPU GTX 1080Ti with that of *FEniCS* solver on Intel(R) Xeon(R) Silver 4108 CPU (there is no GPU version of *FEniCS*) (Table 2).

Table 2. Inference CPU cost

Time (s)	Square	Donut	Polyg.
MGMI	0.912	0.643	7.336
MG-UNet	1.075	0.782	11.312
FEM	173.87	164.35	163.72

For problems on fixed mesh, the computation time of neural networks is about 100 times faster than *FEniCS*, which cannot take advantage of the fixed mesh on this nonlinear problem. When considering problems on variable polygon domains, the sampling operators slow down the graph-based approaches, making the computation time only one order of magnitude faster than *FEniCS*. Also, MGMI has fewer down-sampling operators than MG-UNet and hence allows slightly faster prediction. Finally, note that this work studied a simple problem, though nonlinear, for which FEM solvers are relatively fast. The advantage of graph-based inference for complex PDEs (e.g., 3D CFD) would be even more significant.

Table 3. Relative MAE (%) Results on Polygonal Domains (see text for details)

Models	Graph		CNN	
	MGMI	MG-UNet	MGMI	MG-UNet
GPU cost(s)	169.52	170.46	71.54	71.23
Val	2.19 ± 0.15	2.40 ± 0.20	6.09 ± 0.29	5.24 ± 0.19
CNN error	\	\	1.62 ± 0.15	1.38 ± 0.07
Test	**2.20 ± 0.16**	2.41 ± 0.18	6.14 ± 0.26	5.24 ± 0.15
1200–1600	**2.53 ± 0.17**	2.73 ± 0.21	6.55 ± 0.32	5.90 ± 0.20
1600–2000	**3.71 ± 0.25**	4.05 ± 0.27	7.21 ± 0.41	6.52 ± 0.26
Test 5 vertices	**5.29 ± 0.41**	**5.71 ± 0.60**	6.40 ± 0.72	4.73 ± 0.46
Test 10 vertices	**3.56 ± 0.31**	**3.73 ± 0.22**	6.11 ± 0.54	4.13 ± 0.42
Test 20 vertices	**2.39 ± 0.18**	2.61 ± 0.13	5.72 ± 0.39	5.08 ± 1.26

6 Conclusion

This paper introduced multi-resolution graph-based approaches to learn PDE solutions on unstructured meshes, addressing the up- and down-sampling issues of GNNs spatially, based on a hierarchy of meshes of increasing complexity. Bypassing the projection on a regular mesh and the use of standard CNNs, these approaches thus avoid the resulting interpolation errors. Experiments have shown that these hierarchical models can improve the prediction accuracy on test sets of different source terms and domain shapes, as well as the inference time compared to the classical FEM computation. Furthermore, whereas Out-of-Distribution generalization is satisfactory w.r.t. the source characteristics and the mesh complexity, further work is needed to decrease the dependency w.r.t. the domain shape outside the strict bounds of the training distribution. A short-term perspective is to consider transfer learning approaches to deal with meshes of different resolution on different domains. A longer-term perspective is to port the proposed approaches on 3D problems, for which an unstructured mesh is far more expressive than pixel-like grids.

References

1. Alnæs, M.S., Blechta, J., et al.: The FEniCS project version 1.5. Arch. Numer. Softw. **3**(100) (2015)
2. Atwood, J., Towsley, D.: Diffusion-convolutional neural networks (2016)
3. de Avila Belbute-Peres, F., Economon, T.D., Kolter, J.Z.: Combining differentiable PDE solvers and GNNs for fluid flow prediction. In: 37th ICML (2020)
4. Berg, J., Nyström, K.: A unified deep ANN approach to PDEs in complex geometries. Neurocomputing **317**, 28–41 (2018)
5. Bhatnagar, S., Afshar, Y., et al.: Prediction of aerodynamic flow fields using CNNs. Comput. Mech. **64**(2), 525–545 (2019)

6. Briggs, W., Henson, V., et al.: A Multigrid Tutorial, 2nd edn. SIAM, Philadelphia (2000)
7. Bruna, J., Zaremba, W., Szlam, A., LeCun, Y.: Spectral networks and locally connected networks on graphs (2014)
8. Ciarlet, P.G.: Finite Element Method for Elliptic Problems. Society for Industrial and Applied Mathematics, USA (2002)
9. Defferrard, M., Bresson, X., Vandergheynst, P.: CNNs on graphs with fast localized spectral filtering. In: NeurIPS (2017)
10. Gao, H., Ji, S.: Graph U-nets. In: 36th ICML. PMLR (2019)
11. Kashefi, A., Rempe, D., Guibas, L.J.: A point-cloud deep learning framework for prediction of fluid flow fields on irregular geometries. Phys. Fluids 33(2), 027104 (2021)
12. Kipf, T.N., Welling, M.: Semi-supervised classification with graph convolutional networks. In: 5th ICLR (2017)
13. Monti, F., Boscaini, D., et al.: Geometric deep learning on graphs and manifolds using mixture model CNNs. In: CVPR (2016)
14. Qi, C.R., Su, H., Mo, K., Guibas, L.J.: PointNet: deep learning on point sets for 3D classification and segmentation (2017)
15. Qi, C.R., Yi, L., Su, H., Guibas, L.J.: PointNet++: deep hierarchical feature learning on point sets in a metric space (2017)
16. Raissi, M.: Deep hidden physics models: deep learning of nonlinear partial differential equations. JMLR 19(1), 932–955 (2018)
17. Ronneberger, O., Fischer, P., Brox, T.: U-net: convolutional networks for biomedical image segmentation. In: Navab, N., Hornegger, J., Wells, W.M., Frangi, A.F. (eds.) MICCAI 2015. LNCS, vol. 9351, pp. 234–241. Springer, Cham (2015). https://doi.org/10.1007/978-3-319-24574-4_28
18. Sirignano, J., Spiliopoulos, K.: DGM: a deep learning algorithm for solving PDEs. J. Comput. Phys. 375, 1339–1364 (2018)
19. Tang, W., Shan, T., et al.: Study on a Poisson's equation solver based on deep learning technique. In: IEEE EDAPS, pp. 1–3 (2017)
20. Veličković, P., Cucurull, G., Casanova, A., Romero, A., Liò, P., Bengio, Y.: Graph attention networks. In: ICLR (2018)

Link Prediction on Knowledge Graph by Rotation Embedding on the Hyperplane in the Complex Vector Space

Thanh Le[1,2]([✉]), Ngoc Huynh[1,2], and Bac Le[1,2]

[1] Faculty of Information Technology, University of Science,
Ho Chi Minh City, Vietnam
{lnthanh,lhbac}@fit.hcmus.edu.vn
[2] Vietnam National University, Ho Chi Minh City, Vietnam

Abstract. The large-scale exploitation of knowledge graphs has promoted research efforts on graph construction and completion in many organizations such as Google, Apple. The problem of predicting the missing links in the knowledge graph often depends heavily on the method of embedding the vertices into a low-dimensional space, mostly considering the relations as a translation. Recently, there is an approach based on rotation embedding, which can improve efficiency remarkably. Therefore, in this paper, we propose an approach towards rotation embedding entities on a low-dimensional vector. Specifically, we start by projecting the entities onto the relation-specific hyperplanes before rotating them so that the head entities are as close as possible to the tail entities. Based on that, each relation is a rotation from the head entities to the tail entities on the hyperplane in complex vector space. Experiments on well-known datasets show the improvement of the proposed model compared to other models.

Keywords: Link prediction · Graph embedding · Relational rotation · Hyperplane

1 Introduction

Today's knowledge graphs (KGs) often face a lack of links between entities or incomplete due to the rapid growth of data and no tight constraints. Therefore, link prediction (LP) emerges as an inevitable consequence and attracts the research community's interest. Most current studies focus on embedding a given graph in a low-dimensional vector space. A branch concerned with creating rules from graphs deals with long rule extraction and run time, which is not practical in real life. With the graph embedding method, embedded vectors are learned automatically, based on the interactions occurring in the dataset. Embedding vectors represent features of entities and relations in graphs so that they can describe the semantics of the original graph to predict the missing links. Creating embedding instances and mining them has formed some main groups of methods: matrix factorization (MF), geometric and deep learning (DL) [3,13].

© Springer Nature Switzerland AG 2021
I. Farkaš et al. (Eds.): ICANN 2021, LNCS 12893, pp. 164–175, 2021.
https://doi.org/10.1007/978-3-030-86365-4_14

In the MF, the models view the graph as a matrix, which is decomposed from the combination of low dimensional vectors. The learned embedding can generalize the associations with high-valued entities in the adjacency matrix. The advantage of these models is that there are little or no shared parameters, so they are especially light and have short training times. Some models under this category are Distmult [18], ComplEX [16], SimplE [8] and ANALOGY [9].

For the geometric branch, models mainly use relations as transformations in embedding space. Specifically, the scoring function will be the distance between the head entity after transformating and the tail entity. These models' advantage is few parameters shared, so they are light and easy to train. Some prominent models in this branch are TransE [1], RotaE [15], STranE [11], TransH [17].

The current popular approach is DL due to high results in LP. The DL network uses embedded vectors as input values, performs weight vector learning and becomes more flexible because of sharing the same parameters. On the other hand, it is not easy to train and able to overfitting. Some well known models in this branch are ConvKB [12], CapsE [14] and RSN [6]. The common advantages are automatically extracting the features and generalizing the graph's complex structure based on a large amount of training data. Nevertheless, some methods only focus on the grid structure and can not keep the KG's spatial characteristics.

Although the works with high results in LP often focus on the DL model [7], there are some drawbacks that need to be mentioned such as long training time and hard learning process's explanation. The implementation in practice is, therefore, often complex. Meanwhile, the branch based on geometry allows the application of transformations to be intuitive and easily implemented. In this article, we focus on analyzing and proposing some improvements in this branch.

Our paper begins with an introduction to LP on the KG, presents the different approaches in the geometry branch, including analyzing their advantages and disadvantages. From there, we choose the suitable methods as the background model to improve. The model's foundation and adjustments to make a better prediction are presented in the third section before experiments on well-known datasets are conducted to evaluate the performances of the proposed ideas. Finally, we conclude the accomplishment and some next steps in the future.

2   Related Work

Embedding graph based on geometric transformations starts with an encoder function that converts the original graph's vertices and edges to the embedding space. After that, a relation-specific geometrical transformation is applied to the head entities, which expects a new point closing to the tail entitis. The challenge comes from a number of aspects, such as choosing the encoder function, the transformation method and determining the similarity in the original graph and the embedding space. In this paper's scope, we focus on proposing new geometry transformations to increase the efficiency of the prediction model.

Recently, there are numerous proposed ideas for geometric transformations. The first method that can be mentioned is purely translational transformation.

The most obvious demerit of this approach is the high learning cost with a large number of parameters. The popular method in this branch is TransE [1]. Generally, the head or tail entity of a triplet in the graph, called positive triplet, is replaced by randomly entities. The newly created triplets, called negative triplets, must not exist in the graph. If the distance $\|\mathbf{h} + \mathbf{r} - \mathbf{t}\|$ is within a given threshold, the new triplet will be treated as a prediction one. This method has many advantages such as easy to learn, low complexity and high extensibility. However, the disadvantage need to be considered is the inability to handle symmetric, composed, one-to-many and many-to-one relations.

The translation with additional embedding method has been introduced to improve the performance of TransE. Models in this approach use multiple embedding for the entities and relations. Two popular methods in this group are STransE [11] and CrossE [19]. The main idea of the STransE model is to combine two models, Structured Embeddings [2] and TransE [1]. For each relation, two matrices $\mathbf{W}_{r,1}$ and $\mathbf{W}_{r,2}$ ($\mathbf{W}_{r,1}, \mathbf{W}_{r,2} \in \mathbb{R}^{k \times k}$) are created to define the relational aspects of h and t. After that, the translation vector $\vec{r}$ is used to describe the relationship between $\mathbf{h}$ and $\mathbf{t}$ in the subspace. The main merit is reducing problems of categories of relations of TransE. As regards CrossE, the idea is to create additional relation-specific embedding $\mathbf{c}_r$ and combine $\mathbf{h}$ and $\mathbf{r}$ with $\mathbf{c}_r$. From there, it is possible to represent entities and relations from cross interactions, which calls interaction embedding. The score function applied in this method is $f(h, r, t) = \sigma(\tanh(\mathbf{c}_r \circ \mathbf{h} + \mathbf{c}_r \circ \mathbf{h} \circ \mathbf{r} + \mathbf{b}) \times \mathbf{t}^T$. The main advantages of CrossE are low complexity, richer representations and generalization capability.

Another approach recently introduced is the roto-translational method, which uses rotational or combined transformations to replace the translation. Two methods introduced are: TorusE [5] and RotatE [15]. The idea of the TorusE method is embedding entities and relations in torus spaces to avoid normalization problems, each point $\mathbf{x} \in \mathbb{R}^d$ to a point $[\mathbf{x}]$ on the torus T^d. The main purpose is to make the translation less restrictive than the TransE, i.e. the embedding is not unlimitedly divergent and needless to normalization. Some outstanding advantages of TorusE are scalability, the lowest complexity and reducing computation time without regularization. Turning to RotatE model, each relation is modeled as a rotation in embedding space. After passing the rotation vector, the head entity has a close distance to the tail entity according to the $L1$ norm. This method overcomes the drawbacks of TransE with symmetric relations. The distance function used is $d_r(\mathbf{h}, \mathbf{t}) = \|\mathbf{h} \circ \mathbf{r} - \mathbf{t}\|$. Because of linear space and time complexity, it is scalable to large KGs and more representable than TorusE.

In general, the roto-translational methods have low complexity, scalability with massive KGs. They also solve problems of relations of TransE. Nevertheless, this approach is mostly new and there are still many things that we can improve. Furthermore, generating negative samples effectively in embedding space is also the problem that needs to be considered. Therefore, this paper proposes an approach in the roto-translational system that provides the other embedding for entities and relations and applies a self-adversarial sampling scheme based on the selected model.

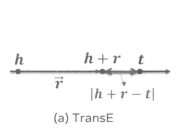

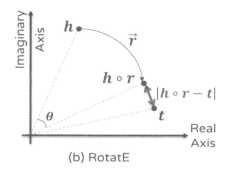

(a) TransE   (b) RotatE

Fig. 1. Translation based embedding on 1 dimension in TransE and RotatE

3   Background

To begin with, we describe some common notations used in the paper. h denotes the head entity, r denotes the relation, and t denotes the tail entity. Bold symbols **h**, **r**, **t** denote the corresponding embedded vector of head entity, relation and tail entity. Δ, Δ' denotes the set of positive and negative triplets.

Introduced in 2013, TransE [1] models each relation r as a translation $\mathbf{r} \in \mathbb{R}^k$ and assumes the distance $\|\mathbf{h} + \mathbf{r} - \mathbf{t}\|$ as low as possible. This embedding method applies well to irreflexive or one-to-one relations, but it does not handle effectively the reflexive or one-to-many, many-to-one and many-to-many relations. Figure 1a illustrates the translation embedding in TransE model.

The basic idea for our proposed method is from two models, RotatE and TransH, because both models have better reflexive relation predictions than TransE and low complexity as well as TransE.

3.1   RotatE

RotatE [15] models each relation r as a rotation vector in embedding space. Figure 1 describes the rotation embedding in RotatE model. The distance function between **h** and **t** is calculated by Fig. 1b.

$$d_r(\mathbf{h}, \mathbf{t}) = \|\mathbf{h} \circ \mathbf{r} - \mathbf{t}\| \tag{1}$$

where $\mathbf{h}, \mathbf{r}, \mathbf{t} \in \mathbb{C}^k$.

To begin with, each head entity in the embedding space is rotated with a relation-specific angle θ, where $\theta \in [0, 2\pi]$, $\mathbf{h}_r$ denoted the coordinate of **h** after rotating. The following step calculates the distance between $\mathbf{h}_r$ and **t** and choosing the negative triplets whose distance lies within the threshold γ. To optimize the model, the loss function is presented in Eq. 2.

$$L = -\log \sigma(\gamma - d_r(\mathbf{h}, \mathbf{t})) - \sum_{i=1}^{n} \frac{1}{k} \log \sigma(d_r(\mathbf{h}_i', \mathbf{t}_i) - \gamma) \tag{2}$$

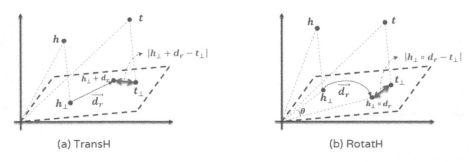

(a) TransH   (b) RotatH

Fig. 2. Embedding by translating on hyperplanes in (a) TransH, (b) RotatH

where γ is fixed margin, σ is sigmoid function and (h'_i, r, t'_i) is i-th negative triplets.

3.2   TransH

TransH [17] models each relation r as a hyperplane with a translation on it (Fig. 2a). The distance function between $\mathbf{h}$ and $\mathbf{t}$ is calculated by Eq. 3.

$$f_r(\mathbf{h}, \mathbf{t}) = \|(\mathbf{h} - \mathbf{w}_r^T \mathbf{h} \mathbf{w}_r) + \mathbf{d}_r - (\mathbf{t} - \mathbf{w}_r^T \mathbf{t} \mathbf{w}_r)\|_2^2 \tag{3}$$

where $\mathbf{w}_r, \mathbf{d}_r \in \mathbb{R}^k$.

The goal of this model is allowing entities to have multiple representations of different relations in embedded space. Specifically, the head and tail entity of each triplet are projected onto the hyperplane $\mathbf{w}_r$ corresponding to each relation ($\mathbf{h}_\perp$ and $\mathbf{t}_\perp$) and the point $\mathbf{h}_\perp$ after the translational vector $\mathbf{d}_r$ is expected to be as close to the point $\mathbf{t}_\perp$ as possible. The distance function can be simply understood as Eq. 4.

$$\|\mathbf{h}_\perp + \mathbf{d}_r - \mathbf{t}_\perp\| \tag{4}$$

This distance is expected to lies within the threshold γ, triplets having a large distance will be considered invalid. To distinguish between positive and negative triplets, the loss function in Eq. 5 is used.

$$L = \sum_{(h,r,t) \in \Delta} \sum_{(h',r',t') \in \Delta'_{(h,r,t)}} [f_r(\mathbf{h}, \mathbf{t}) + \gamma - f_{r'}(\mathbf{h'}, \mathbf{t'})]_+ \tag{5}$$

where $[x]_+$ is RELU function.

The most striking and obvious advantage of these models is well predictions of symmetric, antisymmetric, inverse and composed relations.

The two state-of-the-art models prompt us to combine them into a single model, called the RotatH. In particular, we use the relation-specific hyperplane $\mathbf{w}_r$ generated in the TransH model to identify the relational aspects of h and

t, and use the rotation matrix R in the RotatE model to describe the relationship between $\mathbf{h}$ and $\mathbf{t}$ in the subspace. Specifically, model RotatH will choose $\mathbf{w}_r, \mathbf{h}, \mathbf{d}_r, \mathbf{t}$ to satisfy Eq. 6.

$$(\mathbf{h} - \mathbf{w}_r^T\mathbf{h}\mathbf{w}_r) \circ \mathbf{d}_r \approx (\mathbf{t} - \mathbf{w}_r^T\mathbf{t}\mathbf{w}_r) \tag{6}$$

where $\mathbf{w}_r, \mathbf{h}, \mathbf{d}_r, \mathbf{t} \in \mathbb{C}^k$.

4   Proposed RotatH Model

RotatE and TransH approaches still have some drawbacks that need to be mentioned. While RotatE only represents the head and tail entities in the same way with different relations, the experimental results show that TransH does not work well with 1-to-N and N-to-1 relations.

Our RotatH model is proposed in order to improve the performances of RotatE and TransH and enable entities have a variety of representations depending on their relations and to improve predictive results across relation types. Figure 2b illustrates embedding by rotating on hyperplanes in our model.

For each relation r, we define the relation-specific rotation matrix $\mathbf{d}_r$ on the hyperplane $\mathbf{w}_r$ corresponding to the relation r instead of rotating points in the same space of entity embeddings.

Given a triplet (h, r, t), there are three main steps in RotatH model:

– **Step 1: Projection**
  The embedding $\mathbf{h}$ and $\mathbf{t}$ are first projected to the relation-specific hyperplane $\mathbf{w}_r$, we have:

$$\mathbf{h}_\perp = \mathbf{h} - \mathbf{w}_r^T\mathbf{h}\mathbf{w}_r \qquad\qquad \mathbf{t}_\perp = \mathbf{t} - \mathbf{w}_r^T\mathbf{t}\mathbf{w}_r \tag{7}$$

  where $\mathbf{h}_\perp$ and $\mathbf{t}_\perp$ correspond to points $\mathbf{h}$ and $\mathbf{t}$ projected on the hyperplane, $\mathbf{h}, \mathbf{t}, \mathbf{w}_r \in \mathbb{C}^k$. $\mathbf{w}_r$ is restricted by $\|\mathbf{w}_r\|_2 = 1$
– **Step 2: Rotation**
  After that, $\mathbf{h}_\perp$ is rotated by an angle θ corresponding to each relation:

$$\mathbf{h}_r = \mathbf{h}_\perp \circ \mathbf{d}_\perp \tag{8}$$

  where $\mathbf{h}_r$ is the point $\mathbf{h}_\perp$ after rotated by an angle θ on the hyperplane. By doing these steps, we expect $\mathbf{h}_r$ and $\mathbf{t}$ have a certain similarity.
– **Step 3: Calculating distance**
  In this step, we calculate the distance between $\mathbf{h}_r$ and $\mathbf{t}_\perp$ to consider whether the distance is within a given margin γ:

$$f(h, r, t) = \|\mathbf{h}_r - \mathbf{t}_\perp\|_2^2 \tag{9}$$

  If $f(h, r, t)$ is low, (h, r, t) is a valid triplet.

The overall score function is as Eq. 10.

$$f_r(\mathbf{h}, \mathbf{t}) = \|(\mathbf{h} - \mathbf{w}_r^T \mathbf{h} \mathbf{w}_r) \circ \mathbf{d}_r - (\mathbf{t} - \mathbf{w}_r^T \mathbf{t} \mathbf{w}_r)\|_2^2 \qquad (10)$$

To optimize distance-based model efficiently, we use a loss function (Eq. 11) similar to the negative sampling one [10].

$$L = -\log \sigma(\gamma - f_r(\mathbf{h}, \mathbf{t})) - \sum_{i=1}^{n} \frac{1}{k} \log \sigma(f_r(\mathbf{h}_i', \mathbf{t}_i') - \gamma) \qquad (11)$$

where γ is fixed margin, σ is sigmoid function, (h_i', r, t_i') is i-th negative triplets.

This is a uniform way of sampling negative triplets, which is often ineffective. It is mainly because there are a host of obviously created negative samples, which do not bring meaningful information during the training process. Another approach, therefore, is called self-adversarial negative sampling, which creates negative triplets based on the current embedding model. To be more precise, the negative triplets created are based on the distribution in Eq. 12.

$$p(h_j', r, t_j' | \{(h_i, r_i, t_i)\}) = \frac{\exp \alpha f_r(\mathbf{h}_j', \mathbf{t}_j')}{\sum_i \exp \alpha f_r(\mathbf{h}_i', \mathbf{t}_i')} \qquad (12)$$

where α is the temperature of sampling. The final loss takes the form in Eq. 13.

$$L = -\log \sigma(\gamma - f_r(\mathbf{h}, \mathbf{t})) - \sum_{i=1}^{n} p(h_i', r, t_i') \log \sigma(f_r(\mathbf{h}_i', \mathbf{t}_i') - \gamma) \qquad (13)$$

We choose Adagrad Optimizer [4] to minimize errors. This optimizer adjusts learning rate to the appropriate parameters so Adagrad is suitable for problems with sparse data. To demonstrate the effectiveness of the proposed model, we implement and experiment RotatH on standard datasets used for the LP problem, as well as using common metrics to evaluate the model. Parameters are initially set based on the original models, then altered to find the most suitable parameter. The following section will show the details of this process.

5   Experiments

5.1   Datasets

We experimented our model on four standard datasets: FB15k, FB15k-237, WN18 and WN18RR.

- FB15k, a subset of FreeBase dataset, consists 14,951 entities and 1,345 relations. There are 483,142 triplets in train-set, 50,000 triplets in valid-set and 50,971 triplets in test-set.
- FB15k-237 dataset, introduced by Toutanova and Chen to reduce the effect of test leakage properties, consists of textual descriptions of FreeBase entity pairs and knowledge base relationships. This is a subset of FB15k dataset with 14,541 entities and 237 relations. There are 272,115 triplets in train-set, 17,535 triplets in valid-set and 20,466 triplets in test-set.

- WN18, a subset of WordNet dataset with 40,943 entities and 18 relations, tends to adhere to a strict hierarchy. There are 141,442 triplets in train-set, 5,000 triplets in valid-set and 5,000 triplets in test-set.
- To reduce the influence of test leakage, WN18RR dataset was introduced. 7 relations were removed while the number of entities was unchanged. There are 86,835 triplets in train-set, 3,034 triplets in valid-set and 3,134 triplets in test-set.

5.2 Parameters

Firstly, the parameters of our model are set based on the baseline models. After that, they are adjusted to suit the hardware configuration and the results of the experiment. Table 1 shows details of the parameters we gained for the final result.

Table 1. Parameters in our model with γ is fixed margin, α is learning rate, and adver. is adversarial temperature.

	FB15k	FB15k-237	WN18	WN18RR
Dim	1000	1000	500	500
Norm	1	1	1	1
γ	24.0	9.0	12.0	6.0
α	0.01	0.01	0.01	0.01
#Batch	1,024	1,024	512	512
#Neg.	256	256	1024	1,024
#Test batch	16	16	16	16
Max step	150,000	150,000	100,000	80,000
Valid step	10,000	10,000	10,000	10,000
Adver.	1.0	1.0	0.5	0.5

5.3 Metrics

To evaluate the models, we use standard metrics including MR, MRR, Hits@K. Equation 14, Eq. 15, and Eq. 16 describe these measures.

$$MR = \frac{1}{|Q|} \sum_{q \in Q} rank(q) \tag{14}$$

$$MRR = \frac{1}{|Q|} \sum_{q \in Q} \frac{1}{rank(q)} \tag{15}$$

$$H@K = \frac{|q \in Q : rank(q) \leq K|}{|Q|} \tag{16}$$

5.4   Running Environment

The experiment was conducted on a machine with Ubuntu 18.04 operating system, Intel (X) Xeon (R) CPU E5-2698 v4 @ 2.20 Ghz, 26GB RAM and 32 GB NVIDIA Tesla V100-DGXS GPU. The source code is programmed in Python language with the support of the Pytorch library.

5.5   Results

We inherit and develop the program from the RotatE and TransH code publicly available by author Yanhui Peng. The RotatE and TransH codes we run with are the same parameters as the original models published. Our RotatH model is implemented with the parameters mentioned in the previous section. The remaining models we extracted from the available publications. The results of the detailed comparison between the models are listed in Table 2 and Table 3.

Table 2. Comparing the experimental results of the models on the FB15k and FB15k-237 dataset

	FB15k					FB15k-237				
	MRR	MR	Hits@1	Hits@3	Hits@10	MRR	MR	Hits@1	Hits@3	Hits@10
TransE	0.628	**45**	0.494	–	0.847	0.310	209	0.217	–	0.496
STransE	0.543	69	0.398	–	0.796	0.315	357	0.225	–	0.496
ConvE	0.688	<u>51</u>	0.595	–	<u>0.849</u>	0.305	281	0.219	–	0.476
ConvKB	0.211	324	0.114	–	0.408	0.230	309	0.140	–	0.415
CapsE	0.087	610	0.019	–	0.218	0.160	405	0.073	–	0.356
TransH	0.653	58	0.547	0.729	0.825	0.327	**190**	0.236	0.362	<u>0.510</u>
RotatE	<u>0.698</u>	<u>51</u>	<u>0.609</u>	<u>0.758</u>	<u>0.849</u>	<u>0.330</u>	245	<u>0.240</u>	<u>0.364</u>	0.507
RotatH	**0.707**	**45**	**0.613**	**0.777**	**0.856**	**0.342**	<u>199</u>	**0.250**	**0.378**	**0.526**

Table 3. Comparing the experimental results of the models on the WN18 and WN18RR dataset.

	WN18					WN18RR				
	MRR	MR	Hits@1	Hits@3	Hits@10	MRR	MR	Hits@1	Hits@3	Hits@10
TransE	0.646	279	0.406	–	0.949	0.206	3936	0.028	–	0.495
STransE	0.656	208	0.431	–	0.935	0.226	5172	0.101	–	0.422
ConvE	<u>0.945</u>	413	<u>0.939</u>	–	**0.957**	0.427	4944	0.390	–	0.508
ConvKB	0.709	<u>202</u>	0.529	–	0.949	0.249	<u>3429</u>	0.056	–	0.525
CapsE	0.890	233	0.846	–	0.951	0.415	**720**	0.337	–	<u>0.560</u>
TransH	0.814	**190**	0.701	0.929	**0.957**	0.190	4165	0.031	0.308	0.458
RotatE	0.931	410	0.917	<u>0.945</u>	0.950	**0.476**	3662	<u>0.431</u>	**0.494**	**0.565**
RotatH	**0.947**	316	**0.941**	**0.950**	0.956	<u>0.472</u>	4120	**0.432**	0.484	0.554

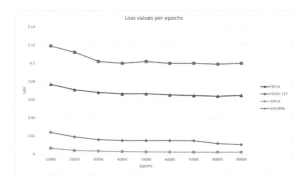

Fig. 3. Loss value per epoch in RotatH training

The results show that our RotatH model outperforms all the state-of-the-art models on the metrics using different datasets compared to other models. Our results on FB15k-237 dataset in Table 2 show the significant improvement.

As can be seen from the results in Table 2 and Table 3, the performances of these models are remarkably different on four common datasets.

- On FB15k dataset, there are mainly symmetry, antisymmetry and inverse relations. It is clearly seen that RotatH well performs at five metrics.
- On FB15k-237 dataset, the main relation instance is composition. We can see that RotatH works well at four out of five used metrics excepts MR.
- On WN18 dataset, there are mainly symmetry, antisymmetry and inverse relations. Results of different models are not much different at Hits@3 and Hits@10. RotatH well performs at MRR, Hits@1, Hits@3 and Hits@10.
- On WN18RR dataset, one of the main relation instances is symmetry. So that the TransE, STransE and TransH models do not well on this dataset since it is not able to model the symmetric relations. RotatH works well at Hits@1, while RotatE has the best results at three out of five metrics.

We also perform experiments to examine the convergence of the loss function (Fig. 3). For the FB15k and FB15k-237 dataset, we found that the loss function tends to converge at epoch 70,000. Meanwhile, the loss function on the WN18 and WN18RR dataset converged earlier at epoch 40,000. The loss function value on the FB15k* was in the range 0.06 to 0.12 while that in the WN18* set was lower about 0.04 and in the range 0.002 to 0.025. The preprocessed dataset has a higher loss value than the original one.

Moreover, we run RotatH on many different relation types, including 1-to-1, 1-to-n, n-to-1, n-to-n through prediction head and prediction tail. The prediction head is processed by taking each of the positive triplets, removing the head entity, and keeping the relation and tail. Then choose some entities randomly to replace and predict if the newly created triplets is valid or not. In short, we need to predict $(?, r, t)$. Prediction tail is made in the same way, but the replaced entity is the tail entity $(h, r, ?)$. The results are summarized in Table 4 and Table 5.

Table 4. Prediction head results of RotatH on datasets by relation category

RotatH	FB15k				FB15k-237				WN18				WN18RR			
	1-to-1	1-to-n	n-to-1	n-to-n	1-to-1	1-to-n	n-to-1	n-to-n	1-to-1	1-to-n	n-to-1	n-to-n	1-to-1	1-to-n	n-to-1	n-to-n
MRR	0.675	0.895	0.371	0.718	0.481	0.464	0.077	0.268	0.940	0.958	0.945	0.935	0.940	0.313	0.084	0.939
MR	127	14	196	26	409	165	702	147	736	121	419	430	306	1651	11849	255
Hits@1	0.538	0.851	0.286	0.615	0.432	0.362	0.039	0.168	0.905	0.953	0.939	0.927	0.904	0.219	0.044	0.928
Hits@3	0.796	0.931	0.408	0.797	0.510	0.514	0.079	0.301	0.976	0.959	0.949	0.941	0.976	0.339	0.091	0.946
Hits@10	0.855	0.959	0.533	0.877	0.542	0.656	0.148	0.476	0.976	0.966	0.951	0.946	0.976	0.522	0.167	0.958

Table 5. Prediction tail results of RotatH on datasets by relation category

RotatH	FB15k				FB15k-237				WN18				WN18RR			
	1-to-1	1-to-n	n-to-1	n-to-n	1-to-1	1-to-n	n-to-1	n-to-n	1-to-1	1-to-n	n-to-1	n-to-n	1-to-1	1-to-n	n-to-1	n-to-n
MRR	0.676	0.467	0.865	0.742	0.484	0.071	0.744	0.381	0.948	0.942	0.960	0.931	0.941	0.111	0.293	0.935
MR	131	179	25	18	418	605	50	103	19	453	119	452	2	3914	3304	309
Hits@1	0.541	0.386	0.814	0.639	0.443	0.036	0.670	0.270	0.929	0.938	0.955	0.922	0.905	0.059	0.225	0.927
Hits@3	0.795	0.510	0.907	0.822	0.505	0.064	0.796	0.431	0.976	0.943	0.962	0.936	0.976	0.120	0.315	0.942
Hits@10	0.857	0.616	0.842	0.904	0.568	0.128	0.874	0.607	0.976	0.947	0.972	0.946	0.976	0.215	0.428	0.950

6   Conclusion

This paper has proposed an improved link prediction approach based on the embedded vector rotation method in RotatE. Our rotation method gives entities a variety of representations depending on their relations. From there, it helps to represent the embedding of samples from the graph more accurately. The implementation process consists of projecting the head and tail entity onto the relation-specific plane. Next, we rotate the prohected head entity by an angle corresponding to that relation so that after rotation, the point will be at a close distance to the projected vector of the tail entity. Experiments show that the proposed method has better results than other models in the data sets FB15k, FB15k-237, and WN18. Except, the WN18RR is only better at Hits@1 compared to the original model. Our model still has some shortcomings in terms of limitations, such as slow training time, projection space not fully showing all the relations. In the future, we will seek some ideas to improve these points.

Acknowledgements. This research is funded by the Faculty of Information Technology, University of Science, VNU-HCM, Vietnam, Grant number CNTT 2021-03 and Advanced Program in Computer Science.

References

1. Bordes, A., Usunier, N., Garcia-Duran, A., Weston, J., Yakhnenko, O.: Translating embeddings for modeling multi-relational data. In: Neural Information Processing Systems (NIPS), pp. 1–9 (2013)
2. Bordes, A., Weston, J., Collobert, R., Bengio, Y.: Learning structured embeddings of knowledge bases. In: Proceedings of the AAAI Conference on Artificial Intelligence, vol. 25, no. 1 (2011)

3. Cai, H., Zheng, V.W., Chang, K.C.C.: A comprehensive survey of graph embedding: problems, techniques, and applications. IEEE Trans. Knowl. Data Eng. **30**(9), 1616–1637 (2018)
4. Duchi, J., Hazan, E., Singer, Y.: Adaptive subgradient methods for online learning and stochastic optimization. J. Mach. Learn. Res. **12**(7) (2011)
5. Ebisu, T., Ichise, R.: Toruse: knowledge graph embedding on a lie group. In: Proceedings of the AAAI Conference on Artificial Intelligence, vol. 32, no. 1 (2018)
6. Hopfield, J.J.: Hopfield network. Scholarpedia **2**(5), 1977 (2007)
7. Ji, S., Pan, S., Cambria, E., Marttinen, P., Yu, P.S.: A survey on knowledge graphs: representation, acquisition and applications. arXiv preprint arXiv:2002.00388 (2020)
8. Kazemi, S.M., Poole, D.: Simple embedding for link prediction in knowledge graphs. In: NeurIPS (2018)
9. Liu, H., Wu, Y., Yang, Y.: Analogical inference for multi-relational embeddings. In: International Conference on Machine Learning, pp. 2168–2178. PMLR (2017)
10. Mikolov, T., Sutskever, I., Chen, K., Corrado, G., Dean, J.: Distributed representations of words and phrases and their compositionality. In: Proceedings of the 26th International Conference on Neural Information Processing Systems, NIPS 2013, vol. 2 (2013)
11. Nguyen, D.Q., Sirts, K., Qu, L., Johnson, M.: Stranse: a novel embedding model of entities and relationships in knowledge bases. In: Proceedings of the 2016 Conference of the North American Chapter of the Association for Computational Linguistics: Human Language Technologies, pp. 460–466 (2016)
12. Nguyen, D.Q., Nguyen, T.D., Nguyen, D.Q., Phung, D.: A novel embedding model for knowledge base completion based on convolutional neural network. In: Proceedings of the 2018 Conference of the North American Chapter of the Association for Computational Linguistics: Human Language Technologies, (Short Papers), vol. 2 pp. 327–333 (2018)
13. Rossi, A., Barbosa, D., Firmani, D., Matinata, A., Merialdo, P.: Knowledge graph embedding for link prediction: a comparative analysis. ACM Trans. Knowl. Discov. Data (TKDD) **15**(2), 1–49 (2021)
14. Sabour, S., Frosst, N., Hinton, G.E.: Dynamic routing between capsules. In: 31st Conference on Neural Information Processing Systems (NIPS 2017) (2017)
15. Sun, Z., Deng, Z.H., Nie, J.Y., Tang, J.: Rotate: knowledge graph embedding by relational rotation in complex space. In: Seventh International Conference on Learning Representations (2019)
16. Trouillon, T., Welbl, J., Riedel, S., Gaussier, É., Bouchard, G.: Complex embeddings for simple link prediction. In: International Conference on Machine Learning, pp. 2071–2080. PMLR (2016)
17. Wang, Z., Zhang, J., Feng, J., Chen, Z.: Knowledge graph embedding by translating on hyperplanes. In: Proceedings of the AAAI Conference on Artificial Intelligence, vol. 28, no. 1 (2014)
18. Yang, B., Yih, W.T., He, X., Gao, J., Deng, L.: Embedding entities and relations for learning and inference in knowledge bases. In: Proceedings of the International Conference on Learning Representations (ICLR) (2015)
19. Zhang, W., Paudel, B., Zhang, W., Bernstein, A., Chen, H.: Interaction embeddings for prediction and explanation in knowledge graphs. In: Proceedings of the Twelfth ACM International Conference on Web Search and Data Mining, pp. 96–104 (2019)

Graph Neural Networks II

Contextualise Entities and Relations: An Interaction Method for Knowledge Graph Completion

Kai Chen[1], Ye Wang[1,2(✉)], Yitong Li[3], Aiping Li[1], and Xiaojuan Zhao[1]

[1] National University of Defense Technology, Changsha 410000, China
{chenkai_,ye.wang,liaiping}@nudt.edu.cn
[2] School of Computer Science and Technology, Harbin Institute of Technology, Shenzhen 518000, China
[3] Huawei Device Co., Ltd., Shenzhen 518000, China
liyitong3@huawei.com

Abstract. The incompleteness of Knowledge Graph (KG) stimulates substantial research on knowledge graph completion, however, current state-of-the-art embedding based methods represent entities and relations in a semantic-separated manner, overlooking the interacted semantics between them. In this paper, we introduce a novel entity-relation interaction mechanism, which learns contextualised entity and relation representations with each other. We feature entity interaction embeddings by adopting a translation distance based method which projects entities into a relation-interacted semantic space, and we augment relation embeddings using a bi-linear projection. Built upon our interaction mechanism, we experiment our idea using two decoders, namely a simple Feed-forward based Interaction Model (FIM) and a Convolutional network based Interaction Model (CIM). Through extensive experiments conducted on three benchmark datasets, we demonstrate the advantages of our interaction mechanism, both of them achieving state-of-the-art performance consistently.

Keywords: Knowledge graph completion · Link prediction · Knowledge inference

1 Introduction

Extensive applications [14,25] of real-world employ knowledge graphs, consisting of abundant facts [1,2,9]. Specifically, each fact is denoted by a triple, (h, r, t), representing a head entity h has relation r with a tail entity t. In real KG applications, annotated facts are sparse and many facts remain unrevealed, thus requiring to be completed or inferred using the existing facts, i.e., Knowledge Graph Completion (KGC) [8,17,23]. One of the most common KGC tasks is link

This work is supported by the National Natural Science Foundation of China (No. 61732004, 61732022).

© Springer Nature Switzerland AG 2021
I. Farkaš et al. (Eds.): ICANN 2021, LNCS 12893, pp. 179–191, 2021.
https://doi.org/10.1007/978-3-030-86365-4_15

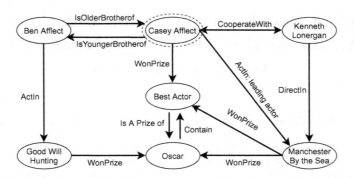

Fig. 1. An example of a knowledge graph. The nodes represent entities while the edges represent relations. The dashed red circle represents the entity to be predicted in a given incomplete triple. (Color figure online)

prediction that infers a missing entity in an incomplete triple, e.g. $(h, r, ?)$, or vise versa $(?, r, t)$.

Generally, tackling link prediction requires KGC model understanding the semantics of entities and relations, as well as the structure information of existing graph. For example, in Fig. 1, when inferring the tail entity in the incomplete fact (*Ben Affleck, IsOlderBrotherof, ?*), one can imply that the tail entity should be a person rather than other type of entity given the semantic information of relation *IsYoungerBrotherof*, i.e. either *Casey Afflect* or *Kenneth Lon* in the current KG. Such semantics can usually be discovered by existing SOTA KGC methods [8,16], however, this is not enough to distinguish these two candidates. In fact, *Casey Afflect* is "younger than" a person, given the semantics of the relation *IsYoungerBrotherof*, which makes *Casey Afflect* more likely to be the candidate. That is the semantics of the relation, as the contextual information of the entity, can provide sufficient information for learning the entity representations, while it is often omitted by the existing embedding methods, e.g. translation-based methods. On the other hand, when learning relation representations, the semantic of context entity can also be helpful. Furthermore, semantics of the mutual learning procedure will be aggregated. The idea of contextualised representations have been successfully applied to NLP applications [5,15], however not well-studied for KGC. Therefore, in this paper, we test the hypothesis that learning contextualised representations of entity and relation can help KGC models better utilise and understand the semantics of surrounding entities and relations.

Recently, [13] considers a intuitive tensor factorization model that describes the semantic relevance of entities via a bi-linear transformation based on the entity relationship. And [22] relaxes the bi-linear transformation with a diagonal matrix. Inspired by their approaches of bi-linear inter-relation, to capture a contextual representation, we extend the idea of bi-linear interaction to entities and relations, where entity and relation are not only represented by their original embeddings but also contextualised with each other within the fact triple. And finally, the model is capable of learning contextualised representations for entity and relation.

Following the above inspirations, in this paper, we propose a novel interaction mechanism to better learn the contextualised entity and relation representations. Our interaction mechanism (1) adopts the idea of translational models [3,8], i.e., we project the relation embedding into the entity space and integrate it with the entity embedding to form an interacted entity embedding, (2) takes advantages of bi-linear models for their semantic interaction [13,20,22], i.e., we take an element-wise *Hadamard product* over entity embedding, relation embedding and entity interactive embedding to form an interacted relation embedding. Based on these two interaction mechanisms, we explore two decoders: a state-of-the-art Convolutional Neural Net (CNN) and a feed-forward neural network, and we experiment with link prediction tasks across different benchmarks.

We summarize our main contributions as follows:

1. We propose a novel entity-relation interaction mechanism and experiment with a CNN and a feed-forward Interaction Models (CIM and FIM) based on the proposed interaction mechanism.
2. Our CIM achieves the SOTA performance on all of FB15k-237, WN18RR and YAGO3-10 datasets for link prediction task. Even without CNN, the simple FIM can achieve comparable performance with previous SOTA methods consistently, demonstrating the advantages of the proposed interaction mechanism.

2 Related Works

Translational Methods. Translational model is an important founder in KGC. Its main idea is based on translation distance, projecting both entities and relations into the same embedding space and utilizing a distance based reductive equation to reflect the translation constraint. Among them, TransE is the origin, which holds a translation distance for the relation between the corresponding head and tail entities for the triple (h, r, t), that is, $\mathbf{h} + \mathbf{r} \approx \mathbf{t}$ [3]. Similarly, TransR also applies the translation distance but by projecting the embeddings of head and tail entities from entity space into relational space, and then uses translation distances for relations $\mathbf{h}_r + \mathbf{r} \approx \mathbf{t}_r$ [8].

Bi-linear Methods. Bi-linear models describe the semantic relevance of entities by a bi-linear transformation based on the relationship between entities, and it can effectively describe the coordination between entities. RESCAL expresses the relation by full rank matrix and defines the scoring function as $f_{\mathbf{r}}(\mathbf{h}, \mathbf{t}) = \mathbf{h}^\top \mathbf{M_r} \mathbf{t}$ [13]. To avoid overfitting, Distmult relaxes the constraint on the relation matrix and replaces it with a diagonal matrix of relation by $f_{\mathbf{r}}(\mathbf{h}, \mathbf{t}) = \mathbf{h}^\top \mathrm{Diag}(\mathbf{M_r}) \mathbf{t}$ [22], however, only symmetric relations can be well studied.

Convolutional Network Methods. Beneficial from the powerful ability of feature extraction, many recent methods are developed upon CNN. ConvE introduces an CNN based model to KGC, which applies a 2D convolution network to extract

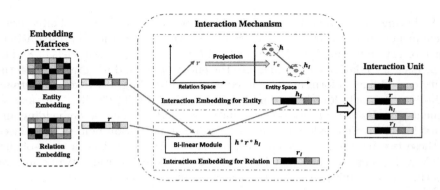

Fig. 2. An illustration of the proposed interaction mechanism. We take two different methods to get the interaction embedding for entity and the interaction embedding for relation, then we construct the interaction unit.

features [4]. Differently, ConvKB deploys 1D convolution filters rather than 2D filters and has been declared to be superior to ConvE [12]. However, the performance of ConvKB has been revealed inconsistent across different datasets and the evaluation protocol of ConKB is concerned [18]. To take advantages of the translation property, Shang et al. proposes ConvTransE [16]. CrossE makes attempts to simulate the crossover interactions between entities and relations [24] by considering the interaction as two parts: the interaction from relations to entities and vice versa. InteractE captures heterogeneous feature interactions through permutations over the embedding structure [21]. It realigns components from both entities and relations to form a so-called feature permutation followed by decoding procedure with ConvE which is quite different from our method that explores extra latent features from real interactions between entities and relations.

Graph Network Methods. Recently, more works [11, 16] aggregate inherent local graph neighbourhood to encode embeddings of entities. SACN [16] builds entity embedding matrix by a weighted GCN encoder but pays little attention on encoding relation embeddings before feeding them into the ConvTransE decoder. KBGAT [11] utilizes a simple transformation to the initial relation embedding for calculating the relative attention value for single triple to compute new embeddings of entities so that contextual semantics can hardly make contribution to relation embeddings beyond 2-hop neighbors. Moreover, the attention mechanism is questioned because of a data leakage problem [18].

3 Methodology

We apply an interaction method to learn contextualised entity and relation representations. Firstly, we define the interaction embeddings for both entity and relation, which constitute an interaction unit as feature of the triple. The interaction unit integrates the superiorities of both translational models and bi-linear models by combining the representations of general embeddings and interaction embeddings. We then feed the interaction unit into the decoder to make a prediction. In this paper, we utilise two types of decoders, a feed-forward based model and a convolutional network based model to test our hypothesis.

3.1 Interaction Mechanism

The interaction mechanism is illustrated in Fig. 2. In this paper, we focus on the link prediction task, that is, given only one entity and the relation of a triple, we need to predict the other entity. We build interaction embeddings for both the given entity and the relation accordingly. For the convenience, we take the head entity h as the known entity and the tail entity t as the predicting entity in the following of this section.

Entity Interaction Embedding. Inspired by translation based models, we notice the strong interrelations among the basic elements of a triple: head entity, relation, and tail entity. For example, aiming at the task of predicting tail entity for a masked triple $(h, r, ?)$, we project the relation embedding $\mathbf{r}$ into the entity space, and use a translation transformation over the embedding of head entity $\mathbf{h}$. The interaction embedding for entity is formulated as:

$$\mathbf{h}_I = \mathbf{h} + \mathbf{W}_e \mathbf{r}, \tag{1}$$

where $\mathbf{W}_e$ denotes a trainable transferring matrix used to project the embedding of relation into the entity space. Intuitively, it also delivers information hidden in $\mathbf{r}$ to $\mathbf{h}$.

We can describe Eq. 1 in terms of semantic spatial features. We divide the whole semantic space into entity space and relation space. When the head entity $\mathbf{h}$ is taken as a central node and the edge corresponding to relation $\mathbf{r}$ is considered, all neighbor nodes connected to the central via the edge should have features similar to $\mathbf{h}_I$ in the entity space, as is illustrated in Fig. 2.

Relation Interaction Embedding. Different from entity interaction embedding, we take inspirations from bi-linear models to construct relation interaction embedding. Here, we utilize *Hadamard product*, an element-wise multiplication operator, to formulate the interaction embedding for relation:

$$\mathbf{r}_I = \mathbf{h} \circ \mathbf{r} \circ \mathbf{h}_I, \tag{2}$$

where $\circ$ denotes *Hadamard product*.

One advantage of applying bi-linear function is that the interacted embedding is capable of representing the potential semantic information of entities and relations, which tends to obtain deep level interactions and inter-relationships between entities and relations. Note that all the embeddings above are vectorised in the same dimension $\mathbf{h}, \mathbf{h}_I, \mathbf{r}, \mathbf{r}_I \in \mathbb{R}^E$, where E is dimension of the embedding.

Interaction Unit. To enhance the features of latent interactions between entities and relations, we concatenate the two general embeddings $\mathbf{h}$ and $\mathbf{r}$ and the two interaction embeddings $\mathbf{h}_I$ and $\mathbf{r}_I$ to preserve more information. Finally, the interaction unit is formulated as:

$$\mathbf{U} = \text{concat}([\mathbf{h}, \mathbf{r}, \mathbf{h}_I, \mathbf{r}_I]) \in \mathbb{R}^{4 \times E}. \tag{3}$$

The interaction unit is further served as an input of the decoder models. By utilizing the interaction mechanism, we aim to make more information interaction of entity and relation directly from the embedding level, so that our models are expected to be more robust than having them separated in their own semantic spaces.

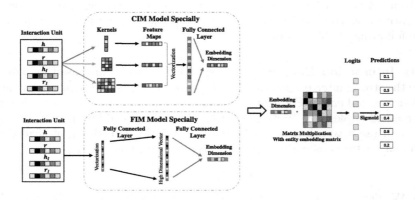

Fig. 3. An illustration of the two proposed methods, CIM and FIM. Both CIM and FIM take the proposed interaction unit as the input and utilize a convolutional neural network and a feed-forward neural network, respectively.

3.2 Interaction Embedding Decoders

Based on our interaction mechanism, we propose two methods to decode the tail entity.

Feed-Forward Neural Network Based Interacted Model (FIM). The first one is a simple feed-forward neural network based interacted model. The overall architecture of FIM is depicted in Fig. 3.

Taking the interaction unit $\mathbf{U}$ as the input, the model firstly reshapes it into an 1d vector, and then puts it into a fully-connected (FC) layer to produce a hidden representation $\mathbf{V}_H$.

$$\hat{\mathbf{U}} = \text{vec}(\mathbf{U}) \tag{4}$$

$$\mathbf{V}_H = \text{FC}(\hat{\mathbf{U}}) = \text{relu}(\mathbf{W}_{fc}\hat{\mathbf{U}} + \mathbf{b}_{fc}), \tag{5}$$

where vec denotes the vectorization operator, FC denotes the fully-connected layer with the activation function relu, producing $\mathbf{V}_H \in \mathbb{R}^D$, where D is the dimension of the hidden layer.

Then we transform $\mathbf{V}_H$ into a predicted embedding $\mathbf{V} \in \mathbb{R}^E$ parameterised by a transformation matrix $\mathbf{W_F} \in \mathbb{R}^{D \times E}$ and a *non-linear* function f:

$$\mathbf{V} = f(\mathbf{V}_H \mathbf{W_F}). \tag{6}$$

And $\mathbf{V}$ is the acquired prediction vector for the target entity of the task.

Finally, we measure the similarity between the prediction embedding and the candidate tail entity embedding using *dot product*, formulated as $\mathbf{V} \cdot \mathbf{t}$, where $\mathbf{t}$ denotes the embedding of a tail entity. And the overall scoring function of a triple is summarised as following:

$$f\left(\mathrm{FC}(\mathrm{vec}([\mathbf{h}, \mathbf{r}, \mathbf{h}_I, \mathbf{r}_I]))\right) \cdot \mathbf{t}. \tag{7}$$

For training, we calculate the scoring function for all entities and minimise the cross-entropy loss between the score logits (with a softmax) and the true label. For inference, we choose the entity with high score as the predicted entity.

CNN Based Interacted Model (CIM). We also propose a novel CNN based interacted model CIM. We take advantages of previous ConvTransE [16], and the main idea of our CIM is also illustrated in Fig. 3.

Based on the interaction unit $\mathbf{U}$, we take advantages of the convolutional neural network for its computation efficiency and powerful ability to learn features. We first apply the convolutional filters on $\mathbf{U}$ and generate the output $\mathbf{C}$ as follow:

$$\mathbf{C} = \mathrm{conv}(\mathbf{U}), \tag{8}$$

where conv denotes a convolution operator. The convolution operator uses N_C channels, each applying a 1D convolutional filter with size $4 \times k$, where k is kernel width. Specifically, the c-th kernel is parameterised by ω_c (ω_c is trainable), and the convolution utilized here is as follows:

$$m_c(n) = \sum_{\tau=0}^{k-1} \sum_{j=0}^{3} \omega_c(\tau, j) \hat{\mathbf{U}}_j(n + \tau), \tag{9}$$

where the $\hat{\mathbf{U}}$ over a vector denotes a padding version of the corresponding vector, and n indexes the entries in the output vector. And the output vector corresponding to the c-th kernel is formulated as $\mathbf{M}_c = [m_c(0), \cdots, m_c(E-1)]$. Considering the channel size N_C, our output of the convolution $\mathbf{C}$ is actually a combination of different $\mathbf{M}_c$, and $\mathbf{C} \in \mathbb{R}^{E \times N_C}$.

To predict the tail entity from a masked triple $(h, r, ?)$, we resize $\mathbf{C}$ to a vector:

$$\mathbf{V} = f(\mathrm{vec}(\mathbf{C}) \mathbf{W_C}), \tag{10}$$

where vec again denotes reshaping operator to reshape a matrix shaped as $\mathbb{R}^{E \times N_C}$ into a vector $\mathbf{V} \in \mathbb{R}^{E N_C}$, $\mathbf{W_C}$ denotes the parameter for the linear transformation ($\mathbf{W_C} \in \mathbb{R}^{E N_C \times E}$), and f denotes a non-linear function.

Similar to FIM, we present the overall scoring function for CIM, formulated as follows:

$$f\left(\text{vec}(\text{conv}([\mathbf{h}, \mathbf{r}, \mathbf{h}_I, \mathbf{r}_I]))\right) \mathbf{t}. \tag{11}$$

Overall, the model aims to minimise the same cross-entropy loss for training.

Note that we only take the head entity h as the known entity as an example, and we can also apply our method to a tail entity t when predicting h.

4 Experiments

4.1 Benchmark Dataset

We experiment link prediction task on three commonly accepted benchmarks: FB15k-237, WN18RR and YAGO3-10.

Table 1. Results on link prediction over FB15k-237, WN18RR and YAGO3-10. The best score is in **bold** and second best score is underlined. Since both CIM and FIM generalize CrossE while CIM generalizes ConvTransE alone, we highlight performance comparison among the four methods specially in the table above. Note that Hits@3 is missing for YAGO3-10, as it is not reported by other methods.

Model	FB15k-237					WN18RR					YAGO3-10			
	Hits			MR	MRR	Hits			MR	MRR	Hits		MR	MRR
	@10	@3	@1			@10	@3	@1			@10	@1		
DistMult	0.419	0.263	0.155	254	0.241	0.491	0.439	0.389	5,110	0.425	0.540	0.240	5,926	0.340
ComplEx	0.419	0.263	0.152	248	0.240	0.507	0.458	0.411	5,261	0.444	0.550	0.260	6,351	0.360
R-GCN	0.417	0.258	0.153	–	0.248	–	–	–	–	–	–	–	–	–
ConvE	0.491	0.350	0.239	246	0.316	0.480	0.430	0.390	5,277	0.460	0.660	0.450	2,792	0.520
RotatE	0.533	0.375	0.241	177	0.338	**0.571**	<u>0.492</u>	0.428	**3,340**	<u>0.476</u>	–	–	–	–
SACN	<u>0.536</u>	<u>0.385</u>	0.261	–	0.352	0.540	0.480	0.430	–	0.470	–	–	–	–
InteractE	0.535	–	<u>0.264</u>	**172**	<u>0.354</u>	0.528	–	0.430	5,202	0.463	0.687	0.462	<u>2,375</u>	0.541
CrossE	0.474	0.331	0.221	–	0.299	–	–	–	–	–	–	–	–	–
ConvTransE	0.513	0.365	0.240	–	0.331	0.520	0.470	0.430	–	0.460	–	–	–	–
FIM (our)	0.534	0.383	0.256	201	0.348	0.530	0.484	<u>0.442</u>	4,332	0.472	<u>0.688</u>	<u>0.473</u>	3,017	<u>0.550</u>
CIM (our)	**0.538**	**0.390**	**0.265**	<u>176</u>	**0.355**	<u>0.543</u>	**0.494**	**0.446**	4,531	**0.478**	**0.693**	**0.485**	**1,969**	**0.559**

The FB15k-237 [19] dataset contains extensive knowledge base triples and has been commonly used in link prediction task. Consisting of $14,541$ entities and 237 relations, the dataset is a subset of FB15k [3] and all inverse relations are removed.

The WN18RR [4] dataset contains $40,943$ entities and 11 relations, derived from WordNet [10] and WN18 [3]. And all inverse relations are removed.

It has been revealed [19] that FB15k and WN18 suffer from test leakage through inverse relations: a large number of test triples can be obtained simply by inverting triples in the training set. To perform the evaluation more rigorously, we prefer FB15k-237 and WN18RR, where inverse relations and inverse triples have been removed.

The YAGO3-10 [9] dataset is a subset of YAGO3 which includes at least 10 relations involved for each entity. YAGO3-10 contains extensive relations with high in-degrees and out-degrees. Since the meanings of these head and tail entities may differ greatly, modeling on YAGO3-10 is more challenging.

4.2   Evaluation Protocol

The reported performance is evaluated on 5 standard metrics: proportion of correct triples ranked at top 1, 3 and 10 (Hits@1, Hits@3, and Hits@10), Mean Rank (MR), and Mean Reciprocal Rank (MRR). The Hits@N and MRR are the higher the better, while the MR is the lower the better. For all experiments, we report averaged results across 5 runs, and we omit the variance on all the metrics as they are not significant.

4.3   Main Results

Performance Comparison. To evaluate our CIM and FIM, we compare them with a range of knowledge graph embedding methods, including current state-of-the-art methods. The results over three benchmark datasets are listed in Table 1.

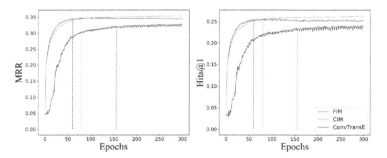

Fig. 4. The convergence study of FIM, CIM and ConvTransE by epochs on FB15k-237 validation set. It takes more than 150 epochs for ConvTransE to reach its convergent performance, but both our proposed CIM and FIM need fewer than 80 epochs. (Color figure online)

Overall, compared to the existing SOTA models, our CIM outperforms them over all three datasets on Hits@N and MRR, and it also achieves comparable performances on MR. On the other hand, FIM is also competitive with these methods on all metrics over all datasets. This demonstrates the advantages of our proposed methods.

Interaction Mechanism. Since the basic idea of our interaction mechanism is similar to CrossE [24], to explore the interaction between entities and relations, we focus on performance comparisons among FIM, CIM and CrossE. On FB15k-237, both CIM and FIM outperform CrossE on all metrics. On average, our CIM has a 17.5% performance improvement, and our FIM has a 15.2% performance improvement. Based on the improvements of the metrics, we can easily find out our novel interaction mechanism is more effective compared to CrossE, and even our FIM with a simple feed-forward neural network can make a huge boost.

We also compare against ConvTransE [16] with the proposed CIM since CIM also utilises the CNN structures. We observe that CIM outperforms ConvTransE across all metrics. On average, it has a 7.4% performance improvement over FB15k-237 and a 4.2% higher performance over WN18RR. In fact, our CIM adopts the same CNN module as ConvTransE does, and the only difference is that CIM takes our proposed interaction mechanism as the input feature, which aims to strengthen the interactions between entities and relations but cannot be fully learnt by the CNN model, empirically. From the metrics comparison, it is easy to find out our innovative interaction mechanism functions well.

On the other hand, we observe that compared to ConvTransE, our FIM also performs well, which only uses a feed-forward net on our interaction embeddings. On average, it has a 5.2% performance improvement over FB15k-237 and a 2.6% higher performance over WN18RR. This shows that our interaction mechanism can actually encode more information, which cannot be captured by CNN, and that our interaction mechanism is still compatible with CNN models. Even for some metrics, our FIM can outperform the strong CNN baseline ConvTransE, which also demonstrates the superiority of our interacted models.

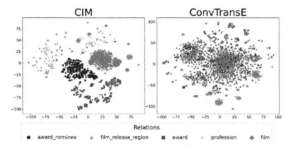

(a) t-SNE plot of tail entity embeddings learned by CIM (left) and ConvTransE (right).

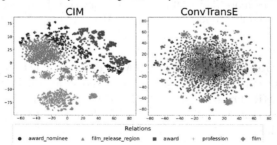

(b) t-SNE plot of concatenation of head and tail entity embeddings learned by CIM (left) and ConvTransE (right).

Fig. 5. t-SNE plots of learned entity embeddings by our CIM and ConvTransE over FB15k-237 dataset under two settings. We plot 5 most frequent relations with 1,000 entities for each relation.

Comparing with GCN-Based SOTA. As shown in Table 1, SACN [16] is also a competitive baseline and even it is the second best on several metrics. It is built on a weighted graph convolutional network (WGCN) as an encoder, which can help improve performance but at an extra computational expense [16] that it needs to load all the nodes and edges of a graph for training, as well as high computational complexity. By contrast, both of our FIM and CIM are computationally friendly and achieve comparable or even better performance as SACN. On the other hand, our methods are in a fully end-to-end manner, which is much easier for re-training when the KG is modified or evolved. Above all, these observations illustrate the practical and advantages of our models from many perspectives.

4.4   Analysis and Discussion

Convergence Analysis. Figure 4 shows the convergence study of FIM (the red line) and CIM (the yellow line) compared to ConvTransE (the green line) on FB15k-237 validation set. For convergence analysis, we utilize the Adam optimizer [6] and the same settings such as learning rate for all three models. We observe that both our CIM and FIM converge faster than ConvTransE, and achieve better performance. It takes more than 150 epochs for ConvTransE to reach its convergent performance, while both our proposed CIM and FIM need fewer than 80 epochs. The converge difference between our models and ConvTransE proves that our interaction mechanism can provide better representations for models. And after a period of training (after 100 epochs), as is depicted in Fig. 4, our FIM tends to descend slightly, which seems to be overfitting, while the CIM does not. Convincingly, the CNN based CIM is empirically better than the fully-connected layer based FIM.

Can Our Methods Learn Better Embeddings? To understand how well our methods learn interactions between entities and relations, we visualise the learned embeddings. We choose the five most frequent relations and randomly sample 1000 corresponding triples for each relation on FB15k-237 test set. To present in a 2D view, we utilize t-SNE [7] on these learned embeddings. Specially, we compare our CIM with ConvTransE since they both generalise a CNN architecture while CIM has an additional interaction mechanism.

Figure 5a shows the results of using the embeddings of tail entities only. Obviously, grouped by relations, tail entity embeddings trained by our CIM can be easily differentiated and separated from each other, while there is no such pattern for ConvTransE. Since tail entities corresponding to the same relation are supposed to have similar features in the entity space, it is easy to evaluate that the embeddings learned by CIM are better than those learned by ConvTransE in reflecting their semantics.

Figure 5b shows the results of using the concatenated embeddings of both head and tail entities, that is, the concatenation of the triples with the relation masked. Evidently, although the scatters plotted only contain information of entities, our CIM implicates information of relations since clusters of entity concatenation embeddings corresponding to different relations separate from each other, while ConvTransE can hardly make it. Because the main difference between CIM and ConvTransE lies in our interaction mechanism, we intuitively show the advantages of our interaction mechanism in the embedding process.

5 Conclusion

Introducing a novel interaction mechanism to learn the contextualised representation of entities and relations, we alleviate the limitations of existing KGC methods. Based on the proposed interaction mechanism, we build two effective models, FIM and CIM, utilizing a feed-forward neural network and a convolutional neural network respectively. Through extensive experiments and sufficient comparisons, we demonstrate that considering the contextualised representations of entity and relation, our models achieve the new SOTA performance in link prediction task. Furthermore, we evaluate and prove the necessity of our interaction mechanism in performance improvement.

References

1. Auer, S., Bizer, C., Kobilarov, G., Lehmann, J., Cyganiak, R., Ives, Z.G.: DBpedia: a nucleus for a web of open data. In: ISWC 2007 + ASWC 2007 (2007)
2. Bollacker, K.D., Evans, C., Paritosh, P., Sturge, T., Taylor, J.: Freebase: a collaboratively created graph database for structuring human knowledge. In: SIGMOD (2008)
3. Bordes, A., Usunier, N., Garcia-Duran, A., Weston, J., Yakhnenko, O.: Translating embeddings for modeling multi-relational data. In: Advances in Neural Information Processing Systems (2013)
4. Dettmers, T., Minervini, P., Stenetorp, P., Riedel, S.: Convolutional 2D knowledge graph embeddings. In: AAAI (2018)
5. Devlin, J., Chang, M., Lee, K., Toutanova, K.: BERT: pre-training of deep bidirectional transformers for language understanding. In: NAACL-HLT (2019)
6. Kingma, D.P., Ba, J.: Adam: a method for stochastic optimization. In: Bengio, Y., LeCun, Y. (eds.) ICLR 2015, Conference Track Proceedings (2015)
7. Laurens, V.D.M., Hinton, G.: Visualizing data using t-SNE. J. Mach. Learn. Res. 9(2605) (2008)
8. Lin, Y., Liu, Z., Sun, M., Liu, Y., Zhu, X.: Learning entity and relation embeddings for knowledge graph completion. In: AAAI (2015)
9. Mahdisoltani, F., Biega, J., Suchanek, F.M.: YAGO3: a knowledge base from multilingual Wikipedias. In: CIDR (2015)
10. Miller, G.A.: WordNet: a lexical database for English. Commun. ACM 38(11) (1995)
11. Nathani, D., Chauhan, J., Sharma, C., Kaul, M.: Learning attention-based embeddings for relation prediction in knowledge graphs. In: ACL (2019)
12. Nguyen, T.D., Nguyen, D.Q., Phung, D., et al.: A novel embedding model for knowledge base completion based on convolutional neural network. In: NAACL-HLT (2018)

13. Nickel, M., Tresp, V.: Tensor factorization for multi-relational learning. In: Blockeel, H., Kersting, K., Nijssen, S., Železný, F. (eds.) ECML PKDD 2013. LNCS (LNAI), vol. 8190, pp. 617–621. Springer, Heidelberg (2013). https://doi.org/10.1007/978-3-642-40994-3_40

14. Nie, Y.P., Han, Y., Huang, J.M., Jiao, B., Li, A.P.: Attention-based encoder-decoder model for answer selection in question answering. Front. Inf. Technol. Electron. Eng. **18**(4), 535–544 (2017)

15. Peters, M.E., et al: Deep contextualized word representations. In: NAACL-HLT (2018)

16. Shang, C., Tang, Y., Huang, J., Bi, J., He, X., Zhou, B.: End-to-end structure-aware convolutional networks for knowledge base completion. In: AAAI (2019)

17. Shi, B., Weninger, T.: Open-world knowledge graph completion. In: AAAI (2018)

18. Sun, Z., Vashishth, S., Sanyal, S., Talukdar, P.P., Yang, Y.: A re-evaluation of knowledge graph completion methods. In: ACL (2020)

19. Toutanova, K., Chen, D., Pantel, P., Poon, H., Choudhury, P., Gamon, M.: Representing text for joint embedding of text and knowledge bases. In: EMNLP (2015)

20. Trouillon, T., Welbl, J., Riedel, S., Gaussier, É., Bouchard, G.: Complex embeddings for simple link prediction. In: ICML. JMLR Workshop and Conference Proceedings (2016)

21. Vashishth, S., Sanyal, S., Nitin, V., Agrawal, N., Talukdar, P.P.: InteractE: improving convolution-based knowledge graph embeddings by increasing feature interactions. In: AAAI (2020)

22. Yang, B., Yih, W., He, X., Gao, J., Deng, L.: Embedding entities and relations for learning and inference in knowledge bases. In: ICLR (2015)

23. Yao, L., Mao, C., Luo, Y.: KG-BERT: BERT for knowledge graph completion. arXiv (2019). http://arxiv.org/abs/1909.03193

24. Zhang, W., Paudel, B., Zhang, W., Bernstein, A., Chen, H.: Interaction embeddings for prediction and explanation in knowledge graphs. In: WSDM (2019)

25. Zhao, X., Jia, Y., Li, A., Jiang, R., Song, Y.: Multi-source knowledge fusion: a survey. World Wide Web **23**(4), 2567–2592 (2020)

Civil Unrest Event Forecasting Using Graphical and Sequential Neural Networks

Zheng Chen[✉][iD] and Yifan Wang[iD]

School of Information and Software Engineering, University of Electronic Science and
Technology of China, Chengdu, China
zchen@uestc.edu.cn

Abstract. Having the ability to forecast civil unrest events, such as violent protests, is crucial because they can lead to severe violent conflict and social instabilities. Civil unrests are comprehensive consequences of multiple factors, which could be related to political, economic, cultural, and other types of historical events. Therefore, people naturally organize such historical data into time-series data and feed it into an RNN-like model to perform the forecasting. However, how to encode discrete historical information into a unified vector space is very important. Different events may have extensive and complex relationships in time, space, and participants. Traditional methods, such as collecting indicators of various fields as features, miss the vital correlation information between events. In this work, we propose a Graph Neural Network based model to learn the representation of correlated historical event information. By using the dates, events, participants, and locations as nodes, we construct an event graph so that the relationship between events can be expressed unambiguously. We organize date-node's representations into time-series data and use an LSTM to predict if there will be a violent protest or demonstration in the next few days. In the experiments, we use historical events from Hong Kong to evaluate our system's forecasting ability in 1-day, 2-day, and 3-day lead-time. Our system achieves recall rates of 0.85, 0.86, 0.88, and precision rates of 0.75, 0.77, 0.75, respectively. We also discussed the impact of longer prediction lead times, and external events in China Mainland, the United States, and the United Kingdom on the Hong Kong civil unrest event prediction.

Keywords: Event forecasting · Civil unrest event · Graph neural network

1 Introduction

Civil unrest is a kind of social problem that includes riots, violent demonstrations, marches, protests, barricades, and strikes [6]. Sometimes it can cause a significant amount of economic and political loss [3]. Thus, predicting the occurrence of violent protests is of interest to policymakers and citizens, as these may lead to civil unrest and regional instability, threatening to life, and property.

Supported by the Sichuan Science and Technology Plan Project 2020YFG0009.

I. Farkaš et al. (Eds.): ICANN 2021, LNCS 12893, pp. 192–203, 2021.
https://doi.org/10.1007/978-3-030-86365-4_16

Factors in the emergence of civil unrest include social interactions and injustices, changes in domestic and international policies cultural awareness, and economic factors, such as poverty, unemployment levels, and food prices [8]. All these factors can be regarded as historical information and found in historical events. In recent years, open-source data, such as social media content and event data, have been used with varying degrees of success to forecast civil unrest [17]. By using traditional machine learning models, Muthiah et al. [11] and Qiao et al. [12] predicted civil unrest events in many countries in Southeast Asia and Latin America. By using neural network models such as LSTM, Cortez et al. [2] have made remarkable achievements in predicting civil disturbance time. Some of these method's f1-scores are in the range of 0.68 to 0.95 [8]. One limitation of many such studies is that the methods only involve limited features extracted from data, thus cannot establish the extensive correlation between events. Besides, maintaining databases manually or obtaining information from social media is complicated and biased. For example, if we want to obtain the daily flow on the topic of protests on Twitter, we need to collect a large number of tweets, select keywords carefully, then count the number of tweets related to these keywords. In this process, the choice of keywords is so vital that it will directly affect the follow-up prediction result. Furthermore, civil unrest events are a complex process that cannot be fully characterized by collecting indicators in some fields isolated.

In this paper, we utilize graph structure to construct the correlation between historical events and then adopt a sequential model to predict future events. We call our **Gra**phical and **S**equential **Net**work the **GasNet**. To the best of our knowledge, this is the first attempt at civil unrest forecasting that combines representation learning of events graph and time-series forecasting using an RNN-like model. First, we construct our event graph with not only event nodes but also date nodes, event actor nodes, and attribute nodes. Then we use graph neural networks to learn the semantic representation of all those nodes. After that, we organize the data nodes, which serve as the readout nodes, in chronological order to use the convolutional neural networks to extract the features in the temporal dimension. Finally, we input the extracted temporal features into a recurrent neural network to predict future events. To predict the civil unrest events in Hong Kong, we exploit the above model to build a verification experiment. Experimental results show that by making an event prediction three days in advance, our method can achieve a precision rate of 0.75 and a recall rate of 0.88. We also study the impact of lead time and external events through experiments.

2   Related Work

2.1   Event Database

Early event databases were built manually. However, even the biggest human team is incapable of fully reading and analyzing billions of words and images posted every day over the whole world. Fortunately, with the development of event extraction technologies, large-scale automated structured event databases, such as ICEWS [5], NewsReader [16], and EMBERS [11], have gradually been established. As the largest open-access event database, GDELT(Global Database of Events, Language, and Tone) uses complex algorithms combined with deep learning tailored for news articles to create a real-time structured record of global events [9]. Each event in GDELT will be parsed into about 60 fields. In this paper, we mainly use *SQLDATE*, *EventBaseCode*, *NumMentions*, *ActorCountryCode*, *ActorTypeCode*, and *ActionGeo_CountryCode*, which represent the date, event type, number of mentions of the event, participant's country, identity, and event's location, respectively.

2.2   Civil Unrest Forecasting

Events database such as GDELT and social media data such as Twitter data are widely used in event prediction. Qiao et al. [12] use GDELT to build a Hidden Markov Models (HMMs) based framework to discover the development mechanism of potential events and predict indicators associated with country instability. Islam et al. [6] filter tweet stream and classifies tweets using linear Support Vector Machine (SVM) classifier. After distributing weights to tweets, use them to predict civil unrest in a location. In order to predict civil unrest events more accurate, heterogeneous data sources are used. Korkmaz et al. [8] use the input data containing predictors extracted from social media sites (Twitter and blogs), news, and requests for Tor to predict the probability of occurrence of civil unrest events. Logistic regression models with Lasso are used to select a sparse feature set from datasets.

In the work described above, various kinds of traditional machine learning methods are used. In recent years, many deep learning methods have also been utilized in civil unrest forecasting [18]. Chen et al. [1] count the number of various types of events in GDELT and use a LSTM-like model to predict future events that will occur between a specific pair of countries. The experiment only provides a coarse-grained prediction that can indicate the future trend of the relationship between the two countries. Meng et al. [10] use historical data, social media data, and economic indicators as structured data; the embedding of related tweets as unstructured data. They use a model that combines convolutional layers and LSTM layers to learn patterns from various data sources and predict civil unrest events.

These systems only collect indicators of possible related fields in isolation. However, we argue that events are universally correlated. This idea motivates us to study various potential civil unrest drivers by using a graph neural network that learns to represent the input event data via a graph structure.

Besides, it is also essential to be able to predict the occurrence of civil unrest earlier. Muthiah et al. [11] develop EMBERS that can capture significant societal unrest with an average lead time of 4.08 days. In this paper, we discussed the influence of the lead time on the prediction results. We also discussed the influence of external events related to China mainland and other areas on the events in Hong Kong.

2.3   Graph Convolutional Networks

Graph neural networks can be understood as special cases of a simple differentiable message-passing framework [13]:

$$h_i^{(l+1)} = \sigma(\sum_{m \in M_i} g_m(h_i^{(l)}, h_j^{(l)})) \tag{1}$$

where $h_i^{(l)} \in R^d(l)$ is the hidden state of node v_i in the l-th layer of the neural network, with $d^{(l)}$ being the dimensionality of this layer's representations. Incoming messages of the form g_m are accumulated and passed through an element-wise activation function $\sigma()$. M_i represents the set of incoming message for node v_i and is usually means the set of incoming edges of v_i. g_m is message passing function. In Kipf and Welling's work [7], g_m is simply a linear transformation: $g_m(h_i, h_j) = Wh_j$ with a weight matrix W.

Duvenaud et al. [4] introduce a convolutional neural network that operates directly on graphs, which have satisfactory performance on fingerprint learning and other tasks. Kipf and Welling [7] present a semi-supervised learning method on graph structured data that learns hidden layer representations that encode both local graph structure and features of nodes. Their work achieve significant progress on citation networks and a knowledge graph dataset. Relational Graph Convolutional Networks are developed specifically to deal with the multi-relational data [13]. The record in the event database can be naturally represented as a graph structure with multi relations. Therefore, we employ this model to operate on event graph.

3   Methodology

The goal of this work is to predict whether civil unrest events will occur in a particular region within the next n days, according to the input historical events.

We consider this task as a classification problem. Our model consists of two parts: (i)representation learning and (ii)prediction. We construct historical event data as event graph G, then learn node representations in the event graph through Graph Convolutional Networks. We take the representation of the date node in the event graph as the feature of this date. Through the Graph Convolutional Network, this date node aggregates information about events connected to that node. Assuming that $x_t \in R^n$ represents t day's features, then we organize these nodes' representations into a sequence data in chronological order. $[x_{t-s}, x_{t-s+1}, ..., x_t]$ is the input of the prediction model, and $y_{t+\Delta t}$ is the output. $y_{t+\Delta t} = 0$ or 1, which means whether there would be protests or demonstrations on day $t + \Delta t$. The task of the model is to learn the representations of the date node x_t, and then use the learned date representation to predict whether there would be protests or demonstrations event in $t + \Delta t$ day.

The overall structure of our model is shown in Fig. 1. The entire forecasting process can be divided into 5 steps.

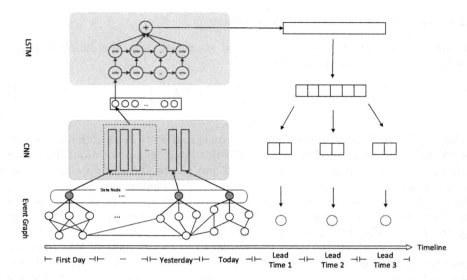

Fig. 1. The overall structure of our Graphical and Sequential Network(GasNet) for civil unrest event forecasting.

Step 1: we collect historical events related to the target area in accordance with specific rules. Since we use GDELT as our dataset, the specific rule is whether the '*ActionGeo_CountryCode*' of the event is target area, which means whether it happened in the area we are concerned about.

Step 2: we structure the historical event data into a graph structure and then train it with the graph neural network.

Step 3: we organize the representation of the date nodes, which serve as the graph's readout, into time-series. Then perform one-dimensional convolution in the time dimension to better extract its temporal features.

Step 4: the output of the convolutional layer is then inputted into a 2-layer LSTM network for sequential learning.

Step 5: finally, we concatenate the output vectors of the LSTM and then produce the prediction results with a linear layer and a softmax layer.

3.1 Construction of the Event Graph

We construct structured event data in GDELT as an event graph, which is the input of the Graph Neural Network. The construction method of the event graph is as follows.

There are three main types of nodes in our event graph: event nodes, attribute nodes, and date nodes. An individual event node represents each event. Event has some attributes. Hence, each event node connects several attribute nodes. In the GDELT event dataset, each event has two participants. Participant has their name, identity, country, and other information. We ignore the participant's

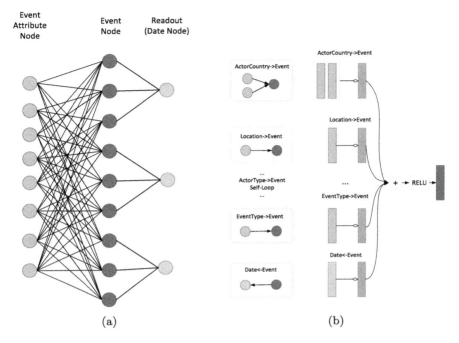

Fig. 2. (a) Construction of the event graph. (b) Update of event node representation. (Color figure online)

specific name, only consider his abstract attributes, especially the 'ActorCountry' and 'ActorType'. In addition to the participants, GDELT also records the event's type and location as 'EventType' and 'Location' attributes. In our event graph, each different value of these attributes also represented by an individual node. Event nodes connect to event attribute nodes by different types of relations. Since there are hundreds of events every day, but types and locations are limited, the number of event nodes is much higher than the number of event attribute nodes. Each event node also connects to the corresponding date node according to the date it occurred. In this way, events indirectly connect by sharing the same date nodes, event type nodes, location nodes, and other attribute nodes. An example of our event graph is shown in Fig. 2a.

3.2 Representation Learning

We employ a Graph Neural Network to learning the representation of the previously constructed event graph. Since there are various directed relations in the graph, we follow the method of the Relational Graph Convolutional Networks(R-GCNs) to perform different linear transformation according to each type of edge.

inherently discrete and does not possess a natural continuous metric, both fundamental properties for defining the Euclidean topology. These issues have cost the machine learning practitioner time and effort to develop feature engineering techniques to represent the data suitably for Euclidean-based learning methods. For instance, circular fingerprints encode a molecule's graph-like structure through a one-hot-encoding of certain pre-established chemical substructures. The steadily increasing number of applications in which graphs naturally represent the data of interest has driven the development of proper graph-based learning [29]. A prime source of applications stems from chemistry, where predictive models for bioactivity or physicochemical properties of a molecule are rapidly gaining relevance in the drug discovery process [21]. Other applications arise in the context of social and biological networks, knowledge graphs, e-commerce, among others [29,33].

A crucial step for defining graph-based learning is to extend the above definition of a graph by considering each element of the sets V, E as feature vectors, that is, $\mathbf{x}_v, \mathbf{e}_{ij} \in \mathcal{M}$, where $\mathcal{M}$ is a suitable manifold. In this context, the field of graph representation learning (GRL) is often divided into spectral [4,14,17] and non-spectral/spatial approaches [8,13,27]. The latter class, to which this works belong, is based on the idea of *local message passing*, where vector messages between connected nodes are exchanged and updated using neural networks [12]. Most of the literature on GNNs has focused on $\mathcal{M} = \mathbb{R}^n$, that is, vertex and edge embeddings are into Euclidean space. Therefore, it is natural to ask whether this choice is again a restriction imposed by history or simplicity and to which extent GRL could benefit from greater freedom in choosing the manifold $\mathcal{M}$. As first step we consider $\mathcal{M} = \mathbb{R}^n$ as a topological space, but generalize its algebra structure, that is, a vector space equipped with a bilinear product, beyond the real numbers. Example of these are the familiar complex and quaternion algebras, and these and more general algebras are often referred to as hypercomplex number systems.

2   Related Work

The present work lies at the intersection of three active research areas: (1) geometric approaches to GNNs, (2) hypercomplex/algebraic generalizations of deep learning methods, and (3) regularization/parameter efficiency techniques. This section illustrates how our work relates to these areas and which new aspects we introduce or generalize.

Geometric deep learning is the discipline that comprises the formalization of learning of data embeddings as functions defined on non-Euclidean domains [3]. Hyperbolic manifolds, for example, constitute an important class of non-Euclidean spaces which has been successfully deployed in deep learning. Here, basic manifold-preserving operations such as addition and multiplication in the context of neural networks have been extended to hyperbolic geometry [10]. Such advances led to the development of hyperbolic GNNs. The works [6,20] have empirically shown that the hyperbolic setting is better suited for representation learning on real-world graphs with scale-free or hierarchical structure.

As mentioned above, another defining property of the embedding function learned by a neural network is its underlying vector space structure. Complex- and hypercomplex-based neural networks have received increasing attention in several applications, from computer vision to natural language processing (NLP) tasks [11,23,25,26]. Hypercomplex representation learning offers promising theoretical properties and practical advantages. It has been argued that, as in the complex case [1], networks possess a richer representational capacity, resulting in more expressive embeddings. Hypercomplex models encompass greater freedom in the choice of the product between the algebra elements: in the case of the quaternion algebra, the Hamilton product naturally incorporates a weight-sharing within the component of the quaternion representation, yielding an additional form of regularization. This approach is, however, virtually unexplored in the graph setting. [22] recently introduced a quaternion based graph neural network, where they showed promising results for node and graph prediction tasks.

The characteristic of the hypercomplex product just mentioned, responsible for heavily reducing the number of parameters (for fixed model depth and width), can be generalized to yield more generic algebras. As a consequence, it is possible to train deeper models, avoiding to overfit the data while supplying more expressive embeddings. The crucial adaption in complex- and hypercomplex-valued neural networks, compared to their real-valued counterpart, lies in the reformulation of the linear transformation, i.e., of the fully-connected (FC) layer. Recent work in the realm of NLP by Zhang et al. [32] introduces the PHM-layer, an elegant way to parameterize hypercomplex multiplications (PHM) that also generalizes the product to n-dimensional hypercomplex spaces. The model benefits from a greater architectural flexibility when replacing fully-connected layers with their alternative that includes the interaction of the constituents of a hypercomplex number.

In this work, we embark on the first extensive exploration of hypercomplex graph neural networks. We benchmark our models in graph property prediction tasks in the OGB and Benchmarking-GNNs datasets [9,15].

In summary, we make the following contributions:

- We propose *Parameterized Hypercomplex Graph Neural Networks* (PHC-GNNs), a class of graph representation learning models that combine the expressiveness of GNNs and hypercomplex algebras to learn improved node and graph representations.
- We study the learning behavior of the hypercomplex product as a function of the algebra dimensions n. We introduce novel initialization and regularization techniques for the PHM-layer, based on our theoretical analyses, and provide empirical evidence for optimal learning at large n.
- We demonstrate the effectiveness of our PHC-GNNs, reaching SOTA performance compared to other GNNs with a much lower memory footprint, making it appealing for further research in GRL to develop even more powerful GNNs with sophisticated aggregation schemes that use the idea of hypercomplex multiplication.

3 Hypercomplex Neural Networks

3.1 Parameterized Hypercomplex Layer

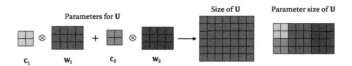

Fig. 1. Illustration of of the PHM layer introduced by Zhang et al. [32]. It uses a sum of Kronecker products of matrices $\mathbf{C}_i$ and $\mathbf{W}_i$ ($i = 1, 2$) to construct the transform matrix $\mathbf{U}$ in Eq. (1) (here $m = 2, k = 6, d = 8$). Best viewed in color.

The parameterized hypercomplex multiplication (PHM) layer introduced by [32] aims to *learn* the multiplication rules defining the underlying algebra, i.e., the interaction between the real and imaginary components of the algebra's product. One obvious advantage of the PHM layer is lifting the restriction on the (pre-defined) algebra dimensionality, otherwise being limited to $n = \{2, 4, 8, 16, ...\}$ as in the case of the algebra of complex, quaternion, octonion, and sedenion numbers, respectively.

The PHM layer takes the same form as a standard affine transformation, that is,

$$\mathbf{y} = \text{PHM}(\mathbf{x}) = \mathbf{U}\mathbf{x} + \mathbf{b} . \tag{1}$$

The key idea is to construct $\mathbf{U}$ as a block-matrix through the sum of Kronecker products. The Kronecker product generalizes the vector outer product to matrices: for any matrix $\mathbf{X} \in \mathbb{R}^{m \times n}$ and $\mathbf{Y} \in \mathbb{R}^{p \times q}$, the Kronecker product $\mathbf{X} \otimes \mathbf{Y}$ is a block matrix with shape $(mp \times nq)$. Now, let n be the dimension of the hypercomplex algebra, and let us suppose that k and d are both divisible by a user-defined hyperparameter $m \in \mathbb{Z}_{>0}$ such that $m \leq n$. Then, the block-matrix $\mathbf{U}$ in Eq. (1) is given by a sum of n Kronecker products

$$\mathbf{U} = \sum_{i=1}^{n} \mathbf{C}_i \otimes \mathbf{W}_i , \tag{2}$$

where $\mathbf{C}_i \in \mathbb{R}^{m \times m}$ are denoted contribution matrices and $\mathbf{W}_i \in \mathbb{R}^{\frac{k}{m} \times \frac{d}{m}}$ are the component weight matrices. In the rest of our discussion, we make the simplifying assumption that $m = n$, for which (2) yields $n(\frac{kd}{n^2} + n^2) = \frac{kd}{n} + n^3$ degrees of freedom. Since k and d correspond to the output- and input-size for a linear transformation, and n determines the user-defined PHM-dimension, the overall complexity of the matrix $\mathbf{U}$ is $\mathcal{O}(\frac{kd}{n})$ under the mild assumption that $kd \gg n^4$. This shows that the PHM-layer enjoys a parameter saving factor of up to $\frac{1}{n}$ compared to a standard fully-connected layer [32] as illustrated in the example in Fig. 1.

4   Hypercomplex Graph Neural Network

4.1   Initialization of Linear Independent Contributions

While the authors [32] introduced the PHM layer, no further details on the initialization of the contribution matrices $\{\mathbf{C}_i\}_{i=1}^{n}$ have been elucidated. In the case of known hypercomplex algebras, these matrices can be chosen to be of full rank – that is, the rows/columns are linearly *independent* –, and whose elements belong to the set $\{-1, 0, 1\}$. Following the same logic, let $\tilde{\mathbf{I}}_n$ be a diagonal matrix with alternating signs on the diagonal elements

$$\tilde{\mathbf{I}}_n = \operatorname{diag}(1, -1, 1, -1, \dots) . \tag{3}$$

In our work, we initialize each contribution matrix $\mathbf{C}_i$ as a product between the matrix $\tilde{\mathbf{I}}_n$ and a power of the cyclic permutation matrix $\mathbf{P}_n$ that right-shifts the columns of $\tilde{\mathbf{I}}_n$, that is,

$$\mathbf{C}_i = \tilde{\mathbf{I}}_n \mathbf{P}_n^{i-1} , \tag{4}$$

where $(\mathbf{P}_n)_{i,j} = 0$ except for $j - i = 1$ and $i = n, j = 1$ where it has value 1. It is immediate to verify that the columns of the constructed $\mathbf{C}_i$'s are linearly independent, as desired. Note that the above construction is not the only one yielding contribution matrices with such properties. In fact, for $n \in \{2, 4\}$ we do not implement (4), but instead we initialize the contribution matrices as in the complex and quaternion algebra.

Learning Dynamics for Larger n. With the initialization scheme defined above, each $\mathbf{C}_i$ in (4) contains n non-zero elements versus $n(n-1)$ zero entries. Hence, the sparsity for each contribution matrix scales quadratically as a function of n, while the number of non-zero entries only linearly. While it is still possible for our model to adjust the parameters of the contribution matrices during training, it is conceivable that initializing too sparsely the fundamental operation of algebra, will deteriorate training. To overcome this issue, we also implement a different initialization scheme

$$\mathbf{C}_i \sim U(-1, 1) , \tag{5}$$

by sampling each element from the contributions matrices uniformly from $U(-1, 1)$. We will show in Sect. 5 that this initialization strategy greatly benefits the training and test performance for models with larger n.

4.2   Hypercomplex Graph Neural Network

Message Passing. We build our PHC message passing layer based on the graph isomorphism network (GIN-0) introduced by [30] with the integration of edge features [16]. The GIN model is a simple, yet powerful architecture that employs injective functions within each message passing layer, obtaining representational power as expressive as the Weisfeiler-Lehman (WL) test [28].

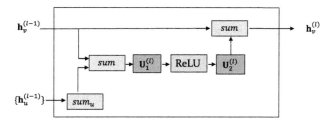

Fig. 2. Computation diagram of the PHC-GNN layer. Here the weight matrices $\{\mathbf{U}_s\}_{s=1}^{2}$ are constructed using the sum of Kronecker products described in Eq. (2).

Before any transformations on the embeddings are made, neighboring node representations are aggregated,

$$\mathbf{m}_v^{(l)} = \sum_{u \in \mathcal{N}(u)} \alpha_{uv}(\mathbf{h}_u^{(l-1)} + \mathbf{e}_{uv}^{(l)}) \,, \tag{6}$$

where the edge-embeddings $\mathbf{e}_{uv}^{(l)}$ are obtained through a learnable lookup-table or linear layer based on initial edge-features [16]. The aggregation weights α_{uv} can be computed using different mechanism as in the GCN, GraphSAGE, GAT and DeeperGCN models [13,17,19,27]. The GIN model, for instance, utilizes the sum-aggregator, i.e., all weights $\alpha_{uv} = 1$. In our class of models we implement several common aggregation strategies, namely, $\alpha_{uv} \sim$ {sum, mean, min, max, softmax}. Such flexibility is crucial for models, as different aggregators learn different statistical property of a graph [30] and generally define the method in the literature. Often, datasets differ regarding the topological properties of graphs, such as density and size, and as a consequence, optimal embeddings for a given dataset are notably sensitive to the choice of message passing aggregation strategy [7]. In our model, we set the default aggregation function to the *sum*-operator. The interpretation of Eq. (6) is that the message received by node v is a variable aggregation of the sum of the neighboring node embeddings and its corresponding edge-embeddings. This message is then the key ingredient in the update strategy of the node v embedding through a Multi-Layer-Perceptron (MLP), adding residual skip-connections to enable better gradient flow when backpropagating.

$$\mathbf{h}_v^{(l)} = \mathbf{h}_v^{(l-1)} + \text{MLP}^{(l)} \left(\mathbf{h}_v^{(l-1)} + \mathbf{m}_v^{(l)} \right) \,. \tag{7}$$

It is in this step that the PHM-layer from Eq. (1) is implemented. The computation diagram in Fig. 2 illustrates the usage of the PHM-weight matrices within the Multi-Layer-Perceptron (biases and edge-features ommited for clarity).

Our proposed message passing layer is a simple generalization of the GIN module, but uses the parameterized hypercomplex multiplication layer from

Eq. (1). For the case we set the hyperparameter $n = 1$, our model reduces to a modified version of GIN-0, where the (block) weight-matrix for each affine transformation consists of the sum of Kronecker products from only one matrix, as shown in Eq. (2).

Graph Pooling. The graph-level representation $\mathbf{h}_G$ is obtained by soft-averaging the node embeddings from the final message passing layer, i.e.,

$$\mathbf{h}_G = \sum_{v \in G} \mathbf{w}_v \odot \mathbf{h}_v^{(L)} \; , \tag{8}$$

where $\mathbf{w}_v$ is a soft-attention weight and $\odot$ denotes element-wise multiplication. We follow the proposal of Jumping-Knowledge GNNs [31] and assign attention scores to each hidden node embedding from the last embedding layer.

Downstream Predictor. The graph-level representations are further passed to a task-based downstream predictor, which can (but does not have to) be a Neural Network [9,15]. In our work we utilize a 2-layer MLP to predict the final logits for classification.

Although we define our GNN as graph classification model, the model can in fact also be utilized for node classification tasks. Such a model can be obtained, by not applying the graph pooling, and instead use the last hidden layer nodes embedding $\mathbf{H}^{(L)}$ to compute the logits for node classification.

5 Experiments

We evaluate the effectiveness of parameterized hypercomplex GNNs on six datasets from two recent graph benchmark frameworks [9,15]. The two recent graph benchmark frameworks address the inadequacy of past benchmark datasets, which are rather small in size, and thus not suitable for proper model evaluation. These issues become even more relevant for real-life graph-based learning applications, where often the datasets are fairly extensive and the issue of out-of-distribution samples is key in assessing the true predictive performance of the algorithm. To demonstrate the architectural advantage and effectiveness of the hypercomplex multiplication, we evaluate the performance of our GNNs for increasing algebra dimension n. We recall that in our framework, this hyperparameter controls the amount of parameter sharing in the PHM layer (1). In all our experiments, we report the test performance evaluated on the model saved from the epoch with the best validation performance.

Increasing n for a Fixed Network Architecture. Table 1 shows results on two molecular property prediction datasets from OGB [15], where all the models share the same *fixed* network architecture. Note that, due to the inherent weight-sharing mechanism, the number of parameters decreases as n increases. We observe an improved performance of our GNN when we adopt the (parameterized) hypercomplex multiplication layers. In fact, all models that were trained with PHM-layer, with the exception of the PHC-5 model, performed better than the "real" baseline PHC-1. This result supports our hypothesis that the employment of hypercomplex multiplication acts as regularizer and aids to better generalization performance on the test set.

Table 1. Results on the OGB graph classification datasets. The PHC-GNN can reduce the total number of model parameters and obtains improved averaged test performance over 10 (ogbg-molhiv) and 5 runs (ogbg-molpcba).

Model	ogbg-molhiv		ogbg-molpcba	
	# PARAMS	ROC-AUC (%) ↑	# PARAMS	PR (%) ↑
PHC-1	313K	78.18 ± 0.94	3.15M	29.17 ± 0.16
PHC-2	178K	79.25 ± 1.07	1.69M	**29.47±0.26**
PHC-2-C	178K	79.13 ± 0.87	1.69M	29.41 ± 0.15
PHC-3	135K	79.07 ± 1.16	1.19M	29.35 ± 0.28
PHC-4	111K	**79.34±1.16**	0.99M	29.30 ± 0.16
PHC-4-Q	111K	79.04 ± 1.89	0.99M	29.21 ± 0.23
PHC-5	101K	78.34 ± 1.64	0.87M	29.13 ± 0.24

For the medium-scale ogbg-molpcba dataset, our models include 7 message passing layers as stated in (7), each of a fixed size of 512. We refer to the SI for further details regarding architecture and hyperparameters. In deep learning, it is often observed that parameter-heavy models tend to outperform parameter-scarce models, but incur the risk of overfitting the training data, as the high number of degrees of freedom tempts the model to simply "memorize" the training data, with the consequential detrimental effect of poor generalization on unseen test data. Consequently, significant effort needs to be invested in regularizing the model, often in an *ad-hoc* manner. This experiment showed that HC-based models offer an elegant and universally-applicable approach to regularization that does not require any extensive hyperparameter tuning. As our baseline PHC-1 model in the ogbg-molpcba benchmark seems to overfit the training data (see SI for learning curves), having more parameter efficient models with the *same* architecture led to overall better performance. To further study the relation between n and model regularization, we trained the same model-architecture but with a much smaller embedding sizes of 64. Within this setting of under-parameterized models, the GNN with $n = 1$ performs best on the train/val/test dataset, followed by the model with increasing PHM-dim. This shows that, in a heavily underfitting setting, merely increasing the HC algebra dimension proves to be detrimental. Additionally, we empirically observe that models that can learn the multiplication rule from the training data (PHC-2 and PHC-4) outperform the complex- and quaternion-valued models (PHC-2-C and PHC-4-Q) in the OGB benchmarks.

Table 2. Results of the PHC-GNNs on the ZINC graph property prediction dataset. Our model can increase its embedding size for a fixed-length network through the inherent weight-sharing component. All shown models are constraint to a capacity budget of approximately 100K (L = 4) and 400K (L = 16) parameters and the performances are averaged over 4 runs [9]. Models with †-suffix are initialized with (5).

MODEL	ZINC, L = 4		ZINC, L = 16	
	# PARAMS	MAE ↓	# PARAMS	MAE ↓
PHC-1	102K	0.198 ± 0.010	403K	0.178 ± 0.007
PHC-2	99K	0.197 ± 0.007	403K	0.170 ± 0.005
PHC-3	101K	0.191 ± 0.005	407K	0.169 ± 0.001
PHC-4	107K	0.188 ± 0.003	399K	0.167 ± 0.006
PHC-5	106K	$\mathbf{0.185 \pm 0.008}$	408K	$\mathbf{0.164 \pm 0.003}$
PHC-8	104K	0.201 ± 0.005	401K	0.177 ± 0.009
PHC-10	104K	0.218 ± 0.010	395K	0.184 ± 0.005
PHC-16	110K	0.225 ± 0.009	412K	0.199 ± 0.008
PHC-8-†	104K	0.193 ± 0.006	401K	0.166 ± 0.005
PHC-10-†	104K	0.195 ± 0.004	395K	0.165 ± 0.005
PHC-16-†	110K	0.210 ± 0.013	412K	0.172 ± 0.003

Increasing n for a Fixed Parameter Budget. For our next experiment we examine the test performance of our models with increasing hyperparameter n, while constraining the parameter budget to approximately 100K and 400K parameters [9]. We design a fixed parameter-budget experiment to explore the expressiveness of the hypercomplex embeddings independently of the regularization effect investigated above, as all models possess the same overfitting capacity. This also constitutes a realistic scenario on the production level, where a constrained and low model memory footprint is crucial [24].

A feature of our proposed PHC-GNN is the ability to increase the embedding size of hidden layers for larger hyperparameter n without increasing the parameter count. Table 2 shows the results of experiments conducted on the ZINC dataset for a fixed-length hypercomplex GNN architecture, with L = {4,16} message passing- and 2 downstream-layers. The models differ merely in the embedding sizes, which are chosen so that the total parameter count respects the fixed budget. We observe that the models making use of the PHM-layer outperform the "real"-valued baseline, that uses standard FC layers. Particularly, being able to increase the embedding size seems to strengthen the performance of PHC-models on the test dataset. Nevertheless, we discover that above a certain value for the PHM-dimension n the performance deteriorates. One possible explanation for this behaviour lies in the learning dynamics between the set of contribution and weight matrices $\{\mathbf{C}_i, \mathbf{W}_i\}_{i=1}^{n}$ through the sum of Kronecker products in each PHM-layer (2). With increasing n, the initialization rule in (4) returns n

(increasingly) sparse contribution matrices, which seem to negatively affect the learning behaviour for the PHC-$\{8, 10, 16\}$ models.

For example, in the $n = 16$ scenario, exactly 16 elements from each $\mathbf{C}_i$ matrix are non-zero, in comparison to the remaining $16 \cdot 15 = 240$ zero elements. This aggravates the learning process as the weight-sharing achieved by the ith Kronecker product in (2) is not fully exploiting the interaction between all "algebra components". Using the initialization described in (5) enhanced the performance as shown in the undermost part of Table 2 Another reason for the performance decline of models with larger n, even when utilizing the different initialization scheme, is related to the complexity ratio of the PHM weight matrix $\mathbf{U}_i$ in (2). Recall that $\mathbf{U}_i$ consists of $\frac{kd}{n} + n^3 = \frac{k^2}{n} + n^3$ trainable parameters, where we assume $k = d$, the two contributions reflecting the trainable weight and contribution matrices, respectively. Now, given a fixed parameter budget, the allocation for the contribution matrices grows on a cubic scale with n, limiting the ability to increase the embedding size k, which plays a crucial role in the feature transformation through the weight matrices. As n grows, an increasingly higher share of parameters are allocated to the contribution matrices, and for large enough n, this negatively affects the learning behaviour of our models, as in the 100K case for $n = \{8, 6, 10\}$ in Table 2.

Finally, we compare our models with the current best performing algorithms on the datasets analyzed above. Table 3 shows that our GNNs are among the top-3 models in all datasets, and it defines a new state-of-the-art on ogbg-molpcba. Particularly significant is the comparison with the GIN+FLAG model. FLAG [18] is an adversarial data augmentation strategy which accomplishes a data-dependent regularization. Since, as we remarked in Sect. 4.2, our models can be considered as a generalization of GIN, we observe that our GNNs outperform the FLAG regularization strategy applied on the same underlying learning strategy.

Table 3. Performance results of our model on molecular property prediction datasets against: DGN [2], PNA [7], GIN, GCN, and DeeperGCN [19] and DeeperGCN/GIN-FLAG [18]. The results for GIN and GCN are reported from [9,15]. Model performances marked with * include a virtual-node [12] in their underlying method.

MODEL	OGBG-MOLHIV		OGBG-MOLPCBA		ZINC	
	ROC-AUC ↑ (%)	# PARAMS	AP ↑ (%)	# PARAMS	MAE ↓	# PARAMS
DGN	**79.70 ± 0.97**	114K	28.85 ± 0.30	6,732K	**0.168 ± 0.003**	98K
PNA	79.05 ± 1.32	326K	28.38 ± 0.35	6,550K	0.188 ± 0.004	95K
GIN	77.07 ± 1.49*	3,336K	27.03 ± 0.23*	3,374K	0.387 ± 0.015	103K
GCN	76.06 ± 0.97	537K	24.24 ± 0.34*	2,017K	0.459 ± 0.006	103K
DeeperGCN	78.58 ± 1.17	532K	27.81 ± 0.38*	5,550K	–	–
GIN+FLAG	77.48 ± 0.96*	3,336K	28.34 ± 0.38*	3,374K	–	–
DeeperGCN+FLAG	79.42 ± 1.20*	531K	28.42 ± 0.43*	5,550K	–	–
PHC-GNN (ours)	79.34 ± 1.16	111K	**29.47 ± 0.26**	1,169K	0.185 ± 0.008	106K

6   Conclusion

We have introduced a model class we named *Parameterized Hypercomplex Graph Neural Networks*. Our class of models extends to the graph setting the expressive power and the flexibility of (generalized) hypercomplex algebras. Our experiments showed that our models implement a powerful and flexible approach to regularization.

We have empirically shown that increasing the dimension of the underlying algebra leads to memory-efficient models (in terms of parameter-saving) and performance benefits, consistently outperforming the corresponding real-valued model, both for fixed architecture and fixed parameter budget. We have studied the learning behaviour for increasing algebra-dimension n, and addressed the sparsity phenomenon that manifests itself for large n, by introducing a different initialization strategy and an additional regularization scheme. Finally, we have shown that our models reach state-of-the-art performance on all graph-prediction benchmark datasets. In this work, we have undertaken the first thorough study on the applicability of higher dimensional algebras in the realm of GNNs. Given the very promising results we have obtained with a relatively simple base architecture, it would be worthwhile to extend to the hypercomplex domain to the recent progresses that have been achieved in "real" graph representation learning. For example, it would be interesting to improve the expressivity of our model by learning the aggregation function for the local message passing.

References

1. Arjovsky, M., Shah, A., Bengio, Y.: Unitary evolution recurrent neural networks. In: International Conference on Machine Learning, pp. 1120–1128 (2016)
2. Beaini, D., Passaro, S., Létourneau, V., Hamilton, W.L., Corso, G., Liò, P.: Directional graph networks (2020)
3. Bronstein, M.M., Bruna, J., LeCun, Y., Szlam, A., Vandergheynst, P.: Geometric deep learning: going beyond Euclidean data. IEEE Signal Process. Mag. **34**(4), 18–42 (2017)
4. Bruna, J., Zaremba, W., Szlam, A., LeCun, Y.: Spectral networks and locally connected networks on graphs (2014)
5. Chami, I., Abu-El-Haija, S., Perozzi, B., Ré, C., Murphy, K.: Machine learning on graphs: a model and comprehensive taxonomy (2021)
6. Chami, I., Ying, Z., Ré, C., Leskovec, J.: Hyperbolic graph convolutional neural networks. In: Wallach, H., Larochelle, H., Beygelzimer, A., d' Alché-Buc, F., Fox, E., Garnett, R. (eds.) Advances in Neural Information Processing Systems, vol. 32, pp. 4868–4879. Curran Associates, Inc. (2019)
7. Corso, G., Cavalleri, L., Beaini, D., Liò, P., Veličković, P.: Principal neighbourhood aggregation for graph nets (2020)
8. Duvenaud, D., et al.: Convolutional networks on graphs for learning molecular fingerprints (2015)
9. Dwivedi, V.P., Joshi, C.K., Laurent, T., Bengio, Y., Bresson, X.: Benchmarking graph neural networks (2020)

10. Ganea, O., Becigneul, G., Hofmann, T.: Hyperbolic neural networks. In: Bengio, S., Wallach, H., Larochelle, H., Grauman, K., Cesa-Bianchi, N., Garnett, R. (eds.) Advances in Neural Information Processing Systems, vol. 31, pp. 5345–5355. Curran Associates, Inc. (2018)
11. Gaudet, C.J., Maida, A.S.: Deep quaternion networks. In: 2018 International Joint Conference on Neural Networks (IJCNN), pp. 1–8 (2018)
12. Gilmer, J., Schoenholz, S.S., Riley, P.F., Vinyals, O., Dahl, G.E.: Neural message passing for quantum chemistry. In: Precup, D., Teh, Y.W. (eds.) Proceedings of the 34th International Conference on Machine Learning. Proceedings of Machine Learning Research, vol. 70, pp. 1263–1272. PMLR, International Convention Centre, Sydney, Australia, 06–11 Aug 2017
13. Hamilton, W., Ying, Z., Leskovec, J.: Inductive representation learning on large graphs. In: Advances in Neural Information Processing Systems, pp. 1024–1034 (2017)
14. Henaff, M., Bruna, J., LeCun, Y.: Deep convolutional networks on graph-structured data (2015)
15. Hu, W., et al.: Open graph benchmark: Datasets for machine learning on graphs (2020)
16. Hu, W., et al.: Strategies for pre-training graph neural networks. In: International Conference on Learning Representations (2020)
17. Kipf, T.N., Welling, M.: Semi-Supervised Classification with Graph Convolutional Networks. In: Proceedings of the 5th International Conference on Learning Representations, ICLR 2017 (2017)
18. Kong, K., et al.: Flag: Adversarial data augmentation for graph neural networks (2020)
19. Li, G., Xiong, C., Thabet, A., Ghanem, B.: DeeperGCN: All you need to train deeper GCNs (2020)
20. Liu, Q., Nickel, M., Kiela, D.: Hyperbolic graph neural networks. In: Wallach, H., Larochelle, H., Beygelzimer, A., d' Alché-Buc, F., Fox, E., Garnett, R. (eds.) Advances in Neural Information Processing Systems, vol. 32, pp. 8230–8241. Curran Associates, Inc. (2019)
21. Montanari, F., Kuhnke, L., Ter Laak, A., Clevert, D.A.: Modeling physico-chemical ADMET endpoints with multitask graph convolutional networks. Molecules **25**(1) 44 (2020)
22. Nguyen, D.Q., Nguyen, T.D., Phung, D.: Quaternion graph neural networks (2020)
23. Parcollet, T., et al.: Quaternion recurrent neural networks. In: International Conference on Learning Representations (2019)
24. Sohoni, N.S., Aberger, C.R., Leszczynski, M., Zhang, J., Ré, C.: Low-memory neural network training: A technical report (2019)
25. Tay, Y., et al.: Lightweight and efficient neural natural language processing with quaternion networks (2019)
26. Trabelsi, C., et al.: Deep complex networks. In: International Conference on Learning Representations (2018)
27. Veličković, P., Cucurull, G., Casanova, A., Romero, A., Liò, P., Bengio, Y.: Graph attention networks. In: International Conference on Learning Representations (2018)
28. Weisfeiler, B.A.L.A.: A reduction of a graph to a canonical form and an algebra arising during this reduction. Nauchno-Technicheskaya Informatsia **2**(9), 12–16 (1968)

29. Wu, Z., Pan, S., Chen, F., Long, G., Zhang, C., Yu, P.S.: A comprehensive survey on graph neural networks. IEEE Trans. Neural Netw. Learn. Syst. **32**(1), 4–24 (2021)
30. Xu, K., Hu, W., Leskovec, J., Jegelka, S.: How powerful are graph neural networks? In: International Conference on Learning Representations (2019)
31. Xu, K., Li, C., Tian, Y., Sonobe, T., Kawarabayashi, K.i., Jegelka, S.: Representation learning on graphs with jumping knowledge networks. In: Dy, J., Krause, A. (eds.) Proceedings of the 35th International Conference on Machine Learning. Proceedings of Machine Learning Research, vol. 80, pp. 5453–5462. PMLR (2018)
32. Zhang, A., et al.: Beyond fully-connected layers with quaternions: Parameterization of hypercomplex multiplications with $1/n$ parameters. In: International Conference on Learning Representations (2021)
33. Zhou, J., et al.: Graph neural networks: A review of methods and applications (2019)

Feature Interaction Based Graph Convolutional Networks for Image-Text Retrieval

Yongli Hu[1], Feili Gao[1], Yanfeng Sun[1(✉)], Junbin Gao[2], and Baocai Yin[1,3]

[1] Faculty of Information Technology, Beijing University of Technology, Beijing, China
{huyongli,yfsun,ybc}@bjut.edu.cn, gaofl@emails.bjut.edu.cn
[2] Discipline of Business Analytics, The University of Sydney Business School,
The University of Sydney, Sydney, NSW, Australia
junbin.gao@sydney.edu.au
[3] Faculty of Electronic Information and Electrical Engineering,
Dalian University of Technology, Dalian, China

Abstract. To solve the challenge of heterogeneous gap between visual and linguistic data in image-text retrieval task, many methods have been proposed and significant progress has been made. Recently, some works use more refined information of the relation between regions in images or the semantic connection between words in text to further improve the representation of text and image data, while the cross-modal relation between image region and text word is not well explored in the representation. The current methods lack feature interaction in the data representation. For this purpose, we propose a novel image-text retrieval method which introduces inter-modal feature interaction in the graph convolutional networks (GCN) of image and text fragments. By the feature interaction between fragments of different modalities and the information propagation of GCN, the proposed method can capture more inter-modal interaction information for image-text retrieval. The experimental results on MS COCO and Flickr30K datasets show that the proposed method outperforms the state-of-the-art methods.

Keywords: Image-text retrieval · Inter-modal feature interaction · Semantic relationship

1 Introduction

In the past decades, many cross-modal representation and learning methods have been proposed due to the needs of cross-modal data processing. In these researches, the cross-modal retrieval is one of the hottest topics. Many cross-modal retrieval methods have been proposed, including [3,5,9,11,12], and been applied in web search, multi-channel interaction and multi-modal data management and service, etc.

Measuring the similarity between the heterogeneous modalities of image and text is the main challenge of image-text cross-modal retrieval. Most of the existing methods extract the global features of image and text independently, and

© Springer Nature Switzerland AG 2021
I. Farkaš et al. (Eds.): ICANN 2021, LNCS 12893, pp. 217–229, 2021.
https://doi.org/10.1007/978-3-030-86365-4_18

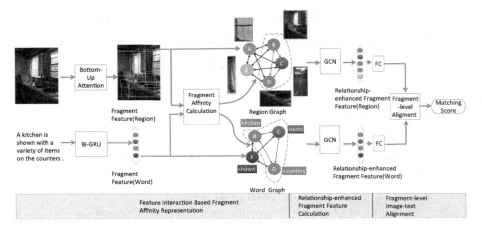

Fig. 1. Framework of our proposed model. It consists of three modules: (a) feature interaction based fragment affinity representation. (b) relationship-enhanced fragment feature calculation. (c) fragment-level image-text alignment. The model extracts the image-text joint information of region graph and word graph. The solid red line indicates strong correlation between fragments, and the solid black line indicates weak correlation. The relationship between image-text joint fragments B, C, and D are enhanced (Best viewed when zoomed in). (Color figure online)

then project the features of the two modalities into a common embedding subspace to calculate their similarity [7]. However, most of the current methods ignore the semantic relationship between the fine-grained fragments in the image or text modality, i.e. the regions in image and the words in text. Recently, some works try to model this structure of fragments of image to improve cross-modal representation [9].

But the influence of the other modal data on the semantic relationship of these fragments has not been explored at present. However, from the view of human, it is natural to establish the semantic relationship between fragments from different modalities and capture their common information by the interaction of these cross-modal fragments through their semantic connections. Inspired from the cross-modal mechanism of human, we propose a novel image-text retrieval method based on feature interaction of fragments from different modalities. The framework of the proposed method is shown in Fig. 1. We first use the fragments features extracted by bottom-up attention model and Bi-GRU on image regions and words in text as the graph nodes of region and word graph respectively. Then a feature interaction module is proposed to utilize the cross-modal feature similarity to represent the affinity between the fragments in region or word graph. The relations between sharing common nodes in different graphs are enhanced and the links connecting to the private nodes in these graphs are suppressed. From the interaction, we further propagate these cross-modal information by the following graph convolutional networks (GCNs) [13] on the image and text mobilities. Based on the relation enhanced fragments features, we utilize a feature alignment module to match the features of different modalities and obtain the final similarity. Our main contributions are summarized as follows:

- Use the interaction information between modalities to influence the semantic relationship between fragments in the image modality or text modality, so that fragments which is semantically irrelevant with the other modality are close to maintain the original feature after passing through the graph convolutional network and the semantic relationship between the common fragments (parts) of different modalities is enhanced.
- Use graph convolutional network to capture the semantic relationship between the key words in the text modality.
- Compared with state-of-the-art method IMRAM [3], our IGCN achieves promising results on two benchmarks.

2   Related Work

In this section, we first review the dominant cross-modal retrieval method: joint subspace. Then we introduce the methods that mine the inter-modal and intra-modal correlations of cross-modal data to improve cross-modal feature representation.

Joint Subspace for Retrieval. The existing image-text retrieval methods use various methods to extract image and text features to ensure that the extracted feature is accurate and comprehensive. Li et al. [10] run multiple text encoding components (bag-of-words, word vector model and GRU) in parallel to encode sentences, in order to capture the interactive information between concepts in the sentence. As for image features extracting, now many methods use bottom-up attention mechanism to extract the salient fragment features in the image [1].

The extracted image and text features are usually projected into the common subspace. Zou et al. [14] impose the l_{21}-norm to the projection matrix, uses the row sparsity feature of the l_{21}-norm to filter out noise and redundant feature. Most image-text retrieval works train the model by triplet ranking loss. Faghri et al. [4] uses hardest negatives instead of all negative pairs in the triplet loss. The hardest negative loss encourages the distance between the positive sample and the query to be less than that of negative sample which is closest to the query.

Mining Inter-modal and Intra-modal Correlations of Cross-modal Data. Mining the information of inter-modal relation is of great help to cross-modal retrieval tasks. Cao et al. [2] use co-attention network to interactively learn cross-modal text and image embedding. In this way, the embedding considers the interactive information between the modalities.

Many researches now start from the fine-grained fragments (regions and words) in the modality to solve the retrieval problem: Wang et al. [12] incorporate cross-modal information into fragment features, and then aggregate these features into global image and text features through simple attention approach.

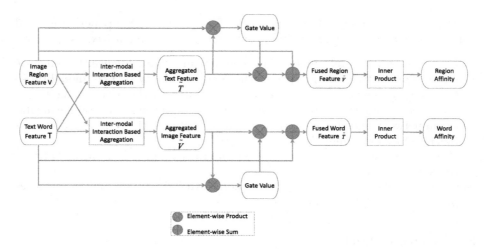

Fig. 2. The details of fragment relationship representation module.

Karpathy et al. [7] extract fragment features of images and text, and then align the region-word pairs. Meanwhile, the semantic association between fragments within the modality should be considered in retrieval task. Huang et al. [6] classified the regions in the image into multi-labels: objects and semantic relations, so that the global image representation obtained can capture the semantic concepts of the local regions.

However, most of the current methods ignore the influence of inter-modal correlations on the semantic relationship between fragments in the modality. In this paper, we will study this problem.

3   Feature Interaction Based Graph Convolutional Networks for Image-Text Retrieval

In this section, we describe the proposed feature interaction based graph convolutional networks, as shown in Fig. 1. The model consists of three modules: fragment affinity representation, relationship-enhanced fragment feature calculation and image-text alignment. In fragment affinity representation module, we add cross modal information to express the relationship between fragments in an image or text sample. In relationship-enhanced fragment feature calculation module, we use graph convolutional network to generate fragment features with semantic relationship between fragments. Finally, in image-text alignment module, we execute fragment-level alignment.

3.1   Feature Interaction Based Fragment Affinity Representation

At the beginning of the work, we extract fragment features of image and text modalities. Similar to some retrieval methods, we also use the bottom-up attention model on the image data G to obtain the region-level image feature $V = \begin{bmatrix} v_1^T \dots v_n^T \end{bmatrix}^T, v_i \in \mathbb{R}^{1*d}$. n is the number of regions detected in the image, and v_i represents the region (fragment) feature. Given a sentence S with m words, we use bi-directional GRU to extract the word-level text features $T = \begin{bmatrix} t_1^T \dots t_m^T \end{bmatrix}^T, t_j \in \mathbb{R}^{1*d}$, where fragment t_j represent the word feature in the sentence S. The dimension of v_i and t_j is equal.

In this module, we calculates the affinity between fragments in the image or text samples, as shown in Fig. 2.

Cross-modal Information Interaction. We project the region features and word features in the image-text pairs into a common space, and calculate the affinity between the region and word as:

$$A = (W_v V)^T (W_t T) \tag{1}$$

where $W_v, W_t \in \mathbb{R}^{d_h * d}$ are the projection matrix, which projects the d-dimensional region or word feature into the space of dimension d_h. $A \in \mathbb{R}^{n*m}$ is the region-word affinity matrix, where A_{ij} represents the affinity between region v_i and word t_j. The purpose of A is to align regions with words. A region has different affinities for different words in a sentence. We use these affinities as attention weights to aggregate all the word features in a sentence and then obtain region-specific global text feature:

$$\widetilde{T} = AT \tag{2}$$

where the ith row of $\widetilde{T} \in \mathbb{R}^{n*d}$ represents the text feature specific to region v_i. Similarly, the word-specific global image feature is defined as:

$$\widetilde{V} = A^T V \tag{3}$$

Gating Function. The rest of this paper will take image modality as example and the processing method of text modality data is the same as that of image modality. Denote the text feature specific to region v_i, i.e., the ith row of $(\widetilde{T})$ as $(\widetilde{T})_i$. We incorporate the aggregated text feature $(\widetilde{T})_i$ specific to original region v_i into v_i. Note that the gating function needs to be set to control the extent to which $(\widetilde{T})_i$ is integrated with the region features, as shown in Fig. 2. Specifically, if there is a match between the region and the text, we expect to incorporate more text information into the region features through a high gate value. Conversely, if the region and text information are not related, the gating function is expected to inhibit the original information from merging with the information of the other modality, so that the fused feature $\overline{V}$ approaches the original feature V. The gate vector corresponding to $(\widetilde{T})_i$ can be formulated as:

$$g_i = \sigma(v_i \otimes (\widetilde{T})_i) \in \mathbb{R}^{1*d} \tag{4}$$

where $\otimes$ denotes element-wise product, $\sigma(.)$ denotes sigmoid function. The set of gate vectors corresponding to all regions can be represented as: $G_v = \begin{bmatrix} g_1^T & g_2^T \dots g_n^T \end{bmatrix}^T \in \mathbb{R}^{n*d}$.

Fused Fragment Feature. The original region feature V is integrated with the text information to obtain the fused region feature $\overline{V}$, in which the gate vector G_v controls how much text information is integrated into the fused region feature:

$$\overline{V} = G_v \otimes \widetilde{T} + V \in \mathbb{R}^{n*d} \tag{5}$$

where $\otimes$ denotes the element-wise product. Similarly, we can obtain the fused word features $\overline{T} \in \mathbb{R}^{m*d}$. The fused region features and word features are sent to the fully connected layer, then we obtain the set of region and word features $\overline{V}, \overline{T}$.

Cross-modal Interaction Based Fragments Affinity Calculation. If two fused fragment features $\overline{v_i}$ and $\overline{v_j}$ are similar, indicating that they incorporate similar sentence information from text, then the two regions are considered to be highly correlated. On the contrary, if an region is not related to text information (given the query text, the text-unrelated region may be a background region in the positive image sample, or it may exist in the negative image sample), then its corresponding fused region feature contains almost no text information, its correlation with other text-related regions will be low. Therefore, we can do inner product between the fused region features to get the affinity R_V between regions in an image:

$$R(v_i, v_j) = norm(\overline{v_i})(norm(\overline{v_j}))^T \tag{6}$$

where $norm(.)$ performs l_2−normalized operation on the vector, $R(v_i, v_j)$ is an element of R_V. In this way, in the graph network constructed based on positive and negative image samples, the semantic relationship between the text-unrelated region (node) and text-related region is very low. As a result, we weaken the interference of the text-unrelated region on the retrieval performance. The affinity between words can be expressed in a similar way.

In other words, as shown in Fig. 1, we enhance the relationship between image-text common fragments in region graph and word graph.

3.2 Relationship-Enhanced Fragment Feature Calculation

We construct a relationship-enhanced fragment feature calculation module to generate fragment features with semantic relationship with other fragments. In Sect. 3.1, we have built affinity matrix R_V and R_T between fragments. $R_V(\overline{v_i}, \overline{v_j})$, the element of matrix R_V, represents the pairwise affinity between region $\overline{v_i}$ and $\overline{v_j}$. Then we use affinity matrix to build a fully-connected fragment relationship graph $G_v = (V, E)$, where V is composed of all detected regions in the image and E is consist of the edge (affinity) $R_V(\overline{v_i}, \overline{v_j})$ of each pair of regions.

Then we perform graph convolutional network on this fragment relationship graph to generate fragment features with relationship information. The response of each graph node is influenced by its' relationship with neighborhood node.

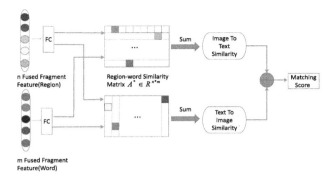

Fig. 3. The detail of bidirectional fragment-level image-text alignment module.

In addition, we apply a residual structure to the proposed graph convolutional network as follows:

$$V^* = W_r(R_V V W_g) + V \qquad (7)$$

where $W_g \in \mathbb{R}^{d*d}$ is the weight matrix of GCN layer, and $W_r \in \mathbb{R}^{n*n}$ is the weight matrix of residual connection. Note that since the text-unrelated region node has low affinity with other regions in the image, it is close to keep it's original feature after passing through the graph convolutional network. In a word, we get the relationship-enhanced region feature $V^* = \begin{bmatrix} v_1^{*T} & ... & v_n^{*T} \end{bmatrix}^T, v_i^* \in \mathbb{R}^{1*d}$ by graph convolutional network. Similarly, we can get relationship-enhanced word feature T^*.

3.3   Fragment-Level Image-Text Alignment

We align the heterogeneous relationship-enhanced fragments v_i^* and t_j^* in the image and text modalities, as shown in Fig. 3. Two matched heterogeneous fragments are required not only to be inherently similar in semantics, but also to have similar semantic relationships with other fragments in their respective samples. Take the matched image-text pair of the example in the third row of Fig. 4 for instance, when the relationship-enhanced region fragment 'man' and word fragment 'man' both incorporate similar semantic relationships with other image-text joint sub-fragments such as glasses and hat, these two heterogeneous fragments are considered to match each other.

Specifically, we send the relationship-enhanced region and word features into the fully connected layer, and compute the cosine similarity between each pair of region feature v_i^* and word feature t_j^* to obtain the final region-word similarity matrix $A^* \in \mathbb{R}^{n*m}$. We calculate the similarity between all the most matching regions and words in the image and text bidirectionally, and then accumulate these fine-grained similarities as the global similarity of image-text pairs. Specifically, we construct this fine-grained similarity bidirectionally. For image to text direction, we search the most matching word in the sentence for each region

Query image Three men are working on a roof .
Two men sitting on the roof of a house while
another one stands on a ladder .
People are fixing the roof of a house .
Three men , one on a ladder , work on a roof .
a construction worker prepping for roof work .
**Ground truth not retrieved in Top5: Two men
on a rooftop while another man stands atop
a ladder watching them**

Query image Five people wearing winter clothing , helmets , and ski goggles
stand outside in the snow .
Five people wearing winter jackets and helmets stand in the
snow , with snowmobiles in the background .
A group of people are climbing in cold weather .
Four people playing hockey in an ice rink .
Group gathered to go snowmobiling .
**Ground truth not retrieved in Top5: Five snowmobile riders all
wearing helmets and goggles line up in a snowy clearing in a
forest in front of their snowmobiles ; they are all wearing black
snow pants and from left to right they are wearing a black coat ,
white coat , red coat , blue coat , and black coat .
A group of snowmobile riders gather in the snow .**

Query text:The man with pierced ears is wearing glasses and an
orange hat .

Query text:A girl kicking a stick that a man is holding in tae kwon
do class .

Fig. 4. Top 5 retrieved results of query image and query text. Green results indicates the ground truth retrieved, and red indicates the wrong results retrieved (Best viewed when zoomed in). (Color figure online)

in an image and calculate region-word similarity. Accumulate these similarities corresponding to all regions as global image to text similarity s_1:

$$s_1^i = max(A_{i1}^*, ..., A_{im}^*) \qquad (8)$$

$$s_1 = \frac{\sum_{i=1}^{n} s_1^i}{n} \qquad (9)$$

where A_i^* represents the ith row of matrix A^*, each element in the ith row of the matrix A^* represents the similarity between region v_i and each word in the sentence. Note that because the relationship-enhanced text-unrelated region feature processed by Eq. 7 basically does not incorporate relationship information, its similarity with the most matching word is much lower than that of text-related region. The text to image similarity s_2 can be obtained by the similar way:

$$s_2^j = max(A_{1j}^*, ..., A_{nj}^*) \qquad (10)$$

Table 1. Quantitative results on Flickr30K.

Method	Text retrieval			Image retrieval			R@sum
	R@1	R@5	R@10	R@1	R@5	R@10	
SCAN [8]	67.4	90.3	95.8	48.6	77.7	85.2	465.0
CAMP [12]	68.1	89.7	95.2	51.5	77.1	85.3	466.9
VSRN [9]	71.3	90.6	96.0	54.7	81.8	88.2	482.6
IMRAM [3]	74.1	93.0	96.6	53.9	79.4	87.2	484.2
IGCN	**75.7**	**93.3**	**97.2**	**55.1**	**82.7**	**89.7**	**493.7**

$$s_2 = \frac{\sum_{j=1}^{m} s_2^j}{m} \tag{11}$$

We assign different weights to s_1 and s_2, then sum them to obtain the image-text similarity s:

$$s = s_1 + \mu s_2 \tag{12}$$

We use triplet ranking loss as loss function. The hardest negative sample is used in the loss as follows instead of all negative samples:

$$L = [\alpha - m(I, S) + m(I, \hat{S})]_+ + [\alpha - m(I, S) + m(\hat{I}, S)]_+ \tag{13}$$

where $[x]_+ = max(x, 0)$, α is a margin parameter. m(.) calculates the similarity between two modal data. $\hat{S}$ and $\hat{I}$ represent the hardest negative sample corresponding to query image I and query text S respectively.

3.4 Datasets and Evaluation Metric

In our experiment, two kinds of datasets are used, (1) MS COCO dataset. Each image in the dataset corresponds to 5 sentences, we use the same data split as [4], that is, a training set of 113287 images, a validation set of 5000 images, a test set of 5000 images. (2) Flickr30K dataset. It consists of 31,000 images and corresponding texts. Each image in the dataset also matches 5 texts. We use the widely adopted split: 29,000 images are used for training, 1000 images are used for verification, and 1000 images are used for testing. We use recall at K (R@K) as the evaluation metric of performance, which is common in retrieval tasks. Recall at K measure the fraction of queries for which the correct item is retrieved in the closest K points to the query. Following [8], we report the results of R@1, R@5 and R@10. In order to express the overall performance of the model, we also report the metric "R@sum", which is the sum of R@1, R@5 and R@10 on image retrieval and text retrieval.

4   Experiment

4.1   Implementation Details

Since all stopwords (such as: the, if) have no related regions in the image, the text data is preprocessed to remove the stopword. We set the dimension of the joint embedding space d to 1024 and the word embedding dimension to 300. We use Adam optimizer to train the model for 34 epochs. The learning rates of the first three epochs are 0.000075, 0.00015 and 0.00025, respectively. The learning rate is reduced to half of the previous epoch at epoch 8, 11, 15, 19, 23, 27 and 31. Except for the above, the learning rate of an epoch is the same as that of the previous epoch. The parameter μ in Eq. 12 is set to 1.5. The margin parameter α in Eq. 13 is set to 0.331. We choose a mini-batch size of 60. In order to prevent overfitting, we choose the model parameter with the best performance on the validation set.

4.2   Comparisons with the State-of-the-Art

In the model VSRN [9], an image region graph is established. However, the model does not consider the important influence of the text modality on the relationship between regions. Model IMRAM [3] adopt an iterative matching scheme with a cross-modal attention unit to align fragments across different modalities and then refine alignment knowledge from early steps to later ones.

Quantitative Results on Flickr30K and MS COCO. The quantitative results of proposed method and previous methods on the Flickr30K are shown in Table 1. IGCN has achieved better performance than the existing state-of-the-art in both text retrieval and image retrieval. Specifically, compared with the state-of-the-art method IMRAM, the performance improvement (Recall@5) of IGCN is 3.3% and 0.3% for image retrieval and text retrieval respectively. The result proves the effectiveness of adding modal interaction information to the fragment relationship mining. We report the quantitative results on the 5 folds of 1k test images of MS COCO in Table 2. The results on MS COCO once again prove the effectiveness of proposed IGCN.

Qualitative Results on Flickr30K. We show the qualitative retrieved results of proposed method in Fig. 4. The top5 retrieved results of image and text queries are displayed respectively. Since an image in the dataset matches 5 texts, we also display ground truth text that does not appear in the top5 retrieved text of query image. Take the first row of Fig. 4 as example, the top5 retrieved image are all related to the query text, but only the top1 image matches the query text in every detail.

Table 2. Quantitative results on MS-COCO.

Method	Text retrieval			Image retrieval			R@sum
	R@1	R@5	R@10	R@1	R@5	R@10	
SCAN [8]	72.7	94.8	98.4	58.8	88.4	94.8	507.9
CAMP [12]	72.3	94.8	98.3	58.5	87.9	95.0	506.8
VSRN [9]	76.2	94.8	98.2	**62.8**	89.7	95.1	516.8
IMRAM [3]	76.7	95.6	98.5	61.7	89.1	95.0	516.6
IGCN	**78.9**	**96.9**	**98.8**	61.9	**90.0**	**95.8**	**522.3**

Table 3. Ablation study on Flickr30K.

Method	Text retrieval			Image retrieval			R@sum
	R@1	R@5	R@10	R@1	R@5	R@10	
IGCN	**75.7**	**93.3**	**97.2**	**55.1**	**82.7**	**89.7**	**493.7**
w/o interaction	74.5	93.2	96.7	54.4	81.7	89.0	489.5
1OGCN	72.3	92.6	96.3	53.6	81.6	88.0	484.4
Baseline	72.8	91.4	96.0	52.6	80.3	87.8	480.9

4.3 Ablation Study

In the baseline model (denoted as "baseline" in Table 3), the image and text fragment features extracted by the bottom-up attention model and the bi-directional GRU are directly sent to the fragment-level image-text alignment module in Fig. 1 to calculate the image-text matching score without passing through the (a) module and (b) module. By comparing the performance of the baseline model and IGCN, we demonstrate the necessity of fragment relationship mining.

Proposed IGCN has three layers of ordinary GCN and one layer of CGCN. CGCN use the module described in Sect. 3.1 to calculate fragment affinity. Ordinary GCN layer calculates fragment affinity based on single-modality information. The affinity between fragments in ordinary GCN is expressed as:

$$R(v_i, v_j) = norm(\varphi(v_i))(norm(\phi(v_j)))^T \tag{14}$$

where $\varphi(v_i) = v_i W_\varphi$ and $\phi(v_j) = v_j W_\phi, W_\varphi \in \mathbb{R}^{d*d}, W_\phi \in \mathbb{R}^{d*d}$ are the embedding of fragment feature v_i and v_j. We change the CGCN layer in model to ordinary GCN layer and retain the rest network structure of IGCN (marked as w/o interaction in Table 3). The experimental result strongly proves that the cross-modal information we used in fragment affinity calculating accurately predicts the relationship between fragments. Then, we study the effect of the number of ordinary GCN layers on the model performance, and mark the result of 1 layer of ordinary GCN as 1OGCN in the Table 3 (proposed model has 3 layers of ordinary GCN). Experimental results show that the model with more layers of ordinary GCN have better performance.

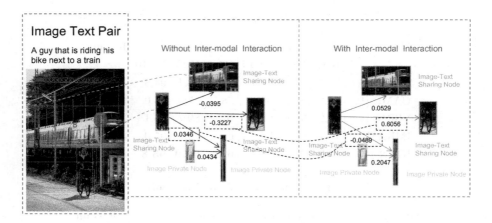

Fig. 5. The visualization of the graphs with or without inter-modal interaction. The edge weights of the two graphs are linked by dashed to show their difference. Compared with the model without interaction module, The model with interaction module has higher weights between image-text sharing nodes, and has lower weights between sharing node and private node, which is indicated by red and green lines respectively (Please zoom in for best view). (Color figure online)

4.4 Visualization

Taking the image modality as an example, we visualize the edge weights between fragments of a sample in the model with and without inter-modal interaction in Fig. 5. The model without interaction module is the 'w/o interaction' introduced in Sect. 4.3. Note that in models with and without interaction module, the range of the edge weight of graph is $[-1, 1]$. As shown in Fig. 5, the inter-modal interaction module can selectively promote the mining of semantic relations between image-text sharing nodes and inhibit the semantic connection between sharing node and private node.

5 Conclusion

We propose IGCN for inferring the semantic relationship between fragments based on modal interaction information. The model captures the semantic relationship between fragments in the image and text modalities, and performs image-text alignment on the fragment-level to complete the image-text matching task. Experimental results on MS COCO and Flickr30K dataset show that the performance of our model surpasses state-of-the-art methods. Our work shows the effectiveness and necessity of introducing the other modal information when exploring the semantic relationship between fragments within a modality.

References

1. Anderson, P., et al.: Bottom-up and top-down attention for image captioning and visual question answering. In: Proceedings of the IEEE Conference on Computer Vision and Pattern Recognition, pp. 6077–6086 (2018)
2. Cao, D., Yu, Z., Zhang, H., Fang, J., Nie, L., Tian, Q.: Video-based cross-modal recipe retrieval. In: Proceedings of the 27th ACM International Conference on Multimedia, pp. 1685–1693 (2019)
3. Chen, H., Ding, G., Liu, X., Lin, Z., Liu, J., Han, J.: IMRAM: iterative matching with recurrent attention memory for cross-modal image-text retrieval. In: Proceedings of the IEEE/CVF Conference on Computer Vision and Pattern Recognition, pp. 12655–12663 (2020)
4. Faghri, F., Fleet, D.J., Kiros, J.R., Fidler, S.: VSE++: improving visual-semantic embeddings with hard negatives. arXiv preprint arXiv:1707.05612 (2017)
5. Gu, J., Cai, J., Joty, S.R., Niu, L., Wang, G.: Look, imagine and match: improving textual-visual cross-modal retrieval with generative models. In: Proceedings of the IEEE Conference on Computer Vision and Pattern Recognition, pp. 7181–7189 (2018)
6. Huang, Y., Wu, Q., Song, C., Wang, L.: Learning semantic concepts and order for image and sentence matching. In: Proceedings of the IEEE Conference on Computer Vision and Pattern Recognition, pp. 6163–6171 (2018)
7. Karpathy, A., Fei-Fei, L.: Deep visual-semantic alignments for generating image descriptions. In: Proceedings of the IEEE Conference on Computer Vision and Pattern Recognition, pp. 3128–3137 (2015)
8. Lee, K.-H., Chen, X., Hua, G., Hu, H., He, X.: Stacked cross attention for image-text matching. In: Ferrari, V., Hebert, M., Sminchisescu, C., Weiss, Y. (eds.) ECCV 2018. LNCS, vol. 11208, pp. 212–228. Springer, Cham (2018). https://doi.org/10.1007/978-3-030-01225-0_13
9. Li, K., Zhang, Y., Li, K., Li, Y., Fu, Y.: Visual semantic reasoning for image-text matching. In: Proceedings of the IEEE International Conference on Computer Vision, pp. 4654–4662 (2019)
10. Li, X., Xu, C., Yang, G., Chen, Z., Dong, J.: W2vv++ fully deep learning for ad-hoc video search. In: Proceedings of the 27th ACM International Conference on Multimedia, pp. 1786–1794 (2019)
11. Nam, H., Ha, J.W., Kim, J.: Dual attention networks for multimodal reasoning and matching. In: Proceedings of the IEEE Conference on Computer Vision and Pattern Recognition, pp. 299–307 (2017)
12. Wang, Z., et al.: Camp: cross-modal adaptive message passing for text-image retrieval. In: Proceedings of the IEEE International Conference on Computer Vision, pp. 5764–5773 (2019)
13. Wu, Z., Pan, S., Chen, F., Long, G., Zhang, C., Philip, S.Y.: A comprehensive survey on graph neural networks. IEEE Trans. Neural Netw. Learn. Syst. **32**, 4–24 (2020)
14. Zou, F., Bai, X., Luan, C., Li, K., Wang, Y., Ling, H.: Semi-supervised cross-modal learning for cross modal retrieval and image annotation. World Wide Web **22**(2), 825–841 (2018). https://doi.org/10.1007/s11280-018-0581-2

Generalizing Message Passing Neural Networks to Heterophily Using Position Information

Wenzheng Zhang[1], Jie Liu[1(✉)], and Liting Liu[2]

[1] College of Artificial Intelligence, Nankai University, Tianjin, China
wzzhang@mail.nankai.edu.cn, jliu@nankai.edu.cn
[2] College of Software, Nankai University, Tianjin, China
liu_liting@mail.nankai.edu.cn

Abstract. Message Passing Neural Networks (MPNNs) is a promising architecture for machine learning on graphs, which iteratively propagates the information among nodes. The existing MPNNs methods are more suitable for homophily graphs in which the geometrically close nodes have similar features and class labels. However, in real-world applications, there exist graphs with heterophily and the performance of MPNNs may be limited when dealing with the heterophily graphs. We analyze the limitations of MPNNs when facing heterophily graphs and owe it to the indistinguishability of nodes during aggregating and combining. To this end, we propose a method under the MPNNs architecture called Position Enhanced Message Passing model (PEMP) that endows the node with position information to make the node distinguishable. Extensive experiments on nine real-world datasets show that our method achieves state-of-the-art performances in most heterophily graphs while preserving the performances of MPNNs on homophily graphs.

Keywords: Message Passing Neural Networks · Graph neural networks · Heterophily graphs · Position information

1 Introduction

Graph (sometimes called network) is a ubiquitous data structure that consists of nodes and edges, which can model objects and their relationships. The current paradigm of machine learning on the graph first encodes the node to a low-dimensional hidden space and then uses a loss function to optimize the entire model in an end-to-end manner. The loss is task-specific, such as semi-supervised node classification [8], graph classification [18], and link prediction [22].

Message Passing Neural Networks (MPNNs) approaches [4] have become the *de facto* standard for machine learning on graphs. Typically, in a layer of MPNNs, each node receives the hidden representation ("message") from its neighborhood. The "messages" of the neighborhood are aggregated into a neighbor-embedding

© Springer Nature Switzerland AG 2021
I. Farkaš et al. (Eds.): ICANN 2021, LNCS 12893, pp. 230–242, 2021.
https://doi.org/10.1007/978-3-030-86365-4_19

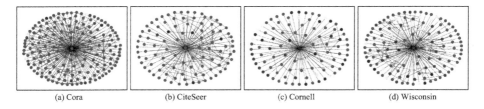

| (a) Cora | (b) CiteSeer | (c) Cornell | (d) Wisconsin |

Fig. 1. Visualizations of four real-world graphs. Different color indicates different class. We visualize the node with the maximum degree and its first-order neighborhood.

by the aggregator. Then, the combinator combines the ego- and the neighbor-embeddings into the representation of the next layer.

However, the existing MPNNs approaches are more suitable for graphs with homophily and they may not perform well on heterophily graphs. Homophily means that the geometrically close nodes, such as the first-order neighborhood, have similar node features and class labels. Figure 1 (a) and (b) show two typical homophily graphs. In this case, the aggregator does not need to distinguish different neighbor nodes, and the combinator does not need to distinguish the ego- and the neighbor-embeddings because all these nodes are similar. However, in practice, there exist graphs not meeting the homophily property, leading to graphs with heterophily: the geometrically close nodes have different classes (as visualized in Fig. 1 (c) and (d)) or dissimilar features. For example, in telecommunications networks, each node corresponds to a telecom user, and the edge denotes the telephone call between users. A fraudster is more likely to connect to normal users than to connect to other fraudsters. Thus, the graph centered on the fraudster is heterophily, as the node has a different label from its neighborhood. Moreover, in the Wikipedia page-page network, the linked web pages may have vastly different content, i.e., dissimilar node features. Most MPNNs approaches fail to generalize to the heterophily setting, and even simple models that completely ignore the graph structure (e.g., MLPs) can outperform many MPNNs methods [25].

The node position can be regarded as distinguishable information because different nodes have different positions. Therefore, the position information can help the aggregator and combinator distinguish different nodes, which is of vital importance in the heterophily graph. Nevertheless, there are two challenges for introducing the position information. Firstly, different from the Euclidean data like text and images with implicit position, the graph is typical non-Euclidean data, in which the node has no pre-defined position information. Secondly, both homophily graphs and heterophily graphs exist in the real world. Therefore, the model enhanced with position information is required to perform well not only on the heterophily graphs but also on the homophily graphs. Besides, the node identification can be deemed as distinguishable information [22], but it is too sparse and difficult to model, which is demonstrated by our experiment.

To tackle the aforementioned challenges, a graph neural networks model under the MPNNs architecture called Position Enhanced Message Passing model

(PEMP) is proposed in this paper. The implicit position in Euclidean data can be regarded as the relative position to some fixed points, and we call these points *anchors*. Motivated by this, we consider to select the nodes as *anchors* on a graph using some strategies. Furthermore, the position encoder is designed to obtain the position-aware node embeddings with respect to each *anchor*. In order to perform well on the homophily graphs, PEMP inherits the two fundamental operators (aggregator and combinator) of MPNNs with some differences. The position-aware node embeddings enable the aggregator and combinator of PEMP to distinguish different nodes, and the combinator further separates the ego- and neighbor-embeddings. The node representation of every intermediate PEMP layer is concatenated to generate the final node representation for the semi-supervised node classification task.

We conduct extensive experiments on nine real-world datasets covering graphs from high homophily to strong heterophily. The experimental results demonstrate that PEMP performs well on the heterophily graphs while being competitive in homophily graphs. In conclusion, the main contributions are as follows:

- We extend the research of MPNNs approaches on homophily graphs and reveal the limitation of existing operations of MPNNs, i.e., the aggregator and combinator when facing the heterophily graphs.
- We analyze the reasons that hinder the generalization of MPNNs to heterophily and propose the Position Enhanced Message Passing model. Our model endows distinguishability with nodes using position information.
- We empirically evaluate the proposed model on real-world graphs. The results show that our model performs well on the heterophily graphs while preserving the performance of MPNNs on homophily graphs.

2   Related Work

PEMP utilizes the position information to augment traditional GNNs to generalize MPNNs to heterophily. We review the above mentioned related work.

To generalize ConvNets to graphs, [2] introduce the spectral graph convolutional neural networks. ChebyNets [1] defines local graph convolutions using Chebyshev polynomials to approximate the computationally expensive eigendecomposition. Graph Convolution Network (GCN) [8] simplifies graph convolution via stacking layers of first-order local Chebyshev polynomial filters. GraphSAGE [5] scales to large graphs by spatial-based sampling and aggregation. Graph Attention Network (GAT) [17] adopts attention mechanisms to learn the relative weights between two connected nodes. Graph Isomorphism Network (GIN) [18] is a graph neural network model with expressive power equal to the WL graph isomorphism test. MPNNs [4] is a general framework of these GNNs.

The existing MPNNs approaches are more suitable for the homophily graphs than for the heterophily graphs. To tackle this limitation, Dual Self-Paced Graph Convolutional Network (DSP-GCN) [20] utilizes node- and edge-level self-paced learning to learn from the simple nodes/edges (homophily ones) to the complex nodes/edges (heterophily ones). Geometric Graph Convolutional Networks (Geom-GCN) [11] utilizes a geometric aggregation scheme that operates in both graph and latent continuous space, which endows the aggregation with distinguishability of neighbor nodes. [25] theoretically justifies a set of key designs in MPNNs and combine them into a model, H_2GCN, that adapts to homophily graphs. In this paper, we analyze the reasons that hinder the performance of MPNNs on heterophily graphs and propose PEMP that generalize MPNNs architecture to heterophily using the node position information.

Position-aware Graph Neural Networks (P-GNNs) [22] is the first work that considers the node position information. However, P-GNNs completely ignores the local structure information as the nodes in each layer do not receive information from their neighborhood. Therefore, the position information in P-GNNs can only be used to boost the performance of link prediction and community detection. Stochastic Message Passing (SMP) [24] augments the existing graph neural networks with stochastic node representations to capture the position information. Many heuristic methods are also helpful to capture position information, such as assigning a one-hot encoding to each node [5,8] as the position encoding used in [3] and using locally assigned node identifiers plus pre-trained transductive node features [23].

3   Problem

A graph can be represented as $\mathcal{G} = (\mathcal{V}, \mathcal{E})$ where $\mathcal{V} = \{v_i : i = 1, \cdots, |\mathcal{V}|\}$ is the node set and $\mathcal{E} = \mathcal{V} \times \mathcal{V}$ is the edge set. The graph can also be represented by its adjacency matrix $A \in \{0,1\}^{|\mathcal{V}| \times |\mathcal{V}|}$ (suppose the graph is undirected, unweighted), and its node feature matrix $\mathcal{X} \in \mathbb{R}^{|\mathcal{V}| \times F}$, where F is the feature dimension and the vector $\vec{x_v} \in \mathbb{R}^F$ corresponds to the initialized feature of node v. The class label of node v is y_v, and $\mathcal{Y}$ denotes the class label set of all nodes in graphs. The i-th order neighborhood of node v is denoted as $\mathcal{N}_i(v)$.

3.1   Indices of Heterophily

Definition 1. Edge-Label Index (ELI). *This index is the fraction of edges in a graph, of which the head node has a different class label from the tail node.*

$$ELI = \frac{1}{|\mathcal{E}|}|\{(u,v) : (u,v) \in \mathcal{E} \land y_u \neq y_v\}|.$$

Definition 2. Neighborhood-Label Index (NLI). *The neighborhood-label index is the average of normalized label diversities in the first-order neighborhood of every node. The NLI is calculated as:*

$$NLI = \frac{1}{|\mathcal{V}||\mathcal{Y}|} \sum \{L(\mathcal{N}_1(u)) : u \in \mathcal{V}\},$$

where $L(\cdot)$ is the function that returns the count of distinct class labels of the inputted nodes, $\sum$ denotes the summation operation of the set.

Algorithm 1: The architecture of PEMP

Input: (1) Graph $\mathcal{G}$; (2) *Anchors*, $\mathcal{A}$; (3) The message computation function, $\mathcal{F}_c^\ell(\cdot, \cdot)$; (4) The aggregator $\text{AGG}_\ell(\cdot)$ and combinator $\text{COMB}_\ell(\cdot, \cdot)$; (5) The reduce function $\text{REDUCE}_\ell(\cdot)$; (6) Total number of layers, L.

Output: The representation h_v for every node v

$h_v^0 \leftarrow \vec{x_v}, \forall v \in \mathcal{V}$

for $\ell \in [1, L]$; **do**

    for $v \in \mathcal{V}$; **do**

        for $i \in [1, 2, \cdots, |\mathcal{A}|]$; **do**

            | $M_v^\ell[i] = \mathcal{F}_c^\ell(v, a_i)^\top$

        end

        $z_v^\ell = \text{REDUCE}_\ell(M_v^\ell)$

        $\widetilde{h_v^\ell} = z_v^\ell \oplus h_v^{\ell-1}$

        $m_v^\ell = \text{AGG}_\ell(\{\widetilde{h_u^\ell} : u \in \mathcal{N}_1(v)\})$

        $h_v^\ell = \text{COMB}_\ell(m_v^\ell, \widetilde{h_v^\ell})$

    end

    $h_v^\ell = h_v^\ell / \|h_v^\ell\|_2, \forall v \in \mathcal{V}$

end

return $h_v = h_v^0 \oplus h_v^1 \oplus \cdots \oplus h_v^L, \forall v \in \mathcal{V}$

Definition 3. *Neighborhood-Feature Index (NFI).* *The neighborhood-feature index is the average of normalized distances from the neighbor nodes to their virtual centrical node. This index is calculated as:*

$$NFI = \frac{\sum\{1 - \cos(\mathcal{F}_m(\mathcal{N}_1(u)), \vec{x_v}) : u \in \mathcal{V}, v \in \mathcal{N}_1(u)\}}{2|\mathcal{E}|},$$

where $\mathcal{F}_m(\mathcal{N}_1(u)) = \frac{1}{|\mathcal{N}_1(u)|} \sum\{\vec{x_k} : k \in \mathcal{N}_1(u)\}$ *returns the feature of virtual centrical node by averaging the inputs.*

These indices range from 0 to 1. A value near 0 implies high homophily, while a value near 1 means high heterophily.

4   Approach

To generalize MPNNs to the heterophily graphs, Position Enhanced Message Passing model (PEMP) is proposed, and the architecture is shown in Algorithm 1. Concretely, each layer of PEMP consists of a position encoder and a representation updater. The position encoder calculates the node position embedding with respect to the *anchors* (some nodes selected by strategies). The aggregator and combinator in the representation updater are able to distinguish the inputs using the position embedding. After L stacking layers, the node representations are inputted into a classifier.

4.1   Anchor Selection

The Euclidean data has natural position information, like texts (1D sequence) and images (2D grid). The classic methods that process these data implicitly encode the position information. For instance, RNN [6] sequentially encodes the texts, and CNN [9] encodes the image patches in order. Transformer [16], an attention-only method, needs to add the "positional encodings" explicitly. However, the graph is typical non-Euclidean data, and the node has no natural position information.

The implicit position in Euclidean data can be regarded as the relative position given some fixed points, and we call these points *anchors*. For example, in the image data, the relative positions of all pixels are determined when the positions of any three non-collinear pixels are fixed. Inspired by this analysis, we consider to select some nodes as *anchors*. The node centrality can evaluate the representativeness of the node. Therefore, we select the *anchors* with high node centrality. The degree centrality, closeness centrality (Eq. 1) [14], and PageRank centrality (Eq. 2) [10] are three centrality metrics. The PageRank centrality is applied as the default metric.

$$C_c(v) = \frac{n-1}{|\mathcal{V}|-1} \frac{n-1}{\sum_{u=1}^{n-1} d_{sp}(v,u)},\tag{1}$$

$$C_p(v) = \alpha \sum_j A_{i,j} \frac{C_p(v)}{\sum_k A_{j,k}} + \frac{1-\alpha}{|\mathcal{V}|},\tag{2}$$

where n is the number of reachable nodes of v, and $d_{sp}(v,u)$ is the shortest path length between the node v and the node u. α is a hyperparameter. The set of the selected *anchors* is denoted as $\mathcal{A}$ and the i-th *anchor* is a_i. The pre-selected *anchors* are fixed during training and testing. After selecting the *anchors*, we compute the shortest path length between node v and each anchor a_i, and transform the distance to $s(v,a_i) = \frac{1}{d_{sp}(v,a_i)+1}$ to map it to $(0,1)$.

4.2   Position Encoder

The position encoder is designed to endow the aggregator and combinator distinguishability when facing different nodes. Node v communicates with each *anchor* to produce a positional message vector. The process can be denoted as the function $\mathcal{F}_c^\ell(v,a_i)$, and

$$\mathcal{F}_c^\ell(v,a_i) = h_v^{\ell-1} \oplus s(v,a_i)h_{a_i}^{\ell-1},\tag{3}$$

where $h_v^{\ell-1} \in \mathbb{R}^{d_{\ell-1}}$ is the output of the $(\ell-1)$-th PEMP layer (also the input of ℓ-th layer), and $d_{\ell-1}$ is the representation dimension of the $(\ell-1)$-th layer. The message vectors are stacked to a message matrix $M_v^\ell \in \mathbb{R}^{|\mathcal{A}| \times 2d_{\ell-1}}$:

$$M_v^\ell = \begin{pmatrix} \mathcal{F}_c^\ell(v,a_1)^\top \\ \mathcal{F}_c^\ell(v,a_2)^\top \\ \vdots \\ \mathcal{F}_c^\ell(v,a_{|\mathcal{A}|})^\top \end{pmatrix}.\tag{4}$$

Then, the message matrix M_v^ℓ is reduced into a position information vector that is denoted as $z_v^\ell \in \mathbb{R}^{|\mathcal{A}|}$ (each message vector is reduced into a scalar). This reduction process is designed as:

$$z_v^\ell = \sigma \left(M_v^\ell \cdot \frac{w_p^\ell}{||w_p^\ell||_2} \right), \tag{5}$$

where $w_p^\ell \in \mathbb{R}^{2d_{\ell-1}}$ is the trainable weight vector, and σ can be any non-linear activation function such as tanh, ReLU, and LeakyReLU. The i-th dimension of z_v^ℓ corresponds to the i-th *anchor* a_i. Therefore, z_v^ℓ captures the relative position information with respect to all the *anchors* in $\mathcal{A}$. The position information vector z_v^ℓ is further concatenated with $h_v^{\ell-1}$, resulting in a position-aware node representation vector $\widetilde{h_v^\ell} \in \mathbb{R}^{d_{\ell-1}+|\mathcal{A}|}$:

$$\widetilde{h_v^\ell} = z_v^\ell \oplus h_v^{\ell-1}. \tag{6}$$

4.3 Representation Updater

In order to preserve the performances of MPNNs on homophily graphs, the representation updater is designed to inherit the two fundamental operators (aggregator and combinator) of MPNNs.

The aggregator aggregates the position-aware representations of v's neighbor nodes into a neighbor-embedding that is denoted as $m_v^\ell \in \mathbb{R}^{d_\ell}$, in the ℓ-th layer. We adopt the mean aggregator parameterized by $W_a^\ell \in \mathbb{R}^{d_\ell \times (d_{\ell-1}+|\mathcal{A}|)}$:

$$m_v^\ell = \sigma \left(W_a^\ell \cdot \mathrm{MEAN}(\{\widetilde{h_v^\ell} : v \in \mathcal{N}_1(v)\}) \right), \tag{7}$$

The combinator further combines the ego- and the aggregated neighbor-embeddings into the representation of the next layer. The combinator has two forms, mix (e.g., summation) and concatenation. The preliminary experiments demonstrate the concatenation combinator performs better, which is consistent with [25]. We adopt the concatenation combinator parameterized by $W_c^\ell \in \mathbb{R}^{d_\ell \times 2d_\ell}$ in our implementation.

$$h_v^\ell = \sigma \left(W_c^\ell \cdot (\widetilde{h_v^\ell} \oplus m_v^\ell) \right), \quad h_v^\ell = \frac{h_v^\ell}{||h_v^\ell||_2}, \tag{8}$$

Inspired by the JK-Net architecture [19], the outputs of all the intermediate layers and the input features are concatenated to generate the final representation $h_v \in \mathbb{R}^{F+d_1+\cdots+d_L}$ where L is the number of layers:

$$h_v = \vec{x_v} \oplus h_v^1 \oplus \cdots \oplus h_v^L. \tag{9}$$

Finally, h_v is inputted into a linear classifier. For semi-supervised multi-class node classification, we evaluate the cross-entropy loss over the training set.

4.4   Complexity Analysis

The computation of the shortest path length in the graph can be finished in a pre-processing step. Here we discuss the complexity of neural network computation. In one PEMP layer, every node communicates with $|\mathcal{A}|$ *anchors*. Therefore, the computational complexity of position encoder is $\mathcal{O}(|\mathcal{V}||\mathcal{A}|)$. Besides, the representation updater has the computational complexity $\mathcal{O}(|\mathcal{V}| + |\mathcal{E}|)$. Thus, the computational complexity of PEMP is $\mathcal{O}(|\mathcal{V}||\mathcal{A}| + |\mathcal{V}| + |\mathcal{E}|)$. PEMP is implemented by the sparse matrix operations, reducing the storage complexity to linear of the number of nodes and edges.

Table 1. The grid search space for the hyperparameters.

Hyperparameter	Range
Learning rate	1e−1, 5e−2, 1e−2, 5e−3, 1e−3, 1e−4
Hidden dimension	8, 16, 32, 64, 128
L2 regularization	1e−2, 1e−3, 1e−4, 1e−5
Head num (for GAT)	2, 4, 8
Layer num	1, 2, 3
Dropout ratio	0, 0.1, 0.3, 0.5
Activation function	Tanh, ReLU, LeakyReLU, ELU

5   Experiments

5.1   Datasets

Nine real-world graph datasets are utilized to validate the proposed PEMP. The characteristics of these datasets are summarized in the top half of Table 2. Cora, CiteSeer, and PubMed are standard homophily citation network benchmark datasets [13]. The rest six datasets are heterophily graphs. Texas, Wisconsin, and Cornell are three subgraphs of the CMU WebKB. Actor [15] is the actor-only subgraph of the film-director-actor-writer network in Wikipedia. Squirrel and Chameleon [12] are page-page networks on specific topics in Wikipedia. The detailed descriptions can be referred to in [11].

5.2   Compared Methods

We compare the PEMP with a number of methods. GAT [17], GCN [8], and GraphSAGE [5] are three MPNNs methods. We further augment the node with the one-hot identifier and denote the MPNNs methods as GCN_{onehot}, GAT_{onehot}, and $\text{GraphSAGE}_{onehot}$. P-GNNs [22] is the position-aware graph neural networks method. PEMP is further compared with the recent proposed approaches for heterophily graphs. These approaches are H_2GCN [25] and Geom-GCN [11]. H_2GCN is the state-of-the-art method.

5.3   Experimental Setup

For the three citation networks, we use the public splits as in [21]: 20 labeled examples per class as the training set, 500 examples as the validation set, and 1,000 examples as the test set. For the rest six datasets, we use the public ten random splits (48%/32%/20% of nodes per class for training/validation/test) as in [11]. We use the same training and hyperparameter-tuning procedures for PEMP and compared methods, and report the mean accuracy and the standard deviation. The training is early stopped if the validation loss does not decrease for continuing 50 epochs, with a maximum of 2,000 epochs. Adam [7] is adopted to train all the methods.

The grid search space is shown in Table 1. The hyperparameter α in Eq. 2 is set as the default value 0.85. The number of *anchors* is set as $\log_2^2 |\mathcal{V}|$, which is sublinear of node number $|\mathcal{V}|$ and consistent with P-GNNs.

5.4   Experimental Results

Table 2 shows the node classification results, from which we can analyze and draw the conclusions as follows.

Firstly, PEMP achieves the best performances on most heterophily datasets (5/6) while preserves the performances of MPNNs on the homophily graphs, which validate the effectiveness of PEMP empirically. The compared results between PEMP and MPNNs methods demonstrate that the effectiveness of position information introduced by PEMP. Secondly, the position-aware graph neural networks method, P-GNNs, also performs well relatively on heterophily graphs, which demonstrates that the node position information is helpful on heterophily graphs. At the same time, MPNNs with one-hot feature augmentation reach slightly better results than the vanilla MPNNs, which also validates the effectiveness of distinguishable information in heterophily graph learning. But the distinguishable information in one-hot features is too sparse and difficult to learn. Thirdly, the three proposed indices, ELI, NLI, NFI, indicate the difficulty of datasets. The three citation networks are relatively straightforward. Almost all the methods reach good performances on these datasets with small training sets (20 examples per class). While the rest six datasets are difficult (Actor, Squirrel, Chameleon are the most difficult), most MPNNs methods are incapable of good classification results. In these six heterophily datasets, PEMP achieves good performances. Geom-GCN and P-GNNs are two exceptional cases in that they perform well on heterophily graphs but not that good on homophily. The reason for P-GNNs is that it completely ignores the local structure information. The reason for Geom-GCN may be that the training set is too small for it to model the graph (we use the public split that selects 20 labeled examples per class as training set, rather than 60% nodes for training in the paper of Geom-GCN). Finally, among the MPNNs methods, the performances of GraphSAGE on heterophily graphs are much better than those of other MPNNs methods because the combinator in GraphSAGE is the concatenation combinator, rather than the mix combinator used in other MPNNs.

Table 2. Overall performances. The best performance per benchmark is highlighted in gray, and the second-best is underlined.

	Cora	Citeseer	Pubmed	Cornell	Texas	Wisconsin	Actor	Squirrel	Chameleon
# Nodes $|\mathcal{V}|$	2,708	3,327	19,717	183	183	251	7,600	5,201	2,277
# Edges $|\mathcal{E}|$	5,429	4,732	44,338	295	309	499	33,544	217,073	36,101
# Classes $|\mathcal{Y}|$	7	6	3	5	5	5	5	5	5
ELI	0.1900	0.2645	0.1976	0.6964	0.8881	0.7940	0.7805	0.7761	0.7688
NLI	0.2018	0.2169	0.4265	0.3519	0.3650	0.3769	0.5616	0.8024	0.7148
NFI	0.4250	0.3440	0.3911	0.2761	0.2580	0.2760	0.4912	0.9837	0.7969
PEMP	79.30±1.84	67.09±0.77	75.00±0.76	82.43±7.67	84.05±5.33	86.07±3.21	35.91±0.95	36.81±1.78	51.27±2.35
H$_2$GCN	80.07±0.73	69.93±1.33	77.77±0.31	79.46±7.56	81.62±7.73	85.48±3.34	35.48±1.13	34.12±1.92	55.61±1.98
Geom-GCN	65.95±3.64	54.34±8.64	67.30±3.43	58.65±3.61	66.22±3.43	64.12±4.14	31.35±1.14	36.80±0.97	55.79±2.88
P-GNNs	58.53±3.02	47.45±2.97	61.29±5.94	70.81±6.92	70.27±10.11	73.33±5.35	35.45±0.86	36.21±1.87	52.19±2.15
GraphSAGE	77.97±2.31	67.39±1.73	75.94±1.29	78.11±6.99	78.38±3.63	79.41±5.96	33.84±1.30	35.52±1.29	50.72±2.00
GraphSAGE$_{onehot}$	78.54±1.25	67.18±1.33	75.81±2.01	78.92±5.24	77.30±6.07	79.61±6.21	34.32±1.27	36.71±1.11	50.92±2.02
GCN	80.10±0.99	67.71±1.51	77.78±2.07	58.15±5.93	60.00±6.02	53.14±6.29	29.59±1.20	25.38±0.83	34.65±2.36
GCN$_{onehot}$	80.07±1.68	66.90±2.34	76.58±2.60	58.38±6.96	60.81±6.86	53.53±2.78	30.03±0.90	26.47±1.65	33.62±2.36
GAT	80.40±1.46	68.01±1.56	78.11±1.81	58.65±3.43	59.46±4.36	50.39±5.48	28.55±0.87	29.38±0.56	43.29±2.71
GAT$_{onehot}$	79.56±1.51	68.04±2.08	77.03±2.50	59.19±3.30	59.46±4.52	50.00±3.85	28.92±1.06	29.51±1.02	43.65±2.48

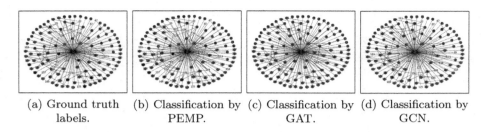

(a) Ground truth   (b) Classification by   (c) Classification by   (d) Classification by
     labels.   PEMP.   GAT.   GCN.

Fig. 2. Visualization of classification of PEMP, GCN, and GAT on Wisconsin dataset. Different color indicates a different node class label. (Color figure online)

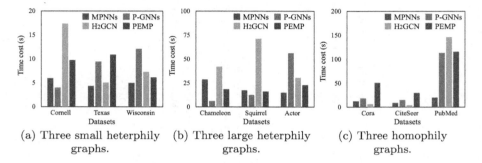

(a) Three small heterphily   (b) Three large heterphily   (c) Three homophily
         graphs.   graphs.   graphs.

Fig. 3. Time cost comparison of different methods on nine datasets. Due to space limitation, the time cost of MPNNs is the average of GraphSAGE's, GCN's, and GAT's. The cost of Geom-GCN is not reported, as that it has a large number of operations on the CPU, which is vastly time-consuming.

5.5   Visualization

In order to deeply analyze the classification performances of PEMP on heterophily graphs and intuitively show the effectiveness of PEMP, we visualize the classification results of PEMP, GCN, and GAT on the Wisconsin dataset. The accuracy of PEMP, GCN, and GAT on this subgraph is 93.50%, 65.47%, and 59.55%, respectively. The NLI and NFI of the visualized subgraph are 1 and 0.4590, respectively, which indicates this subgraph has strong heterophily. Figure 2 shows the visualization results. It can be observed that the two MPNNs methods (GAT and GCN) fail to classify the nodes correctly, especially GAT, while PEMP can classify most nodes. Moreover, the ego node is misclassified as the majority label (the green label) in Fig. 2 (c) and (d), which indicates that GCN and GAT tend to classify the ego node as the most frequent class label in the neighborhood. The reason is that these MPNNs methods are suitable for the homophily graphs in which nodes geometrically close have similar features and class labels.

5.6   Time Cost Analysis

On each dataset, the methods are run with corresponding optimal hyperparameters on ten different splits until convergence (with early stop). The time cost analysis results are summarized in Fig. 3.

Firstly, overall, the proposed PEMP has a similar time cost as the P-GNNs and the H2GCN. Secondly, from Fig. 3 (a) and (b), the time cost of PEMP on graphs with heterophily is similar to that of MPNNs. Although the MPNNs approaches have lower computational complexity than PEMP, they converge slower on these heterophily graphs as these graphs do not meet the homophily property. In contrast, PEMP converges fast in these datasets. At the same time, on the three large and complicated heterophily graphs, PEMP converges faster than H2GCN. Finally, from Fig. 3 (c), the time cost of PEMP and P-GNNs on graphs with homophily is relatively high, which indicates the position information hinders the convergence on homophily graphs to a certain extent. In comparison, MPNNs methods are good at handling homophily graphs. Besides, H2GCN is a method that combines three designs of MPNNs. Therefore its time cost on homophily graphs is close to that of MPNNs. Nevertheless, it can be observed that H2GCN converges slowly in PubMed with the most nodes.

6   Conclusion

In this paper, we extended the research of MPNNs methods on homophily graphs. Based on the analysis, PEMP was proposed to deal with heterophily graphs using the position information, which first encodes the position of the node to make the node distinguishable. To preserve the performances on homophily graphs, PEMP inherits the aggregator and combinator of MPNNs with some differences. Extensive experimental results compared with several methods on real-world datasets demonstrated that PEMP is effective when handling heterophily settings while preserving the ability on homophily graphs.

Acknowledgement. This research is supported by the National Natural Science Foundation of China under the grant No. 61976119 and the Natural Science Foundation of Tianjin under the grant No. 18ZXZNGX00310.

References

1. Defferrard, M., Bresson, X., Vandergheynst, P.: Convolutional neural networks on graphs with fast localized spectral filtering. In: Advances in NIPS (2016)
2. Estrach, J.B., Zaremba, W., Szlam, A., LeCun, Y.: Spectral networks and deep locally connected networks on graphs. In: ICLR (2014)
3. Gehring, J., Auli, M., Grangier, D., Yarats, D., Dauphin, Y.N.: Convolutional sequence to sequence learning. In: Proceedings of ICML (2017)
4. Gilmer, J., Schoenholz, S.S., Riley, P.F., Vinyals, O., Dahl, G.E.: Neural message passing for quantum chemistry. In: Proceedings of ICML (2017)

5. Hamilton, W.L., Ying, Z., Leskovec, J.: Inductive representation learning on large graphs. In: Advances in NIPS (2017)
6. Hochreiter, S., Schmidhuber, J.: Long short-term memory. Neural Comput. **9**(8), 1735–1780 (1997)
7. Kingma, D.P., Ba, J.: Adam: a method for stochastic optimization. In: ICLR (2015)
8. Kipf, T.N., Welling, M.: Semi-supervised classification with graph convolutional networks. In: ICLR (2017)
9. LeCun, Y., Bottou, L., Bengio, Y., Haffner, P.: Gradient-based learning applied to document recognition. Proc. IEEE **86**(11), 2278–2324 (1998)
10. Page, L., Brin, S., Motwani, R., Winograd, T.: The PageRank citation ranking: bringing order to the web. Technical report, Stanford InfoLab (1999)
11. Pei, H., Wei, B., Chang, K.C., Lei, Y., Yang, B.: Geom-GCN: geometric graph convolutional networks. In: ICLR (2020)
12. Rozemberczki, B., Allen, C., Sarkar, R.: Multi-scale attributed node embedding. CoRR abs/1909.13021 (2019)
13. Sen, P., Namata, G., Bilgic, M., Getoor, L., Gallagher, B., Eliassi-Rad, T.: Collective classification in network data. AI Mag. **29**(3), 93–106 (2008)
14. Stephenson, K., Zelen, M.: Rethinking centrality: methods and examples. Soc. Netw. **11**(1), 1–37 (1989)
15. Tang, J., Sun, J., Wang, C., Yang, Z.: Social influence analysis in large-scale networks. In: Proceedings of KDD (2009)
16. Vaswani, A., et al.: Attention is all you need. In: Advances in NIPS (2017)
17. Velickovic, P., Cucurull, G., Casanova, A., Romero, A., Liò, P., Bengio, Y.: Graph attention networks. In: ICLR (2018)
18. Xu, K., Hu, W., Leskovec, J., Jegelka, S.: How powerful are graph neural networks? In: ICLR (2019)
19. Xu, K., Li, C., Tian, Y., Sonobe, T., Kawarabayashi, K., Jegelka, S.: Representation learning on graphs with jumping knowledge networks. In: ICML (2018)
20. Yang, L., Chen, Z., Gu, J., Guo, Y.: Dual self-paced graph convolutional network: towards reducing attribute distortions induced by topology. In: Proceedings of IJCAI (2019)
21. Yang, Z., Cohen, W.W., Salakhutdinov, R.: Revisiting semi-supervised learning with graph embeddings. In: Proceedings of ICML (2016)
22. You, J., Ying, R., Leskovec, J.: Position-aware graph neural networks. In: Proceedings of ICML (2019)
23. Zhang, M., Chen, Y.: Link prediction based on graph neural networks. In: Advances in NeurIPS (2018)
24. Zhang, Z., Niu, C., Cui, P., Zhang, B., Cui, W., Zhu, W.: A simple and general graph neural network with stochastic message passing. CoRR abs/2009.02562 (2020)
25. Zhu, J., Yan, Y., Zhao, L., Heimann, M., Akoglu, L., Koutra, D.: Beyond homophily in graph neural networks: current limitations and effective designs. In: Advances in NeurIPS (2020)

Local and Non-local Context Graph Convolutional Networks for Skeleton-Based Action Recognition

Zikai Gao⬛, Yang Zhao, Zhe Han, Kang Wang, and Yong Dou⁽⊠⁾

National University of Defense Technology, Changsha 410073, Hunan, China
{gaozk18,zhaoyang10,hanzhe18,wangkang,yongdou}@nudt.edu.cn

Abstract. Graph convolutional networks (GCNs) for skeleton-based action recognition have achieved considerable progress recently. However, there are still two unresolved shortages. One is that the input data lacks high-level motion information of discriminant features. The other is that the access to the long-range action features is limited by the local sampling scale. In this work, we propose a new model called local and non-local context graph convolutional networks (LnLC-GCN). The first innovation is a motion enhanced graph containing high-level motion information which is served as the multi-stream input. Secondly, to overcome the limitations of local receptive field, we present a local and non-local context module based on the global context mechanism. Moreover, we use two optimization strategies of front-end fusion and non-local context feedback to further improve the accuracy of LnLC-GCN. For validation of the performance, numerous experiments were deployed on three public datasets, NTU-RGB+D 60 & 120 and Kinetics-Skeleton, strongly demonstrating that our approach achieves state-of-the-art.

Keywords: Skeleton-based action recognition · Graph convolutional networks · Motion enhanced graph · Local context · Non-local context

1 Introduction

As one of the basic tasks of computer vision, action recognition has been widely researched in human-computer interaction, motion analysis and other fields [6, 14,19]. The RGB video is a mainstream data modality for action recognition and methods focus on pixels and optical flow in video sequences [22]. Differently, human skeleton data as a data modality that has attracted much attention recently has fewer vertices and no background noise, which makes the skeleton-based methods more robust with lower computational cost [1].

With the development of deep learning, various convolutional neural networks (CNNs) [2,8] and recurrent neural networks (RNNs) [5,9,10] have been applied to skeleton-based action recognition, but their performance is limited due to the lack of the ability to extract spatial features of human skeleton data. The human skeleton can be modeled as an initial spatiotemporal graph (shown

© Springer Nature Switzerland AG 2021
I. Farkaš et al. (Eds.): ICANN 2021, LNCS 12893, pp. 243–254, 2021.
https://doi.org/10.1007/978-3-030-86365-4_20

in Fig. 1 (a)) by abstracting joints as vertices, natural connections between joints in a frame as spatial edges, and connections between the same nodes between adjacent frames as temporal edges. Graph convolutional networks (GCNs) are generalized from CNNs and can implement spatiotemporal convolutions on the adjacency matrices of graphs, which have made great progress in the task of action recognition. However, there are two shortcomings in the previous approaches [4,12,16,18,20,21]. One is that the discriminant information contained in the initial graph is insufficient, and the other is that the spatiotemporal receptive field of GCNs is constrained by the sampling area.

In this paper, we design the motion enhanced graph to extend the discriminative features contained in graphs by embedding high-level information, such as position and motion vectors of joints and bones. The local and non-local context graph convolutional networks (LnLC-GCN) is presented for skeleton-based action recognition. Before skeleton sequences are input into the networks, we first segment them into clips. To obtain the features of each clip, we use the spatiotemporal local context (STLC) module, and calculate the global response of all clips with the non-local context (nLC) module. In addition, we adopt the front-end fusion strategy to input the fusion information of joints and bones into two backbone networks respectively. The non-local context feedback strategy that transmits context information between two backbone networks and epochs, is used to dynamically adjust the weight of non-local context modules in the training process, so that the weight can be repeatedly concentrated on the discriminant vertices in the graphs.

By doing these, we conclude that our approach has the following contributions:

- A novel motion enhanced graph embedding high-level discriminative information is proposed to extend the spatiotemporal initial graph.
- A new model named local and non-local context graph convolutional networks (LnLC-GCN) with global receptive field is proposed and can extract the discriminative features of vertices in the sequence.
- Two optimization strategies, named front-end fusion and non-local context feedback, are proposed to further improve the feature extraction ability of the model.
- LnLC-GCN achieves state-of-the-art performance according to extensive experiments on the three largest benchmark datasets for skeleton-based action recognition

2   Related Work

2.1   Skeleton Based Action Recognition

Recently, a number of deep learning methods have been proposed to use skeleton data for action recognition, and these methods can be divided into three categories according to the distinct representation of skeleton data, namely, CNN-based, RNN-based and GCN-based methods. CNNs have the recognized ability to extract the features of the image, so the CNN-based methods [2,8] attempt to construct skeletons as pseudo images and the training is greatly simplified by using numerous pre-training models suitable for image processing. With the advantage of processing sequences, RNN-based methods [5,10] construct the skeleton data into sequences of joint-coordinate vectors generally. However, CNN-based and RNN-based methods can not completely retain the spatial relationship of skeletons, which greatly limit their performance and generalization ability. Inspired by the graph neural networks (GNNs), Yan et al. [20] modeled the skeleton sequence as a spatiotemporal graph which can retain the complete information of skeletons, and constructed ST-GCN using spatial and temporal GCNs to extract the spatiotemporal features. However, ST-GCN only studies the basic coordinates and connections in skeleton data, and the receptive field is constrained by the scale of graph convolution kernels which is unable to model long-range dependence. Therefore, recent GCN-based methods [4,12,16–18,21] are presented for above problems to improve the performance of action recognition.

2.2 Embedding High-Level Information in Graphs

There is growing concern that it is not sufficient to use discriminative information contained in the initial graph for action recognition, so several methods enhance the initial graph by embedding high-level information. Shi et al. [16] embedded high-level information in the initial image, including position vectors of bones and motion vectors of joints and bones between adjacent time frames. Song et al. [18] extended the position coordinates relative to the central joint, and calculated the motion velocities of adjacent frames and the information of bones as the input of multi-stream model. By studying the motion of the rigid body in space, we find that the previous methods are inappropriate for the representation of bones. Therefore, we propose a novel motion enhanced graph including both static and dynamic information of the skeleton.

2.3 Modeling Long-Range Dependence

In this task, long-range dependence refers to the possible association between vertices of long distance in space or time. These relationships may have discriminative features for action recognition. Shi et al. [17] decomposed the self-attention mechanism into spatial attention and temporal attention, and completely used the attention features for action recognition. Cheng et al. [4] adopted non-local shift spatial graph convolution in spatial feature extraction. However, it should be noted that the scale of parameters of the models with global receptive field is very sensitive to the scale of input data, so such models face the problem of higher training complexity when dealing with longer action sequences. Due to the continuity of actions, we segment the action sequence into clips with strong correlation. Spatiotemporal local context information is extracted from each clip, and non-local context is processed on all clips to obtain long-range features.

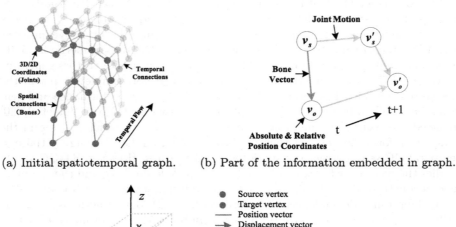

(a) Initial spatiotemporal graph.   (b) Part of the information embedded in graph.

(c) Calculation model of bones motion information.

Fig. 1. Illustration of initial spatiotemporal graph and construction of motion enhanced graph by embedding four kinds of data (joint positions, joint motions, bone positions, bone motions).

3 Method

3.1 Overview

The original skeleton data obtained by motion-capture devices or pose estimation algorithms is usually the sequences of frames, in which each frame includes the spatial coordinates of a group of joints. Skeleton based action recognition is defined as inputting the skeleton sequences into the feature extraction networks to calculate the feature maps, which are classified by the classifier into corresponding action category labels as output. In LnLC-GCN, the original skeleton data is preprocessed to form the motion enhanced graph as input. We use the LnLC modules to construct feature extraction networks, and apply two optimization strategies to enhance the feature extraction ability of networks. The overall architecture of LnLC-GCN is illustrated in Fig. 3. As following, we will introduce the components in LnLC-GCN detailly.

3.2   Motion Enhanced Graph

The spatiotemporal initial graph [20] abstracted from the skeleton sequences only retains the basic spatiotemporal information. For GCN-based methods, constructing graphs with more action related information can improve the performance of the model. Therefore, we construct a graph with more motion information called motion enhanced graph.

Firstly, in basic 3D human skeleton data, the initial information only contains the 3D coordinates of each joint. The joints correspond to the vertices in the graph, and the spatial 3D coordinates of the vertex v_i in frame t can be expressed as $v_{i,t} = (x_{i,t}, y_{i,t}, z_{i,t})$. We extend the relative position coordinates of vertex v_i which is relative to the source vertex v_s, as in $\hat{v}_{i,t} = v_{i,t} - v_{s,t}$, where the source vertex v_s is the adjacent vertex of v_i closer to the central vertex. The absolute and relative coordinates of each vertex are combined into a six-dimensional position coordinates to form a set of positions for all vertices, namely $V_p = [v_{i,t}, \hat{v}_{i,t}]$. We define the motion of the joint as the coordinate difference of the same vertex between the adjacent frames, as shown in Fig. 1 (b). Then the absolute motion vectors and relative motion vectors of joints are defined as $v_{m,i,t} = v_{i,t+1} - v_{i,t}$ and $\hat{v}_{m,i,t} = \hat{v}_{i,t+1} - \hat{v}_{i,t}$. The two sets are combined to form the set of motion vectors for the joints, called $V_m = [v_{m,i,t}, \hat{v}_{m,i,t}]$.

Secondly, we define the natural connection of vertices in human body as bones, and use the coordinates of source vertex $v_{s,t}$ to represent the position of bones and the vector $e_{s,t}$ from source vertex v_s to target vertex v_o to represent the length and direction of bones. The position set of all bones is marked as $E_p = [v_{s,t}, e_{s,t}]$, where the vector $e_{s,t} = v_{o,t} - v_{s,t}$.

Since human bones do not deform during actions, we approximate human bones as rigid bodies to express the motion of bones and it can be divided into two parts as shown in Fig. 1 (c). The first part of the motion is the displacement vector $e_{m,s,t} = v_{s,t+1} - v_{s,t}$ of the source vertex of the bone between the adjacent frames, which represents the distance and direction of the motion of bones in space. The second part is the rotation of the bone in space. Specifically, it refers to the variations $a_{m,s,t}$ in adjacent frames of the angle list $a_{s,t} = [\theta, \phi, \gamma]$ of the bone. The angles of the bone and their variations can be calculated as $a_{s,t} = arccos[\frac{\bar{l}(x)}{\bar{l}(x,y)}, \frac{\bar{l}(y)}{\bar{l}(y,z)}, \frac{\bar{l}(z)}{\bar{l}(x,z)}]$ and $a_{m,s,t} = a_{s,t+1} - a_{s,t}$, where $\bar{l}(x)$ represents the projection length of the bone vector on the x axis and $\bar{l}(x,y)$ represents the projection length onto the x-y plane.

3.3   Local and Non-local Context Module

The local and non-local context (LnLC) module includes three parts: basic spatiotemporal graph convolutional module, local context module and non-local context module. Before feature extraction, we segment the input skeleton sequence into clips with N frames. In each clip, according to [20], we use the spatio-temporal graph convolutional module to extract the spatio-temporal features.

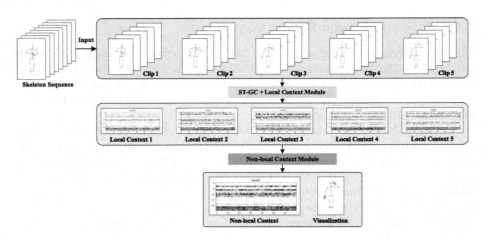

Fig. 2. Illustration of local and non-local context module.

Considering the spatial dimension, the graph convolutional operation on the vertex v_i is equation

$$f_{out}(v_i) = \sum_{v_j \in \mathcal{B}_i} f_{in}(v_j) \cdot w(v_i, v_j) \tag{1}$$

where f represents the feature map, v represents the vertex and $\mathcal{B}_i$ marks the sampling area of v_i, which is defined as the 1-neighborhood adjacent vertices v_j of v_i. w is the weight between the vertices that are recorded in the adjacency matrix. According to the experience of convolutional neural networks, the kernel size is set to 3. For the temporal dimension, since the neighbors of each vertex is fixed to 2 (the corresponding vertex in the two adjacent frames), a 3×1 convolution is performed on the calculated output feature map $\mathbf{f}_{out}$. Batch normalization layers and ReLU layers are inserted after the spatial and temporal convolutional blocks. After sequential splicing of these components, residual branches are added to make up the spatiotemporal graph convolutional (ST-GC) module.

Cao et al. [3] proposed a lightweight global context network (GCNet) based on the global context modeling framework. It establishes global attention pooling for context modeling and uses bottleneck transformation to capture channel-wise dependence. Finally, GCNet broadcasts element-wise addition for feature fusion. In this paper, we use the ST-GC module to extract the spatiotemporal feature map on the clips, and then use the local context module to extract the local context features in each clip. For the vertex v_i, the local context features can be calculated by equation

$$f_{out}(v_i) = f_{in}(v_i) + W_{v2} ReLU \left(LN \left(W_{v1} \sum_{j=1}^{N_p} \frac{e^{W_k f_{in}(v_j)}}{\sum_m^{N_p} e^{W_k f_{in}(v_m)}} f_{in}(v_j) \right) \right) \tag{2}$$

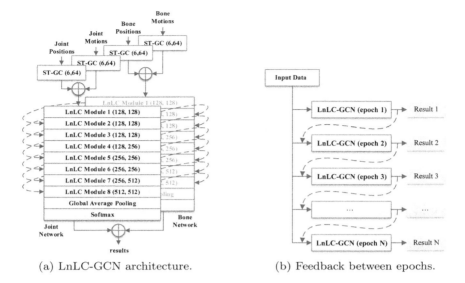

(a) LnLC-GCN architecture.   (b) Feedback between epochs.

Fig. 3. Illustration of the overall architecture of the LnLC-GCN. The feedback flows are marked with dotted lines, in blue for those between layers and in red for those between epochs. (Color figure online)

where $\alpha_j = \frac{e^{W_k f_{in}(v_j)}}{\sum_m^{N_p} e^{W_k f_{in}(v_m)}}$ is the weight used for global attention pooling. 1×1 convolution W_k and SoftMax function are used to obtain attention features, and global context features are obtained after attention pooling. N_p represents the total number of vertices of the current clip. $\delta(\cdot) = W_{v2} ReLU(LN(W_{v1}(\cdot)))$ is the bottleneck transform, which is designed for channel-wise dependencies. The LN represents layer normalization which reduces the optimization difficulty and improves generalization through regularization, W_{v1} and W_{v2} are 1×1 convolutions for transform. $f_{in}(v_i)$ represents residual branch to prevent the networks degradation. After local context features are extracted, their local response values are normalized and filtered. The response values of all vertices within the frame in the clip are summed and sorted. Frames in the top 50% of the response value ranking are treated as key frames containing discriminant information from the current clip. Non-local context feature extraction is executed on key vertices in all clips, which make the model have global receptive field. As shown in Fig. 2.

3.4 Optimization Strategies

Some of the previous methods [12,16] adopt multi-stream network architecture and back-end fusion strategy to get the final results. It should be pointed out that computing networks separately require a large amount of computing resources, and there is no information exchange between different backbone networks. Therefore, we design the front-end fusion strategy when we use four kinds of data (joint positions, joint motions, bone positions, bone motions) provided by the motion enhanced graph as input. Four branches are input respectively and the features divided into joint features and bone features are combined at the first layer and input into two backbone networks, namely joint networks and bone networks. In order to realize the information exchange between two backbone networks, a non-local context feedback strategy is designed, which transfers the non-local context features as hidden information between the backbone networks and attaches them into the next layer. In addition, this strategy includes feeding back the non-local context features of the previous epoch to the next epoch in training as shown in Fig. 3 (b). This feedback strategy dynamically adjusts the current state by exchanging the context features so that the attention can be repeatedly focused on several discriminative vertices in the sequences.

4   Experiment

4.1   Dataset

NTU-RGB+D 60 & 120. This NTU-RGB+D 60 [15] consists of 56,880 skeleton sequences covering 60 action classes on 40 different subjects which is collected by three Kinect cameras for 3D action recognition. As the extension of NTU-RGB+D 60 [15], the NTU-RGB+D [11] is the largest one used for 3D action recognition. It contains 114,480 skeleton sequences and 120 action classes covering 106 different subjects. Each skeleton contains 25 joints and each sequence contains up to 2 actors in both datasets. Following the evaluation protocols in the literatures [11,15], we execute cross-view (xview) and cross-subject (xsub) evaluations on the NTU-RGB+D 60 dataset and cross-subject (xsub) and cross-setup (xset) evaluations on the NTU-RGB+D 120 dataset and report the top-1 accuracy in percentages on each of the four benchmarks.

Kinetics-Skeleton. Kinetics-Skeleton [20] is a large-scale dataset for skeleton-based action recognition. The original Kinetics [7] dataset contains over 300,000 video sequences in 400 categories which are collected from YouTube. It should be noted that the original Kinetics [7] does not contain joints information, so the algorithms for human pose estimation are used in literature [20] to estimate the 2D coordinates and confidence of 18 joints per person in each frame. Each sequence has 300 frames and retains up to 2 subjects. The dataset is divided into a training set (240,000 sequences) and a test set (20,000 sequences). We report the accuracy of top-1 on the dataset and the results are expressed as percentages.

4.2   Implementation Details

In terms of data processing, we follow the design of action enhanced graph to preprocess the 3D skeleton data in NTU-RGB+D 60 & 120 and the 2D skeleton data in Kinetics-Skeleton. For the missing frames in the datasets, the average adjacent frames can be interpolated to ensure the smoothness of the action.

Table 1. The results of the ablation studies.

(a) Motion enhanced graph

Methods	Paras.	xview	xsub
ST-GCN-IG	0.48M	88.0	81.2
ST-GCN-MG	0.50M	89.3	83.7
ST-GCN-VG	0.55M	88.8	84.1
ST-GCN-MEG	0.71M	**91.8**	**88.3**

(b) Local and non-local context module

Methods	Paras.	xview	xsub
LnLC (N = 1)	2.13M	87.2	82.6
LnLC (N = 3)	1.90M	88.7	82.9
LnLC (N = 5)	1.84M	**89.3**	**84.1**
LnLC (N = 10)	**1.78M**	88.9	83.2
LnLC (N = 20)	1.79M	85.0	79.5
LnLC (N = 30)	1.91M	83.1	78.2

(c) Front-end fusion module

Methods	paras.	xview	xsub
LnLC-GCN-BF	3.92M	91.8	86.2
LnLC-GCN-FF	**2.44M**	**93.5**	**90.7**

(d) Non-local context feedback module

Methods	Paras.	xview	xsub
LnLC-GCN-NoF	2.43M	92.6	89.3
LnLC-GCN-BNF	2.66M	93.1	91.0
LnLC-GCN-EF	2.72M	93.3	90.7
LnLC-GCN-NCF	2.74M	**93.9**	**91.4**

The maximum frame number of all sequences is limited to 300 frames, and the missing frames are filled by playing back the action in the same sequences. We deploy parallel training on 8 GPUs and the batch size is set to 64. The initial learning rate is designed to be 0.05, which is reduced by 0.1 times at the 30th, 40th and 50th epochs respectively. The training is completed in 60 epochs. We use SGD as the optimizer and the cross-entropy as the loss function.

4.3   Ablation Study

In this section, we design adequate ablation studies of each component of LnLC-GCN. The study benchmarks are the cross-view (xview) and cross-subject (xsub) evaluations on NTU-RGB+D 60 [15] and the number of parameters.

Motion Enhanced Graph. According to the MSAAGCN [16] and Res-GCN [18], we construct graphs containing two kinds of high-level information, motion displacement and velocity information, labeled as MG (Motion Graph) and VG (Velocity Graph) respectively. The initial graph containing only the 3D coordinates of joints and the basic spatiotemporal edges is labeled as IG. The motion enhanced graph proposed in this paper is labeled as MEG. In Table 1, different graph structure labels are identified as suffixes. To avoid the experimental error caused by network optimization, we choose the basic ST-GCN [20] as the evaluation model. Multi-stream data is input into multiple ST-GCN at the same time, and the final results are obtained by a weighted summation. The evaluation results show that our motion enhanced graph can increase performance by up to 3.8% (xview) and 7.1% (xsub) compared to the initial graph. Compared with other two graphs, such as MG and VG, our motion enhanced graph can still achieve more than 2.5% (xview) and 4.2% (xsub) performance improvements.

Local and Non-local Context Module. First of all, we conducted experiments by using clips with different frames, and compared the number of parameters to balance the number of parameters and accuracy of local and non-local context modules we proposed. In the design of the controlled experiments, we unified the input into the initial graph to avoid interference from other factors. As for the number N of frames, six values of $\{1, 3, 5, 10, 20, 30\}$ can be selected for the experiment, where $N = 1$ represents the setting without segmentation and serves as the baseline. The maximum value of N is 30, considering that at the frame rate of 30 FPS, actions lasting more than 1 s may be complex, and the local context information of the clips is relatively discrete and the calculation is hard. The results in Table 1 show that, compared with the baseline of $N = 1$, the number of parameters with all other values of N has been reduced, in which the setting of $N = 10$ has achieved the least number of parameters. Furthermore, the recognition accuracy of $N = \{3, 5, 10\}$ is improved, among which the setting of $N = 5$ gets the best accuracy. The recognition accuracy of $N = \{20, 30\}$ is relatively lower, indicating that some information is lost when extracting non-local context information due to long clips. For the final architecture of LnLC-GCN, we set $N = 5$ for better action recognition accuracy.

Front-End Fusion Strategy. The final architecture proposed by us consists of two backbone networks, and four input branches as defined in the section Method. The results of the controlled experiments are shown in Table 1. We designed two strategies of front-end fusion and back-end fusion, and added suffixes -FF and -BF as labels respectively. From the results, we can observe that the model with front-end fusion achieves the higher accuracy with 37.8% reduction of parameters, which proves the effectiveness of the proposed strategy.

Non-local Context Feedback Strategy. We designed four controlled experiments: no feedback (NoF), feedback only between backbone networks (BNF), feedback only between epochs (EF) and non-local context feedback (NCF). Table 1 shows that the non-local context feedback strategy achieves the best accuracy with a small increase in the number of parameters. The results demonstrate that the feedback context information strategy is lightweight and can assist in correcting the weights in the network, so that the attention can be focused on key discriminative vertices.

4.4   Comparison with the State-of-the-Art

To validate the performance of skeleton-based action recognition, we compare our LnLC-GCN with the state-of-the-art methods on NTU-RGB+D 60, NTU-RGB+D 120 and Kinetics-Skeleton datasets. The methods for comparisons include CNN-based methods [2,8], RNN-based methods [5,9,10], and GCN-based methods [4,12,13,16,18,20,21]. The results are shown in Table 2. In cross-view evaluation of the NTU-RGB+D 60 dataset, our method demonstrates competitive performance. Nevertheless, it is worth noting that the proposed LnLC-GCN achieves the state-of-the-art in all other evaluations.

Table 2. Comparison of LnLC-GCN and the previous methods on NTU-RGB+D 60 [15], NTU-RGB+D 120 [11] and Kinetics-Skeleton [7] datasets. Empty data in the table represents unreported results.

Methods	NTU-RGB+D 60		NTU-RGB+D 120		Kinetics
	xview	xsub	xset	xsub	Skeleton
Clips+CNN+MTLN [8]	84.8	79.6	–	–	–
ResNet152+3scale [2]	92.3	85.0	–	–	–
H-RNN [5]	64.0	59.1	–	–	–
ST-LSTM+Trust Gate [10]	77.7	69.2	57.9	55.7	–
GCA-LSTM [9]	84.0	76.1	59.2	58.3	—-
ST-GCN [20]	88.3	81.5	–	–	30.7
2S-AGCN+TEM [13]	95.8	88.7	–	–	38.6
MS-AAGCN [16]	96.2	90.0	–	–	37.8
MS-G3D [12]	96.2	91.5	88.4	86.9	38.0
FGCN [21]	96.3	90.2	87.4	85.4	–
DSTA-Net [17]	96.4	91.5	89.0	86.6	–
MS-AAGCN+TEM [13]	**96.5**	91.0	–	–	38.0
Shift-GCN [4]	**96.5**	90.7	87.6	85.9	–
ResGCN [18]	–	–	88.3	87.3	–
LnLC-GCN (ours)	**96.4**	**92.1**	**89.7**	**87.7**	**39.5**

5 Conclusion

In this work, we present the simple yet effective local and non-local context graph convolutional networks (LnLC-GCN) for high performance skeleton-based action recognition. The method obtains the global receptive field through the spatiotemporal local context module and non-local context module. In addition, proposed method uses the motion enhanced graph which contains high-level motion information for better feature representation, and adopts two strategies of front-end fusion and non-local context feedback to further improve the ability of feature extraction. Notably, it is proved that our method achieves state-of-the-art performance compared with the previous works on three public datasets.

References

1. Aggarwal, J.K., Xia, L.: Human activity recognition from 3d data: a review. Pattern Recogn. Lett. **48**(1), 70–80 (2014)
2. Bo, L., Dai, Y., Cheng, X., Chen, H., He, M.: Skeleton based action recognition using translation-scale invariant image mapping and multi-scale deep CNN. In: IEEE International Conference on Multimedia & Expo Workshops (2017)
3. Cao, Y., Xu, J., Lin, S., Wei, F., Hu, H.: GCNet: non-local networks meet squeeze-excitation networks and beyond. In: ICCVW, pp. 1971–1980 (2019)

4. Cheng, K., Zhang, Y., He, X., Chen, W., Cheng, J., Lu, H.: Skeleton-based action recognition with shift graph convolutional network. In: CVPR, pp. 180–189 (2020)
5. Du, Y., Wang, W., Wang, L.: Hierarchical recurrent neural network for skeleton based action recognition. In: CVPR, pp. 1110–1118 (2015)
6. Herath, S., Harandi, M., Porikli, F.: Going deeper into action recognition: a survey. Image Vis. Comput. **60**, 4–21 (2017)
7. Kay, W., Carreira, J., Simonyan, K., Zhang, B., Zisserman, A.: The Kinetics Human Action Video Dataset (2017)
8. Ke, Q., Bennamoun, M., An, S., Sohel, F., Boussaid, F.: A new representation of skeleton sequences for 3d action recognition. In: CVPR 2017 (2017)
9. Liu, J., Gang, W., Ping, H., Duan, L.Y., Kot, A.C.: Global context-aware attention LSTM networks for 3d action recognition. In: CVPR (2017)
10. Liu, J., Shahroudy, A., Xu, D., Wang, G.: Spatio-temporal LSTM with trust gates for 3D human action recognition. In: Leibe, B., Matas, J., Sebe, N., Welling, M. (eds.) ECCV 2016. LNCS, vol. 9907, pp. 816–833. Springer, Cham (2016). https:// doi.org/10.1007/978-3-319-46487-9_50
11. Liu, J., Shahroudy, A., Perez, M., Wang, G., Duan, L.Y., Kot, A.C.: NTU RGB+D 120: a large-scale benchmark for 3d human activity understanding. IEEE Trans. Pattern Anal. Mach. Intell. (TPAMI) **42**(10), 2684–2701 (2020)
12. Liu, Z., Zhang, H., Chen, Z., Wang, Z., Ouyang, W.: Disentangling and unifying graph convolutions for skeleton-based action recognition. In: CVPR, pp. 1971–1980 (2020)
13. Obinata, Y., Yamamoto, T.: Temporal extension module for skeleton-based action recognition. In: 2020 25th International Conference on Pattern Recognition (ICPR) (2021)
14. Poppe, R.: A survey on vision-based human action recognition. Image Vis. Comput. **28**(6), 976–990 (2010)
15. Shahroudy, A., Liu, J., Ng, T.T., Wang, G.: NTU RGB+D: A large scale dataset for 3d human activity analysis. In: CVPR, pp. 1010–1019 (2016)
16. Shi, L., Zhang, Y., Cheng, J., Lu, H.: Skeleton-based action recognition with multi-stream adaptive graph convolutional networks (2019). arXiv:1912.06971
17. Shi, L., Zhang, Y., Cheng, J., Lu, H.: Decoupled spatial-temporal attention network for skeleton-based action recognition (2020). arXiv:2007.03263
18. Song, Y.F., Zhang, Z., Shan, C., Wang, L.: Stronger, faster and more explainable: a graph convolutional baseline for skeleton-based action recognition. In: Proceedings of the 28th ACM International Conference on Multimedia (MM), pp. 1625–1633 (2020)
19. Wang, H., Schmid, C.: Action recognition with improved trajectories. In: ICCV (2014)
20. Yan, S., Xiong, Y., Lin, D.: Spatial temporal graph convolutional networks for skeleton-based action recognition. In: AAAI (2018)
21. Yang, H., et al.: Feedback graph convolutional network for skeleton-based action recognition (2020). arXiv:2003.07564
22. Zhang, J., Li, W., Ogunbona, P.O., Wang, P., Tang, C.: RGB-D-based action recognition datasets: a survey. Pattern Recogn. **60**, 86–105 (2016)

STGATP: A Spatio-Temporal Graph Attention Network for Long-Term Traffic Prediction

Mengting Zhu[1,2], Xianqiang Zhu[1,2(✉)], and Cheng Zhu[1,2]

[1] Science and Technology on Information Systems Engineering Laboratory, Changsha 410073, China
[2] College of Systems Engineering, National University of Defense Technology, Changsha 410073, China
zhuxianqiang@nudt.edu.cn

Abstract. Traffic prediction is essential to public transportation management in cities. However, long-term traffic prediction involves complex spatio-temporal correlations changing dynamically, which is highly challenging to capture in road networks. We focus on these dynamic correlations and propose a spatio-temporal graph modeling method to solve the long-term traffic prediction problem. Our proposed method builds a Spatio-Temporal Graph Attention network for Traffic Prediction (STGATP), exploring and capturing the complex spatial-temporal nature in traffic networks. We apply dilated causal convolution with a gated fusion in the temporal modeling block, and diffusion convolution with the attention mechanism in the spatial modeling block. This results in that STGATP can simultaneously capture spatial dependencies and temporal dependencies in road networks. Finally, we conduct the experiments on public traffic datasets METR-LA and PEMS-BAY, and our method reaches superior performance. In particular, STGATP surpasses state-of-the-art methods by up to 11% improvement of RMSE measure on the PEMS-BAY datasets.

Keywords: Spatio-temporal modeling · Long-term traffic prediction · Graph convolutional network · Attention mechanism

1 Introduction

The ever-increasing number of urban vehicles poses a significant challenge to public transportation management, resulting in a series of problems such as severe road congestion and fuel consumption. Under this background, traffic prediction has been widely studied, aiming to provide valuable traffic information for public transportation management, including flow control and route planning [1,2]. The main idea of traffic prediction is to forecast the future traffic state by analyzing previous traffic data recorded by traffic sensors [3].

As traffic conditions change dynamically, some researchers apply mathematical theories to model these patterns, such as queuing theory. Other researchers

© Springer Nature Switzerland AG 2021
I. Farkaš et al. (Eds.): ICANN 2021, LNCS 12893, pp. 255–266, 2021.
https://doi.org/10.1007/978-3-030-86365-4_21

regard traffic prediction as a time-series problem and apply traditional time-series analysis to address it. These methods utilize historical traffic data and usually observe a certain assumption of time-series. However, traffic data is not always satisfying such assumptions. Almost all of these methods are of certain limits [4].

With the development of machine learning, K-Nearest Neighbors (KNN) and Support Vector Regression (SVR) have been applied in traffic prediction [5,6]. These machine learning-based methods need less prior knowledge about different traffic patterns and can better capture non-linear relationships in traffic data [7]. However, they only concentrate on the time-series correlations, ignoring the spatial correlations in traffic networks. Some researchers have noticed this limitation and proposed to model the spatial correlation with Convolutional Neural Networks (CNN) [8]. Although these methods have made some progress, they only model spatial structure in the Euclidean space, which is unsuitable for graph structure data like road networks. Recent studies applied Graph neural network (GNN) [9–11] to model spatial structure in the non-Euclidean space. GraphWavenet [12] models the spatial structure into a graph and constructs a self-adaptive adjacency matrix that preserves hidden spatial dependencies. Some researchers proposed graph updating strategies to explore the complex spatial-temporal nature of traffic evolution [13]. These methods mainly focus on short-term traffic prediction (within 30 min), long-term traffic prediction (more than 30 min) still lacks sufficient research [14].

To address the limitations mentioned above, we build a novel Spatio-Temporal Graph Attention network for Traffic Prediction (STGATP), an end-to-end solution that captures long-term spatio-temporal dependencies. The main contributions of our work are as follows.

1) We propose a new spatio-temporal graph modeling method, which can simultaneously consider temporal dependencies and spatial dependencies in road networks to explore the complex spatial-temporal nature.
2) We introduce dilated causal convolution and a gated fusion to capture long-range temporal dependencies. In spatial modeling, we propose the pair-wise graph convolution with attention mechanism, which can effectively capture the traffic impact from upstream and downstream, respectively.
3) We conducted experiments on real-world traffic datasets METR-LA and PEMS-BAY. Compared with state-of-the-art methods, STGATP presents superior performances and achieves 11% improvement of RMSE measure on PEMS-BAY datasets.

2   Prior Work

Traffic Prediction is a typical spatio-temporal modeling problem associated with time-series changes and spatial structure. In light of this, the previous traffic prediction methods can be classified into three main categories as follows.

One category of traffic prediction methods focuses on modeling temporal correlations, including traditional time-series models such as Auto-Regressive

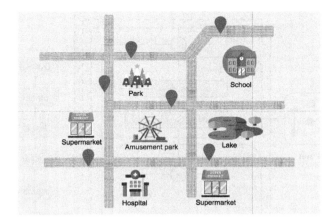

Fig. 1. An example of road networks in which the red dots represent the sensors that can collect traffic data with a specific sampling frequency. The traffic state of each location can be affected by the traffic flow of adjacent roads. (Color figure online)

Integrated Moving Average (ARIMA). Besides, support vector regression [15] have been applied to model temporal correlations. Compared with traditional time-series models, the machine learning-based methods show superior performances in capturing temporal correlations from historical traffic data. Another category is more concerned with spatial structure and utilizes convolutional neural networks to capture the spatial dependencies in Euclidean space [8]. Since the traffic data in the road network is non-Euclidean data, Graph Neural Networks (GNN) are more widely applied in traffic prediction. The other category simultaneously models the spatial and temporal dependencies in traffic networks and makes satisfactory progress in traffic prediction [4,12,16].

In general, these methods evolve from considering spatial and temporal correlations separately to integrating. In light of this, STGATP takes the latter approach to explore spatio-temporal correlations simultaneously. We combine long-range temporal dependencies and pair-wise spatial dependencies, which is more suitable for long-term traffic prediction.

3   Methodology

3.1   Problem Definition

As Fig. 1 shows, the traffic state can be observed by some traffic sensors placed in the road network. Thus we can represent the traffic network as a weighted directed graph $G = (V, E, A)$, where V denotes a set of $N = |V|$ traffic sensors in the road network; E denotes a set of edges which indicates the connectivity among traffic sensors; $A \in R^{N \times N}$ denotes the weighted adjacency matrix. The value of A_{v_i,v_j} represents the proximity between vertex v_i and v_j, usually measured by the road network distance. We regard the traffic state as graph signals

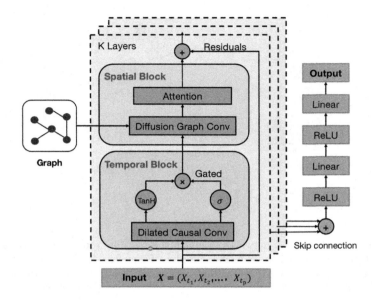

Fig. 2. The framework of Spatio-Temporal Graph Attention network for Traffic Prediction (STGATP), which consists of spatial modeling blocks and temporal modeling blocks.

$X \in R^{N \times M}$, where M is the number of features relevant to traffic conditions. As the graph signals change dynamically, the traffic state at time step t can be represented as $X_t \in R^{N \times M}$. Given a graph G and historical graph signals $X = (X_{t_1}, X_{t_2}, ..., X_{t_k})$, our goal of traffic prediction concerns the learning of a mapping function $f(\cdot)$ which is able to map k historical graph signals to the next l step graph signals, formally denoted as follows,

$$[X_{t_1:t_k}, G] \xrightarrow{f(\cdot)} X_{t_{k+1}:t_{k+l}} \tag{1}$$

3.2   Framework

The framework of STGATP is presented in Fig. 2. It consists of K spatio-temporal layers to simultaneously learn structure information and temporal information in traffic networks. Each spatio-temporal layer can be divided into the spatial convolutional block and temporal convolutional block. We introduce the attention mechanism in the spatial convolutional block to model the dynamic spatial correlations. Besides, a gated mechanism is applied to model complex temporal dependencies in the temporal convolutional block. Each spatio-temporal layer has residual connections and is skip-connected to the output layer. Finally, the output layer generates the L time steps ahead prediction $\hat{X}_{t_{k+1}:t_{k+l}}$.

We take minimizing the mean absolute error (MAE) as our training goal and train this model end-to-end through back-propagation. The mean absolute error in our model is defined as follows,

$$\mathcal{L}(\Theta) = \frac{1}{L \times N \times M} \sum_{s=1}^{L} \sum_{j=1}^{N} \sum_{i=1}^{M} \left| X_{t_{k+s},j,i} - \hat{X}_{t_{k+s},j,i} \right| \tag{2}$$

3.3 Temporal Convolutional Block

At a certain moment, each position's traffic state is closely related to the historical state in a road network, so it is essential to model in the temporal dimension. In order to capture long-term correlations, we adopt dilated causal convolution [17] in the temporal convolutional block, which is derived from the dilated convolution in the computer vision [18,19], as well as the causal convolution in the sequence modeling [20,21]. Fusing these two convolutional operations, dilated causal convolution can perform time-series analysis and enable the network to have larger receiving fields without losing resolution or coverage. This convolutional operation employs a filter to the temporal sequence longer than its length by ignoring parts of certain inputs. In other words, dilated causal convolution pads zeros to the original filter so that the dilated filter has the same length as the temporal sequence. Given a 1D signal $\mathbf{x}$ at time step t and a filter $\mathbf{f}_\theta \in R^D$, the dilated causal convolution with dilated coefficient d is formally denoted as follows,

$$\mathbf{x} \star \mathbf{f}_\theta = \sum_{p=0}^{D-1} \mathbf{f}_\theta(p) \mathbf{x}_{t-p \times d} \tag{3}$$

As illustrated by Fig. 3, the receptive fields and computational efficiency increase rapidly with the convolutional layers increase. In this way, we can capture long-range temporal dependencies with fewer layers in the temporal convolutional block.

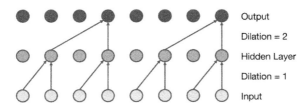

Fig. 3. Dilated casual convolution with dilation coefficient 1 in the bottom layer and dilation coefficient 2 in the middle layer.

Then we introduce a gating mechanism to alleviate the disappearance of gradients, which is widely used in recurrent neural networks to control information propagation [22]. Mathematically, gated fusion over a signal $\mathbf{x}$ is denoted as follows,

$$z = tanh\left(W_1 \star \mathbf{x} + \mathbf{b_1}\right) \odot \sigma\left(W_2 \star \mathbf{x} + \mathbf{b_2}\right) \qquad (4)$$

where W_1, W_2, b_1, b_2 are the learnable parameters, $\sigma(\cdot)$ is a sigmoid function controlling the extent to which the information should be propagated to the subsequent layers.

3.4   Spatial Convolutional Block

Graph Convolution Layer. The traffic conditions in a specific location are easily affected by the traffic conditions of the surrounding roads, so it is necessary to consider the road network's spatial structure when predicting future traffic state. Graph convolutional networks can utilize structure information to effectively mine the hidden feature of graph data, achieving satisfying performance in many machine learning tasks [23]. Thus, we adopt graph convolutional networks to aggregate the effect coming from the roads in the neighborhood.

Even if observed at the exact location, sometimes the traffic conditions on both sides of the road are not balanced. For example, in the morning rush hour, the traffic flow entering the urban area is usually more, and there is less traffic flow away from the urban area. The situation is the opposite during the evening rush hour. Therefore, when considering the impact of space structure, we need to consider the pair-wise traffic changes. To address this problem, we adopt diffusion convolution [4], capable of capturing the influence from both the upstream and the downstream. Given a graph signal $\mathbf{X} \in R^{N \times M}$, the diffusion convolution process of graph signals with C finite steps is formally denoted as follows,

$$\boldsymbol{X} \star f_\theta = \sum_{c=0}^{C-1} \left(\boldsymbol{D}_O^{-1}\boldsymbol{A}\right)^c \boldsymbol{X}\boldsymbol{W}_{c,1} + \left(\boldsymbol{D}_I^{-1}\boldsymbol{A}\right)^c \boldsymbol{X}\boldsymbol{W}_{c,2} \qquad (5)$$

where $\boldsymbol{A} \in R^{N \times N}$ denotes the adjacency matrix with weight, and $\boldsymbol{D}_O^{-1}\boldsymbol{A}$, $\boldsymbol{D}_I^{-1}\boldsymbol{A}$ are the transition matrices of forward transition and backward transition. With the diffusion convolution operation mentioned above, we build a graph convolutional layer that can aggregate neighborhood information from both in-degree and out-degree aspects.

Attention Mechanism. The attention mechanism has been widely applied in many sequence-based tasks, which allows variable-sized inputs and can focus on the most influential proportion [24]. Researchers have introduced this mechanism to process graph-structured data and achieved excellent results in graph classification tasks.

We apply the attention mechanism to capture hidden spatial patterns in the spatial convolutional block because of its fruitfulness. It enables the network to flexibly assign different weights to neighbors at different time steps so that the feature updating process can be formalized as follows,

$$h_i^{(l)} = \sigma \left(\sum_{j \in neig_i} \alpha_{ij} \mathbf{W} h_j^{(l-1)} \right) \tag{6}$$

where $\mathbf{W}$ is the matrix of linear transformation aimed to transform the input features to a higher level, and α_{ij} denotes the masked attention coefficient. Then we just need to compute the attention coefficients of neighbors, which can be achieved through a softmax operation over the whole attention coefficients. The process can be formalized as follows,

$$\alpha_{ij} = \text{softmax}\,(e_{ij}) = \frac{\exp\,(e_{ij})}{\sum_{k \in neig_i} \exp\,(e_{ik})} \tag{7}$$

where attention coefficients e_{ij} are the attention coefficients of one node in the graph, which are computed by the formula as follows,

$$e_{ij} = \text{LeakyReLU}\,(\mathbf{a}\,[\mathbf{W} h_i \| \mathbf{W} h_j]) \tag{8}$$

where $\mathbf{W}$ is the matrix of learnable parameters as mentioned in formula (6). The LeakyReLU is a kind of activation function with nonlinearity, and $\mathbf{a} \in \mathbf{R}^{2F}$ denotes the parameter of a single-layer forward neural network. By introducing the attention mechanism in the spatial convolution block, our proposed method can effectively evaluate the impact of surrounding roads at different time steps.

4 Experiments

4.1 Datasets

We conduct experiments on two real-world traffic datasets, namely METR-LA and PEMS-BAY. As shown in Table 1, METR-LA contains statistics of traffic speed collected by 207 sensors in Los Angeles County. PEMS-BAY reflects the traffic speed information recorded by 325 sensors in the Bay area, and all the sensors gather the information every five minutes.

Following the data preprocessing method in DCRNN, we compute the road network distance processed through a thresholded Gaussian kernel, which acts as the weight of a traffic network's adjacency matrix. All the inputs are processed via Z-score normalization, and 70% data is used for training, 10% for validation, and 20% for testing.

Table 1. Dataset description

Dataset	Nodes	Edges	Duration months	Time steps
METR-LA	207	1515	4	34272
PEMS-BAY	325	2369	6	52116

4.2 Experimental Settings

We conduct the experiments on a workstation with one NVIDIA GeForce RTX 2080Ti GPU. Following the previous works, We set the input sequence length to 12 to predict the traffic state in an hour. In the temporal convolutional block, the dilation coefficient is set as 1 in the first dilated causal layer and 2 in the next layer. In spatial convolutional block, the diffusion step is set as 2, and the dropout is set as 0.2. Finally, we train the model with Adam optimizer and test the performance through three widely applied metrics, namely mean absolute error (MAE), root mean squared error (RMSE) and mean absolute percentage error (MAPE), which are defined as follows

$$\text{MAE} = \frac{1}{n} \sum_{i=1}^{n} \left| X_i - \hat{X}_i \right| \tag{9}$$

$$\text{RMSE} = \sqrt{\frac{1}{n} \sum_{i}^{n} \left(X_i - \hat{X}_i \right)^2} \tag{10}$$

$$\text{MAPE} = \frac{1}{n} \sum_{i=1}^{n} \left| \frac{X_i - \hat{X}_i}{X_i} \right| \times 100\% \tag{11}$$

In order to evaluate the prediction effect, we compare the performance with some typical methods including traditional time-series analysis, machine learning-based methods and deep learning-based methods. These methods are as follows: Auto-regressive integrated moving average (ARIMA) [25]; Support vector regression (SVR) [26]; Feedforward neural network (FNN) [27]; Fully-connected long short-term memory (FC-LSTM) [28]; Spatio-temporal graph convolutional network (STGCN) [29]; Diffusion convolutional recurrent neural network (DCRNN) [4]; Graph WaveNet [12]; Graph Multi-Attention Network (GMAN) [16].

4.3 Experimental Results

Table 2 shows the one-hour traffic prediction effect on the two datasets, and STGATP achieves superior performance compared with other methods. It can be shown that traditional time-series methods such as ARIMA are limited to model complicated temporal and spatial dependencies in traffic prediction. Machine learning-based methods such as FNN can capture non-linear temporal dependencies, so the prediction effect is better than traditional time-series methods. Deep learning-based methods such as STGCN introduce graph data and capture the spatial structure's impact so that the prediction effect improves. Our proposed method introduces dilated causal convolution with a gated fusion and diffusion convolution with attention mechanism so that STGATP can simultaneously model spatio-temporal dependencies. Thus, STGATP achieves superior performance in long-term traffic prediction. As the datasets grow in size, our proposed method realizes better prediction effects. In particular, it achieves 11% improvement of RMSE measure (from 4.32 to 3.81) on PEMS-BAY datasets.

Table 2. Experimental results for traffic prediction **one hour** ahead

Dataset	METR			PEMS		
Model	MAE	RMSE	MAPE	MAE	RMSE	MAPE
ARIMA	6.90	13.23	17.40%	3.38	6.50	8.30%
SVR	6.72	13.76	16.70%	3.28	7.08	8.00%
FNN	4.49	8.69	14.00%	2.46	4.98	5.89%
FC-LSTM	4.37	8.69	13.20%	2.37	4.96	5.70%
STGCN	4.59	9.4	12.70%	2.49	5.69	5.79%
DCRNN	3.60	7.59	10.50%	2.07	4.74	4.90%
Graph WaveNet	3.53	7.37	10.01%	1.95	4.52	4.63%
GMAN	**3.40**	7.21	9.72%	1.86	4.32	4.31%
STGATP	3.41	**6.71**	**9.57%**	**1.73**	**3.81**	**3.94%**

4.4   Supplementary Experiment

Our proposed method has been verified great performances in the long-term traffic prediction (more than 30 min). In order to verify the universality of STGATP, we also conduct experiments on traffic prediction within 30 min. Table 3 and Table 4 show experimental results for traffic prediction thirty minutes ahead and fifteen minutes ahead, respectively. As the results show, STGATP is also suitable for short-term traffic prediction and achieves 17% improvement of RMSE measure (from 2.82 to 2.33) on PEMS-BAY datasets.

Table 3. Experimental results for traffic prediction **thirty minutes** ahead

Dataset	METR			PEMS		
Model	MAE	RMSE	MAPE	MAE	RMSE	MAPE
ARIMA	5.15	10.45	12.70%	2.33	4.76	5.40%
SVR	5.05	10.87	12.10%	2.48	5.18	5.50%
FNN	4.23	8.17	12.90%	2.30	4.63	5.43%
FC-LSTM	3.77	7.23	10.90%	2.20	4.55	5.20%
STGCN	3.47	7.24	9.57%	1.81	4.27	4.17%
DCRNN	3.15	6.45	8.80%	1.74	3.97	3.90%
Graph WaveNet	3.07	6.22	8.37%	1.63	3.70	3.67%
GMAN	3.07	6.34	8.35%	1.62	3.72	3.63%
STGATP	**3.04**	**5.91**	**8.17%**	**1.43**	**3.08**	**3.06%**

Table 4. Experimental results for traffic prediction **fifteen minutes** ahead

Dataset	METR			PEMS		
Model	MAE	RMSE	MAPE	MAE	RMSE	MAPE
ARIMA	3.99	8.21	9.60%	1.62	3.30	3.50%
SVR	3.99	8.45	9.30%	1.85	3.59	3.80%
FNN	3.99	7.94	9.90%	2.20	4.42	5.19%
FC-LSTM	3.44	6.30	9.60%	2.05	4.19	4.80%
STGCN	2.88	5.74	7.62%	1.36	2.96	2.90%
DCRNN	2.77	5.38	7.30%	1.38	2.95	2.90%
Graph WaveNet	**2.69**	5.15	6.90%	1.30	2.74	2.73%
GMAN	2.77	5.48	7.25%	1.34	2.82	2.81%
STGATP	2.70	**5.04**	**6.88%**	**1.16**	**2.33**	**2.34%**

5   Conclusions

In this paper, we propose a novel spatio-temporal graph modeling method for traffic prediction. This method utilizes the historical traffic data and spatial structure information to explore hidden spatio-temporal features. It can effectively model the temporal dependencies while applying a gated fusion to capture the long-range dependencies efficiently. Also, we adopt graph convolutional networks with the attention mechanism to model spatial dependencies. Finally, we conduct the experiments on public traffic datasets, and experimental results verified the superior effect of STGATP. In the future, we will explore the pre-training model over spatio-temporal networks.

Acknowledgments. This work was funded by the National Natural Science Foundation of China (71571186) and the Postgraduate Research Innovation Project of Hunan Province, China (CX20200058).

References

1. Chen, C., Liu, B., Wan, S., Qiao, P., Pei, Q.: An edge traffic flow detection scheme based on deep learning in an intelligent transportation system. IEEE Trans. Intell. Transp. Syst. **22**(3), 1840–1852 (2021)
2. Chen, L., Zheng, L., Yang, J., Xia, D., Liu, W.: Short-term traffic flow prediction: from the perspective of traffic flow decomposition. Neurocomputing **413**, 444–456 (2020)
3. Han, L., Zheng, K., Zhao, L., Wang, X., Shen, X.: Short-term traffic prediction based on deep cluster in large-scale road networks. IEEE Trans. Veh. Technol. **68**(12), 12301–12313 (2019)
4. Li, Y., Yu, R., Shahabi, C., Liu, Y.: Diffusion convolutional recurrent neural network: data-driven traffic forecasting. In: International Conference on Learning Representations (2018)

5. Yang, B., Sun, S., Li, J., Lin, X., Tian, Y.: Traffic flow prediction using LSTM with feature enhancement. Neurocomputing **332**, 320–327 (2019)
6. Zhang, W., Yu, Y., Qi, Y., Shu, F., Wang, Y.: Short-term traffic flow prediction based on spatio-temporal analysis and CNN deep learning. Transportmetrica A Transp. Sci. **15**(2), 1688–1711 (2019)
7. Boukerche, A., Wang, J.: Machine learning-based traffic prediction models for intelligent transportation systems. Comput. Netw. **181**, 107530 (2020)
8. Ma, X., Dai, Z., He, Z., Ma, J., Wang, Y., Wang, Y.: Learning traffic as images: a deep convolutional neural network for large-scale transportation network speed prediction. Sensors **17**(4), 818 (2017)
9. Scarselli, F., Gori, M., Tsoi, A.C., Hagenbuchner, M., Monfardini, G.: The graph neural network model. IEEE Trans. Neural Netw. **20**(1), 61–80 (2008)
10. Xu, K., Hu, W., Leskovec, J., Jegelka, S.: How powerful are graph neural networks? In: International Conference on Learning Representations (2018)
11. Zhou, J., et al.: Graph neural networks: a review of methods and applications. AI Open **1**, 57–81 (2020)
12. Wu, Z., Pan, S., Long, G., Jiang, J., Zhang, C.: Graph WaveNet for deep spatial-temporal graph modeling. In: The 28th International Joint Conference on Artificial Intelligence (IJCAI). International Joint Conferences on Artificial Intelligence Organization (2019)
13. Guo, K., et al.: Optimized graph convolution recurrent neural network for traffic prediction. IEEE Trans. Intell. Transp. Syst. **21**, 3848–3858 (2020)
14. He, Z., Chow, C.Y., Zhang, J.D.: STCNN: a spatio-temporal convolutional neural network for long-term traffic prediction. In: 2019 20th IEEE International Conference on Mobile Data Management (MDM), pp. 226–233. IEEE (2019)
15. Ranjan, N., Bhandari, S., Zhao, H.P., Kim, H., Khan, P.: City-wide traffic congestion prediction based on CNN, LSTM and transpose CNN. IEEE Access **8**, 81606–81620 (2020)
16. Zheng, C., Fan, X., Wang, C., Qi, J.: GMAN: a graph multi-attention network for traffic prediction. In: Proceedings of the AAAI Conference on Artificial Intelligence, vol. 34, pp. 1234–1241 (2020)
17. van den Oord, A., et al.: WaveNet: a generative model for raw audio. In: The 9th ISCA Speech Synthesis Workshop, Sunnyvale, CA, USA, 13–15 September 2016. p. 125. ISCA (2016)
18. Mehta, S., Rastegari, M., Caspi, A., Shapiro, L., Hajishirzi, H.: ESPNet: efficient spatial pyramid of dilated convolutions for semantic segmentation. In: Ferrari, V., Hebert, M., Sminchisescu, C., Weiss, Y. (eds.) ECCV 2018. LNCS, vol. 11214, pp. 561–580. Springer, Cham (2018). https://doi.org/10.1007/978-3-030-01249-6_34
19. Wei, Y., Xiao, H., Shi, H., Jie, Z., Feng, J., Huang, T.S.: Revisiting dilated convolution: a simple approach for weakly-and semi-supervised semantic segmentation. In: Proceedings of the IEEE Conference on Computer Vision and Pattern Recognition, pp. 7268–7277 (2018)
20. Treur, J.: Dynamic modeling based on a temporal-causal network modeling approach. Biol. Insp. Cogn. Architect. **16**, 131–168 (2016)
21. Pandey, A., Wang, D.: TCNN: temporal convolutional neural network for real-time speech enhancement in the time domain. In: ICASSP 2019–2019 IEEE International Conference on Acoustics, Speech and Signal Processing (ICASSP), pp. 6875–6879. IEEE (2019)
22. Dauphin, Y.N., Fan, A., Auli, M., Grangier, D.: Language modeling with gated convolutional networks. In: International Conference on Machine Learning, pp. 933–941. PMLR (2017)

23. Bronstein, M.M., Bruna, J., LeCun, Y., Szlam, A., Vandergheynst, P.: Geometric deep learning: going beyond Euclidean data. IEEE Signal Process. Mag. **34**(4), 18–42 (2017)
24. Shanthamallu, U.S., Thiagarajan, J.J., Spanias, A.: A regularized attention mechanism for graph attention networks. In: ICASSP 2020–2020 IEEE International Conference on Acoustics, Speech and Signal Processing (ICASSP), pp. 3372–3376. IEEE (2020)
25. Makridakis, S., Hibon, M.: ARMA models and the box-Jenkins methodology. J. Forecast. **16**(3), 147–163 (1997)
26. Wu, C.H., Ho, J.M., Lee, D.T.: Travel-time prediction with support vector regression. IEEE Trans. Intell. Transp. Syst. **5**(4), 276–281 (2004)
27. Raeesi, M., Mesgari, M., Mahmoudi, P.: Traffic time series forecasting by feedforward neural network: a case study based on traffic data of Monroe. Int. Archiv. Photogram. Remote Sens. Spat. Inf. Sci. **40**(2), 219 (2014)
28. Sutskever, I., Vinyals, O., Le, Q.V.: Sequence to sequence learning with neural networks. Adv. Neural. Inf. Process. Syst. **27**, 3104–3112 (2014)
29. Yu, B., Yin, H., Zhu, Z.: Spatio-temporal graph convolutional networks: a deep learning framework for traffic forecasting. In: Proceedings of the 27th International Joint Conference on Artificial Intelligence, pp. 3634–3640 (2018)

Hierarchical and Ensemble Models

Integrating N-Gram Features into Pre-trained Model: A Novel Ensemble Model for Multi-target Stance Detection

Pengyuan Chen[iD], Kai Ye, and Xiaohui Cui[✉]

Key Laboratory of Aerospace Information Security and Trusted Computing,
Ministry of Education, School of Cyber Science and Engineering,
Wuhan University, Wuhan, China
xcui@whu.edu.cn

Abstract. Multi-target stance detection in tweets aims to detect the stance of given texts towards a specific target entity. Most existing models on stance detection consider word embedding as input, however, recent developments pointed out that it would be beneficial to incorporate feature-based information appropriately. Motivated by the strong performance of the pre-trained models in many Natural Language Processing field, and n-gram features that have been proved to be effective in prior competition, we present a novel combination module to obtain both advantages. This paper has proposed a pre-trained model integrated with n-gram features module (PMINFM) to better utilize multi-scale feature representation information and semantic features. Then connect it to a Bidirectional Long Short-Term Memory networks with target-specific attention mechanism. The experimental results show that our proposed model outperforms other baseline models in the SemEval-2016 stance detection dataset and achieves state-of-the-art performance.

Keywords: Stance detection · Text classification · N-gram features

1 Introduction

The increasing popularity of social media makes people more inclined to post their opinions online, which allows researchers to measure users' opinions towards a specific target based on these social media texts. In other social media analytical studies, such as rumors detection, stance detection also plays a major role. Stance detection is similar to aspect-based sentiment classification (ABSC), as they both perform text classification for specific aspects or targets, but there are essential differences between them: the same words express the same emotions, but may

Supported by National Key Research and Development Program of China No. 2018YFC1604000, Fundamental Research Funds for the Central Universities No. 2042017gf0035.

express different stances due to the presence of different targets. Therefore, fully integrating the target with texts is particularly important in stance detection.

The first target-specific task of stance detection from tweets is SemEval-2016 Task 6 [13], which defined that the task aims to automatically determine the stance of the given social media texts (like tweets) with corresponding targets. The stance includes being favor of, against, and neutral.

Many difficulties in social media post analysis tasks exist in stance detection. For example, social media posts are often short, usually containing abbreviations, emojis, spelling errors and nonstandard use of words and grammar [6]. Besides, stance detection in tweets has unique difficulties, including some tweets express their opinions in a vague or ironic way, and some tweets' target objects are not explicitly mentioned, which makes the stance detection task very challenging.

Research shows that pre-trained language models like BERT [8], RoBERTa [12] have more powerful performance in many natural language processing (NLP) tasks. In SemEval 2016 task 6A, however, the SVM-ngrams model (using word and character n-grams as features), which is a classic machine learning model proposed as a baseline, has unexpectedly beat all participating models including a variety of different deep neural networks at the time. This demonstrates that handcrafted features such as n-gram can boost performance in a way and combining it with deep neural networks may take the advantages of both since deep neural networks focus on semantics and handcrafted features focus on linguistics [28].

Motivated by the effectiveness of the combination of pre-trained model and handcrafted features in other NLP tasks [16, 28], we propose a novel network structure for stance detection in social media. Specifically, the social media sentences are processed separately to two modules, one is to feed to regression fine-tuned single sequence RoBERTa model to output embedding matrix, and the other is to extract handcrafted features. The concatenation is integrated with the target vector and then connected to a Bidirectional Long Short-Term Memory networks (BiLSTM) [18] with attention mechanism [5] for the final prediction task.

The main contributions of our work are summarized as below:

- To the best of our knowledge, we are the first to use the joint vector of n-gram features and RoBERTa's output to represent sentences for classification in the multi-target stance detection task.
- We propose a novel approach that boosts the performance of stance detection with the help of an ensemble model architecture that combines the pre-trained model integrated with n-gram features module (PMINFM) and the BiLSTM with target-specific attention mechanism.
- Experimental results on the SemEval 2016 stance detection dataset represent remarkable improvements in performance, which demonstrates that our model is competitive.

2   Related Works

In the previous stance detection work, online debate is the main concern of researchers. To solve the problem in this field, lots of handcrafted features such as sentiment lexicon [23], dialogic properties [22], dialogic context [3] have been exploited. Nonetheless, it is found that simple unigram features achieves better results than the relatively complicated sentiment features [19]. This highlights that n-gram features have the ability to better incorporate specific words expressing stance and it is beneficial for classifying social media texts composed of hashtags and other unique elements that may imply their opinions.

With the rise in popularity of the online social media represented by twitter, convenient opinion expression and rich corpus make the research focus of stance detection shift here. Mohammad et al. [13] proposed tweet-based stance detection task in SemEval 2016 which is one of the pioneering works. The competition requires classifying the stance of given target's tweets, which consists of support, opposition, and neutrality. Some participants tried feature-based classical supervised classifiers methods including Support Vector Machines (SVM), Naive-Bayes and so on, while deep learning methods such as Recurrent Neural Networks (RNN) [4] and Convolutional Neural Networks (CNNs) [25] which emerged at the time also presented. It is worth mentioning that an ensemble of features combined with SVM method achieved the best results of the competition [13].

Recent work is mainly based on deep learning models, which improve the results by reconstructing the model structure or incorporating more features. Du et al. [9] proposed the Target-specific Attentional Network (TAN) proving that applying the attention mechanism to learn target-augmented embeddings can improve performance by making full use of target information. In [20,24], they boost performance with the help of the mend of attention mechanism, the HAN proposed by the former introduces a hierarchical attention network consisted of linguistic attention and hyper attention for better extracting the feature, and the TGMN-CR proposed by the latter adds to the attention mechanism memory modules. A new way found by [1] construct a network by acquiring additional user interaction information, and detect stance by network features.

Most recently, the proposal of the pre-trained models such as BERT [8], RoBERTa [12] and GPT [17] promotes further development in many NLP fields. Yang et al. [26] proposed to use GPT to win the first place in the rumor detection task of SemEval 2019 competition Task 7A. Pre-trained language models have also achieved better results in fake news detection [10] and Sentence-Level Propaganda Detection [21]. The effectiveness of incorporating handcrafted features into pre-trained models has also been proven in many studies, wherefore we get the inspiration. The aforementioned Yang's work is an example of combining GPT with features such as emotional words to achieve state-of-the-art results, and the works of [2,16] have proved the availability as well.

3   Model

This section describes the proposed model. The overall architecture of the proposed model is shown in Fig. 1. It consists of two main components: one is a pre-trained model integrated with n-gram features module (PMINFM) and the other is a BiLSTM layer with target-specific attention mechanism. Each part is introduced separately below.

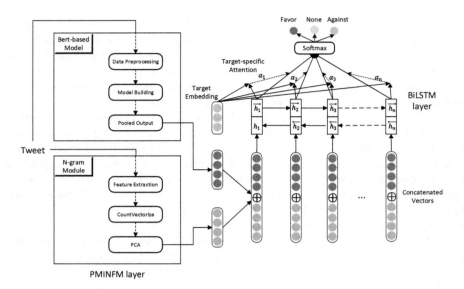

Fig. 1. The overview of the proposed ensemble model.

3.1 PMINFM Layer

BERT is a pre-trained model based on the transformer architecture, which can more thoroughly capture the bidirectional relationship in sentences, and has verified its performance on many NLP tasks. As a BERT-based model, RoBERTa, which is the abbreviation of Robustly Optimized BERT Pretraining Approach, has developed BERT in the training phase mainly by canceling Next Sentence Prediction (NSP) tasks, using dynamic masks and text encoding changes, etc., and has achieved performance improvements on General Language Understanding Evaluation (GLUE). Both BERT and RoBERTa have two sizes called Base and Large with differences in the number of layers, hidden, attention heads and parameters. We have conducted experiments on both sizes of BERT and RoBERTa, and the results show that RoBERTa-Large is the most convincing choice, so as to be selected as the pre-trained model applied in the ensemble architecture.

N-gram is a kind of handcrafted feature widely used in NLP fields. In [14], word and character n-grams are drawn as features to train a linear kernel support vector machine (SVM) model to realize stance classification, which surpasses the best result in SemEval-2016 task 6. Because of its effectiveness in SemEval-2016 task 6, we use the same n-gram features as them, more specifically, the presence or absence of contiguous sequences of 1, 2, and 3 tokens for word n-grams and of 2, 3, 4, and 5 characters for character n-grams.

The input sentences are fed into BERT-based model and n-gram features extraction module respectively. To match the BERT-based model's output with the dimension of n-gram features, we choose the pooled output of the BERT-based model as its output. The pooled output is the output of the last layer of BERT-based model connected to the pooling layer consisting of dense layer with hyperbolic tangent (tanh) activation function. As for extracted n-gram features, it is then vectorized using CountVectorizer from scikit-learn [15]. To reduce noise and unify dimensions, we apply Principal Component Analysis (PCA) to shorten the n-gram vector. It is concatenated with the pooled output, and the concatenated vector is then sent to the BiLSTM layer as its input.

3.2   BiLSTM Layer

We employ BiLSTM to process the input concatenated sequence $V \in R^{n \times (d_1 + d_2)}$ where n is the number of sentences provided as input to the ensemble architecture, d_1 is the dimension of pooled output from BERT-based model, and d_2 is the dimension of extracted n-gram vector. BiLSTM consists of two bidirectional LSTM layers including forward LSTM and backward LSTM, which process input from two opposite directions. Each LSTM cell generates a hidden vector h_i at time step i, which is calculated based on the prior knowledge of the current input x and the previous hidden vector h_{i-1}. Concatenating together two reverse hidden vectors at each time step, we get the resulted hidden vectors $h_i = \left[\overrightarrow{h_i} ; \overleftarrow{h_i} \right]$. Then the embedding of concatenated sequence e_c calculated from the concatenated vector and hidden vector h_i. We adopt the attention mechanism to improve the result of stance classification, and the weight of attention α_i^c is calculated from the following formula:

$$\alpha_i^c = \frac{\exp (e_c)}{\sum_{i=1}^n \exp (e_i)} \tag{1}$$

The obtained vector representation r_c is the sum of the hidden vectors with attention as the weight:

$$r_c = \sum_{i=1}^n \alpha_i^c h_i \tag{2}$$

To enable BiLSTM to capture the part of the sentence related to the target information to make full use of the target information, a target-specific attention mechanism motivated by [29] is applied here. This mechanism integrates the target embedding e_t in the attention layer. The target embedding e_t is derived from the word embedding of the target word using fastText [7]. For a single word target such as "Abortion", the word vector is used directly, while for a multi-word target such as "Climate Change is a Real Concern", it is transformed into the word "Climate" which best summarizes its original meaning. Table 1 shows the corresponding relations presented among the five targets in the dataset. Then the attention weight of target embedding e_t is calculated according to Eq. 1 to get a_t, the target vector representation r_t is calculated according to Eq. 2, and eventually concatenated with r_c to get the final vector representation. Finally, the output of BiLSTM is connected to a fully-connected layer and then apply softmax function to get the final vector representation.

Table 1. Target transformation correspondence

Full name	Atheism	Climate Change is a Real Concern	Feminist Movement	Hillary Clinton	Legalization of Abortion
Shorten form	Atheism	Climate	Feminist	Hillary	Abortion

3.3 Output and Model Training

Finally, the output of BiLSTM layer is connected to a non-linear layer where softmax function is applied to get the final prediction.

In the training phase, because each target subset has a certain degree of imbalanced class sample problem, we utilize weighted cross entropy to increase the attention paid to minority class. The relevant weights for each class are calculated as below:

$$\frac{1}{w_n} = \frac{q_n}{\sum_{t=1}^{n} q_t} \tag{3}$$

where q_n means the sample quantity of class n in training set.

4 Experiment

4.1 Dataset and Evaluation Metrics

As a dataset for stance detection in common usage provided by Semeval-2016 Task 6.A, on which we conducted experiments to validate the performance of our proposed model. In this dataset, 4163 instances are annotated with stance labels ("Favor," "Against" or "None") towards one of five targets containing "Atheism," "Climate Change is a Real Concern" ("Climate"), "Feminist Movement" ("Feminism"), "Hillary Clinton" ("Hillary") and "Legalization of Abortion" ("Abortion"). Table 2 shows the distribution of instances in this dataset.

For each target, the macro-average of F1-score is obtained by the average F1-scores of label "Favor" and "Against":

$$F_{avg} = \frac{F_{\text{favor}} + F_{\text{against}}}{2} \tag{4}$$

Table 2. Distribution of instances in the SemEval-2016 dataset

Target	#total	% of instances in train				% of instances in test			
		#train	Favor	Against	Neither	#test	Favor	Against	Neither
Atheism	733	513	17.9	59.3	22.8	220	14.5	72.7	12.7
Climate Change is Concern	564	395	53.7	3.8	42.5	169	72.8	6.5	20.7
Feminist Movement	949	664	61.6	49.4	19.0	285	20.4	64.2	15.4
Hillary Clinton	984	689	17.1	57.0	25.8	295	15.3	58.3	26.4
Legalization of Abortion	933	653	18.5	54.4	27.1	280	16.4	67.5	16.1
All	4163	2914	25.8	47.9	26.3	1249	24.3	57.3	18.4

Note that "None" class is ignored in evaluation metrics but exists during training. The calculation method of F_{favor} and F_{against} is as follows:

$$F_{\text{favor}} = \frac{2P_{\text{favor}} R_{\text{favor}}}{P_{\text{favor}} + R_{\text{favor}}} \tag{5}$$

$$F_{\text{against}} = \frac{2P_{\text{against}} R_{\text{against}}}{P_{\text{against}} + R_{\text{against}}} \tag{6}$$

where P is precision and R is recall rate.

The micro-average of F1-score calculated across targets is utilized as the evaluation metric of proposed models for Semeval-2016 Task 6.

4.2 Preprocessing and Experimental Settings

The texts sent to BERT-based model have similar preprocessing steps as [16]. The mention (beginning with '#') and URL (beginning with 'http' or 'https') information matching the regular expression in each instance is replaced with the particular token '$MENTION$' and 'URL'. To tune the best hyper-parameters, we apply 5-fold cross validation method on training set. We train the model on each target subset separately sharing the same configuration and take the concatenated prediction as the final result. During the experiments, the training batch size of BERT-based model is set to 4. The dimension for target information initialized with fastText word embeddings [7] is 100. The size of hidden units in BiLSTM is set to 128. The training epoch is located at 10 and the learning rate of Adam optimizer is $2e^{-6}$. The dropout rate between two components is 0.3 and for BiLSTM is 0.1.

4.3 Results

Validity of Model Parts. First, we investigate the impact of each component of our proposed model through ablation experiments that delete one or two components at a time.

– AT-BiLSTM: BiLSTM layer integrated with target-specific attention mechanism.
– RoBERTa: RoBERTa model with large size.

- RoBERTa + AT-BiLSTM: Our proposed model without n-gram module.
- PMINFM: Pre-trained model integrated with n-gram features module (PMINFM) alone without BiLSTM layer and make classification through linear layer.
- PMINFM-AT-BiLSTM: An ensemble model connecting pre-trained model integrated with n-gram features module to BiLSTM with target attention.

Table 3 (top) shows the performance of different component combinations in the ablation study. It is obvious that the performance of RoBERTa or AT-BiLSTM model alone is not performing as well as the ensemble model. In addition, experimental results show that F1-score increased by 2.79% when the n-gram features component combined. Compared with the around 1% increase in the related works, this increase ratio strongly proves that the additional n-gram information is the main source for the improvement of our model performance. And the drop is 0.96% after removing AT-BiLSTM, which indicates this component contributes to stance detection as well.

Table 3. Performance comparison of stance detection on the SemEval-2016 dataset

Model	Atheism	Climate	Feminism	Hillary	Abortion	F_{avg}
	F_{avg}	F_{avg}	F_{avg}	F_{avg}	F_{avg}	
AT-BiLSTM	63.62	56.33	54.66	52.54	61.06	66.04
RoBERTa	68.85	45.53	54.46	61.60	65.65	70.01
RoBERTa + AT-BiLSTM	70.91	45.17	64.94	66.07	60.14	70.98
PMINFM	71.94	43.40	64.43	65.75	63.67	72.81
PMINFM-AT-BiLSTM	**72.66**	44.75	**65.93**	65.61	68.37	**73.77**
SVM-ngrams	65.19	42.35	57.46	58.63	66.42	68.98
TAN	59.33	53.59	55.77	65.38	63.72	68.79
HAN	70.53	49.56	57.50	61.23	66.16	69.79
TGMN-CR	64.60	43.02	59.35	66.21	66.21	71.04
AT-JSS-Lex	69.22	59.18	61.49	**68.33**	**68.41**	72.33
T-DAN	65.37	**64.90**	64.12	63.53	66.74	72.57

Comparison with Baselines. Second, to evaluate the validity, we test our proposed model against the following state-of-the-art baseline methods:

- SVM-ngrams [13]: SVM linear classifier trained with word n-grams and character n-grams features. As the baseline of SemEval-2016 task 6 competition, it exceeded all the competing models.
- TAN [9]: Bidirectional RNN integrates target-specific attention mechanism, and shows the capability to extract the target part of given text which promotes the performance.
- HAN [20]: Hierarchical attention model consisted of linguistic attention for leveraging linguistic features and hyper attention for adjusting the weight of features.

- TGMN-CR [24]: End-to-end neural model combines dynamic memory module and recurrent neural network.
- AT-JSS-Lex [11]: Multi-task learning framework improving performance with the help of sentiment task and lexicon knowledge.
- T-DAN [27]: Two-stage deep neural network with densely connected BiLSTM in each stage.

All the experimental data of the above baselines in the next chapter are from the original paper.

Table 3 (bottom) shows the result of the comparison between our proposed model and baselines. In general, the proposed model has achieved the state-of-the-art level with 1.2% advantage in overall micro-average F1-score. Among five target subsets, we observe that the proposed model obtains the best result on the target "Atheism" and "Feminism", while the performance is competitive on the other targets except "Climate". Specifically, compared with SVM-ngrams model which uses the same n-gram features but is trained with SVM instead of deep neural networks, the proposed model improves by 4.79%. Furthermore, the better performance compared with other classical or novel attention-based models guaranteeing the effectiveness of the ensemble model. The model performs poorly on the "Climate" target because of the extreme label imbalance and the details will be analyzed in the next section.

4.4 Case Study

Table 4. Examples of case study

Sentence	Target	Gold	PM-BiLSTM	PMINFM-BiLSTM
@ dsurman Jesus is favor of all, that they would believe He died for them. Why try to wage a conflict you will lose? #God #SemST	Atheism	Against	Favor	Against
We live in a sad world when wanting equality makes you a troll... #SemST	Feminist Movement	Favor	None	Favor

In this section, we list two test instances in Table 4 to describe how the n-gram features works on stance detection task. For the first instance, the author expresses Jesus' fraternity towards believers to show his respect for God, so the author is obviously against atheism. The classification results show that model without n-gram embedded will be confused by the word "favor" to make misclassification results, while with the word n-gram features can capture the keyword "god" leading to correct result. The situation is not alike in the second instance, the model without n-gram considers the sentence has nothing to do with the target. Different from the PM-BiLSTM, the word "equality" which implies that it is related to the target can be noticed by attention mechanism with the help of n-gram features.

5 Conclusion

In this paper, we propose a novel ensemble model that incorporates RoBERTa's pooled output with n-gram features as the input of attention-based neural network for multi-target stance detection task. Our proposed model outperforms the state-of-the-art baselines with a micro-averaged F1-score of 73.77 on a stance detection benchmark dataset. Moreover, experimental results show that integrating n-gram features obtained substantial improvements. We conclude that integrating effective handcrafted features in one field into a pre-trained model such as RoBERTa help getting better performance in this field. Future work including solving the problem of imbalance samples, classifying stance on large-scale corpus without label and extracting additional knowledge embraced by hashtag compound.

References

1. Aldayel, A., Magdy, W.: Your stance is exposed! analysing possible factors for stance detection on social media. Proc. ACM Hum.-Comput. Interact. **3**(CSCW), 1–20 (2019)
2. Alghanmi, I., Espinosa-Anke, L., Schockaert, S.: Combining BERT with static word embeddings for categorizing social media (2020)
3. Anand, P., Walker, M., Abbott, R., Tree, J.E.F., Bowmani, R., Minor, M.: Cats rule and dogs drool!: classifying stance in online debate. In: Proceedings of the 2nd Workshop on Computational Approaches to Subjectivity and Sentiment Analysis (WASSA 2011), pp. 1–9 (2011)
4. Augenstein, I., Rocktäschel, T., Vlachos, A., Bontcheva, K.: Stance detection with bidirectional conditional encoding. arXiv preprint arXiv:1606.05464 (2016)
5. Bahdanau, D., Cho, K., Bengio, Y.: Neural machine translation by jointly learning to align and translate. arXiv preprint arXiv:1409.0473 (2014)
6. Baly, R., et al.: A characterization study of Arabic twitter data with a benchmarking for state-of-the-art opinion mining models. In: Proceedings of the Third Arabic Natural Language Processing Workshop, pp. 110–118 (2017)
7. Bojanowski, P., Grave, E., Joulin, A., Mikolov, T.: Enriching word vectors with subword information. Trans. Assoc. Comput. Linguist. **5**, 135–146 (2017)
8. Devlin, J., Chang, M.W., Lee, K., Toutanova, K.: BERT: pre-training of deep bidirectional transformers for language understanding. arXiv preprint arXiv:1810.04805 (2018)
9. Du, J., Xu, R., He, Y., Gui, L.: Stance classification with target-specific neural attention networks. In: International Joint Conferences on Artificial Intelligence (2017)
10. Dulhanty, C., Deglint, J.L., Daya, I.B., Wong, A.: Taking a stance on fake news: towards automatic disinformation assessment via deep bidirectional transformer language models for stance detection. arXiv preprint arXiv:1911.11951 (2019)
11. Li, Y., Caragea, C.: Multi-task stance detection with sentiment and stance lexicons. In: Proceedings of the 2019 Conference on Empirical Methods in Natural Language Processing and the 9th International Joint Conference on Natural Language Processing (EMNLP-IJCNLP), pp. 6300–6306 (2019)
12. Liu, Y., et al.: Roberta: a robustly optimized BERT pretraining approach. arXiv preprint arXiv:1907.11692 (2019)

13. Mohammad, S., Kiritchenko, S., Sobhani, P., Zhu, X., Cherry, C.: SemEval-2016 task 6: detecting stance in tweets. In: Proceedings of the 10th International Workshop on Semantic Evaluation (SemEval-2016), pp. 31–41 (2016)
14. Mohammad, S.M., Sobhani, P., Kiritchenko, S.: Stance and sentiment in tweets. ACM Trans. Internet Technol. (TOIT) **17**(3), 1–23 (2017)
15. Pedregosa, F., et al.: Scikit-learn: machine learning in Python. J. Mach. Learn. Res. **12**, 2825–2830 (2011)
16. Prakash, A., Madabushi, H.T.: Incorporating count-based features into pre-trained models for improved stance detection. arXiv preprint arXiv:2010.09078 (2020)
17. Radford, A., Narasimhan, K., Salimans, T., Sutskever, I.: Improving language understanding by generative pre-training (2018)
18. Schuster, M., Paliwal, K.K.: Bidirectional recurrent neural networks. IEEE Trans. Signal Process. **45**(11), 2673–2681 (1997)
19. Somasundaran, S., Wiebe, J.: Recognizing stances in ideological on-line debates. In: Proceedings of the NAACL HLT 2010 Workshop on Computational Approaches to Analysis and Generation of Emotion in Text, pp. 116–124 (2010)
20. Sun, Q., Wang, Z., Zhu, Q., Zhou, G.: Stance detection with hierarchical attention network. In: Proceedings of the 27th International Conference on Computational Linguistics, pp. 2399–2409 (2018)
21. Vlad, G.A., Tanase, M.A., Onose, C., Cercel, D.C.: Sentence-level propaganda detection in news articles with transfer learning and BERT-BiLSTM-capsule model. In: Proceedings of the Second Workshop on Natural Language Processing for Internet Freedom: Censorship, Disinformation, and Propaganda, pp. 148–154 (2019)
22. Walker, M., Anand, P., Abbott, R., Grant, R.: Stance classification using dialogic properties of persuasion. In: Proceedings of the 2012 Conference of the North American Chapter of the Association for Computational Linguistics: Human Language Technologies, pp. 592–596 (2012)
23. Wang, L., Cardie, C.: Improving agreement and disagreement identification in online discussions with a socially-tuned sentiment lexicon. arXiv preprint arXiv:1606.05706 (2016)
24. Wei, P., Mao, W., Zeng, D.: A target-guided neural memory model for stance detection in twitter. In: 2018 International Joint Conference on Neural Networks (IJCNN), pp. 1–8. IEEE (2018)
25. Wei, W., Zhang, X., Liu, X., Chen, W., Wang, T.: pkudblab at SemEval-2016 task 6: a specific convolutional neural network system for effective stance detection. In: Proceedings of the 10th International Workshop on Semantic Evaluation (SemEval-2016), pp. 384–388 (2016)
26. Yang, R., Xie, W., Liu, C., Yu, D.: BLCU_NLP at SemEval-2019 task 7: an inference chain-based GPT model for rumour evaluation. In: Proceedings of the 13th International Workshop on Semantic Evaluation, pp. 1090–1096 (2019)
27. Yang, Y., Wu, B., Zhao, K., Guo, W.: Tweet stance detection: a two-stage DC-BiLSTM model based on semantic attention. In: 2020 IEEE Fifth International Conference on Data Science in Cyberspace (DSC), pp. 22–29. IEEE (2020)
28. Zhang, C., Yamana, H.: WUY at SemEval-2020 task 7: combining BERT and Naïve Bayes-SVM for humor assessment in edited news headlines. In: Proceedings of the Fourteenth Workshop on Semantic Evaluation, pp. 1071–1076 (2020)
29. Zhou, Y., Cristea, A.I., Shi, L.: Connecting targets to tweets: semantic attention-based model for target-specific stance detection. In: Bouguettaya, A., et al. (eds.) WISE 2017, Part I. LNCS, vol. 10569, pp. 18–32. Springer, Cham (2017). https://doi.org/10.1007/978-3-319-68783-4_2

Hierarchical Ensemble for Multi-view Clustering

Fei Gao[iD] and Liu Yang[(✉)][iD]

College of Intelligence and Computing, Tianjin University, Tianjin 300350, China
{g_f,yangliuyl}@tju.edu.cn

Abstract. Multi-view clustering is a challenging task due to the distinct feature distributions among different views. To permit complementarity while exploiting consistency among views, some multi-layer models have been developed. These models usually enforce consistent representation on the top layer for clustering purpose while allowing the other layers to represent various attributes of the multi-view data. However, a single consistent layer is often insufficient especially for complicated real-world tasks. In addition, the existing models often represent different views using the same number of layers without taking the various levels of complexity of different views into account. Furthermore, different views are often considered to be equal in the clustering process, which does not necessarily hold in many applications. To address these issues, in this paper, we present a hierarchical ensemble framework for multi-view clustering (HEMVC). It is superior to the existing methods in three facets. Firstly, HEMVC allows for different views to share more than one consistent layers and implement ensemble clustering on all shared layers. Secondly, it facilitates an adaptive clustering scheme by automatically quantifying the contribution of each layer and each view in the ensemble learning process. Thirdly, it represents different views using different numbers of layers to compensate various complexities of different views. To realize HEMVC, a two-stage algorithm has been derived and implemented. The experimental results on five benchmark datasets illustrate its performance by comparing with the state-of-the-art methods.

Keywords: Multi-view clustering · Ensemble learning · Hierarchical framework

1 Introduction

Multi-view clustering (MVC) [2,5,22,26,27] aims to identify the group structures in multi-view data from different domains [15,28]. In order to unify multi-view features, a series of MVC approaches have been proposed. The first naive way is to directly concatenate the features from different views together and apply traditional single-view learning methods on the concatenated representation. However, different views may naturally be expressed in completely distinct manners, so that simply combining all the features fails to reveal the group structure effectively. The second type of strategies is named late integration or

© Springer Nature Switzerland AG 2021
I. Farkaš et al. (Eds.): ICANN 2021, LNCS 12893, pp. 280–292, 2021.
https://doi.org/10.1007/978-3-030-86365-4_23

late fusion, which is well-known in the regime of ensemble clustering [9,10,16]. It generates basic partitions from each view individually, and fuses them together for final clustering. However, there is no communication among individual partitions until the final consensus stage. Hence, these method only make use of very limited complementary and consistent information in different views.

The third category aims to map the multi-view data from original feature spaces to a common space with the structure preserved. A typical approach is to seek for a shared latent space by constructing similarity graph, such as nearest-neighbor graphs and self-represented graphs [7,11,14,20,21,23,24]. But it is always computationally expensive to build the similarity graph [13]. In addition, canonical correlation analysis (CCA) based methods [3] learn a mapping function to maximize the correlation between two feature spaces, while Joint non-negative matrix factorization (NMF) methods [12,19] exploit the latent space by sharing the consensus matrix. Multi-view clustering in latent embedding space (MCLES) [4] jointly learns latent embedding space, similarity matrix and cluster indicator matrix. In general, these latent space learning methods rely on simple transformation functions to bridge the gap across multiple views, which is often limited by their low expressibility.

To overcome this problem, multi-layer models have been adopted to learn the hierarchical structure for multi-view clustering. Deep CCA-based methods [18] are proposed to learn complicated nonlinear transformations in a layer-wise fashion specifically for two-view problem. Later, deep generalized CCA (DGCCA) method [1] and multi-view deep semi-nonnegative matrix factorization (MDSMF) method [28] were proposed to learn shared representations for general multi-view data. Although clustering performance has been successfully improved, these deep approaches simply rely on only the top layer for consistent latent representation, which is often insufficient for real-world applications where complicated underlying group structure is often embedded among instances. Moreover, these methods often assume equal importance of different layers and views in the clustering process, which does not necessarily hold due to the different levels of expressibility of different layers and views. Furthermore, these methods often represent different views using the same number of layers without taking their different levels of complexity into account. Such formulation is not proper especially when unbalanced dimensions appear among multiple views. For instance, the dimensions of two views are 1750 and 79 respectively in BDGP dataset. As the dimension of the first view is significantly higher than the second one, the required structure for the first view should be more complicated than the second. Enforcing the same deep structure may lead to significant information loss for the first view.

In order to address these limitations, we propose to develop a hierarchical ensemble framework for multi-view clustering (HEMVC). Firstly, HEMVC allows multiple shared layers among different views to facilitate a more comprehensive consistent representation among different layers. As shown in an example in Fig. 1 where neither shared layer 1 nor shared layer 2 is capable of representing the complicated multi-view data by its own, HEMVC provides a more expressive representation on group structural for better clustering performance.

282 F. Gao and L. Yang

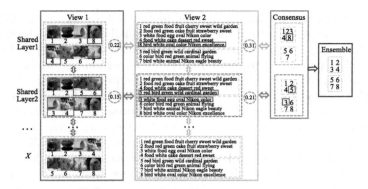

Fig. 1. Illustration of the clustering result learned by the hierarchical ensemble framework HEMVC. Taken the NUS-WIDE dataset ('food' and 'birds') as an example, the original data of two views (image and text) are shown in the bottom layer. The clustering results of two views are illustrated in the left two columns in a layer-by-layer fashion. HEMVC is able to learn a hierarchical structure features, such as color (shared layer 2) and shape (shared layer 1). Moreover, it can automatically learn a weight for each layer and each view to quantify its contribution in clustering process, which is shown in the round box. The clustering result based on the common representation of each shared layer is shown in the third column, and the ensemble clustering based on the shared layers is shown in the right box. The misclassified examples are marked with red boxes. It can be observed that some instances (e.g., eagle, image 8) are misgrouped in one of the shared layers (shared layer 1) while being successfully clustered in another (shared layer 2), but according to the ensemble strategy, all the instances can be clustered correctly. (Color figure online)

One step further, different views and layers, providing the cluster information at different levels, are allowed to contribute differently to the final results. Adaptive weights are updated automatically, and are involved for multi-layer and multi-view integration, so that the ensemble results would achieve better performance. For instance in Fig. 1, layers and views achieving better clustering performance receive larger weights as highlighted by the dashed circular boxes.

Moreover, the HEMVC framework also permits different views to be represented by different numbers of layers to compensate their different levels of complexity.

In summary, our contributions in this work can be concluded as follows:

- HEMVC can obtain comprehensive consensus representations by enforcing consistent constraint on more than one shared layers, and explore the ensemble clustering result of the shared layers from different views.
- HEMVC can automatically learn a weight for each layer and each view to quantify the adaptive contribution, and this weight can be used to combine the clustering result of different shared layers.
- HEMVC can capture the diversity of feature spaces using the unshared layers, which allows the hierarchical structures of different views to be modeled by distinct numbers of unshared layers.

2   The Hierarchical Ensemble Framework

In this section, the hierarchical ensemble framework for multi-view clustering is introduced firstly, followed by a corresponding two-stage learning algorithm.

2.1   The Proposed Model

Given a set of n instances in V views, each instance is represented with d_v features in the v-th view, the data matrix is denoted by $X^{(v)} \in \mathbb{R}^{d_v \times n}$, then the dataset is $\{X^{(v)}\}_{v=1}^{V}$. Multi-view clustering aims to divide n instances into c clusters. For the v-th view, m_v hierarchical layers of latent representations of data matrix $X^{(v)}$ can be given by the following factorization[1]:

$$X^{(v)} \approx Z_{m_v}^{(v)} Z_{m_v-1}^{(v)} \cdots Z_1^{(v)} H_1^{(v)},$$

where m_v is the number of layers in the v-th view, it should be defined in advance based on the dimension d_v. $Z_{m_v}^{(v)} \in \mathbb{R}^{d_v \times r_{m_v}^{(v)}}$ and $Z_l^{(v)} \in \mathbb{R}^{r_{l+1}^{(v)} \times r_l^{(v)}} (1 \leq l < m_v)$ are the basis matrices of the bottom (m_v-th) layer and other layers in the v-th view respectively, $r_l^{(v)}$ is the dimension of the l-th layer latent space. $H_1^{(v)} \in \mathbb{R}^{r_1^{(v)} \times n}$ is the representation of the first layer in the v-th view. The error of multi-layer matrix factorization is evaluated by

$$D(X^{(v)}, Z_{m_v}^{(v)} \cdots Z_1^{(v)} H_1^{(v)}).$$

The implicit representations for a hierarchy of m_v layers can be given by the following factorizations: $H_2^{(v)} \approx Z_1^{(v)} H_1^{(v)}; \cdots; H_l^{(v)} \approx Z_{l-1}^{(v)} \cdots Z_1^{(v)} H_1^{(v)}; \cdots; H_{m_v}^{(v)} \approx Z_{m_v-1}^{(v)} \cdots Z_1^{(v)} H_1^{(v)}$, where $H_l^{(v)} \in \mathbb{R}^{r_l^{(v)} \times n}$. Then for the l-th layer, $X^{(v)}$ is decomposed as $Z_{m_v}^{(v)} Z_{m_v-1}^{(v)} \cdots Z_l^{(v)} H_l^{(v)}$.

In order to effectively exploit data correlation among multi-views, the consistent constraints are enforced to the top μ layers. μ is a parameter to control the number of shared layers and $\mu \leq \min\{m_v\}_{v=1}^{V}$. For μ shared latent layers, the dimension for each of them remains to be constant among all views, that is $r_l^{(1)} = r_l^{(2)} = \cdots = r_l^{(V)} = r_l (1 \leq l \leq \mu)$, then the dimension setting of all layers in the v-th view is $[r_1 \cdots r_\mu \ r_{\mu+1}^{(v)} \cdots r_{m_v}^{(v)}]$. In general, $r_1 < \ldots < r_\mu < r_{\mu+1}^{(v)} < \ldots < r_{m_v}^{(v)} < d_v$. For the l-th shared layer ($1 \leq l \leq \mu$), the disagreement between coefficient matrix of the v-th view $H_l^{(v)}$ and the consensus matrix $H_l^* \in \mathbb{R}^{r_l \times n}$ is evaluated by

$$D(H_l^{(v)}, H_l^*).$$

---

[1] To unify the number of the top shared layers in different views, the layer is numbered from top to bottom, which is opposite with Deep Semi-NMF [17]. It does not affect the rigorousness.

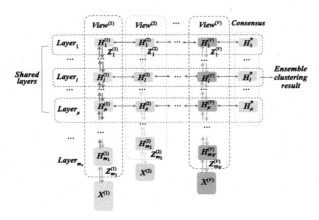

Fig. 2. The proposed framework. Each column represents the multi-layer structure established for one view. Each row represents a layer: the top μ layers indicate the shared layers, the consensus H_l^* is enforced on each shared layer; the bottom layers exploit the diversity of feature spaces with different structures allowed for different views. Ensemble clustering strategy is used to cluster the multi-view data with the new multi-layer representations $\{H_l^*\}_{l=1}^{\mu}$.

For the top μ shared layers, $D(H_l^{(v)}, H_l^*)$ should be involved in the loss function of the hierarchy structure. To sum up, the overall loss function is formulated by

$$\min_{\Omega} \sum_{v=1}^{V} (\omega_l^{(v)})^{\gamma} \left(D(X^{(v)}, Z_{m_v}^{(v)} \cdots Z_1^{(v)} H_1^{(v)}) + \lambda \sum_{l=1}^{\mu} D(H_l^{(v)}, H_l^*) \right) \qquad (1)$$

$$\text{s.t.} \quad H_l^{(v)} \geq 0, \sum_{v=1}^{V} \sum_{l=1}^{\mu} \omega_l^{(v)} = 1, \omega_l^{(v)} \geq 0$$

where $\Omega = \left\{ \left\{ \{Z_l^{(v)}, H_l^{(v)}, \omega_l^{(v)}\}_{l=1}^{m_v} \right\}_{v=1}^{V}, \{H_l^*\}_{l=1}^{\mu} \right\}$ is the set of desired variables. $\omega_l^{(v)}$ is the weighting coefficient for the v-th view and the l-th layer. γ is the parameter to control the weight distribution. λ is the parameter to balance the fitting term and consistent term.

The new representations $\{H_l^*\}_{l=1}^{\mu}$ of the top μ shared layers are used to cluster the data by ensemble clustering methods, such as the weighted multiple kernel method [8]. The adaptive weights of views and layers can be used to unify the clustering results of multiple shared layers. The complete work flow of the proposed framework is depicted in Fig. 2.

Note that any loss function can be incorporated into the proposed objective function. Here we simply employ least-square loss as an example. Also the distance can be easily replaced by nonlinear loss function for the proposed framework. Most of the regularization terms for clustering purpose, such as the Laplacian terms and orthogonal constraints, can be easily integrated into the proposed model. Moreover, various ensemble clustering methods can also be adopted on the new representations.

2.2   The Numerical Scheme

To perform the proposed hierarchical ensemble clustering task, a two-stage strategy including pre-training and fine-tuning has been employed [17].

Pre-training. Similar to [17], in order to have an initial approximation of variables, the input data matrix is decomposed as $X^{(v)} \approx Z_{m^{(v)}}^{(v)} H_{m^{(v)}}^{(v)}$ to perform the pre-training. For each layer ($l > 1$), $H_l^{(v)}$ is updated by $Z_{l-1}^{(v)} \cdots Z_1^{(v)} H_1^{(v)}$ from top to bottom. Weight of each layer and each view $\omega_l^{(v)}$ is initialized to $1/(V \times \mu)$, V is the total number of views.

Fine-Tuning. After the pre-training, the variables are fine-tuned layer by layer in an iterative fashion, in which an alternative scheme is used to update each of the variables by fixing the others for each layer.

(1) **Updating rule for basis matrix $Z_l^{(v)}$:** For the l-th layer, by fixing $\{Z_i^{(v)}\}_{i=l+1}^{m_v}$, and setting $\Phi_{m_v+1}^{(v)} = \phi$ (empty set) and $\Phi_{l+1}^{(v)} = Z_{m_v}^{(v)} Z_{m_v-1}^{(v)} \ldots Z_{l+1}^{(v)} (1 \leq l < m_v)$, the proposed optimization problem for $Z_l^{(v)}$ is

$$\min_{Z_l^{(v)}} \left\| X^{(v)} - \Phi_{l+1}^{(v)} Z_l^{(v)} H_l^{(v)} \right\|_F^2. \tag{2}$$

By setting the derivative to 0, the solution is given as

$$Z_l^{(v)} = (\Phi_{l+1}^{(v)})^\dagger X^{(v)} (H_l^{(v)})^\dagger, \tag{3}$$

where $(\Phi_{l+1}^{(v)})^\dagger$ and $(H_l^{(v)})^\dagger$ indicate the pseudo-inverse of $\Phi_{l+1}^{(v)}$ and $H_l^{(v)}$, respectively.

(2) **Updating rule for representation matrix $H_l^{(v)}$:** For $\mu < l \leq m_v$, the proposed optimization problem for $H_l^{(v)}$ is

$$\min_{H_l^{(v)}} \left\| X^{(v)} - \Phi_l^{(v)} H_l^{(v)} \right\|_F^2. \tag{4}$$

The updating rule is formulated by utilizing a similar proof to [6] as follows:

$$H_l^{(v)} = H_l^{(v)} \odot \sqrt{\frac{A}{B}} \tag{5}$$

where $A = [(\Phi_l^{(v)})^T X^{(v)}]^{pos} + [(\Phi_l^{(v)})^T \Phi_l^{(v)} H_l^{(v)}]^{neg}$, $B = [(\Phi_l^{(v)})^T X^{(v)}]^{neg} + [(\Phi_l^{(v)})^T \Phi_l^{(v)} H_l^{(v)}]^{pos}$. Υ^{pos} is a matrix with all negative elements in Υ replaced by 0, while positive elements are replaced by 0 in Υ^{neg} [17].

For $1 \leq l \leq \mu$, the proposed optimization problem is

$$\min_{H_l^{(v)}} \left\| X^{(v)} - \Phi_l^{(v)} H_l^{(v)} \right\|_F^2 + \lambda \left\| H_l^{(v)} - H_l^* \right\|_F^2. \tag{6}$$

Similarly, the updating rule is formulated by

$$H_l^{(v)} = H_l^{(v)} \odot \sqrt{\frac{A + \lambda P}{B + \lambda Q}} \tag{7}$$

where $P = [H_l^*]^{pos} + [H_l^{(v)}]^{neg}$, $Q = [H_l^*]^{neg} + [H_l^{(v)}]^{pos}$.

(3) **Updating rule for consistent matrix** $H_l^*(1 \leq l \leq \mu)$: By fixing $\{H_l^{(v)}, \omega_l^{(v)}\}_{v=1}^V$, the proposed optimization problem for H_l^* becomes

$$\min_{H_l^*} \sum_{v=1}^{V} (\omega_l^{(v)})^\gamma \|H_l^{(v)} - H_l^*\|_F^2. \tag{8}$$

It is easy to obtain the following rule,

$$H_l^* = \frac{\sum_{v=1}^{V} (\omega_l^{(v)})^\gamma H_l^{(v)}}{\sum_{v=1}^{V} (\omega_l^{(v)})^\gamma}. \tag{9}$$

(4) **Updating rule for weight of each layer and each view** $\omega_l^{(v)}$: For $(1 \leq l \leq \mu)$, let $U_l^{(v)} = \|E_l^{(v)}\|_F^2 + \lambda \|C_l^{(v)}\|_F^2$, where $E_l^{(v)} = X^{(v)} - \Phi_l^{(v)} H_l^{(v)}$ and $C_l^{(v)} = H_l^{(v)} - H_l^*$. When $(\mu + 1 \leq l \leq m_v)$, $U_l^{(v)} = \|E_l^{(v)}\|_F^2$. The objective term with respect to $\omega_l^{(v)}$ can be written as

$$\min_{\omega_l} \sum_{v=1}^{V} \sum_{l=1}^{\mu} (\omega_l^{(v)})^\gamma U_l^{(v)}$$

$$\text{s.t.} \sum_{v=1}^{V} \sum_{l=1}^{\mu} \omega_l^{(v)} = 1, \omega_l \geq 0. \tag{10}$$

Similar to [28], the updating rule is

$$\omega_l^{(v)} = (\gamma U_l^{(v)})^{\frac{1}{1-\gamma}}. \tag{11}$$

In order to set $\sum_{v=1}^{V} \sum_{l=1}^{\mu} \omega_l^{(v)} = 1$, the normalized rule is

$$\omega_l^{(v)} = \frac{(U_l^{(v)})^{\frac{1}{1-\gamma}}}{\sum_{v=1}^{V} \sum_{l=1}^{\mu} (U_l^{(v)})^{\frac{1}{1-\gamma}}}. \tag{12}$$

Up to now, the updating rules for down up have all been conducted, then $H_l^{(v)}$ is updated from top to bottom, they are repeated iteratively. After getting the new representations $\{H_l^*\}_{l=1}^{\mu}$ of the top μ layers, the ensemble clustering method can be used to the new representations.

3 Experiments

In this section, a series of experiments on five real-world datasets have been conducted to demonstrate the performance of the proposed HEMVC model by comparing with the-state-of-the-art multi-view clustering methods.

3.1   Implementation

Datasets. Datasets statistics are listed in Table 1.

Table 1. Description of the datasets.

Dataset	♯views	♯instances	♯clusters	♯dimensions
BDGP	2	2500	5	1750/79
NUS-C10	2	8000	10	500/1000
Yale	3	165	15	4096/3304/6750
YaleB	3	640	10	2500/3304/6750
COIL	3	1440	20	1024/3304/6750

Methodology. For the compared baselines, we have considered a series of methods. Among them, three ensemble methods (**PTGP** [9], **MVEC** [16] and **LWGP** [10]) and two graph-based methods (**ECMSC** [20] and **MLAN** [14]) are selected. And three methods based on multi-layer latent space are compared. **MDSMF** [28] applies Deep Semi-NMF clustering to project each view data to the shared latent subspace. **DCCAE** [18] and **DGCCA** [1] are two CCA-based methods. **MCLES** [4] is a state-of-the-art work which jointly learns latent embedding space, similarity matrix and cluster indicator matrix.

The same spectral clustering method is used for all methods to ensure the fairness of the results. For our model, the weighted linear multiple kernel method is adopted to unify all kernels constructed on $\{H_l^*\}_{l=1}^{\mu}$, where the weight of each layer can be the weight of combined kernels. And then the spectral clustering method is used on the unified kernel. Each method is conducted for ten times.

Six metrics [25] are adopted including accuracy (ACC), normalized mutual information (NMI), adjusted rand index (AR), F-score, Precision and Recall.

3.2   Results and Discussion

Adaptive Weights. The proposed model can set different numbers of layers for different views. Taken BDGP dataset as an example due to the unbalanced dimensions (1750 and 79), Table 2 shows NMI results under different layer size.

In order to illustrate the influence of sharing more than one layers with adaptive weights, MDSMF [28] which only shares the same representation on the top layer is selected for comparison in this part. The dimension of latent space should be smaller than that of the original space for MDSMF, so it cannot be conducted with layer structure of [30, 60, 300] and [15, 50, 100, 500]. Taken the layer sizes [30, 60, 300]/[30, 60] as an example, t-SNE visualization of $H_l^{(v)}$ generated by HEMVC is shown in Fig. 3(a). From Fig. 3(a), we can see the second view and the second layer might give the best result which indicates the second view and layer is more important. This is actually coincident with the learned weights, i.e. the weight for the second view and layer (0.351) is the largest. t-SNE visualization of MDSMF is shown in Fig. 3(b), the instances in the first layer are

Table 2. The adaptive weights learned by HEMVC and clustering results (NMI) of HEMVC and MDSMF under different layer size settings on BDGP dataset.

Layer size setting of each view	Adaptive weight of each layer ω	HEMVC	MDSMF
View1 [30, 60] View2 [30, 60]	[0.153, 0.264] [0.235, 0.348]	0.833	0.491
View1 [30, 60, 300] View2 [30, 60]	[0.106, 0.143, 0.137] [0.263, 0.351]	0.954	–
View1 [15, 50] View2 [15, 50]	[0.117, 0.179] [0.303, 0.401]	0.829	0.552
View1 [15, 50, 100, 500] View2 [15,50]	[0.146, 0.154, 0.112, 0.123] [0.202, 0.263]	0.908	–

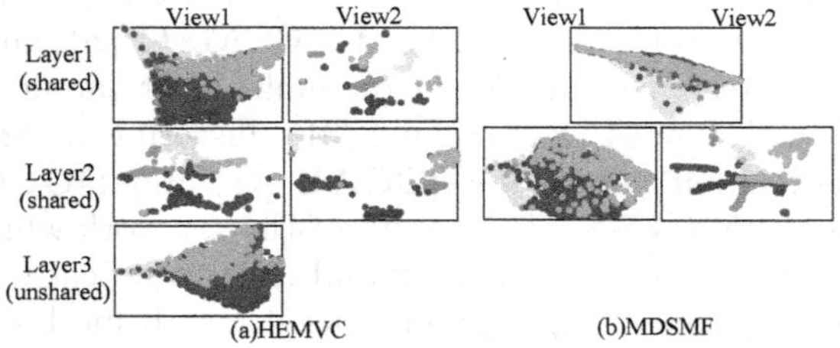

Fig. 3. The t-SNE visualization of $H_l^{(v)}$ generated by (a) HEMVC [30, 60, 300]/[30, 60] and (b) MDSMF [30, 60].

not well clustered for MDSMF, which validates our assumption that it is not reasonable to only share one single layer.

Ensemble Clustering Results. We conduct experiments to evaluate the ensemble strategy on the Yale dataset. Taken the layer size setting [50, 100, 250, 500, 1000] for all views as an example, the first three layers are shared. As shown in Fig. 4, we can see that the instances are well clustered by the ensemble clustering.

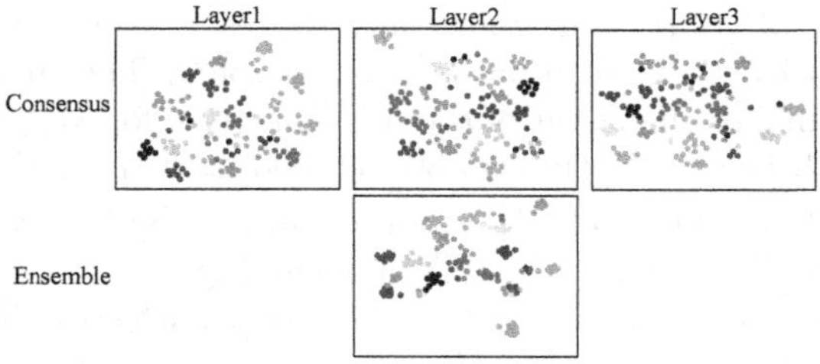

Fig. 4. The clustering result of each shared layer and the ensemble result.

Effect of Parameters. Taken YaleB dataset as an example, the effect of three important parameters (γ, λ, μ) is illustrated in this part. Parameter γ controls the weights distribution of $\omega_l^{(v)}$. The resulting NMIs of different selections of γ are shown in Fig. 5(a). γ is selected from a candidate set of $\{0.002, 0.02, 0.2, 2, 20, 200\}$. From Fig. 5(a), it can be seen that the best clustering performance is obtained when γ is around 2.

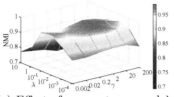
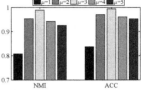

(a) Effect of parameters γ and λ (b) Effect of parameter μ

Fig. 5. Effect of parameter on YaleB dataset

λ balances the contribution of fitting term and consistent term, it is tuned among $\{0.0001, 0.001, 0.01, 0.1, 1, 10\}$. The NMI firstly goes up as λ increases, which suggests that the effectiveness of the consistent term. The optimal results are obtained when $\lambda = 0.01$ and the NMI decreases afterwards as larger λ which enforces too strict consistency in representations to destroy the diversity of multiple views. μ is the number of shared layers, the results on YaleB dataset are shown in Fig. 5(b). When $\mu = 1$, the result is the worst which illustrates the fact that only one layer is not enough to constrain the consistency. The best is for $\mu = 3$, it illustrates that more than one layers are necessary to preserve the consistency among different views. The performance decreases when $\mu > 3$, as too many shared layers may reduce the complementarity of representations.

Comparison of Clustering Performance. The results are listed in Table 3. DCCAE cannot deal with more than two views, so it is not tested on three-view datasets. MCLES is ensitive to parameters, we only list reasonable results on Yale and COIL. As expected, the proposed model consistently outperforms the baselines. For ensemble clustering methods (PTGP, MVEC and LWGP), they do not fully use the hierarchical information in the original data and the interaction between individual partitions. The graph-based methods (ECMSC and MLAN) convert the original feature space into similarity graph while some complicated structures in the original space are possibly ignored. The proposed model outperforms MDSMF and MCLES, as more consistent information can be preserved in more than one shared layers, and the distinct contributions of the shared layers to the clustering task are automatically adjusted. Finally, compared to CCA-based methods (DCCAE and DGCCA) which consider the equal importance for all views, the proposed method can automatically adjust the weights of different views which emphasizes useful information from the important view. Overall, the proposed model benefits from its sufficient amount of information learned with the hierarchical ensemble strategy with all views.

Table 3. The clustering results.

BDGP	ACC	NMI	AR	F-score	Precision	Recall	NUS-C10	ACC	NMI	AR	F-score	Precision	Recall
PTGP	0.799	0.664	0.517	0.624	0.564	0.697	PTGP	0.594	0.443	0.319	0.391	0.360	0.418
MVEC	0.743	0.616	0.498	0.593	0.528	0.654	MVEC	0.579	0.464	0.307	0.362	0.356	0.407
LWGP	0.871	0.740	0.683	0.748	0.720	0.779	LWGP	0.505	0.461	0.275	0.375	0.271	0.401
ECMSC	0.913	0.865	0.826	0.861	0.845	0.879	ECMSC	0.596	0.494	0.327	0.408	0.339	0.512
MLAN	0.948	0.910	0.906	0.924	0.922	0.928	MLAN	0.420	0.372	0.246	0.325	0.321	0.349
MDSMF	0.593	0.572	0.564	0.569	0.564	0.675	MDSMF	0.543	0.454	0.274	0.366	0.286	0.509
DCCAE	0.826	0.732	0.759	0.723	0.735	0.776	DCCAE	0.531	0.433	0.289	0.367	0.335	0.406
DGCCA	0.943	0.863	0.896	0.892	0.888	0.896	DGCCA	0.558	0.462	0.293	0.379	0.336	0.471
HEMVC	**0.989**	**0.954**	**0.969**	**0.981**	**0.979**	**0.975**	HEMVC	**0.643**	**0.535**	**0.349**	**0.431**	**0.362**	**0.543**
Yale	ACC	NMI	AR	F-score	Precision	Recall	**COIL**	ACC	NMI	AR	F-score	Precision	Recall
PTGP	0.593	0.672	0.455	0.491	0.449	0.541	PTGP	0.707	0.845	0.704	0.720	0.670	0.778
MVEC	0.569	0.627	0.412	0.479	0.427	0.493	MVEC	0.739	0.893	0.707	0.725	0.620	0.855
LWGP	0.600	0.671	0.406	0.449	0.384	0.539	LWGP	0.793	0.904	0.777	0.789	0.735	0.851
ECMSC	0.771	0.773	0.590	0.617	0.584	0.621	ECMSC	0.860	0.954	0.827	0.833	0.746	0.944
MLAN	0.558	0.590	0.297	0.348	0.293	0.463	MLAN	0.862	0.961	0.835	0.844	0.758	**0.953**
MDSMF	0.745	0.782	0.579	0.601	0.598	0.613	MDSMF	0.839	0.843	0.832	0.832	0.786	0.843
DGCCA	0.791	0.757	0.591	0.621	0.613	0.637	DGCCA	0.783	0.921	0.771	0.781	0.769	0.891
MCLES	0.721	0.752	0.555	0.584	0.550	0.622	MCLES	0.797	0.911	0.772	0.784	0.725	0.854
HEMVC	**0.867**	**0.849**	**0.732**	**0.749**	**0.721**	**0.769**	HEMVC	**0.912**	**0.969**	**0.862**	**0.863**	**0.851**	0.949
YaleB	ACC	NMI	AR	F-score	Precision	Recall							
PTGP	0.623	0.623	0.404	0.513	0.573	0.578							
MVEC	0.728	0.696	0.436	0.531	0.602	0.572							
LWGP	0.695	0.688	0.465	0.526	0.613	0.630							
ECMSC	0.783	0.759	0.544	0.597	0.513	0.718							
MLAN	0.601	0.641	0.424	0.491	0.417	0.597							
MDSMF	0.763	0.649	0.512	0.564	0.525	0.610							
DGCCA	0.875	0.866	0.763	0.781	0.743	0.825							
HEMVC	**0.994**	**0.989**	**0.989**	**0.988**	**0.989**	**0.989**							

4 Conclusion

In this paper, a hierarchical ensemble approach is proposed for MVC problem. HEMVC can utilize the ensemble consistent information from different views by sharing more than one layers, and automatically estimate the importance of each layer and view in the ensemble learning process. Moreover, it can capture the diversity of distinct feature spaces in the rest unshared layers. Experimental results demonstrate that the proposed model can get better performance compared to the state-of-the-art multi-view clustering methods.

Acknowledgements. This work was supported in part by Beijing Natural Science Foundation under Grant Z180006.

References

1. Benton, A., Khayrallah, H.: Deep generalized canonical correlation analysis. arXiv preprint arXiv:1702.02519 (2017)
2. Chao, G., Sun, S.: A survey on multi-view clustering. arXiv preprint arXiv:1712.06246 (2017)

3. Zhou, Y., Cristea, A.I., Shi, L.: Connecting targets to tweets: semantic attention-based model for target-specific stance detection. In: Bouguettaya, A., et al. (eds.) WISE 2017, Part I. LNCS, vol. 10569, pp. 18–32. Springer, Cham (2017). https://doi.org/10.1007/978-3-319-68783-4_2

4. Chen, M.S., Huang, L.: Multi-view clustering in latent embedding space. In: Proceedings of the AAAI Conference on Artificial Intelligence, vol. 34, pp. 3513–3520 (2020)

5. Cheng, M., Jing, L., Ng, M.K.: Tensor-based low-dimensional representation learning for multi-view clustering. IEEE Trans. Image Process. **28**(5), 2399–2414 (2019)

6. Ding, C.H., Li, T.: Convex and semi-nonnegative matrix factorizations. IEEE Trans. Pattern Anal. Mach. Intell. **32**(1), 45–55 (2010)

7. Gao, H., Nie, F.: Multi-view subspace clustering. In: Proceedings of the IEEE International Conference on Computer Vision, pp. 4238–4246 (2015)

8. Gönen, M., Alpaydın, E.: Multiple kernel learning algorithms. J. Mach. Learn. Res. **12**, 2211–2268 (2011)

9. Huang, D., Lai, J.H.: Robust ensemble clustering using probability trajectories. IEEE Trans. Knowl. Data Eng. **28**(5), 1312–1326 (2016)

10. Huang, D., Wang, C.D.: Locally weighted ensemble clustering. IEEE Trans. Cybern. **48**(5), 1460–1473 (2018)

11. Jing, P., Su, Y.: Learning robust affinity graph representation for multi-view clustering. Inf. Sci. **544**, 155–167 (2021)

12. Liu, J., Wang, C., Gao, J., Han, J.: Multi-view clustering via joint nonnegative matrix factorization. In: Proceedings of the SIAM International Conference on Data Mining, pp. 252–260 (2013)

13. Ng, M.K., Wu, Q.: A fast Markov chain based algorithm for MIML learning. Neurocomputing **216**, 763–777 (2016)

14. Nie, F., Cai, G.: Auto-weighted multi-view learning for image clustering and semi-supervised classification. IEEE Trans. Image Process. **27**(3), 1501–1511 (2018)

15. Sun, S.: A survey of multi-view machine learning. Neural Comput. Appl. **23**(7–8), 2031–2038 (2013)

16. Tao, Z., Liu, H.: From ensemble clustering to multi-view clustering. In: Proceedings of the International Joint Conference on Artificial Intelligence, pp. 2843–2849 (2017)

17. Trigeorgis, G., Bousmalis, K.: A deep matrix factorization method for learning attribute representations. IEEE Trans. Pattern Anal. Mach. Intell. **39**(3), 417–429 (2017)

18. Wang, W., Arora, R.: On deep multi-view representation learning: objectives and optimization. arXiv preprint arXiv:1602.01024 (2016)

19. Wang, X., Zhang, T.: Multiview clustering based on non-negative matrix factorization and pairwise measurements. IEEE Trans. Cybern. **49**(9), 3333–3346 (2019)

20. Wang, X., Guo, X.: Exclusivity-consistency regularized multi-view subspace clustering. In: Proceedings of the IEEE Conference on Computer Vision and Pattern Recognition, pp. 923–931 (2017)

21. Wang, Y., Wu, L.: Multi-view spectral clustering via structured low-rank matrix factorization. arXiv preprint arXiv:1709.01212 (2017)

22. Wen, J., Xu, Y., Liu, H.: Incomplete multiview spectral clustering with adaptive graph learning. IEEE Trans. Cybern. **50**(4), 1418–1429 (2020)

23. Yin, M., Gao, J.: Low-rank multi-view clustering in third-order tensor space. arXiv preprint arXiv:1608.08336 (2016)

24. Zhan, K., Zhang, C.: Graph learning for multiview clustering. IEEE Trans. Cybern. **8**(99), 1–9 (2017)

25. Zhang, C., Fu, H.: Low-rank tensor constrained multiview subspace clustering. In: IEEE International Conference on Computer Vision, pp. 1582–1590 (2015)
26. Zhang, C., Fu, H.: Generalized latent multi-view subspace clustering. IEEE Trans. Pattern Anal. Mach. Intell. **42**(1), 86–99 (2020)
27. Zhang, Y., Yang, Y.: A multitask multiview clustering algorithm in heterogeneous situations based on LLE and LE. Knowl.-Based Syst. **163**, 776–786 (2019)
28. Zhao, H.: Multi-view clustering via deep matrix factorization. In: Proceedings of the Association for Advancement of Artificial Intelligence, pp. 2921–2927 (2017)

Structure-Aware Multi-scale Hierarchical Graph Convolutional Network for Skeleton Action Recognition

Changxiang He[1]🆔, Shuting Liu[1], Ying Zhao[2], Xiaofei Qin[2], Jiayuan Zeng[1], and Xuedian Zhang[2(✉)]

[1] College of Science, University of Shanghai for Science and Technology, Shanghai, China
[2] School of Optical-Electrical and Computer Engineering, University of Shanghai for Science and Technology, Shanghai, China

Abstract. In recent years, graph convolutional neural network (GCNN) has achieved the most advanced results in skeleton action recognition tasks. However, existing models mainly focus on extracting local information from joint-level and part-level, but ignore the global information of frame-level and the relevance between multiple levels, which lead to the loss of hierarchical information. Moreover, these models consider the non-physical connection relationship between nodes but neglect the dependence between body parts. The lose of topology information directly results in poor model performance. In this paper, we propose a structure-aware multi-scale hierarchical graph convolutional network (SAMS-HGCN) model, which includes two modules: a structure-aware hierarchical graph pooling block (SA-HGP Block) and a multi-scale fusion module (MSF module). Specifically, SA-HGP Block establishes a hierarchical network to capture the topological information of multiple levels by using the hierarchical graph pooling (HGP) operation and model the dependence among parts via the structure-aware learning (SA Learning) operation. MSF module fuses information of different scales in each level to obtain multi-scale global structural information. Experiments show that our method achieves comparable performances to state-of-the-art methods on NTU-RGB+D and Kinetics-Skeleton datasets.

Keywords: Skeleton action recognition · Hierarchical graph convolution network · Multi-scale fusion

1 Introduction

Action recognition is a new research topic in recent years, which attracts much attention in academia. It is widely used in human-computer interaction, automatic driving, intelligent health care and video surveillance [1,2]. However, the method of action recognition based on video has a large amount of computation. Moreover, due to the complexity of human behavior environment, when

ⓒ Springer Nature Switzerland AG 2021
I. Farkaš et al. (Eds.): ICANN 2021, LNCS 12893, pp. 293–304, 2021.
https://doi.org/10.1007/978-3-030-86365-4_24

performing action recognition tasks, it is often interfered by background noise, lighting conditions, object occlusion or the change of shooting angle [3,4], which greatly increases the difficulty of action recognition tasks.

Fortunately, with the development of vision sensors such as Microsoft Kinect [5], people can quickly and accurately obtain 3D skeleton coordinates of human body. Due to the strong robustness of skeleton coordinate information to the interference of external environment, skeleton-based action recognition task has been well developed.

Most of the original skeleton-based action recognition methods used recurrent neural networks [6] or convolutional neural networks [7] to treat the skeleton sequence as a pseudo-image for processing, and input it to the neural network for action information extraction. However, these methods ignore the spatial relationship between joints, which results the loss of topological structures in the skeleton frame.

In [8], the graph neural network was first applied to the skeleton action recognition task in order to extract the discriminativeness of human action information. [9] introduced a multi-scale module by increasing the skeleton adjacency to a higher power. [10] used adjacency matrix for multi-scale modeling, and it also generated node connections to enhance spatial graph convolution. [11] utilized bone features, which simultaneously updated joint and bone features through alternate spatial aggregation schemes. [12] introduced a graph adaptation with self-attention and a free-learning graph residual mask.

However, these models ignored the global information of frame-level and the dependence between multiple levels, thus losing a lot of hierarchical structure information. Moreover, these models considered the non-physical connection relationship between nodes but neglected the dependence between body parts. These loss of topology information lead to the poor model performance.

To overcome such limitations, we propose a new structure-aware multi-scale hierarchical graph convolutional network (SAMS-HGCN). We build a multi-scale hierarchical network by sequentially exploring the dependencies between different levels of structural information in the skeleton sequence and capture the local subgraph information hierarchically. On the one hand, in order to better model the topological structure information of skeleton graph, we introduce a structure-aware hierarchical graph pooling block (SA-HGP Block), which adaptively updates the subgraph structure of different levels according to the semantic information of skeleton sequence. On the other hand, we introduce the multi-scale fusion module (MSF module) to integrate the information of different scales in each level to obtain the multi-scale hierarchical information. The main contributions of our work can be included as follows: (1) We propose a data-driven structure-aware hierarchical graph pooling block, which can obtain non-physical connections between different body parts in each level and enhance the ability of GCN to extract information. (2) We propose a multi-scale fusion module which fuse the information of multiple levels in the human skeleton graph to obtain more global information of the human skeleton. (3) Experimental results demonstrate that our method outperforms the existing state-of-the-art methods.

2   Related Works

Skeleton data is widely used in action recognition. Traditional methods for action recognition are developed based on two approaches: the hand-crafted-based and the deep-learning-based. Recently, with the flexibility to exploit the body joint relations, the graph-based approach draws much attention [8, 14].

2.1   Traditional Methods for Action Recognition

Traditional methods rely on manual features for action recognition, which design algorithms to capture action patterns based on physical intuitions, such as local occupancy features [15], temporal joint covariances [16] and Lie group curves [17]. Meanwhile, the deep-learning-based approach automatically learns the action features from data. Some recurrent-neural-network (RNN)-based models capture the temporal dependencies between consecutive frames, such as bi-RNNs [18], deep LSTMs [19], and attention-based model [20]. Convolutional neural networks (CNN) also achieve remarkable results, such as residual temporal CNN [21], information enhancement model [22] and CNN on action representations [7].

2.2   Graph-Based Methods for Action Recognition

In [8], it is the first attempt to apply GCN to skeleton based action recognition. [10] uses adjacency matrix for multi-scale modeling, but it also generates node connections to enhance spatial graph convolution. Similarly, [12] introduces graph adaptation with self-attention, and a free-learning graph residual mask. It also uses a dual-stream network with skeletal features to improve performance. [11] uses bone features, but it updates joint and bone features at the same time through an alternate spatial aggregation scheme. Different from these methods which mainly focus on spatial modeling, [9] proposes a unified method to capture complex node associations directly across time and space. [23] merges every three frames on the skeleton graph sequence and adds sparse edges between adjacent frames.

3   Method

In this section, we mainly introduce our proposed SAMS-HGCN, SA-HGP Block and MSF module in details.

3.1   Graph Convolutional Network

Graph convolutional network (GCN) [24] has been proved to be very effective and has achieved good performance in various challenging tasks. Thus, we choose GCN as our model's building block and briefly review its mechanism in this subsection.

We consider a skeleton graph as $G = (V, E)$, where V is the set of joints and E is the set of skeleton edges. Let $A \in \{0, 1\}^{N \times N}$ is the adjacency matrix of the skeleton graph, where $A_{i,j} = 1$ indicates that there is an edge between nodes i and j. A fully describes the skeleton structure. Let $D \in R^{N \times N}$ be the diagonal degree matrix, where $D_{i,i} = \sum_j A_{i,j}$. Let $X_{in} \in R^{C_{in} \times T \times N}$ be the input features, where C_{in} denotes the number of input channels, T denotes the temporal length, N denotes the number of nodes, and $X_{out} \in R^{C_{out} \times T \times N}$ is the output features, where C_{out} denotes the number of output channels. The spatial graph convolution is as follows

$$X_{out} = \sum\nolimits_{r=1}^{R} M_r \odot \widetilde{A_r} X_{in} W_r, \tag{1}$$

where $\widetilde{A_r} = \Lambda_r^{-\frac{1}{2}} A_r \Lambda_r^{-\frac{1}{2}}$ is the normalized adjacency matrix, $\Lambda_r^{ii} = \sum_j (A_r^{ii})$ is the diagonal degree matrix, $\odot$ denotes the Hadamard product, W_r is a weighting function denoting the feature importance, M_r is a learnable matrix denoting the edge weight, and R denotes the kernel size of the spatial dimension. With the partition strategy designed above, R is 3.

3.2   Pipeline Overview

We propose a new structure-aware multi-scale hierarchical graph convolutional neural network (SAMS-HGCN). The overall architecture of the model is shown in Fig. 1. Our network architecture uses two branches. Their inputs are node sequence and bone sequence, respectively. These two branches are trained independently. We finally fuse the output features of these two branches, and then input the obtained feature vector into the fully connected classifier to generate the corresponding predicted class label.

Let's take the skeleton data of 25 joints as an example. For the skeleton node sequence, we firstly use two graph convolutional layers to extract the local information of the original skeleton. Then, through two SA-HGP Blocks and two HGP Blocks, the original skeleton graph composed of 25 nodes is sequentially pooled into a new graph with 10, 6, 2 super nodes and 1 super node, respectively. Morever, we add a MSF module to fuse information of different scales in multiple levels to obtain multi-scale hierarchical structure information. Finally, we use temporal dilated convolution to extract the spatio-temporal information of the skeleton sequence.

3.3   SA-HGP Block

In this section, we will introduce our structure-aware hierarchical graph pooling block, as shown in Fig. 2 (a). This block implements down-sampling of graph data to obtain subgraphs of different levels, and is data-driven according to the semantic information of the skeleton data. This block can learn the non-physical connections between body parts in different levels, which can obtain more complete graph topology between parts.

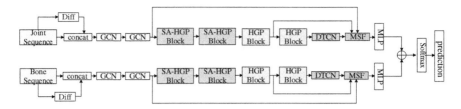

Fig. 1. The illustration of our proposed SAMS-HGCN architecture. GCN is the spatial-temporal graph convolution block. SA-HGP Block is the structure-aware hierarchical graph pooling block. HGP Block is the HGP operation with GCN. DTCN is dilated temporal convolution. MSF is the multi-scale fusion module.

Hierarchical Graph Pooling. As a highly regular figure, the human skeleton graph can be merged simply and effectively in the task of skeleton action recognition. Without loss of generality, we take the skeleton in the NTU-RGB+D dataset as an example to show how to rationally merge the joints of the human body through our strategy. Note that our pooling strategy can be extended to any human skeleton data.

Assume that the human skeleton graph G is decomposed into K parts. That is to say, we divide the skeleton graph G with N nodes into K subgraphs corresponding to K parts of the human body, and each subgraph contains a set of joints J_i ($i \in \{1, 2, ..., k\}$). According to the division of the subgraph, we construct an assign matrix $P \in R^{K \times N}$, where $P_{i,j}$ is defined as

$$P_{i,j} = \begin{cases} 1 & if\ joint\ j \in J_i, \\ 0 & if\ joint\ j \notin J_i. \end{cases} \quad (2)$$

Hierarchical graph pooling (HGP) operation can be expressed as $Y_{out} = M \odot \widetilde{P}X$, where $Y_{out} \in R^{K \times M}$ is the output of HGP operation, $M \in R^{K \times N}$ is the trainable mask matrix to adjust the contribution of each joint to Y_{out}, $X \in R^{N \times d}$ denote the joint feature matrix assuming that each joint has a d-dimensional feature and $\widetilde{P}$ is the normalized form of the assign matrix P. After this HGP operation, we get a new graph, which is composed of K new super nodes, corresponding to K subgraphs.

As shown in Fig. 2 (b), we perform four HGP operations in total, and obtain four new levels of graphs. Specifically, the original skeleton graph composed of 25 nodes is pooled into a new graph with 10, 6, 2 super nodes and 1 super node, respectively.

Structure-Aware Learning. For the new graph G_t obtained by the t-th pooling of the graph G, we take its structure information $A_t \in R^{N_t \times N_t}$ and the hidden representation $H_t \in R^{N_t \times M}$ as input. Our goal is to learn the graph structure of the pooling graph, which encodes the potential pairwise relationship between each pair of super nodes, as shown in Fig. 2 (c). Formally, we use a single layer

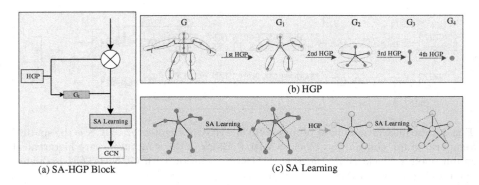

Fig. 2. (a) Illustration of the SA-HGP Block. GCN is the spatial-temporal graph convolution block. G_t ($t = 1, 2, 3, 4$)) is the new graph after the t-th HGP operation. The original skeleton graph G represents the Joint-level, G_1, G_2, G_3 represent 3 types part-level respectively and G_4 represents the frame-level. (b) Illustration of HGP operations. (c) Illustration of SA learning operations.

neural network parameterized by a weight vector $\vec{a} \in R^{1 \times 2M}$. Then, the similarity score of super node v_p and v_q be calculated by the attention mechanism which can be expressed as

$$E_t(p, q) = \sigma(\vec{a}[H_t(p, ;)||H_t(q, ;)]^T) + \lambda \cdot A_t(p, q), \qquad (3)$$

where $\sigma(\cdot)$ is the activation function like $ReLU(\cdot)$ and $||$ represents the concatenation operation. $H_t(p, ;) \in R^{1 \times M}$ and $H_t(q, ;) \in R^{1 \times M}$ indicate the p-th and q-th row of matrix H_t, which denote the representations of node v_p and v_q, respectively. A_t encodes the induced subgraph structure information, where $A_t(p, q) = 0$ if node v_p and v_q are not directly connected. λ is a trade-off parameter between them. We incorporate A_t into our Structure-Aware layer to bias the attention mechanism to give a relatively larger similarity score between directly connected nodes, and at the same time try to learn the underlying pairwise relationships between disconnected super nodes.

To make the similarity score easily comparable across different super nodes, we could normalize them across super nodes using the softmax function

$$S_t(p, q) = \frac{exp(E_t(p, q))}{\sum_{m=1}^{N_t} exp(E_t(p, m))}. \qquad (4)$$

However, the softmax transformation always has non-zero values and thus results in dense fully connected graph, which may introduce lots of noise into the learned structure. Hence, we propose to utilize sparsemax function [25], which retains the most important properties of softmax function and has in addition the ability of producing sparse distributions. The $sparsemax(\cdot)$ function aims to return the Euclidean projection of input onto the probability simplex and can be formulated as follows

$$S_t(p, q) = sparsemax(E_t(p, q)) = [E_t(p, q) - \tau(E_t(p, :))]_+, \qquad (5)$$

where $[x]_+ = max\{0, x\}$, and $\tau(\cdot)$ is the threshold function. Thus, $sparsemax(\cdot)$ preserves the values above the threshold and the other values will be truncated to zeros, which brings sparse graph structure. Similarly to softmax function, $sparsemax(\cdot)$ also has the properties of non-negative and sum-to-one, that's to say, $S_t(p, q) \geq 0$ and $\sum_{q=1}^{N_t} S_t(p, q) = 1$.

3.4   MSF Module

As shown in Fig. 2 (b), since the neural network structure repeatedly performs graph convolution and pooling operations, we can get t new graphs of different scales: G_1, G_2, ..., G_t. In this paper, we set t = 4.

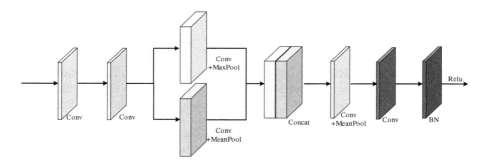

Fig. 3. Illustration of the readout mechanism.

In order to generate a fixed size frame-level representation and integrate the hierarchical structure information of different scales, we design a readout mechanism to aggregate the structure information of multiple scales in different levels, as shown in Fig. 3. Here, we simply use the connection of mean-pooling and max-pooling in each new graph as follows

$$r_t = R(H_t) = \sigma(\frac{1}{N_t}\sum_{p=1}^{N_t} H_t(p, :) \| \max_{q=0}^{M} H_t(:, q)), \tag{6}$$

where $r_t \in R^{2M}$. Then we add up the output of the different levels of the frame-level to form our final graph-level representation: $Z_i = r_1 + r_2 + r_3 + \cdots + r_t$, which summarizes multi-scale graph representations.

Finally, we feed the graph level representation into MLP layer with softmax classifier, and the final loss function is defined as the cross-entropy of predictions over the labels

$$\hat{Y} = softmax(MLP(Z)), \quad L = -\sum_{j=1}^{c} Y_j \log \hat{Y}_j, \tag{7}$$

where $\hat{Y}_j$ represents the predicted probability that graph G belongs to class j, Y_j is the ground truth, and L denotes the training set of dataset that have labels.

4   Experiments

The proposed method is evaluated on two benchmark skeleton-based action datasets: NTU-RGB+D dataset and Kinetics-Skeleton dataset. We compare our SAMS-HGCN with the state-of-the-art methods, and then extensively analyze some network components.

4.1   Datasets

NTU-RGB+D. The NTU-RGB+D dataset [26] is one of the largest indoor action recognition dataset. It contains 56,880 sequences in 60 actions classes, which is concurrently captured by three Microsoft Kincet v2 cameras from different horizontal angles: $-45°$, $0°$, $45°$. We follow the benchmark Cross View (CV) and Cross Subject (CS) evaluation protocol to give top-1 classification accuracy.

Kinetics-Skeleton. Kinetics [27] is a large-scale human action dataset that contains 300,000 videos clips retrieved from YouTube in 400 classes. Since raw video clips have no skeleton data, [8] use the publicly available Open-Pose toolbox [28] to estimate the location of 18 joints on every frame in the clips. We use their released data (Kinetics-Skeleton) to evaluate our model, where 240,000 videos are divided into training set and 20,000 videos are for the validation set.

4.2   Implementation Details

We use PyTorch framework to perform our experiments. Stochastic gradient descent (SGD) algorithm is adopted to train our network. We choose SGD with Nesterov momentum (0.9) as the optimization strategy, set weight-decay to 0.0001, and the batch size is 64. The graph-structure in the forepart of the network is the same as [8], but it is changed after hierarchical graph pooling, as shown in Fig. 2 (b).

For the NTU-RGB+D dataset, we apply cutting and zero-padding to make the number of people in each sample to be 2, and the temporal length of every sample to be 300 frames. The fully connecting layer's dropout rate is set to 0.4. The initial learning rate is 0.1 and decreases 10 times at the 30-th and 40-th epoch. We train our model for 60 epochs. For the Kinetics-Skeleton dataset, we make each video contains 150 frames and two people by cutting and zero-padding. Those frames are randomly chosen from the input sequence and argument with random rotation and translation. The dropout rate of the fully connecting layer is set to 0 because Kinetics-Skeleton is hard to fitting. The initial learning rate is 0.1 and decreases 10 times at the 45th and 55th epoch. We train our model for 80 epochs.

4.3   Comparisons with the State-of-the-Art Methods

We compare our SAMS-HGCN with the state-of-the-art methods. 2s represents the final result of the two-stream fusion. For the NTU RGB+D dataset, we obtain the top-1 accuracies of two protocols in the test phase. As shown in Table 1, the Cross-Subject protocol accuracy and Cross-View protocol accuracy of our method are 91.2(%) and 97.1(%), respectively. The training results during 60 epoch training and loss process are illustrated in Fig. 4 (a). It can be seen from Table 1 that although some methods based on learned graph such as AS-GCN and 2s-SGCN. These methods can also capture the dependencies between joints, but they neglect the dependence between body parts, which lose a lot of topology information and resulting in poor model performance. For the Kinetics-Skeleton dataset, as shown in Table 2, the top-1 and top-5 accuracies on the validation set are 37.5% and 60.3%, respectively. Compared with other graph-based methods, our model achieves the state-of-the-art performances on two benchmark datasets.

Table 1. Comparison of action recognition performance on NTU-RGB+D. The classification accuracies on both CS and CV benchmarks are presented.

Method	CS(%)	CV(%)
Lie Group [17]	50.1	52.8
H-RNN [18]	59.1	64.0
Deep LSTM [26]	60.7	67.3
PA-LSTM [26]	62.9	70.3
ST-LSTM+TS [19]	69.2	77.7
ST-GCN [8]	81.5	88.3
HCN [29]	86.5	91.1
SR-TSL [14]	84.8	92.4
AS-GCN [10]	86.8	94.2
2s-AGCN [12]	88.5	95.1
2s-SGCN [30]	90.1	96.2
SAMS-HGCN (only joint)	90.6	95.9
SAMS-HGCN (only bone)	90.7	96.1
SAMS-HGCN (ours)	**91.2**	**97.1**

4.4   Ablation Study

To verify the effectiveness of the proposed modules in SAMS-HGCN, we perform the following experiments on NTU RGB+D dataset with the Cross-View benchmark.

Evaluating of MSF Module. To evaluate the effectiveness of the proposed MSF module, we perform four groups of contrast tests. As shown in Table 3,

Table 2. Comparison of action recognition performance on Kinetics-Skeleton. We list the top-1 and top-5 classification accuracies.

Method	top-1 Acc	top-5 Acc
Deep LSTM [26]	16.4	35.3
ST-GCN [8]	30.7	52.8
AS-GCN [10]	34.8	56.5
2s-AGCN [12]	36.1	58.7
SAMS-HGCN (only joint)	36.5	59.5
SAMS-HGCN (only bone)	36.7	59.8
SAMS-HGCN (ours)	**37.5**	**60.3**

Table 3. Evaluating the effectiveness of proposed MSF module on the NTU-RGB+D dataset. (%), 'w/' means 'with', 'wo/' means 'without', 'j' means 'joint-level', 'p1', 'p2', 'p3' means '3 types part-level', 'f' means 'frame-level'.

Method	Acc	Method	Acc
wo/MSF	96.0%	w/j+p1+p2+p3	96.7%
w/j	96.2%	w/j+p1+p2+p3+f	96.4%
w/j+p1	96.5%	w/j+p1+f	96.8%
w/j+p1+p2	96.6%	**w/j+p3+f**	**97.1%**

experimental data shows that removing the multi-scale fusion module we proposed, the recognition accuracy is reduced by 1.1%, and in a certain range, with the increase of the number of scales, the recognition accuracy increases gradually, but adding too many scales with small difference will cause information redundancy and reduce the accuracy.

Evaluating of SA-HGP Block. To analyze the effectiveness of the SA-HGP Block, we design five groups of contrast tests. As shown in Fig. 4 (b), experimental data shows that by deleting the entire SA-HGP Block we proposed, the

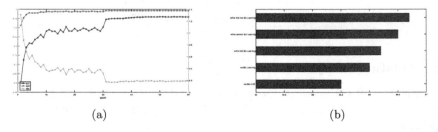

(a)   (b)

Fig. 4. (a) Plots of validation accuracy (the left y-axis) and training loss (the right y-axis) on NTU-RGB+D dataset (Cross View) (%); (b) Evaluating the effectiveness of proposed SA-HGP Block on the NTU-RGB+D dataset. 'w/' means 'with', 'wo/' means 'without'.

recognition accuracy is reduced by 1.6%. If we conduct the experiment without SA Learning operations, the recognition accuracy is reduced by 1.1%, which shows that hierarchical information and non-physical connection information between body parts are very helpful for action recognition tasks.

5   Conclusion

In this paper, we propose a SAMS-HGCN model for improving skeleton-based action recognition. The hierarchical graph structure is obtained through the HGP operation and the SA Learning operation aims to learn the non-physical connection relationship between the parts. The MSF module is used to fuse the graph representations of multiple scales to obtain more complete global information. Experiments on large skeleton based action recognition datasets have shown the superiority of our proposed method as compared to other mainstream approaches.

Acknowledgements. This work was supported by the Artificial Intelligence Program of Shanghai under Grant 2019-RGZN-01077.

References

1. Zhang, Y., Cao, C., Cheng, J., Lu, H.: EgoGesture: a new dataset and benchmark for egocentric hand gesture recognition. IEEE Trans. Multimed. **20**, 1038–1050 (2018)
2. Ziaeefard, M., Bergevin, R.: Semantic human activity recognition: a literature review. Pattern Recognit. **48**, 2329–2345 (2015)
3. Aggarwal, J.K., Xia, L.: Human activity recognition from 3D data: a review. Pattern Recognit. Lett. **48**(1), 70–80 (2014)
4. Han, F., Reily, B., Hoff, W., Zhan, H.: Space-time representation of people based on 3D skeletal data: a review. Comput. Vis. Image Underst. **158**(C), 85–105 (2017)
5. Zhang, Z.: Microsoft kinect sensor and its effect. IEEE Multimed. **19**(2), 4–10 (2012)
6. Zhu, W., Lan, C., Xing, J., Zeng, W., Xie, X.: Co-occurrence feature learning for skeleton based action recognition using regularized deep LSTM networks. In: AAAI 2016 (2016)
7. Ke, Q., Bennamoun, M., An, S., Sohel, F., Boussaid, F.: A new representation of skeleton sequences for 3D action recognition. In: CVPR 2017 (2017)
8. Yan, S., Xiong, Y., Lin, D.: Spatial temporal graph convolutional networks for skeleton-based action recognition. In: AAAI 2018 (2018)
9. Liu, Z., Zhang, H., Chen, Z., Wang, Z., Ouyang, W.: Disentangling and unifying graph convolutions for skeleton-based action recognition. IEEE (2020)
10. Li, M., Chen, S., Chen, X., Zhang, Y., Wang, Y., Tian, Q.: Actional-structural graph convolutional networks for skeleton-based action recognition. In: CVPR 2019 (2019)
11. Shi, L., Zhang, Y., Cheng, J., Lu, H.: Skeleton-based action recognition with directed graph neural networks. In: CVPR 2020 (2020)

12. Shi, L., Zhang, Y., Cheng, J., Lu, H.: Two-stream adaptive graph convolutional networks for skeleton-based action recognition (2018)
13. Luo, W., Li, Y., Urtasun, R., Zemel, R.: Understanding the effective receptive field in deep convolutional neural networks (2017)
14. Si, C., Jing, Y., Wang, W., Wang, L., Tan, T.: Skeleton-based action recognition with spatial reasoning and temporal stack learning. In: Ferrari, V., Hebert, M., Sminchisescu, C., Weiss, Y. (eds.) ECCV 2018, Part I. LNCS, vol. 11205, pp. 106–121. Springer, Cham (2018). https://doi.org/10.1007/978-3-030-01246-5_7
15. Wang, J., Liu, Z., Wu, Y., Yuan, J.: Mining actionlet ensemble for action recognition with depth cameras. Human Action Recognition with Depth Cameras (2014)
16. Hussein, M.E., Torki, M., Gowayyed, M.A., El-Saban, M.: Human action recognition using a temporal hierarchy of covariance descriptors on 3D joint locations. In: International Joint Conference on Artificial Intelligence (2013)
17. Vemulapalli, R., Arrate, F., Chellappa, R.: Human action recognition by representing 3D skeletons as points in a lie group. In: CVPR 2014 (2014)
18. Du, Y., Wang, W., Wang, L.: Hierarchical recurrent neural network for skeleton based action recognition. In: CVPR, pp. 1110–1118 (2015)
19. Liu, J., Shahroudy, A., Xu, D., Wang, G.: Spatio-temporal LSTM with trust gates for 3D human action recognition. In: Leibe, B., Matas, J., Sebe, N., Welling, M. (eds.) ECCV 2016, Part III. LNCS, vol. 9907, pp. 816–833. Springer, Cham (2016). https://doi.org/10.1007/978-3-319-46487-9_50
20. Song, S., Lan, C., Xing, J., Zeng, W., Liu, J.: An end-to-end spatio-temporal attention model for human action recognition from skeleton data (2016)
21. Kim, T.S., Reiter, A.: Interpretable 3D human action analysis with temporal convolutional networks. In: 2017 IEEE Conference on Computer Vision and Pattern Recognition Workshops (CVPRW) (2017)
22. Liu, M., Hong, L., Chen, C.: Enhanced skeleton visualization for view invariant human action recognition. Pattern Recognit. **68**, 346–362 (2017)
23. Gao, X., Hu, W., Tang, J., Liu, J., Guo, Z.: Optimized skeleton-based action recognition via sparsified graph regression. In: The 27th ACM International Conference (2019)
24. Kipf, T.N., Welling, M.: Semi-supervised classification with graph convolutional networks (2016)
25. Martins, A., Astudillo, R.F.: From softmax to sparsemax: a sparse model of attention and multi-label classification. JMLR.org (2016)
26. Shahroudy, A., Liu, J., Ng, T.T., Wang, G.: NTU RGB+D: a large scale dataset for 3D human activity analysis, pp. 1010–1019. IEEE Computer Society (2016)
27. Kay, W., Carreira, J., Simonyan, K., Zhang, B., Zisserman, A.: The kinetics human action video dataset (2017)
28. Zhe, C., Simon, T., Wei, S.E., Sheikh, Y.: Realtime multi-person 2D pose estimation using part affinity fields. In: CVPR 2017 (2017)
29. Li, C., Zhong, Q., Xie, D., Pu, S.: Co-occurrence feature learning from skeleton data for action recognition and detection with hierarchical aggregation. In: Twenty-Seventh International Joint Conference on Artificial Intelligence, IJCAI-2018 (2018)
30. Yang, W., Zhang, J., Cai, J., Xu, Z.: Shallow graph convolutional network for skeleton-based action recognition. Sensors **21**(2), 452 (2021)

Learning Hierarchical Reasoning for Text-Based Visual Question Answering

Caiyuan Li, Qinyi Du, Qingqing Wang, and Yaohui Jin[✉]

Department of Computer Science and Engineering, Shanghai Jiao Tong University, Shanghai 200240, China
{1161313414,xrswhisper,qqwang0723,jinyh}@sjtu.edu.cn

Abstract. Text-based visual question answering (TextVQA) task needs to answer questions based on the objects and text information in image, which involves the joint reasoning over three modalities - question, visual objects, and text in image. Recent approaches on textVQA regard three modalities as joint input of transformers. However, these implicit reasoning methods do not make full use of multi-modal information, especially visual modality. To this end, we propose a novel model for textVQA based on reasoning explicitly in human-like mode. Firstly, the relevance between different objects and question is obtained. Then, the object modality is fused into the text modality weighted by obtained relevance. Finally, the amended text modality is used to predict the answer. In contrast to previous multi-modal free fusion strategy, our method can make the reasoning process more explicit and robust. Moreover, a prior-based loss is proposed to constrain object-question relevance. Extensive experimental results on several benchmark datasets well demonstrate the superior performance of our hierarchical reasoning framework over current state-of-the-art methods.

Keywords: textVQA · Multi-modality · Hierarchical reasoning

1 Introduction

Visual Question Answering (VQA) has received an increasing amount of attention in recent years. However, most VQA datasets [2] and methods [3, 8, 15] tend to ignore an important modality - text in image, which is essential to understand and reason scenes. To this end, some new datasets [4, 20] are proposed to cover this challenge and refer it as textVQA. In contrast to traditional VQA, textVQA datasets provide text information that appears on images additionally. In general, textVQA task requires models to jointly reasoning over three modalities: the input question, the visual objects in the image, and the text in the image.

Recently, some works [9–12, 20] focus on multi-modal reasoning to tackle textVQA challenge. A well-known pioneering work in this domain is M4C [12], which naturally fuses the three input modalities and captures intra- and inter- modality interactions homogeneously within a multi-modal transformer. M4C [12] projects all entities from each modality into a common semantic embedding space and regards them as joint inputs of transformer. Self-attention mechanism is applied to collect relational representations for each entity. Under ideal circumstances, this approach seems to be

© Springer Nature Switzerland AG 2021
I. Farkaš et al. (Eds.): ICANN 2021, LNCS 12893, pp. 305–316, 2021.
https://doi.org/10.1007/978-3-030-86365-4_25

able to fuse multi-modal information and predict accurate answers. However, as shown in Table 1, this fusion method is not really effective. In the case of removing the object modality without modifying any other setting, the answer prediction accuracy improves unexpectedly. The result shows that if the inter-modality information fusion method is not constrained explicitly, even if all entities from each modality are projected into a common embedding space, transformer can not handle multi-modal reasoning effectively.

Table 1. Modality ablation study of M4C [12] on the textVQA dataset. Without visual object modality, the answer prediction accuracy improves unexpectedly.

Method	Input modalities	Acc. on val
M4C [12]	Question + objects + text	39.40
	Question + text	**39.60**

To address this problem, we design a hierarchical reasoning framework for the textVQA task, where the inter-modality fusion can be constrained explicitly based on some priors. When a human being is provided an image and a question related to the text in the image, the reasoning process is hierarchical. First, the object or region most relevant to the question will be captured. Then the OCR tokens near the most relevant object or region will get more attention, and people are more inclined to select these OCR tokens to answer the question. It is obvious that the information of text modality at this time has been fused with the information of visual object modality. We simulate the human being's reasoning logic to handle this task. We decompose the reasoning process into three hierarchical modules, which can be trained end-to-end. The first module is object-question correlation score generator. The question and visual object modalities are used to calculate the score for each object, which means the relevance of the object to the question. The second module is object-score-guided text modality updater. In this module, the text modality features are fused with visual object features under the weighting by obtained object-question correlation score. The final module is the answer predictor. Question modality and amended text modality are used as joint inputs for transformer to predict the answer. In this hierarchical reasoning mechanism, all three modalities are utilized effectively.

Our contributions in this paper are as follows:

1) We find a fatal flaw of previous works on text-based VQA - they can not utilize visual object modality effectively.
2) We propose a hierarchical reasoning network to simulate human being's reasoning logic on text-based VQA task. We decompose the reasoning process into three interpretable modules to predict the answer hierarchically, in which the information of all three modalities is effectively utilized.
3) We evaluate our approach on textVQA dataset and ST-VQA dataset, and achieve state-of-the-art performance.

2   Related Work

Visual Question Answering. VQA task requires model to answer a given question asked about an image. Since the first large-scale VQA dataset was introduced by [2], numerous works [3,8,15] have tried to overcome this challenge. There are two major types of models that exist to tackle VQA. The inchoate methods are based on simple attention mechanisms. Typically, these models [8,15,23,24] can be characterized as top-down approaches, with context provided by a representation of a representation of the question in VQA. [1] introduced an approach which combines top-down and bottom-up attention mechanisms to achieve state-of-the-art performance on image captioning and obtain first place in the VQA 2017 challenge. Recent works [7,17] in the field of NLP have brought to light the positive effects of Language Model pre-training on various downstream tasks. Taking inspiration from such architectures, recent VQA models [6,13,14,21] adopt a BERT [7] style of pre-training for Transformer models. These works apply various attention mechanisms and multi-modal fusion techniques to better locate the image region for a given question to facilitate the answering procedure. Using a Transformer with a pre-training objective is a common theme that runs across all of these models.

Text-Based VQA. Traditional VQA tends to ignore a crucial modality - text in the images and fails catastrophically on questions requiring reading. To this end, some datasets [4,16,20] have been released recently to facilitate studies on text-based VQA. Meanwhile, several approaches [9–12,20] have been proposed. LoRRA [20] extends the Pythia [19] framework for VQA and allows it to copy a single OCR token from the image as the answer. M4C [12] regards all entities from each modality homogeneously with a transformer architecture and predicts answers with a pointer-augmented multi-step decoder. Other works [9–11] are all based on M4C [12] and optimize some components to improve performance. However, all previous works based on M4C [12] have a fatal flaw - they use visual object modality as part of the input, but they can not utilize it at all. Removing the visual object modality has no impact on performance. In this paper, a hierarchical reasoning network are designed to overcame this problem.

3   Method

In this section, we elaborate on the proposed hierarchical reasoning network for answering questions that require reading text in image. Figure 1 shows an overview of our model.

3.1   Multi-modal Embedding Construction

The textVQA task provides inputs from three modalities - question, visual objects in image, and OCR tokens in image. Following M4C [12], We extract feature representations for each modality and project them into a common d-dimensional semantic space as follows.

Question Modality. A question is composed of K words. Using a pre-trained BERT [7] model, we embed these words into a sequence of d-dimensional feature vectors $\{x_k^{ques}\}$

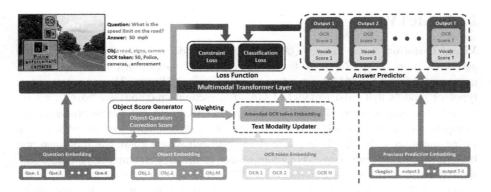

Fig. 1. An overview of our model. We first calculate the object-question correlation score to find out the focus area of question. Then we fuse object modality into text modality under the weight of object-question correlation score to obtain the amended OCR token embedding. Finally, we apply a multi-modal transformer to predict the answer. Moreover, we design a prior-based loss to constrain the object-question correlation score.

(where $k = 1, ..., K$). During training, the BERT parameters are fine-tuned using the question answering loss.

Visual Object Modality. For an image, we obtained M visual object features through a pre-trained Faster R-CNN [18], denoted as $\{x_m^{ft}\}$ (where m = 1, ..., M). The corresponding bounding box coordinates are represented as x_m^b. The final object embedding is as follows:

$$x_m^{obj} = LN\left(W_1 x_m^{ft}\right) + LN\left(W_2 x_m^b\right) \tag{1}$$

Text Modality. After obtaining a set of N OCR tokens from the image, a combination of Faster RCNN [18], Pyramidal Histogram of Characters (PHOC) and FastText embedding is adopted for them, denoted as $\{x_n^{ft}\}$ (where n = 1, ..., N). The corresponding bounding box coordinates are represented as x_n^b. The final OCR tokens embedding is as follows:

$$x_n^{ocr} = LN\left(W_3 x_n^{ft}\right) + LN\left(W_4 x_n^b\right) \tag{2}$$

The above is the mathematical representation of the three modalities, where W_1, W_2, W_3 and W_4 are learned projection matrices and $LN(\cdot)$ is layer normalization. The matrix forms of the three modalities are X^{ques}, X^{obj} and X^{ocr}, where

$$\begin{aligned} X^{ques} &= [x_1^{ques}, ..., x_k^{ques}, ..., x_K^{ques}], k = 1, ..., K \\ X^{obj} &= [x_1^{obj}, ..., x_m^{obj}, ..., x_M^{obj}], m = 1, ..., M \\ X^{ocr} &= [x_1^{ocr}, ..., x_n^{ocr}, ..., x_N^{ocr}], n = 1, ..., N \end{aligned} \tag{3}$$

3.2 Object Score Generator

This module is designed to find out the focus area of the question, which involves question modality and visual object modality. Since visual object modal information consists of M object embeddings $\{x_m^{obj}\}$, we transform finding out the focus area of the question into inferring the correlation degree between M objects and the question.

To represent the whole question, we average the embeddings of K words. The final question embedding is obtained as

$$\bar{X}^{ques} = \frac{1}{K} \sum_{k=1}^{K} x_k^{ques} \tag{4}$$

We calculate the object-question correlation score as

$$S = \text{softmax}((W^{ques}\bar{X}^{ques})^T * W^{obj}X^{obj}) \tag{5}$$

where W^{ques} and W^{obj} are $d \times d$ learned matrices. It can be seen that the object-question correlation score S is a $1 \times M$ normalized vector. S is used to weight the attention scores between visual objects and OCR tokens in Sect. 3.3. Moreover, we design a prior-based loss function to constraint the object-question correlation score S, which is explained in detail in Sect. 3.5.

3.3 Text Modality Updater

In this module, text modal information is amended by fusing visual object modal information, which is in line with human reasoning logic. When we try to understand the text in image, objects around the text will provide auxiliary information to help to reason. Take image in Fig. 1 for example. We deduce that the text "50" represents the limited speed because we notice that the text is on a white circular warning sign with a red border.

The detail computation process is described as follows. Firstly, the object-guided attention score between n-th OCR token and the visual objects is calculated as

$$attn_n = \text{softmax}\left((W^Q x_n^{ocr})^T * (W^K X^{obj})\right) \tag{6}$$

where W^Q and W^K are query projection matrix and key projection matrix respectively. $attn_n$ is a $1 \times M$ normalized vector.

Then the object-question correlation score S is used to amend the attention score $attn_n$ between n-th OCR token and the visual objects. The object information that the question pays more attention to should be more integrated into the text information. The final attention score $\hat{attn}_n$ is calculated as

$$\hat{attn}_n = \frac{attn_n \cdot S}{\sum_{m=1}^{M} (attn_n \cdot S)_m} \tag{7}$$

This weighting mechanism can increase the attention score of objects that the question pays more attention to, and vice versa.

The final amended n-th OCR token embedding $\hat{x}_n^{ocr}$ is represented as

$$\hat{x}_n^{ocr} = X^{obj} * \hat{attn}_n^{T} + x_n^{ocr} \tag{8}$$

It's worth mentioning that the object-question correlation score S is not directly used as attention score to fuse visual object modal information upon text modal information. Independent internal relationships exist between different visual objects and OCR tokens. We apply S to amend the attention score $attn_n$ and force OCR tokens to fuse more information of the object that the question pays more attention to.

The amended text modal information fuse the visual object modal information under the guidance of the question. This makes each new OCR token embedding more robust and contain more effective information to predict the answer of the question.

3.4 Answer Predictor

We fuse the question modal information and amended text information to predict the answer. Following M4C [12], we apply a stack of L transformer layers with a hidden dimension of d over the list of all $K + N$ entities from $\{x_k^{ques}\}$ and $\{\hat{x}_n^{ocr}\}$. We predict an answer to the question through iterative decoding, using exactly the same transformer layers as a decoder. Specifically, we decode the answer word by word for a total of T steps.

The answer candidate set consists of two parts: 1) A vocabulary of V words that frequently appear in the training set answers, which is fixed for different images and questions. 2) N OCR tokens from input image, which is dynamic for different images.

Let $\{z_1^{ocr}, \cdots, z_N^{ocr}\}$ be the transformer outputs of the N OCR tokens. The matrix form of OCR token output embedding is represented as Z^{ocr}, where $Z^{ocr} = [z_1^{ocr}, \ldots, z_N^{ocr}], n = 1, \ldots, N$. At the t-th decoding step, the transformer outputs a d-dimensional vector z_t^{dec}, which is used to predict both V-dimensional scores y_t^{voc} of choosing a word from fixed vocabulary and N-dimensional scores y_t^{ocr} of selecting an OCR token from image as answer. The detail calculation process is as follows

$$
\begin{aligned}
y_t^{voc} &= W^v z_t^{dec} + b^v \\
y_t^{ocr} &= (W^o Z^{ocr} + b^o)^T (W^d z^{dec} + b^d) \\
y_t &= [y_t^{voc}; y_t^{ocr}]
\end{aligned}
\tag{9}
$$

where W^v is $V \times d$ matrix, W^o and W^d are $d \times d$ matrices. y_t is a $(V + N) \times 1$ vector. Multi-label sigmoid loss $\mathcal{L}_{cls}$ is applied over y_t to predict the answer.

3.5 Loss Design

Predicting the answer is a classification task. We use cross-entropy loss to train our model, formulated as

$$
\mathcal{L}_{cls} = -\sum_{t=1}^{T} \widetilde{y}_t^\top \log(\sigma(y_t))
\tag{10}
$$

where σ is a sigmoid function and $\widetilde{Y} = \{\widetilde{y}_t\}_{t=1}^{T}$ is ground truth.

An important prior is that the objects that question pays more attention to tend to be those that are closer to the answer OCR token. Take image in Fig. 1 for example. The object that question pays most attention to is the warning sign, which is closest to the answer OCR token "50". Based on this prior, we can generate a pseudo label to constraint the object-question correlation score S.

As mentioned in Sect. 3.4, the answer word may be either an OCR token in the image or a word from fixed vocabulary. For the first case, the center coordinate c^{ans} of answer OCR token is represented as $c^{ans} = [x_c^{ans}, y_c^{ans}]$. Similarly, the center coordinates c^{obj} of M visual objects are represented as $\{c_m^{obj}\}, m = 1, \ldots, M$. All coordinates are normalized. The distance between visual object and the answer OCR token is used to approximate the object-question correlation. The final pseudo label $\hat{S}$ is formulated as

$$\hat{S} = softmax([\frac{1}{||c_1^{obj} - c^{ans}||_2}, \ldots, \frac{1}{||c_M^{obj} - c^{ans}||_2}]) \tag{11}$$

$\hat{S}$ is regarded as a weak supervision signal to constraint the object-question correlation score S. Since the pseudo label $\hat{S}$ is smoothed innately, cross-entropy loss is applied following [22]. Hence, the optimization function $\mathcal{L}_{cons}$ is formulated as

$$\mathcal{L}_{cons} = -\sum_{m=1}^{M} \hat{s}_m \log(s_m) \tag{12}$$

The final loss function is formulated as

$$\mathcal{L} = \mathcal{L}_{cls} + \alpha \cdot \mathcal{L}_{cons} \tag{13}$$

4   Experiment

To verify the effectiveness of our method, we carry out experiments on two public benchmark datasets, including TextVQA [20] and ST-VQA [4]. We show that our method achieve state-of-the-art performance over both datasets. Moreover, some ablation studies are conducted to investigate each component of our model.

4.1   Datasets and Protocols

TextVQA Dataset. TextVQA [20] is a recently proposed dataset for TextVQA task that requires reading texts in images to answer questions. TextVQA dataset includes 28,408 images with 45,336 questions, and the average question length is 7.18 words. For each image, there are 1–2 questions.

ST-VQA Dataset. The ST-VQA dataset includes three VQA tasks, namely strongly contextualised, weakly contextualised and open vocabulary, which gradually increase in difficulty. The task 3 - open vocabulary (containing 18,921 training-validation images and test 2,971 images) corresponds to the general TextVQA setting where no answer candidates are provided at test time. Following M4C [12], we evaluate our method on task 3. Most questions of the ST-VQA can be unambiguously answered with the text recognized in the image. As the ST-VQA dataset does not have an official split for training and validation, we follow M4C [12] to randomly select 17,028 images as our training set and use the remaining 1,893 images as our validation set.

Table 2. Comparison on TextVQA dataset.

Method	Acc. on Val	Acc. on Test
LoRRA [20]	27.40	27.63
MM-GNN [10]	31.44	31.10
M4C [12]	39.40	39.01
SMA [9]	39.58	40.29
LaAP-Net [11]	40.68	40.54
Ours	**40.72**	**40.88**
Ours + LaAP-Net*	**41.93**	**42.12**

Evaluation Metrics. Following existing works, we use a common VQA accuracy (Acc) as an evaluation metric. In particular, ST-VQA proposes a new evaluation metric, ANLS (average normalized Levenshtein similarity), which focuses on character comparisons between the predicted answer and the ground truth answer. Note that if the ANLS score is below the threshold of 0.5, it is truncated to 0 before averaging.

4.2   Implementation Details

For a fair comparison with the state-of-the-art methods, we follow the same multimodal input as M4C [12]. We set the common dimensionality $d = 768$ and the number of transformer layers $L = 4$. For every image, the total number of detected visual object $M = 100$. In this paper, We use only 10 objects with higher confidence. For final loss function, $\alpha = 0.1$.

4.3   Quantitative Analysis

TextVQA. We compare our result on TextVQA to the newest SOTA method LaAP-Net [11] and other existing works like LoRRA [20] and M4C [12]. The results are shown in Table 2. It can be seen that our model outperforms all considered methods both on the validation set and test set. Since our method is based on M4C [12], the accuracy on validation set and test set significantly rises by 1.32% and 1.77% correspondingly.

ST-VQA. As shown in Table 3, we report the accuracy and ANLS of our method on ST-VQA dataset, where ANLS is the official evaluation metric for this dataset. It can be seen that our model outperforms all considered methods both on the validation set and test set. Since the ST-VQA dataset is collected from six different image datasets (including ImageNet, COCO-text, and VizWiz), the results better reflect the generalization ability of the model.

It is worth mentioning that LaAP-Net [11] not only generates the answer to the question but also predicts a bounding box as evidence of the generated answer. In other words, [11] added a localization loss function to regress bounding box of ground-truth ocr token. We implement this loss function and add it to our model, and the result is represented as *ours+LaAP-Net** in Table 2 and Table 3. It can be seen that our model

Table 3. Comparison on ST-VQA dataset.

Method	Acc. on Val	ANLS on Val	ANLS on Test
MM-GNN [10]	–	–	0.207
VTA [5]	–	–	0.282
M4C [12]	38.05	0.472	0.462
SMA [9]	–	–	0.466
LaAP-Net [11]	39.74	0.497	0.485
Ours	**40.11**	**0.508**	**0.501**
Ours + LaAP-Net*	**41.61**	**0.522**	**0.515**

obviously outperforms LaAP-Net by adding the same addition loss function that LaAP-Net proposed.

4.4 Ablation Study

To verify the validity and investigate each component of our model, we perform elaborate ablation studies. The overall results are shown in Table 4.

Table 4. Ablation study on TextVQA dataset.

	Object modality	O-Q score weighting	$\mathcal{L}_{cons}$	Acc. on Val
#1	×	×	×	39.60
#2	✓	✓	×	39.62
#3	✓	✓	×	40.11
#4	✓	✓	✓	**40.72**

Self-attention mechanism is applied to fuse multi-modal information in M4C [12]. However, M4C [12] provide no ablation study on multi-modal input in its paper. First, we remove the object modal input of M4C [12] without modifying any other setting, which is represented as #1 in Table 4. Combined with Table 1, it can be seen that without visual object object modality, the answer prediction accuracy increases from 39.40 to 39.60 unexpectedly. The result shows that M4C [12] can not use the object modal information at all.

Different from M4C [12], We apply guide attention mechanism to fuse object modality to text modality. The calculation process is Eq. 6 and Eq. 8. The object-guided attention score $attn_n$ is not weighted by object-question correlation score S. This restricted model is represented as #2 in Table 4. It can be seen that the accuracy of #2 has barely improved, which shows that infer-modality fusion mechanism maybe need explicit constraint.

what number is the player looking at the children?
M4C: 1950
ours: **9**
ground truth: **9**

what is the advertisement in the white board?
M4C: fsl
ours: **southern homes**
ground truth: **southern homes**

what does the canister say?
M4C: **FLOUR**
ours: **FLOUR**
ground truth: **FLOUR**

who is the author of the book?
M4C: unanswerable
ours: **gioconda belli**
ground truth: **gioconda belli**

Fig. 2. Qualitative examples of our model on the TextVQA validation set. The red box is the object with the highest object-question correlation score. The number next to it represents the score of the object. As shown, our model can locate the area that the question pays more attention to. Compare with M4C, our model can use visual object modal information effectively and achieve better performance. (Color figure online)

Simulating human reasoning mechanism, we first generate the object-question correlation score S as Eq. 5 and use it to weight the object-guided attention score $attn_n$ as Eq. 7. This model is represented as #3 in Table 4. the accuracy of #3 increases from 39.62 to 40.11, which shows that the designed reasoning process is effective.

Moreover, we design a constraint loss $\mathcal{L}_{cons}$ as Eq. 12 to constrain the object-question correlation score S. This final model is represented as #4 in Table 4. The accuracy increases to 40.72 and achieve the SOTA performance.

4.5   Case Study and Visualization

In this section, we show some visualization examples of our model on TextVQA validation set in Fig. 2. As mentioned above, previous works represented by M4C [12] can not utilize visual object modal information at all. As shown in first image, M4C [12] understand the answer should be a number and select a number OCR token '1950' in image as the answer. However, our model can find the object that question pays more attention to. The object with the highest object-question correlation score is the man on the far left, which is in line with human reasoning. Similarly, our model can locate the area of greatest concern in other images, which make our model more effective to fuse object modal information into text modal information. From the results, our method indeed achieves SOTA performance.

5   Conclusion

In this paper, we propose a hierarchical reasoning network for answering questions based on the texts in images. The alleged multi-modal reasoning in previous works is deceitful because they can not utilize visual object modality effectively. To simulate human being's reasoning logic, our model decomposes the reasoning process into three interpretable modules to predict the answer hierarchically, in which the information of each modality is effectively utilized. Moreover, we design a prior-based loss additionally to improve performance. Our model achieves SOTA performance on both TextVQA dataset and ST-VQA dataset.

Acknowledgements. This work was supported by the National Key R&D Program of China (Grant No. 2020YFC2008700).

References

1. Anderson, P., et al.: Bottom-up and top-down attention for image captioning and visual question answering. In: 2018 IEEE Conference on Computer Vision and Pattern Recognition, CVPR 2018, Salt Lake City, UT, USA, June 18–22, 2018, pp. 6077–6086. IEEE Computer Society (2018)
2. Antol, S., et al.: VQA: visual question answering. In: ICCV (2015)
3. Ben-younes, H., Cadène, R., Cord, M., Thome, N.: MUTAN: multimodal tucker fusion for visual question answering. In: ICCV (2017)
4. Biten, A.F., et al.: Scene text visual question answering. In: ICCV (2019)
5. Biten, A.F., et al.: ICDAR 2019 competition on scene text visual question answering. In: ICDAR, pp. 1563–1570
6. Chen, Y.-C., et al.: UNITER: UNiversal image-TExt representation learning. In: Vedaldi, A., Bischof, H., Brox, T., Frahm, J.-M. (eds.) ECCV 2020, Part XXX. LNCS, vol. 12375, pp. 104–120. Springer, Cham (2020). https://doi.org/10.1007/978-3-030-58577-8_7
7. Devlin, J., Chang, M., Lee, K., Toutanova, K.: BERT: pre-training of deep bidirectional transformers for language understanding. In: NAACL (2019)
8. Fukui, A., Park, D.H., Yang, D., Rohrbach, A., Darrell, T., Rohrbach, M.: Multimodal compact bilinear pooling for visual question answering and visual grounding. In: Su, J., Carreras, X., Duh, K. (eds.) EMNLP (2016)

9. Gao, C., et al.: Structured multimodal attentions for TextVQA. CoRR abs/2006.00753 (2020)
10. Gao, D., Li, K., Wang, R., Shan, S., Chen, X.: Multi-modal graph neural network for joint reasoning on vision and scene text. In: CVPR (2020)
11. Han, W., Huang, H., Han, T.: Finding the evidence: localization-aware answer prediction for text visual question answering. CoRR abs/2010.02582 (2020)
12. Hu, R., Singh, A., Darrell, T., Rohrbach, M.: Iterative answer prediction with pointer-augmented multimodal transformers for TextVQA. In: CVPR (2020)
13. Li, L.H., Yatskar, M., Yin, D., Hsieh, C., Chang, K.: VisualBERT: a simple and performant baseline for vision and language. CoRR abs/1908.03557 (2019)
14. Li, X., et al.: OSCAR: object-semantics aligned pre-training for vision-language tasks. In: Vedaldi, A., Bischof, H., Brox, T., Frahm, J.-M. (eds.) ECCV 2020, Part XXX. LNCS, vol. 12375, pp. 121–137. Springer, Cham (2020). https://doi.org/10.1007/978-3-030-58577-8_8
15. Lu, J., Yang, J., Batra, D., Parikh, D.: Hierarchical question-image co-attention for visual question answering. In: NIPS (2016)
16. Mishra, A., Shekhar, S., Singh, A.K., Chakraborty, A.: OCR-VQA: visual question answering by reading text in images. In: ICDAR (2019)
17. Peters, M.E., et al.: Deep contextualized word representations. In: Walker, M.A., Ji, H., Stent, A. (eds.) Proceedings of the 2018 Conference of the North American Chapter of the Association for Computational Linguistics: Human Language Technologies, NAACL-HLT 2018, New Orleans, Louisiana, USA, June 1–6, 2018, vol. 1 (Long Papers), pp. 2227–2237. Association for Computational Linguistics (2018)
18. Ren, S., He, K., Girshick, R.B., Sun, J.: Faster R-CNN: towards real-time object detection with region proposal networks. In: NIPS (2015)
19. Singh, A., et al.: Pythia-a platform for vision & language research. In: SysML Workshop, NeurIPS, vol. 2018 (2018)
20. Singh, A., et al.: Towards VQA models that can read. In: CVPR (2019)
21. Su, W., et al.: VL-BERT: pre-training of generic visual-linguistic representations. In: 8th International Conference on Learning Representations, ICLR 2020, Addis Ababa, Ethiopia, April 26–30, 2020. OpenReview.net (2020)
22. Szegedy, C., Vanhoucke, V., Ioffe, S., Shlens, J., Wojna, Z.: Rethinking the inception architecture for computer vision. In: CVPR (2016)
23. Xu, H., Saenko, K.: Ask, attend and answer: exploring question-guided spatial attention for visual question answering. In: Leibe, B., Matas, J., Sebe, N., Welling, M. (eds.) ECCV 2016, Part VII. LNCS, vol. 9911, pp. 451–466. Springer, Cham (2016). https://doi.org/10.1007/978-3-319-46478-7_28
24. Yao, T., Pan, Y., Li, Y., Qiu, Z., Mei, T.: Boosting image captioning with attributes. In: IEEE International Conference on Computer Vision, ICCV 2017, Venice, Italy, October 22–29, 2017, pp. 4904–4912. IEEE Computer Society (2017)

Hierarchical Deep Gaussian Processes Latent Variable Model via Expectation Propagation

Nick Taubert$^{(\boxtimes)}$ and Martin A. Giese

Section Computational Sensomotorics, CIN/HIH, University Clinic Tübingen,
Otfried-Müller-Str. 25, 72076 Tübingen, Germany
{nick.taubert,martin.giese}@uni-tuebingen.de

Abstract. Gaussian Processes (GPs) and related unsupervised learning techniques such as Gaussian Process Latent Variable Models (GP-LVMs) have been very successful in the accurate modeling of high-dimensional data based on limited amounts of training data. Usually these techniques have the disadvantage of a high computational complexity. This makes it difficult to solve the associated learning problems for complex hierarchical models and large data sets, since the related computations, as opposed to neural networks, are not node-local. Combining sparse approximation techniques for GPs and Power Expectation Propagation, we present a framework for the computationally efficient implementation of hierarchical deep Gaussian process (latent variable) models. We provide implementations of this approach on the GPU as well as on the CPU, and we benchmark efficiency comparing different optimization algorithms. We present the first implementation of such deep hierarchical GP-LVMs and demonstrate the computational efficiency of our GPU implementation.

Keywords: Deep GP-LVM · Hierarchical probabilistic model · Dimension reduction · Motion synthesis · Expectation propagation

1 Introduction

Many applications, e.g. in computer graphics and robotics, require real-time generative models for complex, high-dimensional, coordinated human motion. One possible solution of this problem is the use of neural networks [10,12]. The generalization properties of such networks are not easy to control, and often they require substantial amounts of training data to accomplish high accuracy and robustness of the generated motion. As an alternative to this approach we propose here probabilistic graphical models [1]. Such models provide an attractive theoretical framework for the construction of modular and hierarchical models, and for inference on arbitrary variables within these models. While probabilistic models have been used extensively for motion synthesis and editing in computer graphics [2,5,13], or robotics [23,30], many of these techniques result in offline models that are not suitable for embedding in online control systems, or the learning from large data sets, due to their high computational complexity.

© Springer Nature Switzerland AG 2021
I. Farkaš et al. (Eds.): ICANN 2021, LNCS 12893, pp. 317–329, 2021.
https://doi.org/10.1007/978-3-030-86365-4_26

Gaussian process latent variable models (GP-LVM) provide a successful framework for the very accurate approximation high-dimensional human motion, where Gaussian processes (GP) can be interpreted as neural networks with infinitely many hidden units [21]. GP-LVMs have been successfully applied for kinematic modeling and motion interpolation [9], inverse kinematics [16], and for the learning of low-dimensional dynamical models [29]. By inclusion of sparse approximation techniques, they can be made suitable for real-time applications [25]. However, they have a tendency to overfit and additional limitations, which make them unsuitable for a variety of applications, e.g. on large data sets. Approximative inference exploiting sparse approximations of Gaussian processes (GP) within a variational free energy (VFE) framework control for overfitting [26]. In addition, they are suitable for the formulation of multi-layer architectures in the form of Deep Gaussian processes (DGP) [14,27]. Such architectures are equivalent to deep neural networks with infinite many hidden units per layer [7]. However, the VFE approach is not parallizable and produces unnecessarily large memory footprints during learning, which makes it specifically unsuitable for GPU implementations.

We propose here to use instead approximate inference exploiting Expectation propagation (EP) [18], resulting in an algorithm that is more suitable for GPU implementations. The use of stochastic expectation propagation (SEP) [17] it also reduces the memory overhead. In addition, the underlying learning scheme of Power EP [19] combines the advantages of VFE and EP within a single algorithm.

Exploiting such DGPs, our main contributions are: a hierarchical probabilistic graphical model in form of *hierarchical* deep GP-LVMs (hDGP-LVM); implementation of this model on the GPU, exploiting approximate inference using SEP. We demonstrate the suitability of this method for the learning of online generative models for complex full-body movements of two interacting humans with 189 degrees of freedom.

The following sections, first develop the underlying mathematical theory. We then discuss briefly the implementation details and present our results, comparing the GPU and CPU implementations, followed by a conclusion.

2   Preliminaries

2.1   GP Regression and Approximation

In the function space view GPs can be considered as nonlinear mapping, $f(\mathbf{x})$, from an input variable $\mathbf{x}$ to a one-dimensional real-valued output variable. The function value $f_n := f(\mathbf{x}_n)$, at a particular input point, $\mathbf{x}_n$ of an input set $\mathbf{X} = [\mathbf{x}_1, \ldots, \mathbf{x}_N]^{\mathrm{T}} \in \mathbb{R}^{N \times Q}$, is a random variable, and a GP is an infinite collection of random variables, any finite number of which have a joint Gaussian distribution [3,22], where N being the sample size and Q the dimensionality of the input space.

A real Gaussian process $f(\mathbf{x})$ is characterized through its mean function $m(\mathbf{x})$ and kernel function $k(\mathbf{x}, \mathbf{x}')$,

$$
\begin{aligned}
m(\mathbf{x}) &= \mathbb{E}[f(\mathbf{x})], \\
k(\mathbf{x}, \mathbf{x}') &= \mathbb{E}[(f(\mathbf{x}) - m(\mathbf{x}))(f(\mathbf{x}') - m(\mathbf{x}'))].
\end{aligned}
\tag{1}
$$

This can be interpreted as $f(\mathbf{x})$ being drawn from a Gaussian process prior with mean function $m(\mathbf{x})$ and kernel function $k(\mathbf{x}, \mathbf{x}')$,

$$
f(\mathbf{x}) \sim \mathcal{GP}(f(\mathbf{x}); m(\mathbf{x}), k(\mathbf{x}, \mathbf{x}')).
\tag{2}
$$

In most cases we assume a zero mean function, $m(\mathbf{x}) = 0$, since for our application the prior knowledge about $f(\cdot)$ can be encoded by the kernel function and its hyperparameters. For our model we used in all layers an automatic relevance determination (ARD) kernel of the form,

$$
k(\mathbf{x}, \mathbf{x}') = \sigma^2 \exp\left(-\frac{1}{2}\sum_{q=1}^{Q}\frac{|x_q - x_q'|^2}{l_q^2}\right),
\tag{3}
$$

where σ is the variance and l_q the length-scale of the q-th input dimension of the kernel. For this particular kernel $\theta = (\sigma, \{l_q\}_{q=1}^{Q})$ are the hyperparameters.

Typically for regression models, a data set $\{y_n\}_{n=1}^{N}$ is defined by an unknown function $f(\cdot) := f$, evaluated at input location $\mathbf{x}_n$ and corrupted by some independent noise ε_n,

$$
y_n = f(\mathbf{x}_n) + \varepsilon_n.
\tag{4}
$$

With the prior $p(\varepsilon_n) = \mathcal{N}(\varepsilon_n; 0, \beta^{-1})$ the probabilistic model can be written as follows,

$$
f|\theta \sim \mathcal{GP}(f; 0, k(\cdot, \cdot)),
\tag{5}
$$

$$
p(\mathbf{y}|f, \beta) = \prod_{n=1}^{N} \mathcal{N}(y_n; f(\mathbf{x}_n), \beta^{-1}),
\tag{6}
$$

where $\mathbf{y}$ specifies the vector of all one dimensional data points. To find the noise free function values $\mathbf{f}$ and the right hyperparameter set $\{\theta, \beta\}$ by hand is quite difficult. The usual Bayesian approach would be to specify a prior over the hyperparameter set to compute the joint posterior $p(\mathbf{f}, \theta, \beta|\mathbf{y})$. For Gaussian processes this inference problem is typically not analytically solvable, due to the intrinsic non-linearity of the GP. A common practice to handle this problem is to optimize the hyperparameter set instead by minimizing the negative log-marginal likelihood,

$$
\mathcal{L}(\theta, \beta) = -\log p(\mathbf{y}|\theta, \beta),
\tag{7}
$$

$$
= -\log \int p(\mathbf{y}|f(\mathbf{x}_n), \beta)p(f|\theta)\,\mathrm{d}f,
\tag{8}
$$

$$
= -\log \mathcal{N}(\mathbf{y}; \mathbf{0}, \mathbf{K_{ff}} + \beta^{-1}\mathbf{I}),
\tag{9}
$$

$$
= -\frac{N}{2}\log 2\pi - \frac{1}{2}\log|\mathbf{K_{ff}} + \beta^{-1}\mathbf{I}| - \frac{1}{2}\mathbf{y}^{\mathrm{T}}(\mathbf{K_{ff}} + \beta^{-1}\mathbf{I})^{-1}\mathbf{y}.
\tag{10}
$$

This allows to derive a conditioned posterior $p(\mathbf{y}_*|\mathbf{y}, \theta, \beta)$, based on Gaussian identities [1], from the joint probability of the prior function of the training set $p(\mathbf{y}|\theta, \beta)$ and the prior function of the test set $p(\mathbf{y}_*|\theta, \beta)$ for the prediction of new test outputs $\mathbf{y}_*$ with given test inputs $\mathbf{x}_*$ and a *fixed* hyperparameter set [15],

$$\tilde{m}(\mathbf{x}_*) = \mathbf{k}_{*,\mathbf{f}}(\mathbf{K}_{\mathbf{ff}} + \beta^{-1}\mathbf{I})^{-1}\mathbf{y}, \tag{11}$$

$$\tilde{k}(\mathbf{x}_*, \mathbf{x}'_*) = k(\mathbf{x}_*, \mathbf{x}'_*) - \mathbf{k}_{*,\mathbf{f}}(\mathbf{K}_{\mathbf{ff}} + \beta^{-1}\mathbf{I})^{-1}\mathbf{k}_{*,\mathbf{f}}^{\mathrm{T}}, \tag{12}$$

which is also a GP. The constructed matrices result from the covariance function evaluations of the training inputs $\{\mathbf{x}_n\}_{n=1}^N$, i.e. $[\mathbf{K}_{\mathbf{ff}}]_{n,n'} = k(\mathbf{x}_n, \mathbf{x}_{n'})$ and similarly between the test inputs $\{[\mathbf{x}_*]_i\}_{i=1}^I$ and training input locations $\{\mathbf{x}_n\}_{n=1}^N$, $[\mathbf{k}_{*,\mathbf{f}}]_{i,n} = k([\mathbf{x}_*]_i, \mathbf{x}_n)$.

This minimization procedure has several disadvantages: First, it often gets stuck at local minima and has a computational cost, due to the inversion of $\mathbf{K}_{\mathbf{ff}} + \beta^{-1}\mathbf{I}$, see Eq. (10), of $O(N^3)$ at each iteration step and a $O(N^2)$ for prediction. Second, one has to store the full observation vector $\mathbf{y}$ for learning and prediction, see Eqs. (10) and (11). These limitations prohibit larger scale learning using this approach, because of time and memory limitations. Especially the memory aspect is critical if optimization is implemented by GPU computing. Further, due to intractability of the posterior joint probability $p(\mathbf{f}, \theta, \beta|\mathbf{y})$, the construction of hierarchical (deep) models is not possible, because of the conditional dependency between the function value sets in the different layers.

In this paper, we show that approximate inference, exploiting Expectation Propagation (EP) framework in combination with sparse approximations of the Gaussian processes, offers an elegant solution for these problems.

2.2 GP Sparse Approximations

In order to implement the proposed GP framework for large data sets it is essential to reduce the computational complexity. This can be accomplished by a the GP sparse approximation approach [4]. For this purpose, the noise-free function value set $\mathbf{f}$, is approximated by selection of a small set of $M \ll N$ pseudo-point inputs $\{[\mathbf{x}_\mathbf{u}]_m\}_{m=1}^M$, mapped to the function values $\mathbf{u}$. It is assumed that training and test points of the Gaussian process are approximately conditionally independent, if conditioned on their pseudo-points so that $f = \{\mathbf{f}, \mathbf{u}, f_{\neq\mathbf{f},\mathbf{u}}\}$. Under this assumption, the GP prior, see Eq. (5), can be approximated as follows:

$$q(f|\theta) = q(\mathbf{f}|\mathbf{u}, \theta)p(\mathbf{u}|\theta)p(f_{\neq\mathbf{f},\mathbf{u}}|\mathbf{f}, \mathbf{u}, \theta), \tag{13}$$

where $p(\mathbf{u}|\theta)$ is the GP prior over $\mathbf{u}$. The conditional relationship between $\mathbf{u}$ and $\mathbf{f}$ is fundamental for this equation. With the GP priors $p(\mathbf{f}|\theta)$ and $p(\mathbf{u}|\theta)$ it is possible to derive from their joint probability the conditional dependency $p(\mathbf{f}|\mathbf{u}, \theta) = \mathcal{N}(\mathbf{f}; \mathbf{K}_{\mathbf{fu}}\mathbf{K}_{\mathbf{uu}}^{-1}\mathbf{u}, \mathbf{D}_{\mathbf{ff}})$, where $\mathbf{D}_{\mathbf{ff}} = \mathbf{K}_{\mathbf{ff}} - \mathbf{Q}_{\mathbf{ff}}$ and $\mathbf{Q}_{\mathbf{ff}} = \mathbf{K}_{\mathbf{fu}}\mathbf{K}_{\mathbf{uu}}^{-1}\mathbf{K}_{\mathbf{uf}}$. The constructed matrices correspond to the covariance function evaluations at the pseudo-point input locations $\{[\mathbf{x}_\mathbf{u}]_m\}_{m=1}^M$, i.e. $[\mathbf{K}_{\mathbf{uu}}]_{m,m'} = k_\mathbf{f}([\mathbf{x}_\mathbf{u}]_m, [\mathbf{x}_\mathbf{u}]_{m'})$ and similarly covariance function evaluations between pseudo-point input and data locations $[\mathbf{K_{fu}}]_{n,m} = k_{\mathbf{f}}(\mathbf{x}_n, [\mathbf{x_u}]_m)$. The matrices of $p(\mathbf{f}|\mathbf{u}, \theta)$ can be approximated by simpler forms using several approaches, compactly summarized [3] by:

$$q(\mathbf{f}|\mathbf{u}, \theta) = \prod_{b=1}^{B} \mathcal{N}(\mathbf{f}_b; \mathbf{K}_{\mathbf{f}_b \mathbf{u}} \mathbf{K}_{\mathbf{uu}}^{-1} \mathbf{u}, \alpha \mathbf{D}_{\mathbf{f}_b, \mathbf{f}_b}). \tag{14}$$

where b indexes B disjoint blocks of data-function values with $\mathbf{f}_b = [f_1, \ldots, f_B]^{\mathrm{T}}$. The Deterministic Training Conditional (DTC) approximation uses $\alpha \to 0$; the Fully Independent Training Conditional (FITC) approximation uses $\alpha = 1$ and $B = N$; the Partially Independent Training Conditional (PITC) approximation uses $\alpha = 1$ [4,24]. This approximation assumes that $f(\mathbf{x})$ is fully determined by the pseudo-point inputs and reduces the computational cost to $O(M^2 N)$ during learning and $O(MN)$ for prediction.

The new prior $q(f|\theta)$ with approximation can be combined with the data likelihood to obtain the modified generative model:

$$q(\mathbf{y}, f|\theta) = q(f|\theta) \prod_{n=1}^{N} p(y_n|f(\mathbf{x}_n), \theta). \tag{15}$$

This modified model is suitable for the construction of hierarchical models, keeping the memory inference steps node-local because each layer is associated with its own GP approximation. However, this formulation still leaves some problems unsolved. One is the intrinsic non-linearity of the data likelihood and its related analytic intractability. The second problem is that, due to GP approximation (especially for DTC), the model tends to overfit [26]. Approximate inference exploiting the EP framework can solve these remaining problems.

3   Methods

3.1   Stochastic Expectation Propagation

Expectation Propagation (EP) is a deterministic Bayesian inference algorithm [18] which allows to approximate intractable, but factorizable joint-distributions. EP returns a tractable form of the model joint-distribution, evaluated on the observed data. In the case of GP regression, the approximation takes the form of an unnormalized process $q^*(f|\theta) \approx p(\mathbf{y}, f|\theta)$ (the superscript $*$ defines an unnormalized process). The basic concept of distributional inference approximations, like Variational Free Energy (VFE) [26], EP [18] and Power EP [19] is the decomposition of the joint-distribution into terms of interest, such that $p(f, \mathbf{y}|\theta) = p^*(\mathbf{y}|f, \theta) = p(\mathbf{y}|\theta)p(f|\mathbf{y}, \theta)$. They are fully reflected by tractable terms of the decomposed approximation $q^*(f|\theta) = Zq(f|\theta)$, where the normalization constant Z approximates the marginal likelihood $p(\mathbf{y}|\theta) \approx Z$ and the posterior is approximated by GP sparse approximation, Eq. (13), so that $p(f|\mathbf{y}, \theta) \approx q(f|\theta)$, i.e. the approximate inference schemes return simultaneously approximations of the posterior and marginal likelihood in form of an unnormalized Gaussian process $q^*(f|\theta)$.

For the implementation of EP we reformulate the unnormalized form $p^*(\mathbf{y}|f, \theta)$ in terms of a dense Gaussian process prior $p(f|\theta)$, see Eq. (5), and the independent likelihoods $\{p(y_n|f, \theta)\}_{n=1}^N$. EP constructs the approximate posterior as a product of *site functions* t_n [20] and employs an approximating family whose form mirrors that of the target [3],

$$p^*(f|\mathbf{y}, \theta) = p(f|\mathbf{y}, \theta)p(\mathbf{y}|\theta) = p(f|\theta) \prod_{n=1}^N p(y_n|f, \theta)$$

$$\approx p(f|\theta) \prod_{n=1}^N t_n(\mathbf{u}) = Z\, q(f|\theta) = q^*(f|\theta), \qquad (16)$$

where $t_n(\mathbf{u})$ is approximated by a simple Gaussian. The site functions were iteratively refined by minimizing an unnormalized Kullback-Leibler divergence, $\overline{\mathrm{KL}}$ [3], between the real posterior and each of the distributions formed by replacing one of the likelihoods by the corresponding approximating factor [17],

$$\arg\min_{t_n(\mathbf{u})} \overline{\mathrm{KL}}\left(p(f, \mathbf{y}|\theta) \,\middle\|\, \frac{p(f, \mathbf{y}|\theta)\, t_n(\mathbf{u})}{p(y_n|\mathrm{f}_n, \theta)}\right)$$

$$= \arg\min_{t_n(\mathbf{u})} \overline{\mathrm{KL}}(p^*_{\backslash n}(f|\theta)p(y_n|\mathrm{f}_n, \theta) \,\|\, p^*_{\backslash n}(f|\theta)\, t_n(\mathbf{u})),(17)$$

Unfortunately, such an update is still intractable as it involves the computation of the full posterior. Instead, EP replaces the leave-one-out posteriors $p^*_{\backslash n}(f|\theta) \propto p(f, \mathbf{y}|\theta)/p(y_n|\mathrm{f}_n, \theta)$ on both sides of KL by approximate leave-one-out posterior $q^*_{\backslash n}(f|\theta) \propto q^*(f|\theta)/t_n(\mathbf{u})$, called the cavity, so that:

$$\overline{\mathrm{KL}}(q^*_{\backslash n}(f|\theta)p(y_n|\mathrm{f}_n, \theta) \,\|\, q^*_{\backslash n}(f|\theta)t_n(\mathbf{u})) = \overline{\mathrm{KL}}(q^*_{\backslash n}(f|\theta)p(y_n|\mathrm{f}_n, \theta) \,\|\, q^*(f|\theta)).$$

The update for the approximating factors are coupled and must be optimized by iterative updating. EP is doing this in four steps. We apply here a generalized version, called Power EP [19], where only a fraction α of the approximate or true likelihood is removed (or included). The steps are as follows:

1. Compute the cavity distribution by removing a fraction of one approximate factor, $q^*_{\backslash n}(f|\theta) \propto q^*(f|\theta)/t_n^\alpha(\mathbf{u})$.
2. Compute a hybrid or tilted distribution, $\tilde{p}(f|\theta) = q^*_{\backslash n}(f|\theta)p^\alpha(y_n|\mathrm{f}_n, \theta)$.
3. Project the hybrid distribution onto the approximate posterior by minimizing unnormalized KL divergence,

$$q^*(f|\theta) \leftarrow \arg\min_{q^*(f|\theta)\in\mathcal{Q}} \overline{\mathrm{KL}}(\tilde{p}(f|\theta) \,\|\, q^*(f|\theta)),$$

where $\mathcal{Q}$ is the set defined in Eq. (16).
4. Update the approximate factor by including the new fraction of the approximate factor, $t_n(\mathbf{u}) = [t_n^{1-\alpha}(\mathbf{u})]_{\mathrm{old}}[t_n^\alpha(\mathbf{u})]_{\mathrm{new}}$, with $[t_n^\alpha(\mathbf{u})]_{\mathrm{new}} = q^*(f|\theta)/q^*_{\backslash n}(f|\theta)$.

The fractional updates are equivalent to running the original EP procedure, but replacing the KL minimisation with an α-divergence minimisation [19,31], where

$$\overline{D}_\alpha(p^*(f|\theta) \parallel q^*(f|\theta)) = \frac{1}{\alpha(1-\alpha)} \int [\alpha p^*(f|\theta) + (1-\alpha)q^*(f|\theta)$$
$$- p^*(f|\theta)^\alpha q^*(f|\theta)^{1-\alpha}] \, df. \quad (18)$$

The α-divergence becomes the inclusive KL divergence, $\overline{KL}(p^*(f|\theta) \parallel q^*(f|\theta))$, when $\alpha = 1$. It becomes the exclusive KL divergence, $\overline{KL}(q^*(f|\theta) \parallel p^*(f|\theta))$, when $\alpha \to 0$. Minimising a set of local exclusive KL divergences is equivalent to minimizing a single global exclusive KL divergence [19] and the Power EP solution is the minimum of a VFE [3]. Since the unnormalized approximation, $q^*(f|\theta)$, consists of the product of independent approximate factors $t_n(\mathbf{u})$, the data can be partitioned in B disjoint blocks $\mathbf{y}_b = \{y_n\}_{n\in\mathcal{B}_b}$. The choice of α and corresponding approximate factors $t_b(\mathbf{u})$ have a strong influence on the GP sparse approximation scheme, see Eq. (14) (and [3] for more details) and enables batch learning, which makes the GP regression task scalable. However, local computation comes at the cost of memory overhead that grows with the number of datapoints, since local approximating factors need to be stored for every datapoint.

Stochastic Expectation Propagation (SEP) reduces the memory complexity of Power EP by a factor of N. This is accomplished by parameterizing a global factor, $t(\mathbf{u})$, that captures the average effect of a likelihood on the posterior $t(\mathbf{u})^N := \prod_{n=1}^N t_n(\mathbf{u})$ and combines the benefits of local approximation (tractability of updates, distributability, and parallelisability) with global approximation (reduced memory demands) [17]. The set of the approximate posterior in Eq. (16) can be rewritten as,

$$p^*(f|\mathbf{y},\theta) = p(f|\mathbf{y},\theta)p(\mathbf{y}|\theta) = p(f|\theta) \prod_{n=1}^N p(y_n|f,\theta)$$

$$\approx p(f|\theta) \prod_{n=1}^N t_n(\mathbf{u}) = p(f|\theta)t(\mathbf{u})^N = q_{\text{SEP}}^*(f|\theta). \quad (19)$$

One method to implement SEP would be to compute the approximate factorizations by the iterative procedure of Power EP and optimize the hyperparameters in an outer loop with Power EP [17]. But, it was shown in [11] that the factor tying approximation turns the optimization problem into a minimization problem, i.e. the approximate Power EP energy can be optimized with standard optimization algorithms (e.g. ADAM, L-BFGS-B) to find the approximate posterior and hyperparameters at the same time for each iteration step. This makes construction of hierarchical deep GP-LVMs feasible.

3.2 DGP-LVM

Standard GP models with sparse approximation have strong limitations in terms of real world data sets with large numbers of training examples. This typically requires a substantial increase of the pseudo-inputs for a good approximation, resulting in a quadratic increase of computational complexity with the number of data points. This renders larger-scale learning not practicable. Constructing a multi-layer GP reduces the computational cost to $O(NLM^2)$, where L is the number of layers. Further, DGPs employ a hierarchical structure of GP mappings and therefore are arguably more flexible, have a greater capacity to generalize, and are potentially able to provide better predictive performance [6].

DGPs have relationships to different kinds of GP models, including GP-LVMs. The basic probabilistic model can be written as,

$$f^{(l)}|\theta^{(l)} \sim \mathcal{GP}(f^{(l)}; 0, k^{(l)}(\cdot, \cdot)), \ l = 1, \ldots, L$$

$$p(\mathbf{h}^{(l)}|f^{(l)}, \mathbf{h}^{(l-1)}, \beta^{(l)}) = \prod_{n=1}^{N} \mathcal{N}(h_n^{(l)}; f^{(l)}(h_n^{(l-1)}), [\beta^{(l)}]^{-1}), \ h_n^{(1)} = \mathbf{x}_n, \ h_n^{(L)} = y_n$$

where $h_n^{(l)}$ is the hidden variable associated to the l-th layer, which forms the output vector $\mathbf{h}^{(l)} := \{h_n^{(l)}\}_{n=1}^{N}$, i.e. $\mathbf{h}^{(L)} = \mathbf{y}$, and $f^{(l)}$ is the function of the l-th layer. In order to infer the posterior distribution over the latent functions mappings, hidden variables and to obtain an estimate for the marginal likelihood for hyperparameter tuning the joint probability can be written as follows,

$$p(\mathbf{h}^{(1:L)}, f^{(1:L)}|\theta^{(1:L)}) = \prod_{n=1}^{N} \prod_{l=1}^{L} p(f^{(l)}|\theta^{(l)}) p(h_n^{(l)}|f^{(l)}, \theta^{(l)}), \tag{20}$$

where $\mathbf{h}^{(1:L)}$ is a short notation for $\mathbf{h}^{(1)}, \ldots, \mathbf{h}^{(L)}$, likewise for $f^{(1:L)}$ and $\theta^{(1:L)}$. Again, the joint probability is analytically intractable, due to the non-linearity of the data likelihoods and also the unknown intermediate outputs of each layer. So we make use of the SEP set for a tied factor constraint, see Eq. (19), in combination with GP sparse approximation to approximate the data likelihood of each layer,

$$q_{\text{SEP}}^{*}(f^{(1:L)}|\theta^{(1:L)}) = Z \prod_{l=1}^{L} q^{(l)}(f^{(l)}|\theta^{(l)}) = \prod_{l=1}^{L} p(f^{(l)}|\theta^{(l)}) t^{(l)}(\mathbf{u}^{(l)})^N, \tag{21}$$

to obtain a scalable, convergent approximate inference method. The model above can be extended for unknown and random inputs $\mathbf{X}$, defining a deep Gaussian process latent variable model (DGP-LVM).

In a GP-LVM regression model, we suppose that each output point $\mathbf{y}_n$ of a high dimensional data set $\mathbf{Y} = [\mathbf{y}_1, \ldots, \mathbf{y}_N]^{\mathrm{T}} \in \mathbb{R}^{N \times D}$ is represented by a corresponding, uncertain instance $\mathbf{x}_n$ of a low dimensional latent input variable, where D is the dimension of the data space. Each dimension of $\mathbf{y}_n = [y_{n,1}, \ldots, y_{n,D}]^{\mathrm{T}}$ is defined by an unknown function $f_d(\cdot) := f_d$, evaluated at input location $\mathbf{x}_n$. The usual generative model can be summarised as follows,

$$p(\mathbf{X}) = \prod_{n=1}^{N} p(h_n^{(1)}) \tag{22}$$

$$f_d|\theta \sim \mathcal{GP}(f_d; 0, k(\cdot, \cdot)), \quad \text{for } d = 1, \ldots, D \tag{23}$$

$$p(\mathbf{Y}|\mathbf{X}, f_1, \ldots, f_D, \beta) = \prod_{n=1}^{N} \prod_{d=1}^{D} \mathcal{N}(y_{n,d}; f_d(\mathbf{x}_n), \beta^{-1}), \tag{24}$$

where $p(\mathbf{X})$ is an isotropic Gaussian and $h_{1,n} = \mathbf{x}_n$. For a DGP-LVM the joint density in Eq. (20) has to be extended with the prior over $\mathbf{X}$ and dimensions D,

$$p(\mathbf{H}^{(1:L)}, f^{(1:L)}|\theta^{(1:L)}) = \prod_{n=1}^{N} p(h_n^{(1)}) \prod_{l=1}^{L} \prod_{d=1}^{D^{(l)}} p(f_d^{(l)}|\theta^{(l)}) p(h_n^{(l)}|f_d^{(l)}, \theta^{(l)}), \tag{25}$$

where $\mathbf{H}^{(l)} = [\mathbf{h}_1^{(l)}, \ldots, \mathbf{h}_N^{(l)}]^{\mathrm{T}} \in \mathbb{R}^{N \times D^{(l)}}$ for $l = 1, \ldots, L$. The approximate joint density takes the following form,

$$q_{\mathrm{SEP}}^*(f^{(1:L)}|\theta^{(1:L)}) = p(\mathbf{H}^{(1)})\gamma(\mathbf{H}^{(1)})^N \prod_{l=1}^{L} \prod_{d=1}^{D^{(l)}} p(f_d^{(l)}|\theta^{(l)}) t_d^{(l)}(\mathbf{u}^{(l)})^N, \tag{26}$$

where $\gamma(\mathbf{H}_1)^N$ is the global site function of $\mathbf{X}$. The prior over $\mathbf{X}$ can be replaced by top-down influences and enables, together with the approximate Power EP energy and the resulting minimization problem, hierarchical structures of multiple DGP-LVMs.

4   Hierarchical Interaction Model

We tested the proposed novel statistical framework by learning of the high dimensional kinematic data of two interacting humans (actors). The interactive motion of a pair of actors was modeled using DGP-LVMs for successive dimension reduction, see Fig. 1. The model is composed of three DGP-LVMs which were learned jointly. Learning includes both the bottom-up and top-down contributions at each hierarchy level. The right part of the figure represents the kinematic data of each actor $a \in \{1; 2\}$ by a DGP-LVM. The left part of the graph corresponds to a top level DGP-LVM that represents the interaction of both actors in a lower-dimensional latent space.

Modeling of the Human Actors. The bottom layers of our model represent the observed kinematic data of each actor $\mathbf{Y}_a$. The dimensionality of each of these data sets is reduced by a DGP-LVM with the same sample size ($N_a = 360$) and dimensionality ($D_a = 159$). Each hidden layer reduces the dimensionality by a factor of two (i.e. $D_a^{(3)} = 80$, $D_a^{(2)} = 40$ and $D_a^{(1)} = 20$), resulting in a dimensionality $Q_a = 10$ on the top layer ($\mathbf{X}_1, \mathbf{X}_2$). The hidden layers are approximated sparsly by a pseudo-input set $[\mathbf{X_u}]_a^{(l)}$ of size $M_a^{(l)} = 30$.

Modeling of the Interaction Between the Human Actors. The top levels of our model represents the interaction of both actors, also with a DGP-LVM with two hidden layers. The mapping function of $\mathbf{h}_3^{(2)}$ maps onto the concatenated set $[\mathbf{X}_1, \mathbf{X}_2]$ with dimension $D_{[\mathbf{X}_1,\mathbf{X}_2]} = 20$. Similarly to the bottom DGP-LVMs each hidden layer reduced the dimensionality by a factor of two ($D_3^{(2)} = 10$, $D_3^{(1)} = 5$). Again, each mapping function is approximated by a pseudo-input set $[\mathbf{X}_\mathbf{u}]_3^{(l)}$ of size $M_3^{(l)} = 100$. The latent inputs $\mathbf{X}_3$ have a dimensionality of $Q_3 = 2$. The unnormalized, approximated process of the whole model can be written as follows,

$$q_{\mathrm{SEP}}^*(f_1^{(1)}, f_1^{(2)}, f_1^{(3)}, f_2^{(1)}, f_2^{(2)}, f_2^{(3)}, f_3^{(1)}, f_3^{(2)} | \theta_1^{(1)}, \theta_1^{(2)}, \theta_1^{(3)}, \theta_2^{(1)}, \theta_2^{(2)}, \theta_2^{(3)}, \theta_3^{(1)}, \theta_3^{(2)})$$

$$= p(\mathbf{X}_3)\gamma_3(\mathbf{X}_3)^N \prod_{l=1}^{L_3} \prod_{d=1}^{D_3^{(l)}} p(f_{3,d}^{(l)}|\theta_3^{(l)}) \, t_{3,d}^{(l)}(\mathbf{u}^{(l)})^N$$

$$\times p(\mathbf{X}_2|f_3^{(2)})\gamma_2(\mathbf{X}_2|f_3^{(2)})^N \prod_{l=1}^{L_2} \prod_{d=1}^{D_2^{(l)}} p(f_{2,d}^{(l)}|\theta_2^{(l)}) \, t_{2,d}^{(l)}(\mathbf{u}^{(l)})^N$$

$$\times p(\mathbf{X}_1|f_3^{(2)})\gamma_1(\mathbf{X}_2|f_3^{(2)})^N \prod_{l=1}^{L_1} \prod_{d=1}^{D_1^{(l)}} p(f_{1,d}^{(l)}|\theta_1^{(l)}) \, t_{1,d}^{(l)}(\mathbf{u}^{(l)})^N. \tag{27}$$

5   Results

We tested our method by modeling of the body movements of two interacting subjects, each with 189 DOFs, performing a 'high five' movement with different emotional expressions. The kinematic data (BVH format) was converted into exponential maps [8], and we computed also velocities within this representation.

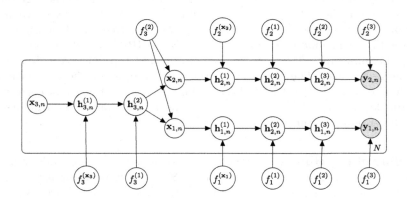

Fig. 1. Graphical model of the hierarchical DGP-LVM for modeling the interactive motion of two actors. The model consists of three DGP-LVMs, where each actor $\in \{1, 2\}$ is represented by a DGP-LVM on the right. The interaction of both actors is represented by the third DGP-LVM on the left side of the graph.

Our GP model was trained on a small set of 360 data points (6 trajectories, each normalized to 60 frames (2 angry, 2 sad, 2 neutral). We varied the α-values (0.1, 0.25, 0.5, 0.75, 0.9) and tested different optimizers: ADAM and L-BFGS-B. The second algorithm was implemented with different line search algorithms: Armijo Backtracking (AB), More Thuente (MT), Wolfe Backtracking (WB).

Learning was implemented on the CPU with an AMD Ryzon Threadripper 1950X 16 core processor 3.4 GHz with 64 GB RAM, and on GPU with a NVIDIA Quadro P600 graphics card with 24 GB RAM. Both implementations were realized in C++ using the ArrayFire framework [28] which allows to implement just one code for CPU and GPU solutions.

For maximal 2000 iteration steps in each learning condition this took in average 3.63 h on CPU and 1,21 h on GPU. ADAM, due to stochastic gradient decent, was always the fastest optimizer in each condition (Table 1 right). The GPU implementation with ADAM was almost seven times faster than the one on the CPU (GPU: 0.48 h vs. CPU: 3.39 h in average). For the L-BFGS-B implementation on the GPU the line search, which includes several internal loops, turned out to be the bottleneck in terms of computation time.

To determine the reconstruction performance of our model we computed the *normalized mean squared error* (NMSE) for the different optimization methods. On the one hand, overall ADAM performed best on average (Table 1 left). We found an increase of NMSE with higher α-values (i.e. the approximation being closer to a Power EP than to a VFE). On the other hand the algorithm converged faster for larger values of α. An α-value of 0.5 seems to be the best trade-of between reconstruction performance and optimization time. Our probabilistic generative motion model is fully real-time capable for computer-animation applications with the GPU implementation, since the computation time is only 0.0035ms per frame. An example movie of the reconstructed data and the corresponding ground truth can be found at https://hih-git.neurologie.uni-tuebingen.de/ntaubert/highfive_icann.

Table 1. *Normalized Mean Square Error (NMSE) and optimization time for different learning conditions.* Reconstructions from a model optimized with ADAM results in the smallest reconstruction error (left) and lowest optimization time (right). The optimization time of the line search algorithms are averaged for L-BFGS-B, due to similarity of inner loops.

	NMSE						Optimization time			
	ADAM	L-BFGS-B					ADAM		L-BFGS-B	
		AB	MT	WB			GPU	CPU	GPU	CPU
α 0.1	0.0210	0.0725	0.0485	0.0645	α	0.1	0.54 h	3.75 h	3.34 h	6.89 h
0.25	0.0213	0.0615	0.0419	0.0766		0.25	0.53 h	3.73 h	2.23 h	4.38 h
0.5	0.0309	0.0733	0.0898	0.0643		0.5	0.51 h	3.66 h	1.83 h	3.79
0.75	0.0900	0.1357	0.2419	0.2238		0.75	0.48 h	3.47 h	1.65 h	3.04
0.9	0.3175	0.3068	0.2408	0.2789		0.9	0.34 h	2.32 h	0.65 h	1.25
Average	**0.0961**	0.1300	0.1326	0.1416		Average	**0.48 h**	**3.39 h**	1.94 h	3.87

6 Conclusion

Combining methods from Bayesian unsupervised learning and inference, we devised a novel real-time-capable method for the realization of Deep Gaussian Process Latent Variable models (DGP-LVMs). Our method combines sparse GP approximations with Stochastic Expectation Propagation, and we provide a GPU implementation of the developed algorithms. To our knowledge, implementations of hierarchical DGP-LVMs have never been developed before. We found that optimization using ADAM results in the highest prediction accuracy of the model and optimization speed. In spite of the sophisticated underlying probabilistic model, we demonstrated that the algorithm is real-time-capable when implemented on the GPU for applications in computer animation.

Future work will extend such architectures by applying a dynamical system in form of a state space model to learn also time evolution. Further we plan to apply our algorithm on bigger data sets, exploiting batch learning on the GPU.

Acknowledgments. This research was funded through The research leading to these results has received funding from HFSP RGP0036/2016; NVIDIA Corp.; BMBF FKZ 01GQ1704, KONSENS-NHE BW Stiftung NEU007/1; DFG GZ: KA 1258/15-1; ERC 2019-SyG-RELEVANCE-856495; SSTeP-KiZ BMG: ZMWI1-2520DAT700.

References

1. Bishop, C.M.: Pattern Recognition and Machine Learning. Springer, Heidelberg (2007)
2. Brand, M., Hertzmann, A.: Style machines. In: Proceedings of SIGGRAPH 2000, pp. 183–192 (2000)
3. Bui, T.D.: Efficient deterministic approximate Bayesian inference for Gaussian process models (September 2017)
4. Quiñonero Candela, J., Rasmussen, C.E.: A unifying view of sparse approximate Gaussian process regression. J. Mach. Learn. Res. **6**, 1939–1959 (2005)
5. Chai, J., Hodgins, J.K.: Performance animation from low-dimensional control signals. ACM Trans. Graph. **24**(3), 686–696 (2005)
6. Dai, Z., Damianou, A.C., Hensman, J., Lawrence, N.D.: Gaussian process models with parallelization and GPU acceleration. CoRR abs/1410.4 (2014)
7. Damianou, A., Lawrence, N.: Deep Gaussian processes. In: Proceedings of Machine Learning Research, vol. 31, pp. 207–215. PMLR, Scottsdale (2013)
8. Grassia, F.S.: Practical parameterization of rotations using the exponential map. J. Graph. Tools **3**(3), 29–48 (1998)
9. Grochow, K., Martin, S.L., Hertzmann, A., Popovic, Z.: Style-based inverse kinematics. ACM Trans. Graph. **23**(3), 522–531 (2004)
10. Harvey, F.G., Pal, C.: Recurrent transition networks for character locomotion (2019)
11. Hernandez-Lobato, D., Hernandez-Lobato, J.M.: Scalable Gaussian process classification via expectation propagation. In: Gretton, A., Robert, C.C. (eds.) Proceedings of the 19th International Conference on Artificial Intelligence and Statistics. Proceedings of Machine Learning Research, vol. 51, pp. 168–176. PMLR, Cadiz (2016)

12. Holden, D., Komura, T., Saito, J.: Phase-functioned neural networks for character control. ACM Trans. Graph. **36**(4), 1–13 (2017)
13. Ikemoto, L., Arikan, O., Forsyth, D.A.: Generalizing motion edits with Gaussian processes. ACM Trans. Graph. **28**(1), 1–12 (2009)
14. Kaiser, M., Otte, C., Runkler, T., Ek, C.H.: Bayesian alignments of warped multi-output Gaussian processes. In: Bengio, S., Wallach, H., Larochelle, H., Grauman, K., Cesa-Bianchi, N., Garnett, R. (eds.) Advances in Neural Information Processing Systems, vol. 31, pp. 6995–7004. Curran Associates, Inc. (2018)
15. Lawrence, N.D.: Probabilistic non-linear principal component analysis with Gaussian process latent variable models. J. Mach. Learn. Res. **6**, 1783–1816 (2005)
16. Levine, S., Wang, J.M., Haraux, A., Popović, Z., Koltun, V.: Continuous character control with low-dimensional embeddings. ACM Trans. Graph. **31**(4), 1–10 (2012)
17. Li, Y., Hernandez-Lobato, J.M., Turner, R.E.: Stochastic expectation propagation (2015)
18. Minka, T.P.: Expectation propagation for approximate Bayesian inference. In: Proceedings of the Seventeenth Conference on Uncertainty in Artificial Intelligence, UAI 2001, pp. 362–369. Morgan Kaufmann Publishers Inc., San Francisco (2001)
19. Minka, T.: Power EP. Technical report (2004)
20. Naish-guzman, A., Holden, S.: The generalized FITC approximation. In: Platt, J., Koller, D., Singer, Y., Roweis, S. (eds.) Advances in Neural Information Processing Systems, vol. 20. Curran Associates, Inc. (2008)
21. Neal, R.: Bayesian learning for neural networks. Ph.D. thesis, Dept. of Computer Science, University of Toronto (1994)
22. Rasmussen, C.E., Williams, C.K.I.: Gaussian processes for machine learning. J. Am. Stat. Assoc. **103**, 429 (2008)
23. Schmerling, E., Leung, K., Vollprecht, W., Pavone, M.: Multimodal probabilistic model-based planning for human-robot interaction. In: 2018 IEEE International Conference on Robotics and Automation (ICRA), pp. 3399–3406 (May 2018)
24. Schwaighofer, A., Tresp, V.: Transductive and inductive methods for approximate Gaussian process regression. In: Advances in Neural Information Processing Systems, vol. 15. pp. 953–960. MIT Press (2002)
25. Taubert, N., Löffler, M., Ludolph, N., Christensen, A., Endres, D., Giese, M.A.: A virtual reality setup for controllable, stylized real-time interactions between humans and avatars with sparse Gaussian process dynamical models. In: Proceedings of SAP 2013, pp. 41–44 (2013)
26. Titsias, M.: Variational learning of inducing variables in sparse Gaussian processes. J. Mach. Learn. Res. - Proc. Track **5**, 567–574 (2009)
27. van der Wilk, M., Dutordoir, V., John, S.T., Artemev, A., Adam, V., Hensman, J.: A framework for interdomain and multioutput Gaussian processes (2020)
28. Yalamanchili, P., et al.: ArrayFire - a high performance software library for parallel computing with an easy-to-use API (2015)
29. Ye, Y., Liu, C.K.: Synthesis of responsive motion using a dynamic model. Comput. Graph. Forum **29**(2), 555–562 (2010)
30. Zhao, X., Robu, V., Flynn, D., Dinmohammadi, F., Fisher, M., Webster, M.: Probabilistic model checking of robots deployed in extreme environments (2018)
31. Zhu, H., Rohwer, R.: Information geometric measurements of generalisation (1995)

Adaptive Consensus-Based Ensemble for Improved Deep Learning Inference Cost

Nelly David[(✉)] and Nathan S. Netanyahu

Department of Computer Science, Bar-Ilan University, 5290002 Ramat-Gan, Israel
nellydavid.biu@gmail.com, nathan@cs.biu.ac.il

Abstract. Deep learning models are continuously improving the state-of-the-art in nearly every domain, achieving increased levels of accuracy. To sustain, however, this performance, these models have become larger and more computationally intensive at a staggering rate. Using an ensemble of deep learning models to improve the accuracy (in comparison to running a single model) is a well-known approach, but using it in real-world settings is challenging due to its exuberant inference computational cost. In this paper we present a novel method for reducing the cost associated with an ensemble of models by ∼50% on average while maintaining comparable accuracy. The method proposed is simple to implement, and is fully agnostic to the model and the problem domain. The experimental results presented demonstrate that our method can be used in a number of configurations, all of which provide a much better "performance per cost" than standard ensembles, whether using an ensemble of N instances of the same model architecture (trained from scratch each time), or an ensemble of completely different models.

1   Introduction

During the past few years deep neural networks have improved the state-of-the-art performance in nearly every domain applied to, e.g., computer vision, speech recognition, language understanding, etc. However, the improved accuracy obtained comes at the expense of a rapidly rising computational cost, since employing many of these models in real-world scenarios becomes infeasible, due to the associated inference cost for models providing the best accuracy. For example, the generative pre-trained transformer 3 (GPT-3), considered the most accurate language model, consists of 175 billion parameters, i.e., 10-fold the number of parameters of Microsoft's Turing natural language generation (NLG) model and 100-fold the number of parameters of GPT-2. In other words, we observe a trend of an exponentially-growing computational cost for smaller accuracy gains. This trend is significant, since in many real-world applications, even the smallest

---

Nathan Netanyahu is also affiliated with the Department of Computer Science at the College of Law and Business, Ramat-Gan 5257346, Israel

I. Farkaš et al. (Eds.): ICANN 2021, LNCS 12893, pp. 330–339, 2021.
https://doi.org/10.1007/978-3-030-86365-4_27

accuracy improvement often results in dramatic impact on the usability of the model.

One of the well-known methods for improving the performance of neural networks, is by using an ensemble of models. This could be done by either training the same model architecture multiple times (with different initial random weights or over different training sets), obtaining thereby N trained models, or by training, alternatively, N different models. A given new sample would be fed during inference through the N models, which output N predictions (typically in the form of softmax vectors). A final average vector of these output vectors represents the combined "knowledge" of all of these N models. Such ensemble methods substantially improve the inference accuracy for any model or problem domain (see, e.g., the experimental results in Sect. 3).

Despite their ubiquitous success in improving model accuracy, such ensemble models incur an exuberant computational cost for inference, which is linear in the number of models in the ensemble. For example, using an ensemble of 10 models results in a computational cost that is 10-fold the computational cost of a single model. Several previous methods benefit from the improved accuracy of ensembles without paying the full computational cost associated with them. However, these methods obtain lower accuracy than a standard ensemble of N models, or may require customized training or fine-tuning.

In this paper we present a novel method for an *adaptive consensus-based ensemble*, which works on ensembles of same model architecture (i.e., the same model trained multiple times with different initialization) or different model architectures, which can be used in ensembles of any size; more importantly, the presented method yields an accuracy level comparable to that of N models at a lower computational cost of $\sim 50\%$, on average, i.e., it runs about twice faster without compromising the accuracy. Additionally, this new adaptive ensemble method is very easy to implement, and can be added on top of any existing set of models using a few lines of code, without having to modify the way by which the models are trained.

The paper is organized as follows: In Sect. 2 we review previous methods using ensembles, various suggested improvements for these methods, and their limitations. Section 3 presents our novel adaptive ensemble method and extensive experimental results, comparing the performance per cost of our method for various ensembles. Finally, Sect. 4 makes concluding remarks.

2 Background

Ensemble methods have been widely used to improve the accuracy of neural networks [4,9,14]. Popular ensemble techniques include, e.g., bagging [1] and boosting [2], which use a single learning algorithm and train each model with a different subset of the training set. Another commonly used ensemble approach applies random initialization to the members of an ensemble, where each member has the same architecture and is trained on the same training set. Training each model with different initial weights produces different classifiers [15]. It has been shown that random initialization is sufficient to create an ensemble that reduces the variance and improves the accuracy of an individual model [10,11,13]. In other words, ensembles formed by training the same model architecture N times (with different initial weights), as well as ensembles composed of N different models have been shown to improve significantly the accuracy for nearly every problem domain.

Even though these ensembles of neural network models improve the accuracy in comparison to using only a single model, their cost is linear in the number of ensemble models. For example, the inference computational cost associated with an ensemble of N models is N times higher than that of a single model.

Several methods have gained advantage by using an ensemble of models, without incurring the full cost of training N models. For example, Huang et al. [7] suggested training a network using cyclic learning rate [12] to allow the network to converge to multiple local minima, each of which is associated with a separate model. Xie et al. [19] proposed a method for creating an ensemble from a range of epochs towards the end of a single training (instead of training multiple times from scratch). Gal and Ghahramani [3] applied dropout as a Bayesian approximation at both train and test time. By running the model multiple times with dropout at inference time, different predictions are obtained which are then averaged to provide a final prediction. Although these models allow for creating an ensemble of N models without incurring the cost of N training cycles from scratch, they do not reduce the inference cost, which remains the main impediment for the application of ensembles in deployment. And while most deep learning models in real-world applications are trained sporadically, they are intensively queried when deployed, i.e., the cost of inference is typically orders of magnitude higher than that of training. A second limitation of the above ensemble types is that they benefit only partially from the notion of an ensemble, as they do not yield the full accuracy improvement obtained by training N models entirely from scratch.

Several works have suggested methods for reducing the inference computational cost of ensembles, while still taking advantage of some of the accuracy gain. Inoue [8] proposed a confidence-based ensemble, where models are used sequentially until the ensemble of the models predicts a class with a confidence level that does not overlap with the confidence level of the other classes. Even though an early exit due to a high confidence level reduces the total cost of inference, the overall accuracy is still inferior to that of a standard ensemble (due to errors with high confidence values). Wen et al. [18] proposed batch ensemble, a method that reduces the test time of ensembles by sharing a subset of weights across the models in the ensemble. However, their method too resulted in lower accuracy gain than that of a standard ensemble. Zhou et al. [20] proposed using only a subset of models from an ensemble of N models by using genetic algorithms. The major limitation of their approach is the extensive fine-tuning needed for each specific set of models.

Finally, the empirical results of Opitz and Maclin [14] suggest that most of the gain due to ensembles is derived from a few combined models. In the spirit of their suggestion, our novel approach uses a subset of models to reduce the inference cost while maintaining the accuracy of a full ensemble of N models.

3   Adaptive Consensus-Based Ensemble and Experiments

In this section we propose a simple modification to existing ensembles, in order to significantly reduce the cost, while benefiting from the full accuracy gain of the ensemble.

Our method relies on the premise that when several classifiers predict the same class, regardless of their assigned softmax confidence scores, the predicted class is likely the correct one. Table 1 illustrates this observation. As indicated, when two randomly selected models agree on a predicted class, they are correct in 96.6% of the cases. A consensus among four models yields even a higher accuracy of above 98%. This insight led us to develop an adaptive model that draws on the consensus established among a subset of models, as far as providing the same class prediction.

Table 1. Accuracy (%) vs. number of randomly selected ResNet-32 models (denoted by N) that form a consensus on CIFAR-10

N	Accuracy (%)
2	96.6
3	97.9
4	98.2
5	98.5
6	99.0
7	99.1
8	99.2
9	99.3

We propose a consensus-based ensemble, where only a subset of models are used if they unanimously predict the same output. If there is no agreement on the output, we consult additional models and average the softmax outputs to get a final prediction. Let N_1 and N_2 denote, respectively, the number of subset models initially queried to check for a unanimous prediction, and the total number of models ensembled otherwise. We performed several experiments to examine the effect of different values of N_1 and N_2.

For each combination of N_1, N_2, where $N_1 \geq 2$ and $N_2 > N_1$, we performed the following steps for each input:

1. Randomly choose N_1 models and run predictions;
2. If the N_1 models predict the same class, then choose this class as the output;
3. Otherwise, randomly choose additional $N_2 - N_1$ models, and average the softmax outputs over all the N_2 models to obtain a final prediction.

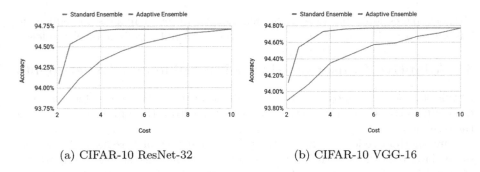

(a) CIFAR-10 ResNet-32   (b) CIFAR-10 VGG-16

Fig. 1. CIFAR-10 accuracy of standard ensemble vs. adaptive ensemble at different costs using (a) ResNet-32 and (b) VGG-16 models.

We experimented with the popular CIFAR-10 and CIFAR-100 datasets. As known, these datasets each consists of 60,000 32×32 RGB images divided, respectively, to 10 classes with 6,000 images per class, and to 100 classes with 600 images per class. For each dataset we performed our experiments using the following three model sets:

1. 10 trained ResNet-32 [6] models;
2. 10 trained VGG-16 [16] models;
3. 10 trained ResNet-32 models + 10 trained VGG-16 models.

To ensure that the results are stable, all of the experiments presented here were repeated 10 times, before reporting the final average value.

3.1   Performance of Standard Ensemble

Before demonstrating the performance of our adaptive ensemble method, we first measure the performance gain due to the use of standard ensembles relatively to a baseline of a single model. Since there are multiple (N) trained models in each experiment, we calculate the baseline accuracy as the average accuracy over the N models.

Using ensembles results in greatly improved accuracy across different models and datasets, as demonstrated by Table 2.

3.2   Performance of Adaptive Consensus-Based Ensemble

We now compare the inference cost of a standard ensemble to the cost incurred by the proposed method. A standard ensemble of size N performs N predictions for each input, and thus, has an inference cost of N. We first compute the accuracy for each standard ensemble size. We then evaluate the performance of our adaptive ensemble method for different value combinations of N_1 and N_2, by calculating the cost incurred.

Table 2. Performance of different ensembles vs. single model baseline; ensembles significantly improve the accuracy over a single model

Dataset	Model	Baseline accuracy (%)	Ensemble size	Ensemble accuracy (%)	ΔAccuracy vs. baseline
CIFAR-10	ResNet-32	92.70	10	94.71	+2.01
CIFAR-10	VGG-16	92.94	10	94.77	+1.83
CIFAR-10	RN-32+VGG-16	92.82	20	95.36	+2.54
CIFAR-100	ResNet-32	69.33	10	76.67	+7.34
CIFAR-100	VGG-16	69.71	10	73.83	+4.12
CIFAR-100	RN-32+VGG-16	69.52	20	77.36	+7.84

We define the inference cost as the average number of predictions performed across all samples. For example, if $N_1 = 3$ and $N_2 = 10$, for each sample we first query a randomly selected subset of three models. If they all agree on the predicted class, we use this as the prediction of the ensemble (without querying the remaining seven models), and the cost would be 3. If there is no consensus, the remaining seven models are queried as well, and the combined prediction is obtained by averaging all the softmax outputs of these 10 models. Thus, the total cost in this case would be 10 (i.e., 3 for the first subset and 7 for the additional models). For each experiment, we measure the average inference cost over all test samples, and compare it to that of the standard ensemble yielding the same accuracy.

Figures 1, 2, and 3 provide comparisons for each of the experiments. For each cost level $< N$, the adaptive ensemble achieves higher accuracy than the standard ensemble with the equivalent cost, and obtains comparable accuracy to that of a standard ensemble of size N at a lower cost (Table 3). This holds true for both ResNet-32 and VGG-16 over CIFAR-10 (Fig. 1), CIFAR-100 (Fig. 2), and ensembles comprising of a combination of ResNet-32 and VGG-16 for both CIFAR-10 and CIFAR-100 (Fig. 3).

Table 3 provides a summary of comparisons over the various experiments. The results indicate that our adaptive ensemble consistently maintains comparable accuracy to that of a standard ensemble, over different configurations, at about half the computational cost, on average. In other words, the proposed method offers a speedup gain of about 2, while maintaining similar accuracy.

Table 4 provides the accuracy of ResNet-32 on CIFAR-10 with different value combinations of N_1 and N_2, and Table 5 gives the cost for each combination. As can be seen, the adaptive ensemble obtains the same accuracy as a standard ensemble of 10 (94.71%) for all combinations of N_1, N_2, where $N_1 \geq 4$ and $N_2 = 10$. Using this configuration, the same accuracy of a full ensemble is obtained using a cost of 4.7 instead of 10. In addition, the inference cost can be further reduced to 3.7 with a small reduction in accuracy.

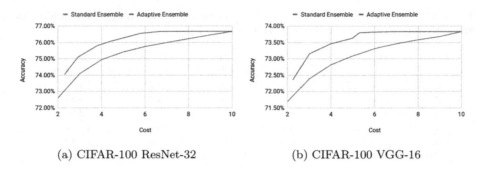

(a) CIFAR-100 ResNet-32   (b) CIFAR-100 VGG-16

Fig. 2. CIFAR-100 accuracy of standard ensemble vs. adaptive ensemble at different costs using (a) ResNet-32 and (b) VGG-16 models.

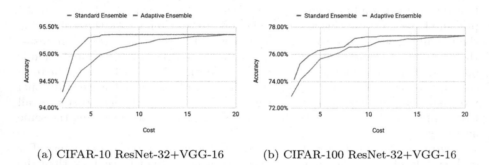

(a) CIFAR-10 ResNet-32+VGG-16   (b) CIFAR-100 ResNet-32+VGG-16

Fig. 3. Accuracy of standard ensemble vs. adaptive ensemble at different costs using a combination of ResNet-32 and VGG-16 models for (a) CIFAR-10 and (b) CIFAR-100 datasets.

Table 3. Adaptive ensemble accuracy (%) is comparable to that of standard ensemble at ∼ half the computational cost

Dataset	Model	Standard cost	Standard accuracy (%)	Adaptive cost	Adaptive accuracy (%)	Speedup vs. standard
CIFAR-10	ResNet-32	10	94.71	4.7	94.71	2.1
CIFAR-10	VGG-16	10	94.77	4.6	94.76	2.2
CIFAR-10	RN-32+VGG-16	20	95.36	7.1	95.36	2.8
CIFAR-100	ResNet-32	10	76.67	6.6	76.67	1.5
CIFAR-100	VGG-16	10	73.83	5.3	73.80	1.9
CIFAR-100	RN-32+VGG-16	20	77.36	11.1	77.34	1.8

Table 4. Accuracy (%) of different combinations of N_1 and N_2 for ResNet-32 on CIFAR-10

N_1/N_2	3	4	5	6	7	8	9	10
2	94.05	94.21	94.31	94.39	94.44	94.44	94.47	94.53
3	–	94.37	94.44	94.54	94.55	94.66	94.67	94.69
4	–	–	94.44	94.53	94.63	94.67	94.69	94.71
5	–	–	–	94.54	94.60	94.66	94.68	94.71
6	–	–	–	–	94.61	94.62	94.69	94.71
7	–	–	–	–	–	94.66	94.68	94.71
8	–	–	–	–	–	–	94.68	94.71
9	–	–	–	–	–	–	–	94.71

Table 5. Inference cost of different combinations of N_1 and N_2 for ResNet-32 on CIFAR-10

N_1/N_2	3	4	5	6	7	8	9	10
2	2.0	2.1	2.2	2.2	2.3	2.4	2.5	2.5
3	–	3.1	3.2	3.3	3.4	3.5	3.6	3.7
4	–	–	4.1	4.2	4.3	4.5	4.6	4.7
5	–	–	–	5.1	5.2	5.4	5.5	5.7
6	–	–	–	–	6.1	6.3	6.4	6.6
7	–	–	–	–	–	7.1	7.3	7.5
8	–	–	–	–	–	–	8.1	8.3
9	–	–	–	–	–	–	–	9.1

The experimental results show that the proposed adaptive ensemble obtains comparable accuracy to that of running N models at a significantly lower cost across different models, datasets, and ensemble sizes. Moreover, the adaptive ensemble method achieves higher accuracy than that of a standard ensemble of size $< N$ with the equivalent cost.

4   Concluding Remarks and Future Work

In this paper we presented a novel method that exploits the powerful potential of ensemble models while incurring only partially their full computational cost. The method presented can be easily implemented on top of any existing set of models, is fully agnostic to the problem domain and type of models, and does not require any customized training or fine tuning.

The experimental results presented in Sect. 3 show that the method works well across different configurations. Another important aspect of the method for real-world scenarios is that it can combine different models, even if some or all of them are based on commercial APIs, with no access to the training process.

The insights regarding this adaptive ensemble approach are also biologically plausible. Our brain's neocortex is comprised of hundreds of millions of cortical columns [17]. There has been growing evidence in recent years, which suggests that for relatively "easy" problems fewer cortical columns are activated, but when these cortical columns "disagree" on the prediction, a larger number of cortical columns are activated (see [5] for an overview of recent works). This insight is very similar to the approach taken here, as the easier samples would activate only a few models and reach a consensus, while more challenging samples would require the activation of additional models.

Nowadays, we often encounter increasingly growing neural networks, containing sometimes over 100 layers and a huge number of parameters. These very large models come at a staggering computational expense for inference, which is justified by the higher accuracy obtained. In this paper we demonstrated that ensemble models not only improve the accuracy, but it is possible to obtain their full accuracy gain without incurring their full computational cost. Thus, for many problems, an ensemble of smaller models may yield comparable accuracy to that of a single huge model (or even higher), at a possibly lower computational cost.

We intend to extend this work to explore the following research directions: (1) State-of-the-art improvement for some problems using our consensus-based ensemble, i.e., obtaining a higher overall accuracy for a smaller (or comparable) inference computational cost; (2) alternative selection of the first subset of models for each sample (instead of randomly selected models), and (3) incorporate softmax information, as a measure of the model's confidence, to further improve the efficiency of the process.

References

1. Breiman, L.: Bagging predictors. Mach. Learn. **24**(2), 123–140 (1996)
2. Freund, Y., Schapire, R.E.: Experiments with a new boosting algorithm. In: International Conference on Machine Learning, vol. 96, pp. 148–156 (1996)
3. Gal, Y., Ghahramani, Z.: Dropout as a Bayesian approximation: representing model uncertainty in deep learning. In: International Conference on Machine Learning, pp. 1050–1059 (2016)
4. Hansen, L.K., Salamon, P.: Neural network ensembles. IEEE Trans. Pattern Anal. Mach. Intell. **12**(10), 993–1001 (1990)
5. Hawkins, J.: A Thousand Brains: A New Theory of Intelligence. Basic Books, New York (2021)
6. He, K., Zhang, X., Ren, S., Sun, J.: Deep residual learning for image recognition. In: Proceedings of IEEE Conference on Computer Vision and Pattern Recognition, pp. 770–778 (2016)
7. Huang, G., Li, Y., Pleiss, G., Liu, Z., Hopcroft, J.E., Weinberger, K.Q.: Snapshot ensembles: train 1, get M for free. arXiv preprint arXiv:1704.00109 (2017)
8. Inoue, H.: Adaptive ensemble prediction for deep neural networks based on confidence level. In: The 22nd International Conference on Artificial Intelligence and Statistics, pp. 1284–1293 (2019)
9. Krogh, A., Vedelsby, J.: Neural network ensembles, cross validation, and active learning. Adv. Neural Inf. Process. Syst. **7**, 231 (1995)

10. Lakshminarayanan, B., Pritzel, A., Blundell, C.: Simple and scalable predictive uncertainty estimation using deep ensembles. arXiv preprint arXiv:1612.01474 (2016)
11. Lee, S., Purushwalkam, S., Cogswell, M., Crandall, D., Batra, D.: Why M heads are better than one: training a diverse ensemble of deep networks. arXiv preprint arXiv:1511.06314 (2015)
12. Loshchilov, I., Hutter, F.: SGDR: stochastic gradient descent with warm restarts. arXiv preprint arXiv:1608.03983 (2016)
13. Naftaly, U., Intrator, N., Horn, D.: Optimal ensemble averaging of neural networks. Netw.: Comput. Neural Syst. **8**(3), 283–296 (1997)
14. Opitz, D., Maclin, R.: Popular ensemble methods: an empirical study. J. Artif. Intell. Res. **11**, 169–198 (1999)
15. Pollack, J.B.: Backpropagation is sensitive to initial conditions. Complex Syst. **4**, 269–280 (1990)
16. Simonyan, K., Zisserman, A.: Very deep convolutional networks for large-scale image recognition. arXiv preprint arXiv:1409.1556 (2014)
17. Tsunoda, K., Yamane, Y., Nishizaki, M., Tanifuji, M.: Complex objects are represented in macaque inferotemporal cortex by the combination of feature columns. Nat. Neurosci. **4**(8), 832–838 (2001)
18. Wen, Y., Tran, D., Ba, J.: Batchensemble: an alternative approach to efficient ensemble and lifelong learning. arXiv preprint arXiv:2002.06715 (2020)
19. Xie, J., Xu, B., Chuang, Z.: Horizontal and vertical ensemble with deep representation for classification. arXiv preprint arXiv:1306.2759 (2013)
20. Zhou, Z.H., Wu, J., Tang, W.: Ensembling neural networks: many could be better than all. Artif. Intell. **137**(1–2), 239–263 (2002)

Human Pose Estimation

Multi-Branch Network for Small Human Pose Estimation

Yuchen Ge[1,2], Zhongqiu Zhao[1,2,3,4](✉), Yao Gao[1,2], Weidong Tian[1,2],
and Hai Min[1,2]

[1] School of Computer Science and Information Engineering,
Institute of Intelligent Manufacturing of Hefei University of Technology,
Hefei 230009, China
z.zhao@hfut.edu.cn
[2] Intelligent Interconnected Systems Laboratory of Anhui Province
(Institute of Intelligent Manufacturing of Hefei University of Technology),
Hefei, China
[3] Key Laboratory of Knowledge Engineering with Big Data
(Institute of Intelligent Manufacturing of Hefei University of Technology),
Ministry of Education, Hefei, China
[4] Guangxi Academy of Science, Nanning 530007, China

Abstract. The task of 2D human pose estimation aims to obtain the
position of the body's articulation points in picture, it is the basis
for many other tasks, but the current human pose estimation network
has shortcomings when dealing with small objects. Due to the ambiguity caused by inadequate expansion, a small human object contains
insufficient semantic information. Therefore, the prediction of coordinate points becomes imprecise. In this paper, to address the problem
of small human pose estimation, we present a novel network structure
called Multi-Branch Network (MBN), consisting of three modules: Multi-
Branch Expansion Module (MBEM), Multi-Branch Downsample Module (MBDM), and Refine Module (RM). MBEM reduces the input bias
before the image enters the backbone network. MBDM adds an extra
downsampling branch to obtain richer semantic information. RM locates
hard joints by the refined operation. The experimental studies on COCO
benchmark show that our approach gains noteworthy enhancements on
the state-of-the-art single-stage models of ResNet and RSN.

Keywords: Computer vision · Neural network · Human pose
estimation

1 Introduction

Human pose estimation has always been an important task in the field of computer vision [5,13,22]. With the growing popularity of neural networks, the methods of human pose estimation have evolved from graphical models to neural
networks [3,20,22]. The main goal has also evolved from the regression of the
coordinates to the generation of the heatmap. As the performance of neural

© Springer Nature Switzerland AG 2021
I. Farkaš et al. (Eds.): ICANN 2021, LNCS 12893, pp. 343–355, 2021.
https://doi.org/10.1007/978-3-030-86365-4_28

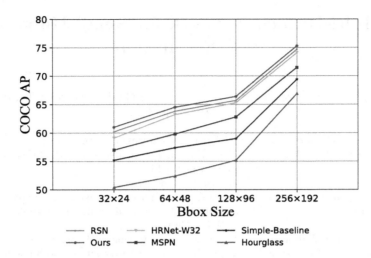

Fig. 1. The influence of different sizes of bounding box (bbox) on various human pose estimation networks, including single-stage MSPN (res50) [11], Simplebaseline (res50) [21], 8-stage Hourglass [14], HRNet-W32 [19], single-stage RSN-50 [1], and Our Method.

networks for single-person pose estimation is gradually saturated, the research hotspots have been transfered to multi-person pose estimation [3,4,14,20]. The approaches of multi-person pose estimation are mainly divided into two categories: top-down approaches [3,11,14,19,21] and bottom-up approaches [2,16]. The top-down approaches convert multi-person pose estimation to single-person pose estimation. Firstly, the object detection network is utilized to locate the people in the image, then the human bounding box (bbox) is fed into the single pose estimation network [3,24], and the heatmap is generated. The bottom-up approaches firstly locate all the keypoints in the image and then perform a cluster-like algorithm [2]. With the development of object detection algorithms, the time performance and accuracy of top-down methods are gradually increasing, so the researchers are paying greater attention to the top-down methods [11].

Fig. 2. Visualization of different bounding box (bbox) sizes and their corresponding results. (a) is expansion from original bbox, the original size is 274×161. (b) is expansion from 128×96. (c) is expansion from 64×48. (d) is expansion from 32×24.

Like object detection, human pose estimation also faces the challenge of small objects [10]. There are two criteria to define small objects. One is relative size, namely, if the length or width of an object is smaller than one-tenth of the whole image size, this object is considered as a small one. The other is absolute size, namely, if the length or width of an object is equal to or smaller than 32 × 32 pixel, this object can be considered a small one [18]. We artificially simulate small objects by changing the size of the human bounding box. The effect of human pose estimation on different bounding box sizes is shown in Fig. 1. For all networks, as the size of the obtained object decreases, the performance is continuously declined. The reasons may come from three aspects. As shown in Fig. 2, firstly, the smaller the bounding box is, the more severe the blurring is caused by sampling. The ambiguity leads to confusion as to what kind of information is valid when entering the backbone network. Our approach resolves the confusion by increasing the diversity of the receptive field through expanding the object to multiple sizes. Secondly, small objects lack much pixel information, which leads to the lack of semantic information. Therefore, to compensate for the lack of semantic information, our approach presents an additional downsampling branch and fuses the features at each step of downsampling. Finally, keypoints are difficult to locate with small bounding boxes due to the image jaggies produced by image expansion. Wrists, elbows, and waists are more difficult. Therefore, our approach proposes a new refinement module to further locate these difficult joints.

In summary, our contributions are as follows:

- We propose a novel network structure called Multi-Branch Network for small human pose estimation. In this network, we propose the MBEM to avoid the confusion by increasing the diversity of inputs, the MBDM to supplement the missing features of small objects, and the RM to localize hard joints.
- Our algorithm has 0.9AP improvement over the state-of-the-art single-stage model, RSN, and 1.0AP improvement over the MSPN which is the best single-stage model using ResNet as the backbone network at the same magnitude of parameters on COCO *test-dev* dataset.

2   Related Work

2.1   Top-Down Approaches

In top-down approaches, the accuracy of the human body detection bounding boxes is very important for human pose estimation [3,11]. An accurate human body bounding box should include the entire human body and important environmental information around it [7]. Therefore, the use of higher accuracy object detection algorithms allows for improved human pose estimation [3]. Another factor to affect the human pose estimation is the mutual occlusion between bounding boxes. To solve the occlusion problem, the current methods [1,3,11,14,19] try to obtain rich semantic information through continuous upsampling and downsampling. There are many top-down approaches which have significant effects on human pose estimation. Newell *et al.* [14] used a stacked modular design that can integrate multiple scales to make the location of key points more accurate, which is named The Stacked Hourglass Network. Chen *et al.* [3] proposed the Cascade Pyramid Network (CPN), which is divided into two parts, one is Globalnet and the other is Refinenet. The network structure of Globalnet is similar to U-net [17] and uses ResNet [8] as its backbone network, The Refinenet contains Online Hard Keypoints Mining (OHKM) by which the occluded and invisible joints can also be accurately predicted. Xiao *et al.* [21] proposed the Simple-Baseline which achieves higher results than CPN by using deconvolution to perform upsampling operations. The Multi-Stage Pose Network (MSPN) proposed by Li *et al.* [11] combines modularization and OHKM [3], which also increases the interactions between modules [6]. In summary, these networks focus on the following issues: obtaining more semantic information, making better use of the semantic information, and passing on semantic information between modules. Sun *et al.* [19] proposed the High-Resolution Network (HRNet) where in contrast to the previous scale fusion routine, the low-resolution and high-resolution features are more closely linked, and only the highest-resolution features are retained for prediction. In all of the above methods, the bottleneck is based on ResNet, and the champion of COCO Keypoint Challenge 2019, Cai *et al.* [1] proposed Residual Steps Network (RSN), which uses a new bottleneck named Residual Steps Blocks (RSB), to increase the acquisition of semantic information. In the RSN, an attention mechanism, Pose Refine Machine (PRM) is newly proposed. PRM introduces both spatial attention and channel attention into human posture estimation. Currently, it is the state-of-the-art on COCO dataset.

2.2 Refined Operation

Refined operation is the application of further detailing to the final result. OHKM [3] proposed by Chen *et al.* uses multiple crude results to rank the difficulty of locating the nodes, and locates difficult keypoints only. The Unbiased Data Processing (UDP) [9] proposed by Huang *et al.* and the Distribution-Aware coordinate Representation of Keypoints (DARK) [23] proposed by Peng *et al.* can be considered as the refinement works. Before the emergence of UDP and DARK, the coordinate points are usually selected from the maximum and the second maximum response points after Gaussian transformation. However, such a selection of coordinating points is not accurate enough. The UDP uses unbiased estimation to improve picking coordinate points [9]. The DARK locates the coordinates by Taylor expansion at sub-pixel accuracy [23]. Both of them achieve more accurate results, but at the same time, they are artificially designed. Therefore, we improve it by applying the idea of Machine Learning [20], which neural networks are used to learn the potential connections between things.

3 Approach

Our approach consists of three modules: Multi-Branch Expansion Module, Multi-Branch Downsample Module, and Refine Module. As illustrated in Fig. 3, MBEM

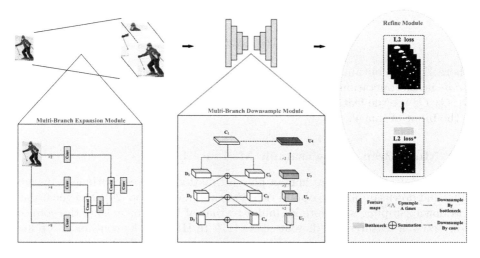

Fig. 3. Overview of our method. MBEM: Given a detected bounding box in the top-left, we amplify it to different magnifications, and fuse it two by two with different convolution operations. MBDM: $C_1 \sim C_4$ are the features extracted by ResNet, $D_1 \sim D_3$ are the features obtained from convolutional downsampling. The extracted feature of each step is preceded by feature fusion. RM: $U_1 \sim U_4$ are the features obtained by upsampling from the previous features. L2 loss* means L2 loss with online hard keypoints mining.

module expands the small objects for entering the backbone network, MBDM module extracts and fuses the features, and RM module locates joints.

3.1 Multi-Branch Expansion Module

The human pose estimation networks have dimensional requirements for feature extraction. Therefore, enlargement of the small bounding box is required. However, using the original single-branch enlargement method will lead to the confusion problem caused by image blurring in extracting features. Our approach is to solve the confusion problem by increasing the diversity of extracted features. The Multi-Branch Expansion Module expands the original small target to different times including ×2, ×4, ×8. The magnification depends on the input size of the backbone network, and we use the single-branch expansion magnified size as the maximum magnified size in multi-branch expansion. The branches adopt different convolution operations to make their outputs dimensionally identical while keeping them diversified. Before entering the backbone network, the features from the branches are fused and the valid feature information is preserved. We adopt the progressive fusion strategy for features at different scales. The features of the ×8 branch and the ×4 branch are firstly fused together and then pass through a 1 × 1 convolutional layer. The resulting features are then fused with the features of the ×2 branch before entering the backbone network. Multi-Branch Expansion Module is defined as follows:

$$Y = Conv(concat(O_1(x), O_2(x))) \tag{1}$$

$$E = Conv(concat(O_3(x), Y)) \tag{2}$$

where Y is the output of the first fusion, E is the output of the second fusion, $Conv$ is the operation of 1×1 convolutional layer, $concat$ is concatenation, O_1, O_2, O_3 are the feature extraction methods used on different branches, and x is the input of image.

3.2 Multi-Branch Downsample Module

Similar to object detection, human pose estimation requires continuous upsampling and downsampling to obtain rich semantic information [20]. The general up and down sampling structure is similar to that of U-Net increasing the connection between features at different scales [17]. In HRNet, the continuous up and down sampling fusion features achieve good results [19], which indicates that it is necessary to increase the connection between different scales in order to obtain more characteristic information. However, for small objects, downsampling with only one branch does not yield enough semantic information. Therefore, to compensate for the loss of information due to small objects, we use multi-branch fusion for downsampling. We design two branches to downsample, performing feature fusion at each downsampling. One of these two branches is with the feature extracted by the original resnet, and the other is with the feature extracted by the 3×3 convolutional layer. The overall structure resembles the fusion of two feature pyramids [12]. This method is defined as follow:

$$C_1 = S^1(E), F_1 = C_1, D_1 = S^2(F_1), \tag{3}$$

$$F_i = add(C_i, D_{i-1}), 2 \le i \le 4 \tag{4}$$

$$C_i = S^1(F_{i-1}), 2 \le i \le 4 \tag{5}$$

$$D_i = S^2(F_i), 2 \le i \le 3 \tag{6}$$

where E is the output of MBEM, $C_1, ..., C_4$ are features generated by ResNet at different scales, $D_1, ..., D_3$ are features generated by 3×3 convolutional downsampling at different scales, $F_1, ..., F_4$ are features of the fusion at different scales, add is elementwise addition, S^1 is the original downsampling operation in ResNet, S^2 is the downsampling by means of 3×3 convolutional operation.

3.3 Refine Module

Various human joints are not equally difficult to locate. Obvious joints can be located by rough treatment, but obscured joints require delicate treatment. The coordinates of the keypoints are obtained through the response points of the heatmaps. Each output channel generates a heatmap through Gaussian transformation, and finally, these heatmaps are combined to generate the predicted joints. In general human pose estimation networks, a convolutional layer is usually used to convert the channels to the heatmaps. Existing methods can be divided into two categories, either by using OHKM [3] to deal with obscured joints, or by using mathematical algorithms to select more precise coordinates on the heatmap. Our approach employs these methods. We first generate rough results with a Gaussian kernel of larger size and perform loss-value calculations to locate obvious keypoints. By ranking the different losses, we obtain difficult keypoints. Then we add additional parameters to these hard points for fitting and calculate the loss for these points only. We use the experimental results from the CPN [3] as the number of difficult points. Finally, in selecting the coordinate points, we follow the convention [14]. The main idea is defined as follow:

$$L2 = \frac{1}{2n} \sum_{x=1}^{n} \left\| y(x) - a^L(x)) \right\|^2 \tag{7}$$

$$L2^* = max_8 \left(\frac{1}{2n} \sum_{x=1}^{n} \left\| y(x) - a^L(x)) \right\|^2 \right) \tag{8}$$

where n is the number of joints, $L2$ loss is used for the simple joints localization, $L2^*$ loss is used for the hard joints localization, $y(x)$ is ground truth coordinate, $a^L(x)$ is the prediction coordinate, x is the input, max_8 is taking the eight largest values, selected by experiments in CPN [3].

$$P = add(3/4R^1, 1/4R^2) \tag{9}$$

$$heatmap = G(W \otimes featuremap) \tag{10}$$

where P is the coordinates of the keypoints, add is the addition operation, R^1 is the coordinate of maximum response point in heatmap, R^2 is the coordinate of second-largest response point in heatmap. Following [14], we fix the weights of R^1 and R^2 as 3/4 and 1/4. Where $featuremap$ is the output of backbone network. $heatmap$ is the basis for the selection of coordinate points. G is Gaussian transformation, W are the additional parameters for the location of hard joints before the Gaussian transformation, $\otimes$ is the multiplication operation.

4   Experiments

It is worth mentioning that the accuracy improvement of human pose estimation usually accompanies with the increase of the amounts of network parameters [1,11,19]. Human pose estimation networks often use a modular design, and can be divided into single-stage networks and multi-stage networks by the number of modules [14]. Therefore, the number of parameters in a multi-stage network is much larger than in a single-stage network, while the real-time performance is much worse [3]. To get rid of this dilemma, our network is designed as a single-stage network and compared with the best single-stage models.

Fig. 4. Comparison of original images and mean scaled images.

4.1 Dataset and Evaluation Metric

MS COCO is adopted to evaluate our method. It consists of three splits: train, validation and test-dev. Similar to [3,11], we aggregate the data of the training and validation parts, and then divide it into a training dataset (nearly 57K images and 150K individual instances) and a val dataset (5K images) for training and evaluation, respectively. OKS-based mAP (AP for short) is used as our evaluation metric.

4.2 Implementation Details

Data Processing. Since there does not exist any dedicated small object human pose datasets, we reduce the human bounding boxes of normal size to small ones by mean scaling. Mean scaling means that adjacent pixels are averaged and the range is determined by the size of output Fig. 4.

Experimental Settings. We use MegDet [15] as the human detecor. Similar to [3,11,19], all the bounding boxes are expanded to the ratio of 4 : 3. The network is trained on 1 Nvidia GTX 2080Ti GPU with mini-batch size 32 without pre-trained model on ImageNet. Adam optimizer is adopted and the linear learning rate gradually decreases from $5e-4$ to 0. The weight decay is $1e-5$. The training runs for 90k iterations.

Each image randomly goes through a series of data augmentation operations including cropping, and instances with more than eight joints are cropped to upper or lower bodies with equal possibility. The scaling range is 0.7–1.35, and the rotation range is $-45°$–$45°$. The bounding box(bbox) size is set 32×24.

A post-Gaussian filter is applied to the estimated heat maps. Following the line of work in [14], we average the predicted heat maps of original image with results of corresponding flipped image. Then, a quarter offset in the direction from the highest response to the second highest response is implemented to obtain the final locations of key point. The pose score is the multiplication of box and average scores of key point [3].

4.3   Ablation Study

In this section, we provide an in-depth analysis of our method: the effects of different backbones, each module and different small bounding box sizes. These experiments are done on COCO *val* dataset.

Different Backbones. Experimental results on different backbones are shown in Table 1. We compare our method with MSPN (1s), and our method gains 1.0 AP higher when backbone network is ResNet-18. As the backbone network is ResNet-50, our method achieves 0.9AP improvement. When the backbone network is ResNet-101, our method achieves 0.7AP improvement. We can see that our approach yields better results with different backbone networks, but as the number of parameters increase, the improvement becomes smaller.

Different Bbox Sizes. We verify the impact of different bounding box sizes on our method, as shown in Table 2. We compare our method with MSPN (1s) and RSN (1s). As the size of the bounding box is 16×12, our method achieves 1.7AP higher than MSPN (1s), 1.6AP higher than RSN (1s). These results illustrate that with smaller human objects, our method can achieve more notable improvement, but with very small human objects, it is very difficult to perform pose estimation.

Table 1. Compared with MSPN (1s) under different ResNet structures, 1s means single-stage, Input size of backbone network is 64×48. Ours (Res) means that bottleneck is Residual block.

Method	Backbone	Bbox size	AP
MSPN (1s)	ResNet-18	32×24	47.6
	ResNet-50	32×24	57.0
	ResNet-101	32×24	59.4
Ours (Res)	ResNet-18	32×24	**48.6**
	ResNet-50	32×24	**57.9**
	ResNet-101	32×24	**60.1**

352   Y. Ge et al.

Table 2. Comparison with MSPN (1s) on different bounding box sizes, 1s means single-stage, Input size of backbone network is 64 × 48. Ours (Res) and Ours (RSB) mean that bottleneck is Residual block and Residual Steps Block, respectively.

Method	Backbone	Bbox size	AP
MSPN(1s)	ResNet-18	16 × 12	19.0
Ours(Res)			**20.7**
RSN(1s)	RSN-18		26.0
Ours(RSB)			**27.6**

Table 3. Ablation study on different modules, 1s means single-stage, Input size of backbone network is 64 × 48. Ours (Res) and Ours (RSB) mean that bottleneck is Residual block and Residual Steps Block, respectively.

MBEM	MBDM	RM	Ours (Res)	Ours (RSB)
			47.6	55.2
		✓	47.9 (+0.3)	55.5 (+0.3)
	✓	✓	48.2 (+0.6)	55.7 (+0.5)
✓	✓	✓	**48.6 (+1.0)**	**56.0 (+0.8)**

Different Modules. We provide an in-depth analysis of each module designed in our framework, as shown in Table 3. The backbone network of our model is ResNet-18 or RSN-18. The RM module brings about 0.3AP in both Res and RSB models. The MBDM strategy brings about 0.3AP in the Res model, and 0.2AP in the RSB model. The MBEM strategy brings about 0.4 AP in the Res model, 0.3AP in the RSB model. These results imply that each of our proposed modules is valid.

4.4   Comparison with State-of-the-art Methods

We compare the effects of different methods on COCO *val* dataset (Table 4) and COCO *test-dev* dataset (Table 5). On COCO *val* dataset, Ours (Res) achieves

Table 4. Comparisons of various methods on COCO *val* dataset, 1s means single-stage, Input size of backbone network is 64 × 48. Ours (Res) and Ours (RSB) mean that bottleneck is Residual block and Residual Steps Block, respectively.

Method	Backbone	Bbox size	#Params	AP	AP (50)	AP (75)	AR
Hourglass [14]	-	32 × 24	25.1M	50.4	80.5	59.4	60.2
CPN [3]	ResNet-50	32 × 24	28.7M	55.3	83.2	61.8	63.5
Simplebaseline [21]	ResNet-50	32 × 24	34.0M	55.2	83.3	61.7	63.5
HRNet-W32 [19]	-	32 × 24	28.5M	59.1	85.5	63.8	66.2
MSPN (1s) [11]	ResNet-50	32 × 24	25.1M	57.0	83.9	63.1	65.0
RSN (1s) [1]	RSN-50	32 × 24	25.7M	60.2	85.9	64.0	67.7
Ours (Res)	ResNet-50	32 × 24	27.1M	**57.9**	**85.3**	**63.9**	**65.4**
Ours (RSB)	RSN-50	32 × 24	28.0M	**61.0**	**86.2**	**64.7**	**68.3**

Table 5. Comparisons of various methods on COCO *test-dev* dataset, 1s means single-stage, Input size of backbone network is 64 × 48. Ours (Res) and Ours (RSB) mean that bottleneck is Residual block and Residual Steps Block, respectively.

Method	Backbone	Bbox size	#Params	AP	AP (50)	AP (75)	AR
Hourglass [14]	-	32 × 24	25.1M	49.3	79.6	59.2	59.8
CPN [3]	ResNet-50	32 × 24	28.7M	54.1	82.7	61.4	63.1
Simplebaseline [21]	ResNet-50	32 × 24	34.0M	54.0	82.6	61.5	63.2
HRNet-W32 [19]	-	32 × 24	28.M	58.0	84.2	63.3	65.5
MSPN (1s) [11]	ResNet-50	32 × 24	25.1M	55.9	83.3	62.9	64.0
RSN (1s) [1]	RSN-50	32 × 24	25.7M	59.1	85.1	66.2	67.4
Ours (Res)	ResNet-50	32 × 24	27.1M	**56.9**	**84.4**	**63.1**	**64.8**
Ours (RSB)	RSN-50	32 × 24	28.0M	**60.0**	**85.8**	**67.0**	**68.2**

0.9AP higher than MSPN (1s) which is the best single-stage model using ResNet as the backbone network, and Ours (RSB) achieves 0.8AP higher than RSN (1s) which is the state-of-the-art single-stage model. On COCO *test-dev* dataset, Ours (Res) achieves 1.0AP higher than MSPN (1s), and Ours (RSB) achieves 0.9AP higher than RSN (1s). These results indicate that our approach is effective for small human pose estimation.

5   Conclusion

In this paper, we explain why the current pose estimation networks are out of work when facing small human objects. Then, we propose a novel network structure called Multi-Branch Network (MBN) and verify its effectiveness on COCO dataset. MBN consists of three modules of MBEM, MBDM and RM. MBEM increases the variety of input, MBDM obtains more semantic information, and RM further locates hard joints. In the future, in order to solve the problem of the ambiguity of small object input, various image restoration methods can be adopted to repair the missing information of the small object.

Acknowledgements. This work was supported in part by the National Natural Science Foundation of China under Grants 61976079, in part by Anhui Natural Science Funds for Distinguished Young Scholar under Grant 170808J08, and in part by Anhui Key Research and Development Program under Grant 202004a05020039.

References

1. Cai, Y., et al.: Learning delicate local representations for multi-person pose estimation. In: Vedaldi, A., Bischof, H., Brox, T., Frahm, J.-M. (eds.) ECCV 2020. LNCS, vol. 12348, pp. 455–472. Springer, Cham (2020). https://doi.org/10.1007/978-3-030-58580-8_27

2. Cao, Z., Simon, T., Wei, S.E., Sheikh, Y.: Realtime multi-person 2D pose estimation using part affinity fields. In: CVPR, pp. 7291–7299 (2017)
3. Chen, Y., Wang, Z., Peng, Y., Zhang, Z., Yu, G., Sun, J.: Cascaded pyramid network for multi-person pose estimation. In: CVPR, pp. 7103–7112 (2018)
4. Fang, H.S., Xie, S., Tai, Y.W., Lu, C.: Rmpe: regional multi-person pose estimation. In: ICCV, pp. 2334–2343 (2017)
5. Felzenszwalb, P., McAllester, D., Ramanan, D.: A discriminatively trained, multi-scale, deformable part model. In: CVPR, pp. 1–8. IEEE (2008)
6. Gkioxari, G., Toshev, A., Jaitly, N.: Chained predictions using convolutional neural networks. In: Leibe, B., Matas, J., Sebe, N., Welling, M. (eds.) ECCV 2016. LNCS, vol. 9908, pp. 728–743. Springer, Cham (2016). https://doi.org/10.1007/978-3-319-46493-0_44
7. He, K., Gkioxari, G., Dollár, P., Girshick, R.: Mask R-CNN. In: ICCV, pp. 2961–2969 (2017)
8. He, K., Zhang, X., Ren, S., Sun, J.: Deep residual learning for image recognition. In: CVPR, pp. 770–778 (2016)
9. Huang, J., Zhu, Z., Guo, F., Huang, G.: The devil is in the details: delving into unbiased data processing for human pose estimation. In: CVPR, pp. 5700–5709 (2020)
10. Li, J., Liang, X., Wei, Y., Xu, T., Feng, J., Yan, S.: Perceptual generative adversarial networks for small object detection. In: CVPR, pp. 1222–1230 (2017)
11. Li, W., et al.: Rethinking on multi-stage networks for human pose estimation. arXiv preprint arXiv:1901.00148 (2019)
12. Lin, T.Y., Dollár, P., Girshick, R., He, K., Hariharan, B., Belongie, S.: Feature pyramid networks for object detection. In: CVPR, pp. 2117–2125 (2017)
13. Lin, T.Y., et al.: Microsoft COCO: common objects in context. In: Fleet, D., Pajdla, T., Schiele, B., Tuytelaars, T. (eds.) ECCV 2014. LNCS, vol. 8693, pp. 740–755. Springer, Cham (2014). https://doi.org/10.1007/978-3-319-10602-1_48
14. Newell, A., Yang, K., Deng, J.: Stacked hourglass networks for human pose estimation. In: Leibe, B., Matas, J., Sebe, N., Welling, M. (eds.) ECCV 2016. LNCS, vol. 9912, pp. 483–499. Springer, Cham (2016). https://doi.org/10.1007/978-3-319-46484-8_29
15. Peng, C., et al.: Megdet: a large mini-batch object detector. In: CVPR, pp. 6181–6189 (2018)
16. Pishchulin, L., et al.: Deepcut: joint subset partition and labeling for multi person pose estimation. In: CVPR, pp. 4929–4937 (2016)
17. Ronneberger, O., Fischer, P., Brox, T.: U-Net: convolutional networks for biomedical image segmentation. In: Navab, N., Hornegger, J., Wells, W.M., Frangi, A.F. (eds.) MICCAI 2015. LNCS, vol. 9351, pp. 234–241. Springer, Cham (2015). https://doi.org/10.1007/978-3-319-24574-4_28
18. Singh, B., Davis, L.S.: An analysis of scale invariance in object detection snip. In: CVPR, pp. 3578–3587 (2018)
19. Sun, K., Xiao, B., Liu, D., Wang, J.: Deep high-resolution representation learning for human pose estimation. In: CVPR, pp. 5693–5703 (2019)
20. Toshev, A., Szegedy, C.: Deeppose: human pose estimation via deep neural networks. In: CVPR, pp. 1653–1660 (2014)
21. Xiao, B., Wu, H., Wei, Y.: Simple baselines for human pose estimation and tracking. In: ECCV, pp. 466–481 (2018)
22. Yang, W., Li, S., Ouyang, W., Li, H., Wang, X.: Learning feature pyramids for human pose estimation. In: ICCV, pp. 1281–1290 (2017)

23. Zhang, F., Zhu, X., Dai, H., Ye, M., Zhu, C.: Distribution-aware coordinate repre-sentation for human pose estimation. In: CVPR, pp. 7093–7102 (2020)
24. Zhao, Z.Q., Zheng, P., Xu, S.T., Wu, X.: Object detection with deep learning: a review. IEEE Trans. Neural Netw. Learn. Syst. **30**(11), 3212–3232 (2019)

PNO: Personalized Network Optimization for Human Pose and Shape Reconstruction

Zhijie Cao[1], Min Wang[4], Shanyan Guan[2], Wentao Liu[4], Chen Qian[4], and Lizhuang Ma[1,3(✉)]

[1] Department of Computer Science and Engineering, Shanghai Jiao Tong University, Shanghai, China
caozhijie_sjtu@sjtu.edu.cn
[2] Department of Electronic Engineering, Shanghai Jiao Tong University, Shanghai, China
shyanguan@cs.sjtu.edu.cn
[3] School of Computer Science and Technology, East China Normal University, Shanghai, China
ma-lz@cs.sjtu.edu.cn
[4] SenseTime Research, Shatin, Hong Kong
{wangmin,liuwentao,qianchen}@sensetime.com

Abstract. Most previous human pose and shape reconstruction methods focus on the generalization ability and learn a prior of the general pose and shape, however the personalized features are often ignored. We argue that the personalized features such as appearance and body shape are always consistent for the specific person and can further improve the accuracy. In this paper, we propose a Personalized Network Optimization (PNO) method to maintain both generalization and personality for human pose and shape reconstruction. The general trained network is adapted to the personalized network by optimizing with only a few unlabeled video frames of the target person. Moreover, we specially propose geometry-aware temporal constraints that help the network better exploit the geometry knowledge of the target person. In order to prove the effectiveness of PNO, we re-design the benchmark of pose and shape reconstruction to test on each person independently. Experiments show that our method achieve the state-of-the-art results in both 3DPW and MPI-INF-3DHP datasets.

Keywords: Human pose and shape reconstruction · Human mesh recovery · Personalized Network Optimization

1 Introduction

Monocular human pose and shape reconstruction is important for computers to understand human in images and videos. With the large scale human datasets and powerful deep neural networks, great progress in human analysis has been made in recent years [10,14]. However, the *general networks* trained on large scale datasets may lose the personality of different cases.

© Springer Nature Switzerland AG 2021
I. Farkaš et al. (Eds.): ICANN 2021, LNCS 12893, pp. 356–367, 2021.
https://doi.org/10.1007/978-3-030-86365-4_29

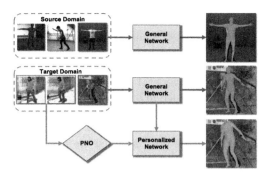

Fig. 1. General networks trained on the source domain suffer performance drop when applied to unseen person in the target domain. With a few unlabeled video frames of the target person, the Personalized Network Optimization (PNO) can adapt a general network into a personalized network that is located on the target domain. The personalized network can produce much more accurate results.

As shown in Fig. 1, when the input image contains a target person that is quite different from training data, the general network tends to predict inaccurate pose and shape. The general solution of labeling more target domain data is not suitable for 3D human reconstruction due to the expensive cost of obtaining 3D ground truth. In this paper, we propose a method to get the personalized network located in the target domain which is more suitable than the general network for pose and shape reconstruction for a particular person.

Most previous works intend to enlarge the domain of training data to cover the target domain, including data augmentation [19], exploiting 2D annotations as weak supervision [10], and integrating synthesis data [5]. However, fitting a neural network to various in-the-wild data is quite challenging and somehow not feasible. Conversely, there is another way that we can narrow down the domain of the network to focus on the specific person in the video, such as post-optimizing the 3D pose [3]. The problem is these methods require access to the whole test data during the post-processing. Our insight is: we can infer ones pose accurately when we are familiar with his or her somatotype and appearance. Therefore, we aim to employ only a part of unlabelled test data and we optimize the weights of a general network into a personalized network. The domain of the personalized network contains the general information of poses and shapes, and the personal information distilled with the partial yet sufficient samples. Therefore, the network can obtain the superior performance on the specific person with the personalized feature.

In this work, we propose the Personalized Network Optimization (PNO) framework to reconstruct the pose and shape of the specified person from an offline video or an online video stream. Given a test video, we sample a part of unlabeled video frames and obtain their 2D keypoints by a 2D pose estimator [4]. Then we take an off-the-shelf human pose and shape reconstruction network [14] as the basic network. The personalized network has a fusion architecture which is integrated by two duplicated basic networks, where one is for general features extraction, the other is for personalized features learning. We named them as general branch and personalized branch respectively. The fitting process is supervised by the 2D re-projection constraint and pose plausibility constraint. Since we fix the weights of the general branch, a critical characteristic of our method is that it learns the knowledge of the personalized feature of the specific person without losing the memories of the general 3D prior. Therefore, the proposed network decreases the reconstruction error not only in the sampled data, but also in those data of the same person which are not sampled before. We also introduce the geometry-aware temporal constraint based on the assumption that the somatotype of the person is invariant in the video. It is applied on each pair of the sampled frames so that the personalized network tends to output stable shape parameters over time.

To evaluate the effectiveness of our method, we re-design the benchmark that separate the test sets of 3DPW [18] and MPI-INF-3DHP [19] into different subsets for each specific person. We experimentally evaluate the effect with different proportions of test data for PNO, and it shows that using only part of the test data achieves the competitive performance compared with 100% of them on 3D pose and shape estimation. We also find that the human shape which is predicted by the personalized network is more steady than the one predicted by the general network. It is a reliable evidence to prove that personalized feature is remembered by the personalized network.

We summarize the contributions of our approach below:

- We propose a novel Personalized Network Optimization (PNO) framework for human pose and shape reconstruction. To our knowledge, it is the first work to personalize the neural network for a specific person for human pose and shape reconstruction.
- We propose an integrated architecture called Fusion Network to learn the personalized feature without losing 3D priors.
- We employ the geometry-aware temporal constraints that keep the body shape consistency of the specified person to help the network learn the geometry knowledge prior.
- We raise a novel benchmark that evaluates individual human pose and shape estimation on 3DPW and MPI-INF-3DHP. We achieve the state-of-the-art results, and we demonstrate the effectiveness of the Personalized Network Optimization through extensive experiments.

2   Related Work

Human Mesh Reconstruction. SMPL [17] is a popular parametric model for 3D human pose and shape reconstruction, which is also used in this work. Generally, the early works [3,6,15] adopt the optimization scheme. A T-pose SMPL template is gradually fit to given images according to the silhouettes [15], 2D keypoints [3], or multi-view constraints [6]. These optimization approaches are time-consuming since they need thousands of iteration to fit an image. Recently, many works [10, 12, 14, 21] shift the spotlight to train a neural network to directly obtain the parameters of the SMPL model, which is more efficient. The major drawback of CNN-based works is the scalability for new domains. For example, a model trained on indoor data generally fails to get satisfactory results on outdoor data. To tackle this problem, [10] propose an adversarial framework to facilitate the training on in-the-wild data. [14] use a hybrid framework, combining CNN and optimization module, to enable training on 2D datasets without 3D pose annotation. However, since there will always be some test data that is distinguishable from the training data, the principled challenges still exist.

In this work, we tackle this problem from a completely novel view. Specifically, instead of taking efforts to improve generalization ability during training, we optimize the network at test time to improve scalability for unseen data.

Unsupervised Network Optimization. Unsupervised network optimization refers to optimizing a pre-trained model to test data before the inference stage in an unsupervised manner. It is an effective technique to prevent performance drop when test data vary from the training data. Previous works [2, 20, 22] apply it for many tasks, such as tracking [20], image super-resolution [22], image manipulation [2]. However, none of them present a pilot work of unsupervised network optimization for human pose and shape reconstruction.

3 Method

First, we formulate the problem in Sect. 3.1. Then we introduce the details of vanilla PNO and the design of the network architecture in Sect. 3.2. Next, we describe the temporal PNO framework in Sect. 3.3, which integrates geometry-aware temporal constraints into the optimization procedure.

3.1 Problem Formulation

Human pose and shape reconstruction based on SMPL refers to that given an input image, a deep neural network regresses its SMPL parameters $\{\theta, \beta\}$ and the parameters of a weak-perspective camera model π. In order to chase a well-trained network which is general to various environments and people with different body size and appearance, previous works [10, 12] train the deep network in a large-scale of datasets. Although the deep network is well trained, it still collapses when the test data has a significant difference from the training data, *e.g.* training on indoor data and test on outdoor data. In this work, we instead choose to adapt the general network to the domain of a specific person, and this personalized network can accurately reconstruct this person. Given a test video V_t of a single person, we first sample video frames V_s from it. Then we aim to optimize the general network Φ_g into the personalized network Φ_p by utilizing the unlabeled frames in V_s. The personalized network Φ_p is then used to produce more accurate 3D reconstruction results on the whole test video V_t.

Discussion. Some techniques such as domain adaptation, network fine-tuning are also designed to adapt the network to the test domain. However, domain adaptation requires training with the training data and test data together, which is infeasible to our problem that supposing the data of the specific person is accessible at inference stage. Fine-tuning a model is hard to be applied in our problem, since it typically requires paired labels of the input images. Conversely, we propose the personalized network optimization (PNO) framework which can adapt the model to the test domain at inference stage, without paired 3D labels.

3.2   Personalized Network Optimization

Utilizing the powerful off-the-shelf 2D pose estimator [4] which has strong robustness against appearance distribution shift, we can provide pseudo-2D annotations of the unlabeled target frames. Then we can optimize the network in a weakly-supervised way. Since only part of the test data is available to the optimization routine, we need to keep the generalization ability of the neural network. Therefore, we take the parameters of the general network as our initialization and fine-tune the network using a small learning rate α. The routine of the single-frame based unsupervised optimization framework can be described as follows. For image I_i in the sampled video $V_s = \{I_i\}_{i=1}^N$, we first use a 2D pose estimator to get the 2D keypoints $\hat{x}_i = f_{2d}(I_i)$. Our target objective function for the optimization can be described as:

$$\Phi_p^* = \arg\min_{\Phi_p} \frac{1}{N} \sum_{i=1}^N \mathcal{L}(\Phi_p(I_i)). \tag{1}$$

The loss function $\mathcal{L}$ for vanilla PNO is design as:

$$\mathcal{L} = \mathcal{L}_{2d} + \gamma_1 \mathcal{L}_{prior}, \tag{2}$$

where

$$\mathcal{L}_{2d} = \sum_{k=1}^K \omega_k \left(\left\| x_i^k - \hat{x}_i^k \right\|_2 \right)$$

In Eq. 2, x_i^k represents the kth keypoint in the projected SMPL joints for image I_i and ω_k is the corresponding confidence given by the 2D pose estimator. The $\mathcal{L}_{prior}$ term is a mixture of Gaussians pose loss learnt from separate 3D data to avoid non-plausible 3D pose with the same usage of [3]. Note that the $\mathcal{L}_{prior}$ is an unpaired 3D pose prior which does not take the image as input. Finally, γ_1 is the coefficients here.

Network Architecture. To keep the 3D prior we design the fusion network architecture as Fig. 2 shows. We take an off-the-shelf network for human pose and shape reconstruction [14] as the basic network. The fusion network is integrated by two duplicated basic networks. The fusion network is designed in the encoder-regressor manner. The general feature $h_g \in \mathbb{R}^{2048}$ is extracted by a ResNet-50

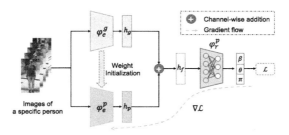

Fig. 2. Fusion Network Architecture. General feature and personal feature are fused at the fusion layer. The general encoder will not be updated in the optimization.

feature encoder φ_e^g and the personal feature $h_p \in \mathbb{R}^{2048}$ is extracted by another feature encoder φ_e^p whose weights are initialized by φ_e^g. Then the features will be sent into the fusion layer which conducts a channel-wise addition with a balance ratio $\tau = 0.5$. The fusion layer outputs the fused feature $h_f \in \mathbb{R}^{2048}$. We apply a regressor φ_r^p to interpret fused feature h_f into SMPL parameters $\{\theta, \beta\}$ and camera parameter π. Personalized regressor φ_r^p is also initialized by general regressor φ_r^g. To avoid prior forgetting problem, we keep the parameters of the general encoder φ_e^g fixed during PNO. In summary, we have two parts of learnable parameters in the fusion network: $\Phi_p = \{\varphi_e^p, \varphi_r^p\}$

3.3 Geometry-Aware Temporal Constraints

Weak-supervision with 2D keypoints has the inherent ill-posed problem in training the 3D pose estimation network. The reason is that weak-supervision cannot constrain the 3D keypoint in the depth direction. Human geometry knowledge such as bone lengths and body somatotype can help to solve this ambiguity. However, exploiting human geometry knowledge is quite hard in a single-frame setting due to the uncertainty of the camera pose. We develop two geometry-aware temporal constraints: the cross-frame shape consistency loss $\mathcal{L}_{beta}$ which serves as the long-term constraint and the temporal skeleton consistency loss $\mathcal{L}_{skel}$ which serves as the short-term constraint. As human body geometry keeps constant cross frames, we can learn the personalized geometry knowledge from temporal information. The supervision of $\mathcal{L}_{beta}$ is penalizing the network to keep a consistent shape across frames in long term as the following formulation:

$$\mathcal{L}_{beta} = \left\| \beta_t - \overline{\beta}_t \right\|_2 , \tag{3}$$

where

$$\overline{\beta}_t = \delta \overline{\beta}_{t-1} + (1 - \delta)\beta_t.$$

β_t is the predicted SMPL shape parameter at step t. The $\overline{\beta}_t$ is the current consistent shape parameter which is updated by a moving average with rate δ.

The supervision of $\mathcal{L}_{skel}$ is to solve the depth-ambiguity problem by the motion continuity of 3D skeleton in a short-term. The formulation could be written as:

$$\mathcal{L}_{skel} = \|X_t - X_{t-1}\|_2 , \tag{4}$$

where X_t is the predicted 3D joints at step t. Our insight is the two losses should be used together. $\mathcal{L}_{beta}$ provides the constraint on bone length from long-term consistency while $\mathcal{L}_{skel}$ provides the constraint on camera translation and rotation from short-term continuity. Ablation in Sect. 4.2 analysis this claim in details.

The overall network optimization loss function $\mathcal{L}$ can be rewritten as:

$$\mathcal{L} = \mathcal{L}_{2D} + \gamma_1 \mathcal{L}_{prior} + \gamma_2 \mathcal{L}_{beta} + \gamma_3 \mathcal{L}_{skel}, \tag{5}$$

where γ_2 and γ_3 are balance coefficients.

4   Experiments

Datasets. We evaluate the PNO on 3DPW and MPI-INF-3DHP respectively. Considering the setting of our paper, we collect the images having the same person ID in the test set as subsets, then we evaluate our method on each subset separately. The reported accuracy is the weighted mean of each subset. Next, we introduce the details of two datasets.

- **3DPW** is an outdoor dataset that is captured by a hand-held camera. We only evaluate on the test set, which has five subjects (denoting from H0-H4).
- **MPI-INF-3DHP** is a dataset that is captured in both outdoor and indoor environments. Compared with 3DPW, MPI-INF-3DHP has less images for optimizing a general model, which increases the optimization difficulty. We evaluate on the test set, which has six subjects (denoting from S1-S6).

We report the statistics of re-organized dataset in Table 1. The general network is specified as a pretrained model from SPIN [14], which is trained on various datasets, including Human3.6M [7], MPI-INF-3DHP [19], LSP [8], LSP-Extended [9], MPII [1] and COCO [16].

Optimization Details. We first split the dataset into person-specific subsets. For each subset, we use the foremost λ percent of video frames as input for PNO and test on the whole subset. For 3DPW, we combine different video clip of one single person into a long video and we select $\lambda = 25\%$. And for MPI-INF-3DHP, since the video frames are much less than 3DPW, we select $\lambda = 40\%$. We use the Adam optimizer with a learning rate of 2×10^{-5}. We set $\gamma_1 = 3.2 \times 10^{-5}$ for $\mathcal{L}_{prior}$, $\gamma_2 = 3.2 \times 10^{-3}$ for $\mathcal{L}_{beta}$, $\gamma_3 = 1 \times 10^{-4}$ for $\mathcal{L}_{skel}$ and moving average rate $\delta = 0.9$.

Table 1. Dataset Statistics for 3DPW and MPI-INF-3DHP. We report the number of frames for each subset.

MPI-INF-3DHP	S1	S2	S3	S4	S5	S6
#Frames	603	540	506	558	276	452
3DPW	H0	H1	H2	H3	H4	–
#Frames	19929	13089	789	768	939	–

Evaluation Metrics. We use mean per joint position error (MPJPE) and Procrustes-aligned MPJPE (PA-MPJPE) to evaluate our method, which was reported in [11]. We also take the Percentage of Correct Keypoints (PCK) with a threshold at 150 mm as one of the evaluation metrics on MPI-INF-3DHP as [12] does. Besides, we analyze the bone stability which indicated by the mean square error (MSE) of the predicted bone lengths across frames along time.

Table 2. Quantitative evaluation on 3DPW and MPI-INF-3DHP datasets. HMR-PNO and SPIN-PNO are the personalized networks optimized from the original HMR and SPIN network.

Models	3DPW		MPI-INF-3DHP		
	PA-MPJPE ↓	MPJPE ↓	3DPCK ↑	PA-MPJPE ↓	MPJPE ↓
Metha *et al.* [19]	–	–	64.7	–	–
Zhou *et al.* [23]	–	–	69.2	–	–
HMR [10]	70.5	122.6	68.7	88.3	135.2
CMR [13]	70.2	–	–	–	–
SPIN [14]	59.2	96.9	72.7	78.2	126.1
HMR-PNO	61.8(8.7↓)	98.0(24.6↓)	71.0(2.3↑)	79.0(9.3↓)	128.6(6.6↓)
SPIN-PNO	**52.7**(6.5↓)	**82.8**(14.1↓)	**76.5**(3.8↑)	**71.3**(6.9↓)	**114.7**(11.4↓)

4.1 Comparing with the State-of-the-Arts Methods

Quantitative Evaluation. Quantitative comparison on 3DPW and MPI-INF-3DHP are reported on Table 2. HMR-PNO and SPIN-PNO are the personalized networks optimized from the original HMR and SPIN network. Although our method exploit human geometry knowledge from temporal consistency in the network optimization stage, the personalized network is not constrained on temporal input and can be used in a single frame manner. Here we compare several previous state-of-the-art single frame based methods. Note that these methods do not use the training set of 3DPW and MPI-INF-3DHP. For fair comparison, we retrain the general network HMR and SPIN without using 3DPW and MPI-INF-3DHP training set. We can see that SPIN-PNO achieves better performance than previous methods by a large margin. Compare the personalized networks with the general networks, we can see that the PNO method greatly improve

Table 3. Ablation Study on 3DPW in terms of losses we used. The network is SPIN-PNO. We can see that joint-use of the two temporal geometry losses can achieve better performance than single-use of each.

Method	MPJPE↓	PA-MPJPE↓
$\mathcal{L}_{2d} + \mathcal{L}_{prior}$	85.5	53.6
$\mathcal{L}_{2d} + \mathcal{L}_{prior} + \mathcal{L}_{beta}$	83.3	52.8
$\mathcal{L}_{2d} + \mathcal{L}_{prior} + \mathcal{L}_{skel}$	84.2	53.1
$\mathcal{L}_{2d} + \mathcal{L}_{prior} + \mathcal{L}_{beta} + \mathcal{L}_{skel}$	**82.8**	**52.7**

Fig. 3. Qualitative comparison between SPIN (*the second row*) and SPIN-PNO (*the third row*). The left four cases are sampled from 3DPW while the right four cases from MPI-INF-3DHP. Here, we observe that SPIN-PNO produces more accurate predictions compared to SPIN in challenging scenarios with occlusion and self-occlusion.

performance. That indicates the PNO method is effective and can be applied on different general networks.

4.2 Ablation Study

Ablation on Losses. In Table 3 we evaluate the effectiveness of the different constraints on 3DPW dataset. Comparing the first row and the second row, the cross-frame shape consistency loss $\mathcal{L}_{beta}$ enables the network to exploit human geometry knowledge better since there is a large margin improvement on PA-MPJPE. Comparing the third and the fourth row, we can found that only with the temporal skeleton consistency loss $\mathcal{L}_{skel}$ can not achieve great improvement. The $\mathcal{L}_{skel}$ serves as a short-term constraint does not gain sufficient long-term information of bone length. Therefore, the joint-use of the two geometry-aware losses has a better ability to mine the geometry of the target human and achieves lower reconstruction error.

Ablation on the Amount of Sampled Data. In Table 4 we report PA-MPJPE of both the fusion network and the basic network with the sample ratio λ on the 3DPW

Table 4. Ablation on the amount of sampled data. We report PA-MPJPE of both fusion architecture and basic architecture with the sample ratio λ on the 3DPW dataset. The network is SPIN-PNO. The more data we use, the better result we can achieve. The fusion architecture has more improvements than the basic architecture when less data is sampled.

λ	5%	15%	25%	35%	45%	55%	75%	100%
Basic	58.5	55.3	53.7	53.4	52.3	52.1	51.3	50.4
Fusion	**56.9**	**54.5**	**52.7**	**53.0**	**52.1**	**51.9**	**51.2**	**50.4**

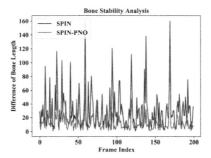

Fig. 4. Bone Stability Analysis between SPIN and SPIN-PNO. We randomly select 200 frames for H0 in 3DPW and calculate the MSE of bone length between current frame and the last frame.

dataset. We only use the sampled data as our unlabeled input video frames to the personalized network optimization module while we test our method on the whole test video. Results show that the more data we can use for the PNO module the lower reconstruction error we can achieve. Since it is not feasible to collect all the data of a target person, we can use part of the data in the target domain and generalize it well. In this paper, 25% for 3DPW is the trade-off setting we use. Results show that using only 25% can achieve competitive performance compared with 100% of them. Comparing the fusion network and the basic network for each data percentage, the fusion network achieves better results than the basic network when using less sampled data. This ability indicates the fusion network has a better ability to keep the prior from the general feature.

Analysis on Geometry Information Mining. To evaluate the effectiveness of the geometry information mining in the PNO, we design the bone stability metric which calculates the mean square error (MSE) of the bone length (in mm) between the current predicted skeleton and the last predicted skeleton in temporal. In Fig. 4, we compare the bone stability of the general network SPIN and the personalized network on randomly selected 200 frames (No. 2250 to No. 2450) of one target person in 3DPW. Result shows that the personalized network can produce much more stable result than the general network across frames while the max amplitude is much lower.

Table 5. Cross-human evaluation on 3DPW. SPIN-PNO(H*) indicates the model is optimized on the subset of H*. The performance of SPIN-PNO on another person is much more worse. This indicates that the SPIN-PNO indeed captures personalized feature and adapt a general model to the specific person.

	H0		H1	
	MPJPE↓	PA-MPJPE↓	MPJPE↓	PA-MPJPE↓
SPIN	94.4	57.3	100.7	62.9
SPIN-PNO (H0)	**77.0**	**49.6**	99.3	60.6
SPIN-PNO (H1)	90.0	58.3	**89.9**	**57.5**

Cross-Human Evaluation. As shown in Table 5, we conduct cross-human evaluation to examine whether the SPIN-PNO has fit on the domain of a specific person. From the Table 5, we can observe that the model optimized on ego-person outperforms its results on another person. For example, the model optimized on the data of H0 performs much better on H0 than that on H1. This result suggests that the SPIN-PNO can capture personalized feature and achieve better reconstruction results for a specific person, comparing with the general model.

4.3 Qualitative Evaluation

Figure 3 shows the qualitative evaluation. Compared to the previous state-of-the-art method SPIN which is trained with general datasets, the personalized network SPIN-PNO can produce more accurate predictions including better human shape estimation, 3D pose estimation, and better camera translation and rotation estimation. Results show that the personalized network has a stronger robustness to occlusions.

5   Conclusion

In this paper, we present the problem of domain shift for training and test in the human pose and shape reconstruction networks. We propose the PNO framework to adapt a general network into the personalized network using a few video frames of the target person. We design two temporal geometry constraints to help the network to mine the geometry knowledge of the target. Experiments show that our method achieves the state-of-the-art results on 3D pose benchmarks.

Acknowledgements. This work is supported by the National Key Research and Development Program of China (No. 2019YFC1521104) and Shanghai Municipal Science and Technology Major Project (No. 2021SHZDZX0102).

References

1. Andriluka, M., Pishchulin, L., Gehler, P., Schiele, B.: 2D human pose estimation: new benchmark and state of the art analysis. In: CVPR (2014)

2. Bau, D., et al.: Semantic photo manipulation with a generative image prior. ACM TOG (2019)
3. Bogo, F., Kanazawa, A., Lassner, C., Gehler, P., Romero, J., Black, M.J.: Keep it SMPL: automatic estimation of 3D human pose and shape from a single image. In: Leibe, B., Matas, J., Sebe, N., Welling, M. (eds.) ECCV 2016. LNCS, vol. 9909, pp. 561–578. Springer, Cham (2016). https://doi.org/10.1007/978-3-319-46454-1_34
4. Cao, Z., Simon, T., Wei, S.E., Sheikh, Y.: Realtime multi-person 2D pose estimation using part affinity fields. In: CVPR (2017)
5. Doersch, C., Zisserman, A.: Sim2real transfer learning for 3D human pose estimation: motion to the rescue. In: NeurIPS (2019)
6. Huang, Y., et al.: Towards accurate marker-less human shape and pose estimation over time. In: 3DV (2017)
7. Ionescu, C., Papava, D., Olaru, V., Sminchisescu, C.: Human3. 6m: large scale datasets and predictive methods for 3D human sensing in natural environments. PAMI **36**(7), 1325–1339 (2013)
8. Johnson, S., Everingham, M.: Clustered pose and nonlinear appearance models for human pose estimation. In: BMVC (2010)
9. Johnson, S., Everingham, M.: Learning effective human pose estimation from inaccurate annotation. In: CVPR (2011)
10. Kanazawa, A., Black, M.J., Jacobs, D.W., Malik, J.: End-to-end recovery of human shape and pose. In: CVPR (2018)
11. Kanazawa, A., Zhang, J.Y., Felsen, P., Malik, J.: Learning 3D human dynamics from video. In: CVPR (2019)
12. Kocabas, M., Athanasiou, N., Black, M.J.: Vibe: video inference for human body pose and shape estimation. In: CVPR (2020)
13. Kolotouros, N., Pavlakos, G., Daniilidis, K.: Convolutional mesh regression for single-image human shape reconstruction (2019)
14. Kolotouros, N., Pavlakos, G., Black, M.J., Daniilidis, K.: Learning to reconstruct 3D human pose and shape via model-fitting in the loop. In: ICCV (2019)
15. Lassner, C., Romero, J., Kiefel, M., Bogo, F., Black, M.J., Gehler, P.V.: Unite the people: closing the loop between 3D and 2D human representations. In: CVPR (2017)
16. Lin, T.-Y., et al.: Microsoft COCO: common objects in context. In: Fleet, D., Pajdla, T., Schiele, B., Tuytelaars, T. (eds.) ECCV 2014. LNCS, vol. 8693, pp. 740–755. Springer, Cham (2014). https://doi.org/10.1007/978-3-319-10602-1_48
17. Loper, M., Mahmood, N., Romero, J., Pons-Moll, G., Black, M.J.: SMPL: a skinned multi-person linear model. ACM TOG **34**(6), 1–16 (2015)
18. von Marcard, T., Henschel, R., Black, M., Rosenhahn, B., Pons-Moll, G.: Recovering accurate 3D human pose in the wild using IMUs and a moving camera. In: ECCV (2018)
19. Mehta, D., et al.: Monocular 3D human pose estimation in the wild using improved CNN supervision. In: 3DV (2017)
20. Park, E., Berg, A.C.: Meta-tracker: fast and robust online adaptation for visual object trackers. In: ECCV (2018)
21. Pavlakos, G., Zhu, L., Zhou, X., Daniilidis, K.: Learning to estimate 3D human pose and shape from a single color image. In: CVPR (2018)
22. Shocher, A., Cohen, N., Irani, M.: "Zero-shot" super-resolution using deep internal learning. In: CVPR (2018)
23. Zhou, X., Huang, Q., Sun, X., Xue, X., Wei, Y.: Towards 3D human pose estimation in the wild: a weakly-supervised approach. In: ICCV (2017)

JointPose: Jointly Optimizing Evolutionary Data Augmentation and Prediction Neural Network for 3D Human Pose Estimation

Zhiwei Yuan and Songlin Du$^{(\boxtimes)}$

Southeast University, Nanjing, China
sdu@seu.edu.cn

Abstract. 3D human pose estimation plays important roles in various human-machine interactive applications, but lacking diversity in existing labeled 3D human posture dataset restricts the generalization ability of deep learning based models. Data augmentation is therefore an important method to solve this problem. However, data augmentation and pose estimation network training are usually treated as two isolated processes, limiting the performance of pose estimation network. In this paper, we developed an improved data augmentation method which jointly performs pose network estimation and data augmentation by designing a reward/penalty strategy for effective joint training, making model training and data augmentation improve each other. In particular, an improved evolutionary data augmentation method is proposed to generate the distribution of nodes in crossover and rotation angles in mutation through the process of the evolution. Extensive experiments show that our approach not only significantly improves state-of-the-art models without additional data efforts but also is extremely competitive with other advanced methods.

Keywords: 3D human pose estimation · Evolutionary data augmentation · Joint neural network

1 Introduction

Human pose estimation (HPE) aims to restore the human body posture and build human body representation (such as, body skeleton and body shape) from input data such as images and videos. And 3D HPE has been applied to a wide range of applications, (e.g., motion recognition and analysis, human-computer interaction, virtual reality(VR), security identification, etc.). However, due to the limited information provided by a single image and the complexity and diversity of 3D human pose estimation, this task is extremely challenging. Thanks to their representation learning power, the deep learning method greatly improves the accuracy of the model [9, 11, 12, 14, 15], and makes deep learning based human pose estimation have a better prospect.

Despite such success, the training of deep learning model requires a large amount of labeled data hence the training data directly determines the upper limit of accuracy of the model. In particular, this is more severe for 3D HPE as during the process of obtaining the human body posture dataset, collecting accurate 3D pose annotation of the human dataset require a lot of manpower and time cost, and the collection of human

© Springer Nature Switzerland AG 2021
I. Farkaš et al. (Eds.): ICANN 2021, LNCS 12893, pp. 368–379, 2021.
https://doi.org/10.1007/978-3-030-86365-4_30

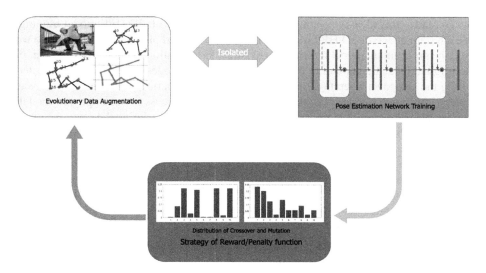

Fig. 1. Data augmentation and network training are usually isolated. We propose to bridge the two by designing a reward/penalty strategy online. In train epoch of 3D HPE model, we use the pre-trained model information (e.g., the value of loss function) to adjust the operation distribution of evolutionary data augmentation.

posture is under the fixed scene. Therefore, the problem of 3D human posture dataset has become a major bottleneck restricting the performance improvement of the depth model.

In order to solve the limitation caused by lack of labeled data, Li *et al.* [7] proposed a method to synthesize massive amount of 3D human skeletons with evolutionary computation. Human postures are first represented as tree-like structures, and new samples are then synthesised by crossover (exchanging two parts of two parental generations) and mutation (randomly rotating local bones). The synthesised evolutionary data is then used to train the pose estimation network, achieving the state-of-the-art performance. However, the data augmentation process and pose estimation network training are carried out separately. This paper investigates whether these two parts can be combined together to jointly train a more effective network.

In this paper, we answer the above question by proposing a new approach that jointly optimizes 3D HPE network and data augmentation by designing a reward/penalty strategy for effective joint training [17]. In original data augmentation, the operation parameters of crossover and mutation are randomly selected, which makes the effect of the algorithm very unsatisfactory. Given the priori knowledge of human pose, there is a natural beauty of symmetry between the joints of different individuals. The random exchange destroys this pattern, so we use the pre-trained information to generate cross-distribution in the evolutionary algorithm to minimize the impact. Similarly, there is a harmonious beauty to the length between the various parts of the human posture, and we use the distribution of variation rather than random parameters to maintain this pattern. Compared with original method, the pose synthesised by our approach is more diverse and efficient.

To realize this idea, we combined data augmentation with 3D HPE model training. In each train epoch of 3D HPE model, there is a pre-trained 3D HPE model, and the we used the pre-training model information to adjust the operation of data augmentation. In the original data augmentation, the human pose's cross nodes were randomly selected during the crossover operation, on the contrary the distribution of the cross nodes was generated through the performance of the pre-training process in our improved model. Similarly, the rotation of bone vectors was selected randomly during the mutation operation, while the distribution of bone vectors in our improved model was also generated using the performance of the pre-training process. Then the data obtained by the improved data augmentation method are trained in the 3D HPE network. In this way, we combine the data augmentation process with the pose estimation network training process. Figure 1 shows our approach jointly performs pose network estimation and data augmentation by designing a reward/penalty strategy. The main contributions of this paper are summarized as follows:

- To the best of our knowledge, we are the first to investigate the joint optimization of evolutionary data augmentation and network training in 3D human pose estimation.

- The pose estimation and data augmentation in network training are combined to jointly improve the performances of both data augmentation and model training.

- Strong performance on the 3D HPE network using the data synthesised by the improved evolutionary data augmentation method, which validate our method substantially.

2   Related Work

3D Human Pose Estimation: Using the identification method to estimate 3D human posture is a direct mapping from image observation to 3D pose. The related and latest depth 3D pose estimation networks mainly adopt two frameworks: the one-stage methods and the two-stage methods. The one-stage methods directly map from the image to 3D pose, while the two-stage methods [3,24] first extract the 2D pose from the image, and then establishes the mapping from 2D pose to 3D pose. In this paper, we take a two-stage approach. In the first stage, in the process of extracting 2D pose from images, the training dataset is not deficient compared with the 3D human pose data set, and the regression accuracy has been relatively ideal, so we directly adopted the model completed by pre-training. The focus of this paper is on the improved data augmentation in the second stage. New 2D-3D data pairs are synthesised by improving the method of evolutionary data augmentation. See Sect. 3 for details.

Human Pose Data Augmentation: There are many methods for data augmentation. For example, in [19,22], new indoor images can be synthesized to augment as to extend additional training dataset. During training with synthetic images, domain adaption was performed in [2]. Adversarial rotation and scaling were used in [17] to augment data for 2D HPE. These works produce augmented images, on the contrary, our approach focus on data augmentation for 2D-to-3D networks and produce the distribution of data augmentation operations for geometric 2D-3D pairs.

Hard Example Mining: The idea is widely used in training SVM models for object detection [21]. It aims to perform an alternative optimization between model training and data selection. Contrary to this idea, the proposed method focuses on mining the distribution P that synthesizes more efficient data in evolutionary data augmentation, rather than hard example for network training, in order to improve the evolutionary data augmentation algorithm. The reasons are as follows: 1) Considering the special structure of the human body, it is unreasonable to randomly select crossover and mutation nodes, so the probability distribution is used to select the operated nodes. 2) As a parameter of the evolutionary data augmentation algorithm, the improved probability distribution directly makes the synthesized data more efficient for network training.

3 Evolutionary Data Augmentation (EDA)

In this section, we use evolutionary algorithm for data augmentation, then combine the pose estimation network training process and data augmentation process and finally generate the distribution of augmentation operations, so as to propose an improved evolutionary data augmentation method.

3.1 3D Human Skeleton Representation

We represent a 3D human skeleton with a set of bones organized hierarchically in a kinematic tree, as shown in Fig. 2. For a given 3D human skeleton, we use a set of vectors $\{b_1, b_2, \cdots b_w\}$ to represent it, and the definition of skeleton vector is

$$b^k = p^{child\_node(k)} - p^{parent\_node(k)}, \tag{1}$$

where b^i is the ith bone in the 3D bone vector, and the direction of the ith bone vector is from the ith child node to the ith parent node. At the same time, for convenience, each skeleton vector is further transformed locally to spherical coordinate system, i.e.

$$b^k_{local} = \{r_k, \theta_k, \phi_k\}, \tag{2}$$

where $\{(\theta_k, \phi_k)\}^\omega_1$ represents the direction of the bone vector, and $\{(r_k)\}^\omega_1$ represents the length of the bone vector. Such a 3D representation of the human skeleton of a tree structure provides convenience for our data-augmentation evolutionary manipulation. In the data evolution operation, the representation of skeleton vector provides the possibility of crossover operation, and the transformation to the local spherical coordinate system makes the mutation operation more convenient.

3.2 Evolutionary Data Augmentation

We use evolutionary data augmentation (EDA) [7] to synthesise a new dataset, as shown in Fig. 2. The original dataset is set as the initial population. A new generation is obtained by go through tectonic evolutionary operators, and then natural selection and the evolution of the generation after generation. Finally, the augmented data can be used for training, in the evolutionary algorithm of 3D human body posture, evolutionary operations are designed as follows.

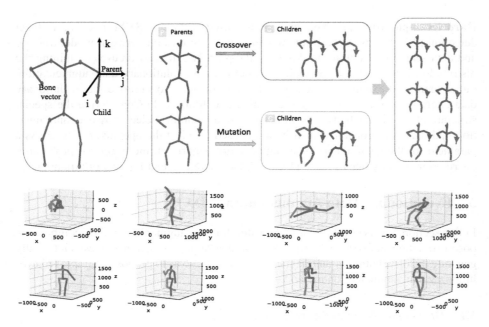

Fig. 2. Top: The human skeleton vector is converted to local spherical coordinates (Left). The process of evolutionary data augmentation. For example, the arms of the two parents are exchanged in crossover; the right and left legs of the two parents are rotated respectively in mutation (Right). **Bottom:** Visualize of initial population (Left) and evolved population (Right) in EDA.

Crossover Operator: Given two parents, we choose a node as a cross node. For example, when the node we choose is the right shoulder, we exchange the bone vector corresponding to the right arm of the two parents. Therefore, the definition the vector selected for crossover operation is

$$\{b^k : parent(k) = q \ and \ F(parent(k), q)\}, \tag{3}$$

where the selection of cross joint k is not random, but based on the result of pre-training, the enhanced distribution is generated. When the performance of a cross node in pre-training is better, the corresponding distribution of this node will be higher.

Mutation Operator: The mutation operation refers to the rotation of bone vectors to increase the diversity of data. In the local spherical coordinate system, $\{(\theta_k, \phi_k)\}$ represents the direction of the bone vector, and the mutation operator is to change the direction of the bone vector, so the definition of the mutation operator is

$$\theta'_k = \theta_k + g, \ \phi'_k = \phi_k + g, \tag{4}$$

where the selection of g is not random, but an enhanced distribution generated according to the information of pre-training model. Similarly, the better the performance of a rotation angle in pre-training model, the higher the distribution of corresponding rotation angle will be.

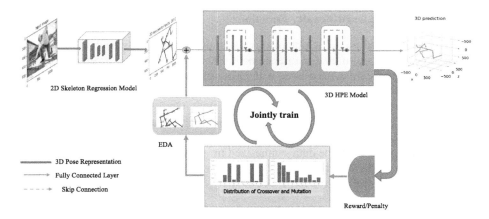

Fig. 3. Overview of our proposed model architecture of jointly optimize improved evolutionary data augmentation and 3D HPE network training. We propose a strategy of reward and penalty functions to jointly train EDA and 3D HPE models.

Natural Selection: We design a simple yet effective way to select the generations. In particular, we use a fitness function to evaluate the rationality of 3D human pose [1]. When 3D human posture is not reasonable, the fitness function $v(p) = -\infty$.

4   Joint Training of EDA and HPE

In this section, we propose a strategy of using reward/penalty function to jointly train EDA and 3D HPE models, as shown in Fig. 3. The proposed traning strategy which jointly optimizing EDA and 3D HPE not only enhances EDA, but also improves the generalization performance of the 3D HPE model.

4.1   Pre-training of HPE Model

In order to enhance the diversity and efficiency of the data synthesised by EDA, a numerical indicator is needed to evaluate these data. Generally, the data synthesised by EDA is a long-tailed distribution, that is, the data that is very effective for the training of the 3D HPE model does not often appear in the synthesized data. If a method can be designed to discover these valid data, then the efficiency of EDA can be improved.

The pre-trained model just meets these requirements. Therefore, using a pre-trained 3D HPE model to back-check the data that is highly efficient for 3D HPE model training. In particular, the proposed method not directly generates the pixels of the 3D human pose picture, but fits the distribution of the nodes of the crossover and mutation operations in the EDA, which greatly reduces the complexity of the algorithm and the consumption of computing resources.

4.2 Strategy of Reward/Penalty Function

When the pre-trained model is obtained, we can optimize the efficiency of the distribution of crossover and mutation operations in EDA. In the training process of the 3D HPE model, after the model is trained with a dataset, if the performance of the 3D HPE model is improved, that is, the loss function of the 3D HPE model on the training dataset is relatively small, then this dataset is highly efficient. On the contrary, if the 3D HPE model is trained with a set of data, its loss function on the training dataset is relatively large, then this dataset is not highly efficient. The strategy we propose is to reward and penalize based on whether the data synthesized by a distributed is efficient. In a certain training process of the 3D HPE model, if the pre-trained 3D HPE model finds that the data synthesized by the distribution P is efficient, then we update P by rewarding

$$P_i' = P_i + \alpha, P_j' = P_j - \frac{\alpha}{n-1}, \forall j \neq i, \tag{5}$$

Similarly, if the pre-trained 3D HPE model finds that the data synthesized by the distribution P is not efficient, then we update P by penalizing

$$P_i' = P_i - \beta, P_j' = P_j + \frac{\beta}{n-1}, \forall j \neq i, \tag{6}$$

where $0 < \alpha, \beta \leq 1$ are hyperparameters that controls the amount of reward and penalty. The greater the value of α and β, the greater the degree of reward and penalty. And n is the number of synthetic data distributions in a set of 3D HPE model training.

Discussion. In reward/penalty strategy, it is important to determine the reference for judging whether synthetic data is efficient. The loss function value of the 3D HPE model on the training dataset is a usable indicator. However, in different training stages, the numerical changes of the loss function are different. For example, the same set of data will cause a rapid decline in the loss function value in early stage of model training, but can only cause a slow decline in later stage of training. Therefore, we use the average of the loss function values of different groups at the same stage as a reference. In addition, when evaluating the efficiency of the distribution, a set of data is used as a unit instead of an individual, which reduces the deviation that may be caused by randomness. Algorithm 1 shows the details of the distribution update process with strategies of reward/penalty function. During the training process, the EDA and 3D HPE model training are alternately carried out, so that the two can improve their own efficiency while also making the other's effect better. Algorithm 2 shows the details of training scheme for joint optimization of EDA and 3D HPE model.

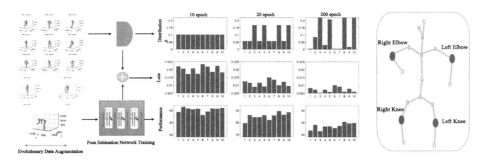

Fig. 4. Network training status visualization: **Left:** distribution of crossover and mutation operation nodes in EDA (**Top**), loss function of 3D HPE model (**Middle**) and performance of 3D HPE model (**Bottom**). **Right:** Location of 4 nodes with high distribution in EDA.

Algorithm 1:
Strategies of reward/penalty
Input: The distribution **P**,
      loss function **Loss**.
Output: The updated distribution **P'**.

---

1 $Loss_{average} = \frac{1}{n} \sum_{i=1}^{n} Loss_i$
2 for i = 1 : n
3   if $Loss_i < Loss_{average}$
4       $P'_i = P_i + \alpha$
5       $P'_j = P_j - \frac{\alpha}{n-1}, \forall j \neq i$
6   if $Loss_i > Loss_{average}$
7       $P'_i = P_i - \beta$
8       $P'_j = P_j + \frac{\beta}{n-1}, \forall j \neq i$
9 Return P'

Algorithm 2:
Scheme for joint optimization
Input: Dataset **X**, Model **HPE**,
      Distribution **P**.
Output: New synthesised dataset **X'**,
      New model **HPE'**,
      New distribution **P'**.

---

1 Train HPE using X;
2 Calculate the Loss of X in HPE;
3 Update P to P' according to algorithm 1;
4 Perform EDA with P' to get X';
5 Train HPE using X'.

---

5 Experiments

In this section, we first show the visualization of network training states to verify the motivation of jointly optimizing EDA and 3D HPE network training. Then we quantitatively evaluate the effectiveness of the method in different scenes and further compare with state-of-the-art approaches.

5.1 Datasets, Evaluation Metrics and Implementation Details

H36M is the largest and most accurate body posture dataset with 3D annotation, which is the body posture of 11 people collected by motion sensor [4,5]. The H36M dataset has 7 subject ID (1, 5, 6, 7, 8, 9, 11), we denote a collection of data by appending subject ID to S, e.g., S1 denotes data from subject 1, S15678 denotes data from subject 1, 5, 6, 7 and 8. Mean Per Joint Position Error (MPJPE) was used as the performance index to evaluate the 3D pose estimation model, as follows

$$MPJPE = \frac{1}{N} \sum_{i=1}^{N} \|J_i - J_i^*\|_2, \tag{7}$$

where N is the number of all joints, J_i and J_i^* are respectively the ground truth position and the estimated position of the ith joint. P1 was directly calculated, P2 was calculated with the ground-truth of 3D pose and the predicted value after rigid transformation. P1* is the second-stage model performance without considering the impact of the first-stage model performance and directly using the 2D key points as input. In our experiment, P1 and P2 refer to average MPJPE over all 15 actions for H36M under protocols P1 and P2. P1* is to use ground truth 2D key points for evaluation under Protocol 1.

We jointly optimize EDA and 3D HPE. The train is performed on RTX 2080 Ti GPU and takes about 336 h. To perform EDA, the parameters α and β gradually decrease from 0.1 to 0.01, and it takes about 40 min to get a new synthetic dataset. To train 3D HPE network, we train the cascade model using Adam optimizer with learning rate 0.001 for 200 epochs. Every 20 epochs we perform a data augmentation operation update based on the penalty and reward function strategy. During the test, our model runs at an average of 31.4 fps.

5.2   Comparison with State-of-the-Art Methods

In this set of experiments, we sequentially simulate the situation of data scarcity and data-rich. S1 and S15678 is used as the initial data respectively. The improved EDA method is then used to synthesis new more datasets for jointly optimization in the training model. In 3D HPE network, we directly adopt the network trained on COCO [10] in the first stage, while in the second stage, we use a deep network consisting of three residual modules and a full connection layer. Compared with others, our approach is also applicable to the case with more data, as shown in Table 1 and Table 2.

5.3   Visualization of the Training Status

In this experiment, we are interested in how the strategies of reward/penalty function deal with the influence of loss function. Taking the experiment of the 3D HPE model on S1 of H36M dataset as an example, Fig. 4 visualizes the distribution in the EDA, the loss function value and the performance of the 3D HPE model in different training stages. In EDA, the distribution of 4 nodes (left elbow, right elbow, left knee and right knee) has been significantly increased, as shown in Fig. 4(Right). Our proposed approach believes that crossover and mutation operations on these nodes can synthesize efficient data. Figure 5 shows some examples of our method applied to 3D HPE.

Table 1. The model performance compared with SOTA methods. Best performance of model is marked with bold font.

Supervision	Method Authors	Performance		
		P1	P1*	P2
Weakly	Use Multi-view			
	Rhodin et al. (CVPR18) [18]	–	–	64.6
	Kocabas et al. (CVPR19) [6]	65.3	–	57.2
	Use Temporal information			
	Pavllo et al. (CVPR19) [16]	64.7	–	–
	Single-Image Method			
	Li et al. (ICCV19) [8]	88.8	–	66.5
	Li et al. (CVPR20) [7]	62.9	50.5	47.5
	Ours	**61.4**	**48.5**	**47.3**
Fully	Martinez et al. (ICCV17) [12]	62.9	45.5	47.7
	Yang et al. (CVPR18) [23]]	58.6	–	37.7
	Zhao et al. (CVPR19) [24]	57.6	43.8	–
	Sharma et al. (ICCV19) [20]	58.0	–	40.9
	Moon et al. (ICCV19) [13]	54.4	35.2	–
	Li et al. (CVPR20) [7]	50.9	34.5	38.0
	Ours	**50.4**	**32.1**	**37.7**

Table 2. Performance on S1 of H36M dataset compared with SOTA method over all 15 actions under weakly supervision.

Method Authors	Performance							
	Direct	Discuss	Eat	Greet	Phone	Photo	Pose	Purchase
Rhodin et al. (CVPR18) [19]	78.90	92.80	82.09	86.34	94.10	113.21	83.75	110.55
Li et al. (ICCV19) [11]	70.44	83.61	76.59	77.91	85.43	106.14	72.26	102.93
Ours	**53.86**	**57.78**	**57.17**	**58.21**	**63.55**	**73.51**	**54.73**	**60.26**
	Sit	SitDown	Smoke	Wait	WalkDog	Walk	WalkPair	**Average**
Rhodin et al. (CVPR18) [18]	125.45	185.76	90.57	82.24	99.83	67.04	79.86	97.72
Li et al. (ICCV19) [20]	115.79	164.99	82.43	74.34	94.61	60.15	70.65	88.77
Ours	**65.18**	**81.48**	**59.13**	**57.05**	**68.10**	**52.03**	**59.11**	**61.41**

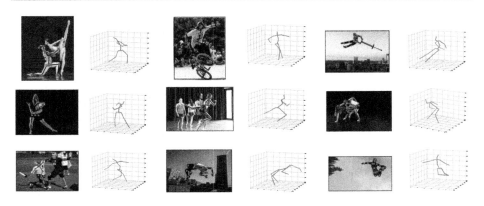

Fig. 5. Some 3D human pose estimation examples of our model. In each example, from left to right are the input image with 2D node coordinates and 3D human pose predicted by the model.

6   Conclusion

In this paper, a joint training strategy with reward and penalty function is proposed to optimize EDA and 3D HPE network during training. Sufficient results on publicly available datasets show that the proposed approach achieves higher performance compared with state-of-the-art methods. In the future research, the proposed method can be extended to other aspects of human pose estimation, such as time-series pictures, multi-person scenes, and multi-view pose estimation. Meanwhile, the data augmentation process and the pose estimation network training process can be further integrated to improve the performance of the pose estimation network.

Acknowledgements. This work was jointly supported by the National Natural Science Foundation of China under grant 62001110, the Natural Science Foundation of Jiangsu Province under grant BK20200353, the Guangdong Basic and Applied Basic Research Foundation under grant 2020A1515110145, the Shenzhen Science and Technology Program under grant RCBS20200714114858072, and the Fundamental Research Funds for the Central Universities under grant 2242021R10115.

References

1. Akhter, I., Black, M.J.: Pose-conditioned joint angle limits for 3D human pose reconstruction. In: Proceedings of the IEEE Conference on Computer Vision and Pattern Recognition, pp. 1446–1455 (2015)
2. Chen, W., et al.: Synthesizing training images for boosting human 3D pose estimation. In: 2016 Fourth International Conference on 3D Vision (3DV), pp. 479–488. IEEE (2016)
3. Cheng, Y., Yang, B., Wang, B., Yan, W., Tan, R.T.: Occlusion-aware networks for 3D human pose estimation in video. In: Proceedings of the IEEE/CVF International Conference on Computer Vision, pp. 723–732 (2019)
4. Ionescu, C., Li, F., Sminchisescu, C.: Latent structured models for human pose estimation. In: 2011 International Conference on Computer Vision, pp. 2220–2227. IEEE (2011)
5. Ionescu, C., Papava, D., Olaru, V., Sminchisescu, C.: Human3. 6m: Large scale datasets and predictive methods for 3D human sensing in natural environments. IEEE Trans. Pattern Anal. Mach. Intell. **36**(7), 1325–1339 (2013)
6. Kocabas, M., Karagoz, S., Akbas, E.: Self-supervised learning of 3d human pose using multiview geometry. In: Proceedings of the IEEE/CVF Conference on Computer Vision and Pattern Recognition, pp. 1077–1086 (2019)
7. Li, S., Ke, L., Pratama, K., Tai, Y.W., Tang, C.K., Cheng, K.T.: Cascaded deep monocular 3D human pose estimation with evolutionary training data. In: Proceedings of the IEEE/CVF Conference on Computer Vision and Pattern Recognition, pp. 6173–6183 (2020)
8. Li, Z., Wang, X., Wang, F., Jiang, P.: On boosting single-frame 3D human pose estimation via monocular videos. In: Proceedings of the IEEE/CVF International Conference on Computer Vision, pp. 2192–2201 (2019)
9. Lin, M., Lin, L., Liang, X., Wang, K., Cheng, H.: Recurrent 3d pose sequence machines. In: Proceedings of the IEEE Conference on Computer Vision and Pattern Recognition, pp. 810–819 (2017)
10. Lin, T.Y., et al.: Microsoft COCO: common objects in context. In: Fleet, D., Pajdla, T., Schiele, B., Tuytelaars, T. (eds.) ECCV 2014. LNCS, vol. 8693, pp. 740–755. Springer, Cham (2014). https://doi.org/10.1007/978-3-319-10602-1_48

11. Luvizon, D.C., Picard, D., Tabia, H.: 2D/3D pose estimation and action recognition using multitask deep learning. In: Proceedings of the IEEE Conference on Computer Vision and Pattern Recognition, pp. 5137–5146 (2018)
12. Martinez, J., Hossain, R., Romero, J., Little, J.J.: A simple yet effective baseline for 3D human pose estimation. In: Proceedings of the IEEE International Conference on Computer Vision, pp. 2640–2649 (2017)
13. Moon, G., Chang, J.Y., Lee, K.M.: Camera distance-aware top-down approach for 3D multi-person pose estimation from a single RGB image. In: Proceedings of the IEEE/CVF International Conference on Computer Vision, pp. 10133–10142 (2019)
14. Nie, B.X., Wei, P., Zhu, S.C.: Monocular 3D human pose estimation by predicting depth on joints. In: 2017 IEEE International Conference on Computer Vision (ICCV), pp. 3467–3475. IEEE (2017)
15. Pavlakos, G., Zhou, X., Derpanis, K.G., Daniilidis, K.: Coarse-to-fine volumetric prediction for single-image 3D human pose. In: Proceedings of the IEEE Conference on Computer Vision and Pattern Recognition, pp. 7025–7034 (2017)
16. Pavllo, D., Feichtenhofer, C., Grangier, D., Auli, M.: 3D human pose estimation in video with temporal convolutions and semi-supervised training. In: Proceedings of the IEEE/CVF Conference on Computer Vision and Pattern Recognition, pp. 7753–7762 (2019)
17. Peng, X., Tang, Z., Yang, F., Feris, R.S., Metaxas, D.: Jointly optimize data augmentation and network training: adversarial data augmentation in human pose estimation. In: Proceedings of the IEEE Conference on Computer Vision and Pattern Recognition, pp. 2226–2234 (2018)
18. Rhodin, H., et al.: Learning monocular 3D human pose estimation from multi-view images. In: Proceedings of the IEEE Conference on Computer Vision and Pattern Recognition, pp. 8437–8446 (2018)
19. Rogez, G., Schmid, C.: Mocap-guided data augmentation for 3D pose estimation in the wild. In: Advances in Neural Information Processing Systems, pp. 3108–3116 (2016)
20. Sharma, S., Varigonda, P.T., Bindal, P., Sharma, A., Jain, A.: Monocular 3D human pose estimation by generation and ordinal ranking. In: Proceedings of the IEEE/CVF International Conference on Computer Vision, pp. 2325–2334 (2019)
21. Uijlings, J.R., Van De Sande, K.E., Gevers, T., Smeulders, A.W.: Selective search for object recognition. Int. J. Comput. Vis. **104**(2), 154–171 (2013)
22. Varol, G., et al.: Learning from synthetic humans. In: Proceedings of the IEEE Conference on Computer Vision and Pattern Recognition, pp. 109–117 (2017)
23. Yang, W., Ouyang, W., Wang, X., Ren, J., Li, H., Wang, X.: 3D human pose estimation in the wild by adversarial learning. In: Proceedings of the IEEE Conference on Computer Vision and Pattern Recognition, pp. 5255–5264 (2018)
24. Zhao, L., Peng, X., Tian, Y., Kapadia, M., Metaxas, D.N.: Semantic graph convolutional networks for 3D human pose regression. In: Proceedings of the IEEE/CVF Conference on Computer Vision and Pattern Recognition, pp. 3425–3435 (2019)

DeepRehab: Real Time Pose Estimation on the Edge for Knee Injury Rehabilitation

Bruno Carlos Dos Santos Melício[✉], Gábor Baranyi, Zsófia Gaál, Sohil Zidan, and András Lőrincz

Eötvös Loránd University, Budapest, Hungary
{a1w636,bagtabi,mpeeho,lorincz}@inf.elte.hu

Abstract. Human pose estimation is a crucial step towards understanding and characterizing people's behavior in images and videos. Current state of the art results on human pose estimation were achieved by large Deep Learning models that are restricted to cloud computing for real time applications. However, with the development of edge computing, Deep Learning is moving more from the cloud to the edge. In this work we present DeepRehab, a Deep Learning based 2D pose estimator optimized for Edge TPU processing. We first improve an existing Edge TPU compatible model named PoseNet by refining its predictions with filtering methods. Subsequently, as the performance of the filters is limited by the model's inaccuracies, specifically on the lower body parts, we developed DeepRehab, trained on 23 keypoints from the COCO-WholeBody dataset. We achieve 0.65 AP with DeepRehab and quantize it, such that, losing only 3% of AP it runs at a speed of 15 FPS on the Coral USB Accelerator that suits real time evaluations.

Keywords: Deep Learning · Human pose estimation · Edge TPU · Rehabilitation · Real-time evaluation

1 Introduction

Human pose estimation is the task of localizing human joints in images and videos. It has enjoyed substantial attention in the Computer Vision community due to its application in areas such as health care, entertainment and Human Computer Interaction. Despite a protracted history of analysis, human pose estimation remains a difficult task due to the variety of poses, occlusions of joints and different lighting conditions present in images and videos.

Researchers have been focusing on enriching the representational power of models, that have been greatly reshaped by Convolutional Neural Networks (CNNs). With the introduction of DeepPose [1], research on human pose estimation began to shift from classical approaches to Deep Learning. Most recent pose estimation systems [2–6] have universally adopted CNNs as their main building block, yielding drastic improvements on standard benchmarks [8,9].

© Springer Nature Switzerland AG 2021
I. Farkaš et al. (Eds.): ICANN 2021, LNCS 12893, pp. 380–391, 2021.
https://doi.org/10.1007/978-3-030-86365-4_31

Although revolutionary, Deep Learning methods are usually trained on massive datasets resulting on large models with lots of parameters that restricts them to cloud computing for real time applications, which raises data privacy issues. With the emergence of Edge TPU devices, which contain co-processors optimized for running Neural Networks computations locally rather than sending data to the cloud, Deep Learning is moving more from the cloud to the edge. Quantization, is a common technique that makes it possible to fit these models in such limited resources devices. It reduces the model size and improves latency by converting the range of all floating-point tensors in the model to a smaller bit representation (8-bits). Google Coral developed PoseNet[1], a quantized version of PersonLab [10] for human pose estimation that runs on Edge TPU devices.

In this work, we focus on the estimation of human poses to be applied in rehabilitation centers for the analysis of exercises performed by people with knee injuries, hence high precision estimation and real time performance is needed. We address the limitations of PoseNet by: 1) refining PoseNet's outputs using filtering methods as a post-processing step, that remove the outliers generated by inaccurate predictions; 2) developing DeepRehab, a 2D pose estimator optimized to run locally and in real time on Edge TPU devices, which uses ResNet101 as backbone for feature extraction instead of PoseNet's MobileNet and ResNet50 backbones, making it more accurate, specifically at lower body parts. In addition, our model is a bottom up approach which eliminates the dependence of a person detector and uses an association algorithm from [10] that uses mid-range offsets to provide more information about the relationship between keypoints.

The paper continues with a section on Related Works (Sect. 2), Methods (Sect. 3), Experiments (Sect. 4), and Results (Sect. 5). The paper concludes with a brief Discussion and Summary (Sect. 6)

2   Related Works

There have been great advancements in human pose estimation research, with High-Resolution Network (HRNet) [4] outperforming all previous 2D methods in the COCO dataset. Nonetheless, HRNet is a rather big model and is not optimized for Edge TPU processing. Google Coral made available PoseNet quantized models with MobileNet and ResNet50 as backbones, compatible with Edge TPU.

The work proposed by Pardos et al. [12] uses PoseNet for edge processing. They developed an edge-native platform for exercises using the Coral USB Accelerator that estimates in real-time the body pose of patients in a rehabilitation center. However, they use the MobileNet based model which has noisy estimations, specifically at lower body keypoints, as it sacrifices accuracy for speed.

Filtering is a common method used in the literature as a post processing step to remove outliers such as mispredicted keypoints. Kim et al. [13] present an approach for estimating pose to find key video frames in a full golf swing to assist in providing feedback for improvements. For the computations, they utilize PoseNet with MobileNet as backbone on the Google Coral Dev Board.

---

[1] Coral PoseNet - an open source repository containing PoseNet models optimized for Edge TPU (https://github.com/google-coral/project-posenet).

The pose estimation limitations and inaccuracies are identified and compensated for by using a Savitzky-Golay filter, which is able to remove outliers from the data. Nonetheless, the filtering methods are limited by the model's performance. When PoseNet mispredicts keypoints in a short period of time (on consecutive frames), the filters are negatively influenced as the amount of outliers increase.

A different approach is taken by Mao et al. [7], where they formulate the pose estimation task into a regression-based sequence prediction problem that can be solved by transformers. Taking as inputs the feature maps of CNNs, the transformer sequentially predicts keypoint coordinates. With the attention mechanism, their framework is able to adaptively attend to the features most relevant to the target keypoints and can inherently take advantages of the structured relationship between keypoints. However, their approach is not optimized for Edge TPU. Having an architecture which uses both CNNs for visual information and transformers for temporal information would result in a big model that may not fit the constraints of real time computations on the edge.

In our work, we present DeepRehab, an Edge TPU compatible model able to predict 23 keypoints (17 for body and 6 for feet). By using a ResNet101 as backbone, adding additional mid-range offset vectors and reducing the image resolution, we achieve a good trade-off between speed and accuracy on the edge.

3   Methods

In order to remove outliers generated by the inaccuracies of PoseNet we apply noise filtering, which reduces the errors to some extent. To address the model limitations that filtering can't handle, we developed DeepRehab.

3.1   Refined PoseNet Outputs with Filtering Methods

Given a video, each frame is input to PoseNet that generates 17 keypoints. We define a window size parameter ω such that each frame input to PoseNet is stacked until we have n frames, with $n \geq \omega$. The filtering methods are then applied to the $n \times 17$ keypoints to refine them over time, removing outliers. The process is illustrated in Fig. 1. Three filtering methods were studied:

1. **Median Filter** [14], given a set of keypoints in an ordered array of pixels x, it replaces a coordinate by the median of all elements in a neighborhood given by a window-size ω, centered around location m.

$$y[m] = \text{median}\{x[i], i \in \omega\} \qquad (1)$$

2. **Savitzky-Golay** [15,16], performs a least squares fit of a small set of consecutive keypoints to a polynomial and takes the calculated central point of the fitted polynomial curve as the new smoothed keypoint $(y_k)_s$. In the following equation, A is the predicted set of integers and ω is the window-size.

$$(y_k)_s = \frac{\sum\limits_{i=-M}^{M} A_i y_{k+i}}{\sum\limits_{i=-M}^{M} A_i}, \quad M = \frac{\omega - 1}{2} \qquad (2)$$

3. **Chebyshev** [17] low pass filter was used, which has the gain (amplitude) response given by

$$G_n(f) = \frac{1}{\sqrt{1 + \epsilon^2 T_n^2(\frac{f}{f_0})}} \tag{3}$$

where ϵ is the ripple factor, f_0 is the cutoff frequency and T^n is a Chebyshev polynomial of the nth order. The passband exhibits equiripple behavior, with the ripple determined by the ripple factor ϵ.

In the experiments section, we indicate all filtering configurations used.

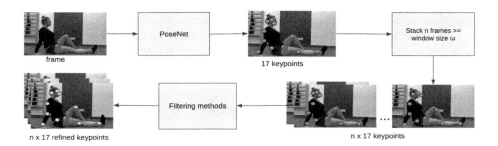

Fig. 1. Refined PoseNet outputs with filtering methods

3.2 DeepRehab for Pose Estimation on the Edge

DeepRehab is a bottom up model that estimates a set of keypoints which are grouped into person instances using a person decoder algorithm. We use a Fully Convolutional architecture with ResNet101 as a backbone for feature extraction. Similar to PoseNet, DeepRehab estimates keypoints by predicting heatmaps and short-range offsets, but also additional mid-range offsets that describe the relationship between keypoints. We trained our model on images of size $224 \times 224 \times 3$ and on 23 keypoints, the same 17 as PoseNet plus 6 additional feet keypoints from the new COCO-Whole Body dataset [11]. Figure 2 shows the differences between PoseNet and our proposed DeepRehab, which is described as follows:

- an image is input to the ResNet101 backbone that extracts features forwarded to 3 convolutional layers (heatmaps, short and mid-range offsets).
- $1 \times 1 \times K$ convolutional filters which output heatmaps of size $H \times W \times K$, where K is the number of keypoints and $H \times W$ is the image resolution.
- $1 \times 1 \times 2 \times K$ convolutional filters that output short-range offsets (displacement vectors) of size $H \times W \times 2 \times K$, in the (X,Y) direction, hence $2 \times K$.
- $1 \times 1 \times 4 \times (K-1)$ convolutional filters that output mid-range offsets of size $H \times W \times 4 \times (K-1)$. These are similar to the previous, however they are represented in pairs of different keypoints, thus $2 \times 2 \times (K-1)$ (for example, mid-range offset from right knee (x,y) to right ankle (x,y)).

- From the outputs of DeepRehab, we form the person poses following Papandreau et al. [10] approach. We aggregate the heatmaps $p_k(x)$ and short-range offsets $S_k(x)$ via Hough voting generating 2D Hough score maps $h_k(x), k = 1, ..., K$, using independent Hough accumulators for every keypoint type. Each image position contributes to each keypoint channel k with weight adequate to its activation probability,

$$h_k(x) = \frac{1}{\pi R^2} \sum_{n=1}^{N} p_k(x_i)B(x_i + S_k(x_i) - x) \qquad (4)$$

where B is the bilinear interpolation kernel, x_i the 2D position within the image, where $i = 1, ...N$ is indexing the position in the image and N is the number of pixels and R is the radius of the keypoint.
- Then, we combine the Hough score maps and mid-range offsets to get person instances. First, a priority queue is created, shared across all K keypoint, in which we insert the position x_i and keypoint k of all local maxima in the Hough score maps $h_k(x)$ which have score above a threshold. We then pop elements out of the queue in descending score order. Next, we follow the mid-range offsets along the edges of the kinematic person graph to greedily connect pairs (k, l) of adjacent keypoints, setting $y_{j,l} = y_j, k + M_k, l(y_j, k)$, in which $y_{j,k}$ is the 2D position of the kth keypoint of the jth person instance, with $j = 1, ..., M$, where M is the number of person instances [10].

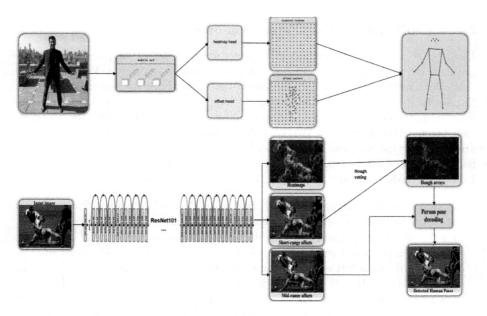

Fig. 2. PoseNet (top) versus our DeepRehab model (bottom). Modified from [10]

4   Experiments

To evaluate the effect of filtering on PoseNet's outputs, data in the temporal domain is needed, hence we used videos and 2D annotations from the test set of MPI-INF-3DHP dataset [9]. It provides 28 keypoints, so we had to map our keypoints with theirs, resulting on a comparison of only 12 keypoints: (left and right for all) shoulders, elbows, wrists, hips, knees and ankles.

For DeepRehab we train and evaluate on the new COCO-Whole Body dataset [11]. It uses the same image base as COCO but it has additional keypoints. We use 17 for the body and 6 for the feet (See Fig. 3). In addition, in a partnership with Emineo clinic, we collected 60 videos that capture specific rehabilitation exercises for the knee, which can't be found in publicly available datasets. We named the dataset as Rehabset and in Sect. 5 we show some results on it.

All the experiments were made using a Coral USB accelerator and a laptop with a CPU of Intel Core i5 10300H and an NVIDIA GeForce GTX 1650 Ti GPU.

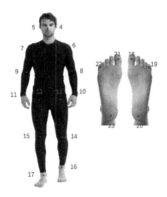

Fig. 3. Keypoints used from COCO-WholeBody dataset [11]

4.1   Filtering Configurations

- **Median** filter has one parameter, the window-size. We tried odd values between 5 and 23 to see its impact on the filtered results. The value of 15 was selected.
- **Savitzky-Golay** filter's window-size was tested similarly to Median filter, with the value 15 yielding the best results. Polynomial degree was set to 3.
- **Chebyshev** Low-Pass filter was tested with all combinations of the following parameters: - order $\in [2, 3, 4, 5, 7, 9, 11]$; - ripple $\in [2, 3, 4]$; - cutoff $\in [0.1, 0.2, 0.3, 0.4, 0.5, 0.6, 1]$. The parameters that presented the best results are: order of 3; ripple of 1; cutoff frequency of 0.2.

Filters are applied on X and Y coordinates separately. For the evaluation of PoseNet + filtering, we use the Root Mean Squared Error (RMSE):

$$RMSE = \sqrt{(X_{GT} - X_{Pred})^2 + (Y_{GT} - Y_{Pred})^2} \tag{5}$$

where X_{GT} and Y_{GT} are the ground truth values and X_{pred} and Y_{pred} are the predictions from PoseNet, unfiltered in case of the original error and filtered when applied filtering.

4.2 PoseNet and DeepRehab Configurations

Google Coral made PoseNet publicly available with MobileNet and ResNet50 based models trained on different image resolutions. In our case, we experimented with different backbones all sharing the same hyperparameters and using image resolution of $224 \times 224 \times 3$. We chose lower image resolution as it reduces the number of computations which contribute for faster inference on the edge. It also has less information, but because we are using high feature extractors as ResNet101, we are able to achieve better precision. The properties of each model can be seen in Table 1. The following are the hyperparameters used for the training of our models: - number of epochs: 50; - steps per epoch: 5000; - Adam optimizer; - learning rate: 0.001; - batch size: 16; - keypoint radius: 16; - keypoint score threshold: 0.4;

Early stopping and learning rate decay were used. The loss function L is a weighted sum of the individual losses of the heatmap, short-range and mid-range offsets:

$$L = \alpha * \text{heatmap\_loss} + \beta * \text{short\_offset\_loss} + \epsilon * \text{mid\_offset\_loss}, \tag{6}$$

where $\alpha = 0.75, \beta = 0.2, \epsilon = 0.1$, heatmap loss is the binary cross entropy and the offset losses are the absolute difference.

DeepRehab was evaluated on COCO-Whole Body validation set using the Average Precision (AP) of all keypoints as the metric. We evaluate the speed performance using Frames Per Second (FPS) and Inference Time in milliseconds.

Table 1. Edge TPU models from Google Coral (PoseNet) and ours (DeepRehab)

Model	Backbone	Resolution (px)	# of parameters	Size
PoseNet	MobilenetV1	$481 \times 353 \times 3$	4.5 M	1.47 MB
PoseNet	MobilenetV1	$641 \times 353 \times 3$	4.5 M	1.6 MB
PoseNet	MobilenetV1	$1281 \times 721 \times 3$	4.5 M	2.35 MB
PoseNet	ResNet50	$416 \times 288 \times 3$	23.7 M	23.2 MB
PoseNet	ResNet50	$768 \times 496 \times 3$	23.7 M	25.6 MB
PoseNet	ResNet50	$960 \times 736 \times 3$	23.7 M	36.7 MB
DeepRehab	MobileNetV2	$224 \times 224 \times 3$	2.5 M	3 MB
DeepRehab	ResNet50	$224 \times 224 \times 3$	24.5 M	24.2 MB
DeepRehab	ResNet101	$224 \times 224 \times 3$	45.2 M	36.7 MB

5 Results

5.1 Refined PoseNet Outputs with Filtering Methods

In our experiments, the Savitzky-Golay filter achieves the best results on average of all keypoints, reducing 5.2% of the PoseNet errors. But, as we focus on the lower body, we choose the Median filter as a baseline, as it reduces PoseNet's error on the knee and ankle joints by 5.4% and 5%, respectively (See Table 2).

In Fig. 4(a) we show the Ground Truth (green), PoseNet estimation (red) and PoseNet estimation + Median (blue) of the ankle keypoints for the video TS1 of MPI-INF-3DHP test set. PoseNet predictions can be noisy, i.e. between frames 10–30, but the Median filter is able to remove such outliers. However, filtering is limited by the performance of PoseNet's predictions. In 4(b) we can observe that when PoseNet inaccurately predicts the ankle keypoint in consecutive frames, i.e. between frames 300 and 340, the filter is negatively influenced as there are too many temporally correlated outliers in a short time interval.

Table 2. RMSE on MPI-INF-3DHP test set. For each joint, we average the error of the left and right keypoints. We apply different filters to reduce PoseNet's errors: Med - Median, SavGol - Savitzky Golay, Cheby - Chebyshev

Joint	PoseNet	Med	Cheby	SavGol	Med+ SavGol	Med+ Cheby	Med+ SavGol+ Cheby
Shoulders	4.6	4.6	4.4	**4.4**	4.5	4.6	4.6
Elbows	8.4	8.1	8.1	**8.1**	8.1	8.2	8.2
Wrists	10.7	10.3	10.2	**10.1**	10.2	10.4	10.4
Hips	6.6	6.3	6.3	6.3	**6.2**	6.3	6.3
Knees	7.4	**7.0**	7.2	7.2	7.0	7.1	7.1
Ankles	8.0	**7.6**	7.8	7.7	7.7	7.7	7.7
All (Average)	7.61	7.32	7.33	**7.30**	7.28	7.38	7.38

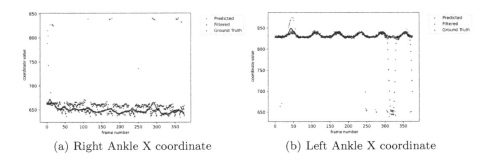

(a) Right Ankle X coordinate   (b) Left Ankle X coordinate

Fig. 4. Plot of PoseNet estimations and Median filtering on the ankle joints.

5.2   DeepRehab for Pose Estimation on the Edge

DeepRehab was trained for 50 epochs and achieved a loss of 0.109 on the training set and 0.172 on validation set. The weights for the base network were initialized with ImageNet weights, which provided a good start for the training and helped to reach convergence faster.

Figure 5(a) shows the results of the 23 predicted keypoints, Fig. 5(b) shows the right knee heatmap, where the highlighted region is an overlay of all the possible right knee keypoints over the image, Fig. 5(c) depicts the right knee short-range offset vectors, and Fig. 5(d) shows the mid-range offset vectors from the right knee to the right ankle.

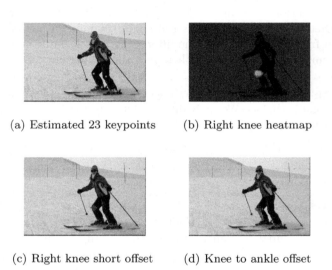

(a) Estimated 23 keypoints   (b) Right knee heatmap

(c) Right knee short offset   (d) Knee to ankle offset

Fig. 5. Visualization of DeepRehab outputs

With DeepRehab we find a good trade-off between speed and accuracy using the ResNet101 based model as a baseline. It achieves a Body Average Precision (Body AP) of 0.65 and a Foot Average Precision (Foot AP) of 0.61, while achieving a 7.5 FPS rate. We quantized the model using post-quantization technique such that the model is optimized to run in real time, reaching 15 FPS and losing only 3% of the Average Precision. In Table 3 we can see a comparison between the Edge TPU compatible models, DeepRehab (ours) and PoseNet (Google Coral). Our quantized model with ResNet101 surpasses the accuracy of all other models, while performing at a desirable speed for real time applications.

DeepRehab is able to predict keypoints in more complex positions as seen in Fig. 6. In Table 4 we show that our DeepRehab model is faster than the state of the art 2D pose estimators, while presenting competitive precision.

Table 3. Results on COCO-Whole Body validation set (Edge TPU). Average Precision (AP) - higher is better; FPS (Frames Per Second) - higher is better; Inference Time in miliseconds - lower is better.

Model	Backbone	Resolution	AP	FPS	Inference Time
PoseNet	MobilenetV1	$481 \times 353 \times 3$	0.49	**68.0**	**9.6 ms**
PoseNet	MobilenetV1	$641 \times 353 \times 3$	0.51	41.5	17.5 ms
PoseNet	MobilenetV1	$1281 \times 721 \times 3$	0.56	15.5	54.9 ms
PoseNet	ResNet50	$416 \times 288 \times 3$	0.54	14.3	61.2 ms
PoseNet	ResNet50	$768 \times 496 \times 3$	0.58	7.4	129 ms
PoseNet	ResNet50	$960 \times 736 \times 3$	0.61	1.3	762.5 ms
DeepRehab	MobileNetV2	$224 \times 224 \times 3$	0.51	45.3	15.8 ms
DeepRehab	ResNet50	$224 \times 224 \times 3$	0.54	20.5	37.8 ms
DeepRehab	ResNet101	$224 \times 224 \times 3$	**0.62**	15.2	61.4 ms

(a) PoseNet predictions: none from 17 keypoints were found

(b) DeepRehab 23 keypoints estimation

Fig. 6. PoseNet versus DeepRehab keypoint predictions on data from Rehabset.

Table 4. Results on COCO-Whole Body validation set. N/A - not applicable. N/A* - not available

Model	Resolution	Body AP	Foot AP	FPS (GPU)	FPS (Edge TPU)
HrNet-w32 [4]	256×192	0.70	0.567	**11.6**	N/A
HrNet-w32 [4]	384×288	0.70	0.587	11.5	N/A
HrNet-w48 [4]	256×192	0.70	0.672	7.6	N/A
HrNet-w48 [4]	384×288	**0.72**	**0.694**	7.6	N/A
OpenPose [5]	368×368	0.62	N/A*	8.8	N/A
DeepRehab	224×224	0.65	0.61	7.5	N/A
DeepRehab-Edge	224×224	0.62	0.60	N/A	**15.2**

6   Discussion and Summary

Human Pose estimation is a challenging task that has been driven by Convolutional Neural Networks (CNNs). The emergence of Edge TPU devices such as the Coral USB accelerator sparked a new wave of Deep Learning models that are optimized to run in real time on edge devices, which is the focus of this study. We provide two key contributions:

1. We show that using simple filtering techniques as post-processing step can reduce up to 5% of keypoints errors produced by the inaccuracies of PoseNet's pose estimations. In our results, Savitzky-Golay filter achieves a better performance overall, but the Median filter is the best option for the lower body parts.
2. We developed DeepRehab, an Edge TPU compatible model with a ResNet101 based network trained on 23 keypoints, including 6 additional feet keypoints that reduces critical errors of PoseNet and increases accuracy. Our quantized model is the fastest 2D pose estimator in comparison to the SOTA, running at 15 FPS.

The main advantages of our model over PoseNet are as follows: DeepRehab uses a ResNet101 backbone which has higher feature extractor capabilities at the cost of being bigger and having more parameters. Because of that, we reduce the image resolution of the model to $224 \times 224 \times 3$ as a tradeoff between speed and accuracy. Our model uses (i) a more complex but fast pose decoder algorithm backed by additional vectors, the mid-range offsets, which allow for associations of joints that are further apart from each other and (ii) it predicts 23 keypoints, which include 6 additional feet keypoints. Points (i) and (ii) together give rise to higher precision.

Our work is intended to advance real-time applications in the rehabilitation domain on the edge, an example of pose estimation based future applications in health and wellbeing.

Contributions. BCDSM,GB,SZ: Conceptualization, Methodology, Software, Validation, Writing - original draft, Visualization. **ZsG**: Physiotherapist expert, video recordings **AL**: Conceptualization, Writing, Supervision.

Acknowledgements. This research was funded by the "Application Domain Specific Highly Reliable IT Solutions" project, implemented with the support provided from the National Research, Development and Innovation Fund of Hungary, financed under the Thematic Excellence Programme no. 2020-4.1.1.-TKP2020 (National Challenges Subprogramme) funding scheme and by the Hungarian Ministry of Innovation and Technology NRDI Office within the framework of the Artificial Intelligence National Laboratory Program.

References

1. Toshev, A., Szegedy, C.: DeepPose: human pose estimation via deep neural networks. In: 2014 IEEE Conference on Computer Vision and Pattern Recognition, pp. 1653–1660 (2014). https://doi.org/10.1109/CVPR.2014.214

2. Tompson, J., Goroshin, R., Jain, A., LeCun, Y., Bregler, C.: Efficient object localization using convolutional networks. In: 2015 IEEE Conference on Computer Vision and Pattern Recognition (CVPR), pp. 648–656 (2015). https://doi.org/10.1109/CVPR.2015.7298664
3. Newell, A., Yang, K., Deng, J.: Stacked hourglass networks for human pose estimation. In: Leibe, B., Matas, J., Sebe, N., Welling, M. (eds.) ECCV 2016. LNCS, vol. 9912, pp. 483–499. Springer, Cham (2016). https://doi.org/10.1007/978-3-319-46484-8_29
4. Wang, J., Sun, K., Cheng, T., Jiang, B., et al.: Deep High-Resolution Representation Learning for Visual Recognition. arXiv (2020)
5. Cao, Z., Hidalgo, G., Simon, T., Wei, S., Sheikh, Y.: OpenPose: Realtime Multi-Person 2D Pose Estimation Using Part Affinity Fields. arXiv (2019)
6. Artacho, B., Savakis, A.: OmniPose: A Multi-Scale Framework for Multi-Person Pose Estimation. arXiv (2021)
7. Mao, W., Ge, Y., Shen, C., Tian, Z., Wang, X., Wang, Z.: TFPose: Direct Human Pose Estimation with Transformers. arXiv (2021)
8. Lin, T.Y., et al.: Microsoft COCO: common objects in context. In: Fleet, D., Pajdla, T., Schiele, B., Tuytelaars, T. (eds.) ECCV 2014. LNCS, vol. 8693, pp. 740–755. Springer, Cham (2014). https://doi.org/10.1007/978-3-319-10602-1_48
9. Mehta, D., Rhodin, H., Casas, D., Fua, P., et al.: Monocular 3D human pose estimation in the wild using improved CNN supervision. In: 2017 International Conference on 3D Vision (3DV), pp. 506–516 (2017). https://doi.org/10.1109/3DV.2017.00064
10. Papandreou, G., Zhu, T., Chen, L.-C., Gidaris, S., Tompson, J., Murphy, K.: PersonLab: person pose estimation and instance segmentation with a bottom-up, part-based, geometric embedding model. In: Ferrari, V., Hebert, M., Sminchisescu, C., Weiss, Y. (eds.) Computer Vision – ECCV 2018. LNCS, vol. 11218, pp. 282–299. Springer, Cham (2018). https://doi.org/10.1007/978-3-030-01264-9_17
11. Jin, S., Xu, L., Xu, J., Wang, C., et al.: Whole-Body Human Pose Estimation in the Wild. arXiv (2020)
12. Pardos, A., Menychtas, A., Maglogiannis, I.: Introducing an edge-native deep learning platform for exergames. In: Artificial Intelligence Applications and Innovations, pp. 88–98 (2020). https://doi.org/10.1007/978-3-030-49186-4_8
13. Kim, T., Zohdy, M., Barker, M.: Applying pose estimation to predict amateur golf swing performance using edge processing. IEEE Access **8**, 143769–143776 (2020). https://doi.org/10.1109/ACCESS.2020.3014186
14. Devarajan, G., Aatre, V., Sridhar, C.: Analysis of median filter. ACE '90. In: Proceedings of [XVI Annual Convention and Exhibition of the IEEE In India, pp. 274–276 (1990). https://doi.org/10.1109/ACE.1990.762694
15. Gallagher, N.: Savitzky-Golay Smoothing and Differentiation Filter (2020). https://www.researchgate.net/publication/338518012_Savitzky-Golay_Smoothing_and_Differentiation_Filter
16. Signal Smoothing Algorithms. http://195.134.76.37/applets/AppletSmooth/Appl_Smooth2.html. Accessed 20 Nov 2020
17. Chavan, M., Agarwala, R., Uplane, M., Mikhael, W., et al.: A comparison of Chebyshev I and Chebyshev II filter applied for noise suppression in ECG signal (2008)

Image Processing

Subspace Constraint for Single Image Super-Resolution

Yanlin Zhang, Ding Qin, and Xiaodong Gu$^{(\boxtimes)}$ ⓘ

Department of Electronic Engineering, Fudan University, Shanghai 200438, China
xdgu@fudan.edu.cn

Abstract. Recently, single image super-resolution (SISR) algorithms based on convolutional neural networks (CNN) have proliferated and achieved significant success. However, most of them use the same constraint to both low-frequency and high-frequency features in the loss function. They do not discriminate between high-frequency details and low-frequency information, which limits the representation capacity of high-frequency information. This paper presents a subspace constraint approach for SISR to discriminate between high-frequency information and low-frequency information and enhance the reconstruction of high-frequency features. In our approach, the constraint is introduced in wavelet domain. Meanwhile, our approach adopts the multi-level residual learning to improve the training efficiency. Extensive experimental results on five benchmark datasets show that our model is superior to those state-of-the-art methods for both accuracy and visual comparisons.

Keywords: Image super-resolution · Convolutional neural network · Wavelet transform

1 Introduction

Single image super-resolution (SISR) aims to reconstruct a super-resolution (SR) image from a low-resolution (LR) image. It is significant for most image-related applications like face recognition, surveillance imaging and satellite imaging. Since SISR has various applications, it attracts a lot of researchers' attention.

Most current SISR algorithms [1, 2] process the low-resolution images in image space to push the outputs pixel-wise closer to ground-truth high-resolution (HR) images in training phase. Dong et al. [14] introduced convolutional neural network to learn the nonlinear mapping. Kim et al. proposed VDSR [1] and DRCN [17] to alleviate gradients vanishing. However, the results of their reconstruction are not ideal for it is hard to discriminate between high-frequency details and low-frequency information in spatial domain. Therefore, SISR remains an open and challenging task.

Wavelet Transform (WT) can depict the contextual and texture information of an image at different levels [3], which motivates us to design a subspace constraint for SISR. We transfer images to wavelet subspace through WT and design a novel loss function named Waveloss to enhance the reconstruction of high-frequency details. Our

© Springer Nature Switzerland AG 2021
I. Farkaš et al. (Eds.): ICANN 2021, LNCS 12893, pp. 395–407, 2021.
https://doi.org/10.1007/978-3-030-86365-4_32

network consists of 3 modules: feature embedding module, image reconstruction module and subspace constraint module. The feature embedding module transforms the low-resolution image into a series of feature maps, and then the reconstruction module will up-sample these feature maps and reconstruct them to high-resolution image. Finally the subspace constraint module will improve the model's reconstruction performance (Fig. 1).

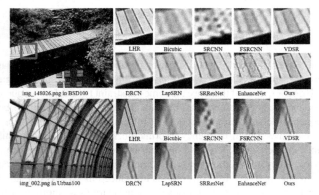

Fig. 1. Comparison between our model and other state-of-the-art networks.

Overall, our main contributions are as follows.

(1) A plug-and-play subspace constraint module is proposed to distinguish between high-frequency information and low-frequency information and strengthen constraint to high-frequency information.
(2) The reconstruction module is combined with residual learning to improve the training efficiency.

2   Related Work

As a conventional image process technique, WT represents and stores images in a highly-efficient and brief way [3, 4] and describe semantic and texture information of images. Many researchers have proposed SR algorithms based on WT [5, 6] and the majority of them focused on multiple image SR algorithms. For single image super resolution, WT is often applied in interpolation-based [7] or statistics-based [8] methods. Anbarjafari et al. [9] used bicubic linear difference algorithm to up-sample the subspace obtained by wavelet transform, and then inverse wavelet transform (IWT) is applied to the subspace to obtain the final high-resolution images. Many other researchers [28, 29] utilized the sparse coding method to optimize the details of the image. However due to the limited training data and fixed models, these methods are not able to reconstruct the optimal SR images, especially for those deep learning algorithms requiring large dataset and variable model structures.

With the development of CNN, some researchers proposed algorithms that combine deep learning and WT. Guo et al. [10] combined ResNet with WT to predict the residual of high-resolution wavelet sub-bands. Huang et al. [11] proposed Wavelet-SRNet for face super resolution construction, which greatly improved the reconstruction effect. Since the process of WT is reversible, Liu et al. [12] replaced the pooling layer in neural network with WT to avoid information loss in the pooling layer. However, a large number of wavelet sub-band channels are generated through operating WT on feature maps continuously, which delays the training speed. Besides, all these methods cannot realize end-to-end algorithms. Meanwhile, LR images need to be up-sampled first will consume lots of computing resources.

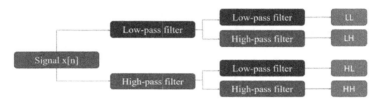

Fig. 2. Two-dimensional discrete wavelet process.

Based on above analysis, we apply WT to the loss function rather than transform the network structure. In this way, our model can fully utilize features in wavelet subspace and avoid the effects of WT on network training.

3   The Proposed Method

3.1   Wavelet Transform

In one-dimensional discrete WT, supposing a one-dimensional signal $x[n] \in R^N$ passes through a high-pass filter $G_H[n]$ and a low-pass filter $G_L[n]$, which are defined as:

$$G_H[n] = \begin{cases} 1, & n = 0 \\ -1, & n = 1 \\ 0 & otherwise \end{cases}, \tag{1}$$

$$G_L[n] = \begin{cases} 1, & n = 0, 1 \\ 0, & otherwise \end{cases}, \tag{2}$$

then $x[n]$ can be decomposed to approximation coefficients and detail coefficients. The approximation coefficients are the mean value of two adjacent signals, while the detail coefficients are the difference between two adjacent signals. The approximation coefficients contain the overall information of $x[n]$, while the detail coefficients contain the difference of $x[n]$.

Any digital image is two-dimensional signal. Let $I(n, m)$ be the pixel value of an image at row n, column m. $I(n, m)$ also means a one-dimensional column signal in row

n or a one-dimensional row signal in column m. The steps of two-dimensional Discrete Wavelet Transform (2dDWT) are shown in Fig. 2. We first wavelet transform the two-dimensional signal along the row direction and make it pass through the low-pass and high-pass filters to get the low-frequency and high-frequency subspace respectively, then we do the same thing along the column direction to get four subspaces: Approximate coefficients LL; Horizontal details LH; Vertical details HL and.

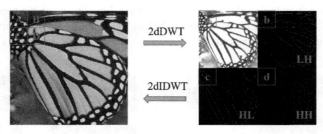

Fig. 3. Schematic diagram of two-dimensional discrete wavelet decomposition

Diagonal details HH. As shown in Fig. 3, four pictures on the right represent four sub-bands after 2dDWT. The LL sub-band represents the semantic information of the image, and the other three sub-bands show the image's details and texture information along different directions.

In SISR, we can take the low-resolution image as the LL sub-band, the other three sub-bands LH, HL and HH are the lost high frequency information of LL sub-band on which our model should focus. As shown in Fig. 3, **A, B, C, D** are four schematic pixel values of a 2 * 2 region in the upper left corner of the high-resolution image, and **a, b, c, d** are schematic pixel values of the upper left corner of LL, HL, LH and HH sub-bands respectively. We get the pixel values of four sub-bands through 2dDWT:

$$
\begin{cases}
a = \frac{1}{4}(A + B + C + D) \\
b = \frac{1}{4}(A - B + C - D) \\
c = \frac{1}{4}(A + B - C - D) \\
d = \frac{1}{4}(A - B - C + D)
\end{cases}
\tag{3}
$$

and we can do the two-dimensional Inverse Discrete Wavelet Transform (2dIDWT).

$$
\begin{cases}
A = a + b + c + d \\
B = a - b + c - d \\
C = a + b - c - d \\
D = a - b - c + d
\end{cases}
\tag{4}
$$

Therefore we can transform images into wavelet domain.

3.2 Design of the WaveLoss Function

The goal of the single-image super resolution is to learn a mapping $f(x, \theta)$ from a low-resolution image to a high-resolution image, where θ represents the parameters to be optimized by the model. In general, most models adopt MSE as loss function like this:

$$L_{SR}(\theta) = \|I_{HR} - I_{SR}\|^2, \tag{5}$$

However, as most research mentioned [30, 31], the model cannot effectively get high-frequency texture information if the model is only optimized by minimizing MSE loss. In order to improve the reconstruction performance of high frequency details, we propose the WaveLoss function (Fig. 4).

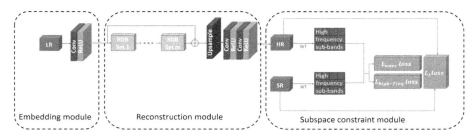

Fig. 4. Network architecture.

First consider an n order wavelet decomposition where n determines the depth of decomposition d and the number of sub-bands N. Here $N = 4^d$. Supposing $Y = (y_1, y_2, \cdots, y_N)$ represents the N sub-bands of labeled high-resolution images, $\widehat{Y} = (\widehat{y_1}, \widehat{y_2}, \cdots, \widehat{y_N})$ represents the N sub-bands of reconstructed high-resolution images. Similar to the MSE loss in the original spatial domain, we first propose a weighted loss function in the wavelet domain. It is defined as:

$$L_{wave}(\theta) = \sum_{i=1}^{N} \lambda_i \|y_i - \hat{y}_i\|^2, \tag{6}$$

where N represents the number of sub-bands and $W = (\lambda_1, \lambda_2, \cdots)$ represents weight vector of a sub-bands to show the importance of different sub-bands in training process. We predict that if we give higher weights to sub-bands that contains high-frequency information, the model will pay more attention to local details and texture information so that the result of the reconstruction will be better.

Meanwhile, since the high-frequency sub-bands are sparser than low-frequency sub-bands, if they are optimized in the same way, the high-frequency sub-bands will easily converge to zero. As a result, the model cannot update the information in high-frequency sub-bands. So we design a content loss function to punish this situation:

$$L_{high-freq} = \sum_{i \in H} \gamma_i \max\left(\tau \|y_i\|^2 - \|\hat{y}_i\|^2 + \epsilon, 0\right), \tag{7}$$

where H includes the serial number of the high-frequency sub-bands to be punished, γ adjusts the penalty weight of each sub-band, and τ and ϵ are the relaxation variables.

This loss function make the loss value of the high-frequency sub-band far away from zero value, thus avoiding the degradation of the extracted texture information.

To balance the model stability and texture information, we still adopt the loss function L1 to constrain the reconstruction result in the spatial domain of the image. Here we get WaveLoss function:

$$L_{waveloss} = L_{l1} + \alpha L_{wave} + \beta L_{high-freq}, \tag{8}$$

So.

$$L_{waveloss} = \|I_{HR} - I_{SR}\|^1$$
$$+\alpha \sum\nolimits_{i=1}^{N} \lambda_j \|y_i - \hat{y}_i\|^2$$
$$+\beta \sum\nolimits_{i \in H} \gamma_i \max\left(\tau \|y_i\|^2 - \|\hat{y}_i\|^2 + \epsilon, 0\right) \tag{9}$$

where α and β adjust the importance of L_{wave} and $L_{high-freq}$. The $L_{waveloss}$ strengthens the model's learning in high-frequency wavelet sub-bands, which further promotes the effectiveness of SR reconstruction.

3.3   Network Architecture

Features Embedding Module. The input of the features embedding module is a single low-resolution image (LR). The LR is first convolved through a standard convolution layer to increase the number of channels of the feature image, then the result is directly connected to the output of the feature embedding module through cross-layer connection to realize a global residual learning. The size of the convolutional kernel of all convolutional layers in the feature embedding network is 3 * 3, the step size of the convolution is 1, and the padding coefficient is 1. According to the formulation of the size of the feature map:

$$W_{out} = \frac{W_{in} + 2 * padding - F}{stride} + 1, \tag{10}$$

where W_{in} and W_{out} represents the size of the input and output feature maps respectively, F represents the size of convolutional kernel, *padding* represents the size of the zero filling coefficient and stride represents the step size. We set $F = 3$, *padding* = 1 and *stride* = 1, so the output feature maps can keep the same size with the input feature maps. A number of densely connected convolutional modules are stacked in series and the structure of each densely connected convolutional modules is the same.

Reconstruction Module. The reconstruction module converts a series of feature maps into high-resolution images. We first up-sample the deep features which contain more high-frequency details via up-sampling module. Two convolutional layers are applied to finish the reconstruction of the SR image. The size of HR is $3 * (r * H) * (r * W)$, where r represents the scaling coefficient.

Subspace Constraint Module. During the training phrase, the SR image will be sent to the subspace constraint network, and the features of each channel will be transformed to the wavelet domain to get four sub-bands. Now we can use L_{wave} and $L_{high-freq}$ to calculate the sub-band weighted loss function and the content-loss function described in (6) and (7). In order to make the loss value can be back propogated, we use convolution layer with fixed weight to simulate the operation of WT. The fixed weight are set according to the WT formula mentioned in (3) and (4).

4 Experiment and Analysis

4.1 Datasets and Metrics

In our experiment, DIV2k dataset is the training set, which contains 800 2k-resolution training images. To increase datasets and reduce the resolution of a single training sample, we crop these 800 images to 480 * 480 and use these cropped images as HR. Then the bicubic down-sampling function of MATLAB generates the corresponding LR images, which are the input of our model. During the training phrase, the LR images are first randomly clipped to 48 * 48 to increase the generalization performance of the model and avoid over fitting, and the HR images are clipped to the corresponding area to obtain the label of the sample. In the experiment, the batch size is 16 due to the GPU memory limitation. Meanwhile, Adam optimizer is applied to update the model parameters with $\beta_1 = 0.9, \beta_2 = 0.999, \epsilon = 10^{-8}$. Our subspace constraint network is built under Pytorch framework, training in Intel Core i7-6700K CPU (4.00 GHz), 32 GB of memory, NVIDIA GeForce Ti GPU machines.

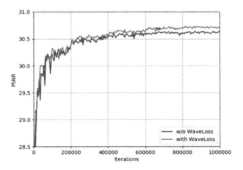

Fig. 5. Model's convergence curve in the training process with or without sub-space constraint

We test the performance on five extensively used benchmark datasets: Set5, Set14, BSD100, Urban100, Manga109, which totally have 328 images. For SISR task, peak signal-to-noise ratio (PSNR) and structural similarity index (SSIM) are commonly used to measure the reconstruction quality. As commonly done in SISR, the results are evaluated with PSNR and SSIM only on Y channel of YCbCr space.

Fig. 6. Visualization of model's feature maps with and without subspace constraint module.

4.2 Effectiveness of Subspace Constraint

To demonstrate the effectiveness of subspace constraint, we also train the model without subspace constraint. Figure 5 compares the model's convergence curve in the training process with and without sub-space constraint. It is obvious that PSNR increases 0.1 dB when adding the space constraint module. To verify that the subspace constraint can guide the model to learn more high-frequency information, we visualize the feature map of the last layer in the feature embedding module, and plot the result in Fig. 6. It is obvious that the model with subspace constraint can effectively improve the reconstruction of high-frequency information and recover more detailed information.

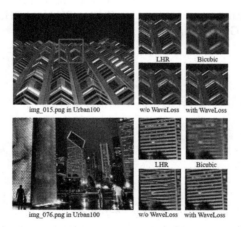

Fig. 7. The visual comparisons between the model with or without Waveloss.

Figure 7 shows the model's evaluation on img_015.png and img_076.png from Urban100. It can be found that model with subspace constraint generate more faithful results for the reconstructed building texture lines are more accurate. However, the model without subspace constraint produces unreliable result for strips in reconstructed images are blurry and distorted. All the above results indicate that our subspace constraint module can indeed make our network pay more attention to high-frequency information.

Table 1. Quantitative evaluations of state-of-the-art methods with PSNR and SSIM.

Methods	Scale	Set5		Set14		BSD100		Urban100		Manga109	
		PSNR	SSIM	PSNR	SSIM	PSNR	SSIM	PSNR	SSIM	PSNR	SSIM
Bicubic	× 4	28.43	0.8109	26.00	0.7027	25.96	0.6678	23.14	0.6574	24.89	0.7866
SRCNN		30.48	0.8628	27.50	0.7513	26.90	0.7103	24.53	0.7226	27.58	0.8555
FRSRCNN		30.70	0.8657	27.59	0.7535	26.96	0.7128	24.60	0.7258	27.90	0.8610
VDSR		31.35	0.8838	28.01	0.7674	27.29	0.7251	25.18	0.7524	28.83	0.8870
DRCN		31.53	0.8854	28.02	0.7670	27.23	0.7233	25.14	0.7510	28.98	0.8860
LapSRN		31.54	0.8866	28.19	0.7694	27.32	0.7270	25.21	0.7553	29.09	0.8900
MemNet		31.74	0.8893	28.26	0.7723	27.40	0.7281	25.50	0.7630	29.42	0.8942
SRDenseNet		32.02	0.8934	28.50	0.7782	27.53	0.7337	26.05	0.7819	–	–
IDN		31.82	0.8903	28.25	0.7730	27.41	0.7297	25.41	0.7632	29.40	0.8936
SRMDNF		31.96	0.8925	28.35	0.7787	27.49	0.7337	25.68	0.7731	30.09	0.9024
D-DBPN		<u>32.47</u>	0.8980	<u>28.82</u>	0.7860	<u>27.72</u>	0.7400	26.38	0.7946	30.91	0.9137
SRFBN		<u>32.47</u>	<u>0.8983</u>	28.81	<u>0.7868</u>	<u>27.72</u>	<u>0.7409</u>	26.60	<u>0.8015</u>	<u>31.15</u>	<u>0.9160</u>
Ours		**32.65**	**0.9000**	**28.96**	**0.7903**	**27.83**	**0.7446**	**27.02**	**0.8134**	**31.58**	**0.9195**

4.3 Comparisons with the State-of-the-Art Methods

To demonstrate the performance of our model, our experimental results are quantitatively compared with several state-of-the-art methods, including SRCNN [14], FSRCNN [15], VDSR [16], DRCN [17], LapSRN [18], MemNet [19], SRDenseNet [20], IDN [21], SRMDNF [22], D-DBPN [23] and SRFBN. Table 1 shows the summaries of the quantitative evaluations under × 4 scale factors on five extensively used five datasets: Set5 [24], Set14 [25], BSD100 [26], Urban100 [27] and Manga109 [32]. The best performance is highlighted and the second is underlined. It is obvious that our model achieves the best performance on five benchmark data sets, particularly on the Urban100 dataset. The comparisons indicate the superiority of our model.

Meanwhile, the visual comparisons of several state-of-the-art methods are also illustrated in Fig. 8. In img_087.png from Urban100, it's obvious that compared methods suffer from blurring artifacts and severe distortions, but our model can not only alleviate the artifacts but also produce sharp edges and abundant details. In img_093.png from Urban100, there are lots of side-by-side zebra crossings and unacceptably the compared methods can't reconstruct these edges of crossings accurately. Only our method can generate the more faithful result. These visual comparisons further demonstrate the necessity of the special constraint module and the powerful representational ability of our model.

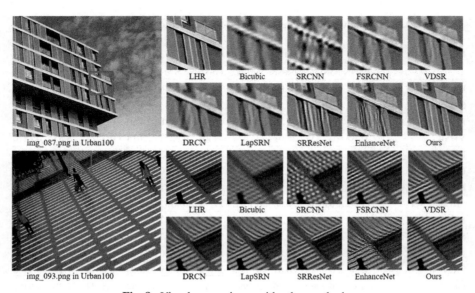

Fig. 8. Visual comparisons with other methods.

4.4 Object Recognition Performance

Image super-resolution is always utilized as the pre-processing step to improve the performance of some high-level computer vision tasks such as object detection and classification. So objection recognition tests are conducted to further demonstrate the superior performance of our model.

As commonly done in [13], ResNet-50 is used as the objection recognition model and the first 1000 images in the CLS-LOC is used as the validation dataset. The original images are resized to 256×256 and then center-cropped to 224×224. Next, these images are down-sampled to 56×56 with MATLAB bi-cubic kernel function.

Table 2. Resnet-50 object recognition performance

Evaluation	Bicubic	VDSR	LapSRN	SRResNet	SRDenseNet	Ours	Baseline
Top-1 error	0.360	0.329	0.329	0.306	0.317	**0.291**	0.238
Top-5 error	0.146	0.133	0.119	0.107	0.104	**0.088**	0.066

In our comparisons, Bi-cubic, VDSR, LapSRN, SRResNet and SRDenseNet algorithms are used to upscale the images. The up-sampled images are then used to calculate their mean top-1 and top-5 errors. The results are shown in Table 2 and the best performance is **highlighted.** Our model achieves the lowest mean top-1 and top-5 errors, which further demonstrate the effectiveness of our model.

5   Conclusion

In this paper, we apply the wavelet subspace constraint module to single image super-resolution (SISR) to achieve additional constraints on high-frequency details. We verify that the subspace constraint module can effectively obtain the high-frequency details of the features by transforming the HR images into wavelet domain and making the SR images as close to the HR images as possible. Since this constraint module only takes effect during the training phrase, it will not delay the predicting speed. The extensive evaluations on benchmark datasets indicate our model outperforms those state-of-the-art methods on both quantitative results and visual performance.

Acknowledgments. This work was supported in part by National Natural Science Foundation of China under grant 61771145. Thanks Mr. Qingrong Chen for his valuable revision advice.

References

1. Kim, J., Kwon Lee, J., Mu Lee, K.: Accurate image super-resolution using very deep convolutional networks. In: Proceedings of the IEEE Conference on Computer Vision and Pattern Recognition, pp. 1646–1654 (2016)
2. Lai, W.S., Huang, J.B., Ahuja, N., et al.: Fast and accurate image super-resolution with deep laplacian pyramid networks. IEEE Trans. Pattern Anal. Mach. Intell. **41**(11), 2599–2613 (2018)
3. Mallat, S.: Wavelets for a vision. Proc. IEEE **84**(4), 604–614 (1996)
4. Stankovićr, S., Falkowski, B.J.: The haar wavelet transform: its status and achievements. Comput. Electr. Eng. **29**(1), 25–44 (2003)
5. Chan, R.H., Chan, T.F., Shen, L., et al.: Wavelet algorithms for high-resolution image reconstruction. SIAM J. Sci. Comput. **24**(4), 1408–1432 (2003)
6. Robinson, M.D., Toth, C.A., Lo, J.Y., et al.: Efficient fourier-wavelet super resolution. IEEE Trans. Image Process. **19**(10), 2669–2681 (2010)
7. Nguyen, N., Milanfar, P.: A wavelet-based interpolation-restoration method for super resolution (wavelet super resolution). Circ. Syst. Sig. Process. **19**(4), 321–338 (2000)
8. Zhao, S., Han, H., Peng, S.: Wavelet-domain hmt-based image super-resoltion. In: Proceedings 2003 International Conference on Image Processing, vol. 2, pp. 2–953 (2003)
9. Anbarjafari, G., Demirel, H.: Image super resolution based on interpolation of wavelet domain high frequency subbands and the spatial domain input image. ETRI J. **32**(3), 390–394 (2010)
10. Guo, T., Seyed Mousavi, H., Huu Vu, T., et al.: Deep wavelet prediction for image super-resolution. In: Proceedings of the IEEE Conference on Computer Vision and Pattern Recognition Workshops, pp. 104–113 (2017)
11. Huang, H., He, R., Sun, Z., et al.: Wavelet-srnet: a wavelet-based cnn formulti scale face super resolution. In: Proceedings of the IEEE International Conference on Computer Vision, pp. 1689–1697 (2017)
12. Liu, P., Zhang, H., Zhang, K., et al.: Multi-level wavelet-CNN for image restoration. In: Proceedings of the IEEE Conference on Computer Vision and Pattern Recognition Workshops, pp. 773–782 (2018)
13. Sajjadi, M. S., Scholkopf, B., Hirsch, M.: Enhancenet: single image super resolution through automated texture synthesis. In: Proceedings of the IEEE International Conference on Computer Vision, pp. 4491–4500 (2017)

14. Dong, C., Loy, C.C., He, K., Tang, X.: Super-resolution using deep convolutional networks. IEEE Trans. Pattern Anal. Mach. Intell. **38**, 295–307 (2016). https://doi.org/10.1109/TPAMI.2015.2439281

15. Dong, C., Loy, C.C., Tang, X.: Accelerating the super-resolution convolutional neural network. In: Leibe, B., Matas, J., Sebe, N., Welling, M. (eds.) ECCV 2016. LNCS, vol. 9906, pp. 391–407. Springer, Cham (2016). https://doi.org/10.1007/978-3-319-46475-6_25

16. Kim, J., Lee, J.K., Lee, K.M.: Accurate image super-resolution using very deep convolutional networks. In: 2016 IEEE Conference on Computer Vision and Pattern Recognition (CVPR). pp. 1646–1654. IEEE, Las Vegas (2016)

17. Kim, J., Lee, J.K., Lee, K.M.: Deeply-recursive convolutional network for image super-resolution. In: 2016 IEEE Conference on Computer Vision and Pattern Recognition (CVPR), pp. 1637–1645. IEEE, Las Vegas (2016)

18. Lai, W.-S., Huang, J.-B., Ahuja, N., Yang, M.-H.: Deep laplacian pyramid networks for fast and accurate super-resolution. In: 2017 IEEE Conference on Computer Vision and Pattern Recognition (CVPR), pp. 5835–5843. IEEE, Honolulu (2017)

19. Tai, Y., Yang, J., Liu, X., Xu, C.: MemNet: a persistent memory network for image restoration. In: 2017 IEEE International Conference on Computer Vision (ICCV), pp. 4549–4557. IEEE, Venice (2017)

20. Tong, T., Li, G., Liu, X., Gao, Q.: Image super-resolution using dense skip connections. In: 2017 IEEE International Conference on Computer Vision (ICCV), pp. 4809–4817. IEEE, Venice (2017)

21. Hui, Z., Wang, X., Gao, X.: Fast and accurate single image super-resolution via information distillation network. In: 2018 IEEE/CVF Conference on Computer Vision and Pattern Recognition, pp. 723–731. IEEE, Salt Lake City (2018)

22. Zhang, K., Zuo, W., Zhang, L.: Learning a single convolutional super-resolution network for multiple degradations. In: 2018 IEEE/CVF Conference on Computer Vision and Pattern Recognition, pp. 3262–3271. IEEE, Salt Lake City (2018)

23. Haris, M., Shakhnarovich, G., Ukita, N.: Deep back-projection networks for super-resolution. In: 2018 IEEE/CVF Conference on Computer Vision and Pattern Recognition, pp. 1664–1673. IEEE, Salt Lake City (2018)

24. Bevilacqua, M., Roumy, A., Guillemot, C., Morel, M.A.: Low-complexity single-image super-resolution based on nonnegative neighbor embedding. In: Procedings of the British Machine Vision Conference 2012, pp. 135.1–135.10. British Machine Vision Association, Surrey (2012)

25. Zeyde, R., Elad, M., Protter, M.: On single image scale-up using sparse-representations. In: Boissonnat, J.-D., et al. (eds.) Curves and Surfaces 2010. LNCS, vol. 6920, pp. 711–730. Springer, Heidelberg (2012). https://doi.org/10.1007/978-3-642-27413-8_47

26. ArbelÁEz, P., Maire, M., Fowlkes, C., Malik, J.: Contour detection and hierarchical image segmentation. IEEE Trans. Pattern Anal. Mach. Intell. **33**, 898–916 (2011). https://doi.org/10.1109/TPAMI.2010.161

27. Huang, J.-B., Singh, A., Ahuja, N.: Single image super-resolution from transformed self-exemplars. In: 2015 IEEE Conference on Computer Vision and Pattern Recognition (CVPR), pp. 5197–5206. IEEE, Boston (2015)

28. Mallat, S., Yu, G.: Super-resolution with sparse mixing estimators. IEEE Trans. Image Process. **19**(11), 2889–2900 (2010). https://doi.org/10.1109/TIP.2010.2049927

29. Dong, W., Zhang, L., Shi, G., Xiaolin, W.: Image deblurring and super-resolution by adaptive sparse domain selection and adaptive regularization. IEEE Trans. Image Process. **20**(7), 1838–1857 (2011). https://doi.org/10.1109/TIP.2011.2108306

30. Lim, B., Son, S., Kim, H., et al.: Enhanced deep residual networks for single image super resolution. In: Proceedings of the IEEE Conference on Computer Vision and Pattern Recognition Workshops, pp. 136–144 (2017)

31. Hui, Z., Wang, X., Gao, X.: Fast and accurate single image super-resolution via information distillation network. In: Proceedings of the IEEE Conference on Computer Vision and Pattern Recognition, pp. 723–731 (2018)
32. Fujimoto, A., Ogawa, T., Yamamoto, K., et al: Manga109 dataset and creation of metadata. In: Proceedings of the 1st International Workshop on Comics Analysis, Processing and Understanding, pp. 1–5 (2016)

Towards Fine-Grained Control over Latent Space for Unpaired Image-to-Image Translation

Lei Luo[1]([✉]), William Hsu[1], and Shangxian Wang[2]

[1] Kansas State University, Manhattan, KS 66506, USA
{leiluoray,bhsu}@ksu.edu
[2] Johns Hopkins University, Baltimore, MD 21210, USA
wshangx1@jhu.edu

Abstract. We address the open problem of unpaired image-to-image (I2I) translation using a generative model with fine-grained control over the latent space. The goal is to learn the conditional distribution of translated images given images from a source domain without access to the joint distribution. Previous works, such as MUNIT and DRIT, which simply keep content latent codes and exchange the style latent codes, generate images of inferior quality. In this paper, we propose a new framework for unpaired I2I translation. Our framework first assumes that the latent space can be decomposed into content and style sub-spaces. Instead of naively exchanging style codes when translating, our framework uses an interpolator that guides the transformation and is able to produce intermediate results under different strengths of translation. Domain specific information, which might still exist in content codes, is excluded in our framework. Extensive experiments show that the translated images using our framework are superior than or comparable to state-of-the-art baselines. Code is available upon publication.

Keywords: Unpaired image-to-image translation · Latent space · Content codes · Style codes · Fine-grained control

1 Introduction

Image-to-image (I2I) translation refers to translating images from one domain to another with different properties. An example is the task of turning images of cartoon sketches into real-life graphs. Many tasks in computer vision can be posed as I2I translation, such as image inpainting [1], style and attribute transfer [2,3], and super-resolution [4]. Paired I2I transfer tasks require paired data sets that are costly to acquire, and such tasks are relatively easier to solve than their unpaired counterparts. Chen and Koltun translated paired images of semantic map to photographic images by taking a regression approach [5]. Isola et al. framed paired I2I translation tasks using conditional generative models [6]. Our work addresses the more challenging unpaired I2I task, where no paired data sets are available. Most of works on unpaired I2I translation draw inspiration

© Springer Nature Switzerland AG 2021
I. Farkaš et al. (Eds.): ICANN 2021, LNCS 12893, pp. 408–420, 2021.
https://doi.org/10.1007/978-3-030-86362-3_33

from CycleGANs using the cycle consistency constraint [7], and have achieved impressive results. These models, however, often have little control over the translation strength and can only provide a single translated image as output. Furthermore, they often disentangle latent space into domain-invariant (content codes) and domain-specific parts (style codes). When translating, content codes are kept while style codes are exchanged. Domain-specific information, however, might still exist in content codes, which leads to unnatural translation results if they are not removed [8].

In this work, we show a need for fine-grained control over latent space by demonstrating the inferior translation capability in previous works that solely depend on the cycle consistency constraint or translate images by simply exchanging style codes. Fine-grained control over latent space are manifested in three aspects: 1) latent codes can be decomposed into content and style, much like DRIT [9] and MUNIT [10]; 2) an interpolator, which is a neural network, is employed to guide the transformation of style codes instead of simply exchanging them; and 3) domain-specific information in content codes is removed before translation for better translation results. Similar to DRIT and MUNIT, our framework assumes that the latent space can be decomposed into content space and style space by the content encoder and the style encoder, respectively. Before decoding the latent codes to obtain translated results, redundant domain-specific information that exists in content codes is removed. Furthermore, another set of modules, which we call the interpolator, smoothly guide the transition of style codes and allow us to generate intermediate images under different degrees of transformation. In the end, our framework differentiates translated images by using a discriminator. Extensive experiments demonstrate that our method is superior than or comparable to state-of-the-art (SOAT) baselines in unpaired I2I translation.

2   Related Work

Generative Adversarial Networks. Ideally, generative models learn how data is distributed, thus allowing data synthesis from the learned distribution. Since the advent of GANs [11], generative models have achieved impressive results in various tasks like image editing [12] and style transfer [3]. GANs try to learn the data distribution by approximating the similarity of distributions between the training data and the fake data produced by the learned model. GANs usually comprise a generator and a discriminator. The entire model learns by playing a minimax game: the generator tries to fool the discriminator by gradually generating realistic data samples, and the discriminator, in turn, tries to distinguish real samples from fake ones. GANs have been improved in various ways. To produce more realistic samples, an architecture of stacked GANs have been proposed: the laplacian pyramid of GANs [13]; layered, recursive GANs [28]; and style-based GANs [2,3]. Several studies have attempted to solve the instability training of GANs using energy-based GANs [14], Wasserstein GANs [15], and boundary equilibrium GANs [16]. In this study, we use GANs with their improved techniques to learn the distribution of image data and translate them among different domains.

Unpaired I2I Translation. Unpaired I2I translation translates images from one domain to another without paired data supervision. Much success in unpaired I2I translation is due to the cycle consistency constraint, proposed in three earlier works: CycleGANs [7], DiscoGANs [17], and DualGANs [18]. Recent systems such as MUNIT [10] and DRIT [9] were developed to perform multimodal I2I translation, which refers to producing images with the same content but different contexts. For example, a winter scene could be translated into many different summer scenes depending on weather or lighting. To translate more than two domains, StarGAN-V2 [19] and ModularGANs [20] were proposed. I2I translation methods using GANs that merely rely on cycle consistency constraints usually suffer from the issue of discreteness, which refers to inability to continuously control the transformation strength. In this study, we use an interpolator to guide the translation, which allows us to generate visually appealing intermediate translation results.

Our framework is closely related to MUNIT on that the latent space can be decomposed into a style sub-space and a content sub-space. Our framework, however, differs from MUNIT in four aspects: 1. Instead of having to train $n(n-1)$ sets of encoder-decoder for translating images between n domains, our framework consists of only one such set that works for multi-domains; 2. Our framework does not impose a Gaussian prior distribution for style codes, and instead learns the distributions during training; 3. Our framework removes redundant domain-specific information in content codes before translation, thus generating more natural-looking results; 4. Most unpaired I2I translation models that depend on the cycle-consistency loss cannot generate sequences of intermediate translation results. We employ an interpolator module that helps smoothly translate the latent codes of different domains and produces visually satisfying intermediate translation results.

3 Methods

3.1 Preliminaries

Let $x_m \in X_m$ and $x_n \in X_n$ be two images from domain X_m and domain X_n. Our goal is to estimate the conditional distributions $p(x_m|x_n)$ and $p(x_n|x_m)$ using the learned distribution $p(x_{n \to m}|x_n)$ and $p(x_{m \to n}|x_m)$, given the marginal distribution of $p(x_m)$ and $p(x_n)$ but without requiring access to the joint distribution of $p(x_m, x_n)$. Figure 1 shows an overview of our model. Our framework starts with an encoder $E = (E_s, E_c)$ that maps images from image space to latent space, where E_s is the style encoder and E_c is the content encoder. The latent codes consist of style latent codes (s_m, s_n) and content latent codes (c_m, c_n), where $(c_m, s_m) = (E_c(x_m), E_s(x_m))$ and $(c_n, s_n) = (E_c(x_n), E_s(x_n))$. After style codes are obtained, an interpolator I helps transform the style codes across different domains. The translated style codes $s_{m \to n}$ and $s_{n \to m}$ are obtained by calculating $s_m + \alpha * I_{mn}(s_n - s_m)$ and $s_n + \alpha * I_{nm}(s_m - s_n)$, where α is the transformation

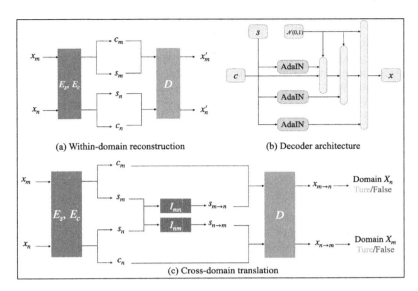

Fig. 1. The structure of our framework. (a) shows within-domain image reconstruction; (b) shows key components of the decoder. The number of convolutional layers are more than what the graph shows; (c) shows cross-domain translation.

strength. Style is injected into the decoder by AdaIN [21] operations. Before injecting the style of the target domain, we remove domain-specific information by injecting the negative style of the same domain, and the strength of the negative style is learned during training. Inspired by StyleGAN [2], we introduce stochastic variation into our model by injecting noise into the decoder. After the transformed style codes are obtained, the decoder D decodes the style and content codes back to image space, thus generating translated images x_{mn} and x_{nm}, where $x_{mn} = D(c_m, s_{m \to n})$ and $x_{nm} = D(c_n, s_{n \to m})$. Finally, the discriminator C tries to differentiate real images from fake ones.

3.2 Framework Architecture

In this section, we outline the architecture of different modules in our framework.

Encoder. Our encoder has two sub-encoders: the style encoder and the content encoder. The content encoder consists of three convolutional layers and four residual blocks [22]. All the layers use ReLU activation function and are followed by an instance normalization (IN) operation [23]. The style encoder starts with five convolutional layers, which are followed by an adaptive average pooling layer and a 1×1 convolutional layer. All layers in the style encoder use ReLU activation function except for the pooling layer.

Decoder. The decoder maps latent codes, which consist of style codes and content codes, to the original image space. The style codes go through a mapping network and are then injected into the decoder by AdaIN [21] operations. The mapping network is a three layer multi-layer perceptron network. Each layer except for the last one is followed by ReLU. Before injecting the style of the target domain, we remove redundant domain-specific information by injecting the negative style of the source domain, and the strength of the negative style is learned via training. Taking transferring the image x_m from the domain X_m to the domain X_n as an example. We first remove domain specific information in content codes c_m by using AdaIN$(-\beta_m * s_m)$, where β_m is learned via training. Then, we inject the style codes s_n of image x_n by using AdaIN again, which is AdaIN(s_n). Inspired by StyleGAN [2], we introduce stochastic variation into our model by injecting Gaussian noise into the decoder. Our decoder consists of four residual blocks using AdaIN, and two sets of upsample and convolution layers. The last layer is a convolution layer with hyperbolic tangent activation function.

Interpolator. Our framework has an interpolator to guide style codes transiting from one domain to another. The interpolator has three convolutional blocks. The first two use ReLU activation function, and the last one does not have any activation function.

Discriminator. We use a multi-scale discriminator, whose architecture is similar to the one proposed by [29], to distinguish real images from fake ones. At each scale, images go through five convolutional layers before being downsampled. The losses at three scales are accumulated for calculating the final discriminator loss. The discriminator also works as a domain predictor, which consists of a three layer multi-layer perceptron with ReLU activation function except for the last one.

3.3   Loss Functions

In this section, we discuss the loss functions and the training algorithm of our framework.

Image Reconstruction Loss. After images are encoded to style and content codes, the decoder can map them back to the image space and reconstruct the image. Therefore, the image reconstruction loss of x_m is formulated as:

$$L_{recon}^{x_m} = \|D(E_c(x_m), E_s(x_m)) - x_m\|_1,\tag{1}$$

and $L_{recon}^{x_n}$ is expressed similarly. After images are translated from one domain to another, the images in the source domain can be reconstructed by inverting the process. For example, x_{mn} has the content of image x_m and the style from domain X_n. x_{mn} is obtained by evaluating $D(c_m, s_n)$. Encoding x_{mn} again produces (c'_m, s'_n), and by decoding $D(c'_m, s_m)$, we can reconstruct x_m, which is now denoted by x_{mnm}. Thus, we calculate $L_{recon}^{x_{mnm}}$ as follows:

$$L_{recon}^{x_{mnm}} = \|x_{mnm} - x_m\|_1 = \|D(E_c(x_{mn}), E_s(x_m)) - x_m\|_1.\tag{2}$$

Similarly, $L_{recon}^{x_{nmn}} = \|x_{nmn} - x_n\|_1$. The reconstructed images should be consistent with the semantics of the original images, so we penalize perceptual loss to minimize the semantic difference:

$$L_{perc}^{x_m} = \|\Phi_3(D(E_c(x_m), E_s(x_m))) - \Phi_3(x_m)\|^2,\tag{3}$$

where Φ_3 denotes the ReLU3_1 layer of a pretrained VGG network [27]. We can similarly calculate the perceptual loss for $L_{perc}^{x_n}$, $L_{perc}^{x_{mnm}}$, and $L_{perc}^{x_{nmn}}$.

Latent Code Reconstruction Loss. By encoding the translated images, we can obtain a new set of content and style codes. For example, encoding the translated image x_{mn} produces (c'_m, s'_n). We construct the latent code reconstruction loss as follows:

$$L_{recon}^c = \|c'_m - c_m\|_1 \, ; L_{recon}^s = \|s'_n - s_n\|_1 \, . \tag{4}$$

Interpolation Loss. Given latent codes of two domains one can interpolate latent codes in a linear fashion. For example, $s_m + \alpha * (s_n - s_m)$ translates s_m to s_n under translation strength α. This approach, however, does not guarantee smooth-looking results as the translation path might not be linear. We employ an interpolator to smoothly transit style codes of different domains, which is calculated as $s_m + \alpha * I_{mn}(s_n - s_m)$. α controls the translation strength and is a random value that is uniformly sampled from 0 to 1. Regarding to domain labels, however, we adopt a linear interpolation strategy. That is to say, we linearly interpolate the domain labels using the same α and use the interpolated domain label as ground truth. The intuition behind this is that linearly interpolated images are supposed to have linearly interpolated labels, but linearly interpolated images are not guaranteed to be smooth-looking. Therefore, an interpolator network is trained to guide the translation. The discriminator C is trained to produce realistic fake images and also to also predict domains of images, and we use the binary cross entropy (BCE) loss and adversarial loss jointly to train the interpolator. The BCE loss function for the interpolator I_{mn} is calculated as:

$$L_{I_{mn}} = \text{BCE}(C(x_{mn}), gt\_domain), \tag{5}$$

where x_{mn} is a translated image via $D(c_m, s_m + \alpha * I_{mn}(s_n - s_m))$ and gt_domain is the ground truth domain label, which is linearly interpolated via $label_m + \alpha * (label_n - label_m)$. $L_{I_{nm}}$ can be calculated similarly.

Regularizers on Style and Content Codes. To further encourage style codes being domain-variant and content codes being domain-invariant, we add regularizers on style and content codes. The style regularizer forces style codes of different domains to be different by minimizing L_{regu}^s, which is calculating as:

$$L_{regu}^s = -\|D(c_m, s_m) - D(c_m, s_n)\|_1 - \|D(c_n, s_m) - D(c_n, s_n)\|_1 \, . \tag{6}$$

The content regularizer encourages content codes of different domains to be similar by minimizing L_{regu}^c, which is formulated as:

$$L_{regu}^c = \|D(c_m, s_m) - D(c_n, s_m)\|_1 + \|D(c_m, s_n) - D(c_n, s_n)\|_1 \, . \tag{7}$$

Adversarial Loss. GANs are used to match the distribution of translated results to real image samples, so the discriminator finds real and fake samples indistinguishable. The loss for learning the discriminator C is formulated as:

$$L_C^{x_{mn}} = \mathbb{E}_{c_m \sim p(c_m), s_{m \to n} \sim p(s_n)}[log(1 - C(D(c_m, s_{m \to n})))] + \mathbb{E}_{x_n \sim p(X_n)}[logC(x_n)],$$

(8)

where the discriminator C tries to differentiate real images from X_n and translated images x_{mn}. $L_C^{x_{nm}}$ is obtained similarly.

Model Training. We alternately train our discriminator and the rest of modules, which are encoders, decoder, mapping network, and the interpolator. The training procedure of our framework is illustrated in Algorithm 1 using a convergence bound B that is empirically calibrated at 1,000,000.

Algorithm 1: Model training

Result: style encoder $\boldsymbol{E}_s$, content encoder $\boldsymbol{E}_c$, interpolators $\boldsymbol{I}_{mn}$, $\boldsymbol{I}_{nm}$, decoder $\boldsymbol{D}$, and β_m, β_n that control the strength of negative style injected for removing domain dependent information.

$n = 0$;

while $n < B$ **do**

  Calculate $L_C^{x_{mn}}, L_C^{x_{nm}}$ according to (8);
  Update the discriminator $\boldsymbol{C}$;
  Calculate $L_{recon}^{x_m}, L_{recon}^{x_n}, L_{recon}^{x_{mnm}}, L_{recon}^{x_{nmn}}$ according to (1), (2);
  Calculate $L_{perc}^{x_m}, L_{perc}^{x_n}, L_{perc}^{x_{mnm}}, L_{perc}^{x_{nmn}}$ according to (3);
  Calculate L_{recon}^c, L_{recon}^s according to (4);
  Calculate $L_{I_{mn}}, L_{I_{nm}}$ according to (5);
  Calculate L_{regu}^s, L_{regu}^c according to (6), (7);
  Update the decoder $\boldsymbol{D}$, the style encoder $\boldsymbol{E}_s$, the content encoder $\boldsymbol{E}_c$, β_m, β_n, and the interpolator $\boldsymbol{I}_{mn}$, $\boldsymbol{I}_{nm}$;
  $n{+}{+}$;

end

---

4   Experiments

In this section we talk about the data sets, baselines, and evaluation metrics that we use for testing our framework.

Data Sets. As in previous research [6,10,12], we use images of shoes and their edge map images, which are generated by [24]. There are 100,000 images of shoes ↔ edges, and 400 images of them are used for testing; the rest are used as the training data set. The cats ↔ dogs data set is provided in [10], which contains about 2,300 images of cats and dogs. We retain 100 images of cats and 100 images of dogs for testing with rest for training.

Baselines. We compare our framework against three baseline models developed in recent years. Our framework is closely related to DRIT and MUNIT, which we use as baseline models. StarGAN-V2 [19] was recently proposed and achieved SOTA results on unpaired I2I translation. Therefore, we use StarGAN-V2 as another baseline in our study.

Evaluation Metrics. We evaluate the visual quality using Frechét inception distance (FID) [25] and the diversity of translated images with learned perceptual image patch similarity (LPIPS) [26]. FID measures the discrepancy between two sets of images. For each test image in the source domain, we translate it into a target domain using 10 reference images randomly sampled from the test set of the target domain. We then calculate FID between the translated images and test images in the target domain. We calculate FID for every pair of image domains (e.g. cat ↔ dog) and report the average value. LPIPS measures the diversity of generated images using the L_1 distance between features extracted from the pretrained AlexNet [30]. For each test image from a source domain, we generate 10 outputs of a target domain using 10 reference images randomly sampled from the test set of the target domain. Then, we compute the average of the pairwise distances among all outputs produced from the same input, which are 45 image pairs. Finally, we report the average of the LPIPS values over all test images. Lower FID values indicate that the two sets of images have similar distributions. Higher values of LPIPS indicate higher diversity of generated images.

Freché't inception distance (FID) [25] and the diversity of translated images with learned perceptual image patch similarity (LPIPS) [26] are commonly used for evaluating I2I translation performance. FID measures the distribution similarity between translation results and test set. LPIPS measures the diversity of generated images. Lower FID values indicate that the two sets of images have similar distributions. Higher values of LPIPS indicate higher diversity of generated images.

5   Results

In this section, we provide the qualitative and quantitative results of the experiments. Ablation study is also provided for evaluating the effectiveness of several key design choices.

Qualitative Results. We show several example translation results by different models in the graph (a) of Fig. 2. To evaluate visual quality of translation results, we utilize the Amazon Mechanical Turk (AMT) to compare our results against the baselines based on user preferences. Given a source image and a reference image, we instruct AMT workers to select the best transfer result among all models. We ask 60 questions for all ten workers. As shown in Table 1, our method slightly outperforms StarGAN-V2 [19] and exceed MUNIT [10] and DRIT [9] for a large margin. Unlike the baselines, which suffer from the issue of discreteness and can only produce one final translation image, our framework can generate sequences of intermediate translation results by interpolating style codes using different translation strengths. The graph (b) in Fig. 2 shows results of translating between the cat and dog domain under different strengths of translation.

Our framework uses $s_m + \alpha * I_{mn}(s_n - s_m)$ during interpolation, which generates smooth-looking intermediate results. Other baselines cannot produce intermediate translation results by default. If we interpolate the style codes linearly using $s_m + \alpha * (s_n - s_m)$, we can see that the translation results by StarGAN-V2 and MUNIT contain artifacts, and the results by DRIT only differ in lighting.

Quantitative Results. The qualitative observations above are confirmed via quantitative evaluations. As Table 2 shows, StarGAN-V2 achieves the lowset FID and highest LPIPS on the `cat2dog` data set among all models, but results by our model are comparable to StarGAN-V2. Translated images by our model on the `edges2shoes` have lower FID and higher LPIPS values than all the baselines.

Table 1. Votes from ATM workers for most preferred style transfer results.

Models	Performance ($\uparrow$)
MUNIT	13.22%
DRIT	15.06%
StarGAN-V2	35.11%
Ours	**36.61%**

Table 2. Quantitative evaluation of image translation using FID and LPIPS. Cat images are translated to dog images, and edges are translated to shoe images.

Metric	Data set	DRIT	MUNIT	StarGAN-V2	Ours
FID ($\downarrow$)	cat2dog	148.87	122.04	**18.81**	21.53
FID ($\downarrow$)	edge2shoes	273.93	274.11	63.78	**61.33**
LPIPS ($\uparrow$)	cat2dog	0.251	0.263	**0.355**	0.341
LPIPS ($\uparrow$)	edge2shoes	0.108	0.110	0.114	**0.126**

Ablation Studies. To further validate effects of key loss functions and design choices in our framework, we carry out ablation studies on the `cat2dog` data set. Let the model without domain-specific information removal (β_m, β_n), interpolators, latent codes regularizers, and noise injection be the naive model. We incrementally add modules to the naive model and calculate FID and LPIPS values. The quantitative evaluations are shown in Table 3, and qualitative results are in Fig. 3.

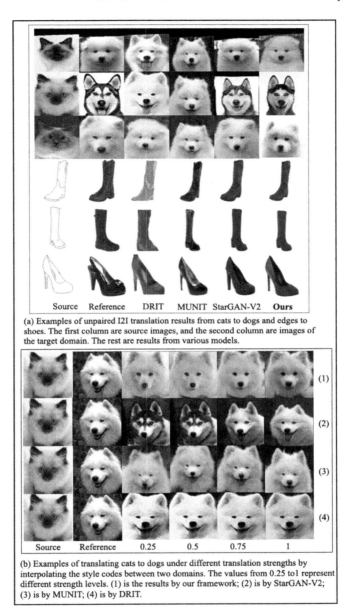

(a) Examples of unpaired I2I translation results from cats to dogs and edges to shoes. The first column are source images, and the second column are images of the target domain. The rest are results from various models.

(b) Examples of translating cats to dogs under different translation strengths by interpolating the style codes between two domains. The values from 0.25 to1 represent different strength levels. (1) is the results by our framework; (2) is by StarGAN-V2; (3) is by MUNIT; (4) is by DRIT.

Fig. 2. Examples of translating results by our framework. (a) compares translation results by different baselines; (b) shows examples of interpolation by all models.

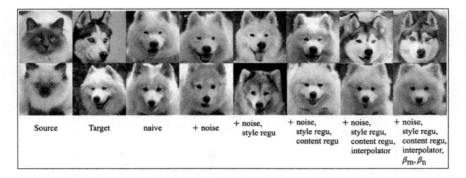

Fig. 3. Ablation study of our framework, which shows examples of translating cats to dogs by incrementally adding modules.

Table 3. FID and LPIPS results of incrementally adding modules to our framework. LPIPS values for the naive model are not reported as it is a deterministic model.

Modules	FID ($\downarrow$)	LPIPS ($\uparrow$)
Naive model	103.30	—
+ Noise injection	76.88	0.326
+ Style regularization	59.21	0.329
+ Content regularization	47.70	0.331
+ Interpolators	30.45	0.333
+ Domain-specific Information elimination	**21.53**	**0.341**

6   Conclusions

In this research, we have presented a new framework for unpaired I2I translation. Our framework proposes fine-grained control over latent codes for achieving better translation results. We show that removing redundant domain-specific information during cross-domain translation helps produce better results. We also show that rather than simply exchanging style codes, an interpolator can help guide the transformation to generate more visually appealing images, which also allows us to produce intermediate translation results. The qualitative results and quantitative evaluations show that our framework is superior than or comparable to the SOTA baselines in unpaired I2I translation.

References

1. Wang, Y., Tao, X., Qi, X., Shen, X., Jia, J.: Image inpainting via generative multi-column convolutional neural networks. In: Advances in Neural Information Processing Systems, Montréal, Canada, pp. 331–340. Curran Associates Inc (2018)

2. Karras, T., Laine, S., Aila, T.: A style-based generator architecture for generative adversarial networks. In: Proceedings of the IEEE/CVF Conference on Computer Vision and Pattern Recognition (CVPR), Long Beach, pp. 4401–4410. IEEE (2019)

3. Karras, T., Laine, S., Aittala, M., Hellsten, J., Lehtinen, J., Aila, T.: Analyzing and improving the image quality of StyleGAN. In: Proceedings of the IEEE/CVF Conference on Computer Vision and Pattern Recognition (CVPR), Seattle, WA, pp. 8110–8119. IEEE (2020)

4. Wang, Z., Chen, J., Hoi, S.C.H.: Deep learning for image super-resolution: a survey. IEEE Trans. Pattern Anal. Mach. Intell. 1 (2020)

5. Chen, Q.-F., Koltun, V.: Photographic image synthesis with cascaded refinement networks. In: Proceedings of the IEEE/CVF Conference on Computer Vision and Pattern Recognition (CVPR), Honolulu, Hawaii, pp. 1511–1520. IEEE (2017)

6. Isola, P., Zhu, J.-Y., Zhou, T.-H., Efros, A.A.: Image-to-image translation with conditional adversarial networks. In: Proceedings of the IEEE/CVF Conference on Computer Vision and Pattern Recognition (CVPR), Honolulu, Hawaii, pp. 5967–5976. IEEE (2017)

7. Zhu, J.-Y., Park, T., Isola, P., Efros A.A.: Unpaired image-to-image translation using cycle-consistent adversarial networks. In: 2017 IEEE International Conference on Computer Vision (ICCV), Venice, Italy, pp. 2242–2251. IEEE (2017)

8. Chang, H.-Y., Wang, Z., Chuang, Y.-Y.: Domain-specific mappings for generative adversarial style transfer. In: Vedaldi, A., Bischof, H., Brox, T., Frahm, J.-M. (eds.) ECCV 2020. LNCS, vol. 12353, pp. 573–589. Springer, Cham (2020). https://doi.org/10.1007/978-3-030-58598-3_34

9. Lee, H.-Y., Tseng, H.-Y., Huang, J.-B., Singh, M., Yang, M.-H.: Diverse image-to-image translation via disentangled representations. In: Ferrari, V., Hebert, M., Sminchisescu, C., Weiss, Y. (eds.) ECCV 2018. LNCS, vol. 11205, pp. 36–52. Springer, Cham (2018). https://doi.org/10.1007/978-3-030-01246-5_3

10. Huang, X., Liu, M.-Y., Belongie, S., Kautz, J.: Multimodal unsupervised image-to-image translation. In: Ferrari, V., Hebert, M., Sminchisescu, C., Weiss, Y. (eds.) ECCV 2018. LNCS, vol. 11207, pp. 179–196. Springer, Cham (2018). https://doi.org/10.1007/978-3-030-01219-9_11

11. Goodfellow, I.J., et al.: Generative adversarial nets. In: Proceedings of the 27th International Conference on Neural Information Processing Systems, pp. 2672–2680. MIT Press, Montreal (2014)

12. Zhu, J.-Y., Krähenbühl, P., Shechtman, E., Efros, A.A.: Generative visual manipulation on the natural image manifold. In: Leibe, B., Matas, J., Sebe, N., Welling, M. (eds.) ECCV 2016. LNCS, vol. 9909, pp. 597–613. Springer, Cham (2016). https://doi.org/10.1007/978-3-319-46454-1_36

13. Denton, E.L., Chintala, S., Szlam, A., Fergus, B.: Deep generative image models using a laplacian pyramid of adversarial networks. In: Proceedings of the 28th International Conference on Neural Information Processing Systems, Montreal, Canada, pp. 1486–149. MIT Press (2015)

14. Zhao, T, Mathieu, M., LeCun, Y.: Energy-based generative adversarial networks. In: 5th International Conference on Learning Representations (ICLR), Toulon, France (2017). OpenReview.net

15. Arjovsky, M., Chintala, S., Bottou, L.: Wasserstein generative adversarial networks. In: Proceedings of the 34th International Conference on Machine Learning (ICML), Stockholm, Sweden, pp. 214–223. PMLR (2017)

16. Berthelot, D., Schumm, T., Metz, L.: BEGAN: boundary equilibrium generative adversarial networks. CoRR abs (1703.10717) (2017)

17. Kim, T., Cha, M., Kim, H., Lee, J.-K., Kim, J.: Learning to discover cross-domain relations with generative adversarial networks. In: Proceedings of the 34th International Conference on Machine Learning (ICML), Sydney, NSW, Australia, pp. 1857–1865. PMLR (2017)

18. Yi, Z.-L., Zhang, H., Tan, P., Gong, M.-L.: DualGAN: unsupervised dual learning for image-to-image translation. In: 2017 IEEE International Conference on Computer Vision (ICCV), Venice, Italy, pp. 2868–2876. IEEE (2017)

19. Choi, Y., Uh, Y.-J., Yoo, J., Ha, J.-W.: StarGAN v2: diverse image synthesis for multiple domains. In: Proceedings of the IEEE/CVF Conference on Computer Vision and Pattern Recognition (CVPR), Seattle, WA, pp. 8185–8194. IEEE (2020)

20. Zhao, B., Chang, B., Jie, Z., Sigal, L.: Modular generative adversarial networks. In: Ferrari, V., Hebert, M., Sminchisescu, C., Weiss, Y. (eds.) Computer Vision – ECCV 2018. LNCS, vol. 11218, pp. 157–173. Springer, Cham (2018). https://doi.org/10.1007/978-3-030-01264-9_10

21. Huang, X., Belongie, S.-J.: Arbitrary style transfer in real-time with adaptive instance normalization. In: 2017 IEEE International Conference on Computer Vision (ICCV), Venice, Italy, pp. 1510–1519. IEEE (2017)

22. He, K.-M., Zhang, X.-Y., Ren, S.-Q., Sun, J.: Deep residual learning for image recognition. In: Proceedings of the IEEE/CVF Conference on Computer Vision and Pattern Recognition (CVPR), Las Vegas, NV, pp. 770–778. IEEE (2016)

23. Ulyanov, D., Vedaldi, A., Lempitsky, V.S.: Improved texture networks: maximizing quality and diversity in feed-forward stylization and texture synthesis. In: Proceedings of the IEEE/CVF Conference on Computer Vision and Pattern Recognition (CVPR), Honolulu, HI, pp. 4105–4113. IEEE (2017)

24. Xie, S.-N., Tu, Z.-W: Holistically-nested edge detection. In: 2015 IEEE International Conference on Computer Vision (ICCV), Santiago, Chile, pp. 1395–1403. IEEE (2015)

25. Heusel, M., Ramsauer, H., Unterthiner, T., Nessler, B., Hochreiter, S.: GANs trained by a two time-scale update rule converge to a local nash equilibrium. In: Advances in Neural Information Processing Systems, Long Beach, CA, pp. 6626–6637. Curran Associates Inc (2017)

26. Zhang, R., Isola, P., Efros, A.A., Shechtman, E., Wang, O.: The unreasonable effectiveness of deep features as a perceptual metric. In: Proceedings of the IEEE/CVF Conference on Computer Vision and Pattern Recognition (CVPR), Salt Lake City, UT, pp. 586–595. IEEE (2018)

27. Johnson, J., Alahi, A., Fei-Fei, L.: Perceptual losses for real-time style transfer and super-resolution. In: Leibe, B., Matas, J., Sebe, N., Welling, M. (eds.) ECCV 2016. LNCS, vol. 9906, pp. 694–711. Springer, Cham (2016). https://doi.org/10.1007/978-3-319-46475-6_43

28. Yang, J.-W., Kannan, A., Batra, D., Parikh, D.: LR-GAN: layered recursive generative adversarial networks for image generation. In: 5th International Conference on Learning Representations (ICLR), Toulon, France (2017). OpenReview.net

29. Wang, T.-C., Liu, M.-Y., Zhu, J.-Y., Kautz, J., Catanzaro, B.: High-resolution image synthesis and semantic manipulation with conditional GANs. In: Proceedings of the IEEE/CVF Conference on Computer Vision and Pattern Recognition (CVPR), Salt Lake City, UT, pp. 8798–8807. IEEE (2018)

30. Krizhevsky, A., Sutskever, I., Hinton, G.: ImageNet classification with deep convolutional neural networks. In: Proceedings of the 25th International Conference on Neural Information Processing Systems, Lake Tahoe, Nevada, pp. 1106–1114. MIT Press (2012)

FMSNet: Underwater Image Restoration by Learning from a Synthesized Dataset

Xiangyu Yin[1]([✉]) [ID], Xiaohong Liu[2] [ID], and Huan Liu[2]

[1] Guilin University of Electronic Technology, Guilin, China
`yinx36@mcmaster.ca`
[2] McMaster University, Hamilton, Canada

Abstract. Underwater images suffer from various degradation, which can significantly lower the visual quality and the accuracy of subsequent applications. Moreover, the artificial light source tends to invalidate many image restoration algorithms. In this paper, an underwater image restoration (UIR) method using a novel Convolutional Neural Network (CNN) architecture and a synthesized underwater dataset is proposed. We discuss the reason for the over enhancement that exists in current UIR methods and revise the underwater image formation model (IFM) to alleviate the problem. With the revised IFM, we proposed an underwater image synthesizing method that can create a realistic underwater dataset. In order to effectively conduct end-to-end supervised learning, we design a network based on the characteristics of image restoration tasks, namely FMSNet. Different from existing networks, the decomposition and fusion operation in FMSNet can process the feature maps more efficiently and improve the contrast more prominently. The UIR method built by FMSNet can directly recover the degraded underwater images without the need of any pre-processing and post-processing. The experimental results indicate that FMSNet performs favorably against the widely used network architectures and our UIR method can outperform the state-of-the-art methods on both qualitative and quantitative evaluations. Comparing with the original underwater images, the experiments carried out by subsequent mission shows that 285% more feature points can be detected in the restored images by using our method.

Keywords: Neural network · Image restoration · CNN architecture · Image formation model

1 Introduction

Underwater Image restoration (UIR) can significantly improve image quality and the performance of computer vision algorithms in the underwater environment. Developed UIR algorithms can also contribute to the development of marine robotics, marine geology, marine biology, and many marine industries. Although countless UIR algorithms are proposed to achieve the restoration, many of them tend to give rise to partly over enhancement, because of the influence of artificial illumination sources. Thus, Lu et al. [1] consider absorption, scattering, and artificial lighting as three major distortion issues

© Springer Nature Switzerland AG 2021
I. Farkaš et al. (Eds.): ICANN 2021, LNCS 12893, pp. 421–432, 2021.
https://doi.org/10.1007/978-3-030-86365-4_34

in the underwater environment. Through experimental observations, we discover that many cases can cause the over-enhancement issue despite no extra artificial luminance used. We attribute the over-enhancement issue to the nonhomogeneous background light, which particularly can be induced by artificial illuminance sources. Nonhomogeneous background light may also appear in other circumstances, such as the underwater land-forms where can shelter the light and the wide-angle photographs where the certain area of the water body is brighter than the seabed.

The underwater image formation model (IFM) developed in [2] and [3] is a prevalently used mathematical model demonstrating the underwater imaging process:

$$I_c(x) = J_c(x)T_c(x) + A_c(1 - T_c(x)) \tag{1}$$

where x is the coordinate of a pixel and $c \in \{R, G, B\}$ is a color channel. $J_c(x)$ and $I_c(x)$ denote the clear object scene radiance and the degraded underwater image. A_c denotes the global ambient light. $T_c(x)$ is the transmission map that represents the residual energy ratio of the scene radiance after the transmission. In this IFM (1), the ambient light A_c is a global value where people assume that the background light is uniform in the whole scene. The neglection of the nonhomogeneous light is one of the reasons that model-based UIR methods tend to suffer from over enhancement.

In addition, most of the deep learning networks are mainly designed by inheriting the classic architectures proposed for the task of image classification or target detection, such as the VGG and the Inception network. There are relatively few CNN architectures partic-ularly designed for end-to-end image transformation. Hence, it is meaningful to design a network architecture that is suitable for the characteristics of image transformation tasks, like image restoration based on supervised learning.

In this paper, we aim to propose a novel CNN network architecture, namely FMSNet, by which we can create a systematic method to recover underwater images with the ability to circumvent the problem of over enhancement and improving the performance of UIR. We revised the traditional underwater IFM by adding an extra item to denote the nonhomogeneous light. And an underwater image synthesizing method is designed to simulate various degraded underwater environments and create an underwater dataset. With the synthesized underwater dataset, we establish a supervised learning framework to train the FMSNet. The FMSNet with frequency-based feature separation and fusion structure is designed based on the characteristics of image restoration tasks and the human visual optimization behaviors. By the convolutional operation with frozen Gaussian convolution kernel, the feature maps can be decomposed into low and high-frequency components and processed efficiently and pertinently.

2   Related Work

Model-Based Underwater Image Restoration. Most model-based methods [4–7] fol-low the scheme of estimating the variables, like ambient light A_c and transmission map $T_c(x)$, then calculate the restored images by the underwater IFM (1). As the estimations from a single degraded image is considered as an ill-post inverse problem, effective prior information tends to be necessary for these methods. The underwater light atten-uation prior (ULAP) [4] is proposed for the estimation of the depth map and A_c. The underwater dark channel prior (UDCP) [5] modifies the Dark channel prior (DCP) [6] by the consideration of the divergency of underwater light attenuation to estimate the $T_c(x)$. Li et al. [7] estimate the variables by minimizing the information loss in the red channel. Model-based methods can markedly improve the contrast and reduce the scattering effect. However, specific priors will inevitably fail in certain cases and lead to incorrect estimation. Moreover, the reliance on the traditional IFM often results in over-enhancement or over compensatory failure for these methods.

Learning-Based Underwater Image Restoration. Learning-based methods [8-12] tend to train a neural network to learn the map between the distorted images and its corresponding clear version from a large amount of data. Hence, the main issue to resolve is the requirement of the paired datasets. Fabbri et al. [8] use real underwater images to train a CycleGAN [9], which can generate the degraded version of good quality underwater images. Furthermore, Islam et al. [10] apply a dataset generated by the method of [8] to their proposed FUnIE-GAN network architecture to obtain the recovered results. However, generating datasets using the style-transform ability of GAN is extremely inefficient, because one well-trained GAN can only generate one type of distortion. On the contrary, Li et al. [11] synthesize underwater images directly from the simplified underwater IFM, and the UWCNN network is designed to achieve better restoration performance with end-to-end training. Wang et al. [12] fuse the prior information into the process of the image synthesizing and two CNN frameworks are designed to learn the estimation of the A_c and $T_c(x)$ respectively. Learning-based methods are relatively robust, but the performance of the results is restrained by the quality of datasets and the performance of the CNN architectures.

3   Proposed Method

3.1   Synthesizing Underwater Dataset

Our dataset synthesizing method roughly follows the process of [11], by which we can efficiently simulate underwater data from a clear depth map dataset (RGBD dataset). In our method, the randomly generated variables for IFM can ensure the diversity of synthesized data. To synthesize underwater datasets that take nonhomogeneous light conditions into account, we revise the underwater IFM by adding an extra item to simulate the nonhomogeneous background light. Once the synthesized underwater dataset can simulate the appearance of the nonhomogeneous light, the neural network trained by the dataset will be able to learn the way to eliminate the effect:

$$I_c(x) = J_c(x)T_c(x) + A_c(1 - T_c(x)) + \eta N(x) \qquad (2)$$

where $N(x)$ denotes the nonhomogeneous light component, η is the weight of the $N(x)$. Considering that the nonhomogeneous light should be a smoothed signal with a gentle changed gradient, we use Perlin noise to simulate it. The Perlin noise is configured as 2-dimension noise with only one noise cycle. We randomly generate 1000 Perlin noises as the set for $N(x)$. Besides, we randomly generate η in the range of (0.2, 0.4) with uniform distribution. In some cases, the nonhomogeneous background light does not exist, so we set 30% of the η as 0. A_c is the ambient light scattered into the sight, which is considered as the homogeneous component of background light with three global values for RGB channels. For the best simulation of A_c, we propose to use the ambient light values from real-world underwater images. Specifically, we use the ULAP [4] to calculate the ambient light in a real-world underwater dataset that can comprehensively cover various water types. Therefore, nearly 1000 groups of ambient light values, A_r, A_g, A_b, are obtained. Before using these values in the synthesizing process, we multiply them by a random jittering generated from a Gaussian distribution. The transmission map $T_c(x)$ is important, which can be expressed as:

$$T_c(x) = e^{-p_\lambda^c d(x)} \tag{3}$$

where p_λ^c is the attenuation coefficient and the $d(x)$ is the distance between the object and the camera. We followed the approach in [7] to generate $T_c(x)$, in which we generated the p_λ^c of the blue channel in the uniform distribution between 1 and 3.

We randomly draw an $N(x)$ and A_c in the set of nonhomogeneous background light and the set of ambient light. Based on Eq. (2) and the variables mentioned above, we can synthesize the underwater images from any RGBD images. To avoid the overexposure phenomenon brought by the additional $N(x)$, an adaptive rule is applied to the value of η. To be specific, we calculate the proportion of white pixels before and after adding the $\eta N(x)$, and mark them as p_o and p_N. If $p_N - p_o \geq 0.1$, we reset the $\eta = \eta * 0.6$ until the $p_N - p_o < 0.1$ or $\eta < 0.1$. We visually illustrate the images synthesized by our method in Fig. 1. The synthesized images can simulate both the color characteristics and the light conditions of realistic underwater scenes.

Fig. 1. The synthesized underwater images of our method

3.2   Proposed FMSNet CNN Framework

The advanced visual system of humans can easily distinguish objects from distorted scenes. Goffaux et al. [18] found that the effect of a low-pass filtered object on the holistic face perception for humans is significantly larger than the high-pass filtered object. On the other hand, most of the hazy and turbid distortions are appeared in the low-frequency components of an underwater photograph, while most information expected to be preserved, like edges and textures, exists in the high-frequency components. Hence, if we hope a neural network can do the restoration job as well as humans, we should guide low spatial frequencies and high spatial frequencies to different paths. We propose a novel CNN structure, namely FMSNet, which embodies the frequency-based decomposition and fusion operations for feature maps. The FMSNet consists of three parts: downsampling, backbone, and upsampling.

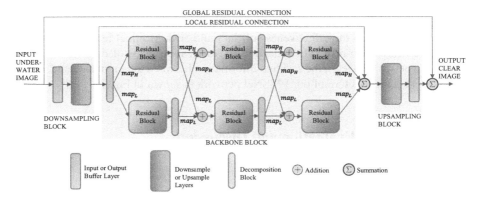

Fig. 2. Architecture of the proposed network

Downsampling and Upsampling Block. The downsampling and upsampling blocks roughly follow the architecture of [14], where there is a convolutional buffer layer with a large receptive field of the inputs for performing the trainable pre-processing and post-processing. In the sampling blocks, we use two stride-2 convolutional layers for downsampling and two stride-1/2 transposed convolutional layers for upsampling of the feature maps. With these blocks, we can save the computational cost and lay the foundation for the subsequent processing. All the convolutional layers use 3∗3 kernels, except for the buffer layers who use 9∗9 kernels.

Decomposition Block. In the backbone of the FMSNet, we introduce the operation of Gaussian filtering to partition the feature maps into low and high-frequency components. The filtering is performed by a convolutional operation with a pre-set Gaussian kernel. The configuration of the Gaussian kernel is treated as a hyperparameter. In our implementation, we set the kernel size as $15 * 15$ pixels and the gaussian standard deviation as 2.75 for both x and y-directions. The parameters in the kernel are frozen, which will not affect the gradient descent process. With the reflected padding, the filtering will not change the shape of the feature maps. The results of the filtering are the low-frequency components of the feature maps, denoted by map_L. To refrain from the information loss, map_L is subtracted by the original feature maps synchronously to receive the high-frequency feature maps, denoted by map_H. The operation above is merged as a decomposition block in the backbone block.

Backbone Block. Since the output image should share structure with the input for the image restoration task, the residual learning is employed in the backbone block. As the certified performance, we adopt the residual block designed in [15] for feature processing, where there are two convolutional layers with residual connection. All the convolutional layers use $3 * 3$ kernels. We adjust the batch normalization to instance normalization which can significantly improve the quality of feedforward. The body of FMSNet thus consists of the alternate decomposition blocks and residual blocks. The map_L and map_H from decomposition blocks will be processed by different residual blocks and crosswise fused to reduce the number of maps. The output of the last pair of residual blocks are summed and propagated to the upsampling block.

In addition, due to the effectiveness of the multi-scale residual learning presented in [16], we design two residual connection for the feature maps of different levels to enforce the network to learn the residual information between the input side and output side. The exact architecture of our FMSNet network is shown in Fig. 2.

4   Experimental Evaluation and Discussion

4.1   Datasets and Training Strategy

Training and Testing Dataset. Synthesizing realistic underwater images to compose a training and testing dataset with high generalization capability is a crucial step. We use the RGBD dataset from [17] with 600 outdoor in-street scenes to synthesize the underwater dataset. On the other hand, the network will learn the explicit/implicit statistical relationship between the degraded images and their ground truth [18]. If there are too many scenes with different features in the ground-truth targets, the network may confuse about the features of its output, which is not conducive to the one-way training of the network. Hence, we only select 200 images that have consistent features of high contrast and appropriate luminance among the RGBD dataset. We synthesize 8 underwater images with different parameters for each RGBD image. Thus, there are only 1600 underwater images in our training and testing dataset.

Training Strategy. We use the summation of L1 loss and the weighted multi-scale structural similarity (MS-SSIM) loss in [19] as the loss functions to achieve supervised learning for the FMSNet. We randomly set 80% of the synthesized data as the training set, and the others as the testing set. For the augmentation of the training set, we crop a patch of $400 * 400$ pixels at a random position of the training samples, and we resize the images who smaller than the size to $400 * 400$. Moreover, we set three types of transforms to augment the training set: horizontal flipping, vertical flipping, and rotate $90°$. Each of them may happen in a probability of 30% on the training set.

The network is initialized by the normal distribution. We set the batch size as 10 and train the network for 100 epochs. The Adam optimizer with β_1 and β_2 of default values is used to accelerate the training. The learning rate is set as 0.002 initially, and we decrease it by half when the epoch number reaches the milestones of 25, 45, 60, 70, 80, 90. The process of the training is performed on a PC with two NVIDIA GeForce GTX 1080Ti GPU and Xeon(R) Gold 5218 CPU.

4.2 Network Performance

To demonstrate the performance of the FMSNet, we reimplement the widely used network architectures, the ResNet [14] and the GridDehazeNet [18], as baselines. All the models are trained by our synthesized training set for 100 epochs. Since the loss function is the summation of L1 loss and MS-SSIM loss, we compare the PSNR and SSIM metrics on both the training set and the testing set to show the loss function minimizing process of the three networks. Figure 3(left) depicts the PSNR curves, where the PSNR of both the training set and testing set for FMSNet are significantly higher than the other models all over the epochs. In Fig. 3(right), the GridDehazeNet achieves highest SSIM curve because of its multi-scale structure. The SSIM curves of the other networks are extremely similar, where FMSNet's SSIM curves are slightly higher. The experimental results demonstrate that the proposed FMSNet performs favorably against the widely used baseline networks for end-to-end training. With the help of the decomposition and fusion structure, the FMSNet is particularly sensitive to the pixel-level loss function, like L1, which leads to the rapid convergence and the best PSNR of 26.8 dB on the training set and 26.2 dB on the testing set.

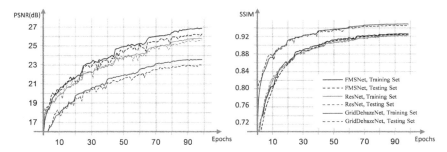

Fig. 3. The PSNR and SSIM curves trained by our network and the baseline networks

4.3 Evaluation on Synthesized Underwater Images

The FMSNet trained by our synthesized underwater dataset can directly recover any degraded underwater images. By which, we can conveniently construct a UIR method without the need of any pre-processing or post-processing. For the evaluation of the restoring performance, we synthesize extra underwater images from the OTS dataset in RESIDE [20], which is never observed by our model. We use the synthesized underwater images to evaluate the restoring results of our method and several state-of-the-art UIR methods, including ULAP in [4], UDCP in [5], the method in [7], FUnIE-GAN in [10], and UWCNN in [11]. We compare the restoring results in Fig. 4.

According to Fig. 4, although the clarity can be improved, the results of [7] and UDCP prone to over enhancement the light and overcompensate the color. Similarly, the first image of column (e) can be restored by ULAP, but it is nearly invalid for the other images. (f) and (g) are from learning-based methods, thus their performances in different scenarios are relatively stable. The contrast ratio of every result from UWCNN gets increased, while the original color saturation is completely dropped. The FUnIE-GAN's restoration can correct the color significantly, nevertheless, the hazy effect cannot be eliminated completely. In contrast, the results of our method in (h) can produce the best clarity and free of the major turbid distortion.

We treat the images before appending the underwater effect as the reference to evaluate the restoration ability of the methods. The Peak Signal-to-Noise Ratio (PSNR), Structural Similarity (SSIM), and Color-Difference Formula CIEDE2000 are used as the quantitate metrics. Table 1 shows the comparison of the metrics and the best numbers are bolded. Our method performs the best result for all the metrics.

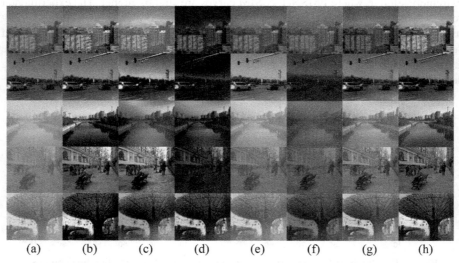

(a)   (b)   (c)   (d)   (e)   (f)   (g)   (h)

Fig. 4. Comparison on synthesized images: (a) the synthesized images; (b) the corresponding reference images; (c) the method of [7]; (d) the method by UDCP; (e) the method by ULAP; (f) the method by UWCNN; (g) the method by FUnIE-GAN; (h) our proposed method

Table 1. Comparison of the methods on quantitate metrics

Method	Method [7]	UDCP	ULAP	FUnIE-GAN	UWCNN	Our method
PSNR	14.44	12.24	11.01	14.99	12.87	**18.70**
SSIM	0.75	0.69	0.66	0.78	0.58	**0.87**
CIEDE 2000	20.63	23.17	28.39	20.80	22.84	**14.14**

4.4 Evaluation on Real-World Underwater Images

Evaluating the algorithms on real-world underwater images is the hinge to validate their performance and generalization ability. We collect 80 various real underwater images carrying serious distortion. 60 of them are from the challenging dataset of [13] and the rest are collected from the internet. Figure 5 presents the visual comparison of the restoration results on the real-world underwater images.

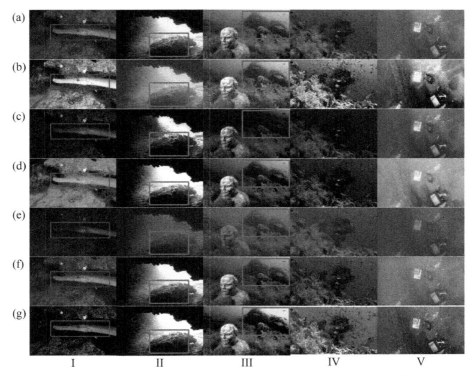

(a)

(b)

(c)

(d)

(e)

(f)

(g)

I   II   III   IV   V

Fig. 5. Evaluation on the real-word images: (a) the real-world underwater images; (b) the method of [7]; (c) the method by UDCP; (d) the method by ULAP; (e) the method by UWCNN; (f) the method by FUnIE-GAN; (g) our proposed method

According to the images in the row (b), the results of [7] can balance the color distribution and the contrast ratio to a large extent. But the manifest over enhancement and oversaturation are also produced in images I, II, and III because of the ignoration of the nonhomogeneous light in their model. The prior of UDCP and ULAP in the row of (c) and (d) succeed in removing the foggy noise utterly but tend to drastically change the original color distribution and darken the brightness. The loss of their effectiveness is due to the fact that their specific priors can hardly adapt to these lighting conditions. Comparing with UDCP, the method by UWCNN in (e) can maximumly eliminate the color distortion, but the beneficial color information is destroyed too. Owing to the using of a real underwater dataset in the method of FUnIE-GAN, the results in (f) look limpid and natural, whereas the degree of removing scattering effect is still not enough. The reason is maybe relative to the architecture of their neural network. By contrast, our method can enhance the best visibility and the relatively pleasing color distribution.

Thanks to the consideration of the nonhomogeneous light condition in our method, we have fewer over-enhancement areas. By the comparison of the marked region of I, II, and III, we can figure out much more haze-free details and actual information in (g), which is contributed by the FMSNet architecture. For the quantitate evaluation of the results, we use two non-reference metrics, Underwater Image Quality Metric (UIQM) and Blind/Referenceless Image Spatial Quality Evaluator (BRISQUE), on the 80 restoration results. Smaller BRISQUE means better naturalness and larger UIQM means better comprehensive quality. In Table 2, we list the average scores of the different methods and bold the best scores. Our method gets the best score for UIQM and the second-best score for BRISQUE.

Table 2. Comparison on real-world testing set with non-reference metrics and feature points matching

Algorithms	Non-reference Metrics		Matched feature points number				
	UIQM	BRISQUE	Image I	Image II	Image III	AVG	INC (%)
Original	1.24	39.17	64	134	32	76	0%
Method [7]	2.76	34.00	412	226	83	240	213.71%
UDCP	2.15	40.02	187	99	60	115	50.52%
ULAP	1.83	38.17	217	180	53	150	95.82%
UWCNN	2.11	43.78	91	80	24	65	−15.14%
FUnIE-GAN	2.16	**23.59**	209	184	64	152	98.82%
Our method	**3.13**	23.78	**489**	**272**	**119**	**293**	**285.52%**

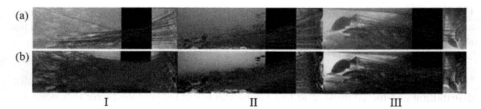

Fig. 6. Experiment of SIFT feature points matching: (a) is for the original underwater images; (b) is for the restoration results of our method

4.5 Evaluation by the Subsequent Application

In this experiment, we indirectly measure and compare the quality of the restorations by observing that how much the restoring results can improve the performance of the subsequent algorithm. The feature point detecting and matching by SIFT algorithm [21] is implemented on the restoration results of Sect. 4.4. We choose three typical underwater scenes with fish groups and rugged seabed as testing objections (I, II, III). These images are rotated and zoomed in to format the paired targets for feature points matching. Figure 6. shows the matching lines on the original underwater images and the restored images of our method. The more feature points that can be detected and matched means the more information is reserved in the image. Therefore, we list the matched number of the feature points of each image in Table 2. The AVG is the average number for the three examples and the INC shows the improvement comparing with the original underwater images. From Table 2, our method gets the highest number of feature points for all the examples, which shows that the results of our method can grab more detailed information. After the restoration by our method, the average number of the matched feature points increased by 285.52%.

5 Conclusion

In this paper, we presented an underwater image restoration method based on an end-to-end CNN model and a synthesized underwater dataset. The proposed CNN architecture, FMSNet, showed promising performance on image restoration tasks. Comparing with the baseline models, the FMSNet can efficiently perform supervised learning. We also gave an explanation about the over enhancement caused by artificial luminance for the existed methods. To circumvent the effect of nonhomogeneous background light, we revised the IFM and designed a new underwater image synthesizing method, by which we can create realistic underwater datasets for network training. The experimental evaluations indicate that our restoration method can significantly improve the quality of underwater images and refrain from the effect of over enhancement. The experiment by SIFT algorithm shows that our restoration method can increase the matched feature points number by 285%.

In the FMSNet, we designed a decomposition block to separate the feature maps into two components by fixed Gaussian filtering, which sheds some light on future works about more appropriate ways to modify the decomposition block, such as introducing the multi-scale Gaussian filtering or random-scale Gaussian filtering.

Acknowledgements. The work is supported by the study abroad program for graduate student of Guilin University of Electronic Technology.

References

1. Lu, H., et al.: Underwater image enhancement method using weighted guided trigonometric filtering and artificial light correction. J. Vis. Commun. Image Represent. **38**, 504–516 (2016). https://doi.org/10.1016/j.jvcir.2016.03.029
2. Chiang, J.Y., Chen, Y.-C.: Underwater image enhancement by wavelength compensation and dehazing. IEEE Trans. Image Process. **21**(4), 1756–1769 (2012). https://doi.org/10.1109/TIP.2011.2179666
3. Schechner, Y.Y., Karpel, N.: Recovery of underwater visibility and structure by polarization analysis. IEEE J. Oceanic Eng. **30**, 570–587 (2005). https://doi.org/10.1109/JOE.2005.850871

4. Song, W., Wang, Y., Huang, D., Tjondronegoro, D.: A rapid scene depth estimation model based on underwater light attenuation prior for underwater image restoration. In: Hong, R., Cheng, W.-H., Yamasaki, T., Wang, M., Ngo, C.-W. (eds.) PCM 2018. LNCS, vol. 11164, pp. 678–688. Springer, Cham (2018). https://doi.org/10.1007/978-3-030-00776-8_62

5. Drews, Jr., P., Nascimento, E., Moraes, F., Botelho, S., Campos, M.: Transmission estimation in underwater single images. In: 2013 IEEE International Conference on Computer Vision Workshops, pp. 825–830 (2013)

6. He, K., Sun, J., Tang, X.: Single image haze removal using dark channel prior. IEEE Trans. Pattern Anal. Mach. Intell. **33**, 2341–2353 (2011). https://doi.org/10.1109/TPAMI.2010.168

7. Li, C.-Y., Guo, J.-C., Cong, R.-M., Pang, Y.-W., Wang, B.: Underwater image enhancement by dehazing with minimum information loss and histogram distribution prior. IEEE Trans. on Image Process. **25**, 5664–5677 (2016). https://doi.org/10.1109/TIP.2016.2612882

8. Fabbri, C., Islam, M.J., Sattar, J.: Enhancing underwater imagery using generative adversarial networks. In: 2018 IEEE International Conference on Robotics and Automation (ICRA), pp. 7159–7165. IEEE, Brisbane (2018)

9. Zhu, J.-Y., Park, T., Isola, P., Efros, A.A.: Unpaired image-to-image translation using cycle-consistent adversarial networks. In: 2017 IEEE International Conference on Computer Vision (ICCV), pp. 2242–2251 (2017)

10. Islam, M.J., Xia, Y., Sattar, J.: Fast underwater image enhancement for improved visual perception. IEEE Robot. Autom. Lett. **5**, 3227–3234 (2020). https://doi.org/10.1109/LRA.2020.2974710

11. Li, C., Anwar, S., Porikli, F.: Underwater scene prior inspired deep underwater image and video enhancement. Pattern Recogn. **98**, 107038 (2020). https://doi.org/10.1016/j.patcog.2019.107038

12. Wang, K., Hu, Y., Chen, J., Wu, X., Zhao, X., Li, Y.: Underwater image restoration based on a parallel convolutional neural network. Remote Sens. **11**, 1591 (2019). https://doi.org/10.3390/rs11131591

13. Li, C., et al.: An underwater image enhancement benchmark dataset and beyond. arXiv:1901.05495 (2019)

14. Johnson, J., Alahi, A., Fei-Fei, L.: Perceptual losses for real-time style transfer and super-resolution. In: Leibe, B., Matas, J., Sebe, N., Welling, M. (eds.) ECCV 2016. LNCS, vol. 9906, pp. 694–711. Springer, Cham (2016). https://doi.org/10.1007/978-3-319-46475-6_43

15. He, K., Zhang, X., Ren, S., Sun, J.: Deep residual learning for image recognition. In: 2016 IEEE Conference on Computer Vision and Pattern Recognition (CVPR), pp. 770–778 (2016)

16. Zhang, Y., Tian, Y., Kong, Y., Zhong, B., Fu, Y.: Residual dense network for image super-resolution. arXiv:1802.08797 (2018)

17. Li, R., Cheong, L.-F., Tan, R.T.: Heavy rain image restoration: integrating physics model and conditional adversarial learning. In: 2019 IEEE/CVF Conference on Computer Vision and Pattern Recognition (CVPR), pp. 1633–1642. IEEE, Long Beach (2019)

18. Liu, X., Ma, Y., Shi, Z., Chen, J.: GridDehazeNet: attention-based multi-scale network for image dehazing. In: 2019 IEEE/CVF International Conference on Computer Vision (ICCV), pp. 7313–7322. IEEE, Seoul (2019)

19. Zhao, H., Gallo, O., Frosio, I., Kautz, J.: Loss functions for neural networks for image processing. arXiv:1511.08861 (2018)

20. Li, B., et al.: Benchmarking single-image dehazing and beyond. IEEE Trans. Image Process. **28**, 492–505 (2019). https://doi.org/10.1109/TIP.2018.2867951

21. Dai, C., Lin, M., Wang, Z., Zhang, D., Guan, Z.: Color compensation based on bright channel and fusion for underwater image enhancement. Acta Optica Sinica. **38**, 1110003 (2018)

Towards Measuring Bias in Image Classification

Nina Schaaf[1]([⊠]) [iD], Omar de Mitri[1,3], Hang Beom Kim[1],
Alexander Windberger[2], and Marco F. Huber[1,4] [iD]

[1] Fraunhofer IPA, Stuttgart, Germany
{nina.schaaf,omar.de.mitri,hang.beom.kim,marco.huber}@ipa.fraunhofer.de
[2] IDS Imaging Development Systems GmbH, Obersulm, Germany
r.windberger@ids-imaging.de
[3] CNR Institute of Applied Sciences and Intelligent Systems, Lecce, Italy
[4] Institute of Industrial Manufacturing and Management IFF,
University of Stuttgart, Stuttgart, Germany

Abstract. Convolutional Neural Networks (CNN) have become *de facto* state-of-the-art for the main computer vision tasks. However, due to the complex underlying structure their decisions are hard to understand which limits their use in some context of the industrial world. A common and hard to detect challenge in machine learning (ML) tasks is data bias. In this work, we present a systematic approach to uncover data bias by means of attribution maps. For this purpose, first an artificial dataset with a known bias is created and used to train intentionally biased CNNs. The networks' decisions are then inspected using attribution maps. Finally, meaningful metrics are used to measure the attribution maps' representativeness with respect to the known bias. The proposed study shows that some attribution map techniques highlight the presence of bias in the data better than others and metrics can support the identification of bias.

Keywords: Interpretability · Image classification · Data bias

1 Introduction

Repeatedly, cases surface in which algorithms have made biased decisions. One example are biased models for the detection of diseases[1]. Algorithmic bias, when undetected, can have unwanted and potentially severe consequences—most often for humans that are directly or indirectly affected. If the data used to train an ML algorithm is biased this will be reflected in the final result. For these reasons it is necessary to extensively validate ML models before deploying them.

Support by the State Ministry of Baden-Wuerttemberg for Economic Affairs, Labour and Housing Construction under the grant KI-Fortschrittszentrum "Lernende Systeme", grant No. 036-170017.

[1] https://medium.com/@jrzech/what-are-radiological-deep-learning-models-actually-learning-f97a546c5b98, accessed on March 25, 2021.

© Springer Nature Switzerland AG 2021
I. Farkaš et al. (Eds.): ICANN 2021, LNCS 12893, pp. 433–445, 2021.
https://doi.org/10.1007/978-3-030-86365-4_35

However, especially deep neural networks, are of opaque nature due to their non-linear structures (*black boxes*). In order to interpret these black box models, they can for example be analyzed through feature attribution techniques. Attribution maps can help to understand image classification models, such as CNNs, by visualizing the importance of each individual pixel of the input image for the prediction. For example, data bias can manifest by diverting the CNNs' attention towards irrelevant background contents or unintended image objects. Such biases can be rather subtle in the training data and can be detected much more efficiently if highlighted by attribution maps.

This work switches means and goals: Both, background and object biases are artificially generated in reference datasets. These biases are verified within two accordingly trained CNN architectures to exclude systematic effects caused by architectural features. Several feature attribution map techniques are then statistically evaluated by adequate metrics to put a number on the question: How efficient are attribution maps in detecting data bias?

2   Related Work

Semi-automatic Bias Detection. With *SpRaY* Lapuschkin et al. [4] present an approach to identify learned decision behaviors of a neural network based by clustering attribution maps. For example, *SpRaY* is used to detect so-called "Clever Hans" behavior, i.e., the inspected model makes correct predictions based on the wrong inputs. Zhang et al. [14] introduce another method for semi-automatic bias detection with the objective to uncover non-semantic relationships between different image attributes such as "smile" and "hair". For this purpose, relationships between different attributes are mined and compared with manually defined ground truth attribute relationships. However, this method is not based on attribution maps. Instead, the attributes are represented by the feature maps of a convolutional layer.

Attribution Map Evaluation. Usually, the evaluation of attribution maps is performed manually and rather qualitatively. Yet, in order to be able to provide reliable evidence about the capabilities of the heatmaps, quantitative results are needed. Yang and Kim [13] present an approach to compare the quality of different feature attribution methods. For this purpose, an artificial dataset with a priori knowledge about relative feature importances is created. Using the introduced metrics, it can be tested how well the different methods recognize the actual feature importance. Similarly, Osman et al. [6] perform an analysis of different explanation methods based on an artificially created dataset. Together with their dataset they introduce metrics that are used to check to what extent the image areas marked as relevant by the attribution maps actually correspond to known ground truth areas.

In this work, we partially build on the approach described in [6]. However, the metrics will not be used primarily to evaluate whether feature attribution methods identify the *correct* image regions. Instead, we intend to investigate whether the introduced metrics reliably indicate the attribution maps' capability to detect data bias.

3   An Approach for Measuring Data Bias

In order to evaluate the ability of attribution maps to indicate algorithmic bias, a four-step procedure is performed: (1) generation of artificial datasets with a *known* bias, (2) training of biased CNNs, (3) generation of attribution maps using different attribution techniques, (4) quantitative evaluation of the results.

3.1   Dataset Generation

Synthetic data is a notable approach to generate datasets that meet certain needs or specific conditions [5]. In this work, synthetic datasets are generated to visualize how attribution maps perform on different types of biased inputs. For this purpose, two use cases are defined: (1) "Cat vs. Dog" and (2) "Fruits". Two datasets are generated for each of the two use cases[2]. One dataset includes a known bias, the second dataset is generated without a bias and serves as a reference. The purpose of the "Cat vs. Dog" dataset is to introduce an object bias in a concentrated area into the trained CNNs. The "Fruits" data, in contrast, introduces a diffuse background bias across the whole image.

Cat vs. Dog. The reference dataset contains unbiased cat and dog images from ImageNet [7] and Kaggle "cat-and-dog"[3] dataset. For generating a biased dataset, this unbiased dataset is modified by systematically adding a ball in all Cat images using randomly generated positions (named "Cat + Ball vs. Dog"). Here, the aim is that the prediction for the class "Cat" is made based on the ball instead of the animal itself. The information about the ball's position is saved in form of a bounding box for every image. In order to avoid errors in the evaluation process, the ball does not overlap with the main image object (Cat). From the 8,545 synthetically generated images, 6,333 are used for model training, 288 for model validation and the remaining 1,924 images as test sets.

Fruits. Images of five different fruits (Apple, Banana, Corn, Peach, Pineapple) from the "Fruits 360"[4] dataset are used for generating a synthetic dataset. The fruits are placed on different backgrounds, e.g., apple trees, plates and desks. In total, 3,224 images, equally distributed among the five classes, are generated, where 1,810 images are used for training, 604 as validation set and 810 images for testing. For all images, binary ground truth (GT) masks are generated that indicate the position of the objects in the image. Again, two datasets are created: (1) a *biased* dataset, where apples are solely placed on apple tree backgrounds and the other fruits are placed on different backgrounds—here, the intention is to have the prediction for the class "Apple" based on the apple tree in the background, not based on the fruit itself; (2) an *unbiased* reference dataset where all fruits (including apples) are placed on different backgrounds.

---

[2] The datasets are available under: https://s.fhg.de/measuring-bias-in-classification.
[3] https://www.kaggle.com/tongpython/cat-and-dog, accessed on March 21, 2021.
[4] https://www.kaggle.com/moltean/fruits, accessed on March 21, 2021.

3.2   Attribution Methods

Starting point for the attribution map generation is a real-valued prediction function $f_c(\cdot)$ for some target class c that computes a prediction y_c, given input $\mathbf{x} \in \mathbb{R}^{W \times H \times C}$, where C is the number of input channels and W and H are the image width and height, respectively. An explanation method provides an attribution map $R \in \mathbb{R}^d$. Depending on the method, the result can be a matrix or a tensor. For a single image $\mathbf{x}$, R has either the same dimensions as the original image or is of size $W \times H$. In case a 3-dimensional map of size $W \times H \times C$ is generated, the relevances can be pooled along the C-axis to obtain a heatmap of the size $W \times H$ using L2-norm squared pooling, as introduced in [6].

Grad-CAM. The Gradient-weighted Class Activation Mapping (GC) [9] computes the gradients of the score y^c before the softmax function with respect to the feature maps of the last convolutional layer in order to produce a coarse class-discriminative 2D-localization map $R_{GC}^c \in \mathbb{R}^{W \times H}$.

Score-CAM. With Score-CAM (SC), Wang et al. [12] present another class-discriminative activation mapping approach. Unlike Grad-CAM, Score-CAM does not depend on gradients to compute an attribution map. Instead, the approach computes score-based weights for each activation map. The attribution map $R_{SC}^c \in \mathbb{R}^{W \times H}$ is then obtained as a linear combination of the score-based weights and activation maps.

Integrated Gradients. Integrated Gradients (IG) [10] generates an attribution map $R_{IG} \in \mathbb{R}^{W \times H \times C}$ based on the gradients of the model output with respect to the input while addressing gradient saturation. IG for an input $\mathbf{x}$ is defined as $R_{IG} = (\mathbf{x}_i - \mathbf{x}_i') \times \int_0^1 \frac{\partial f(\mathbf{x}' + \alpha \cdot (\mathbf{x} - \mathbf{x}'))}{\partial \mathbf{x}_i} \, d\alpha$, where $\mathbf{x}'$ is a baseline input that represents the absence of the feature in the original input $\mathbf{x}$.

For Integrated Gradients, 64 steps for approximating the integral were used together with a black baseline image.

epsilon-LRP. Layer-wise relevance propagation (LRP) [2] computes an attribution map $R_{LRP} \in \mathbb{R}^{W \times H \times C}$ by propagating the prediction back through the network with the help of specific propagation rules. The so-called epsilon rule is defined as $R_j = \sum_k \frac{a_j w_{jk}}{\sum_j a_j w_{jk} + \epsilon \operatorname{sign} \sum_j a_j w_{jk}} R_k$, where j and k are neurons of two consecutive layers of the neural network and $a_j w_{jk}$ is the weighted activation between the neurons of two consecutive layers.

In this work, ϵ-LRP is parameterized with an ϵ-value of 10, using the software library *DeepExplain* [1].

3.3   Metrics

This Section briefly introduces the three metrics used for the quantitative evaluation of attribution maps' ability to detect bias.

Relevance Mass Accuracy. The relevance mass accuracy (RMA), introduced in [6], is defined as the fraction between the relevance values R that lie inside a ground truth mask GT and all relevance values. Intuitively, RMA measures how much of the relevance's "mass" lies within the GT area and is defined as

$$\text{RMA} = \sum_{\substack{k=1 \\ \text{s.t. } p_k \in GT}}^{K} R_{pk} \cdot z, \tag{1}$$

where z is $\frac{1}{\sum_{k=1}^{N} R_{pk}}$, N is the total number of image pixels, K is the number of pixels within GT and R_{pk} is the relevance value at pixel p_k.

Relevance Rank Accuracy. The relevance rank accuracy (RRA) [6], measures the fraction of the high intensity relevances that lie within the GT. For computing RRA, a set of top-K relevance locations $S_{top-K} = \{s_1, s_2, ..., s_K | R_{s_1} > R_{s_2} > .... > R_{s_K}\}$ is obtained, where K is the GT mask's size. Each location s_p is a 2-D vector encoding the horizontal and vertical positions in a pixel grid. Thus, locations in the image that are most relevant for the classifier's prediction are found at the beginning of the set. RRA is defined as

$$\text{RRA} = \frac{|S_{top-K} \cap GT|}{|GT|} . \tag{2}$$

Area over the Perturbation Curve (AOPC). The metric proposed by Samek et al. [8] relies on systematic pixel perturbation, i.e., in several successive steps, the pixel values of the most relevant image regions are perturbed and the effect on the prediction accuracy is observed. This process is quantified as the AOPC and formalized as

$$\text{AOPC} = \frac{1}{1+P} \sum_{p=0}^{P} f(\mathbf{x}'^{(0)}) - f(\mathbf{x}'^{(p)}) , \tag{3}$$

where P defines the number of perturbation steps and $\mathbf{x}'^{(p)}$ is the perturbed image after the pth perturbation step. A large AOPC value means that perturbation results in a steep decrease in prediction accuracy, indicating that the attribution method efficiently detects the relevant image regions. In our experiments we follow the approach described in [8] and perform 100 perturbation steps, where we replace the pixel values around a 9×9 region with random values sampled from a uniform distribution.

4   Experimental Results

This section first describes the training process and performance results for the networks used in the experiments. Afterwards, the results for the quantitative bias evaluation are presented.

4.1   Models

For the experiments two different CNN architectures are used: EfficientNet-B0 [11] and MobileNetV1 [3]. We train eight different models in total, i.e., one biased and one unbiased network for each architecture and use case, respectively. All networks are trained by fine-tuning, using ImageNet pre-trained models. In order to preserve already trained geometrical features, the first 70 layers

N. Schaaf et al.

of EfficientNet and the first 26 layers of MobileNet are frozen. For training, a small learning rate ($1e^{-5}$ for "Cat vs. Dog", $2e^{-5}$ for "Fruits") and *RMSProp* as optimization algorithm are chosen together with *EarlyStopping* to prevent overfitting. The results are summarized in Table 1.

It can be observed that the networks trained on the biased datasets achieve high test accuracies when tested together with the biased datasets, just like the unbiased networks when tested together with the unbiased datasets. Applying the unbiased dataset to the biased networks, though, results in a drop in the prediction accuracy between 17 and 25 percent points (*pp*). On the other hand, when applying the biased datasets to the unbiased networks the prediction accuracy is hardly affected—the loss in accuracy ranges between 0 and 8 *pp*. Thus, we conclude that the biased networks indeed contain the intended bias, i.e., for "Cat vs. Dog" the Ball is used as a feature for the Cat class and for "Fruits" the apple tree background is used as a feature for the Apple class.

4.2 Measure Bias Based on Metrics

Having confirmed that the CNNs contain the desired bias based on the prediction accuracy, the analysis is continued by means of the attention maps. For this purpose, attribution maps are generated for the different datasets and CNNs by applying the four attribution techniques presented in Sect. 3.2.

Specifically, for each dataset and CNN we first apply the validation ("Cat vs. Dog", i.e., 288 images) and test ("Fruits", i.e., 810 images) images to the network to get predictions and then generate the attribution maps. We only consider images for which a correct prediction is made. Then, the resulting attribution maps are analyzed by means of the metrics described in Sect. 3.3. For both use cases, the GT areas (Ball, Fruits) are extended by 50% of their original area. This is due to the fact that those areas are quite small and some attribution methods provide rather fuzzy attribution maps (SC and GC).

Cat vs. Dog. For this use case, we compare the attribution maps created for the four different CNNs based on the "Cat + Ball vs. Dog" dataset.

Relevance Mass and Rank Accuracy. Using the datasets' bounding boxes, RMA and RRA can be computed for the three GT areas *Cat, Dog* and *Ball*. The RMA results are displayed in Fig. 1. It is evident that across all attribution

Table 1. Prediction test accuracy for all networks trained for the two use cases "Cat vs. Dog" and "Fruits".

Dataset	EfficientNet		MobileNet	
	Bias	No bias	Bias	No bias
Cat + Ball vs. Dog (Bias)	0.99	0.97	0.97	0.86
Cat vs. Dog (No Bias)	0.74	0.97	0.80	0.89
Fruits (Bias)	0.97	0.82	0.98	0.95
Fruits (No Bias)	0.77	0.90	0.77	0.96

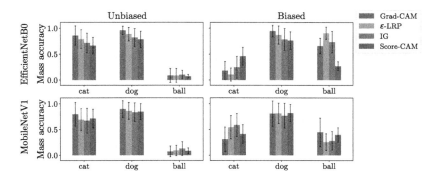

Fig. 1. Use Case "Cat vs. Dog": Mean RMA and standard deviation (error bars) for *Cat*, *Dog* and *Ball* for all CNNs and attribution techniques.

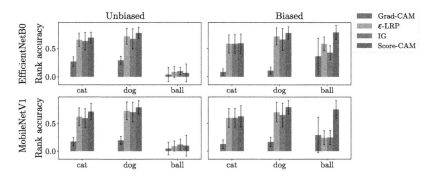

Fig. 2. Use Case "Cat vs. Dog": Mean RRA and standard deviation (error bars) for *Cat*, *Dog* and *Ball* for all CNNs and attribution techniques.

techniques the RMA values for *Cat* and *Dog* are very high for the unbiased CNNs, whereas values for *Ball* are close to zero. For the biased networks the RMA values for *Dog* are similar to those of the unbiased networks, while the RMA values for *Cat* have dropped significantly: from 0.7–0.9 to 0.2–0.5. At the same time, the values for the *Ball* have increased from approximately 0.05–0.1 to up to 0.3–0.8. This indicates that the attention actually shifts from *Cat* to *Ball* for the biased networks, but remains the same for *Dog*. However, this effect is more significant for EfficientNet than for the MobileNet architecture. If those results together with the stronger accuracy drop for the biased EfficientNet (see Table 1) are considered, it can be concluded that MobileNet is less biased. Similar patterns can also be found for RRA (Fig. 2). As for the RMA values, for the biased CNNs the values for *Ball* increase compared to the unbiased CNNs, while the RRA values for *Cat* decrease slightly. A possible explanation could be that the bounding box for *Cat* often covers a large portion of the image. Hence, the chance of relevance values randomly lying within this large image portion is accordingly high. Nevertheless, it can be observed that in the biased networks the attention shifts from the *Cat* to the *Ball*.

Table 2. Use Case "Cat vs. Dog": t-test between the RMA and RRA values of the biased and unbiased CNNs. The p-value for each GT object and attribution method is shown.

CNN architecture	Metric	Cat				Dog				Ball			
		GC	LRP	IG	SC	GC	LRP	IG	SC	GC	LRP	IG	SC
EfficientNet	RMA	0.00	0.00	0.00	0.00	0.30	0.33	0.07	0.17	0.00	0.00	0.00	0.00
	RRA	0.00	0.00	0.06	0.00	0.00	0.89	0.48	0.83	0.00	0.00	0.00	0.00
MobileNet	RMA	0.00	0.00	0.01	0.00	0.00	0.07	0.02	0.33	0.00	0.00	0.00	0.00
	RRA	0.00	0.29	0.91	0.00	0.00	0.47	0.04	0.61	0.00	0.00	0.00	0.00

Looking at the RMA and RRA values of the attribution methods, an interesting phenomenon can be observed. The RMA values of the different methods are relatively evenly distributed: in most cases the difference is about 0.1 to 0.2 points—with GC often achieving the highest values. When considering the RRA results, however, GC under performs consistently. This indicates that most of its relevance values seem to be within the bounding boxes, but the top-K features are located outside and away from the center of mass.

To determine whether the shift in attention observed using RMA and RRA between the biased and unbiased networks is statistically significant, Welch's t-test is performed. For this purpose, the null hypothesis is made that there is no difference between the expected RMA/RRA values of the biased and unbiased CNNs. For both metrics, the test is performed separately for each combination of GT object and attribution method. The results are listed in Table 2. We choose the usual significance level $\alpha = 0.05$, which means that if $p \leq \alpha$ the null hypothesis is rejected. It is noticeable that for *Ball* the p-values are always zero, leading to a rejection of the null hypothesis. Except for the RRA values for LRP and IG, this also applies to *Cat*. For *Dog* $p > 0.05$ holds for most cases.

AOPC. The AOPC results are summarized in Table 3. In order to analyze the effect of the bias, the results are split between the Cat and Dog class. In general, the results show that IG and LRP outperform the other two methods as they consistently achieve higher AOPC values. However, for all methods an unexpected effect can be observed. For the biased CNNs, IG and LRP get high AOPC values for the Cat class, indicating that the attribution maps efficiently highlight the relevant image regions. Considering the RRA results (high values for Cat and Ball), we can presume the Cat and Ball features are relevant for decision making. In contrast, the AOPC values for the Dog class are relatively small, between 0 and 0.15. From the RRA analysis, it is evident that a majority of the relevant pixels for the Dog class lie within the Dog region. However, since perturbing these pixels has no appreciable effect on the prediction accuracy, we can assume that the marked pixels have low relevance for the class decision. One explanation could be that the induced bias causes the trained models to base their decisions almost entirely on the prominent Ball feature in the Cat class. In comparison, the Dog class' features seem to be irrelevant such that the respective AOPC values do not exceed the random values. This effect seems

Table 3. Use Case "Cat vs. Dog": AOPC values for the systematic perturbation using the attribution maps and a random perturbation as a baseline.

Network	Grad-CAM		ε-LRP		IG		Score-CAM		Random
	Cat	Dog	Cat	Dog	Cat	Dog	Cat	Dog	
EfficientNet (Bias)	0.12	0.01	0.67	0.00	**0.72**	0.00	0.11	0.01	0.04
MobileNet (Bias)	0.07	0.14	0.29	0.14	**0.35**	0.15	0.07	0.13	0.10
EfficientNet (No Bias)	0.02	0.35	0.05	0.20	0.04	0.18	0.00	**0.36**	0.04
MobileNet (No Bias)	0.03	0.39	0.02	**0.50**	0.02	**0.50**	0.02	0.34	0.17

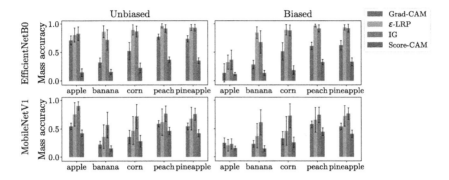

Fig. 3. Use Case "Fruits": Mean RMA and standard deviation (error bars) for each class for all CNNs and attribution techniques.

lifted and even reversed for models trained without bias, turning the Dog class into the dominant one.

Fruits. As for the previous use case, the results for the three metrics RMA, RRA and AOPC are presented.

Relevance Mass and Rank Accuracy. The RMA and RRA results are summarized in Fig. 3 and 4. Specifically, for EfficientNet an almost equal pronouncement of RMA and RRA values across all five classes can be observed for the unbiased networks. In contrast, for the biased networks, the RMA and RRA values of the Apple class are significantly lower: for RMA the decrease is ∼50 pp, for RRA ∼30 pp. For MobileNet, the RMA and RRA vary more significantly between the different classes. Nevertheless, it can also be observed here that the values for Apple are significantly lower for the biased than for the unbiased networks. The results suggest that all attribution maps detect the induced bias diverting the CNNs' attention away from the actual Apple objects towards the diffuse background.

An analysis of the RMA and RRA results provides three interesting observations regarding the performance of the four feature attribution methods. First, as in the "Cat vs. Dog" use case GC achieves high RMA but comparatively poor RRA values. Second, the exact opposite effect can be observed for SC. For both methods this means that the highest relevance values do not necessarily

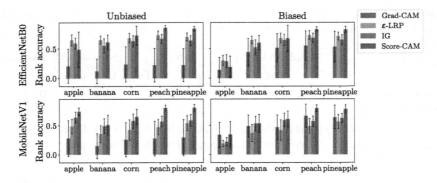

Fig. 4. Use Case "Fruits": Mean RRA and standard deviation (error bars) for each class for all CNNs and attribution techniques.

Table 4. Use Case "Fruits": *t*-test between the RMA and RRA values of the biased and unbiased CNNs. The p-value for each GT object and attribution method is shown.

CNN Architecture	Attribution Method	Apple RMA	Apple RRA	Banana RMA	Banana RRA	Corn RMA	Corn RRA	Peach RMA	Peach RRA	Pineapple RMA	Pineapple RRA
EfficientNet	Grad-CAM	0.00	0.07	0.00	0.00	0.48	0.00	0.00	0.00	0.00	0.00
	ε-LRP	0.00	0.00	0.12	0.71	0.95	0.90	0.12	0.93	0.52	0.14
	IG	0.00	0.00	0.06	0.02	0.25	0.25	0.82	0.98	0.34	0.10
	Score-CAM	0.00	0.00	0.00	0.50	0.00	0.16	0.00	0.00	0.00	0.00
MobileNet	Grad-CAM	0.00	0.04	0.13	0.00	0.30	0.00	0.13	0.00	0.94	0.00
	ε-LRP	0.00	0.00	0.66	0.41	0.46	0.44	0.11	0.21	0.02	0.07
	IG	0.00	0.00	0.09	0.01	0.90	0.45	0.16	0.84	0.33	0.00
	Score-CAM	0.00	0.00	0.56	0.14	0.03	0.01	0.01	0.34	0.09	0.00

lie within the mass of relevance values. This effect should also be kept in mind for the visual analysis as those methods usually provide heatmaps that are concentrated strongly on one area. Thus, it is difficult or even impossible to find single outlying pixels with high relevance by visual inspection only. Third, it is noticeable that IG and LRP provide the most stable results. For these methods, usually the highest RMA and RRA values are obtained and a positive correlation between the RMA and RRA values is observable.

As for the previous use case, we apply a *t*-test to evaluate the statistical significance of the attribution shifts, summarized in Table 4. Again, it is noticeable that the null hypothesis can be rejected for the biased object, i.e., Apple, since the p-values for each attribution map are zero, except for a single case (GC + RRA). For EfficientNet, the null hypothesis is mostly rejected for GC and SC, whereas it holds for IG and LRP. The results for MobileNet are more unstable, leading to a rejection of the null hypothesis for several combinations of GT object and attribution method. However, the p-values reflect the results observable in Fig. 3 and 4. One explanation for the "volatile" p-values could be that the bias does not only influence the biased class (Apple) but also other classes which leads to different attribution maps across the biased/non-biased networks. Nevertheless, no other class except Apple shows such a clear shift between the RMA/RRA values of the biased and unbiased networks.

Table 5. Use Case "Fruits": AOPC values for the systematic perturbation using the attribution maps and a random perturbation as a baseline.

Network	Grad-CAM		ϵ-LRP		IG		Score-CAM		Random
	Apple	Rest	Apple	Rest	Apple	Rest	Apple	Rest	
EfficientNet (Bias)	0.03	**0.51**	0.03	**0.51**	0.01	0.47	0.07	0.50	0.13
MobileNet (Bias)	0.02	0.50	0.06	0.54	0.04	**0.59**	0.01	0.51	0.13
EfficientNet (No Bias)	0.61	0.52	**0.64**	0.54	0.63	0.50	0.49	0.53	0.03
MobileNet (No Bias)	0.75	0.50	0.83	0.54	**0.85**	0.60	0.78	0.53	0.19

AOPC. Table 5 displays the AOPC results—split between the Apple class and the remaining four classes, named as "Rest". For the biased CNNs, perturbation has a nearly no effect on the prediction accuracy for the Apple class, resulting in low AOPC values. More specifically, the systematic perturbation performs worse than the random perturbation. This indicates that the networks do not decide based on small-scale object features, but on large-scale features—here, the apple tree background. For the other classes, however, the AOPC values are much higher compared to random perturbation, suggesting that in this case small image regions are used for decision making, i.e., the fruits themselves. As expected, the attribution maps for the unbiased networks exhibit high AOPC values across all classes, including Apples. This leads to the conclusion that all attribution maps successfully detect the diffuse background bias.

5 Discussion and Conclusion

Through the analytical approach followed in this work, we were partly able to measure attribution maps' explanation capability and found quantitative evidence that these techniques detect data biases, both diffuse and focused. Beyond that, the experiments revealed significant differences between the feature attribution methods. However, the analyses have also shown that attribution maps can sometimes provide misleading explanations.

Specifically, the results obtained for the use case "Cat vs. Dog" underline some inconsistency between the metrics RMA/RRA and AOPC. From the AOPC values it can be seen that, contrary to human expectations, the CNNs do not always use the features of both classes equally for the binary classification. Instead, they mainly rely on the features of one class. Consequently, the features of the other class are irrelevant for the classification decision. Nevertheless, even for the "irrelevant" class, the attribution maps provide results that seem valid at first sight (high RMA and RRA values), but are not confirmed by AOPC results. For this reason, we recommend that the evaluation of attribution maps should not be based on visual inspection and/or one metric alone, especially when applying attribution-map-based methods for industrial use cases. Rather, several different metrics should be used for evaluation for improving the robustness of the results.

The results also motivate a further expansion of the study's scope in three directions: First, new datasets as well as further CNN architectures can be added modularly to generate a scalable and generic test bench for attribution techniques. Second, further investigation into the inconsistency between the RMA/RRA and AOPC metrics should be conducted to investigate why, although the attribution maps highlight certain image regions as relevant, it may be that these are not actually involved for the prediction. Finally, the observation that some CNN architectures might be more vulnerable to bias than others can be studied in detail in future work.

References

1. Ancona, M., Harkous, H., Zhang, Y.: Deepexplain: attribution methods for deep learning (2020), https://github.com/marcoancona/DeepExplain
2. Bach, S., Binder, A., Montavon, G., Klauschen, F., Müller, K.R., Samek, W.: On pixel-wise explanations for non-linear classifier decisions by layer-wise relevance propagation. PLoS ONE 10(7), e0130140 (2015). https://doi.org/10.1371/journal.pone.0130140
3. Howard, A.G., et al.: MobileNets: efficient convolutional neural networks for mobile vision applications (2017). arXiv:1704.04861
4. Lapuschkin, S., Wäldchen, S., Binder, A., Montavon, G., Samek, W., Müller, K.R.: Unmasking clever HANS predictors and assessing what machines really learn. Nat. Commun. 10(1), 1096 (2019). https://doi.org/10.1038/s41467-019-08987-4
5. Nikolenko, S.I.: Synthetic data for deep learning (2019). arXiv:1909.11512
6. Osman, A., Arras, L., Samek, W.: Towards ground truth evaluation of visual explanations (2020). arXiv:2003.07258v1
7. Russakovsky, O., et al.: ImageNet large scale visual recognition challenge. Int. J. Comput. Vis. 115(3), 211–252 (2015). https://doi.org/10.1007/s11263-015-0816-y
8. Samek, W., Binder, A., Montavon, G., Lapuschkin, S., Muller, K.R.: Evaluating the visualization of what a deep neural network has learned. IEEE Trans. Neural Netw. Learn. Syst. 28(11), 2660–2673 (2017). https://doi.org/10.1109/TNNLS.2016.2599820
9. Selvaraju, R.R., Cogswell, M., Das, A., Vedantam, R., Parikh, D., Batra, D.: Grad-CAM: visual explanations from deep networks via gradient-based localization (2016). arXiv:1610.02391v3
10. Sundararajan, M., Taly, A., Yan, Q.: Axiomatic attribution for deep networks. In: Proceedings of the 34th International Conference on Machine Learning, ICML2017, vol. 70, pp. 3319–3328. JMLR.org (2017)
11. Tan, M., Le, Q.V.: EfficientNet: rethinking model scaling for convolutional neural networks. In: 36th International Conference on Machine Learning, ICML 2019, June 2019, pp. 10691–10700 (2019)

12. Wang, H., Du, M., Yang, F., Zhang, Z.: Score-CAM: Improved visual explanations via score-weighted class activation mapping (2019). arXiv:1910.01279
13. Yang, M., Kim, B.: Benchmarking attribution methods with relative feature importance (2019). arXiv:1907.09701v2
14. Zhang, Q., Wenguan, W., Zhu, S.C.: Examining CNN representations with respect to dataset bias. In: McIlraith, Sheila A., Weinberger, Kilian Q. (eds.) Proceedings of the Thirty-Second AAAI Conference on Artificial Intelligence, (AAAI 2018), New Orleans, Louisiana, USA, 2–7 February 2018, pp. 4464–4473. AAAI Press (2018)

Towards Image Retrieval with Noisy Labels via Non-deterministic Features

Hengwei Liu, Jinyu Ma, and Xiaodong Gu[✉]

Department of Electronic Engineering, Fudan University, Shanghai 200438, China
xdgu@fudan.edu.cn

Abstract. For large image retrieval applications, collecting images from the Internet is a relatively low-cost way to obtain labeled training data. However, images from the Internet are often falsely annotated, which may lead to unsatisfying performances of trained models. To alleviate the impact of label noise, our work adopts non-deterministic features for training deep convolutional neural networks. Suppose that non-deterministic features of images obey multi-dimensional Gaussian distribution, and a feature is represented by its mean and variance. During the training, when images are mapped to non-deterministic features, the model will tend to assign large variance to mislabeled samples, suggesting low confidence levels, instead of causing negative optimization by directly changing estimation of mean value. During the test, mean value of non-deterministic features are used for image retrieval. This method increases redundancy by adding variance term of features, so the model has stronger tolerance to label noise. Experimental results and analysis show that on datasets with label noise, using non-deterministic features leads to better image retrieval results than using deterministic features.

Keywords: Image retrieval · Label noise · Non-deterministic feature

1 Introduction

Deep learning is data-driven. With applications of image retrieval becoming more large-scale and widely-used, the demand for training data is growing rapidly. For supervised learning, manually annotating data is undoubtedly painstaking. Webly supervised learning [3] solves this problem by directly utilizing widespread data on the Internet, like searching for images of different keywords and download them in bulk. However, quality of acquired data is never ensured, as there can be labeling errors, i.e., label noise. For example, searching for ⟨chimpanzee⟩ may not only get images containing chimpanzees, but also maps of chimpanzee habitats, which are irrelevant if one aims to retrieve only animals. Besides, images containing gorillas might also be falsely returned, and that will confuse the model if label ⟨gorrila⟩ also exists in the retrieval system. Due to the strong fitting capability of deep neural networks, all the label noise will be learned and this will affect trained models. We introduce data uncertainty learning to deal with label noise.

© Springer Nature Switzerland AG 2021
I. Farkaš et al. (Eds.): ICANN 2021, LNCS 12893, pp. 446–456, 2021.
https://doi.org/10.1007/978-3-030-86365-4_36

While deep learning models are good at embedding high-dimensional data to low-dimensional feature spaces, they are not capable to measure qualities of embeddings, namely confidence levels of resulted features. In this paper, based on theory of data uncertainty learning, we grant deep learning models capability to estimate confidence levels of its mappings, which helps robust training on datasets with label noise. Assuming that for each category of labeled data, there is a class center in the feature space. All the data samples can be considered as observations of corresponding class centers, and they are biased to different extents, not only because of varying image contents, but also different degrees of label noise. Models based on deterministic features attempt to embed these corrupted observations to the same point in the feature space. When it comes to mislabeled samples, loss will be large and the model will likely be falsely penalized. Correspondingly, models based on non-deterministic features tend to embed observations from the same category to the same mean value, while the label noise is characterized by variance. The variance is higher for false labels, indicating that these labels are not that trustworthy, and help prevent from overfitting to some extent.

2   Related Work

Webly supervised learning [3] refers to training model directly using data collected from the Internet. Problem follows that how to exploit unreliable labels. In the presence of label noise, deep neural networks are considered unreliable because a large number of parameters make them easy to fit any complex function [16]. [20] proves that deep neural networks can fit wrong labels of any proportion in the training set, resulting in low generalization capability.

Regularization is a class of methods to resist label noise. Frequently used regularization techniques include data augmentation, weight decay, batch normalization [8], etc. Regularizations reduce the impact of noisy labels by preventing models from overfitting to specific samples, but as they are not designed to deal with label noise, they only show limited effects. Another class of methods [3,6] maintain a label transition matrix whose elements are probabilities of one label being mistaken for another. By applying the label transition matrix on predicted labels, it projects clean predictions to noisy ones to match noisy groundtruths. Such methods strongly rely on some assumptions about noise types and thus are unable to deal with complex noise that do not conform to those assumptions. [1] finds memorization effect: deep neural networks are prone to learn clean samples first and then gradually noisy samples. Therefore, clean samples tend to cause small losses, and noisy ones larger losses. According to this, [7,11] pick training samples to update.

Uncertainty is a metric of model reliability. [12] divides uncertainty into epistemic uncertainty and aleatoric uncertainty. Epistemic uncertainty is also known as model uncertainty [5], which comes from the ambiguity of model parameters caused by insufficient training data. Aleatoric uncertainty, also known as data uncertainty, comes from the noise born with training data, and unlike model uncertainty, it cannot be eliminated by providing enough data. In the field of deep learning in computer vision, uncertainty learning has been introduced to many tasks to enhance robustness and interpretability of models, such as object detection [4], semantic segmentation [9], face recognition [2,16], etc. Our work is inspired by [2] in face recognition, based on which we improve the model to make it easier to converge, and use it on image retrieval with label noise. Experiments show that the model based on non-deterministic features can effectively deal with label noise problems in image retrieval.

3 Proposed Model

3.1 Non-deterministic Features

Let $\mathcal{X}$ be the sample space, $\mathcal{H} \subset \mathbb{R}^D$ be the corresponding feature space. For a category of training samples, assume that there is an "ideal" feature $h_c \in \mathcal{H}$ representing the class center. Then, samples $x_1, x_2, \cdots$ belonging to this category can be viewed as observations sampled from the distribution $p(X|h_c)$. Sampling brings error, causing bias on samples. The bias comes from two parts. One is variations of samples, caused by changing perspectives, positions and lightings from sample to sample on the same object or scene. The other one is noise, or more precisely for this paper, label noise. The essence of model training is to find a universal feature space $\mathcal{H}$ for all training samples and feature distributions $p(H|x)$ given samples. For sample x_i, when adopting deterministic features, the ideal feature distribution can be expressed as

$$p(H|x_i) = \delta(h_i - h_c) = \delta(f(x_i) - h_c), \tag{1}$$

where f is the model and $\delta(\cdot)$ is Dirac delta function. For each x_i, its feature h_i is expected to be precisely embedded to the class center h_c. However, considering label noise, a sample labeled as one category may actually be a sample of another category. So, the sample may deviate significantly from the class center. In this case, for multiple i, it is difficult to find the exact h_c that meets the above requirements. Even if such h_c is found, the model is definitely corrupted, because it maps samples with both correct labels and wrong labels to a similar position in the feature space. To solve the problem, we adopt non-deterministic feature $H_{n,i}$ instead of h_i. $H_{n,i}$ is a random variable following D-dimensional Gaussian distribution

$$\mathcal{N}\left(\mu_i, \sigma_i \sigma_i^\top I\right), \tag{2}$$

where $\mu_i \in \mathbb{R}^D$, $\sigma_i \in \mathbb{R}^D$, and assuming that the covariance matrix is a diagonal matrix. Both μ_i and σ_i will be learned by the model. Then, sample fixed feature $h_{n,i}$ from $H_{n,i}$ for further computations. Compared with Dirac delta function, the covariance of Gaussian distribution brings redundancy to the model. When there come falsely labeled samples, by predicting large variance of them, the model can reduce losses caused by them, therefore avoid biasing mean values of features.

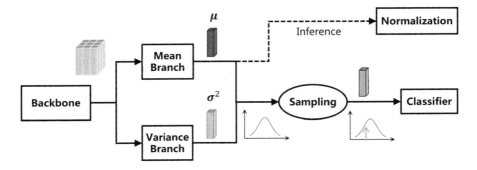

Fig. 1. A diagram of the overall model structure.

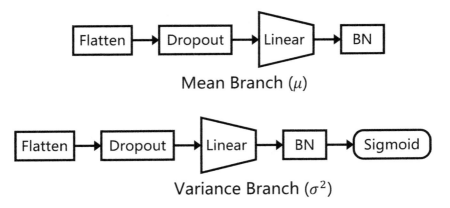

Fig. 2. The structure of mean branch and variance branch.

3.2   Model Structure

The proposed model structure is shown in Fig. 1. Firstly, a CNN backbone processes input images and outputs convolutional features. Then, convolutional features are forwarded through the mean branch and variance branch respectively and we obtain μ and σ, which together represent non-deterministic features. Afterwards, by sampling distribution of non-deterministic features, we get fixed feature vectors that suitable for further computations. At last, a classifier takes in these features and outputs predicted class probabilities. For testing, the variance branch is skipped and mean values are normalized (following the dotted line) as final features for retrieval.

Structures of mean branch and variance branch is shown in Fig. 2. Different backbones have different output sizes, nevertheless, their output features will be flattened as vectors first. Then, vectors sequentially go through a dropout layer and a linear layer and are batch normalized. The mean branch finally outputs this result as μ. For variance branch, because $\sigma^2 > 0$, and also $\sigma^2 < 1$ according to explanations in Sect. 3.4, we append a sigmoid layer on top of the variance branch to restrict its outputs.

The classifier is basically a linear layer without bias. Its weights and input features will be $L2$-normalized before calculating inner products. Outputs of the classifier will be multiplied by a length factor s $(s > 1)$ and then transformed to class probabilities by a softmax function.

3.3 Sampling Non-deterministic Features

Non-deterministic features are probability distributions, and we cannot directly calculate loss from distributions. They need to be sampled once to participate in subsequent calculations. However, sampling operation is not differentiable, preventing the backpropagation of the model. We use re-parameterization [13] trick to let the model still take gradients as usual. Specifically, a random factor ϵ is sampled from a standard D-dimensional Gaussian distribution, and the equivalent sampling representation is as follows:

$$h_n = \mu + \epsilon \cdot \sigma. \tag{3}$$

3.4 Relative Entropy Loss Function

We use cross entropy as task-related loss function. The existence of variance makes sampled features randomized around mean values. In order to converge, the model will tend to predict small variance to reduce cross entropy loss. To prevent the variance from being too small so that it degenerates into deterministic features, a relative entropy loss is incorporated. Relative entropy is also known as Kullback-Leibler divergence, which is a measure of how one probability distribution is different from another. The larger the relative entropy, the greater the difference between two probability distributions. The relative entropy loss function is formulated as the relative divergence from standard D-dimensional Gaussian distribution to distribution of $\boldsymbol{H}_n$:

$$
\begin{aligned}
\mathcal{L}_{KLD} &= \frac{1}{D} \cdot D_{KL}\left(p\left(\boldsymbol{H}_n\right) \| \mathcal{N}\left(\boldsymbol{0}, \boldsymbol{I}\right)\right) \\
&= \frac{1}{D} \cdot D_{KL}\left(\mathcal{N}\left(\boldsymbol{\mu}, \boldsymbol{\sigma}\boldsymbol{\sigma}^T \boldsymbol{I}\right) \| \mathcal{N}\left(\boldsymbol{0}, \boldsymbol{I}\right)\right) \\
&= -\frac{1}{2D} \cdot \sum_{d=1}^{D}\left(1 + \log \sigma_d^2 - \sigma_d^2 - \mu_d^2\right),
\end{aligned}
\tag{4}
$$

where μ_d and σ_d are the d-th element in vector $\boldsymbol{\mu}$ and $\boldsymbol{\sigma}$, respectively. For each σ_d, $\mathcal{L}_{KLD}$ is monotonically increasing in $(0, 1)$ and monotonically decreasing in $[1, +\infty)$. It takes the minimum value if and only if $\sigma_d = 1$. That is why we wish to restrict σ_d in $(0, 1)$ with a sigmoid function. The whole loss function is the sum of cross entropy loss $\mathcal{L}_{CE}$ and relative entropy loss $\mathcal{L}_{KLD}$ with a weight factor λ:

$$\mathcal{L} = \mathcal{L}_{CE} + \lambda\mathcal{L}_{KLD}. \tag{5}$$

During the training, $\mathcal{L}_{CE}$ attempts to penalize large σ to reduce the randomness of features, while $\lambda\mathcal{L}_{KLD}$ attempts to makes it larger. They are expected to reach an equilibrium when the model finally converges.

4   Experiments and Analysis

4.1   Datasets

We train and test our model on Noisy Mini-ImageNet and Noisy Stanford-cars provided by [10]. They are respectively based on Mini-ImageNet [18] and Stanford-cars [14], and extended by data collected from the Internet. The collected images are manually voted to determine whether the labels are correct, and they are mixed with original datasets in different proportions of falsely labeled images. Finally, there are a series of training sets with different noise levels: 0%, 5%, 10%, 15%, 20%, 30%, 40%, 50%, 60%, 70% and 80%, and a clean test set. Noise level is the percentage of images with false labels. For example, a 20% noise level means that, in each category, there are an average of 20% images not labeled correctly. In [10], synthetic label noise is called blue noise, while real world label noise is called red noise. The two types of noise have different properties. We only use red noise because we focus on noise from real world.

Noisy Mini-ImageNet contains 100 categories, 50,000 training images and 5,000 testing images.

Noisy Stanford-cars consists of 196 categories, 8,144 training images and 8,041 testing images.

4.2   Settings and Implementation Details

We pick up ResNet18 pre-trained on ImageNet as backbone and its 512-layer convolutional feature map after global pooling layer as backbone output. Feature dimension $D = 256$. Length factor $s = 64$. The value of λ is key to the performance, so we searched for appropriate values in a certain scope, and show results in later sections. Input size of images are 224×224. Batch size is 256, and each setting is trained for 80 epochs. We use SGD for optimization, with momentum equals to 0.9 and $L2$ weight decay equals to 0.0001. The base learning rate is set to 0.02, and it linearly warms up in the first two epochs, and gradually decays to 0.0002 following cosine function. Our code is implemented in Pytorch framework. We run all experiments on a single NVIDIA Tesla V100 GPU.

4.3   Comparison with Deterministic Features

Figure 3 is the comparison between models based on deterministic features and non-deterministic features. With the increase of noise level, recall@1 is on a downward trend. Although the descending speed is not the same for both datasets and models, performance of the model based on non-deterministic features is consistently better than that based on deterministic features at the

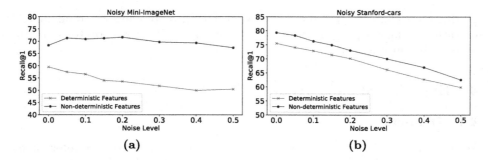

Fig. 3. Comparison between models based on deterministic features and non-deterministic features.

same noise level. Specifically, when noise level increases from 0% to 20% on Mini-ImageNet, recall@1 for the model based on non-deterministic features does not decrease at all, which indicates that the model may completely eliminate the adverse effect of slight label noise.

4.4 Influence of λ

Table 1. Performances under different values of λ.

λ	Noise Level							
	0%	5%	10%	15%	20%	30%	40%	50%
0	75.56	74.06	72.88	71.42	70.12	66.11	62.64	59.79
0.001	78.30	77.14	76.31	74.14	72.04	69.07	65.44	61.27
0.01	79.01	77.20	76.01	74.13	72.43	69.22	66.32	61.68
0.1	78.56	78.34	75.92	74.97	72.54	69.99	65.89	61.52
0.25	79.17	77.49	76.26	74.51	72.73	69.83	66.94	62.48
0.5	79.32	77.70	75.66	74.70	73.05	69.92	66.26	61.45
0.75	77.96	76.06	74.58	72.90	71.64	68.91	64.56	60.25
0.9	76.10	74.92	73.49	71.06	69.13	66.15	62.63	57.93

The influence of λ on retrieval performance is shown in Table 1. The first row $\lambda = 0$ represents deterministic features. From the second row, the proportion of relative entropy loss grows as λ increases. From the table we find that, for every noise level, with the increase of λ, the retrieval performance always first gets better and then gets worse. When λ is close to 0, variance of features is small and non-deterministic features nearly degenerate into deterministic features, which makes retrieval performance also close to using deterministic features. When λ is

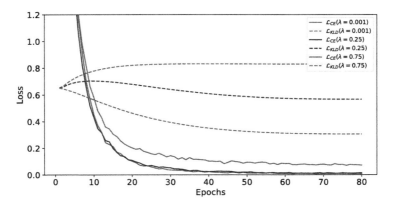

Fig. 4. Losses under different values of λ in training.

too large, the variance is constrained around 1, which hampers the convergence of cross entropy loss, causing poor performance. Figure 4 shows how the two losses vary with training epochs under different values of λ. If λ is small, relative entropy loss will increase at the beginning of training because the value of the cross entropy loss is very large at this time, and optimizing the cross entropy loss makes the variance smaller. With the decrease of cross entropy loss, the two losses gradually reach a equilibrium. When $\lambda = 0.75$, the cross entropy loss converges to a much larger value than in the case of $\lambda = 0.001$ or $\lambda = 0.25$, thus the final retrieval result is not as good as the latter two.

4.5 Analysis on Feature Variance

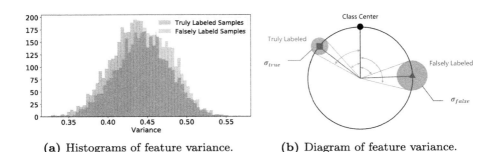

(a) Histograms of feature variance.   (b) Diagram of feature variance.

Fig. 5. Analysis on feature variance.

$\boldsymbol{\sigma}^2$ is a vector that cannot be compared directly. To compare feature variance among different samples, we use harmonic mean of elements in $\boldsymbol{\sigma}^2$ as scalarized variance. We predict variance of Noisy Stanford-cars of 50% noise level with the model trained under $\lambda = 0.1$, and draw histograms of variance, as shown in Fig. 5a. Both histograms approximately follow normal distributions, with the vast majority of variances spread over a narrow range of 0.35 to 0.55, and most part of the two histograms are overlapped. The main difference of them is that, the mean variance of the falsely labeled samples is greater than that of truly labeled samples. This is in line with expectations. By assigning large feature variance to noisy samples, the model prevents itself from overfitting on noisy samples, thereby reducing the harm of noisy samples.

The classifier on top of the model essentially calculates cosine similarities between all the features and all the class centers, as shown in Fig. 5b. When model parameters are initialized, σ predicted by the model is random, and mean variance of the truly and falsely labeled samples are the same. As the training goes, according to the memorization effect described earlier, the model tends to learn easier samples first. So, it first narrows the angle between the truly labeled sample and the class center, while the falsely labeled sample is considered "hard" and its angle with the class center shrinks slowly. For a specific σ, the random oscillations of the angles are relatively greater on small angles than on large angles. Therefore, to converge the cross entropy loss as quick as possible, the model prefers to decrease variance of truly labeled samples first. As a result, this mechanism ensures that simple (often clean) samples are prioritized by the model, which is similar to the conception of curriculum learning.

4.6   Comparison with Hard Mining

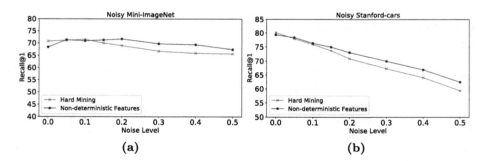

Fig. 6. Comparison between models based on non-deterministic features and hard mining.

Hard mining is an effective sample selection strategy widely adopted in metric leaning [15,17,19]. The general practice of hard mining is to compose hard image pairs or triplets on which the model is likely to make mistakes. By increasing weights of such pairs or triplets in losses, the model converges faster and achieves better image retrieval performance. We find that, the idea of hard mining is exactly opposite of that in the data uncertainty learning or curriculum learning, where models are usually better if easy samples are given more weights in training. It is obvious that mislabeled samples are likely to be deemed as hard samples in hard mining. Thus, we speculate that hard mining on noisy datasets could result in poor performance. We choose multi-similarity, a representative hard mining method, and compare it with the model based on non-deterministic features. The result is shown in Fig. 6. When the noise level is low, the results are similar. Hard mining is sometimes better, possibly because models based on non-deterministic features do not make good use of information in hard samples. However, when the noise level is high, the model based on non-deterministic features gets better results than hard mining. This case suggests that hard samples are not always informative. They could be erroneous. In the presence of heavy noise in training datasets, it might be a better choice to discard hard samples.

5   Conclusion

In order to achieve better image retrieval performance on datasets with label noise, we introduce a model based on non-deterministic features according to the theory of data uncertainty. The model represents image features as multi-dimensional Gaussian distributions, and predicts their mean and variance in the same time. The deviation between samples and class centers caused by label noise is reflected as variance of features in feature space. The trained model tends to predict small variance for clean samples and large variance for noisy ones, thus reducing the fit of the model to mislabeled samples and making the model more resistant to noisy training data. Experimental results and analysis show that, the model based on non-deterministic features obtains better image retrieval results than the model based on deterministic features.

Acknowledgments. This work was supported in part by National Natural Science Foundation of China under grant 61771145.

References

1. Arpit, D., et al.: A closer look at memorization in deep networks. In: International Conference on Machine Learning, pp. 233–242. PMLR, Sydney (2017)
2. Chang, J., Lan, Z., Cheng, C., Wei, Y.: Data uncertainty learning in face recognition. In: Proceedings of the IEEE/CVF Conference on Computer Vision and Pattern Recognition, pp. 5710–5719. IEEE, Seattle (2020)
3. Chen, X., Gupta, A.: Webly supervised learning of convolutional networks. In: Proceedings of the IEEE International Conference on Computer Vision, pp. 1431–1439. IEEE, Santiago (2015)
4. Choi, J., Chun, D., Kim, H., Lee, H.J.: Gaussian YOLOv3: an accurate and fast object detector using localization uncertainty for autonomous driving. In: Proceedings of the IEEE/CVF International Conference on Computer Vision, pp. 502–511. IEEE, Seoul (2019)

5. Gal, Y., Ghahramani, Z.: Dropout as a Bayesian approximation: representing model uncertainty in deep learning. In: International Conference on Machine Learning, pp. 1050–1059. PMLR, New York (2016)
6. Goldberger, J., Ben-Reuven, E.: Training deep neural-networks using a noise adaptation layer (2016)
7. Han, B., et al.: Co-teaching: robust training of deep neural networks with extremely noisy labels. arXiv preprint arXiv:1804.06872 (2018)
8. Ioffe, S., Szegedy, C.: Batch normalization: accelerating deep network training by reducing internal covariate shift. In: International Conference on Machine Learning, pp. 448–456. PMLR, Lille (2015)
9. Isobe, S., Arai, S.: Deep convolutional encoder-decoder network with model uncertainty for semantic segmentation. In: 2017 IEEE International Conference on INnovations in Intelligent SysTems and Applications (INISTA), pp. 365–370. IEEE, Gdynia (2017)
10. Jiang, L., Huang, D., Liu, M., Yang, W.: Beyond synthetic noise: deep learning on controlled noisy labels. In: International Conference on Machine Learning, pp. 4804–4815. PMLR (2020)
11. Jiang, L., Zhou, Z., Leung, T., Li, L.J., Fei-Fei, L.: MentorNet: learning data-driven curriculum for very deep neural networks on corrupted labels. In: International Conference on Machine Learning, pp. 2304–2313. PMLR, Stockholm (2018)
12. Kendall, A., Gal, Y.: What uncertainties do we need in Bayesian deep learning for computer vision? arXiv preprint arXiv:1703.04977 (2017)
13. Kingma, D.P., Welling, M.: Auto-encoding variational Bayes. arXiv preprint arXiv:1312.6114 (2013)
14. Krause, J., Stark, M., Deng, J., Fei-Fei, L.: 3D object representations for fine-grained categorization. In: 4th International IEEE Workshop on 3D Representation and Recognition (3DRR-13). IEEE, Sydney (2013)
15. Oh Song, H., Xiang, Y., Jegelka, S., Savarese, S.: Deep metric learning via lifted structured feature embedding. In: Proceedings of the IEEE Conference on Computer Vision and Pattern Recognition, pp. 4004–4012. IEEE, Las Vegas (2016)
16. Shi, Y., Jain, A.K.: Probabilistic face embeddings. In: Proceedings of the IEEE/CVF International Conference on Computer Vision, pp. 6902–6911. IEEE, Seoul (2019)
17. Sohn, K.: Improved deep metric learning with multi-class N-pair loss objective. In: Advances in Neural Information Processing Systems, pp. 1857–1865. Curran Associates Inc., Red Hook (2016)
18. Vinyals, O., Blundell, C., Lillicrap, T., Kavukcuoglu, K., Wierstra, D.: Matching networks for one shot learning. In: Proceedings of the 30th International Conference on Neural Information Processing Systems, NIPS 2016, pp. 3637–3645. Curran Associates Inc., Red Hook (2016)
19. Wang, X., Han, X., Huang, W., Dong, D., Scott, M.R.: Multi-similarity loss with general pair weighting for deep metric learning. In: Proceedings of the IEEE/CVF Conference on Computer Vision and Pattern Recognition, pp. 5022–5030 (2019)
20. Zhang, C., Bengio, S., Hardt, M., Recht, B., Vinyals, O.: Understanding deep learning requires rethinking generalization. arXiv preprint arXiv:1611.03530 (2016)

Image Segmentation

Improving Visual Question Answering by Semantic Segmentation

Viet-Quoc Pham(✉)[iD], Nao Mishima[iD], and Toshiaki Nakasu[iD]

Corporate Research and Development Center, Toshiba Corporation, Kawasaki, Japan
{quocviet.pham,nao.mishima,toshiaki.nakasu}@toshiba.co.jp

Abstract. Most recent visual question answering (VQA) methods extract object regions (bounding-boxes) by Faster R-CNN and use these region features in the visual encoder. Because extracted bounding-boxes are often located around things (countable objects), information on stuff (amorphous background regions such as grass and sky) is not reflected well in the visual encoder. Because stuff is amorphous and uncountable, it is common to use semantic segmentation to extract its features. In this work, we extend conventional thing-centric regions-of-interest (ROIs) by adding ROIs distributed around stuff regions and use semantic segmentation labels to encode stuff features in the visual encoder. The results of our experiments revealed that our method improved on existing VQA models and produced state-of-the-art results on VQA-v2 val, even though this dataset was not designed specifically for evaluating stuff, and most of its questions are thing-centric.

Keywords: VQA · Semantic segmentation

1 Introduction

Visual question answering (VQA) [3] is a task to predict an answer, given an input image and a question about it. In this study, we investigate image and language recognition, which lie at the crucial intersection of computer vision and natural language processing. Earlier works such as [18] used a regular CNN to extract a grid of image features and then used a recurrent neural network to encode the question. Since the development of the Bottom-Up and Top-Down (BUTD) model [2], thing-centric features have become the most commonly used visual representations.

A VQA model usually comprises a visual encoder that extracts the image representation, a language encoder that encodes the question, and a multi-modal fusion module that derives the answer. Most recent VQA methods use Faster R-CNN to extract object regions (bounding-boxes) [22], the features of which are used in the visual encoder. However, because extracted bounding-boxes are located around things (countable objects such as people and animals), information on stuff (amorphous background regions such as grass and sky) is not reflected well in the visual encoder. For example, in Fig. 1, understanding only things ("bicycle" in this case)

© Springer Nature Switzerland AG 2021
I. Farkaš et al. (Eds.): ICANN 2021, LNCS 12893, pp. 459–470, 2021.
https://doi.org/10.1007/978-3-030-86365-4_37

Question: Is a bicycle near the water?

Fig. 1. While most VQA methods only focus on things, we address both things and stuff in the VQA problem. In this example, both the thing ("bicycle") and stuff ("water") must be understood to answer the question.

cannot answer the question of whether the bicycle is near the water; the stuff "water" is also important for inferring the correct answer.

Recognizing things and stuff remains one of the key problems in scene understanding. Most of the large-scale datasets, such as ImageNet [10] and Visual Genome [15], annotate a large number of thing classes, but only provide labels for bounding boxes. Some semantic segmentation dataset, such as Cityscapes [9], Mapillary Vistas [19] and ADE20k [29], provide dense annotations where all pixels are labeled, but the number of stuff classes is limited. A recent research called panoptic segmentation [14,20] challenges to recognize both thing and stuff classes in a framework. Panoptic segmentation unifies the typically distinct semantic and instance segmentation tasks. The aim is to generate coherent scene segmentations that are rich and complete.

In this work, we address both thing and stuff classes in the VQA problem. Given that stuff is generally amorphous and uncountable, it is common to use semantic segmentation [17,29] to extract stuff information. In our method, we extend conventional thing-centric regions-of-interest (ROIs) by adding ROIs distributed around stuff regions and use their semantic segmentation labels to encode stuff features in the visual encoder.

Our method is easy to implement and can be used as a generic visual encoder to boost model performance in VQA. We conducted experiments using the VQA-v2 dataset [3], which contains 1.1 million questions with 11.1 million answers relating to real images. We show that our method improves on existing VQA models and produces state-of-the-art (SOTA) results on VQA-v2 val, even though this dataset is not designed specifically for evaluating stuff, and most of its questions are thing-centric.

2 Related Work

VQA. The most common VQA framework comprises a visual encoder, a question encoder, and multimodal fusion. The BUTD model [2] involves a combined bottom-up and top-down visual attention mechanism in which the bottom-up mechanism uses Faster R-CNN to extract object regions, the features of which are used in the visual encoder [22]. ReGAT [16] involves a relation encoder that captures inter-object relations beyond static object/region detection. In this approach, images are represented as graphs, whereas interactions between objects are captured via a graph attention mechanism. Taking another approach, [24] generated visual and textual adversarial examples as augmented data to train a VQA model. Other models, including GVQA [1], AReg [21], RUBI [4], and CSS [8], used learning strategies in order to reduce biases in VQA models.

Pre-training for VQA. Recently, the joint pre-training of models for vision and language tasks has attracted intense interest. A common approach is to view regions and words as tokens for their respective domains and to pre-train a variant of BERT [11] for masked token prediction. LXMERT [23] builds a large-scale Transformer [25] model comprising an object-relationship encoder, a language encoder, and a cross-modality encoder. The model is pre-trained with large amounts of image-and-sentence pairs by using several diverse representative pre-training tasks, and then fine-tuned to the VQA task. MUTANT [13] introduces mutation of inputs by modifying semantic parts of the input question and image. A pair-wise training protocol is used to ensure consistency between answer predictions for the original and mutant samples.

Semantic Segmentation. Recognizing and segmenting things and stuff at the pixel level remains one of the key problems in scene recognition. Whereas object detection methods detect objects at only the bounding-box level [6,22], the task of semantic image segmentation involves labeling each pixel of an image with a corresponding class [17,29]. Most semantic segmentation methods use a fully-convolutional network (FCN) with an encoder-decoder architecture [7,27]. A recent method [28] replaces the FCN by a Transformer architecture to encode an image as a sequence of patches. It achieves SOTA performances on various segmentation datasets. Related to semantic segmentation, a recent approach called panoptic segmentation [14,20] combines both instance segmentation (segmenting instance masks from bounding-boxes) and semantic segmentation in the same framework for a more complete scene recognition. The SOTA method [26] proposed a mask transformer to boost the performance.

Fig. 2. Conventional thing-centric ROIs (red bounding-boxes) and additional ROIs distributed around stuff regions (yellow bounding-boxes). (Color figure online)

Gan *et al.* [12] linked the instance segmentations to the questions and answers in the VQA dataset. Their work still focused on thing-centric VQA, and did not address the stuff classes.

3   Proposed Method

A VQA model usually comprises a visual encoder that extracts the image representation, a language encoder that encodes the question, and a multi-modal fusion module that derives the answer. Since the development of BUTD model [2], thing-centric features have become the most commonly used visual representations. Most recent VQA methods use Faster R-CNN to extract object regions [22], the features of which are used in the visual encoder. Because extracted bounding-boxes are located around things (countable objects such as people and animals), information on stuff (amorphous background regions such as grass and the sky) is not reflected well in the visual encoder. Stuff classes are important as they often determine the type of a scene, and provide context helping for recognizing things [5].

Because stuff is amorphous and uncountable, it is common to use semantic segmentation to extract stuff features. This task is defined as simply assigning a class label to each pixel in an image. In this work, we extend conventional thing-centric ROIs by adding ROIs distributed around stuff regions (Fig. 2) and use semantic segmentation labels to encode stuff features in the visual encoder.

3.1 Semantic Segmentation for the Visual Encoder

Faster R-CNN operates in two stages. In the first stage, a region proposal network is used to generate ROIs as object proposals. The network predicts a class-agnostic objectness score for each ROI. In the second stage, RoI pooling is used to extract a small feature map for each box proposal. Then, a feature vector v with 2,048 dimensions is extracted for each ROI r.

In this work, we use the first stage of Faster R-CNN to generate ROI proposals and select N ROIs with the top objectness scores (typically $N = 36$), as in [2]. As stated above, these N ROIs tend to be located around thing regions in the image. To encode stuff features, we use semantic segmentation to select additional M ROIs based on their semantic scores, which are defined as follows:

$$SC(r) = \max_i r \cap S_i \tag{1}$$

where S_i is an image region obtained by semantic segmentation, $r \cap S_i$ is the intersection area of ROI r and S_i, and $SC(r)$ is the largest intersection area of ROI r and a segmented region by semantic segmentation. For example, in Fig. 3(b), the semantic score of the highlighted ROI (yellow bounding-box) is the area of the "floor" region inside it.

The selection algorithm is as follows: we iteratively choose the ROI r^t with the largest semantic score among the remaining ROI proposals; find S_i, which has the largest intersection area with r^t ($i = \arg \max r^t \cap S_i$); remove pixels of S_i inside r^t from S_i; and select the next one r^{t+1}. The reason for removing pixels of S_i inside r^t before selecting r^{t+1} is to prevent the selected ROIs from being located around the same segmented regions. We note that the additional ROIs are often not used in conventional works due to their low objectness scores, but their large overlaps with stuff regions are useful for extracting stuff information.

After selecting these M ROIs, we send the total $N + M$ ROIs to the second stage of Faster R-CNN and extract a mean-pooled convolutional feature vector v for each ROI r. To encode stuff information, we assign a semantic label $SL(r)$ to each ROI r as follows.

$$SL(r) = L(\arg \max_i r \cap S_i) \tag{2}$$

Here, $L(i)$ is the label of the segmented region S_i (i.e., "floor", "grass"), and $SL(r)$ is the label of largest intersection region inside r. For example, the semantic label of the yellow ROI in Fig. 3(b) is "floor". Next, we followed [23] to project each label $SL(r)$ to a vector s by embedding sub-layers:

$$s = \text{WordEmbed}(SL(r)) \tag{3}$$

We use this vector s as a semantic feature for the ROI r.

Finally, each ROI r has a visual feature v obtained by object detection and a semantic feature s obtained by semantic segmentation.

(a)

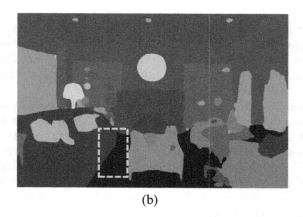

(b)

Fig. 3. Semantic segmentation result (b) from an input image (a). The semantic score of the yellow dotted ROI is the area of the brown region ("floor") inside it. (Color figure online)

3.2   Application to Existing Models

Our method can be used as a generic visual encoder to boost the model performance of a VQA and is easy to apply. In this work, we choose two representative models, namely, ReGAT [16] and LXMERT [23], as our baselines and describe the application of our encoder to these models (Fig. 4).

ReGAT uses Faster R-CNN to generate ROIs, and a question encoder for question embedding (Fig. 4 (a)). The ROI features and position features are then injected into the relation encoder, which uses a graph attention model to encode object relation. Each node of the graph is represented by a concatenation vector of the ROI feature v and the question embedding q. This concatenation helps the graph learn the semantic information from the question. The output features from the graph and the question embeddings are then fed into a cross-modality

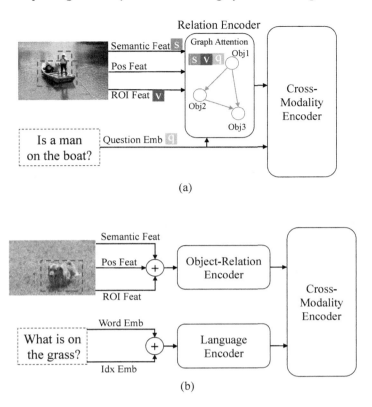

Fig. 4. Application of our encoder to ReGAT (a) and LXMERT (b). We extend ROIs based on their semantic scores, and extract for each ROI a semantic feature.

encoder, which produces the joint representation for the answer predictor. In this work, we apply our encoder to ReGAT by extending ROIs based on their semantic scores, and extracting for each ROI a semantic feature s, as explained in Sect. 3.1. We then concat this semantic feature s to the concatenation vector of the visual feature v and the question embedding q in the graph attention model. This helps the graph learn the semantic information from the stuff regions.

To demonstrate that our method can work with Transformer-based VQA models, we show how to combine LXMERT [23] with our visual encoder in Fig. 4 (b). In LXMERT, the words split from the input question and their indices are projected to word embeddings and index embeddings, and then added to the index-aware word embeddings. For image embeddings, they also use Faster R-CNN to generate ROIs, and extract for each ROI a visual feature and a position feature. The two features are then added to a position-aware embedding. Word embeddings and image embeddings are fed to a language encoder and an object-relation encoder, respectively. The output of the two encoders are then fed to a cross-modality encoder. These three encoders are built based on the Transformer architecture [25], which contains two kinds of attention layers: self-attention layers and cross-attention layers. We apply our encoder to LXMERT by extending original ROIs, and extracting for each ROI a semantic feature s. This semantic feature is then added to the image embedding, before being fed to the object-relation encoder. This process does not change the three Transformer encoders, so that we can fine-tune the LXMERT pre-trained model on the VQA task.

4 Experiments

We conducted experiments on the VQA-v2 dataset [3], which contains 443K training, 214K validation, and 453K test examples. We trained our models on the train split and evaluated them using the val split. We used the VQA accuracy [3] as the evaluation metric.

We used ReGAT [16] and LXMERT [23] as our baselines. LXMERT is a SOTA model among Transformer-based models using pre-training, while ReGAT gave best results among non-pretrained models. We also compared our results with those obtained using GVQA [1], AReg [21], RUBI [4], CSS [8], BUTD [2], Augmentation [24], and MUTANT [13].

For fair comparisons, we re-implemented the two baselines on our system but kept their original parameter settings. The both baselines use a Faster R-CNN model [22] which was trained from Visual Genome [15]. For ReGAT, we chose the implicit relation from the three types of relation (implicit, semantic and spatial) to implement the relation encoder. For LXMERT, we fine-tuned the VQA model from the pre-trained snapshot which was provided in their source code. To implement our visual encoder, we used the semantic segmentation model in [29], which was trained from their proposed ADE20K scene parsing dataset. All training was done on four NVIDIA Tesla V100 SXM2 32 GB GPUs.

The performance on VQA-v2 is shown in Table 1. We demonstrated that our method improves on two SOTA models (ReGAT and LXMERT) and outperforms all the other models mentioned above. Although VQA-v2 val was not specifically designed for evaluating stuff and most of its questions are thing-centric, we were still able to improve the performance of the baseline models.

We believe that evaluation on stuff-centric VQA dataset (which is not available) should give much better improvements. In Fig. 5, we show some qualitative comparisons between the baseline ReGAT [16] and the model combining the baseline with our method (ReGAT + Ours). In Fig. 5 (a) and (b), the baseline does not understand the stuff "grass", and thus gives the wrong answer "person", which has a strong bias for this question pattern. We find the same problems with the baseline in Fig. 5 (d) and (f). Our method shows improvements because it encodes stuff information in the model. As in Fig. 5 (f), distinguishing the stuff "field" from other regions ("sky", "tree") helps the model answer the correct color.

Ablation Study. Our visual encoder has two main components: ROI extension for adding ROIs around stuff regions, and label encoding for extracting for each

Table 1. Accuracy on the VQA-v2 val set. The upper half of the table shows non-pretrained models. The lower half shows pre-trained models based on the Transformer architecture.

Model	Pre-trained	Accuracy (%)
GVQA [1]		48.24
AReg [21]		62.75
RUBI [4]		63.10
CSS [8]		59.91
Augmentation [24]		65.16
BUTD [2]		63.48
ReGAT [16]		65.88
ReGAT + Ours		**66.25**
MUTANT [13]	✓	70.24
LXMERT [23]	✓	74.00
LXMERT + Ours	✓	**74.57**

ROI a semantic feature. We show the efficiency of each component in Table 2. Compared to the baseline models, we can observe consistent performance gain for the both baselines after adding each component. These results demonstrate that our method is a generic approach that can be used to improve VQA models.

Table 2. Efficiency of ROI extension and label encoding. We can observe consistent performance gain for the both baselines after adding each component.

Model	ROI ext.	Label enc.	Acc. (%)
ReGAT			65.88
ReGAT + ours1	✓		66.18
ReGAT + ours2	✓	✓	**66.25**
LXMERT			74.00
LXMERT + ours1	✓		74.43
LXMERT + ours2	✓	✓	**74.57**

There are two important parameters in our encoder: the number N of original ROIs, and the number M of additional ROIs. We show the accuracies for different values of (N, M) in Table 3. We observe that $(36, 36)$ gave the best result, while too small or too large values of them caused performance loss.

(a) Q: What is on the grass?
     Baseline: person
     Ours: dog

(b) Q: What is on the grass?
     Baseline: person
     Ours: truck

(c) Q: What is flying in the sky?
     Baseline: plane
     Ours: plane

(d) Q: Is a bicycle near the water?
     Baseline: no
     Ours: yes

(e) Q: What's the background color?
     Baseline: green
     Ours: green

(f) Q: What color is the field?
     Baseline: green
     Ours: yellow

Fig. 5. Qualitative comparison results between ReGAT (Baseline) and the model combining ReGAT with our method (Ours). The questions are related to stuff ("grass", "sky", "water", "background", "field"). Wrong answers are indicated in red. (Color figure online)

Table 3. Accuracies (%) for different values of (N, M)

(N, M)	$(18, 18)$	$(36, 36)$	$(36, 72)$
ReGAT + ours	65.36	**66.25**	66.21
LXMERT + ours	73.40	**74.57**	74.33

Application. We show a potential application of our method to the domain of street scene understanding in Fig. 6. Images of street scenes are full of stuff, so that most of the large semantic segmentation datasets are related to street scenes [9,19]. In our opinion, stuff information is crucially important for solving the VQA problem in this domain.

Q: Are any persons in the middle of the street?
A: No

Q: Are any persons in the middle of the street?
A: Yes

Q: What color is the car in the middle of the street?
A: White

Q: What is on the right sidewalk?
A: Bike

Fig. 6. VQA results by applying LXMERT + ours to Cityscapes images [9].

5   Conclusion

In this work, we extended conventional thing-centric ROIs by adding ROIs distributed around stuff regions and used semantic segmentation labels to encode stuff features in the visual encoder. We demonstrated that our method improves on the SOTA models ReGAT and LXMERT on VQA-v2 val. This improvement is even clearer when applied to questions related to stuff. Our future work will focus on creating a dataset that can be used to evaluate stuff-centric questions.

References

1. Agrawal, A., Batra, D., Parikh, D., Kembhavi, A.: Dont just assume; look and answer: overcoming priors for visual question answering. In: CVPR (2018)
2. Anderson, P., et al.: Bottom-up and top-down attention for image captioning and visual question answering. In: CVPR (2018)
3. Antol, S., et al.: VQA: visual question answering. In: ICCV (2015)
4. Cadene, R., Dancette, C., Ben-younes, H., Cord, M., Parikh, D.: Rubi: reducing unimodal biases in visual question answering. In: NeurIPS (2019)
5. Caesar, H., Uijlings, J., Ferrari, V.: Coco-stuff: thing and stuff classes in context. In: CVPR (2018)
6. Carion, N., Massa, F., Synnaeve, G., Usunier, N., Kirillov, A., Zagoruyko, S.: End-to-end object detection with transformers. In: Vedaldi, A., Bischof, H., Brox, T., Frahm, J.-M. (eds.) ECCV 2020. LNCS, vol. 12346, pp. 213–229. Springer, Cham (2020). https://doi.org/10.1007/978-3-030-58452-8_13

7. Chen, L.C., Papandreou, G., Kokkinos, I., Murphy, K., Yuille, A.L.: DeepLab: semantic image segmentation with deep convolutional nets, atrous convolution, and fully connected CRFs. TPAMI (2018)
8. Chen, L., Yan, X., Xiao, J., Zhang, H., Pu, S., Zhuang, Y.: Counterfactual samples synthesizing for robust visual question answering. In: CVPR (2020)
9. Cordts, M., et al.: The cityscapes dataset for semantic urban scene understanding. In: CVPR (2016)
10. Deng, J., Dong, W., Socher, R., Li, L.J., Li, K., Fei-Fei, L.: ImageNet: a large-scale hierarchical image database. In: CVPR (2009)
11. Devlin, J., Chang, M.W., Lee, K., Toutanova, K.: BERT: pre-training of deep bidirectional transformers for language understanding. In: NAACL (2019)
12. Gan, C., Li, Y., Li, H., Sun, C., Gong, B.: VQS: linking segmentations to questions and answers for supervised attention in VQA and question-focused semantic segmentation. In: ICCV (2017)
13. Gokhale, T., Banerjee, P., Baral, C., Yang, Y.: MUTANT: a training paradigm for out-of-distribution generalization in visual question answering. In: EMNLP (2020)
14. Kirillov, A., He, K., Girshick, R., Rother, C., Dollar, P.: Panoptic segmentation. In: CVPR (2019)
15. Krishna, R., et al.: Visual genome: connecting language and vision using crowd-sourced dense image annotations. arxiv preprint (2016)
16. Li, L., Gan, Z., Cheng, Y., Liu, J.: Relation-aware graph attention network for visual question answering. In: ICCV (2019)
17. Long, J., Shelhamer, E., Darrell, T.: Fully convolutional networks for semantic segmentation. In: CVPR (2015)
18. Lu, J., Yang, J., Batra, D., Parikh, D.: Hierarchical question-image co-attention for visual question answering. In: NeurIPS (2016)
19. Neuhold, G., Ollmann, T., Bulo, S.R., Kontschieder, P.: The Mapillary vistas dataset for semantic understanding of street scenes. In: ICCV (2017)
20. Pham, V.Q., Ito, S., Kozakaya, T.: BiSeg: simultaneous instance segmentation and semantic segmentation with fully convolutional networks. In: BMVC (2017)
21. Ramakrishnan, S., Agrawal, A., Lee, S.: Overcoming language priors in visual question answering with adversarial regularization. In: NeurIPS (2018)
22. Ren, S., He, K., Girshick, R., Sun, J.: Faster R-CNN: towards real-time object detection with region proposal networks. In: NeurIPS (2015)
23. Tan, H., Bansal, M.: LXMERT: learning cross-modality encoder representations from transformers. In: EMNLP (2019)
24. Tang, R., Ma, C., Zhang, W.E., Wu, Q., Yang, X.: Semantic equivalent adversarial data augmentation for visual question answering. In: Vedaldi, A., Bischof, H., Brox, T., Frahm, J.-M. (eds.) ECCV 2020. LNCS, vol. 12364, pp. 437–453. Springer, Cham (2020). https://doi.org/10.1007/978-3-030-58529-7_26
25. Vaswani, A., et al.: Attention is all you need. In: NeurIPS (2017)
26. Wang, H., Zhu, Y., Adam, H., Yuille, A., Chen, L.C.: Max-DeepLab: end-to-end panoptic segmentation with mask transformers. arxiv preprint (2020)
27. Zhao, H., Shi, J., Qi, X., Wang, X., Jia, J.: Pyramid scene parsing network. In: CVPR (2017)
28. Zheng, S., et al.: Rethinking semantic segmentation from a sequence-to-sequence perspective with transformers. arxiv preprint (2020)
29. Zhou, B., et al.: Semantic understanding of scenes through the ade20k dataset. Int. J. Comput. Vis. **127**, 302–321 (2018)

Weakly Supervised Semantic Segmentation with Patch-Based Metric Learning Enhancement

Patrick P. K. Chan[1(✉)], Keke Chen[1], Linyi Xu[1], Xiaoman Hu[1],
and Daniel S. Yeung[2]

[1] School of Computer Science and Engineering,
South China University of Technology, Guangzhou, China
patrickchan@scut.edu.cn
[2] Hong Kong, China

Abstract. Weakly supervised semantic segmentation (WSSS) methods
are more flexible and less costly than supervised ones since no pixel-level
annotation is required. Class activation maps (CAMs) are commonly
used in existing WSSS methods with image-level annotations to identify
seed localization cues. However, as CAMs are obtained from a classification network that mainly focuses on the most discriminative parts of
an object, less discriminative parts may be ignored and not identified.
This study aims to improve the local visual understanding on objects
of the classification network by considering an additional metric learning task on patches sampled from each CAM-based object proposal. As
the patches contain different object parts and surrounding backgrounds,
not only the most discriminative object parts but the entire objects are
learned through leveraging the patch similarity. After the joint training
process with the proposed patch-based metric learning and classification
tasks, we expect more discriminative local features can be learned by the
backbone network. As a result, more complete class-specific regions of an
object can be identified. Extensive experiments on the PASCAL VOC
2012 dataset validate the superiority of our method. Our proposed model
achieves improvement compared with the state-of-the-art methods.

Keywords: Semantic segmentation · Fully convolutional neural
networks · Weakly supervised learning · Metric learning

1 Introduction

The quality and quantity of labeled samples play an essential role in achieving
satisfactory performance for deep learning. However, obtaining sufficient training samples with labels is expensive and time-consuming, especially for supervised semantic segmentation since pixel-level annotation is required. In contrast,
WSSS requires only lower-level annotations, like bounding boxes [1], scribbles
[2], and image-level labels [3]. Compared to other kinds of annotation, image-
level annotation is more economical and easily to be obtained since it is available
in many open large-scale image datasets, *e.g.*ImageNet [4].

© Springer Nature Switzerland AG 2021
I. Farkaš et al. (Eds.): ICANN 2021, LNCS 12893, pp. 471–482, 2021.
https://doi.org/10.1007/978-3-030-86365-4_38

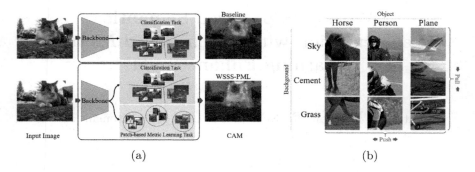

Fig. 1. (a) Examples of CAMs generated by the baseline (only relying on the classification task) and our proposed WSSS-PML (relying on both the classification and patch-based metric learning tasks). (b) Examples of the patches sampled from CAM-based object proposals. The proposed patch-based metric learning task pulls patch pairs with the same objects closer and pushes patch pairs with different objects away. More class-specific object regions can be learnt.

Most of the advanced WSSS methods with image-level annotations follow the pipeline with three steps. The localization cues for each object class are identified by the response maps, *e.g.*Classification Activation Map (CAM) [5], inferred from a multi-label classification network trained with image-level labels. The localization cues, which are treated as the seed areas, are then expanded and refined as the Pseudo Masks. Finally, a standard fully-supervised semantic segmentation model is trained by using the Pseudo Masks as the ground truth and is used in the inference stage. The first step of the three-step pipeline is the most important since it serves as supervision. The CAM is a prevailing method to obtain seed localization cues identified according to the contribution of a pixel to the decision of the classification network. However, directly relying on the classification network may cause incomplete and sparse seed areas. Since an image can be classified correctly by only focusing on most discriminative parts, the contribution of less discriminative regions may be similar to the surrounding background in CAM, *i.e.*less discriminative regions cannot be identified precisely in the seed areas. Figure 1(a) illustrates an example of a cat image in the PASCAL VOC 2012 dataset. If only the classification task is considered, the activation scores on the cat's body are small as the surrounding background since its head provides necessary discriminant information.

A patch-based metric learning task for weakly supervised semantic segmentation (WSSS-PML) which considers the standard classification task and also patch-based metric learning task is devised. The similarity of the patches sampled from the CAM-based object proposals is learnt in the metric learning task in which the same-category patches are pulled together while the different-category patches are pushed away in the latent feature space. As some patches contain different objects and similar backgrounds, shown in Fig. 1(b), this mechanism forces the backbone network to focus on local patterns of the target objects and ignore the backgrounds. As both global and local features are learnt by the classification task and patch-based metric learning task respectively, it is expected that object regions should be explored more thoroughly in our model.

The shared backbone network of the proposed WSSS-PML is first learnt from the classification task to obtain reliable CAM-based object proposals. Patches are selected with non-overlapping sliding window to completely cover the object proposals generated by the trained backbone network. The hard sampling strategy [6], which pushes the closest negative patch pairs and pulls the furthest positive patch pairs to form a denser response to the target object, is applied to form triplets in each mini-batch. The backbone network is then updated by both classification and patch-based metric learning tasks. The framework of our proposed model is shown in Fig. 2. Extensive experiments have been conducted on the PASCAL VOC 2012 dataset to demonstrate the effectiveness of our WSSS-PML. The results confirm that the high quality of seed localization cues provided by our method. Furthermore, overall semantic segmentation is better by using generated seed localization cues compared to state-of-the-arts.

The main contributions of this paper are summarized as follows:

- A novel patch-based metric learning task in addition to the classification task is proposed to enhance the visual understanding on local object parts from the sampled patches to identify more complete seed areas.
- The patch-based metric learning task forces the backbone network to learn on object parts by minimizing the triplet loss with the hard sampling strategy. It is expected more class-specific object regions can be identified.
- The experimental results on PASCAL VOC 2012 dataset demonstrate the outstanding performance of our method on improving the seed area quality, and the performance boost is achieved compared to state-of-the-art methods.

2   Related Work

2.1   Weakly Supervised Semantic Segmentation

Most of WSSS methods with image-level annotations follow a three-step pipeline. The studies of the first two steps, the seed areas identification and refinement methods for generating Pseudo Masks, are introduced.

Seed Areas Identification: CAM [5] is widely used in seed areas identification stage. The contribution of each pixel to the image classification task is quantified to localize the object regions. Several methods aiming at generating high-quality seed areas have been proposed and can be categorized into two types. The first type of the methods pays extra attention on the less discriminative regions by ignoring the knowledge of the network [7,8]. However, the object parts may not be targeted since the dropout units are chosen randomly, *i.e.*there is no guarantee that less discriminative regions of an object can be learnt better. Another kind considers additional constraints in the training of the classification network. Siamese network (SSENet) [9] forces the same CAM should be output on the images with different spatial transformation due to its equivariance. SEAM [10] extends SSENet by considering a pixel correlation module (PCM) additionally to refine CAM. Sub-Category Exploration [11] (SC-CAM) exploits the sub-category relations between object classes through iteratively clustering on image features. More object parts are expected to be indicated by applying a more challenging sub-category classification task. However, an unstable clustering process may require additional iterations for training in SC-CAM. Different from the methods mentioned above, our method enforces the backbone network to identify local object parts from the sampled patches by using metric learning.

Seed Areas Refinement: Seed areas refinement aims to expand and constraint the coarse response map to cover whole object areas precisely. AffinityNet [12], one of the most common refinement methods recently, learns the semantic affinity between adjacent pixel pairs and propagates local activation scores to an entire object through random walk. Another pixel-level affinity method, IRNet [13], aims at detecting accurate object boundaries and propagating activation scores within the boundaries. DSRG [14] reveals more complete areas by integrating the seed region growing algorithm with a deep segmentation network to expand the seed areas iteratively. Moreover, the cross-image relationship is investigate by CIAN [15] and ICD [16], which propose end-to-end framework to indicate more class-specific pixels. Context Adjustment (CONTA) [17] is an external mechanism for seed areas refinement which reconsiders the seed areas after the pipeline is completed by removing the confounding bias of context in classification.

2.2   Metric Learning

Metric Learning has been widely used in computer vision tasks, *e.g.*landmark recognition, face recognition and person re-identification [18]. It aims to learn an embedding space in which samples belong to the same class are close together and those of different classes are far apart. The triplet loss [19], which is a popular objective function used in Metric Learning, minimizes intra-class variations and maximizes inter-class variations simultaneously by using triplets generated by positive and negative samples of an anchor. In order to enhance the training efficiency, a hard sampling [6] is proposed to choose the farthest positive sample and nearest negative sample in a triplet.

3   Weakly Supervised Semantic Segmentation with Patch-Based Metric Learning Enhancement

Our proposed WSSS-PML focuses on seed areas identification in the WSSS pipeline. The backbone network is first trained on a standard classification task to generate reasonable object proposals (Sect. 3.1). CAM of each class is calculated from the trained backbone network. The object proposals are identified according to the seed localization cues calculated by using the CAMs

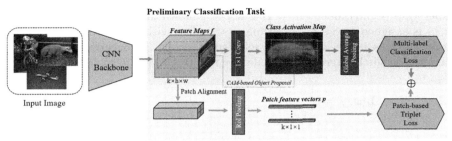

Preliminary Classification Task

Patch-based Metric Learning Task

Fig. 2. Framework of our proposed model. The network is first initialized by minimizing the classification loss. Both the proposed triplet loss of the metric learning on the patches and the classification loss are then optimized.

(Sect. 3.2). To enhance the learning on less discriminative regions, patches are sampled from each CAM-based object proposal for the patch-based metric learning task (Sect. 3.3). The backbone network is adjusted according to the triplet loss ($Loss^p_{tri}$) using the hard sampling strategy [6] jointly with the loss ($Loss_{cls}$) of the standard classification task (Sect. 3.4). The trained backbone network is used in inference to identify seed areas. The framework of our model is shown in Fig. 2.

3.1   Classification Task

A convolutional neural network containing a global average pooling and fully-connected classification layers is used as the classification network. Given an image I, the feature map output by the backbone network is denoted as $f = \phi(I) \in \mathbb{R}^{k \times h \times w}$, where ϕ denotes the function of the backbone network, f denotes the output feature map, k, h and w represent the channels, height and width of the feature map respectively.

The backbone network is updated by minimizing the multi-label classification loss $Loss_{cls}$ of the preliminary classification task. The CAM of object class c can be obtained according to the trained classification network as follows:

$$M_c(x,y) = \theta_c^\top f(x,y) \tag{1}$$

where (x,y) denotes the coordinate on f, θ_c indicates the classification weight of c, and $^\top$ represents the inner product of two vectors. $M_c(x,y)$ which represents the activation score of (x,y) belonging to c is normalized linearly to $[0,1]$. CAMs are then upsampled to meet with the height H and width W of I by the bilinear interpolation, defined as $M \in \mathbb{R}^{C \times H \times W}$, where C is the object class number.

3.2   CAM-Based Object Proposal

As the training data of the patch-based metric learning task, the object proposals are extracted from CAMs during the forward pass of the network in each mini-batch. To extract the object proposals, the CAM is first transformed to the Class

Label Map (CLM), denoted by $\mathbf{L} \in \mathbb{R}^{H \times W}$, shown in Eq. (2). Each coordinate (x, y) is assigned to $c \in C$ according to the class with the maximum activation score which is larger than a pre-selected threshold β, otherwise, the pixel is classified as the background class denoted by 0. CLM is formulated as:

$$\mathbf{L}(x, y) = \begin{cases} \arg\max_{1 \leq c \leq C} M_c(x, y), & \max_{1 \leq c \leq C} M_c(x, y) > \beta \\ 0, & \text{otherwise} \end{cases} \tag{2}$$

where $\mathbf{L}(x, y)$ denotes the class label of the coordinate (x, y) on the CAM, while $M_c(x, y)$ denotes the activation score that the coordinate (x, y) belongs to the class c. β serves as a hard threshold to separate the background and foreground objects, $i.e.$ a coordinate with an activation score smaller than β is classified as the background; otherwise, it is classified as a foreground object.

The quality of the object proposal from which the patches are sampled in our model is affected by β significantly. If β is small, some over-activated background areas will be identified wrongly as a foreground object. On the other hand, non-discriminative object areas may be excluded when β is large. The minimum bounding box containing the connected pixels with the same class label is defined as an object proposal. As an image may contain more than one bounding box for a class, Non-Maximum Suppression (NMS) [20] is adopted to remove proposals of the same class with a large overlapping rate. Moreover, an object proposal with a small size or large aspect ratio is filtered in order to reduce the noise influence.

3.3 Patch-Based Metric Learning

p patches are sampled from each CAM-based object proposal with a non-overlapping sliding window to cover the entire object proposal. A sampled patch is aligned back to the feature map f as the Region of Interest (RoI). As a result, a k-dimensional feature vector $P \in \mathbb{R}^k$ is obtained from f via the RoI pooling for each patch. The label of a patch is then set as the class of its object proposal.

Hard Sampling Strategy in Mini-Batch. Let $\mathcal{P} = \{P^i\}_{i=1}^M$ be the set of patch feature vectors in a mini-batch, where M is the number of the sampled patches. The hard sampling strategy [19] is applied to select the triplet from each $\mathcal{P}$. Unlike the random sampling method, the furthest patch of the same class and the closest patch of a different class are chosen to form a triplet in the hard sampling method in order to obtain a more condensed feature space. The training objective of the patch-based metric learning task is shown in Eq. (3).

$$Loss_{tri}^p = \frac{1}{M} \sum_{i=1}^M \max\{0, D(P_a^i, P_+^i) - D(P_a^i, P_-^i) + \alpha\} \tag{3}$$

where P_+^i and P_-^i denote the positive and negative pathes of the anchor patch P_i^a, α represents the margin, D denotes the distance measure, and the Euclidean distance is used in our study.

3.4   Joint Training Scheme

The losses of the proposed patch-based metric learning and standard classification tasks are minimized simultaneously in our model, shown as follows:

$$Loss = Loss_{cls} + \lambda Loss_{tri}^{p} \qquad (4)$$

where λ denotes the tradeoff between two losses and aims to balance them.

4   Experiment

4.1   Experimental Setting

Dataset: The PASCAL VOC 2012 segmentation benchmark [21] containing 20 object and 1 background classes is considered in our study. 1,464, 1,449 and 1,456 images are contained in training, validation and test sets respectively. The augmentation training set which includes 10,582 images from SBD [22] is applied to enlarge the training set as the common practice. Only image-level labels are used during training.

Evaluation: Mean intersection over union (mIoU), recall and precision are for evaluation following previous works.

Implementation Details: The revised ResNet38 pre-trained on ImageNet is used as the backbone network of our model by following AffinityNet [12]. The data augmentation strategy of [12] is considered in the training process. The default parameters of [12] are applied to train the preliminary classification task. The multi-label soft margin loss is adopted as $Loss_{cls}$ for the classification task in our model. The learning rate r is set to 0.1 with 0.0005 as weight decay in Adam optimizer in the first training on the classification task. During the joint training of the patch-based metric learning and the classification tasks, the learning rate is set to 0.01 and halved every epoch with adam optimizer. The number of patches p is set to 4 in the triplet loss $Loss_{tri}^{p}$. λ in Eq. (4) is set as 0.05 to balance $Loss_{cls}$ and $Loss_{tri}^{p}$. β in Eq. (2) is set as 0.2.

Reproducibility: All experiments are implemented with PyTorch and carried out on 2 NVIDIA GTX 1080 Ti GPUs.

4.2   CAM Analysis

CAMs generated by WSSS-PML and the baseline which only considers classification task are compared in this section in terms of mIoU, recall, precision and visualization. It should be noted that in Epoch#0 of WSSS-PML, the backbone network is trained by the classification task which is identical to the baseline.

As illustrated in Table 1, our WSSS-PML outperforms the baseline (Epoch#0) significantly. With only one epoch of joint optimization in Epoch#1, the mIoU, recall and precision of CAMs generated by our method increases 2.6%, 3.3% and 1.5% respectively. The improvement of our method are mainly caused

Table 1. Quality of CAM generated by WSSS-PML with different epoches on PASCAL VOC 2012 training set

Epoch	mIoU (%)	Recall (%)	Precision (%)
Epoch#0 (*baseline*)	47.7	67.4	61.4
Epoch#1	$50.3_{+2.6}$	$70.7_{+3.3}$	$\mathbf{62.9_{+1.5}}$
Epoch#2	$\mathbf{50.8_{+3.1}}$	$72.6_{+5.2}$	$62.3_{+0.9}$
Epoch#3	$\mathbf{50.8_{+3.1}}$	$\mathbf{72.7_{+5.3}}$	$62.3_{+0.9}$

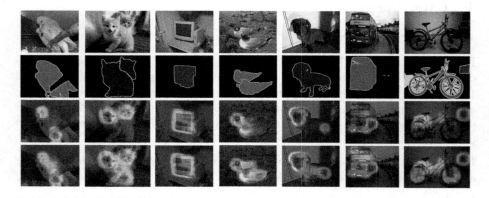

Fig. 3. Visualization examples of CAMs on PASCAL VOC 2012 training set. From the top to bottom, the rows represent the original images, the ground truth, the CAMs generated by the baseline and the CAMs generated by our WSSS-PML respectively.

by the increase of the recall, which means class-specific object parts ignored by the standard classification task are learnt by our WSSS-PML. The performance of our method becomes stable on Epoch#3. For the rest of the experiments, Epoches#2 is adopted considering both the computation efficiency and the performance.

The visualization examples of the generated CAMs on three training images are shown in Fig. 3. The CAM is represented with a heatmap in which the color closer to red means the higher activation score. The results indicate that the baseline tends to activate on the most discriminative regions. Through learning from both classification and patch-based metric learning tasks, the CAM generated by WSSS-PML is capable to cover more complete object regions than the baseline which only considers the classification task.

4.3   State-of-the-Art Methods Comparison

To further evaluate the effectiveness of our model, the AffinityNet [12] is adopted as the seed areas refinement method to generate the Pseudo Masks. One should be noted that WSSS-PML only focuses on the seed areas identification stage. Therefore, any advanced seed areas refinement framework [14–17] could be

Table 2. Comparison of state-of-the-art WSSS seed areas identification methods. 'S' and 'I' denote the saliency map and image level label, while 'val' and 'test' denote the validation and test sets of PASCAL VOC 2012 dataset.

Methods	Supervision	Backbone	mIoU (val)	mIoU (test)
AffinityNet (baseline) [12]	I	ResNet-38	61.7%	63.7%
AffinityNet (baseline)* [12]	I	ResNet-101	**61.9%**	**62.3%**
FickleNet [8]	I+S	ResNet-101	64.9%	65.3%
OAA [23]	I	ResNet-101	63.9%	65.6%
SEAM [10]	I	ResNet-38	64.5%	65.7%
SEAM* [10]	I	ResNet-101	64.4%	64.9%
SC-CAM [11]	I	ResNet-101	66.1%	65.9%
WSSS-PML	I	ResNet-101	**66.5%**	**66.5%**

* Our re-implemented results with DeepLab-v2 (ResNet-101) as the segmentation network.

Fig. 4. Visualization results of segmentation mask on PASCAL VOC 2012 validation set. From the top to bottom, the rows represent the original images, the ground truth and the final segmentation mask of our method respectively.

embedded and is not considered in this comparison. For a fair comparison, we adopt the classical DeepLab-v2 with ResNet-101 as the backbone. Some examples of the final semantic segmentation results are illustrated in Fig. 4, which verifies that our results are close to the ground truth segmentation masks.

State-of-the-art seed areas identification methods of WSSS using the ResNet-based backbone are compared with WSSS-PML in Table 2. Our method achieves the highest mIoU on the validation and test sets against all the advanced methods including those using saliency maps as additional supervision. The baseline, *i.e.*AffinityNet, is 4.6% and 4.2% lower than WSSS-PML on validation and test sets respectively, which suggests that the quality of the identified seed areas improves significantly. Table 3 compares the category performance on the validation set of WSSS-PML with AffinityNet [12], SEAM [10], and SC-CAM [11], which adopted the same seed areas refinement method [12]. Our method performs better on 16 out of the 20 categories comparing to the baseline, *i.e.*AffinityNet,

Table 3. Category performance comparisons with advanced seed areas identification methods that adopted AffinityNet as the seed areas refinement method on PASCAL VOC 2012 validation set.

Score	Areo	Bike	Bird	Boat	Bottle	Bus	Car	Cat	Chair	Cow	Table	Dog	Horse	Motor	Person	Plant	Sheep	Sofa	Train	Tv	mIoU
AffinityNet	68.2	30.6	81.1	49.6	61.0	77.8	66.1	75.1	29.0	66.0	40.2	80.4	62.0	70.4	73.7	42.5	70.7	42.6	68.1	51.6	61.7
SEAM	68.5	33.3	85.7	40.4	67.3	78.9	76.3	81.9	29.1	75.5	48.1	79.9	73.8	71.4	75.2	48.9	79.8	40.9	58.2	53.0	64.5
SC-CAM	51.6	30.3	82.9	53.0	75.8	88.6	74.8	86.6	32.4	79.9	53.8	82.3	78.5	70.4	71.2	40.2	78.3	42.9	66.8	58.8	66.1
WSSS_PML	53.5	32.0	84.4	51.8	69.9	88.9	77.9	88.4	34.1	82.5	53.2	84.0	81.4	73.3	71.1	40.7	79.1	44.4	61.3	56.0	66.5

Table 4. CAMs Quality of the baseline, WSSS-PML$_{Ran}$, and WSSS-PML.

Model	PML	Sampling	mIoU (%)
Baseline	–	–	47.7
WSSS-PML$_{Ran}$	✓	Random	49.6
WSSS-PML	✓	Hard	**50.8**

which demonstrates the effectiveness of our model on different object classes. Our model also achieves the highest and second highest times, at 9 and 6 respectively among all the methods.

All the results confirm that our proposed patch-based metric learning task in the multi-task framework improves the understanding of the backbone network on each part of objects.

4.4   Ablation Study on Hard Sampling Strategy

We analyse the effect of the hard sampling strategy in the proposed patch-based metric learning on the quality of generated CAM. In addition to the baseline, WSSS-PML$_{Ran}$ representing the random sampling in triplet generation of our method is also compared with WSSS-PML using the hard sampling. Table 4 illustrate the mIoU of the generated CAMs. WSSS-PML$_{Ran}$ achieves 1.9% mIoU higher than the baseline, which indicates that the patch-based metric learning enhances the complete understanding on objects of the backbone network. The hard sampling strategy also plays an important role in learning since mIoU of WSSS-PML$_{Ran}$ improves from 49.6% to 50.8% when the hard sampling strategy is used.

4.5   Computation Complexity

Compared to the baseline, WSSS-PML only requires two more epoches for joint training on the classification and patch-based metric learning tasks. the average training time on each image of WSSS-PML is 0.629 sec/img, which is similar to the baseline (0.628 sec/img). It suggests that the patch-based metric learning does not significantly increase the training time complexity. Besides, the inference computation complexity of our approach is the same as the baseline since the backbone networks are the same.

5   Conclusion

One major problem of seed areas identification methods in the WSSS pipeline is that the less discriminative regions of an object may be neglected due to their weak contribution to the classification task. In this paper, we propose a patch-based metric learning task integrated with the classification task for revealing a complete seed areas in WSSS. Our method aims to strengthen the visual understanding on different regions of an object by forcing the backbone network to distinguish object's parts represented by patches of the CAM-based object proposals. With low computation cost, the objects are identified more completely by our proposed method compared with the baseline classification task in the experiments. By using the AffinityNet as seed areas refinement method and DeepLab-v2 as the segmentation model, our method achieves the better performance than the state-of-the-art seed areas identification methods of WSSS on PASCAL VOC 2012 dataset. The experimental results confirm that WSSS-PML improves the understanding of the backbone network on the objects successfully.

Acknowledgments. This paper is supported by the Natural Science Foundation of Guangdong Province, China (No. 2018A030313203).

References

1. Dai, J.F., He, K.M., Sun, J.: BoxSup: exploiting bounding boxes to supervise convolutional networks for semantic segmentation. In: Proceedings of the IEEE International Conference on Computer Vision, pp. 1635–1643. IEEE (2015)
2. Lin, D., Dai, J.F., et al.: ScribbleSup: scribble-supervised convolutional networks for semantic segmentation. In: Proceedings of the IEEE Conference on Computer Vision and Pattern Recognition, pp. 3159–3167. IEEE (2017)
3. Kolesnikov, A., Lampert, C.H.: Seed, expand and constrain: three principles for weakly-supervised image segmentation. In: Leibe, B., Matas, J., Sebe, N., Welling, M. (eds.) ECCV 2016. LNCS, vol. 9908, pp. 695–711. Springer, Cham (2016). https://doi.org/10.1007/978-3-319-46493-0_42
4. Deng, J., Dong, W., Socher, R., Li, L.J., Li, K., Li, F.F.: ImageNet: a large-scale hierarchical image database. In: Proceedings of the IEEE Conference on Computer Vision and Pattern Recognition, pp. 248–255. IEEE (2009)
5. Zhou, B.L., Khosla, A., Lapedriza, A., Oliva, A., Torralba, A.: Learning deep features for discriminative localization. In: Proceedings of the IEEE Conference on Computer Vision and Pattern Recognition, pp. 2921–2929. IEEE (2016)
6. Wu, C., Manmatha, R., Smola, A.J., Krahenbuhl, P.: Sampling matters in deep embedding learning. In: Proceedings of the IEEE International Conference on Computer Vision, pp. 2859–2867. IEEE (2017)
7. Wei, Y.C., Feng, J.S., Liang, X.D., Cheng, M.M., Zhao, Y., Yan, S.C: Object region mining with adversarial erasing: a simple classification to semantic segmentation approach. In: Proceedings of the IEEE Conference on Computer Vision and Pattern Recognition, pp. 6488–6496. IEEE (2017)
8. Lee, J., Kim, E., et al.: FickleNet: weakly and semi-supervised semantic image segmentation using stochastic inference. In: Proceedings of the IEEE Conference on Computer Vision and Pattern Recognition, pp. 5267–5276. IEEE (2019)

9. Wang, Y.D., Zhang, J., Kan, M.N., Shan, S.G., Chen, X.L.: Self-supervised scale equivariant network for weakly supervised semantic segmentation. arXiv: Computer Vision and Pattern Recognition (2019)

10. Wang, Y., Zhang, J., Kan, M., Shan, S., Chen, X.: Self-supervised equivariant attention mechanism for weakly supervised semantic segmentation. In: Proceedings of the IEEE Conference on Computer Vision and Pattern Recognition, pp. 12272–12281. IEEE (2020)

11. Chang, Y.T., Wang, Q.S., Hung, W.C., Robinson, P.: Weakly-supervised semantic segmentation via sub-category exploration. In: Proceedings of the International Conference on Computer Vision, IEEE (2020)

12. Ahn, J., Kwak, S.: Learning pixel-level semantic affinity with image-level supervision for weakly supervised semantic segmentation. In: Proceedings of the IEEE Conference on Computer Vision and Pattern Recognition, pp. 4981–4990. IEEE (2018)

13. Ahn, J., Cho, S., Kwak, S.: Weakly supervised learning of instance segmentation with inter-pixel relations. In: Proceedings of the IEEE Conference on Computer Vision and Pattern Recognition, pp. 2204–2213. IEEE (2019)

14. Huang, Z.L., Wang, X.G., Wang, J.S., Liu, W.Y., Wang, J.D.: Weakly-supervised semantic segmentation network with deep seeded region growing. In: Proceedings of the IEEE Conference on Computer Vision and Pattern Recognition, pp. 7014–7023. IEEE (2018)

15. Fan, J.S., Zhang, Z.X., Tan, T.N., Song, C.F., Xiao, J.: CIAN: cross-image affinity net for weakly supervised semantic segmentation. In: Proceedings of the AAAI Conference on Artificial Intelligence, pp. 10762–10769 (2020)

16. Fan, J., Zhang, Z., Song, C., Tan, T.: Learning integral objects with intra-class discriminator for weakly-supervised semantic segmentation. In: Proceedings of the IEEE Conference on Computer Vision and Pattern Recognition, pp. 4282–4291. IEEE (2020)

17. Zhang, D., Zhang, H.W., Tang, J.H., Hua, X.S., Sun, Q.R.: Causal intervention for weakly-supervised semantic segmentation. In: Proceedings of the Conference on Neural Information Processing Systems (2020)

18. Boiarov, A., Tyantov, E.: Large scale landmark recognition via deep metric learning. In: Proceedings of the ACM International Conference, pp. 169–178 (2019)

19. Schroff, F., Kalenichenko, D., Philbin, J.: FaceNet: a unified embedding for face recognition and clustering. In: Proceedings of the IEEE Conference on Computer Vision and Pattern Recognition, pp. 815–823. IEEE (2015)

20. Neubeck, A., Van Gool, L.: Efficient non-maximum suppression. In: Proceedings of the International Conference on Pattern Recognition, pp. 850–855. IEEE (2006)

21. Everingham, M., Eslami, S.M., Van Gool, L., Williams, C.K.I., Winn, J., Zisserman, A.: The pascal visual object classes challenge: a retrospective. Int. J. Comput. Vision 111(1), 98–136 (2015)

22. Everingham, M., Van Gool, L., Williams, C.K.I., Winn, J., Zisserman, A.: The pascal visual object classes (VOC) challenge. Int. J. Comput. Vision 88(2), 303–338 (2010)

23. Jiang, P.T., Hou, Q.B., Cao, Y., Cheng, M.M., Wei, Y.C., Xiong, H.K.: Integral object mining via online attention accumulation. In: Proceedings of the International Conference on Computer Vision. IEEE (2019)

ComBiNet: Compact Convolutional Bayesian Neural Network for Image Segmentation

Martin Ferianc[1]([✉]), Divyansh Manocha[3], Hongxiang Fan[2], and Miguel Rodrigues[1]

[1] University College London, London WC1E 7JE, UK
{martin.ferianc.19,m.rodrigues}@ucl.ac.uk
[2] Imperial College London, London SW7 2AZ, UK
h.fan17@imperial.ac.uk
[3] Cambridge, UK
divyanshmanocha@gmail.com

Abstract. Fully convolutional U-shaped neural networks have largely been the dominant approach for pixel-wise image segmentation. In this work, we tackle two defects that hinder their deployment in real-world applications: *1)* Predictions lack uncertainty quantification that may be crucial to many decision-making systems; *2)* Large memory storage and computational consumption demanding extensive hardware resources. To address these issues and improve their practicality we demonstrate a few-parameter compact Bayesian convolutional architecture, that achieves a marginal improvement in accuracy in comparison to related work using significantly fewer parameters and compute operations. The architecture combines parameter-efficient operations such as separable convolutions, bilinear interpolation, multi-scale feature propagation and Bayesian inference for per-pixel uncertainty quantification through Monte Carlo Dropout. The best performing configurations required fewer than 2.5 million parameters on diverse challenging datasets with few observations.

Keywords: Two-dimensional image segmentation · Convolutional neural networks · Bayesian probabilistic modelling

1 Introduction

Image segmentation is the pixel-level computer vision task of segregating an image into discrete regions semantically. Among various algorithms, convolutional neural networks (CNNs) have been key to this task, demonstrating outstanding performance [1,8–12,15,22,29]. CNNs are able to express predictions as pixel-wise output masks by learning appropriate feature representations in an end-to-end fashion, while allowing processing inputs with various size. This is especially useful in inferring object support relationships for robotics, autonomous driving or healthcare, as well as scene geometry [12,16,23].

A practical drawback of regular CNNs is that they are unable to capture their uncertainty which is crucial for many safety-critical applications [6]. Bayesian

© Springer Nature Switzerland AG 2021
I. Farkaš et al. (Eds.): ICANN 2021, LNCS 12893, pp. 483–494, 2021.
https://doi.org/10.1007/978-3-030-86365-4_39

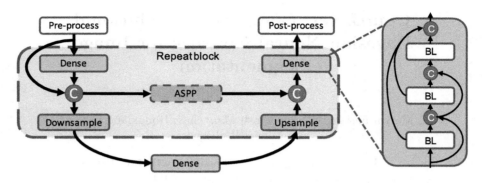

Fig. 1. *ComBiNet* an U-Net [11,22] like architecture consisting of Repeat blocks with different input scales and dilation rates in an Atrous Spatial Pyramid Pooling (ASPP) module. The block contains Dense feature extracting blocks, Downsampling to reduce the spatial dimensionality by 2× and Upsampling for restoring it back after processing the features from a lower dimensionality. The context is transferred through an optional ASPP module and concatenated (C), pairing the same spatial resolution. On the right is the detail of the Dense block consisting of Basic Layers (BLs). The arrows represent data flow.

CNNs [5] adopt Bayesian inference to provide a principled uncertainty estimation on top of the segmentation masks. However, as the research community seeks to improve accuracy and better capture information in a wider range of applications, potential CNN architectures become deeper and further connection-wise complicated [8,11,14,29]. As a result they are increasingly more compute and memory demanding and a regular modern CNN architecture cannot be easily adopted for Bayesian inference. As an analytical prediction of uncertainty is not tractable with such architectures, it is required to approximate it through Monte Carlo sampling with multiple runs through the network. The increased runtime cost, primarily due to sampling, has been a limiting factor of Bayesian CNNs in real-world image segmentation.

To address the aforementioned issues of lacking uncertainty quantification in regular CNNs and extensive execution cost, the contribution of this work is in improving the hardware performance of two-dimensional (2D) Bayesian CNNs for image segmentation, while also considering an efficient pixel-wise uncertainty quantification. Our approach builds on recent successes to improve software-hardware performance [3,8,9,11,12,22,27] and extends these into a novel 2D Bayesian CNN architectural template as shown in Fig. 1. Specifically, we focus on few-parameter/few-operation models which decrease the runtime cost of each feedforward pass, and present a compact design named *ComBiNet*. Monte Carlo Dropout [6] is used for Bayesian inference. The novelty of our work is in demonstrating that it is possible to develop compressed models for 2D image segmentation while preserving uncertainty estimation capabilities, without compromising accuracy. We demonstrate ComBiNet's fine performance on the few-samples video-based CamVid [2] dataset and a database of darkfield microscopy images [20]. On the account of the results obtained, we demonstrate designs that achieve accuracy comparable to the state-of-the-art [1,7,11,12,17,19,26,28], but requiring only a fraction of the parameters or operations. Code for the implementation is at: https://git.io/JmhTo.

2   Related Work

CNN-based architectures for image segmentation comprise of an encoder-decoder network, which first encodes the input into features and an upsampler that then recovers the output from the features as the decoder [1,15]. The decoder is usually hierarchically opposite to the encoder, although both consist of multiple levels of computationally-expensive convolutions. Based on this encoder-decoder structure, the input is thereby refined to obtain the segmentation mask.

Long et al. [15] first proposed the idea of Fully Convolutional Network (FCN) for this task, which outputs a segmentation mask in any given spatial dimensionality. Further improvements were achieved using bipolar interpolation and skip connections [8]. However, FCN is limited to few-pixel local information and therefore prone to lose global semantic context. SegNet [1] was the first CNN trained end-to-end for segmentation. The novelty of the architecture was in eliminating the need for learning to upsample using fixed bilinear interpolation for resolution recovery. Ronneberger et al. [22] introduced a contracting and expansive pathway to better capture context and improve localisation precision, forming the characteristic "U"-shaped network.

Atrous convolutions [3,29] have also been key to recent advancements, as they allow increasing the receptive field without changing the feature map resolution. Multiple such convolutional layers, that can accept the input in parallel, allow us to better account for multi-scale contextual information across images. This is termed Atrous Spatial Pyramid Pooling (ASPP) [29].

The downsampling of input images in deep classification networks can be hardware-inefficient, and several works have addressed this in the context of embedded vision applications. MobileNets [9] introduced the idea of factorising the standard convolution into depth-wise/kernel-wise separable convolutions, formed of a depth-wise convolution layer that filters the input and a 1×1 convolution that combines these to create new features. In [21], the authors employed kernel-wise separable convolutions to construct a compact model with the objective of enabling efficient real-time semantic segmentation. ESPNet [17] used a hierarchical pyramid of dilated and 1×1 convolutions to reduce the architecture size. Nekrasov et al. [19] developed an automatic way to find extremely light-weight architectures for image segmentation.

Bayesian neural networks [5,7,12,13,16] assign a probability distribution on the network weights instead of point estimates, to provide uncertainty measurements in the predictions. Employing this Bayesian mathematical grounding for CNNs enables us to obtain both the mask and uncertainty associated with it in the context of image segmentation. To the best of our knowledge, there are only two works focusing on 2D Bayesian CNNs in image segmentation for robust uncertainty quantification. Both of these approaches use Monte Carlo Dropout (MCD) [6], in which Gal and Ghahramani cast dropout [24] training in a NN as Bayesian inference without the need for additional parametrisation. In [12] the authors searched and utilised dropout positioning in a SegNet [1]. In [7] the authors learned the dropout rates with respect to a DenseNet-like architecture [11].

In comparison to the related work, our work repurposes existing approaches [3,8,9,11,12,22] to construct hardware-efficient 2D segmentation networks by decreasing the number of parameters and multiply-add-accumulate (MAC) operations while also providing improvements in accuracy. Furthermore, unlike previous hardware-efficient works, we use MCD for uncertainty quantification.

3   ComBiNet

The 2D network architecture of ComBiNet is presented in Fig. 1, which is based on a "U"-net-like architecture [11,22] that divides itself into upsampling and downsampling paths as briefly described in Sect. 2. Skip connections connecting the paths preserve sharp edges by reducing the coarseness of masks and as a result contextual information from the input images can be preserved. The general building unit of the network is a Repeat block. A Dense block at the bottom of the network is used to capture global image features in addition to the optional ASPP blocks that are placed with skip connections. The input is processed using a 3×3 2D convolution Pre-processing block, while the output is processed through a 1×1 2D convolution Post-processing block.

3.1   Repeat Block

Repeat blocks have the dual purpose of extracting features, through the Dense block, and extracting contextual information, through an optional ASPP block. Each block spatially downsamples the input by a factor of 2 and later upsamples it back to the block's input resolution.

The Repeat block is reusable, such that multiple blocks can be appended to one another to extract contextually richer features. The output of the Downsampling block is the input into the next Repeat block. This means the features and the input are processed at different spatial sizes. It is important to highlight there is a connection between the input of the Repeat block and the output of its encoding Dense block, prior to Downsampling. The input is concatenated to the output of the block, without being processed through the feature extracting Dense block, to enable propagation of local and global contextual information.

Basic Building Blocks. The Dense block is inspired by [10,11] and shown expanded in Fig. 1 on the right. It is a gradual concatenation of previous features allowing for feature-map changes processed through a Basic Layer (BL). A BL accepts inputs from all previous layers in a Dense block. The output channel number of the BL is restricted to a growth rate of k, which is constant for all BLs in the network, to avoid exponential increase in the channels propagated. More intuitively, it regulates the amount of new information each layer can contribute to the global state. For similar reasons, the output of the Dense block does not automatically include the original input, unless considering the downsampling path. The Dense block can have an arbitrary number of BLs and their counts are increased towards smaller spatial input size. Efficient gradient and feature propagation is ensured by concatenations between all previous stages and the current stage. Details of the serially connected individual operations of BL, Downsampling and Upsampling are given below.

Basic Layer: Batch normalisation; ReLU; 3×3 Completely separable convolution; Dropout
Downsample: Batch normalisation; ReLU; 1×1 Convolution; Dropout; 2×2 Max-pooling with stride 1; 2×2 Blur with stride 2
Upsample: Bilinear interpolation; 1×1 Convolution

The BL first performs batch normalisation (BN) which pre-processes the inputs coming from the different BLs. This operation is followed by ReLU and a 3×3 completely separable convolution for feature extraction. It consists of serially connected $1 \times 3; 3 \times 1$ convolutions with the output channel size same as the input, while being channel-wise separated, followed by a reshaping pointwise 1×1 convolution. We use completely separable convolutions for their parameter and MAC operation count efficiency. In particular, when paired with an appropriate k, BL can be an extremely compact feature extractor. The convolution is followed by a 2D dropout to provide regularisation and perform Bayesian inference [5].

The Downsampling extracts coarse semantic features. The combined operations include BN, ReLU, 1×1 convolution, dropout and 2×2 max-pooling with stride 1 and 2×2 blurring with stride 2. We used additional blurring with max-pooling to preserve shift-invariance of convolutions [27].

The Upsampling uses the parameter-less bilinear interpolation to save computational and memory resources. Furthermore, it also preserves shift invariance of objects in the input images and avoids aliasing [27]. We add a 1×1 2D convolution to the output of the interpolation to refine the upsampled features.

Atrous Spatial Pyramid Pooling (ASPP). ASPP [3,29], as briefly introduced in Sect. 2, has been successfully used in various segmentation models to capture contextual information. It consists of atrous (dilated) convolutions which enables the preservation of shift-invariance while at the same time increasing the receptive field and enhancing the robustness to augmentations [27]. Specifically, it is composed of 4 convolutions interleaved with BN and ReLU to extract information over a wide spatial range though setting wider dilation rates in convolutions. Global average pooling and 1×1 convolution are used for global feature aggregation at the given scale. Each part accepts inputs from all channels, downscales them such that the output is only 32 channels. These are concatenated with all other in the channel-dimension and refined to the output channel dimension by 1×1 convolution. Finally, we regularise by applying dropout. In our work we use ASPP blocks in all Repeat blocks, except the first and the last one. We also changed the original ordering of the dilated convolutions to place BN first, instead of the convolution, for better regularisation. We kept the partial channel numbers to 32 to limit computation.

3.2 Bayesian Inference

MCD [5,6] provides a scalable way to learn a predictive distribution, by applying dropout [24] to the output of convolutions at both training and test time. This leads to Bayesian inference over the network's weights. The sampled distribution provided by the dropout is used to sample models from the learnt variational posterior distribution. Although this can be achieved without additional parameters, it requires sampling and repeating S feedforward steps through the network with the same input. The S repeated steps linearly increase the compute demand, such that the runtime computational or memory complexity scales with $\mathcal{O}(S)$, and hence it is of further importance that the network is hardware efficient both in terms of memory consumption as well as the number of operations for the individual runs. A pixel-wise entropy can be derived, based on the repeated runs, that quantifies uncertainty as $\mathbb{H}(\hat{\boldsymbol{y}}) = -\sum_c^C \hat{y}_c \log(\hat{y}_c)$. The $\hat{\boldsymbol{y}} \in \mathbb{R}^C$ is the pixel-wise mean of the softmax outputs across the S runs with respect to C output classes. The dropout rate presents a trade-off between data fit and uncertainty estimation. For convenience of hardware implementation, we use a dropout rate of 0.05 across the entire network for all experiments.

4 Experiments

This Section first discusses our experimentation settings and then presents an assessment of the results on the CamVid and bacteria datasets. We did not perform pre-training on additional image data or post-training fine-tuning. We introduce three ComBiNet models: ComBiNet-S, ComBiNet-M, ComBiNet-L: small, medium or large depending on the MAC count or the number of parameters, with the aim to trade-off computational complexity, accuracy and uncertainty quantification capabilities. We evaluated uncertainty through the mean per-pixel entropy of networks trained on CamVid or bacteria with respect to a random subset of 250 PascalVOC images [4]. We initalised the weights of all ComBiNets with respect to the He-Uniform initialisation [8]. To train, we used Adam for 800 epochs with an initial learning rate of 0.001 and an exponential decrease with a factor 0.996. We trained ComBiNets with respect to a batch size of 2 and with BN applied to each batch individually, as we found it essential to not use train-time statistics during evaluation. We set $S = 30$ for the quantitative and qualitative software evaluation. For quantitative evaluation we measured the standard per-pixel mean intersection over union (mIoU), entropy, MACs and number of trainable parameters. The number of MACs was calculated with respect to $224 \times 224 \times 3$ input size and $S = 1$. We repeated each experiment 3 times from which we report mean and $\pm$ a single standard deviation in following Tables.

Fig. 2. Qualitative evaluation. (from left) The first column depicts the input image, the second column is the ground-truth segmentation mask, the remaining columns are with respect to predictions of ComBiNet-L, DenseNet-103 + CD and DeepLab-v3+-ResNet50.

4.1 CamVid

The CamVid road scenes dataset [2] originates from fully segmented videos from the perspective of a driving car. It consists of 367 frames for training, 101 frames for validation and 233 frames for testing of RGB images with a 480×360 input resolution. There are 11 manually labelled classes that include roads, cars, signs etc. and a background that is usually ignored during training and evaluation. To augment the dataset we carried out channel-wise normalisation and the following randomly: re-scale inputs between a factor of 0.5 to 2.0; change aspect ratios between 3/4 to 4/3; crop with a square size of 360; horizontal flips; and random colour changes with respect to contrast, saturation and hue for training. We used the combo loss function [25], and weighted it proportionally to class-pixels in the images as CamVid is unbalanced. A weight decay of $1e^{-3}$ was applied.

We summarise the performance of the different ComBiNets in Table 1, comparing to the other state-of-the-art 2D segmentation networks that include those focused on hardware efficiency with respect to their number of parameters and those considering Bayesian inference. The results show all ComBiNets obtained competitive results on mIoU with significantly fewer parameters and MACs. One result that stands out is [30] which used video, fine-tuning and an over-parametrised architecture. ComBiNet-L is the most accurate of ComBiNets with approximately $3\times$ fewer parameters and MACs than its current equivalent with $S = 1$. ComBiNet-S is the most hardware efficient with $42\times$ fewer parameters and $7\times$ fewer MACs than the Bayesian SegNet when $S = 1$, while achieving an accuracy that is still close to the related works. We also compared the entropy pixel-wise, in which ComBiNets are marginally better in comparison to [7,12]. In Figs. 2 and 3 we demonstrate the qualitative results. In general, the model is more uncertain in the objects that are more distant, occluded or surrounded by the background class (black), which was ignored during training and evaluation. The results of the segmentation showed that the most problematic classes were fence and sign/symbol, whilst roads and the sky were most accurately distinguished. Figure 2 demonstrates on one sample that the model is accurate also in comparison to the related work consisting of a non-Bayesian or a Bayesian model.

Table 1. Comparison with respect to other networks on the CamVid test dataset, † notes training and testing with respect to 960×720 images instead of 480×360, ‡ denotes Bayesian approaches. Arrows denote desired trends. - denotes not reported. * were replicated in this work and not officially reported.

Method	mIoU [%] ↑	Params [M] ↓	MACs [G] ↓	Entropy [nats] ↑
SegNet [1]	55.6	29.7	–	–
Bayesian SegNet‡ [12]	63.1	29.7	30.8*	0.68*
DenseNet-103 [11]	66.9	9.4	24.9*	–
DenseNet-103 + CD‡ [7]	67.4	9.4	24.9*	0.47*
ESPNet [17]	55.6	0.36	–	–
BiSeNet† [26]	65.6	5.8	–	–
ICNet† [28]	67.1	6.7	–	–
Compact Nets [19]	63.9	**0.28**	–	–
DeepLab-v3+-ResNet50 [3]	57.6*	16.6*	13.2*	–
Video-WideResNet38† [30]	**79.8**	137.1	–	–
ComBiNet-S‡	66.1 ± 0.3	0.7	**4.2**	$\mathbf{0.69 \pm 0.02}$
ComBiNet-M‡	66.9 ± 0.2	1.3	7.9	0.68 ± 0.01
ComBiNet-L‡	67.9 ± 0.1	2.3	9.4	0.65 ± 0.02

4.2 Bacteria

The bacteria dataset [20] comprises of 366 darkfield microscopy images with manually annotated masks for segmentation. The task is to detect bacteria of the phylum Spirochaetes in blood. This therefore leads to a problem of segmenting two classes corresponding to the bacteria and red blood cells - Spirochaetes and Erythrocytes respectively. This is a challenging task due to both the nature of the problem, a heavily unbalanced dataset, and the collection methodology which results in considerable noisy RGB input images of varying sizes from 1000×1000 to 300×300 pixels. We randomly split the dataset into sizes 219, 73, 74 images for training, validation and test respectively. We then apply the same augmentations as those mentioned in Sect. 4.1 for the CamVid dataset, extended further with vertical flips. We train with respect to the Combo loss function and added a log-dice coefficient. Weight decay was set to $1e^{-4}$.

Table 2 shows that all ComBiNets obtain better accuracy with significantly fewer parameters and MACs. ComBiNet-S is the most hardware efficient with $13\times$ fewer parameters and $6\times$ fewer MACs than DenseNet when $S = 1$. We note that ComBiNet-87 achieves a worse accuracy than ComBiNet-M in our experiments with this dataset, showing that a bigger network is not always the best. All ComBiNets infer that all unrecognisable objects should be classified as a background resulting in smaller entropy than the related work. The qualitative evaluation of Figs. 3 and 4 demonstrates the ability of the architecture to segment noisy images, while comparing it to DenseNet with Concrete Dropout (CD) [7] and Bayesian SegNet. We further depict the corresponding predictive uncertainty of this sample in Fig. 5, which helps us understand the portions of the image

Table 2. Comparison with respect to other networks on the bacteria test dataset, ‡ denotes Bayesian approaches. Arrows denote desired trends. * were replicated in this work and not officially reported.

Method	mIoU [%] ↑	Params [M] ↓	MACs [G] ↓	Entropy [nats] ↑
Bayesian SegNet[‡,*] [12]	76.1	29.7	30.8	0.19
DenseNet-103 + CD[‡,*] [7]	75.8	9.4	24.9	**0.32**
U-Net* [22]	71.4	31.0	41.9	–
DeepLab-v3+-ResNet50* [3]	80.4	16.6	13.2	–
ComBiNet-S[‡]	82.3 ± 0.4	**0.7**	**4.2**	0.18 ± 0.02
ComBiNet-M[‡]	$\mathbf{83.0 \pm 0.4}$	1.3	7.9	0.16 ± 0.01
ComBiNet-L[‡]	82.3 ± 0.2	2.3	9.4	0.16 ± 0.02

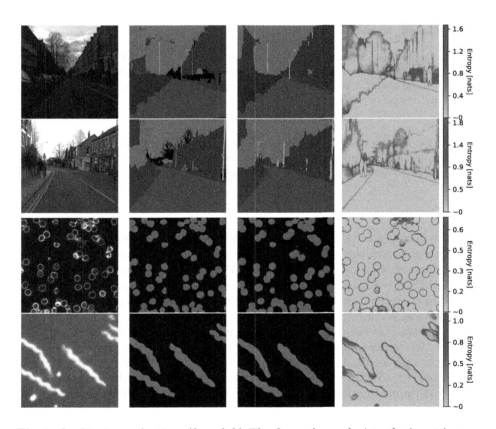

Fig. 3. Qualitative evaluation. (from left) The first column depicts the input image, the second column are the ground-truth segmentation masks, the third column are the predictions and the fourth column are the per-pixel uncertainties measured through the predictive entropy of ComBiNet-L and ComBiNet-M. The two top rows are with respect to CamVid models and the bottom two rows are with respect to bacteria models.

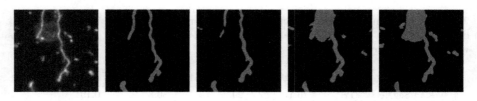

Fig. 4. Qualitative evaluation. (from left) The first column depicts the input image, the second column is the ground-truth segmentation mask, the remaining columns are with respect to predictions of ComBiNet-M, DenseNet-103 + CD and Bayesian SegNet.

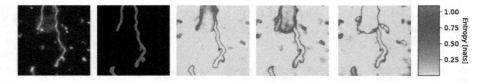

Fig. 5. Qualitative evaluation of predictive uncertainty. (from left) The first column depicts the input image, the second column is the ground-truth segmentation mask and the remaining columns are with respect to predictions of ComBiNet-M, DenseNet-103 + CD and Bayesian SegNet.

where the architecture was less certain in its given predictions. It can be seen that the network is uncertain about suspicious bacteria bodies, which can further help practitioners to better understand their samples.

4.3   Discussion

With respect to the qualitative results in Fig. 3 along with the quantified uncertainty measured by per-pixel entropy we observe that, due to the skip connections and gradual downsampling and upsampling, the model retains sharp edges and detail in the predictions. Additionally, through feature reuse and detailed construction of efficient modules, e.g. BL, the model was able to provide favourable performance, despite smaller parameter or operation counts.

The main bottleneck of this work lies in its use of MCD for Bayesian inference, as it requires multiple feedforward runs, but no extra network weights, to obtain an uncertainty estimate in the output mask. These runs multiply the MAC cost $\times S$ and hence S represents a trade-off between hardware demand and quality of approximation of the predictive distribution. For this reason lowering MACs at the individual feedforward pass level was the focus of this work. Additionally, in hardware it is possible to simply parallelise these runs [18]. Lastly, if uncertainty estimation is not needed, the presented networks can still guarantee high accuracy with respect to weight averaging, disabling dropout and setting $S = 1$, which was relatively lower by approximately one standard deviation as shown in the Tables 1 and 2 for CamVid or bacteria respectively.

5 Conclusion

We propose a compact 2D Bayesian architecture, ComBiNet, that re-purposes hardware efficient operations for the task of image segmentation. We demonstrated that good accuracy along with predictive uncertainties can be achieved with significantly fewer parameters and MACs, lowering hardware resources and computational costs. We show that ComBiNet performs well with an imbalanced dataset, as well as the established CamVid dataset, showing higher uncertainty in misclassified sections. Furthermore, it was not necessary to perform any pre-training or post-training fine-tuning to reach the observed accuracy. For the future, we would like to measure and optimise the architectures with respect to other hardware performance metrics such as power consumption or structured instance-wise uncertainty estimation instead of pixel-wise.

Acknowledgements. We thank the ICANN 2021 reviewers for useful feedback. Martin Ferianc was sponsored through a scholarship from ICCS at UCL.

References

1. Badrinarayanan, V., Kendall, A., Cipolla, R.: SegNet: a deep convolutional encoder-decoder architecture for image segmentation. IEEE Trans. Pattern Anal. Mach. Intell. **39**(12), 2481–2495 (2017)
2. Brostow, G.J., Shotton, J., Fauqueur, J., Cipolla, R.: Segmentation and recognition using structure from motion point clouds. In: Forsyth, D., Torr, P., Zisserman, A. (eds.) ECCV 2008. LNCS, vol. 5302, pp. 44–57. Springer, Heidelberg (2008). https://doi.org/10.1007/978-3-540-88682-2_5
3. Chen, L.-C., Zhu, Y., Papandreou, G., Schroff, F., Adam, H.: Encoder-decoder with Atrous separable convolution for semantic image segmentation. In: Ferrari, V., Hebert, M., Sminchisescu, C., Weiss, Y. (eds.) ECCV 2018. LNCS, vol. 11211, pp. 833–851. Springer, Cham (2018). https://doi.org/10.1007/978-3-030-01234-2_49
4. Everingham, M., Van Gool, L., Williams, C.K., Winn, J., Zisserman, A.: The pascal visual object classes (VOC) challenge. Int. J. Comput. Vision **88**(2), 303–338 (2010)
5. Gal, Y., Ghahramani, Z.: Bayesian convolutional neural networks with Bernoulli approximate variational inference. arXiv preprint arXiv:1506.02158 (2015)
6. Gal, Y., Ghahramani, Z.: Dropout as a Bayesian approximation. arXiv preprint arXiv:1506.02157 (2015)
7. Gal, Y., Hron, J., Kendall, A.: Concrete dropout. In: NeurIPS pp. 3581–3590 (2017)
8. He, K., Zhang, X., Ren, S., Sun, J.: Deep residual learning for image recognition. In: CVPR, pp. 770–778. IEEE (2016)
9. Howard, A.G., et al.: MobileNets: efficient convolutional neural networks for mobile vision applications. arXiv preprint arXiv:1704.04861 (2017)
10. Huang, G., Liu, Z., Van Der Maaten, L., Weinberger, K.Q.: Densely connected convolutional networks. In: CVPR, pp. 4700–4708. IEEE (2017)
11. Jégou, S., Drozdzal, M., Vazquez, D., Romero, A., Bengio, Y.: The one hundred layers tiramisu: Fully convolutional DenseNets for semantic segmentation. In: CVPR Workshops, pp. 11–19 (2017)
12. Kendall, A., Badrinarayanan, V., Cipolla, R.: Bayesian SegNet: model uncertainty in deep convolutional encoder-decoder architectures for scene understanding. arXiv preprint arXiv:1511.02680 (2015)

13. Liang, F., Li, Q., Zhou, L.: Bayesian neural networks for selection of drug sensitive genes. J. Am. Stat. Assoc. **113**(523), 955–972 (2018)
14. Liu, C., et al.: Auto-Deeplab: hierarchical neural architecture search for semantic image segmentation. In: CVPR, pp. 82–92. IEEE (2019)
15. Long, J., Shelhamer, E., Darrell, T., Berkeley, U.: Fully convolutional networks for semantic segmentation. arXiv preprint arXiv:1411.4038 (2014)
16. McAllister, R., et al.: Concrete problems for autonomous vehicle safety: advantages of Bayesian deep learning. In: IJCAI, IJCAI 2017, p. 4745–4753. AAAI Press (2017)
17. Mehta, S., Rastegari, M., Caspi, A., Shapiro, L., Hajishirzi, H.: ESPNet: efficient spatial pyramid of dilated convolutions for semantic segmentation. In: Ferrari, V., Hebert, M., Sminchisescu, C., Weiss, Y. (eds.) ECCV 2018. LNCS, vol. 11214, pp. 561–580. Springer, Cham (2018). https://doi.org/10.1007/978-3-030-01249-6_34
18. Myojin, T., Hashimoto, S., Ishihama, N.: Detecting uncertain BNN outputs on FPGA using monte Carlo dropout sampling. In: Farkaš, I., Masulli, P., Wermter, S. (eds.) ICANN 2020. LNCS, vol. 12397, pp. 27–38. Springer, Cham (2020). https://doi.org/10.1007/978-3-030-61616-8_3
19. Nekrasov, V., Shen, C., Reid, I.: Template-based automatic search of compact semantic segmentation architectures. In: The IEEE Winter Conference on Applications of Computer Vision, pp. 1980–1989. IEEE (2020)
20. Nguyen, L.: Bacteria detection with darkfield microscopy (2020). Data retrieved from work at Hochschule Heilbronn. www.kaggle.com/longnguyen2306/bacteria-detection-with-darkfield-microscopy/metadata
21. Romera, E., Alvarez, J.M., Bergasa, L.M., Arroyo, R.: ErfNet: efficient residual factorized convnet for real-time semantic segmentation. IEEE Trans. Intell. Transp. Syst. **19**(1), 263–272 (2017)
22. Ronneberger, O., Fischer, P., Brox, T.: U-net: convolutional networks for biomedical image segmentation. In: Navab, N., Hornegger, J., Wells, W.M., Frangi, A.F. (eds.) MICCAI 2015. LNCS, vol. 9351, pp. 234–241. Springer, Cham (2015). https://doi.org/10.1007/978-3-319-24574-4_28
23. Ruiz-del Solar, J., Loncomilla, P., Soto, N.: A survey on deep learning methods for robot vision. arXiv preprint arXiv:1803.10862 (2018)
24. Srivastava, N., Hinton, G., Krizhevsky, A., Sutskever, I., Salakhutdinov, R.: Dropout: a simple way to prevent neural networks from overfitting. J. Mach. Learn. Res. **15**(1), 1929–1958 (2014)
25. Taghanaki, S.A., et al.: Combo loss: handling input and output imbalance in multi-organ segmentation. Comput. Med. Imaging Graph., 24–33 (2019)
26. Yu, C., Wang, J., Peng, C., Gao, C., Yu, G., Sang, N.: BiSeNet: bilateral segmentation network for real-time semantic segmentation. In: Ferrari, V., Hebert, M., Sminchisescu, C., Weiss, Y. (eds.) ECCV 2018. LNCS, vol. 11217, pp. 334–349. Springer, Cham (2018). https://doi.org/10.1007/978-3-030-01261-8_20
27. Zhang, R.: Making convolutional networks shift-invariant again. arXiv preprint arXiv:1904.11486 (2019)
28. Zhao, H., Qi, X., Shen, X., Shi, J., Jia, J.: ICNet for real-time semantic segmentation on high-resolution images. In: Ferrari, V., Hebert, M., Sminchisescu, C., Weiss, Y. (eds.) ECCV 2018. LNCS, vol. 11207, pp. 418–434. Springer, Cham (2018). https://doi.org/10.1007/978-3-030-01219-9_25
29. Zhao, H., Shi, J., Qi, X., Wang, X., Jia, J.: Pyramid scene parsing network. In: CVPR, pp. 2881–2890. IEEE (2017)
30. Zhu, Y., et al.: Improving semantic segmentation via video propagation and label relaxation. In: CVPR, pp. 8856–8865. IEEE (2019)

Depth Mapping Hybrid Deep Learning Method for Optic Disc and Cup Segmentation on Stereoscopic Ocular Fundus

Gang Yang[1], Yunfeng Du[2], Yanni Wang[1], Donghong Li[2], Dayong Ding[2], Jingyuan Yang[4], and Gangwei Cheng[3,4(✉)]

[1] School of Information, Renmin University of China, Beijing, China
[2] Vistel AI Lab, Visionary Intelligence Ltd., Beijing, China
[3] Peking Union Medical College Hospital, Chinese Academy of Medical Sciences, Beijing, China
[4] Peking Union Medical College, Beijing, China
ChengGW@pumch.cn

Abstract. Optic disc and cup segmentation on ocular fundus images is an important prerequisite for diagnosing glaucoma. For the segmentation of optic disc (OD) and optic cup (OC), many previously proposed deep learning methods typically utilize monoscopic view images that lack spatial depth information, limiting their diagnostic ability and overall performance. According to ophthalmologists' clinical insights, stereoscopic view of ocular fundus contains great potential to improve optic cup segmentation. We propose a depth mapping hybrid (DeMaH) deep learning method that effectively adopts depth mappings to segment OD and OC (ODC) on ocular fundus images. Experimental results demonstrate that our method achieves significant improvement on ODC segmentation, especially OC segmentation, validating the effectiveness of our method to incorporate clinical prior knowledge.

Keywords: Optic disc · Optic cup · Stereoscopic view · Segmentation

1 Introduction

Recent advances in Artificial Intelligence (AI) based diagnosis have led to wide usage and exciting prospects in automating the assessment of ophthalmic diseases on ocular images. To detect optic nerve diseases on ocular, CDR (cup-to-disc ratio) is an important biomarker especially for glaucoma screening, which is mainly calculated by the ratio of vertical cup diameter (VCD) to vertical disc diameter (VDD) [15]. Glaucoma is one of the common causes of blindness all over the world, with approximately 79 million cases in 2020 [16]. In general, a larger CDR suggests a higher risk of glaucoma and according to [22], eye with CDR of at least 0.65 is usually considered as glaucomatous in clinical practice. Therefore, segmentation of optic disc (OD) and optic cup (OC) on ocular images becomes an important prerequisite for glaucoma screening.

ⓒ Springer Nature Switzerland AG 2021
I. Farkaš et al. (Eds.): ICANN 2021, LNCS 12893, pp. 495–506, 2021.
https://doi.org/10.1007/978-3-030-86365-4_40

However, most existing methods of OD and OC (ODC) segmentation are based on monoscopic fundus images[1,5,9,16], which no longer meets the modern standard for ophthalmic disease diagnosis and limits the validity of further assessment. With the development of medical equipment and diagnostic technology, ophthalmic disease diagnosis based on stereoscopic fundus images has won high popularity and wide approval of ophthalmologists.

Moreover, some prior work in ophthalmology demonstrate that stereoscopic view images can support more sensitive diagnosis. Morgan et al. [18] show that stereoscopic assessments can give higher CDR values in temporal, superior, nasal, and inferior aspects of OD for glaucoma diagnosis. Chan et al. [3] illustrate that a great improvement in accuracy can be obtained with stereoscopic view of conventional mammograms.

The advantages of using stereoscopic view images mainly lie in the spatial depth information that they contain [2,4,13,17,25]. As a result, stereoscopic ocular fundus can be used for recognizing the boundaries of ODC effectively.

In spite of the advantages and potentials, stereoscopic fundus images are normally prone to noise brought by blood vessels, which will affect the assessment of ODC depth. To investigate the difference that blood vessels can make in terms of ODC segmentation, we conducted a control experiment (removing vessels versus keeping vessels in stereoscopic fundus images). Some existing segmentation networks [26] can be used to detect blood vessels, and the nearest neighbor interpolation can be used to substitute them. In our research, we discover that removing blood vessels from stereoscopic fundus images could effectively mitigate the reverse effect on ODC segmentation.

In this paper, we propose a deep learning method named Depth Mapping Hybrid (DeMaH) to segment ODC on stereoscopic view images, fully utilizing the spatial depth information. Meanwhile, the effect of blood vessels on ODC segmentation is also discussed. A custom dataset and a public dataset are used to demonstrate the superiority of our method. Several different backbone architectures are incorporated into the DeMaH, which makes it a plug-and-play method. Extensive experimental results show that our method can achieve significant performance gains on OC segmentation.

The main contributions of this paper are as follows:

1. In contrast with commonly used methods based on monoscopic view fundus, our DeMaH method firstly utilizes the depth information of stereoscopic fundus images for the task of ODC segmentation.
2. Our DeMaH method verifies that stereoscopic fundus images contain rich extra information that can support eye disease diagnosis for ophthalmologists and machine learning system.
3. Most existing methods utilizing spatial depth information are based on image processing technology in stereoscopic fundus images, but our DeMaH method is the first to incorporate it in deep learning. So, DeMaH constructs a baseline method of segmenting ODC on stereoscopic fundus images for computer-aided medical systems.

2   Related Work

2.1   Optic Disc and Cup Segmentation

ODC segmentation on ocular fundus images is a fundamental prerequisite for glaucoma diagnosis. Previous segmentation methods are mostly based on image processing technology. Noor et al. [19] propose color multi-thresholding segmentation method to segment ODC. Gopal Datt et al. [16] integrate the local image information around each point of interest in multidimensional feature space to provide robustness against variations found in and around the OD region for OD segmentation. Traditional machine learning algorithms have also been explored for ODC segmentation. Neeraj Sharma et al. [24] employ K-means clustering algorithm to segment OD, where the cluster regions with highest intensity are considered as the OD.

In recent years, due to the availability of massive labelled data and significantly improved computing power, deep learning has been widely used for the task of ODC segmentation. Sevastopolsky [22] adopts a convolutional neural network based on a modified model of U-Net for automatic ODC segmentation. Shankaranarayana et al. [23] propose a novel improved architecture called ResU-Net, which is built upon FCNs (Fully Convolutional Networks) and meanwhile incorporates the notion of residual learning. Ding et al. propose a High-order Attention Network (HANet) to capture global context information of fundus using an adaptive receptive field and dynamic weights, which could obtain high performance on medical image segmentation [6,7].

2.2   Retinal Vessel Segmentation

Compared with the ODC segmentation, retinal vessel segmentation is a more challenging task due to the thin boundary. Roychowdhury et al. propose a unsupervised iterative blood vessel segmentation algorithm [20] based on a global thresholding. Goatman et al. [12] employ shape, position, orientation, brightness, contrast and line density as the segmentation foundation to automatically detect vessels on the OD.

Recently, many deep learning methods have also been explored. Xiao et al. propose a U-Net-like model [26] with a weighted attention mechanism and a skip connection scheme. Fu et al. propose a deep learning architecture [10] which combines the Convolutional Neural Network(CNN) and Conditional Random Field(CRF) layers into an integrated deep network called DeepVessels. Feng et al. propose a cross-connected convolutional neural network (CcNet) [8], which extracts multi-scale features and fuses them to segment vessels on ocular images.

2.3   Multi-view Stereo Depth

3D reconstruction on stereoscopic view images is one of the most important topics of computer vision. Central to the task of 3D reconstruction is the calculation of depth. Zhu et al. [28] propose a hybrid setup in which a single polarization image is augmented by a second image from a standard RGB camera.

Saxena et al. [21] apply a Markov Random Field (MRF) learning algorithm to capture some of these monocular cues, and incorporated them into a stereo system. Khamis et al. [17] propose a StereoNet that achieves a higher sub-pixel matching precision than those of traditional stereo matching approaches. In multi-view stereo (MVS), one major limitation is that the memory-consuming cost volume regularization makes the learned MVS models hard to be applied to high-resolution scenes. To address this problem, a scalable multi-view stereo framework is proposed by Yao et al. based on the recurrent neural network [27].

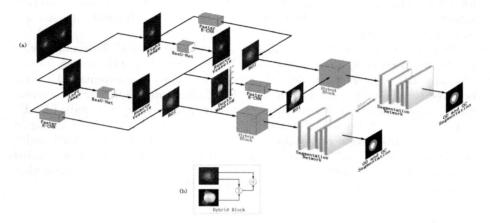

Fig. 1. The proposed depth mapping hybrid deep learning (DeMaH) method. (a) The overall pipeline. (b) The hybrid block in DeMaH.

3   Depth Mapping Hybrid Deep Learning Method for ODC Segmentation

Inspired by the process of generating stereoscopic view when ophthalmologists analyze stereoscopic ocular fundus, we propose our method named DeMaH for ODC segmentation. DeMaH mainly involves four steps: blood vessels removing, depth mapping generation, feature mapping fusing, and segmentation network embedding. In the first step, vessels are removed and substituted using the nearest neighbor interpolation. In the second step, we compute depth mapping from stereoscopic view images. For the feature mapping fusion hybrid, the original image RGB features are enhanced by the generated depth mapping. And finally in the last part, some state-of-the-art deep neural networks could be embedded into our DeMaH to segment ODC with an appropriate loss function. Figure 1(a) illustrates the overall process of our DeMaH method.

In DeMaH, the Hybrid Block shown in Fig. 1(b) produces effective feature enhancement to improve the performance. Referring to the attention theory of deep learning, a multiply and addition operation is introduced to increase the spatial depth information of fundus images in both left and right images.

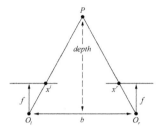

Fig. 2. Illustration of the computation of the depth mappings from stereoscopic view images. O_l and O_r represent the centers of two cameras separately. b represents the baseline length. f represents focal length. P represents a point in the observed object. x^l and x^r represent the imaging points of P in two cameras, and *depth* represents the depth of P.

3.1   Vessel Removing and Depth Computation

In clinical settings, ophthalmologists generally ignore blood vessels when segmenting ODC. Inspired by this domain insight, we speculate that computation of the depth mappings of stereoscopic fundus is error-prone due to noise incurred by blood vessels regions. To verify our hypothesis and to investigate the blood vessels' influence on ODC segmentation, we conduct a control experiment on stereoscopic fundus images (removing blood vessels versus keeping blood vessels).

To detect and remove pixels relevant to blood vessels, we employ ResU-Net, an existing segmentation network proposed by prior researchers [26]. Then we adopt the nearest neighbor interpolation to repaint the removed regions.

The depth mappings are calculated by the image processing method proposed in [28]. As shown in Fig. 2, according to the stereoscopic vision theory, the depth is directly proportional to the baseline length and the focal length of cameras after camera calibration, and it is inversely proportional to the disparity of x^l and x^r. The depth of ocular fundus is calculated as follows:

$$disparity = x^l - x^r \quad depth = \frac{b \times f}{disparity} \tag{1}$$

where x^l and x^r represent the horizontal ordinates of matching points in left and right images respectively, b and f denote the baseline length and focal length of cameras respectively.

Generally speaking, different cameras have different baseline lengths and focal lengths. In order to eliminate the influence of camera variation, the depth is normalized into $[0, 255]$ and rounded down.

$$depth'_i = \left\lfloor \frac{255 \times (depth_i - depth_{min})}{depth_{max} - depth_{min}} \right\rfloor \tag{2}$$

$depth_i$ represents the depth of pixel i ($i = 1 \sim n$). $depth_{max}$ and $depth_{min}$ denote the maximum depth and the minimum depth in the depth mapping respectively, and the total number of pixels in each left and right fundus image is n.

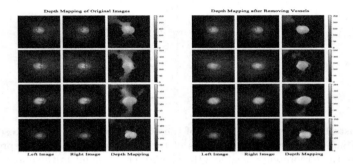

Fig. 3. Illustration of depth mapping, where each row represents a pair of stereoscopic view images. Brighter areas indicate larger depth.

Figure 3 shows the difference that blood vessels introduce in generating depth mappings. The third column shows the depth mapping of the original stereoscopic images, and the sixth column shows the depth mapping of the stereoscopic images after removing the blood vessels. Without the noisy depth information that blood vessels bring, the generated depth mappings are able to focus on ODC regions and reveal the actual spatial relationships of OC and OD.

3.2 Fusion of ROI Features and Depth Mapping

Depth is an important basis for segmenting ODC. Based on this, we fuse the depth mappings of stereoscopic fundus images into the left and right images by a Hybrid Block referring to the attention theory of deep learning, as shown in Fig. 1(b). Using the hybrid block, our DeMaH method can enhance the image features of ODC regions, and meanwhile highlight the boundaries between foreground and background. The operations are shown as follows:

$$r'_i = r_i \times \left(1 + \frac{depth'_i}{255}\right) \quad g'_i = g_i \times \left(1 + \frac{depth'_i}{255}\right) \quad b'_i = b_i \times \left(1 + \frac{depth'_i}{255}\right) \quad (3)$$

where r_i, g_i, and b_i ($i = 1 \sim n$) denote the ith pixel values of RGB channels respectively. The depth of ith pixel is $depth_i$. r'_i, g'_i, and b'_i represent the new i^{th} pixel features of the enhanced RGB channels.

3.3 Loss Function

In our DeMaH method, the pixels that fall into the categories of background, OD, and OC are labeled 0, 1, and 2 respectively. We define a balanced loss as follows to guild the training of DeMaH:

$$Loss^l = -\frac{1}{N} \sum_{i=1}^{N} \sum_{k=0}^{2} y_{ik}^l \log_2 p_{ik}^l \qquad (4.1)$$

$$Loss^r = -\frac{1}{N} \sum_{i=1}^{N} \sum_{k=0}^{2} y_{ik}^r \log_2 p_{ik}^r \qquad (4.2)$$

$$Loss = \alpha Loss^l + (1 - \alpha) Loss^r \qquad (4.3)$$

where $Loss^l$, $Loss^r$ and $Loss$ denote the left image loss, right image loss and the balanced loss respectively. α is the loss function fusion-weight ($\alpha = 0.5$ in our work). $k \in \{0, 1, 2\}$ represents the class of background, OD and OC respectively. The ith pixel true class of left and right image is y_{ik}^l and y_{ik}^r respectively, where y_{ik}^l, $y_{ik}^r \in \{0, 1\}$. 0 represents that the ith pixel is not in the kth class, and 1 represents that the ith pixel is in the kth class. p_{ik}^l, $p_{ik}^r \in [0, 1]$ denote the possibility of the ith pixel predicted to be k^{th} class of the left and right image respectively.

4   Experiments

4.1   Implementation

Our DeMaH method is implemented with Python 2.7 based on PyTorch 1.1.0. During training, the stochastic gradient descent (SGD) is used to optimize the deep model, and the learning rate is set to $1/10^3$. The momentum is 0.99 and the weight decay is 0.0005. These parameters of SGD optimization for OD and OC segmentation are based on our experience and experiments. The optic disc and depth mapping ROIs are all resized into 256×256 pixels. The training batch size is set to 8.

4.2   Datasets and Networks

We test our method on two datasets: a private dataset named XieHe2K and a public dataset named Rim-One-R3. The XieHe2K dataset contains 2084 stereoscopic view images of 2144×1424 pixels from our hospital partners. The ground truth masks are labeled by professional ophthalmologists. There are 1668 images for training, 208 images for validation and 208 images for test. The Rim-One-R3 [11] dataset contains 159 stereoscopic fundus images of 2144×1424 pixels. Because Rim-One-R3 is too small a dataset to train a deep learning algorithm stably, it is only used as test data. Table 1 shows how we divide the two datasets.

In our experiment, four state-of-the-art segmentation networks were embedded into our DeMaH method: U-Net [22], ResU-Net [23], M-Net [9] and CE-Net [14]. In order to compare the effectiveness of DeMaH reasonably, all of these four networks use the *same training parameters* and data partitioning.

4.3 Evaluation Metrics

To evaluate the segmentation performance of our method, we use four metrics as follows:

$$IoU = \frac{Area(S \bigcap G)}{Area(S \bigcup G)} \quad Recall = \frac{TP}{TP + FN} \tag{5}$$

$$Precision = \frac{TP}{TP + FP} \quad Dice = \frac{2 \times Area(S \bigcap G)}{Area(S) + Area(G)} \tag{6}$$

where S and G represent the predicted region and the ground truth respectively. Area() denotes area of the region in parentheses. TP, FN and FP represent the number of true positives, false negatives and false positives respectively.

Table 1. The Distribution of XieHe2K and Rim-One-R3

Data Set	Training	Validation	Testing	Total
XieHe2K	1668	208	208	2084
Rim-One-R3	0	0	159	159

Table 2. Performance Comparison of Different Networks for Segmenting ODC on XieHe2K Dataset

Method	Optic Disc				Optic Cup			
	IoU	Recall	Precision	Dice	IoU	Recall	Precision	Dice
U-Net	**0.9317**	**0.9693**	0.9596	**0.9644**	0.7257	0.8466	0.8831	0.8237
U-Net_DeMaH	0.9213	0.9568	**0.9613**	0.9590	0.7601	0.8412	**0.8874**	0.8637
U-Net_DeMaH$_{rv}$	0.9227	0.9641	0.9556	0.9598	**0.7601**	**0.8469**	0.8812	**0.8637**
ResU-Net	**0.9335**	0.9684	0.9623	**0.9652**	0.7285	0.8580	**0.8672**	0.8314
ResU-Net_DeMaH	0.9292	0.9597	**0.9669**	0.9633	**0.7669**	**0.8734**	0.8628	**0.8681**
ResU-Net_DeMaH$_{rv}$	0.9294	**0.9704**	0.9565	0.9634	0.7482	0.8488	0.8633	0.8560
M-Net	**0.9347**	**0.9669**	**0.9651**	**0.9660**	0.7359	**0.8782**	0.8602	0.8337
M-Net_DeMaH	0.9246	0.9596	0.9620	0.9608	0.7536	0.8421	**0.8775**	0.8595
M-Net_DeMaH$_{rv}$	0.9244	0.9607	0.9607	0.9607	**0.7604**	0.8702	0.8577	**0.8639**
CE-Net	**0.9411**	**0.9758**	**0.9634**	**0.9695**	0.7275	0.8532	**0.8858**	0.8250
CE-Net_DeMaH	0.9248	0.9672	0.9547	0.9609	**0.7582**	**0.8944**	0.8327	**0.8625**
CE-Net_DeMaH$_{rv}$	0.9263	0.9727	0.9510	0.9617	0.7480	0.8372	0.8753	0.8558

4.4 Results and Analysis

On XieHe2K. The results are shown in Table 2. The depth of stereoscopic is fused into left and right images on four segmentation networks. For each network, we make three groups of control experiments containing different segmentation networks: original network, network with DeMaH, and network with DeMaH$_{rv}$ (rv means removing vessels).

The results show that the metrics IoU and Dice of OC are greatly improved in networks with DeMaH compared with those without it. Recall and Precision are slightly improved. However, the depth mappings blur boundaries of OD. In U-Net, ResU-Net and M-Net, the performance decreases less than 1% in most cases, except that the IoU in CE-Net decreases by 1.63%. Similarly, in the case of DeMaH$_{rv}$, the metrics IoU and Dice of OC are greatly improved. Recall and Precision have slightly risen. But, the metrics of OD are slightly decreased.

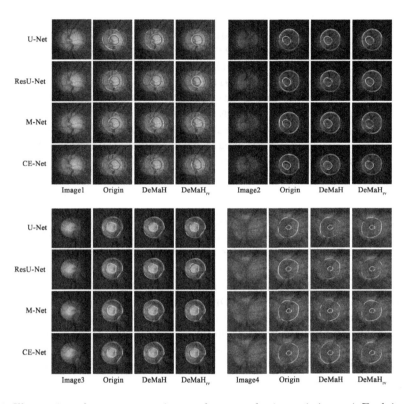

Fig. 4. Illustration of our segmentation results on ocular image1 ~ image4. Each image is tested on four segmentation networks respectively. For each image, the second column represents the segmentation results of ODC without depth. The third column and fourth column represent the results predicted by DeMaH and DeMaH$_{rv}$ separately. The green lines are the true contours ophthalmologists labelled, and the red lines are the predicted contours by deep learning methods. (Color figure online)

Some segmentation results of ODC on dataset XieHe2K are shown in Fig. 4. For each image, the second column represents the segmentation results of ODC without depth mapping. The third column represents the segmentation results of using depth mapping in stereoscopic fundus images. The fourth column represents the results of networks with DeMaH$_{rv}$. The green lines are the ground truth labelled by ophthalmologists, and the red lines are the predicted.

Table 3. Performance Comparison of Different Networks for Segmenting ODC on Rim-One-R3 Dataset

Method	Optic Disc				Optic Cup			
	IoU	Recall	Precision	Dice	IoU	Recall	Precision	Dice
U-Net	**0.8828**	0.9576	**0.9184**	**0.9361**	0.5612	0.7323	0.7438	0.6864
U-Net_DeMaH	0.8785	**0.9826**	0.8924	0.9353	**0.6330**	**0.7581**	**0.7932**	**0.7752**
U-Net_DeMaH$_{rv}$	0.8754	0.9768	0.8940	0.9336	0.6214	0.7418	0.7929	0.7665
ResU-Net	0.8816	0.9514	0.9242	0.9303	0.6290	0.8064	0.7606	0.7484
ResU-Net_DeMaH	**0.9155**	**0.9864**	**0.9271**	**0.9559**	**0.7071**	**0.8238**	**0.8330**	**0.8284**
ResU-Net_DeMaH$_{rv}$	0.9014	0.9790	0.9192	0.9482	0.6793	0.8238	0.7948	0.8090
M-Net	**0.9007**	0.9864	**0.9111**	**0.9475**	0.5502	**0.7580**	0.7703	0.6631
M-Net_DeMaH	0.8804	**0.9890**	0.8892	0.9364	**0.6165**	0.7405	**0.7864**	**0.7628**
M-Net_DeMaH$_{rv}$	0.8827	0.9871	0.8930	0.9377	0.6081	0.7419	0.7712	0.7563
CE-Net	0.8981	**0.9932**	0.9028	0.9461	0.5939	0.7483	**0.8282**	0.7068
CE-Net_DeMaH	**0.9077**	0.9772	**0.9273**	**0.9516**	**0.6744**	**0.8804**	0.7424	**0.8055**
CE-Net_DeMaH$_{rv}$	0.8930	0.9857	0.9047	0.9435	0.6711	0.8074	0.7990	0.8032

There is a significant performance improvement for segmenting OC and a slight performance degradation for segmenting OD. Generally, the improvements on OC segmentation outweigh the degradation for segmenting OD, and our DeMaH method yields an acceptable performance for ODC segmentation.

On Rim-One-R3. Because the number of Rim-One-R3 is too small to train a stable model, we use all of Rim-One-R3 images as test data to evaluate the robustness of our method. The experimental results are shown in Table 3.

Similar to the previous analysis on dataset XieHe2K, Table 3 shows that the metrics of OC segmentation have witnessed significant improvement in the networks with our method on stereoscopic fundus images. In each network, the metrics of IoU and Dice increase by more than 6%. From the experimental results on Rim-One-R3 dataset, we can conclude that our method has better generalization ability and robustness for segmenting OC on stereoscopic fundus images.

5   Conclusion

In this paper, we propose a novel depth mapping hybrid (DeMaH) deep learning method based on spatial depth information of stereoscopic view images. As an efficient and practical method, DeMaH fully utilizes the depth information in stereoscopic fundus images to segment ODC. However, stereoscopic fundus images are normally prone to noise brought by blood vessels, so we conduct a control experiment under two scenarios, namely DeMaH (reserving vessels) and DeMaH$_{rv}$ (removing vessels) to investigate the blood vessels' impact. Results demonstrate that blood vessels on ROIs have little effect on the ODC segmentation. The experiments on two datasets (XieHe2K dataset and Rim-One-R3 dataset) reveal that our DeMaH method yields great performance improvement on OC segmentation.

Acknowledgement. This work was supported by the Beijing Natural Science Foundation (No. 4192029), and the National Natural Science Foundation of China (61773385, 61672523).

References

1. Aquino, A., Gegúndez-Arias, M.E., Marín, D.: Detecting the optic disc boundary in digital fundus images using morphological, edge detection, and feature extraction techniques. IEEE Trans. Med. Imaging **29**, 1860–1869 (2010)
2. Berger, K., Voorhies, R., Matthies, L.H.: Depth from stereo polarization in specular scenes for urban robotics. In: 2017 IEEE International Conference on Robotics and Automation (ICRA), pp. 1966–1973. IEEE, Singapore (2017)
3. Chan, H.P., et al.: Assessment of breast lesions on stereoscopic and monoscopic digital specimen mammograms: an roc study. In: SPIE Medical Imaging, p. 428. SPIR, San Diego (2004)
4. hen, Z., Sun, X., Wang, L., Yu, Y., Huang, C.: A deep visual correspondence embedding model for stereo matching costs. In: IEEE International Conference on Computer Vision, pp. 972–980. IEEE, Santiago (2015)
5. Cheng, J., et al.: Superpixel classification based optic disc and optic cup segmentation for glaucoma screening. IEEE Trans. Med. Imaging **32**, 1019–1032 (2013)
6. Ding, F., et al.: Hierarchical attention networks for medical image segmentation. CoRR abs/1911.08777
7. Ding, F., et al.: High-order attention networks for medical image segmentation. In: Martel, A.L., et al. (eds.) MICCAI 2020. LNCS, vol. 12261, pp. 253–262. Springer, Cham (2020). https://doi.org/10.1007/978-3-030-59710-8_25
8. Feng, S., Zhuo, Z., Pan, D., Tian, Q.: Ccnet: a cross-connected convolutional network for segmenting retinal vessels using multi-scale features. Neurocomputing **392**, 268–276 (2020)
9. Fu, H., Cheng, J., Xu, Y., Wong, D.W.K., Liu, J., Cao, X.: Joint optic disc and cup segmentation based on multi-label deep network and polar transformation. IEEE Trans. Med. Imaging **37**, 1597–1605 (2018)
10. Fu, H., Xu, Y., Lin, S., Kee Wong, D.W., Liu, J.: DeepVessel: retinal vessel segmentation via deep learning and conditional random field. In: Ourselin, S., Joskowicz, L., Sabuncu, M.R., Unal, G., Wells, W. (eds.) MICCAI 2016. LNCS, vol. 9901, pp. 132–139. Springer, Cham (2016). https://doi.org/10.1007/978-3-319-46723-8_16
11. Fumero, F., Alayón, S., Sanchez, J.L., Sigut, J., Gonzalez-Hernandez, M.: RIM-ONE: an open retinal image database for optic nerve evaluation. In: 24th International Symposium on Computer-Based Medical Systems (CBMS), pp. 1–6. IEEE, Bristol (2011)
12. Goatman, K.A., Fleming, A.D., Philip, S., Williams, G.J., Olson, J.A., Sharp, P.F.: Detection of new vessels on the optic disc using retinal photographs. IEEE Trans. Med. Imaging **30**(4), 972–979 (2011)
13. Graber, G., Balzer, J., Soatto, S., Pock, T.: Efficient minimal-surface regularization of perspective depth maps in variational stereo. In: Proceedings of the IEEE Conference on Computer Vision and Pattern Recognition, pp. 511–520. IEEE, Boston (2015)
14. Gu, Z., et al.: CE-Net: context encoder network for 2D medical image segmentation. IEEE Trans. Med. Imaging **38**(10), 2281–2292 (2019)

15. Jonas, J.B., Bergua, A., Schmitz-Valckenberg, P., Papastathopoulos, K.I., Budde, W.M.: Ranking of optic disc variables for detection of glaucomatous optic nerve damage. Invest. Ophthalmol. Vis. Sci. **41**, 1764–1773 (2000)
16. Joshi, G.D., Sivaswamy, J., Krishnadas, S.: Optic disk and cup segmentation from monocular color retinal images for glaucoma assessment. IEEE Trans. Med. Imaging **30**(6), 1192–1205 (2011)
17. Khamis, S., Fanello, S., Rhemann, C., Kowdle, A., Valentin, J., Izadi, S.: StereoNet: guided hierarchical refinement for real-time edge-aware depth prediction. In: Ferrari, V., Hebert, M., Sminchisescu, C., Weiss, Y. (eds.) ECCV 2018. LNCS, vol. 11219, pp. 596–613. Springer, Cham (2018). https://doi.org/10.1007/978-3-030-01267-0_35
18. Morgan, J.E.: Digital imaging of the optic nerve head: mono-scopic and stereoscopic analysis. Br. J. Ophthalmol. **89**(7), 879–884 (2005)
19. Noor, N., Khalid, N., Ariff, N.: Optic cup and disc color channel multi-thresholding segmentation, pp. 530–53. IEEE, Penang (2013)
20. Roychowdhury, S., Koozekanani, D.D., Parhi, K.K.: Iterative vessel segmentation of fundus images. IEEE Trans. Biomed. Eng. **62**(7), 1738–1749 (2015)
21. Saxena, A., Schulte, J., Ng, A.Y., et al.: Depth estimation using monocular and stereo cues. In: Proceedings of the 20th international joint conference on Artificial intelligence (IJCAI 2007), pp. 2197–2220. Morgan Kaufmann Publishers Inc., San Francisco (2007)
22. Sevastopolsky, A.: Optic disc and cup segmentation methods for glaucoma detection with modification of U-Net convolutional neural network. Pattern Recognit Image Anal. **27**, 618–624 (2017)
23. Shankaranarayana, S.M., Ram, K., Mitra, K., Sivaprakasam, M.: Joint optic disc and cup segmentation using fully convolutional and adversarial networks. In: Cardoso, M.J., et al. (eds.) FIFI/OMIA -2017. LNCS, vol. 10554, pp. 168–176. Springer, Cham (2017). https://doi.org/10.1007/978-3-319-67561-9_19
24. Sharma, N., Verma, A.: Segmentation and detection of optic disc using k-means clustering. Int. J. Sci. Eng. Res. **6**(8), 237–240 (2015)
25. Shi, B., Matsushita, Y., Wei, Y., Xu, C., Tan, P.: Self-calibrating photometric stereo. In: 2010 IEEE Computer Society Conference on Computer Vision and Pattern Recognition, pp. 1118–112. IEEE, San Francisco (2010)
26. Xiao, X., Lian, S., Luo, Z., Li, S.: Weighted Res-UNet for high-quality retina vessel segmentation. In: 2018 9th International Conference on Information Technology in Medicine and Education (ITME), pp. 327–331. IEEE, Hangzhou (2018)
27. Yao, Y., Luo, Z., Li, S., Shen, T., Fang, T., Quan, L.: Recurrent MVSNet for high-resolution multi-view stereo depth inference. In: Proceedings of the IEEE Conference on Computer Vision and Pattern Recognition, pp. 5525–5534 (2019)
28. Zhu, D., Smith, W.A.: Depth from a polarisation + RGB stereo pair. In: Proceedings of the IEEE Conference on Computer Vision and Pattern Recognition, pp. 7586–7595. IEEE, Long Beach (2019)

RATS: Robust Automated Tracking and Segmentation of Similar Instances

László Kopácsi[1]([envelope]), Árpád Dobolyi[2], Áron Fóthi[1], Dávid Keller[3],
Viktor Varga[1], and András Lőrincz[1]

[1] Department of Artificial Intelligence, Eötvös Loránd University, Budapest, Hungary
{kopacsi,fa2,vv,lorincz}@inf.elte.hu
[2] Department of Physiology and Neurobiology, Eötvös Loránd University,
Budapest, Hungary
dobolyi.arpad@ttk.elte.hu
[3] MTA-ELTE Laboratory of Molecular and Systems Neurobiology Eötvös Loránd
University, Budapest, Hungary

Abstract. Continuous identification of objects with identical appearance is crucial to analyze the behavior of laboratory animals. Most existing methods attempt to avoid this problem by excluding direct social interactions or facilitating it by implants or artificial markers. Unfortunately, these techniques may distort the results as they can affect the behavior of the observed animals. In this paper, we present a simple, deep learning-based approach that can overcome these problems by providing reliable segmentation and tracking of similar instances. Recognition of frames where the system could not reliably locate the objects and mark them suggests human supervision is central to the system since there should be no mistake in instance tracking. Manual annotation of these data improves tracking and decreases annotation needs quickly. The proposed method achieves higher segmentation accuracy and more stable tracking than previous methods despite requiring only a small set of manually annotated data.

Keywords: Video instance segmentation · Tracking · Identical objects · Deep neural networks

The research has been supported by the European Institute of Innovation and Technology. Á.D., Á.F., D.K. and A.L. were supported by Thematic Excellence Programme 2020 (TKP 2020-IKA-05) of the National Research, Development and Innovation Fund of Hungary. A.L. was supported by the Thematic Excellence Programme (Project no. ED_18-1-2019-0030 titled Application-specific highly reliable IT solutions) by the same Fund. V.V. was supported by the Ministry of Innovation and Technology NRDI Office within the framework of the Artificial Intelligence National Laboratory Program. The authors thank to Robert Bosch, Ltd. Budapest, Hungary for their generous support to the Department of Artificial Intelligence.

© Springer Nature Switzerland AG 2021
I. Farkaš et al. (Eds.): ICANN 2021, LNCS 12893, pp. 507–518, 2021.
https://doi.org/10.1007/978-3-030-86365-4_41

1   Introduction

High throughput research broke into many parts of neuroscience including e.g. gene expressional studies and in vitro drug discovery and animal studies became a bottleneck to understand neuronal functions. The major output of the nervous system in animals is their behavior, consequently, automated behavioral analysis is a major unsolved problem. The most basic information on the behavior of animals is their location. Tracking of animals has been successful for a large number of small animals when individual identification is not essential [1] or tracking single mice or rats [2]. However, several neuropsychiatric disorders, such as schizophrenia and depression include pathological social interactions while it is the primary problem in others, such as social anxiety disorder and autism spectrum disorder [3]. The study of these disorders as well as understanding the normal brain mechanisms responsible to regulate social interactions require the behavioral analysis of more than one animal. In such cases, genetically modified rats are utilized, which look identical to the human eye, but switching them up can invalidate the findings. Some studies avoid the problem of continuous identification of the animals by excluding direct social interactions [4], but this is not the natural way how animals perform their social behaviors. Therefore, further research is required for automated analysis of social behaviors when direct interactions are allowed even though the continuous identification of similarly looking mice and rats remains a challenge: a common problem in video tracking is the inability to maintain the identity of the animals whenever they are in close proximity. Radio frequency-based methods offer a solution [5,6], but in this technique transducers have to be implanted into the animals, information other than the position of the animals is hard to obtain, sensors are necessary in the relative proximity of the animals [7], and the need to isolate the animals during their recovery from surgery may have unwanted effects on their behavior. Thus, automated video analysis seems ideal, but the problem of continuous identification of the otherwise similar animals has to be solved. Artificial markers on them, e.g., coloring of the fur may be occluded and may disturb the natural behavior of the animals. Separation of the animals based on the videos only became possible with recent advances in deep learning techniques, which outperformed traditional approaches in tracking single rodents [8,9]. There have been attempts to use deep learning technologies for quantifying image similarity [10], detecting objects [11], tracking [12,13], and combining velocity of movement with inter-individual distance of rat pairs [14] as well.

In the present study, we developed a combination of algorithms *and* a software package for reliable continuous identification of animals with identical appearance by temporally extending the results of the pre-trained Mask R-CNN [15] model and iteratively fine-tuning on erroneous predictions. Although our solution provides a general framework for neurobiological applications, its parameters are tuned to solve the problem described above. The method begins with synthetic data generation. To this end, we automatically generate overlapping instance annotations with figure-ground segmentation and through various augmentation techniques. After we pre-trained the model, we repeat the following steps. (1) We propagate the predictions of the model and mark frames where the system may have made a mistake in accurately locating the instances. (2) Then we check these samples, annotate if necessary and use the new annotations to fine-tune the system. This way, the performance of the overall system can be improved while minimizing the need for hand-annotation *and* our warning system eliminates errors of instance tracking.

To verify that the proposed method can reliably track instances, we count the number of id switches that may have occurred without our warning system. We also measure the instance segmentation capabilities of the system by calculating the mean of region similarity and contour accuracy ($\mathcal{J}\&\mathcal{F}$) measure proposed in the DAVIS benchmark [16]. Due to pre-training, fine-tuning the system on only 30 samples, we found that it can track objects without switching up the instance ids and achieving 0.833 of $\mathcal{J}\&\mathcal{F}$ mean. Therefore, it outperforms previous methods while using a simpler architecture and fewer ground truth samples.

Our contributions are listed below:

- We propose a simple yet efficient method for reliably tracking and segmenting laboratory animals with identical appearance.
- We extended the Tracktor method [12] with instance segmentation.
- We reduce the need to manually annotate a large set of samples by detecting erroneous predictions during tracking.
- Our method achieves state-of-the-art results even though it requires significantly fewer training samples than previous methods.
- The proposed warning method enables high reliability error-free instance tracking from start[1].

2   Methods

Our proposed method consists of several steps (Fig. 1). We start by pre-training Mask R-CNN [15] via synthetic data generation. Then, we extend the model to track objects by propagating the results through time. Meanwhile, we mark samples for annotation by checking the consistency of the predictions between subsequent frames. Lastly, manual annotation and fine-tuning take place. These steps are repeated until the model converges.

2.1   Pre-training

We follow the training method proposed in [17].

Assume a sequence of images $I = [I_1, I_2, \ldots, I_T]$, where $I_t \in [0, 255]^{H \times W \times 3}$ ($t \in [1, T]$). If the camera is stationary and the background is (relatively) constant, we can extract the background $B \in [0, 255]^{H \times W \times 3}$ by taking the most frequently occurring value at each pixel location:

$$B_{h,w,c} = \text{mode}\left(I_{.,h,w,c}\right),$$

---

[1] Our implementation is available here https://github.com/lkopi/rat_tracking.

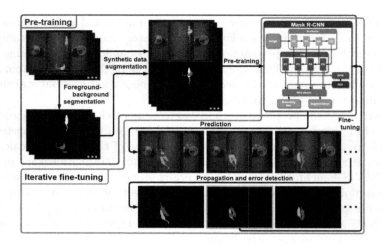

Fig. 1. The pipeline of the proposed method. The method can be divided into two phases. In the first phase, we pre-train the model on the generated synthetic data. While in the second phase, we repeat the following steps until the model converges. We propagate the predictions and detect frames where the model performs poorly. Then use these frames to fine-tune the model. For more information, see Sect. 2.

where $h \in [1, W], w \in [1, W], c \in [1, 3]$ and mode(.) is the statistical mode operation. Then the foreground-background mask at time step $t \in [1, T]$ can be estimated by

$$M_t = |I_t - B| > \epsilon,$$

where ϵ is an appropriate threshold parameter.

We keep frames where the foreground objects do not occlude each other, then apply various augmentation techniques commonly used in the video segmentation literature [18,19], such as rotation, scaling, thin-plat-spline warping [20]. This way, we can generate a synthetic dataset and train an instance segmentation method without ground truth data. As our deep neural network architecture, we chose Mask R-CNN [15] with ResNet50 backbone because it is highly modular and can be easily integrated into Tracktor [12].

2.2 Temporal Extension Using Tracktor

For temporal extension, we used 2 distinct methods. (1) As a baseline, we extended Tracktor [12] to handle instance segmentation. (2) In addition, we propose a simple propagation method described in more details in Sect. 2.3.

Tracktor is a multi-object tracking method. It predicts the position of the objects by feeding bounding box predictions from the previous frame to the bounding box regression layer of the object detector. Consequently, it accomplishes tracking without requiring further training of the underlying model.

Under the hood, Tracktor is using Faster R-CNN [21] to propagate the bounding box proposals. Mask R-CNN extends Faster R-CNN with an additional segmentation head. Therefore, by replacing Faster R-CNN with Mask R-CNN enables Tracktor to produce instance segmentation as well. This way, we can use our models to track and segment objects.

2.3 Propagation and Error Detection

We propose a simple algorithm for propagating instance proposals and detecting frames where the model performs poorly.

The method starts with a pre-processing step. Here we remove small regions and apply morphological closing (a dilation followed by erosion) to fill small holes. Then we do various checks to make sure that the predictions are correct:

- We check the number of instances by counting the number of unique ids. We drop the predictions if the number of instances does not equal 2.
- Then, we check whether the sizes of each rat are similar. We estimate the ratio of the area of the rats. If $\frac{\min(area)}{\max(area)} \leq 0.4$, we drop the smaller instance.
- And lastly, we eliminate intertwined predictions. We calculate the overlap between the convex hull of one of the rats and the predicted mask of the other rat. We remove the prediction if the overlap exceeds τ.

After we obtained the filtered result, we propagate instances using bipartite (Hungarian) matching [22]. If we cannot match an instance, we keep the prediction from the preceding frame and mark the frame for further annotation.

Keeping predictions from the previous time step ensures that we do not lose track of objects even when the model could not locate them for several frames. Meanwhile, it provides an adequate segmentation because instances do not change much in such a short time. Moreover, it eliminates the need for re-identification methods, which may struggle when the objects look identical.

2.4 Annotation Needs and Fine-Tuning

By annotating frames marked in the previous step and using them to fine-tune the model, we can increase the accuracy of the system and reduce the id switches during propagation. The annotation need can be mitigated by incrementally tuning the model. During each training cycle, we only provide ground truth for a small subset of samples, then repeat the propagation and error detection step (see Sect. 2.3) till the model converges. In this phase, we select the frames randomly, and the annotation is done by a human observer, who provides instance segmentation by correcting the predicted masks.

2.5 Benchmark Measures

To evaluate our results, we are counting the track switches (TS) and using the region ($\mathcal{J}$) and boundary ($\mathcal{F}$) measure proposed in DAVIS 2017 [16].

Track Switches (TS) measures the number of id switches during tracking. We use it as our primary metric in this paper, as it is crucial to reliably maintain the identity of instances to do further analysis on them.

Let P and $G \in [0, K]^{T \times H \times W}$ be the proposed predictions and ground truth instance masks, respectively. $K = 2$ is the maximum number of instances present on the scene and 0 is kept for the background. We introduce $\tilde{P}_t = [2/P_t]$ which is identical to P_t but the instance ids are switched up.

Now, let $o(X, Y) = \sum_{h \in [1,H] \wedge w \in [1,W]} \mathbf{1}(X_{h,w} = Y_{h,w})$ measures the overlap between X and Y, and $\mathbf{1} : \mathbb{L} \to \{0, 1\}$ is the indicator function defined as

$$\mathbf{1}(l) = \begin{cases} 1, & \text{if } l \text{ is } true \\ 0, & \text{otherwise} \end{cases}.$$

This way, we can calculate the track switches (TS) as in Algorithm 1.

Algorithm 1: Calculation of track switches.

Result: TS
$TS \leftarrow 0$;
if $o(P_1, G_1) < o(\tilde{P}_1, G_1)$ **then**
 | $P, \tilde{P} \leftarrow \tilde{P}, P$;
end
for $t = 2, 3 \ldots, T$ **do**
 | **if** $o(P_t, G_t) < o(\tilde{P}_t, G_t)$ **then**
 | | $TS \leftarrow TS + 1$;
 | | $P, \tilde{P} \leftarrow \tilde{P}, P$;
 | **end**
end

Region Similarity ($\mathcal{J}$) is defined as the Intersection over Union (IoU). IoU measures the similarity between the estimated $\mathcal{M}$ and the ground truth $\mathcal{G}$ segmentation. As the name implies it is calculated the following way: $\mathcal{J} = \frac{|\mathcal{M} \cap \mathcal{G}|}{|\mathcal{M} \cup \mathcal{G}|}$.

Contour Accuracy ($\mathcal{F}$) is defined as $\mathcal{F} = \frac{2 P_c R_c}{P_c + R_c}$, where P_c and R_c measures the contour-based precision and recall, respectively between the contour points of the proposed mask $c(\mathcal{M})$ and the ground truth mask $c(\mathcal{G})$. Pixel tolerance is set to the benchmark measure [23].

Region and Boundary ($\mathcal{J}\&\mathcal{F}$) **measure** is used to evaluate the performance of each method. It is defined as the mean of the region similarity ($\mathcal{J}$) and the contour accuracy ($\mathcal{F}$).

3 Results

3.1 Experimental Setup

We used the Mask R-CNN implementation of Detectron2[2] with a ResNet50 backbone pre-trained on the COCO instance segmentation dataset [24].

---

[2] https://github.com/facebookresearch/detectron2.

Table 1. Comparison of results on the test set. Methods where "GT" is ✗ are trained without using any hand-annotated samples, only on synthetic ones generated by the process described in Sect. 2.1. Tracktor and Proposed used the same weights.

Method	GT	$\mathcal{J}\&\mathcal{F}$ mean ↑	$\mathcal{J}$ mean ↑	$\mathcal{J}$ recall ↑	$\mathcal{J}$ decay ↓	$\mathcal{F}$ mean ↑	$\mathcal{F}$ recall ↑	$\mathcal{F}$ decay ↓	TS ↓
Cluster R-CNN [13]	✗	0.633	0.560	0.645	0.135	0.706	0.763	0.129	45
Tracktor [12]	✗	0.587	0.517	0.584	0.056	0.657	0.759	0.049	174
Proposed	✗	0.787	0.737	0.882	−0.038	0.837	0.932	−0.047	14
Cluster R-CNN [13]	✓	0.743	0.678	0.790	0.028	0.808	0.813	0.027	23
Tracktor [12]	✓	0.568	0.495	0.575	0.076	0.641	0.722	0.091	112
Proposed	✓	**0.876**	**0.831**	**0.972**	**−0.005**	**0.922**	**0.987**	−0.004	**0**

For pre-training, we trained the model for 50,000 iterations on an NVIDIA GeForce GTX 1080 graphics card with a batch size of 512 for the heads and a batch size of 4 for the rest of the network. The initial learning rate was set to 0.00025. During the evaluation, the confidence threshold was set to 70%. All other parameters were left as default.

During fine-tuning, we trained the model for 30 epochs on the given subset, and set τ to 1. The rest of the hyper-parameters were left unchanged.

3.2 Database

The database consists of a single video where two identical white rats are interacting in a black container. It was recorded by a stationary camera fixed on the top of the container. The whole video is 58,994 frame-long, and the original resolution was 1280 × 720, from which we cropped a 640 × 420 region containing only the box.

For pre-training, we ran the figure-ground segmentation proposed in Sect. 2.1 on the first 15,000 frames. We kept only frames where instances could be clearly separated, i.e., no occlusion was present. The resulting training set consists of 4,625 images, which we dilated to 27,654 by applying augmentation.

For the test set, we selected 18 200-frame-long clips where the rats are interacting with each other. These samples have been hand-annotated using the VGG Image Annotator [25].

3.3 Temporal Extension

We started the experiments by testing the capabilities of each method. We tested each with and without fine-tuning on ground truth samples. We compared the temporal extension techniques described in Sect. 2.2 and Sect. 2.3. We pre-trained Mask R-CNN on the training set, then we fine-tuned it on 2,215 hand-annotated samples. We also tested the Cluster R-CNN architecture [13] trained only on synthetic data and after fine-tuning on the ground truth data. In the former case, we used an additional 15,000 frames to pre-train the model as it requires continuous sequences. And in the latter case, it was fine-tuned on 3,000 ground truth samples. The results can be seen on Table 1.

The proposed method performed better on every benchmark measure regardless of the training process. Cluster R-CNN can separate objects even within a

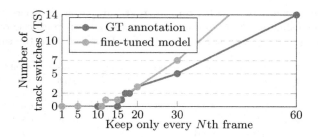

Fig. 2. Robustness of the propagation method. We keep only every Nth ground truth annotation (blue) or prediction (green) and count the track switches. By keeping only every 15th GT or every 11th prediction, the system could maintain stable tracking. (Color figure online)

single bounding box, but it suffers from sudden id switches. In some scenarios, the id of the opposite instance may flow through, thereby spoiling the tracklet. Although Tracktor utilizes the same models, its inferior performance was caused by the non-maximum suppression used during tracking as it may fuse detections close to each other, thereby losing track of objects. Meanwhile, in such cases, the proposed method could maintain tracking by propagating previous predictions.

3.4   Robustness

To evaluate the robustness of the proposed temporal extension method, we took the test sequences and kept only every Nth frame. Then propagated the instance segmentation of these frames and counted the track switches (TS). We tested the method using the ground truth annotation and using the best model presented in Sect. 3.3. Figure 2 show how the number of TS changes respect to N. As the results show, the system is robust enough to reliably track objects, even if only every 15th ground truth annotation or every 11th prediction was available.

3.5   Error Detection and Fine-Tuning

After we pre-trained the model on the synthetic dataset, we test the performance of the method when it is fine-tuned on samples marked by the system. In every case, we start with pre-trained weights then fine-tune the model for several training cycles. During each training cycle, we randomly select a fixed number of marked samples to tune the model. The results can be seen in Table 2.

As the results show, after training on only 30 samples, the performance of the model increased notably. The $\mathcal{J}\&\mathcal{F}$ mean improved by 6% from 0.787 to 0.833, and the number of track switches reduced to 0. Therefore, the model can learn to track objects with little human effort.

Figure 3 shows how the number of track switches changes over each iteration. Initially, we started with the pre-trained model, which made 14 TS, then with each iteration, it gradually decreased to 0.

Table 2. Performance of the fine-tuned method. Apart from the "pre-trained" model, "Model" names consist of two numbers: the number of fine-tuning iterations and the number of ground truth samples used during each iteration. The samples were randomly selected from the marked frames.

Model	$\mathcal{J}\&\mathcal{F}$ mean ↑	$\mathcal{J}$ mean ↑	$\mathcal{J}$ recall ↑	$\mathcal{J}$ decay ↓	$\mathcal{F}$ mean ↑	$\mathcal{F}$ recall ↑	$\mathcal{F}$ decay ↓	TS ↓
Pre-trained	0.787	0.737	0.882	−0.038	0.837	0.932	−0.047	14
25 × 1	0.828	0.780	0.947	−0.014	0.877	0.979	−0.005	0
3 × 10	0.833	0.785	0.946	−0.000	0.881	0.976	−0.010	0
1 × 100	0.820	0.778	0.935	−0.012	0.861	0.977	−0.006	0
1 × 505	0.846	0.797	0.950	−0.018	0.895	0.983	−0.008	0
1 × 2215	0.876	0.831	0.972	−0.005	0.922	0.987	−0.004	0

Figure 4 demonstrates how the length of the marked sequences are distributed. After fine-tuning the model on a few samples, the number of long sequences decreases significantly.

Note that depending on the training method, upon 10-to-15 training samples, the system could reliably track the instances without switches. Hence, there is considerable freedom for the experimenter on risk considerations, checking the potential errors on system warnings, the error types, and the samples that need to be annotated (see, Fig. 2). Optimization of requesting annotations from the experimenter is beyond the present work.

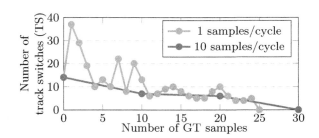

Fig. 3. Performance of the proposed method over the training cycles. "N samples/cycle" denotes that the system was fine-tuned on N randomly selected samples during each training cycle.

Finally, Fig. 5 presents some qualitative results. The proposed method can produce high-quality instance segmentation with minor artifacts. The mask does not capture some fine details, such as the end of the tail and the tip of the nose. Furthermore, when the rats are heavily occluded, the segmentation may extend out to the other mask, but these mistakes vanish when they move away from each other. Nonetheless, the tracking is reliable, and results are adequate to study the animals in an automated way.

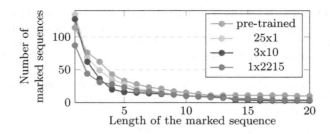

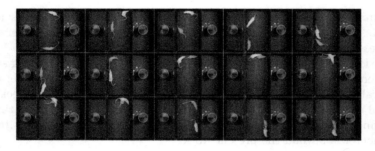

Fig. 4. Distribution of the length of each marked sequence. The plot shows the duration (in frames) of the marked sequences using different models. The notations are the same as in Table 1. Compare with Fig. 2 and see text concerning the role of the experimenter.

Fig. 5. Qualitative results. Visualization of the propagated predictions on 4 different sequences.

4   Summary

In this paper, we presented a simple and efficient deep learning-based approach to track and segment objects with identical appearance. The proposed method can reliably locate instances with little human effort. We reduced the annotation requirement by marking frames where the system could not provide accurate segmentation. Then we use these frames to fine-tune the model. We repeat these steps until the performance is not sufficient. We evaluated the system concerning its segmentation and tracking accuracy using the region and boundary ($\mathcal{J}\&\mathcal{F}$) measure and track switches, respectively. We showed that it outperforms previous approaches, and it is robust even when the model is unable to locate instances for several frames. Relatively small number of human annotations give rise to (a) switching free tracking of the similar animals in our architecture, while also providing warning signals that can be checked, e.g., by sampling means.

The method becomes suitable for the precise analysis of the social behaviors of rats under the condition that components, such as head, body and tail are recognized. This work is in progress. Our method eliminates the need for direct interactions, introducing implants, or artificial markers. The system could also be applied on other domains with slight modifications.

Although the proposed method performed better than previous ones, the combination of the different approaches could improve the overall performance. Moreover, the utilization of reinforcement learning to optimize the pipeline should also be considered. We note that Mask R-CNN architecture has some shortcomings that could be improved for better localization. Finally, other strategies for propagating masks could increase the robustness, such as using optical flow.

Author contributions. L.K. and A.L. conceived and designed the research, L.K. and V.V. designed and combined augmentation procedures, L.K. and Á.F. performed computational analyses, Á.D. and D.K. provided the dataset.

References

1. Henry, J., Wlodkowic, D.: High-throughput animal tracking in chemobehavioral phenotyping: current limitations and future perspectives. Behav. Process., 104226 (2020)
2. Catarinucci, L., et al.: An animal tracking system for behavior analysis using radio frequency identification. Lab Anim. **43**(9), 321–327 (2014)
3. Porcelli, S., et al.: Social dysfunction in mood disorders and schizophrenia: clinical modulators in four independent samples. Progress Neuro Psychopharmacol. Biol. Psychiatry **99**, 109835 (2020)
4. Toth, I., Neumann, I.D.: Animal models of social avoidance and social fear. Cell Tissue Res. **354**(1), 107–118 (2013)
5. de Chaumont, F., et al.: Real-time analysis of the behaviour of groups of mice via a depth-sensing camera and machine learning. Nat. Biomed. Eng. **3**(11), 930–942 (2019)
6. Mitchell, E.J., Brett, R.R., Armstrong, J.D., Sillito, R.R., Pratt, J.A.: Temporal dissociation of phencyclidine: Induced locomotor and social alterations in rats using an automated homecage monitoring system-implications for the 3Rs and preclinical drug discovery. J. Psychopharmacol., 709–715 (2020)
7. Peleh, T., Bai, X., Kas, M.J., Hengerer, B.: RFID-supported video tracking for automated analysis of social behaviour in groups of mice. J. Neurosci. Methods **325**, 108323 (2019)
8. Sturman, O., et al.: Deep learning-based behavioral analysis reaches human accuracy and is capable of outperforming commercial solutions. Neuropsychopharmacology **45**(11), 1942–1952 (2020)
9. Mathis, A.: DeepLabCut: markerless pose estimation of user-defined body parts with deep learning. Nat. Neurosci., 1281–1289 (2018)
10. Charpiat, G., Girard, N., Felardos, L., Tarabalka, Y.: Input similarity from the neural network perspective. In: Advances in Neural Information Processing Systems, vol. 32, pp. 1–10. Curran Associates Inc. (2019)
11. Kang, D., Emmons, J., Abuzaid, F., Bailis, P., Zaharia, M.: NoScope: optimizing neural network queries over video at scale. Proc. VLDB Endow. **10**(11), 1586 (2017)
12. Bergmann, P., Meinhardt, T., Leal-Taixe, L.: Tracking without bells and whistles. In: Proceedings of the IEEE International Conference on Computer Vision, pp. 941–951 (2019)

13. Fóthi, Á., Faragó, K.B., Kopácsi, L., Milacski, Z.Á., Varga, V., Lőrincz, A.: Multi object tracking for similar instances: a hybrid architecture. In: Yang, H., Pasupa, K., Leung, A.C.-S., Kwok, J.T., Chan, J.H., King, I. (eds.) ICONIP 2020. LNCS, vol. 12532, pp. 436–447. Springer, Cham (2020). https://doi.org/10.1007/978-3-030-63830-6_37

14. Peters, S.M., Pinter, I.J., Pothuizen, H.H., de Heer, R.C., van der Harst, J.E., Spruijt, B.M.: Novel approach to automatically classify rat social behavior using a video tracking system. J. Neurosci. Methods **268**, 163–170 (2016)

15. He, K., Gkioxari, G., Dollár, P., Girshick, R.: Mask R-CNN. In: Proceedings of the IEEE International Conference on Computer Vision, pp. 2961–2969 (2017)

16. Pont-Tuset, J., Perazzi, F., Caelles, S., Arbeláez, P., Sorkine-Hornung, A., Van Gool, L.: The 2017 DAVIS challenge on video object segmentation. arXiv preprint arXiv:1704.00675, pp. 1–6 (2017)

17. Kopácsi, L.: A self-supervised method for body part segmentation and keypoint detection of rat images. In: 13th Joint Conference on Mathematics and Informatics Collection of Abstracts, pp. 102–103 (2020)

18. Perazzi, F., Khoreva, A., Benenson, R., Schiele, B., Sorkine-Hornung, A.: Learning video object segmentation from static images. In: Proceedings of the IEEE Conference on Computer Vision and Pattern Recognition, pp. 2663–2672 (2017)

19. Khoreva, A., Benenson, R., Ilg, E., Brox, T., Schiele, B.: Lucid data dreaming for video object segmentation. Int. J. Comput. Vision **127**(9), 1175–1197 (2019)

20. Bookstein, F.L.: Principal warps: thin-plate splines and the decomposition of deformations. IEEE Trans. Pattern Anal. Mach. Intell. **11**(6), 567–585 (1989)

21. Ren, S., He, K., Girshick, R., Sun, J.: Faster R-CNN: towards real-time object detection with region proposal networks. IEEE Trans. Pattern Anal. Mach. Intell. **39**(6), 1137–1149 (2016)

22. Bewley, A., Ge, Z., Ott, L., Ramos, F., Upcroft, B.: Simple online and realtime tracking. In: 2016 IEEE International Conference on Image Processing (ICIP), pp. 3464–3468. IEEE (2016)

23. Perazzi, F., Pont-Tuset, J., McWilliams, B., Van Gool, L., Gross, M., Sorkine-Hornung, A.: A benchmark dataset and evaluation methodology for video object segmentation. In: Proceedings of the IEEE Conference on Computer Vision and Pattern Recognition, pp. 724–732 (2016)

24. Lin, T.-Y., et al.: Microsoft COCO: common objects in context. In: Fleet, D., Pajdla, T., Schiele, B., Tuytelaars, T. (eds.) ECCV 2014. LNCS, vol. 8693, pp. 740–755. Springer, Cham (2014). https://doi.org/10.1007/978-3-319-10602-1_48

25. Dutta, A., Zisserman, A.: The VIA annotation software for images, audio and video. In: Proceedings of the 27th ACM International Conference on Multimedia, MM 2019, p. 2276. ACM (2019)

Knowledge Distillation

Data Diversification Revisited: Why Does It Work?

Yuheng Song[1], Tianyi Liu[1], and Weijia Jia[1,2(✉)]

[1] Department of Computer Science and Engineering, Shanghai Jiao Tong University, Shanghai 200240, China
[2] BNU-UIC Institute of Artificial Intelligence and Future Networks Beijing Normal University (BNU Zhuhai) Guangdong Key Lab of AI and Multi-Modal Data Processing, BNU-HKBU United International College Zhuhai, Guangdong, People's Republic of China
jiawj@uic.edu.cn

Abstract. *Data Diversification* is a recently proposed method of data augmentation for Neural Machine Translation (NMT). While it attracts broad attention due to its effectiveness, the reason for its success is unclear. In this paper, we first establish a connection between data diversification and knowledge distillation, and prove that data diversification reduces the modality complexity. We also find knowledge distillation has a lower complexity of data modality than data diversification, but challenging to boost performance. Our analysis reveals that knowledge distillation has a negative impact on the word frequency distribution where increasing rare words with unreliable representations. Furthermore, data diversification trains multiple models to further decrease the modality complexity, suffering from unbearable computational expenses. To reduce the computational cost, we propose *adjustable sampling*, which samples a model multiple times instead of training multiple models. Different from other sampling methods, our method introduces entropy to adjust the quality and diversity of the generated sentences, achieving the goal of reducing modality complexity and noise introduction. Extensive experimental results show our method dramatically reduces the computational cost of data diversification without loss of accuracy, and achieves improvements over other strong sampling methods.

Keywords: Neural Machine Translation · Data diversification · Knowledge distillation

1 Introduction

Neural Machine Translation (NMT) [15,16] has achieved significant progress due to the strong capability of learning representations from data. While its remarkable success, NMT models are particularly susceptible to the quality and scale of the corpora. Generally, NMT models favor high-quality and large-scale corpora. However, the availability of such corpora is no mean feat. One key trick to alleviate this problem is creating more training data through data augmentation techniques, such as back translation [13] and word replacements [23].

© Springer Nature Switzerland AG 2021
I. Farkaš et al. (Eds.): ICANN 2021, LNCS 12893, pp. 521–533, 2021.
https://doi.org/10.1007/978-3-030-86365-4_42

Recently, Nguyen et al. [8] proposed a novel data augmentation method (*Data Diversification*), delivering impressive gains over strong NMT models. It uses multiple models to translate the original data to obtain pseudo parallel data. Then, the combination of pseudo data and original data is used to train the NMT model. While its success, the reason why it improves NMT models is unclear. We find data diversification is analogous to sequence-level knowledge distillation [5]. The basic idea of sequence-level knowledge distillation is training the model on the corpus generated from a teacher model. It is observed that both methods train the model using pseudo parallel data. Therefore, we take exploring the relationship between these two methods as the starting point for understanding data diversification. In this paper, we aim to answer the following specific questions:

- **Q1**: How does data diversification benefit NMT models, and what is the relationship between data diversification and knowledge distillation? (Sect. 3)
- **Q2**: Does the performance improvement in data diversification come from knowledge distillation? (Sect. 4)
- **Q3**: Is it necessary to train multiple models in data diversification, and is there a way to reduce the computational cost without loss of accuracy? (Sect. 5)

To answer **Q1**, we first conduct a comparative analysis of knowledge distillation and data diversification, and find that they are closely related. As implied in previous works [22], knowledge distillation reduces the modality of data. Accordingly, we reasonably propose two hypotheses: (i) Data diversification can also reduce the complexity of data modality. (ii) The reduction in modality complexity leads to the improvement of performance. We verify these hypotheses through measuring the modality complexity of the data and multimodal experiments. For **Q2**, we show that knowledge distillation has difficulty in boosting performance, thus the improvement in data diversification does not come from knowledge distillation. Moreover, we pinpoint the reason is that knowledge distillation leads to an increase in the number of rare words with unreliable representation, resulting in performance degradation. For **Q3**, we demonstrate that the purpose of introducing multiple models is to make the modality complexity lower. Therefore, we propose *adjustable sampling* to sample a model multiple times instead of training multiple models, which dramatically reduces the computational cost. Our method leverages entropy to adjust the quality and diversity of the generated sentences, achieving the goal of reducing complexity while reducing noise introduction. Experimental results show that our method obtains competitive results compared to data diversification, and achieves improvements over other strong sampling methods. The contributions are summarized as follows:

- We prove that data diversification reduces modality complexity, and quantify the correlation between modality complexity and performance.
- We find that knowledge distillation increases the number of rare words with unreliable representations, resulting in performance degradation.
- We propose *adjustable sampling*. Experimental results show that it is superior to other strong sampling methods, and as effective as data diversification, but the computational cost is significantly reduced.

2   Background

Neural Machine Translation. NMT has attracted the attention of both industry and academy. Numerous architectures are proposed with the goal of improving the NMT model, including recurrent networks [15], convolution networks [2], and transformer networks [16]. Recently, Transformer model [16] has become the de facto method to solve translation tasks due to its efficiency and effectiveness. More and more researchers focus on improving the Transformer model, including model architecture [20], attention mechanism [21]. In this paper, we conduct all the experiments on the vanilla Transformer model [16].

Data Diversification. Data diversification is one of the data augmentation techniques for NMT. As described in Algorithm 1, given the parallel corpus $\mathcal{D} = (S, T)$, where S and T denote source side corpus and target side corpus respectively, multiple forward models $\left(M_{S \to T}^1, \ldots, M_{S \to T}^k\right)$ and multiple backward models $\left(M_{T \to S}^1, \ldots, M_{T \to S}^k\right)$ are first trained, where k denotes a factor. Then, forward models are used to translate source side corpus S of the corpus $\mathcal{D}$ to obtain multiple synthetic target side corpora $\left(M_{S \to T}^1(S), \ldots, M_{S \to T}^k(S)\right)$. Similarly, multiple synthetic source side corpora $\left(M_{T \to S}^1(T), \ldots, M_{T \to S}^k(T)\right)$ are obtained by backward models. Last, synthetic corpora and original corpus are concatenated to train the final NMT model. While its simplicity and effectiveness, it is unclear why this method benefits models.

Sequence-Level Knowledge Distillation. Sequence-level knowledge distillation [5] was proposed for neural network compression, which trains the student model using "hard" labels generated from the teacher model. Explicitly, a teacher model is first trained, and then the sampled translations from the teacher model, out from source side sentences, are used as a new parallel dataset to train the student model. Sequence-level knowledge distillation has a strong correlation with data diversification. The training data for both methods contains synthetic corpus produced by the trained model.

Algorithm 1. Data Diversification

Input: Parallel corpus $\mathcal{D} = (S, T)$, a diversification factor k
Output: Translation model $\hat{M}_{S \to T}$
1: $\mathcal{D}_1 \leftarrow \mathcal{D}$
2: **for** $i \in 1, \ldots, k$ **do**
3:      Train randomly initialized forward model $M_{S \to T}^i$ on corpora $\mathcal{D} = (S, T)$
4:      Train randomly initialized backward model $M_{T \to S}^i$ on corpora $\mathcal{D}' = (T, S)$
5:      $\mathcal{D}_1 \leftarrow \mathcal{D}_1 \cup \left(S, M_{S \to T}^i(S)\right)$
6:      $\mathcal{D}_1 \leftarrow \mathcal{D}_1 \cup \left(M_{T \to S}^i(T), T\right)$
7: Train model $\hat{M}_{S \to T}$ on corpora $\mathcal{D}_1$ until convergence
8: **return** $\hat{M}_{S \to T}$

---

3   How Does Data Diversification Benefit NMT Models?

3.1   Comparative Analysis and Hypothesis

As mentioned above, data diversification has a strong correlation with sequence-level knowledge distillation. The training data for both methods contains synthetic corpus generated from the trained model. Recent works [3, 22] suggest that sequence-level knowledge distillation reduces the modality (Given a sentence, there might be multiple valid translations.) of the dataset, making the synthetic data more deterministic. **Since data diversification has many similarities with knowledge distillation, we reasonably assume that it helps reduce the modality, enabling NMT model learning with less difficulty.** Before verifying this hypothesis, we first illustrate how the modality of the data affects performance. While some works mention the impact of modality [9, 19], to our best knowledge, we are the first to attempt to quantify this impact.

3.2   Preliminary Study for Modality

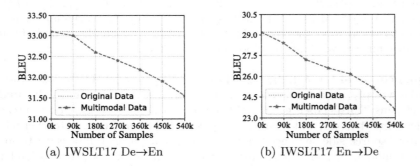

(a) IWSLT17 De→En   (b) IWSLT17 En→De

Fig. 1. BLEU scores on IWSLT17 De → En and En → De. Original data and multimodal data denote training the model on original data and multimodal data.

To quantify the impact of modality, we experiment on the IWSLT[1]17 English ↔ German translation task. We extract sentence pairs aligned with English-German (En-De) dataset from IWLST17 English-Japanese (En-Ja), English-Korean (En-Ko) and English-Chinese (En-Zh) data, and create an En-Ja/Ko/Zh corpus to simulate multi-modality. To explore the relation between modality complexity of the data and performance, we incrementally add these data to En-De training data to simulate the increase in modality complexity. Note that our experiments are similar to multilingual translation [4], but in our case we do not add a language tag to each sentence to help the model distinguish different languages. We take tst2013 and tst2014 as the validation set and choose tst2015 as the test set. We follow the setting *transformer_iwslt* in fairseq [10] to train the model.

---

[1] https://wit3.fbk.eu.

As shown in Fig. 1(a), we find that model accuracy decreases gradually with the increase of source side data modality complexity, and the model obtains the worst performance when all the corpora are mixed together. Similarly, we observe that increasing the modality complexity of the target side data leads to performance degradation from Fig. 1(b). Compared with the source side, target side modality complexity has a more severe impact on model accuracy. **From our observation, we can conclude that reducing the modality complexity of data enables the model to achieve better results without the difficulty of coping with modality uncertainty.**

3.3 Metric for Data Modality Complexity

To prove the hypothesis (Sect. 3.1), we need a metric for measuring the data modality complexity. Inspired by Zhou et al. [22], we leverage conditional entropy to measure the data modality complexity. Different from their work, we take both side modality complexity into consideration, as Nguyen et al. [8] mentioned that modality of source side is as vital as that of target side. Specifically, given a dataset $\mathcal{D} = \{(s_1, t_1) \dots (s_N, t_N)\}$, where (s, t) denotes a sentence pair of the dataset, and $s \in S$, $t \in T$, the modality complexity $C(\mathcal{D})$ is defined as follows:

$$C(\mathcal{D}) = \frac{1}{2}(C_s(D) + C_t(D)) = \frac{1}{2}(\mathcal{H}(\mathbf{S} \mid \mathbf{T}) + \mathcal{H}(\mathbf{T} \mid \mathbf{S})) \tag{1}$$

$$= \frac{1}{2}(\sum_{t \in T} p(t)\mathcal{H}(\mathbf{S} \mid \mathbf{T} = t) + \sum_{s \in S} p(s)\mathcal{H}(\mathbf{T} \mid \mathbf{S} = s)) \tag{2}$$

where $C_s(D)$ and $C_t(D)$ denote the modality complexity of the source side and the target side, respectively. $C_s(D)$ is calculated by the entropy of source sentences conditioned on the target sentences. Similarly, we define the entropy of target sentences conditioned on source sentences as $C_t(D)$. Following the definition of the entropy, the condition entropy $\mathcal{H}(\mathbf{T} \mid \mathbf{S} = s)$ is defined as:

$$\mathcal{H}(\mathbf{T} \mid \mathbf{S} = s) = -\sum_{t \in T} p(t \mid s) \log p(t \mid s) \tag{3}$$

$$\approx -\frac{1}{I_s} \sum_{i=1}^{I_s} \sum_{t \in \mathcal{A}(s_i)} p(t \mid s_i) \log p(t \mid s_i) \tag{4}$$

$$= \frac{1}{I_s} \sum_{i=1}^{I_s} \mathcal{H}(t \mid s = s_i) \tag{5}$$

However, it is intractable to calculate $p(t \mid s)$. To tackle this problem, an alignment model is introduced, then the sentence-level entropy can be approximated by the averaging of the token-level entropy, as shown in Eq. 4, where t and s denote a word in target and source vocabulary, respectively. I_s denotes the length of the source sentence, and $\mathcal{A}(s)$ denotes an aligned word corresponding to the source word s. With the above deduction, we can easily calculate the modality complexity of $C_s(\mathcal{D})$ and $C_t(\mathcal{D})$. However, it is worth pointing out that the modality complexity is prone to being dominated by frequent words, leading to unfair comparison. Therefore, we use the averaging entropy of target words conditioned on a source word to calculate $C_t(\mathcal{D})$, denoted $\frac{1}{|\mathcal{V}_s|}\sum_{s\in\mathcal{V}_s}\mathcal{H}(t\mid s)$. Similarly, $C_s(\mathcal{D})$ can be calculated by $\frac{1}{|\mathcal{V}_t|}\sum_{t\in\mathcal{V}_t}\mathcal{H}(s\mid t)$. $\mathcal{V}_t$ and $\mathcal{V}_s$ denote the vocabulary of the target and the source. Then $C(\mathcal{D})$ is approximated as:

$$C(\mathcal{D}) = \frac{1}{2}\Big(\frac{1}{|\mathcal{V}_s|}\sum_{s\in\mathcal{V}_s}\mathcal{H}(t\mid s) + \frac{1}{|\mathcal{V}_t|}\sum_{t\in\mathcal{V}_t}\mathcal{H}(s\mid t)\Big) \qquad (6)$$

3.4 Hypothesis Verification

To verify our hypothesis, we compute the data modality complexity $C(\mathcal{D})$ on three IWSLT translation datasets (see Sect. 5.3 for more details), including original training data and synthetic training data through data diversification method with different diversification factor k. As shown in Table 1, we observe that the data modality complexity is gradually reduced with the increasing of k. (Note that the computational cost increases linearly with k.) These observations confirm our hypothesis: **Data diversification helps reduce the data modality complexity.**

Table 1. Statistics of $C(\mathcal{D})$ ($\uparrow$ more complex) on three IWSLT data sets.

Tasks	Original data	Data diversification		
	$k = 0$	$k = 1$	$k = 2$	$k = 3$
IWSLT14 De → En	3.96	3.38	3.26	3.20
IWSLT15 En → Fr	3.09	2.61	2.55	2.49
IWSLT17 Zh → En	4.79	4.39	4.35	4.33

4 Does the Performance Improvement Come from Knowledge Distillation?

As analyzed in Sect. 3.1, data diversification is built on sequence-level knowledge distillation. Recent work [3] shows that sequence-level knowledge distillation improves non-autoregressive translation models. Therefore, it is important to test whether the improvement in data diversification comes from knowledge distillation. To verify this, we conduct experiments on IWSLT14 De → En and IWSLT17 Zh → En with different settings: (i) training models on the original data (baseline), (ii) training models using data distilled by knowledge distillation (target distillation), (iii) training models using data augmented through data diversification ($k = 1$). Moreover, we extend knowledge distillation to the source side (source distillation). Specifically, we use a target-to-source model to translate the original data, and then the distilled data is used to train the final model. We use the same test sets as described in Sect. 5.3, and BLEU [11] to measure the performance. We also compute $C(\mathcal{D})$ for each dataset.

Table 2. BLEU scores and $C(\mathcal{D})$ on IWLST14 De $\to$ En and IWSLT17 Zh $\to$ En.

Datasets	Baseline	Source distillation	Target distillation	Data diversification
De $\to$ En($C(\mathcal{D})$)	34.7 (3.96)	33.3 (2.67)	35.0 (2.81)	**36.4** (3.38)
Zh $\to$ En($C(\mathcal{D})$)	21.8 (4.79)	19.8 (3.50)	21.5 (3.70)	**23.0** (4.39)

As shown in Table 2, source distillation does not bring improvements, and target distillation only achieves marginal improvement on the De $\to$ En task. However, data diversification significantly improves the performance while it has higher data modality complexity than source distillation and target distillation, conflicting with the above conclusion (Sect. 3.2). To investigate this, we study the word frequency distribution of each dataset. Select the words that have fewer than R occurrences as rare words. Note that we remove the duplicate samples before counting to reduce the statistical bias. We set $R = 50$ for English and German, and $R = 20$ for Chinese. As shown in Fig. 2, we observe that the number of rare words in source distillation and target distillation is much larger than baseline. However, data diversification significantly reduces the number of rare words. The following explains the reason for this phenomenon.

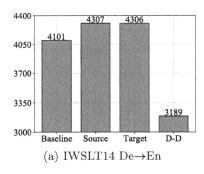
(a) IWSLT14 De$\to$En

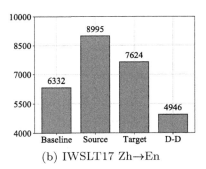
(b) IWSLT17 Zh$\to$En

Fig. 2. Rare words statistics on two IWSLT data sets. Source and Target denote source distillation and target distillation respectively, and D-D denotes data diversification.

Assume that the vocabulary of the target side has only three words, two of which are synonyms. The word frequency is 50, 25 and 15 respectively, denoted $\{A : 50, A' : 25, B : 15\}$. As suggested in previous work [7], NMT favors choosing the one with higher frequency as output when faced with two words with similar meanings. Therefore, after target distillation, the target side vocabulary may be changed into $\{A : 60, A' : 15, B : 15\}$. If we take words with fewer than 20 occurrences as rare words, the number of rare words changes from 1 to 2 after target distillation. Hence, knowledge distillation increases the rare words. The source distillation is analogous to the target distillation. Data diversification utilizes source and target distilled data and original data, thus the target side vocabulary may turn into $2 \times \{A : 50, A' : 25, B : 15\} + \{A : 60, A' : 15, B : 15\}$. Therefore, the number of rare words can be reduced through data diversification.

Existing work [1] shows that rare words have a significant impact on the model, which make the parameter estimation unreliable. The performance of the model deteriorates with the increase of rare words. Therefore, affected by rare words, the performance of knowledge distillation close to or worse than the baseline, even if its modal complexity is lower than data diversification. However, data diversification simultaneously reduces the modal complexity and the number of rare words, which is the reason why it significantly improves the performance. To sum up, we can conclude that the improvement in data diversification does not come from knowledge distillation.

5 How to Reduce the Computational Cost of Data Diversification?

As mentioned in Sect. 3.4, the purpose of introducing multiple models in data diversification is to enable the modality complexity much lower, suffering from unbearable computational cost. The problem becomes serious when it is applied to deep models [18]. To this end, we propose *adjustable sampling*, which introduces appropriate randomness to the sampling process, achieving the goal of reducing cost and noise introduction. Therefore, instead of training multiple models, we sample a model multiple times to obtain the synthetic data.

Algorithm 2. Adjustable Sampling

Input: Maximum length N, width B, threshold r, sampling topk K. **Output**: Sampling solution.

1: $score_{0,i} \leftarrow 0, i = 1 \ldots B$
2: **for** $i \in 1 \ldots B$ **do**
3:      $state_{0,i} \leftarrow$ DECODER-INIT(i)
4: **for** time step $t \in 0 \ldots N$ **do**
5:      **for** $i \in 1 \ldots B$ **do**
6:          **for** all $v \in V_T$ **do**
7:              $p_{t,i,v} \leftarrow$ DECODER-STEP$(state_{t,i})$
8:          $\mathcal{H} \leftarrow -\sum_{v \in V} p_{t,i,v} * \log p_{t,i,v}$
9:          $p_{t,i,*} \leftarrow 1.0$
10:         **if** $\mathcal{H} > r$ **then**
11:             $p_{t,i,*} \leftarrow$ topk-sampling$(p_{t,i}, K)$
12:         **for** all $v \in V_T$ **do**
13:             **if** $p_{t,i,v} > p_{t,i,*}$ **then**
14:                 $sc\hat{o}re_{t,i,v} \leftarrow score_{t,i} + (-\infty)$
15:             **else**
16:                 $sc\hat{o}re_{t,i,v} \leftarrow score_{t,i} + \log p_{t,i,v}$
17:     $score_{t+1} \leftarrow$ max-k$(sc\hat{o}re_t, k = B)$
18:     $state_{t+1} \leftarrow$ UPDATE$($argmax-k$(sc\hat{o}re_t, k = B))$
19: **return** $state_{N+1}[0]$

5.1 Adjustable Sampling

In adjustable sampling (Algorithm 2), the decoder maintains B elements at each time step and expands each of the B elements to find B-best candidates for the next time step. We will obtain B hypotheses when the last time step N is decoded, and take the highest scoring one as the solution. Define the sum of log probability $\log p_{t,i}$ of the selected word at each time step as the score $score_i$ of hypothesis i. In our notation, $score_{t,i}$ and $state_{t,i}$ denote the cumulative score and corresponding state at step t for active hypothesis i, respectively. $s\hat{c}ore_t \in \mathbb{R}^{B \times |V_T|}$ is cumulative candidate score matrix used to determine the state $state_{t+1}$ and score $score_{t+1}$ for the next step, which is obtained by adding log probability $\log p_{t,i,v}$ in the vocabulary V_T to the current step score $score_t$. max-k and $argmax$-k denote the functions which return the value and index of the k largest elements (sorted), respectively. To introduce appropriate randomness to the sampling process, we measure the entropy of each time step to determine whether random sampling is applied to the step. If the entropy $\mathcal{H}$ exceeds a threshold r, we perform random sampling on the current step, otherwise we do not perform it. The idea behind this is that when the entropy is small, the current time step is relatively certain. If we replace it with other words, it may result in significant changes in semantics. Moreover, to guarantee the quality of the solution, we consider sampling restricted to the K most likely words, denoted *topk-sampling*. Actually, the widely used algorithm beam search and top-k sampling can be served as special cases of adjustable sampling.

5.2 Clean Tuning

Noise is inevitably introduced to the data obtained through adjustable sampling. To reduce the impact of noise, we fine tune the model on the clean data. The clean data is composed of the original training data and the data obtained from the trained model through the beam search method. Note that adjustable sampling and beam search are performed on the same trained model.

5.3 Experiments

Datasets. We carry out experiments on seven benchmarks: IWSLT14 De $\leftrightarrow$ En, IWSLT15 En $\leftrightarrow$ Fr, IWSLT17 Zh $\leftrightarrow$ En, and WMT14 En $\rightarrow$ De [16]. For IWSLT14 De $\leftrightarrow$ En, it contains 160k and 7k sentence pairs for training and validation respectively, and we concatenate *tst2010, tst2011, tst2012, dev2010, dev2012* as the test set. For IWSLT15 En $\leftrightarrow$ Fr and IWSLT17 Zh $\leftrightarrow$ En, they contain 202k and 235k parallel data for training, respectively. We choose *tst2012/tst2013* as validation/test set for IWSLT15 En $\leftrightarrow$ Fr. We concatenate *tst2013, tst2014, tst2015* as validation set and utilize *tst2017* as test set for IWSLT17 Zh $\leftrightarrow$ En. As for WMT14 En $\rightarrow$ De, the training set consists of 4.5M sentence pairs. *newstest2013* and *newstest2014* are used as the validation and test set, respectively. We use *jieba*[2] segmenter for Chinese word segmentation

---

[2] https://github.com/fxsjy/jieba.

and Moses [6] for English, French and German tokenization. For each dataset, we apply BPE[14] to split words into subwords. The numbers of BPE merge operations for IWSLT De $\leftrightarrow$ En, En $\leftrightarrow$ Fr, Zh $\leftrightarrow$ En, and WMT14 En $\rightarrow$ De is 10k, 32k, 20k, and 32k, respectively. We share the source and target vocabulary for all tasks.

Model. We choose Transformer [16] as the default model. For IWSLT tasks, we adopt the *transformer_iwslt* setting ($d_{\text{hidden}} = 512$, $d_{\text{ffn}} = 1024$, $n_{\text{head}} = 4$), and *transformer_big* ($d_{\text{hidden}} = 1024$, $d_{\text{ffn}} = 4096$, $n_{\text{head}} = 16$) setting for the WMT task. For adjustable sampling, we set $B = 5$, $r = 2.5$, $K = 5$ for forward model $M_{S \rightarrow T}$, and $B = 5$, $r = 0.0$, $K = 5$ for backward model $M_{T \rightarrow S}$. To reduce the difficulty of tuning these parameters, we set $K = 5$ empirically and tune other parameters on the IWSLT De $\rightarrow$ En task, applying them to other tasks directly. We perform adjustable sampling on the forward model and the backward model three times respectively to keep consistent with [8]. We employ Adam as the default optimizer, and follow the same configurations as suggested by *fairseq* [10]. For inference, we use beam search with a beam width of 5 and a length penalty of 0.6/2.5 for WMT14 En $\rightarrow$ De/IWSLT15 Fr $\rightarrow$ En, respectively. For other tasks, we use width 5 and length penalty 1.0. We measure SACRE-BLEU [12] for IWSLT17 Zh $\leftrightarrow$ En, and case-sensitive tokenized BLEU [11] for other tasks. We train the model with 4/1 GPUs on the WMT datasets and IWSLT dataset respectively, where each GPU is filled with 4096 tokens. Following previous work [8], we accumulate the gradients for 32 updates. To manifest the advances of our sampling method, we also prepare some strong sampling methods for reference, including:

- **Top-5 Sampling.** It samples restricted to the 5 most likely words for each time step.
- **Diverse Beam Search (DBS).** It adds a regularization item in beam search to increase the translation diversity [17].

Table 3. BLEU scores of each method on seven translation tasks. "-" indicates slightly larger than above. FLOPs is the number of floating-point operations. DD denotes data diversification. Top-5 denotes Top-5 sampling. AS and CT denote adjustable sampling and clean tuning, respectively.

Methods	IWSLT14		IWSLT15		IWSLT17		WMT14	
	En $\rightarrow$ De	De $\rightarrow$ En	Fr $\rightarrow$ En	En $\rightarrow$ Fr	En $\rightarrow$ Zh	Zh $\rightarrow$ En	En $\rightarrow$ De	FLOPs
Transformer	28.6	34.7	43.0	44.3	26.5	21.8	29.3	1$\times$
+ DD	**30.6**	37.0	44.4	46.1	28.0	**23.4**	30.7	**7$\times$**
+ Top-5	29.8	36.4	44.2	45.3	27.5	22.8	30.2	3$\times$
+ DBS	29.7	36.5	44.2	45.3	28.0	22.9	30.5	3$\times$
+ AS	30.2	37.0	44.4	45.7	28.0	23.1	30.8	3$\times$
+ CT	**30.6**	**37.3**	**44.7**	**46.2**	**28.2**	**23.4**	**31.0**	-

Main Results. The evaluation results on seven translation tasks are reported in Table 3. As we can see, our method achieves better results than data diversification while dramatically reducing computational cost (from 7× to 3×). Our method achieves improvements from 1.6 to 2.0 over baselines on different tasks. Compared to other sampling methods, our method outperforms them with margins from 0.2 to 0.9, illustrating the superiority of our method. Moreover, we can see that clean tuning further brings improvements (up to 0.5 BLEU scores) on all the tasks, confirming its effectiveness.

Study of B and r. To study the effect of B and r on model accuracy, we separately perform our sampling method with different width B and threshold r on the source-to-target model $M_{S \to T}$ (forward model) and the target-to-source trained model $M_{T \to S}$ model (backward model). The results are reported in Fig. 3. For the forward model, both B and r prefer large values and obtain the best performance when $B = 5$, $r = 2.5$. Note that when B and r are larger, the generated sentences are less noisy. For the backward model, the performance decreases with the growth of r, and a large B is better than a small one. Therefore, we choose $B = 5$, $r = 0.0$ as the best configuration for the backward model.

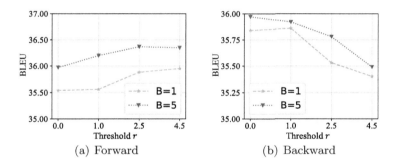

(a) Forward   (b) Backward

Fig. 3. BLEU scores of our method on IWSLT14 De → En task with different B and r. Forward denotes performing our method on the source-to-target model individually, and Backward denotes applying our method to the target-to-source model.

6 Conclusion

In this work, we quantify the correction between data modality complexity and performance, and prove that data diversification reduces the complexity of data modality, benefiting NMT models. We also connect data diversification with knowledge distillation, and find that knowledge distillation has lower modality complexity but hard to boost performance. Our conclusion is that knowledge distillation increases the number of rare words, leading to performance degradation. Furthermore, we propose adjustable sampling to reduce the computational cost. Experimental results show that our method is as effective as data diversification while consuming less computing resources, and confirm the superiority of our method compared to other sampling methods.

Acknowledgements. This work is supported by Guangdong Key Lab of AI and Multi-modal Data Processing, Chinese National Research Fund (NSFC) Project No. 61872239; BNU-UIC Institute of Artificial Intelligence and Future Networks funded by Beijing Normal University (Zhuhai) and AI-DS Research Hub, BNU-HKBU United International College (UIC), Zhuhai, Guangdong, China.

References

1. Fadaee, M., Bisazza, A., Monz, C.: Data augmentation for low-resource neural machine translation. In: ACL, pp. 567–573 (2017)
2. Gehring, J., Auli, M., Grangier, D., Yarats, D., Dauphin, Y.N.: Convolutional sequence to sequence learning. arXiv preprint arXiv:1705.03122 (2017)
3. Gu, J., Bradbury, J., Xiong, C., Li, V.O., Socher, R.: Non-autoregressive neural machine translation. In: ICLR (2018)
4. Johnson, M., et al.: Google's multilingual neural machine translation system: enabling zero-shot translation. TACL (2017)
5. Kim, Y., Rush, A.M.: Sequence-level knowledge distillation. In: Proceedings of EMNLP, pp. 1317–1327 (2016)
6. Koehn, P., et al.: Moses: open source toolkit for statistical machine translation. In: ACL, pp. 177–180 (2007)
7. Nguyen, T.Q., Chiang, D.: Improving lexical choice in neural machine translation. In: Proceedings of NAACL, pp. 334–343 (2018)
8. Nguyen, X., Joty, S.R., Wu, K., Aw, A.T.: Data diversification: a simple strategy for neural machine translation. In: NeurIPS (2020)
9. Ott, M., Auli, M., Grangier, D., Ranzato, M.: Analyzing uncertainty in neural machine translation. In: ICLR, pp. 3956–3965 (2018)
10. Ott, M., et al.: fairseq: a fast, extensible toolkit for sequence modeling. In: NAACL-HLT (2019)
11. Papineni, K., Roukos, S., Ward, T., Zhu, W.J.: BLEU: a method for automatic evaluation of machine translation. In: Proceedings of ACL, pp. 311–318 (2002)
12. Post, M.: A call for clarity in reporting bleu scores. In: WMT 2018, p. 186 (2018)
13. Sennrich, R., Haddow, B., Birch, A.: Improving neural machine translation models with monolingual data. In: Proceedings of ACL, pp. 86–96 (2016)
14. Sennrich, R., Haddow, B., Birch, A.: Neural machine translation of rare words with subword units. In: Proceedings of ACL, pp. 1715–1725 (2016)
15. Sutskever, I., Vinyals, O., Le, Q.V.: Sequence to sequence learning with neural networks. Adv. Neural. Inf. Process. Syst. **27**, 3104–3112 (2014)
16. Vaswani, A., et al.: Attention is all you need. In: NeurIPS, pp. 5998–6008 (2017)
17. Vijayakumar, A.K., et al.: Diverse beam search for improved description of complex scenes. In: AAAI (2018)
18. Wang, Q., et al.: Learning deep transformer models for machine translation. In: Proceedings of ACL (2019)
19. Wei, X., Yu, H., Hu, Y., Weng, R., Xing, L., Luo, W.: Uncertainty-aware semantic augmentation for neural machine translation. In: EMNLP (2020)
20. Wu, F., Fan, A., Baevski, A., Dauphin, Y.N., Auli, M.: Pay less attention with lightweight and dynamic convolutions. In: ICLR (2019)

21. Xu, M., Wong, D.F., Yang, B., Zhang, Y., Chao, L.S.: Leveraging local and global patterns for self-attention networks. In: Proceedings of ACL, pp. 3069–3075 (2019)
22. Zhou, C., Gu, J., Neubig, G.: Understanding knowledge distillation in non-autoregressive machine translation. In: ICLR (2020)
23. Zhu, J., et al.: Soft contextual data augmentation for neural machine translation. arXiv preprint arXiv:1905.10523 (2019)

A Generalized Meta-loss Function for Distillation Based Learning Using Privileged Information for Classification and Regression

Amina Asif[1,2]([⊠]), Muhammad Dawood[1], and Fayyaz ul Amir Afsar Minhas[1]

[1] Department of Computer Science, University of Warwick, Coventry, UK
amina.asif@warwick.ac.uk
[2] Department of Computer Science, Pakistan Institute of Engineering and Applied Sciences (PIEAS), Islamabad, Pakistan

Abstract. Learning using privileged information (LUPI) is a powerful heterogeneous feature space machine learning framework that allows models to learn from highly informative (privileged) features which are available during training only. These models then generate test predictions using input space features which are available during both training and testing. LUPI can significantly improve prediction performance in a variety of machine learning problems. However, existing large margin and neural network implementations of learning using privileged information are mostly designed for classification tasks. In this work, we propose a simple yet effective formulation that allows general application of LUPI to classification, regression, and other related problems. We have verified the correctness, applicability, and effectiveness of our method on regression and classification problems over different synthetic and real-world problems. To test the usefulness of the proposed model in real-world problems, we have further evaluated our method on the problem of protein binding affinity prediction where the proposed scheme has shown to outperform the current state-of-the-art predictor.

Keywords: Classification · Regression · Neural networks · Distillation · Learning using privileged information

1 Introduction

In conventional supervised machine learning, a model requires the same set of features for generating test predictions as the ones used during training [1]. That is, in classical supervised learning, training and testing are performed in the same feature space. One of the limitations of such methods is that even if we have access to some very important and informative features for training examples, they cannot be used for training a model unless the same features can be extracted for test examples as well. Learning methods over different or heterogeneous spaces in training and testing are needed in many practical scenarios. Consider the development of an automated medical diagnosis system using features derived from a patient's current condition (such as temperature, histopathology images, etc.) as input to diagnose his/her disease. One may have access to other important

© Springer Nature Switzerland AG 2021
I. Farkaš et al. (Eds.): ICANN 2021, LNCS 12893, pp. 534–545, 2021.
https://doi.org/10.1007/978-3-030-86365-4_43

knowledge as well, that may be available for training examples but not for test examples, e.g., the doctor's notes, recovery information, condition after a surgery, etc. in this case.

Vapnik et al. proposed a learning paradigm called Learning Using Privileged Information (LUPI) [2] for scenarios where certain features, called privileged information, are available during training only, whereas, input space features are available for both training and testing examples. Using LUPI, privileged information can be used during training along with regular input space features to get a better classifier in the input space that can generate predictions using input space features alone. Results have shown that LUPI based classification models can perform better than models trained using input space features only in a number of machine learning problems including image and object classification [3–9].

LUPI has been formulated for a number of learning methods such as Support Vector Machines (SVMs) [2, 10], Neural Networks [11, 12], Extreme Learning Machines [13], Random Forests [14], etc. However, most of the existing formulations of LUPI based large-margin models and neural networks have been shown to work for classification tasks only. As discussed in more detail in the next section, this limitation is primarily due to the use of label softening as a means of regularization [15]. In this work, we propose a very simple but generalized formulation that can be used to perform regression using privileged information in addition to classification. We provide a complete mathematical formulation as well as implementation of the proposed scheme. We have also performed extensive performance assessment of the proposed scheme over both toy datasets as well as a practical problem of predicting protein binding affinity from sequence and structure information. It is important to note that we have presented performance results for both classification and regression tasks and to the best of our knowledge this is the first generalized implementation of learning using privileged information that can be integrated with neural network models for practically any type of machine learning problem.

2 Methods

2.1 Proposed Formulation

In order to formulate the problem underlying generalized learning using privileged information for classification and regression, consider a dataset of N training examples given by $\left\{ \left(x_i, x_i^* , y_i \right) | i = 1 \ldots N \right\}$ with input space features (x_i), privileged space feature (x_i^*) and target values y_i for examples $i = 1 \ldots N$. The objective of LUPI is to transfer knowledge contained in the privileged space into a machine learning model operating in the input space. Previous solutions for LUPI based classification such as the one by Lopez-Paz et al. [16] work by modelling the LUPI classification problem as a distillation problem (see [17] and [18–21]) wherein knowledge is transferred from a teacher model $f_t(x_i^*) \in \mathcal{F}_t$ trained in the privileged space [22] to a student model $f_s(x_i) \in \mathcal{F}_s$ trained in the input space [15]. The student model can then be used for generating predictions for test examples in the input feature space (Fig. 1). Knowledge transfer from the teacher to the student is achieved by utilizing a meta-loss function that penalizes classification errors of the student model in comparison with the given classification labels as well as the 'softened' or regularized prediction output of the teacher for a given

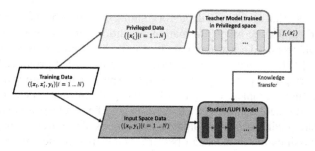

Fig. 1. Illustration of concept of LUPI using distillation.

example. As discussed below, the construction of the meta-loss function in this formulation restricts the application of this approach to classification problems only and we overcome this restriction by proposing a simple yet effective alternative meta-loss function. Specifically, given a non-negative classification loss function $l_{cls}(y, u)$ that gives the classification error of the prediction u of a model and the labels y, the distillation based solution to LUPI can be written as [16]:

$$f_s = \arg\min_{f \in \mathcal{F}_s} \frac{1}{N} \sum_{i=1}^{N} \left[(1 - \lambda)l_{cls}(y_i, \sigma(f(x_i))) + \lambda l_{cls}\left(\sigma\left(f_t(x_i^*)/T\right), \sigma(f(x_i))\right) \right]$$

(1)

Here, $l_{cls}(y_i, \sigma(f(x_i)))$ represents the loss between the actual labels y_i and the input space output $f(x_i)$ whereas $l_{cls}\left(\sigma\left(f_t(x_i^*)/T\right), \sigma(f(x_i))\right)$ is the loss between softened predictions by the teacher model and the student's prediction. $\sigma(\cdot)$ is the soft-max function and the hyper-parameter $\lambda(0 \leq \lambda \leq 1)$ controls the trade-off between learning directly from the target values and learning from the teacher. The division of the teacher's prediction by a temperature hyper-parameter $T > 0$ is called softening and is performed to smooth out the predicted class probabilities. This acts as a regularization factor and can be used to control transfer of knowledge from the teacher to the student. The objective of softening is preventing the student from mimicking the teacher if the teacher is in error. However, the use of division in the above formulation prevents the application of this approach directly in regression problems as dividing by T and applying soft-max becomes meaningless in problems other than classification. This limits the applicability of LUPI to other learning problems [16, 21].

Our proposed scheme generalizes the distillation based solution to LUPI for problems beyond classification. This is achieved by controlling knowledge transfer from the teacher to the student by weighting the generalized loss between the outputs of the student and the teacher $l(f(x_i), f_t(x_i^*))$ by a factor $e^{-Tl(f_t(x_i^*), y_i)}$ which is inversely related to the loss between the teacher's output and the actual targets, i.e., $l(f_t(x_i^*), y_i)$. The complete mathematical formulation thus becomes:

$$f_s = \arg\min_{f \in \mathcal{F}_s} \frac{1}{N} \sum_{i=1}^{N} \left(1 - e^{-Tl(f_t(x_i^*), y_i)}\right) l(f(x_i), y_i) + e^{-Tl(f_t(x_i^*), y_i)} l(f(x_i), f_t(x_i^*))$$

(2)

Here, T is the temperature hyper-parameter that controls the extent to which student should mimic the teacher. For small values of T such as $T = 0$ or when the teacher's prediction is close to the target value with small $l\left(f_t\left(x_i^*\right), y_i\right)$, the student will try to mimic the teacher by putting more emphasis on the reduction of $l\left(f\left(x_i\right), f_t\left(x_i^*\right)\right)$ in comparison to $l(f\left(x_i\right), y_i)$ and, as a result, student predictions will be close to the teacher's output. For large values of T such as $T \rightarrow \infty$ or when the loss $l\left(f_t\left(x_i^*\right), y_i\right)$ is large, there would be limited or no knowledge transfer from the teacher and the student model will try to learn by minimizing the empirical loss between its outputs and the target values only. Consequently, the input space model will learn from the privileged space model only when predictions from the teacher (privileged space) are more reliable. Thus, the proposed model can achieve the same effect as softening for knowledge transfer as Eq. (1) but without involving any soft-max or division of the model's output by T. This makes the proposed formulation more generalized and amenable to several machine learning problems like classification, ranking, regression, etc. The degree of knowledge transfer can be controlled by a single hyper-parameter T. Furthermore, it is also possible to add domain knowledge by setting T for individual examples to reflect our confidence in the given targets or the correctness of predictions generated by the teacher model.

2.2 Experiments

To assess the correctness and effectiveness of our method, we have evaluated its performance on three different types of datasets: 1) the synthetic data used by Lopez-Paz et al. [16], 2) MNIST number classification, and 3) protein binding affinity dataset. Lopez-Paz et al. [16] have performed experiments for classification only. Our focus in this study is to solve regression problems using privileged information, but to prove the applicability of the proposed formulation in different machine learning tasks, we have performed analysis in both classification and regression settings for the synthetic datasets. To further prove its effectiveness in real-world classification problems, we have evaluated the proposed method over the MNIST classification dataset. We have tested our method over a real-world regression problem of predicting protein binding affinity. All the teacher/student models have been implemented as multi-layered perceptron neural networks in pyTorch [23]. The code for reconstructing all experiments is available at: https://gitlab.com/muhammad.dawood/lupi_pytorch.

Synthetic Datasets. As discussed earlier, to prove the correctness of our formulation we tested the method over artificially generated datasets by Lopez-Paz et al. [16]. The study in [16] has performed experiments for classification only. To demonstrate the effectiveness of our scheme in regression settings in addition to classification problems, we assign continuous labels to the data samples and evaluate our method over the resulting regression problem. Four experiments using the artificial data have been carried out, each representing a possible privileged-input space configuration. In each of the experiments, 50-dimensional input space feature vectors drawn from normal distribution are used. The examples are projected onto a hyperplane sampled from a normal distribution to generate target values. For each of these experiments, 200 training examples and 1000 test examples are used. To perform a fair performance comparison with [16], a simple single layer neural network with linear activations is used for each dataset. We have used Binary Cross-Entropy (BCE) and Mean Squared Error (MSE) losses for classification and regression, respectively. Each experiment is repeated 10 times and the

Table 1. Details of synthetic datasets used for performance evaluation in classification and regression settings.

Clean Labels as Privileged Information. Noise-free true targets are used as privileged information while some noise is added to the targets. Mathematically, $$x_i \sim \aleph(0, I_d), d = 50$$ $$\alpha \sim \aleph(0, I_d)$$ $$x_i^* \leftarrow \alpha^T x_i$$ $$\varepsilon_i \sim \aleph(0,1)$$ $$\varepsilon_i \sim \aleph(0,1)$$ For classification, the true labels are obtained using the indicator function $\mathbb{I}(\cdot)$: $$y_i \leftarrow \mathbb{I}((x_i^* + \varepsilon_i) > 0)$$ For regression, the target values are set as: $$y_i \leftarrow (x_i^* + \varepsilon_i)$$	***Clean Features as Privileged Information.*** Here, we use noisy features as input space samples and pass clean features as privileged space features. Mathematically, $$x_i^* \sim \aleph(0, I_d), d = 50$$ $$\alpha \sim \aleph(0, I_d)$$ $$\varepsilon_i \sim \aleph(0, I_d)$$ $$x_i \leftarrow (x_i^* + \varepsilon_i)$$ For classification, the targets are obtained as: $$y_i \leftarrow \mathbb{I}(\alpha^T x_i > 0)$$ For regression, the targets are given by: $$y_i \leftarrow \alpha^T x_i$$
Relevant Features as Privileged Information. Here, we use relevant features as privileged information. From 50 dimensions, a random index set J of size 3 is sampled randomly. For all examples, feature values at these three indices are used as privileged information, i.e., $$x_i \sim \aleph(0, I_d)$$ $$x_i^* \leftarrow x_{iJ}$$ $$\alpha \sim \aleph(0, I_{d^*}), d^* = 3$$ For classification, the labels are generated by: $$y_i \leftarrow \mathbb{I}(\alpha^T x_i > 0)$$ For regression, the targets are: $$y_i \leftarrow \alpha^T x_i$$	***Sample-Dependent Relevant Features as Privileged Information.*** 3 features are selected randomly from the input features for each sample to be used as privileged information. These three features determine the target value for each of the sample and are different for each example. That is, there are no globally important features, each the data is sampled as follows, $$x_i \sim \aleph(0, I_d), d = 50$$ $$x_i^* \leftarrow x_{iJ_i}$$ $$\alpha \sim \aleph(0, I_{d^*}), d^* = 3$$ For classification, $$y_i \leftarrow \mathbb{I}(\alpha^T x_i > 0)$$ For regression, $$y_i \leftarrow \alpha^T x_i$$

average and standard deviation of accuracy (for classification) and Root Mean Squared Error (RMSE) (for regression) is reported. Further details of each of the privileged-input space configuration employed is given Table 1.

MNIST Hand-Written Digit Image Classification. We imitate the experiment carried out on MNIST handwritten digits [24] in [16] to further verify the effectiveness of our meta-loss function for real-world classification. LUPI is usually effective if privileged space is more informative than the regular input space and there is a relationship between the privileged and input spaces. Based on this premise, input and privileged sets are created from MNIST dataset in the same manner as done in [16]. The dataset contains 28×28 pixel images. The original images, being more informative, are used as privileged information and images downscaled to 7×7 are used as input space examples. In this experiment, 500 examples are chosen randomly for training. All the three networks: teacher, input space and LUPI, consist of two hidden layers, the first with 16 rectified linear units, and the second with 32 rectified linear units. Testing is performed over the complete 10,000 image test dataset with classification accuracy as performance evaluation metric.

Protein Binding Affinity Prediction. To test the performance of our method in real-world regression problems, we applied it for prediction of protein binding affinity. Proteins are macromolecules responsible for carrying out most of the activities in cells of living organisms [25]. Proteins usually interact with each other and form protein complexes to perform these activities. These interactions depend on the binding affinity between them [26]. The study of protein interactions and binding affinity is an area of great interest for biologists and pharmaceutical experts due to its direct application in a number of biologically significant problems. However, experimental determination of binding affinity of proteins in an interaction for the formation for a protein complex is difficult [27]. Development of machine learning models for predicting binding affinity of proteins is a very active area of research [28]. Most of the existing machine learning models for the problem use either protein structure information [29] or protein sequences [30] for generating their predictions. 3D structures of proteins are more informative but are not available for every protein due to the significant cost and effort involved in protein structure determination [31]. In contrast, sequence information, though not as informative, is easily available. As a consequence, development of a LUPI model that uses both sequence and structure information in training while requiring protein sequence information only in testing is ideally suited for this problem. The task of binding affinity prediction is a regression problem with real-valued free energy values as targets, i.e., given a pair of proteins, predict the binding affinity between them. In an earlier study, we used large margin classification LUPI [2] for developing a protein binding affinity predictor for complexes [32]. We first remodeled the task as a classification problem. This was done by labeling complexes with target values less than -10.86 as positive class (+1). Although the nature of the problem had to be modified for using the classification LUPI solution, a considerable improvement in performance of the predictor as compared to the previous state-of-the-art was observed.

In contrast to the previous LUPI classification approach, the proposed meta-loss function allows us to perform regression without changing the nature of the task to classification. The dataset used in this experiment is the protein binding affinity benchmark dataset version 2.0 [33]. It comprises of 144 non-redundant protein complexes with both sequence and 3D structure information available for each of the constituent proteins in a complex. For a given protein pair, 2-mer counts i.e., counts of all possible substrings of length 2 in both the proteins, have been used as input features. Moal Descriptors for representing protein structure as proposed by Moal et al. in [34] together with sequence features have been used as privileged information. Length of feature vectors for input and privileged space is 800 and 1000 respectively. Back-propagation Neural Networks with one hidden layer have been used for both input and privileged space models. The hidden layers in both the nets comprise of the same number of neurons as the respective features space dimensions. Linear activation has been used in both the hidden and the output layers. LUPI model has the same architecture as the input space model. Leave One Complex Out cross-validation has been performed to evaluate our method. Root Mean Squared Error (RMSE), Spearman correlation coefficient, Area under the Precision-Recall and Receiver Operating Characteristic Curves have been computed for comparing the method with the previous state-of-the-art classification based LUPI model [32].

Table 2. Performance results on synthetic data using clean labels as privileged information.

Feature space	Lopez-Paz et al. [16]	Proposed meta-loss	
	Class. accuracy	Class. accuracy	Regression (RMSE)
Privileged	0.96 ± 0.00	0.95 ± 0.01	0.31 ± 0.01
Input	0.88 ± 0.01	0.87 ± 0.01	0.36 ± 0.01
LUPI	0.95 ± 0.01	0.95 ± 0.01	0.31 ± 0.01

3   Results and Discussion

3.1   Synthetic Datasets

Here, we discuss the results for applying LUPI based on our formulation over artificially generated datasets. We discuss results for each of the datasets as follows.

Clean Labels as Privileged Information. In this experiment clean labels have been used as privileged space features with some noise added to the given labels. We set $T = 0$ to ensure maximum knowledge transfer from the teacher. The results are presented in Table 2 and compared to the results reported in the work by Lopez-Paz et al. over the same dataset [16]. It can be seen that, LUPI based model outperforms the model trained over input space in both classification and regression settings. This shows that incorporating privileged information improves the input space predictor for both classification and regression tasks as the privileged space information is more reliable in comparison to given labels. In addition to a near perfect reconstruction of classification results in comparison to [16], the proposed scheme is able to perform LUPI based regression as well. To further analyze the behavior of the proposed meta-loss over different values of the control parameter T we present a plot of the mean and standard deviation of RMSEs for teacher, input-space and LUPI models in Fig. 2. It can be seen that, for small values of T, the LUPI based model copies the teacher model and for very high values, there is no knowledge transfer from the teacher, i.e., the performance of LUPI based model and

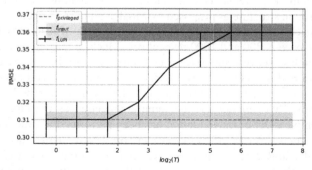

Fig. 2. RMSE of the proposed model over varying values of T. For lower values of T, LUPI tends to mimic the teacher's behavior. For high values, no knowledge is transferred from the teacher.

Table 3. Performance results when clean features are used as privileged information.

| Feature space | Lopez-Paz et al. [16] | Proposed meta-loss | |
	Class. accuracy	Class. accuracy	Regression RMSE
Privileged	0.90 ± 0.01	0.89 ± 0.02	0.03 ± 0.01
Input	0.68 ± 0.01	0.68 ± 0.02	5.78 ± 0.59
LUPI	0.70 ± 0.01	0.68 ± 0.02	5.78 ± 0.59

simple input space model are almost same. This trend verifies the effective control of hyper-parameter T on the extent of knowledge transfer from the teacher.

Clean Features as Privileged Information. In this experiment, noise has been added to the input samples and clean features have been used as privileged information. The results for this experiment are presented in Table 3. Since the additive feature noise is independent of the privileged information, no useful knowledge can be transferred. Therefore, no improvement in the input space performance has been observed. However, it is interesting to note that the LUPI based model gives the same level of classification and regression performance as the input space model. Here again, the trend for both classification and regression based on our formulation is the same as that presented in [16].

Relevant Features as Privileged Information. For this experiment, only relevant features are used as privileged information. We present the results for this experiment in Table 4. A considerable improvement in classification performance is seen for learning using privileged information. However, in case of regression, the problem becomes very easy to learn even for the input space classifier since the privileged information is a subset of the input features and labels are directly dependent on the privileged information. Therefore, RMSE for the input space is already very low and not much improvement can be seen due to application of LUPI. The problem is relatively harder in case of classification due to binarization of labels. Therefore, the usefulness of LUPI is more prominent in classification settings for this problem. We have also tested the performance of predicting classification labels using Mean Squared Error (MSE) as a loss function which further illustrates this point (see column 4 in Table 4).

Table 4. Performance results when relevant features are used as privileged information.

| Space | Lopez-Paz et al. [16] | Proposed meta-loss | | |
	Class. accuracy	Class. accuracy	Regression RMSE	Regression (binary) RMSE
Priv.	0.98 ± 0.00	0.99 ± 0.01	0.01 ± 0.00	0.30 ± 0.00
Input	0.89 ± 0.01	0.87 ± 0.03	0.14 ± 0.04	0.38 ± 0.02
LUPI	0.97 ± 0.01	0.98 ± 0.01	0.14 ± 0.03	0.34 ± 0.02

542   A. Asif et al.

Table 5. Performance results for Sample-dependent relevant features used as privileged information.

Feature space	Lopez-Paz et al. [16]	Proposed meta-loss	
	Classification accuracy	Classification accuracy	Regression RMSE
Privileged	0.96 ± 0.02	0.97 ± 0.02	0.01 ± 0.00
Input	0.55 ± 0.03	0.50 ± 0.03	2.12 ± 1.01
LUPI	0.56 ± 0.04	0.51 ± 0.01	2.12 ± 1.01

Sample-Dependent Relevant Features as Privileged Information. In this experiment, features relevant for each of the example were passed as privileged information. Although the problem can be modelled linearly in privileged space, there is no globally important information that can be transferred from the teacher to student. Therefore, LUPI in this case does not help in improving performance. Results are presented in Table 5. Performance results presented above show that the proposed scheme is effective whenever a relationship exists between input and privileged spaces and the latter is more informative in comparison to the former. Furthermore, these classification results are in agreement with the work by Lopez-Paz et al. [16]. However, the proposed scheme can also perform regression and can possibly be used for other machine learning problems as well with an appropriate loss function.

3.2 MNIST Handwritten Digit Image Classification

This experiment was performed using 500 randomly chosen training examples from MNIST dataset [24]. Original, full resolution images were used as privileged space examples and their downscaled versions as input space examples. Testing was performed over complete 10,000 image dataset. Classification accuracy using both our proposed formulation and formulation in [16] have been presented in Table 6. Our method produces a similar improvement in LUPI as [16]. It can be seen that, given the privileged net is trained properly, i.e., it does not over/under-fit, LUPI improves performance. Here, the use of privileged information in training has produced an improvement of 9% classification accuracy. These results clearly show that the proposed scheme is as effective as the original classification formulation by Lopez-Paz et al.

3.3 Protein Binding Affinity Prediction

In this experiment, we used the proposed LUPI formulation for a practical regression problem: prediction of protein binding affinity. We compare the performance of our regression based modeling with the previous state of the art classification based modeling of the problem [32]. The results are presented in Table 7. It is interesting to note that LUPI gives a significant improvement in both classification and regression tasks in comparison to input features alone. Furthermore, the proposed regression based LUPI outperforms classification LUPI in all performance metrics. An improvement of 7% in AUC-PR and 1% in AUC-ROC has been observed as compared to the LUPI-SVM solution of the problem. A major improvement in Spearman Correlation from 0.48 to 0.56 has also been observed demonstrating the effectiveness of the proposed regression based modeling of the problem.

Table 6. Classification Accuracy for MNIST dataset.

Feature space	Lopez-Paz et al. [16]	Proposed formulation
Privileged	0.84	0.81
Input	0.59	0.67
LUPI	0.75	0.76

Table 7. Leave One Complex Out cross-validation results including Area under the ROC and PR curves, correlation and RMSE for Binding Affinity Problem. Bold values indicate optimal performance.

Method	Space	AUC-ROC	AUC-PR	Corr.	RMSE
Class. LUPI [32]	Input	0.72	0.68	0.40	–
	Priv.	0.73	0.68	0.43	–
	LUPI	0.78	0.73	0.48	–
Proposed Regression LUPI	Input	0.70	0.70	0.41	3.14
	Priv.	0.75	0.75	0.50	3.07
	LUPI	**0.79**	**0.80**	**0.56**	**3.03**

4   Conclusion

In this work, we have addressed a limitation of existing large margin and neural network formulations of learning using privileged information (LUPI) that are restricted to classification only. We propose a simple yet effective meta-loss function for distillation based LUPI that allows effective modeling of both regression and classification problems. The proposed formulation is generalized in that it can be easily extended to model other machine learning problems such as ranking and recommender systems. In contrast to previous formulations, the proposed meta-loss is relatively simpler with a single control hyper-parameter to regulate the contribution of privileged space and performing softening. We have demonstrated correctness and effectiveness of the proposed loss by performing several classification and regression experiments on both synthetic and real-world datasets. Our LUPI model has shown to outperform state of the art predictor of protein binding affinity in complexes. Our work opens the avenues for further application of learning using privileged information and distillation in various machine learning problems.

References

1. Kotsiantis, S.B., Zaharakis, I., Pintelas, P.: Supervised machine learning: a review of classification techniques. Emerg. Artif. Intell. Appl. Comput. Eng. **160**, 3–24 (2007)
2. Vapnik, V., Izmailov, R.: Learning using privileged information: similarity control and knowledge transfer. J. Mach. Learn. Res. **16**, 2023–2049 (2015)
3. Yang, X., Wang, M., Tao, D.: Person re-identification with metric learning using privileged information. IEEE Trans. Image Process. **27**, 791–805 (2017)
4. Gao, Z., et al.: Learning the implicit strain reconstruction in ultrasound elastography using privileged information. Med. Image Anal. **58**, 101534 (2019)
5. Li, Y., Meng, F., Shi, J., Initiative, A.D.N.: others: Learning using privileged information improves neuroimaging-based CAD of Alzheimer's disease: a comparative study. Med. Biol. Eng. Compu. **57**, 1605–1616 (2019)
6. Chevalier, M., Thome, N., Hénaff, G., Cord, M.: Classifying low-resolution images by integrating privileged information in deep CNNs. Pattern Recogn. Lett. **116**, 29–35 (2018)
7. Duan, L., En, Q., Qiao, Y., Cui, S., Qing, L.: Deep feature representation based on privileged knowledge transfer. Pattern Recogn. Lett. **119**, 62–70 (2019)
8. Lee, W., Lee, J., Kim, D., Ham, B.: Learning with privileged information for efficient image super-resolution. In: Vedaldi, A., Bischof, H., Brox, T., Frahm, J.-M. (eds.) ECCV 2020. LNCS, vol. 12369, pp. 465–482. Springer, Cham (2020). https://doi.org/10.1007/978-3-030-58586-0_28
9. Li, X., Du, B., Xu, C., Zhang, Y., Zhang, L., Tao, D.: Robust learning with imperfect privileged information. Artif. Intell. **282**, 103246 (2020)
10. Burnaev, E., Smolyakov, D.: One-class SVM with privileged information and its application to malware detection. In: 2016 IEEE 16th International Conference on Data Mining Workshops (ICDMW), pp. 273–280. IEEE (2016)
11. Vapnik, V., Izmailov, R.: Knowledge transfer in SVM and neural networks. Ann. Math. Artif. Intell. **81**, 3–19 (2017). https://doi.org/10.1007/s10472-017-9538-x
12. Bisla, D., Choromanska, A.: VisualBackProp for learning using privileged information with CNNs. arXiv preprint arXiv:1805.09474. (2018)
13. Zhang, W., Ji, H., Liao, G., Zhang, Y.: A novel extreme learning machine using privileged information. Neurocomputing **168**, 823–828 (2015)
14. Yang, H., Patras, I.: Privileged information-based conditional structured output regression forest for facial point detection. IEEE Trans. Circuits Syst. Video Technol. **25**, 1507–1520 (2015)
15. Hinton, G., Vinyals, O., Dean, J.: Distilling the knowledge in a neural network (2015)
16. Lopez-Paz, D., Bottou, L., Schölkopf, B., Vapnik, V.: Unifying distillation and privileged information. In: International Conference on Learning Representations (ICLR), San Juan, 2–4 May 2016
17. Akhlaghi, M.I., Sukhov, S.V.: Knowledge fusion in feedforward artificial neural networks. Neural Process. Lett. **48**(1), 257–272 (2017). https://doi.org/10.1007/s11063-017-9712-5
18. Howard, A.G., et al.: Mobilenets: efficient convolutional neural networks for mobile vision applications. arXiv preprint arXiv:1704.04861. (2017)
19. Papernot, N., McDaniel, P., Wu, X., Jha, S., Swami, A.: Distillation as a defense to adversarial perturbations against deep neural networks. In: 2016 IEEE Symposium on Security and Privacy (SP), pp. 582–597. IEEE (2016)
20. Anil, R., Pereyra, G., Passos, A., Ormandi, R., Dahl, G.E., Hinton, G.E.: Large scale distributed neural network training through online distillation. arXiv preprint arXiv:1804.03235. (2018)
21. Chen, G., Choi, W., Yu, X., Han, T., Chandraker, M.: Learning efficient object detection models with knowledge distillation. In: Advances in Neural Information Processing Systems, pp. 742–751 (2017)

22. Phuong, M., Lampert, C.: Towards understanding knowledge distillation. In: International Conference on Machine Learning, pp. 5142–5151. PMLR (2019)
23. Paszke, A., et al.: Pytorch: tensors and dynamic neural networks in python with strong gpu acceleration, May 2017
24. LeCun, Y., Cortes, C., Burges, C.J.: The MNIST database of handwritten digits (1998). http://yan.lecun.com/exdb/mnist
25. Creighton, T.E.: Proteins: Structures and Molecular Properties. Macmillan, Basingstoke (1993)
26. Du, X., et al.: Insights into protein–ligand interactions: mechanisms, models, and methods. Int. J. Mol. Sci. **17**, 144 (2016)
27. Dourado, D.F., Flores, S.C.: A multiscale approach to predicting affinity changes in protein–protein interfaces. Proteins Struct. Funct. Bioinf. **82**, 2681–2690 (2014)
28. Siebenmorgen, T., Zacharias, M.: Computational prediction of protein–protein binding affinities. WIREs Comput. Mol. Sci. **10**, e1448 (2020). https://doi.org/10.1002/wcms.1448
29. Xue, L.C., Rodrigues, J.P., Kastritis, P.L., Bonvin, A.M., Vangone, A.: PRODIGY: a web server for predicting the binding affinity of protein–protein complexes. Bioinformatics **32**, 3676–3678 (2016)
30. Gromiha, M.M., Yugandhar, K., Jemimah, S.: Protein–protein interactions: scoring schemes and binding affinity. Curr. Opin. Struct. Biol. **44**, 31–38 (2017)
31. Geng, C., Xue, L.C., Roel-Touris, J., Bonvin, A.M.J.J.: Finding the $\Delta\Delta G$ spot: are predictors of binding affinity changes upon mutations in protein–protein interactions ready for it? Wiley Interdisc. Rev. Comput. Mol. Sci. **9**, e1410 (2019)
32. Abbasi, W.A., Asif, A., Ben-Hur, A.: Learning protein binding affinity using privileged information. BMC Bioinf. **19**, 425 (2018)
33. Kastritis, P.L., et al.: A structure-based benchmark for protein–protein binding affinity. Protein Sci. **20**, 482–491 (2011)
34. Moal, I.H., Agius, R., Bates, P.A.: Protein–protein binding affinity prediction on a diverse set of structures. Bioinformatics **27**, 3002–3009 (2011)

Empirical Study of Data-Free Iterative Knowledge Distillation

Het Shah[1]([✉]), Ashwin Vaswani[1], Tirtharaj Dash[1], Ramya Hebbalaguppe[2], and Ashwin Srinivasan[1]

[1] Department of CS & IS and APPCAIR, BITS Pilani, K. K. Birla Goa Campus, Goa, India
[2] TCS Research, New Delhi, India

Abstract. Iterative Knowledge Distillation (IKD) [20] is an iterative variant of Hinton's knowledge distillation framework for deep neural network compression. IKD has shown promising model compression results for image classification tasks where a large amount of training data is available for training the teacher and student models. In this paper, we consider problems where training data is not available, making it impractical to use the usual IKD approach. We propose a variant of the IKD framework, called Data-Free IKD (or DF-IKD), that adopts recent results from data-free learning of deep models [2]. This exploits generative adversarial networks (GANs), in which a readily available pre-trained teacher model is regarded as a fixed discriminator, and a generator (a deep network) is used to generate training samples. The goal of the generator is to generate samples that can obtain a maximum predictive response from the discriminator. In DF-IKD, the student model at every IKD iteration is a compressed version of the original discriminator ('teacher'). Our experiments suggest: (a) DF-IKD results in a student model that is significantly smaller in size than the original parent model; (b) the predictive performance of the compressed student model is comparable to that of the parent model.

Keywords: Model compression · Data-free learning · Efficient ML

1 Introduction

Deep Neural Networks are remarkably successful in various real-world applications such as image classification [15], object detection [14], activity recognition [17], machine translation [21]. It is well-known that deep networks are (a) 'data-hungry': requiring a large amount of data to learn insights and construct meaningful internal transformed representations; and (b) 'depth-hungry': many state-of-the-art deep models have complex structures both in terms of depth and width. Therefore, it is imperative to see high training and inference time due to the deep network's underlying complex machinery. Furthermore, a complex neural network is likely to have a higher carbon footprint [1] than a simple

H. Shah and A. Vaswani—Equal contribution.

I. Farkaš et al. (Eds.): ICANN 2021, LNCS 12893, pp. 546–557, 2021.
https://doi.org/10.1007/978-3-030-86365-4_44

model. This imposes a substantial limitation on their applicability to various real-world situations, which offer lesser memory storage, faster processing, and high predictive accuracy. Real-time devices such as the ones under the category of Internet-of-Things (IoT) fall under this category. One possible solution to adopt deep networks for resource-limited situations is model compression. Some examples of model compression can be found in the literature such as in [3–5,8]. Among various methods of model compression, Hinton's knowledge distillation (KD) is a simple loss-based method for compressing deep networks. Recently, an iterative variant of KD (called IKD) demonstrated promising model compression performance for various deep neural network architectures [20]. Although model compression reduces the requirement for computational resources and storage in low-cost devices, these methods still require a large amount of data to learn an initial deep model. However, there are real-world situations (such as those arising due to data privacy, data protection regulations) where either available data is limited or not available at all.

In this paper, we investigate an iterative model compression method without requiring to use any training data. To this end, we are motivated by the two recent model compression works: (a) the iterative variant of KD [20], called IKD to obtain a deep model with possibly smallest number of parameters; and (b) a data-free learning method proposed in [2] that compresses models without requiring additional training data. Our method is a combination of IKD with data-free learning of teacher and student models. We call our proposed approach Data-Free Iterative Knowledge Distillation or DF-IKD.

The rest of the paper is organized as follows: We explain the DF-IKD framework in Sect. 2. Experimental results of DF-IKD are presented in Sect. 3. Section 4 provides some methods that are relevant to our present approach. The paper is concluded in Sect. 5.

2   DF-IKD

DF-IKD is a Data Free method to train the student network using an Iterative application of the DAFL approach [2]. We note that the results in Yalburgi *et al.* [20] suggest that it is sufficient to use the model obtained on one iteration as a teacher for the student model in the next iteration (that is, "parental" training is sufficient). This is used in Procedure 1. We note that any model M_i is represented as a pair of (σ_i, π_i), where, σ_i is the structure of the model and π_i is the set of parameters for the model. The exact structure σ will depend on the architecture chosen, but all σ's will consist of a convolutional backbone followed by a multi-layered perceptron (MLP). We assume structures are elements from some set Σ and parameters are elements of some set Π. Models are therefore elements of $M = \Sigma \times \Pi$.

In Procedure 1, $DAFL$ denotes a data-free learning algorithm. We use a variant of the approach proposed in [2], (a different loss-function is used to improve convergence: details are provided later in the paper). Conceptually $DAFL$ is a function $M \times \Sigma \to M$. As in [20], we define a refinement operator $\rho : \Sigma \to \Sigma$. Step 3 in Procedure 1 is therefore $(\sigma_i, \pi_i) = DAFL((\sigma_{i-1}, \pi_{i-1}), \rho(\sigma_{i-1}), \cdot)$.

Algorithm 1: Proposed DF-IKD Procedure

Input: (a) Pre-trained teacher model M_0; (b) number of iterations k; (c) σ_1 for the first student model; (d) Refinement operator ρ;

Output: A compressed model

1 $i := 1$;
2 **while** $i \leq k$ **do**
3 $\quad$ | $\quad M_i = DAFL(M_{i-1}, \sigma_i, \cdot)$;
4 $\quad$ | $\quad \sigma_{i+1} = \rho(\sigma_i)$;
5 $\quad$ | $\quad increment\ i$;
6 **end**
7 **return** M_k;

The $DAFL$ procedure used in this paper is shown below in Procedure 2. We assume a loss-function $\mathcal{L}$, and a generator-function G, and a validation set $\mathcal{D}_{val}$. The description includes some hyper-parameters that are not part of the functional specification of $DAFL$. Data for all models are taken to be from $\Re^d$, where d is some (problem-specific) dimension. We assume a prediction function $Pred : \mathcal{M} \times \Re^d \rightarrow V$, where V is the set of tuples consisting of: softmax scores, labels, and feature map from the final convolutional feature extractor layer in the network architecture. The description of the loss function is provided in the following sub-section. Figure 1 summarises the DF-IKD process.

2.1 Refinement Operator ρ

We define a refinement operator $\rho : \Sigma \rightarrow \Sigma$. Specifically, given a student model's structure, the refinement operator ρ returns a smaller structure (that is, one with fewer parameters). The refinement operator ρ for our training procedure is as follows:

$$\rho(\sigma_i) = \frac{\sigma_i}{2} \tag{1}$$

For instance:

- ρ for ResNet reduces the number of units of each Residual layer by a factor of 2. Thus, For a ResNet-18 structure σ with the set of initial units as $S_i = \{64, 64, 128, 256, 512\}$, then $\sigma_j = \rho(\sigma_i)$, where σ_j's set of units will be reduced to $S_j = \{32, 32, 64, 128, 256\}$
- ρ for VGG reduces the number of units in each non-pooling layer of the given configuration by a factor of 2. For example, for a given VGG-16 structure σ with configuration (Number of units in each layer) as $S_i = \{64, M, 128, M, 256, 256, M, 512, 512, M, 512, 512, M\}$ where M represents MaxPool, then $\sigma_j = \rho(\sigma_i)$, where σ_j's configuration will be reduced to $S_j = \{32, M, 64, M, 128, 128, M, 256, 256, M, 256, 256, M\}$

Algorithm 2: Data-Free Learning (DAFL) based on [2]

Input: (a) A teacher model $M_t = (\sigma_t, \pi_t)$; (b) A student structure σ_s; and (c) Hyperparameters of $\mathcal{L}$: $\boldsymbol{p} = [\alpha, \beta, \gamma]$, (d) $MaxEpochs$; and (e) $MaxSteps$

Output: Trained student model

1 $epoch := 0$;
2 $i := 0$;
3 Initialize π_s;
4 $M^* := (\sigma_s, \pi_s)$;
5 **while** $epoch < MaxEpochs$ **do**
6 $\quad$ $M_s := M^*$;
7 $\quad$ **while** $i < MaxSteps$ **do**
8 $\quad\quad$ Draw $\mathbf{z} \sim \mathcal{N}(0, 1)$;
9 $\quad\quad$ $\mathbf{x} = G(\mathbf{z})$;
10 $\quad\quad$ $O_t = Pred(M_t, \mathbf{x})$;
11 $\quad\quad$ $O_s = Pred(M_s, \mathbf{x})$;
12 $\quad\quad$ Calculate the loss $\mathcal{L}(O_t, O_s, \boldsymbol{p})$;
13 $\quad\quad$ Update G and π_s;
14 $\quad\quad$ increment i;
15 $\quad$ **end**
16 $\quad$ Let $Acc :=$ Accuracy of M_s on $\mathcal{D}_{val}$;
17 $\quad$ **if** $Acc > BestAcc$ **then**
18 $\quad\quad$ $M^* = M_s$;
19 $\quad\quad$ $BestAcc = Acc$;
20 $\quad$ Increment $epoch$;
21 **end**
22 **return** M^*

2.2 Loss Functions

The loss function for the training procedure is broken down into 2 major parts:

$$\mathcal{L} = \mathcal{L}_{Total} + \mathcal{L}_{KD} \qquad (2)$$

The first term $\mathcal{L}_{Total}$ is the loss function for the Generator G. This is computed as:

$$\mathcal{L}_{Total} = \mathcal{L}_{oh} + \alpha \mathcal{L}_a + \beta \mathcal{L}_{ie} \qquad (3)$$

Each individual loss components are described below:

1. $\mathcal{L}_{oh}$: This is calculated as follows. We take a random vector z and generate outputs x using the Generator network G, where $x^i = G(z^i)$. Next, we use these as inputs to the teacher network M_t to produce outputs $y_T^i = M_t(x^i)$. Predicted labels are calculated using $t^i = \arg\max_j (y_T^i)_j$. So,

$$\mathcal{L}_{oh} = \frac{1}{n} \sum_i H_{cross}(y_T^i, t^i) \qquad (4)$$

Here, H_{cross} is the cross entropy loss.

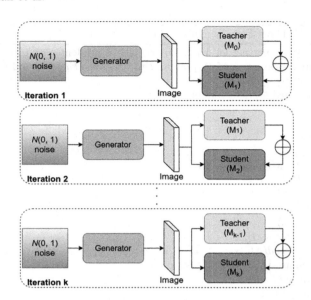

Fig. 1. An overview of the DF-IKD process. It starts with an initial teacher model M_0 and performs DAFL with a student M_1. In the next iteration, M_1 becomes the teacher and we reduce the parameters using ρ to get M_2. This is continued for a given k iterations. In the figure, $\oplus$ represents knowledge distillation.

2. $\mathcal{L}_a$ is calculated as

$$\mathcal{L}_a = -\frac{1}{n} \sum_i |f_T^i|_1 \qquad (5)$$

where, f_T^i are the features extracted by passing x^i to the teacher network M_t and $|\cdot|_1$ is the L_1 norm.

3. $\mathcal{L}_{ie}$ is calculated as

$$\mathcal{L}_{ie} = -H_{info}\left(\frac{1}{n}\sum_i y_T^i\right) \qquad (6)$$

where, H_{info} is the information entropy, measures the degree of confusion, and is calculated as $\mathcal{H}_{info}(p) = -\frac{1}{k}\sum_i p_i log(p_i)$.

The second term in the loss function $\mathcal{L}$ is the KD-loss $\mathcal{L}_{KD}$ that represents the loss function for the student model. Below we describe two variants of $\mathcal{L}_{KD}$: one that is used in [2], and a modified version of it that we introduce in this work.

KD-Loss by Chen *et al.* Chen *et al.* use the KD-loss function given as:

$$\mathcal{L}_{KD} = \frac{1}{m}\sum_{i=1}^{m} \mathcal{H}_{cross}(y_s^i, y_t^i) \qquad (7)$$

where, $\mathcal{H}_{cross}$ is the cross-entropy loss. $y_s^i = M_s(x^i)$ and $y_t^i = M_t(x^i)$ are the outputs of the student network, M_s and teacher network, M_t respectively. However, cross-entropy loss does not capture the entire teacher-student interaction.

Our Modified KD-Loss. Our modified loss function, adapted from [20] is given below:

$$\mathcal{L}_{KD}^+ = \frac{1}{m} \sum_{j=1}^{m} \left(2T^2 \gamma KL(P^{(j)}||Q^{(j)}) + (1 - \gamma) \sum_{i=1}^{c} \mathcal{H}_{cross}(y_s^i, y_t^i) \right) \qquad (8)$$

Here KL is the KL-divergence between the output probabilities of teacher and student network M_t and S_t. P^j and Q^j are the Temperature(T)-softened class probability distributions from the teacher and student networks, respectively. T-softening helps in smoothing out the probability distribution, Fig. 2 gives an example of how T-softening softens the distribution. $y_s^i = M_s(x^i)$ are the one-hot vectors predicted by the student network M_s, and y_t^i are the labels predicted by the teacher network M_t. The KL-Divergence term of the loss acts as a regularising term to the loss function proposed by Chen *et al.* [2]. The parameter γ behaves as a factor affecting the relative importance of KL-divergence and teacher-student outputs in the loss.

Therefore, the new loss function becomes:

$$\mathcal{L} = \mathcal{L}_{Total} + \mathcal{L}_{KD}^+ \qquad (9)$$

Fig. 2. An example of Temperature softening, distribution to the left is the original distribution, distribution to the right is after we soften the distribution.

3   Empirical Evaluation

3.1   Aim

Our aim in this section is to investigate the trade-off between performance and compression with increasing iterations of DF-IKD.

3.2   Materials

We conduct our experiments on 2 standard computer vision datasets MNIST [11], FMNIST [19]. Note that both these datasets are single-channel datasets. We conduct an additional experiment with a multi-channel dataset: CIFAR-10 [10]. We perform model compression on ResNet [7] on all the datasets and on VGG [15] for MNIST and FMNIST dataset. We use Adam optimizer for the generator and the student network with 0.2 and 0.3 learning rates, respectively. We set the latent dimension size to 1000 for the generator. All the experiments are conducted in a Python environment in a machine with 64 GB main memory, 16-core Intel Xeon CPU, and 8 GB NVIDIA P4000 graphics processor.

3.3   Method

Our method is a simple extension to the works on DAFL [2] and IKD [20]. For each architecture and dataset:

1. Start with a pre-trained teacher network $M_0 = (\sigma_0, \pi_0)$ with size $|\pi_0|$, and an initial student structure σ_1, and a refinement operator ρ
2. Construct a validation-set $\mathcal{D}_{val}$ (details below)
3. For $k = 1, 2, \ldots, n$:
   (a) Construct $M_k = DF\text{-}IKD(M_0, k, \sigma_1, \rho)$
   (b) Compare the accuracies of M_0 and M_k on $\mathcal{D}_{val}$
   (c) Compare the sizes $|\pi_0|$ and $|\pi_k|$

We clarify some additional details:

- The architectures used are ResNet and VGG. The datasets used are MNIST, FMNIST, and CIFAR-10.
- The teacher model M_0 for the ResNet experiment is ResNet-34, and for the VGG experiment, it is VGG-19;
- The student model's structure σ_1 for the ResNet architecture is the structure of ResNet-18 with five residual layers with the number of units in each layer being $64, 64, 128, 256, 512$. For the VGG architecture, σ_1 is the structure of VGG-16 with a configuration number of units in each layer being $64, M, 128, M, 256, 256, M, 512, 512, M, 512, 512, M$ where M represents Max-Pool. These are the default configurations for ResNet-18 and VGG-16;
- We set the number of iterations n to 5;
- DF-IKD calls DAFL, which assumes a loss function $\mathcal{L}$. We consider 2 possible loss functions: (a) The function used in [2]. (b) An alternative function proposed in this paper. Both these functions are already described in Sect. 2.2. In all our experiments, the hyperparameters for the loss function are set as: $\alpha = 0.1$ and $\beta = 5$. The parameters for our modified version of the KD loss are set as: $T = 20$ and $\gamma = 0.9$ for all the experiments.
- The batch size is set to 64 for the MNIST and FMNIST datasets and 512 for the CIFAR-10 dataset. In the results reported in [2] for both CIFAR and MNIST, batch sizes of 1024 are used: memory constraints restrict us to at most 512.

3.4 Results

Results for our experiments on ResNet and VGG are tabulated in the Table 1 and Table 2 respectively. The principal findings are: (a) As expected, an increase in iterations decreases accuracy and increases the compression ratio of the model; (b) Other than for CIFAR-10, substantial compressions are achievable with little loss in accuracy, for both loss-functions examined (see Sect. 2.2); (c) In general, the modified loss function has higher accuracy than the original loss function for the same level of compression. In some instances, this difference can be very substantial; (d) The number of epochs needed for convergence is approximately twice for the original loss function; (e) The outlier dataset appears to be CIFAR-10, where compressions of a factor of about 8 (over the original model) are achievable, with a loss in accuracy of about 10%. (f) The losses in accuracy with the original loss function in [2] are substantial, and appear to offset any gains in compression; and (g) The losses in accuracy with the modified loss function appear to perform better than the old loss function: in all the cases for MNIST and FMNIST datasets and 4 out of 5 cases in CIFAR-10 dataset; (h) The modified loss enabled approximately 1.6× faster convergence for each student as compared to the old loss, improving accuracy at the same time.

Table 1. Results for the ResNet model: Column 'S' stands for student model. Column 'CR' denotes the compression ratio between the base model and the current student model M_0/M_j. A denotes accuracy obtained by the student model using the old loss function mentioned [2] and A' denotes accuracy obtained by the student model using the modified loss function in Sect. 2.2.

Model	S	CR	Datasets			
			MNIST		FMNIST	
			A	A'	A	A'
Base	M0	1×	99.40	99.40	98.76	98.76
DF-IKD	M1	1.9×	98.46	**98.64**	96.16	**96.39**
	M2	7.9×	98.21	**98.40**	95.32	**95.80**
	M3	30.3×	98.01	**98.30**	94.16	**95.04**
	M4	120.6×	97.65	**98.17**	93.42	**94.59**
	M5	479.6×	97.21	**97.76**	92.15	**93.50**

We now consider some of these findings in more detail:

Why is the modified loss function better? The modified loss-function is based on the Knowledge Distillation loss, where we have true labels in the cross-entropy term. Here, we replace the true labels with the labels predicted by the teacher network. This acts as a regularising term to the original loss function used in [2]. Moreover, our modified loss uses softened versions of the class probability distributions from the teacher and the student network (Table 3).

Table 2. Results for the VGG model: Column 'S' stands for student model. Column 'CR' denotes the compression ratio between the base model and the current student model M_0/M_j. A denotes accuracy obtained by the student model using the old loss function mentioned [2] and A' denotes accuracy obtained by the student model using the modified loss function in Sect. 2.2

Model	S	CR	Datasets			
			MNIST		FMNIST	
			A	A'	A	A'
Base	M0	1×	99.55	99.55	98.76	98.76
DF-IKD	M1	1.1×	96.01	**96.98**	96.16	**96.72**
	M2	4.1×	94.94	**96.91**	95.32	**96.38**
	M3	16.6×	93.46	**96.74**	94.16	**96.03**
	M4	66.3×	88.16	**96.49**	93.42	**95.21**
	M5	264.5×	79.56	**95.54**	92.15	**90.62**

Table 3. Number of epochs required by the student models to converge. E denotes the epochs using the old loss function [2]; and E' denotes the epochs using the modified loss function in Sect. 2.2

Dataset	E	E'
MNIST	500	200
FMNIST	500	200
CIFAR-10	4000	2500

Why is the performance bad on CIFAR-10? The compression results for ResNet architecture for CIFAR-10 dataset is provided in Table 4. CIFAR-10 is a multi-channel dataset as compared to the single-channel data available in MNIST and FMNIST. This makes the task of the generator more complex. We believe this may be one reason for the drop in accuracy.

What is bad about DF-IKD? Unlike IKD, the DF-IKD procedure additionally employs a generative model. The parameters of this model also require estimation, which requires more time and may require bigger a batch size. The additional computation means that DF-IKD, will in general, be slower than IKD.

4 Related Work

Recently there have been several proposals for compression of deep neural networks. Among various methods, Hinton's knowledge distillation (KD) framework for model compression stands out as it is simple and a loss-driven approach [8]. Following this, there have been approaches such as the iterative method of KD in audio event detection application by Koutini et al. [9], progressive blockwise

Table 4. Results for the ResNet model on CIFAR-10 dataset: Column 'S' stands for student model. Column 'CR' denotes the compression ratio between the base model and the current student model M_0/M_j. A denotes accuracy obtained by the student model using the old loss function mentioned [2] and A' denotes accuracy obtained by the student model using the modified loss function in Sect. 2.2.

Model	S	CR	CIFAR-10	
			A	A'
Base	M0	1×	94.69	94.69
DF-IKD	M1	1.9×	64.66	**91.13**
	M2	7.9×	53.22	**84.91**
	M3	30.3×	52.63	**69.03**
	M4	120.6×	**44.49**	44.40
	M5	479.6×	28.88	**30.02**

KD framework for teacher-student model distillation at the sub-network block level [18]. A very recent study on KD is an exciting proposal for an iterative variant of KD called IKD by Yalburgi *et al.* [20] that provides interesting compression results for various deep network architectures and image classification benchmarks. The goal of IKD is to progressively compress a student model in a hierarchical fashion. However, it was shown that only an immediate predecessor (parental-training) is sufficient. This forms a basis for our present work. Another interesting finding by [6] demonstrates that discarding over 85% of weights in a given neural network would not obviously damage its performance, showing high redundancy in representations learned by Deep Neural Networks.

There are a few methods that focus on compressing deep neural networks without the original training data. For example: Lopes *et al.* [12] attempted reconstructing the original data from 'meta-data' and utilize the KD approach to learn a smaller network. Another data-free approach focuses on removing redundant neurons of a neural network by merging them together [16]. In another work, the data impressions were first synthesized from a complex teacher model. They utilized these as surrogates for the original training data samples to transfer its learning to a student by KD [13]. Another data-free learning of student network was recently proposed by Chen *et al.* [2] that uses a GAN type framework (except the adversarial loss component). Here a generator generates data samples, and a pre-trained teacher network acts as a discriminator. This work forms the second basis for our present work.

5 Conclusion

In this paper, we have looked at a "data-free" approach to iterative knowledge distillation or DF-IKD. We achieve this by combining techniques developed in data-free learning [2] with iterative knowledge-distillation [20]. Our results suggest that data-free iterative knowledge-distillation is achievable, with good compression and little loss in accuracy. An important role in achieving this is played by a modified loss-function that we have proposed, which results in reasonably efficient convergence. Despite the modified loss-function, there is a price to pay for data-free learning: training times are longer than would be needed if data were available. This is due primarily to the use of a generative model in the procedure.

Why is DF-IKD important? The principal motivation for any form of knowledge distillation is the need for small models for use on devices with limited computational power (the usual examples are edge-sensitive and portable devices). The motivation for data-free learning is that training data may not always be available, especially if privacy-preserving applications are involved.

There are a number of ways in which the work here can be extended. Clearly, results on additional architectures and datasets are needed. A gain in efficiency may result by employing a more effective generator. This may be achieved by either using a different architecture (like a variational auto-encoder), or if some amount of training data were available, or more interestingly, if we can incorporate some form of domain-dependent prior information. Finally, the initial choice of student structure to the DF-IKD procedure could be more informed, perhaps by a form of transfer-learning from a related DF-IKD task.

Acknowledgements. This work is supported by "The DataLab" agreement between BITS Pilani, K. K. Birla Goa Campus and TCS Research, India.

References

1. Anderson, M., Gómez-Rodríguez, C.: Distilling neural networks for greener and faster dependency parsing. arXiv preprint arXiv:2006.00844 (2020)
2. Chen, H., et al.: Data-free learning of student networks. In: Proceedings of the IEEE/CVF International Conference on Computer Vision (ICCV), October 2019
3. Chen, W., Wilson, J.T., Tyree, S., Weinberger, K.Q., Chen, Y.: Compressing neural networks with the hashing trick. In: ICML (2015)
4. Denton, E.L., Zaremba, W., Bruna, J., LeCun, Y., Fergus, R.: Exploiting linear structure within convolutional networks for efficient evaluation. arXiv:1404.0736 (2014)
5. Gong, Y., Liu, L., Yang, M., Bourdev, L.D.: Compressing deep convolutional networks using vector quantization. arXiv:1412.6115 (2014)
6. Han, S., Mao, H., Dally, W.J.: Deep compression: compressing deep neural networks with pruning, trained quantization and Huffman coding (2016)
7. He, K., Zhang, X., Ren, S., Sun, J.: Deep residual learning for image recognition. In: 2016 IEEE Conference on Computer Vision and Pattern Recognition (CVPR), pp. 770–778 (2016). https://doi.org/10.1109/CVPR.2016.90
8. Hinton, G., Vinyals, O., Dean, J.: Distilling the knowledge in a neural network (2015)
9. Koutini, K., Eghbal-zadeh, H., Widmer, G.: Iterative knowledge distillation in R-CNNs for weakly-labeled semi-supervised sound event detection. In: Proceedings of the Detection and Classification of Acoustic Scenes and Events (DCASE) (2018)
10. Krizhevsky, A.: Learning multiple layers of features from tiny images. University of Toronto (2012)

11. LeCun, Y., Cortes, C., Burges, C.: MNIST handwritten digit database. ATT Labs (2010). http://yann.lecun.com/exdb/mnist
12. Lopes, R.G., Fenu, S., Starner, T.: Data-free knowledge distillation for deep neural networks. arXiv preprint arXiv:1710.07535 (2017)
13. Nayak, G.K., Mopuri, K.R., Shaj, V., Babu, R.V., Chakraborty, A.: Zero-shot knowledge distillation in deep networks. In: ICML (2019)
14. Ren, S., He, K., Girshick, R.B., Sun, J.: Faster R-CNN: towards real-time object detection with region proposal networks. IEEE Trans. Pattern Anal. Mach. Intell. **39**, 1137–1149 (2015)
15. Simonyan, K., Zisserman, A.: Very deep convolutional networks for large-scale image recognition. CoRR arxiv:1409.1556 (2015)
16. Srinivas, S., Babu, R.V.: Data-free parameter pruning for deep neural networks. arXiv preprint arXiv:1507.06149 (2015)
17. Tran, D., Wang, H., Torresani, L., Feiszli, M.: Video classification with channel-separated convolutional networks. In: 2019 IEEE/CVF International Conference on Computer Vision (ICCV), pp. 5551–5560 (2019)
18. Wang, H., Zhao, H., Li, X., Tan, X.: Progressive blockwise knowledge distillation for neural network acceleration. In: Proceedings of the 27th International Joint Conference on Artificial Intelligence (IJCAI 2018), pp. 2769–2775. AAAI Press (2018)
19. Xiao, H., Rasul, K., Vollgraf, R.: Fashion-MNIST: a novel image dataset for benchmarking machine learning algorithms. CoRR arxiv:1708.07747 (2017)
20. Yalburgi, S., Dash, T., Hebbalaguppe, R., Hegde, S., Srinivasan, A.: An empirical study of iterative knowledge distillation for neural network compression. In: Proceedings of the European Symposium on Artificial Neural Networks, Computational Intelligence and Machine Learning (2020)
21. Zhu, J., et al.: Incorporating BERT into neural machine translation. arXiv:2002.06823 (2020)

Adversarial Variational Knowledge Distillation

Xuan Tang[1] and Tong Lin[1,2]([✉])

[1] The Key Laboratory of Machine Perception (MOE), School of EECS,
Peking University, Beijing, China
{xuantang,lintong}@pku.edu.cn
[2] Peng Cheng Laboratory, Shenzhen, China

Abstract. Knowledge Distillation (KD) is one of the most popular and effective techniques for model compression and knowledge transfer. However, most existing KD approaches are heavily relying on the labeled training data, which is usually unavailable due to privacy concerns. Thus, data-free KD focus on restoring the training data with Generative Adversarial Networks (GANs) by either catering the pre-trained teacher or fooling the student. In this paper we introduce Adversarial Variational Knowledge Distillation (AVKD), a framework that formulates the restoring process as Variational Autoencoders (VAEs). Different from vanilla VAEs, AVKD is specified by a pre-trained teacher model $p(y|x)$ of the visible labels y given the latent x, a prior $p(x)$ over the latent variables and an approximate generative model $q(x|y)$. In practice, we refer the prior $p(x)$ as an alternate unlabeled data distribution from other related domains. Similar to Adversarial Variational Bayes (AVB), we estimate the KL-divergence term between $p(x)$ and $q(x|y)$ by introducing a discriminator network. Although the original training data are unavailable, we argue that the prior data drawn from other related domains can be easily obtained to learn the knowledge distillation efficiently. Extensive experiments testify that our method outperforms the state-of-the-art algorithms in the absence of the original training data, with performance approaching the case where the original training data are provided.

Keywords: Data-free knowledge distillation · Variational autoencoders · Generative Adversarial Networks

1 Introduction

Knowledge Distillation (KD) [8] is a machine learning approach that transfers knowledge from a larger capacity teacher model (or ensembles) into a more compact student model. Given a pre-trained teacher model, a student aims to learn knowledge from the teacher on the training data. Through distillation, one hopes to obtain a student model that not only inherits better performance from

This work was supported by NSFC Tianyuan Fund for Mathematics (No. 12026606), and National Key R&D Program of China (No. 2018AAA0100300).

I. Farkaš et al. (Eds.): ICANN 2021, LNCS 12893, pp. 558–569, 2021.
https://doi.org/10.1007/978-3-030-86365-4_45

the teacher, but is also more efficient in the inference stage. In recent years, the knowledge distillation community has made great achievements with respect to model architecture and several application domains [19–21,23].

In spite of the significant progress, classical distillation methods heavily rely on sufficient training data, which is often unavailable due to privacy, confidentiality, property, size or transience. Hence, it is necessary to explore data-free knowledge distillation algorithms which are independent of the original training data.

Most existing data-free approaches concentrate on modeling the data distribution via GANs but are insufficient in theoretical derivations. In this work, we formulate the data generation process from the perspective of Variational Autoencoders (VAEs) [11].

Contrary to vanilla VAEs, we regard the input feature (e.g. images) as the latent variables instead of visible variables while the output labels are viewed as observations (i.e. visible variables). Here, we denote x as the feature and y as the labels, respectively. As a result, we first propose a principled framework named **Variational Knowledge Distillation** (VKD), which is composed of a classification model $p(y|x)$ of the visible variables y given the latent variables x, a prior $p(x)$ over the latent variables and an approximate generative model $q(x|y)$. Specifically, the classification model $p(y|x)$ is implemented with a well-trained teacher model $p_\theta(y|x)$ with fixed parameters θ. Taking the prior $p(x)$ as Gaussian (e.g. $\mathcal{N}(0, \mathbf{I})$) will cause poor performance in experiments since the generative model $q(x|y)$ can only produce ill-conditioned images that are harmful for distillation.

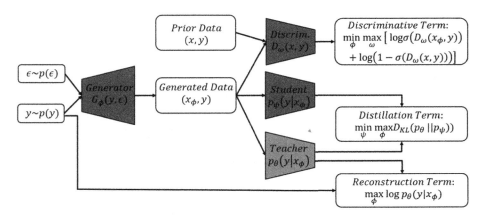

Fig. 1. Overview of our proposed Adversarial Variational Knowledge Distillation (AVKD) framework.

To address this problem, we employ some unlabeled data that can be easily obtained from other related domains as the prior. However, computing the Kullback–Leibler divergence term between $q(x|y)$ and $p(x)$ is intractable since the unlabeled data have no explicit analytic expressions. To this end, we borrow the idea from Adversarial Variational Bayes (AVB) [15] and propose a refined framework called **Adversarial Variational Knowledge Distillation** (AVKD), which can estimate the Kullback–Leibler divergence based on a new discriminator network. The purpose of the discriminator is to determine if an example (x, y) is drawn from $p(y)p(x)$ or from $p(y)q(x|y)$. Here $p(y)$ denotes the real distribution of labels which are categories in a typical classification task. The AVKD framework is shown in Fig. 1.

Experiments in Sect. 4 on various image classification datasets shows that the student networks trained with our framework outperform existing state-of-the-art methods in the absence of the original training data, with performance approaching the settings where the original training data are provided.

2 Related Works

2.1 Knowledge Distillation

Knowledge Distillation is a popular model compression technique that transfers the knowledge of a large-capacity model or an ensemble of models into a small one. Buciluǎ et al. [3] first proposed the idea of training a network with another network's outputs on a large-scale unlabeled dataset. Ba et al. [2] later trained shallow neural networks to mimic deep neural networks via regressing logits (outputs of a neural network before the softmax activation) with mean square error (MSE). Hinton et al. [8] further trained student neural networks with "soft targets" produced by the teacher and first proposed the concept of *Knowledge Distillation*.

2.2 Data-Free Knowledge Distillation

The data-free knowledge distillation, i.e. optimizing the student model without the original training data, becomes more challenging than vanilla knowledge distillation. Most existing approaches focus on synthetic images generation. Lopes et al. [13] first utilized the "meta-data" (e.g. means and standard deviation of activations from each layer) stored the teacher networks to generate fake samples that can produce similar activations. Following-up works [17,22] intended to use less "meta-data" or design different training objectives. A similar strategy [5,7,14] is to exploit the means and variances statistics stored in the batch normalization layers [9] of neural networks. However, these "meta-data" or batch normalization statistics are not always provided by the teacher networks, indicating that related approaches would failed sometimes. Another strategy [1,4] proposed to train a generator network for data generation, which enables the teacher network to produce predictions with high confidence, significantly relying on large batch size and training steps to produce large amount of diverse images. Micaelli et al. [16] developed a new generation scheme via adversarial learning. Specifically, a generator is employed to produce samples that maximize the knowledge distillation loss [8] between the teacher and student networks. Similarly, Fang et al. [6] replaced the knowledge distillation loss with mean average error (MAE) and achieved better performance. These two methods aim to search hard samples for the student throughout the whole input space, which are easily to fall into a suboptimal solution due to the high dimensions of the searching space.

3   Method

3.1   Problem Formulation

Knowledge Distillation. In typical knowledge distillation form of classification tasks, given a pre-trained teacher model $p_\theta(y|x)$ parameterized by θ, a student model $p_\psi(y|x)$ parameterized by ψ aims to solve the following problem:

$$\min_\psi E_{p_{data}(x,y)} \left[D_{KL}(p_\theta(y|x) \parallel p_\psi(y|x)) \right], \tag{3.1}$$

where D_{KL} refers to the Kullback–Leibler divergence that evaluates the discrepancy between the distributions produced by the teacher and student models. Here $p_{data}(x, y)$ denotes joint distribution of the original training samples and labels. Note that the D_{KL} term is independent with labels y, so we can reformulate problem (3.1) as

$$\min_\psi E_{p_{data}(x)} \left[D_{KL}(p_\theta(y|x) \parallel p_\psi(y|x)) \right]. \tag{3.2}$$

Data-Free Knowledge Distillation. Optimization (3.1) can be also rewritten as

$$\min_\psi E_{p_{data}(y)} [E_{p_{data}(x|y)} [D_{KL}(p_\theta(y|x) \parallel p_\psi(y|x)))]], \tag{3.3}$$

where $p_{data}(y)$ is a categorical distribution in classification tasks. However, optimizing either (3.2) or (3.3) requires the knowledge of the data distribution $p_{data}(x)$ or $p_{data}(x|y)$, which is unavailable in the data-free setting. Most existing data-free approaches concentrate on modeling the distribution $p_{data}(x)$ or $p_{data}(x|y)$ directly via GANs without any derivations.

In this work, we focus on approximating $p_{data}(x|y)$ with generative model $q_\phi(x|y)$ parameterized by ϕ. Then, the data-free knowledge distillation problem can be reformulated as

$$\min_\psi E_{p_{data}(y)} [E_{q_\phi(x|y)} [D_{KL}(p_\theta(y|x) \parallel p_\psi(y|x)))]]. \tag{3.4}$$

Thus in the rest of this paper, we concentrate on modeling and learning the generative model $q_\phi(x|y)$.

3.2   Variational Knowledge Distillation (VKD)

Given a pre-trained teacher $p_\theta(y|x)$, our goal is to approximate the true generative model $p_\theta(x|y)$ via a approximate parametric model $q_\phi(x|y)$. In this work, we consider x as the latent variables of features (such as images) and y as the visible variables of labels. As a result, following VAEs, it can be shown as

$$\log p_\theta(y) \geq -D_{KL}(q_\phi(x|y) \parallel p(x)) + E_{q_\phi(x|y)}\left[\log p_\theta(y|x)\right], \qquad (3.5)$$

where $p(x)$ denotes the prior distribution over the latent variables. The right hand side of (3.5) is called the **evidence lower bound** (ELBO).

When performing maximum-likelihood training, the goal of VAEs is to optimize the marginal log-likelihood

$$E_{p_{data}(y)}\left[\log p_\theta(y)\right]. \qquad (3.6)$$

However, computing $\log p_\theta(y)$ requires marginalizing out x in $p_\theta(y,x)$ which is usually intractable. Instead, VAEs use inequality (3.5) to rephrase the intractable problem of optimizing (3.6) into optimizing the ELBO:

$$\max_\theta \max_\phi E_{p_{data}(y)}\left[-D_{KL}(q_\phi(x|y) \parallel p(x)) + E_{q_\phi(x|y)}\left[\log p_\theta(y|x)\right]\right]. \qquad (3.7)$$

In the knowledge distillation setting, the teacher model $p_\theta(y|x)$ has been trained well on the original data distribution $p_{data}(x,y)$. Consequently, we fix the weight θ of teacher while optimizing (3.7), then the training objective becomes

$$\max_\phi E_{p_{data}(y)}\left[-D_{KL}(q_\phi(x|y) \parallel p(x)) + E_{q_\phi(x|y)}\left[\log p_\theta(y|x)\right]\right]. \qquad (3.8)$$

Note that the term $D_{KL}(q_\phi(x|y) \parallel p(x))$ is an expectation on $q_\phi(x|y)$ according to its definition, then we can rewrite the optimization problem in (3.8) as

$$\max_\phi E_{p_{data}(y)}\left[E_{q_\phi(x|y)}\left[\log p(x) - \log q_\phi(x|y) + \log p_\theta(y|x)\right]\right]. \qquad (3.9)$$

When we have an explicit representation of $q_\phi(x|y)$ and $p(x)$ such as Gaussian, (3.9) can be optimized using the reparameterization trick [11, 18] and Stochastic Gradient Descent (SGD).

3.3   Adversarial Variational Knowledge Distillation (AVKD)

One significant drawback of VKD, however, is that samples drawn from the $q_\phi(x|y)$ are ill-formed since it is almost impossible to find a perfect explicit expression for $p(x)$ to model real data such as images. Thus, the performance provided by the student model trained with $q_\phi(x|y)$ might be very poor. To this end, we replace the prior $p(x)$ with large amount unlabeled data in real scenarios from other related domains. For ease of description, we term the unlabeled data as *prior data* in this work. Using the *prior data* the student model can produce much better performance and experiments details are described in Sect. 4.

However, it is intractable to optimize (3.9) when only given *prior data* sampled from an implicit prior $p(x)$. Following the Adversarial Variational Bayes (AVB) [15], we therefore introduce an auxiliary discriminative network to rephrase the maximum-likelihood-problem as a two-player game, as described in the following.

The main idea of AVB is to implicitly representing the term in (3.9)

$$\log p(x) - \log q_\phi(x|y) \tag{3.10}$$

as the optimal value of an additional real-valued discriminator network $D_\omega(x,y)$ parameterized by ω.

Specifically, when given $q_\phi(x|y)$, the objective of the discriminator is

$$\max_\omega E_{p_{data}(y)}[E_{q_\phi(x|y)} \log \sigma(D_\omega(x,y)) + E_{p(x)}\log(1 - \sigma(D_\omega(x,y)))], \tag{3.11}$$

where $\sigma(t) := 1/(1 + e^{-t})$ is the sigmoid function. As shown in literature [15], it turns out that the optimal is given as

$$D^*(x,y) = \log q_\phi(x|y) - \log p(x). \tag{3.12}$$

Here, $D^*(x,y)$ denotes the function that maximizes (3.11) and the right hand side of (3.12) is the negative of (3.10). The detail proof can be found in [15].

We can rewrite the objective in (3.8) as

$$\max_\phi E_{p_{data}(y)}[E_{q_\phi(x|y)}[-D^*(x,y) + \log p_\theta(y|x)]]. \tag{3.13}$$

Optimizing (3.13) requires to calculate the gradient w.r.t ϕ, which is difficult since we have defined $D^*(x,y)$ as the solution of problem (3.11) that itself depends on ϕ. Fortunately, the literature [15] has proved that

$$E_{q_\phi(x|y)}[\nabla_\phi D^*(x,y)] = 0, \tag{3.14}$$

which indicates that it is unnecessary to take the gradient w.r.t the explicit occurrence of ϕ in $D^*(x,y)$.

Adversarial Training. Inspired by the idea of [6,16], we introduce an auxiliary objective for the generative model $q_\phi(x|y)$ that maximizes the discrepancy between the teacher and student model, resulting in a two-player game between the generative model and the student model. With adversarial training, the goal of $q_\phi(x|y)$ changes to maximize objective in (3.13) and adversarial objective jointly:

$$\max_\phi E_{p_{data}(y)}[E_{q_\phi(x|y)}[-D^*(x,y) + \log p_\theta(y|x)$$
$$+ D_{KL}(p_\theta(y|x) \parallel p_\psi(y|x))]]. \tag{3.15}$$

The objective of the generator consists of three terms:

- The $-D^*(x,y)$ is the discriminative term that allows the generator to produce similar samples to *prior data* by fooling the discriminator $D(x,y)$.
- The second term $\log p_\theta(y|x)$ is called the reconstruction log-likelihood for the input labels y.
- The adversarial term $D_{KL}(p_\theta(y|x) \parallel p_\psi(y|x))$ encourages the generator to generate hard training samples for the student.

Training Objectives. Using the reparameterization trick [11,18], we can rewrite the objective of the generative model $q_\phi(x|y)$ in (3.15) as

$$\max_\phi E_{p_{data}(y)}[E_{p(\epsilon)}[-D^*(G_\phi(y,\epsilon),y) + \log p_\theta(y|G_\phi(y,\epsilon)) \\ + D_{KL}(p_\theta(y|G_\phi(y,\epsilon)) \parallel p_\psi(y|G_\phi(y,\epsilon)))]], \tag{3.16}$$

where $p(\epsilon)$ is a Gaussian and $G_\phi(y,\epsilon)$ is a learnable generator network parameterized by ϕ. Similarly, the objective of the discriminator model in (3.11) and the objective of the student model in (3.4) can be rewritten in the form

$$\max_\omega E_{p_{data}(y)}[E_{p(\epsilon)} \log \sigma(D_\omega(G_\phi(y,\epsilon),y)) \\ + E_{p(x)} \log(1 - \sigma(D_\omega(x,y)))] \tag{3.17}$$

and

$$\min_\psi E_{p_{data}(y)}[E_{p(\epsilon)}[D_{KL}(p_\theta(y|G_\phi(y,\epsilon)) \parallel p_\psi(y|G_\phi(y,\epsilon)))]], \tag{3.18}$$

respectively.

Note that applying SGD on the objective of (3.16) requires keep $D^*(x,y)$ optimal which might be very time-consuming. Therefore, we treat the optimization problems in (3.16) and (3.17) as a two-player game following AVB [15]. An overview of our proposed AVKD is shown in Fig. 1.

3.4   Algorithm

In practice, we applying SGD jointly to (3.16), (3.18) and (3.17), see Algorithm 1. Here, η and m denote the learning rate and batch size, respectively. Note that we apply n SGD-updates to the student model at each iteration to distill the teacher model more efficiently.

4   Experiments

4.1   Experiments Setup

CIFAR. The CIFAR10 dataset [12] consists of 50K training and 10K testing RGB images with resolution 32×32 of 10 categories. For the CIFAR10 classification task, we use the CIFAR100 [12] and Tiny-ImageNet datasets as the *prior data* respectively. Since the CIFAR100 dataset contains two coarse classes (i.e. vehicles1 and vehicles2) related with two fine-grained classes (i.e. automobile and truck) of CIFAR10, we therefore remove the 10 fine-grained classes of vehicles1 and vehicles2 in CIFAR100, resulting in a modified dataset termed as CIFAR90. Thus, we train the AVKD with various *prior data* such as CIFAR90, CIFAR100 and Tiny-ImageNet of 32×32 image size, respectively.

Similar to CIFAR10, CIFAR100 [12] consists of 50K training and 10K testing RGB images except that all images are distributed over 100 categories. In this experiment, the CIFAR10 and Tiny-ImageNet of 32×32 image size are employed as *prior data* respectively.

Algorithm 1: Adversarial Variational Knowledge Distillation (AVKD)

---

1 **for** *1,2,...,N* **do**

2   Sample $\{x^{(1)}, ..., x^{(m)}\}$ from *prior data*

3   Sample $\{y^{(1)}, ..., y^{(m)}\}$ from $p_{data}(y)$

4   Sample $\{\epsilon^{(1)}, ..., \epsilon^{(m)}\}$ from $\mathcal{N}(0, \mathbf{I})$

5

6   Compute ϕ-gradient for generator (eq. 3.16):

7     $g_\phi \leftarrow \frac{1}{m} \sum_{k=1}^{k=m} \nabla_\phi [-D^*(G_\phi(y^{(k)}, \epsilon^{(k)}), y^{(k)}) + \log p_\theta(y^{(k)}|G_\phi(y^{(k)}, \epsilon^{(k)}))$

8                      $+ D_{KL}(p_\theta(y^{(k)}|G_\phi(y^{(k)}, \epsilon^{(k)})) \parallel p_\psi(y^{(k)}|G_\phi(y^{(k)}, \epsilon^{(k)})))]$

9   Update parameters of generator:

10     $\phi \leftarrow \phi + \eta \times g_\phi$

11

12   Compute ω-gradient for discriminator (eq. 3.17):

13     $g_\omega \leftarrow \frac{1}{m} \sum_{k=1}^{k=m} \nabla_\omega [\log \sigma(D_\omega(G_\phi(y^{(k)}, \epsilon^{(k)}), y^{(k)}))$

14                     $+ \log(1 - \sigma(D_\omega(x^{(k)}, y^{(k)})))]$

15   Update parameters of discriminator:

16     $\omega \leftarrow \omega + \eta \times g_\omega$

17

18   **for** *1,2,...,n* **do**

19   Sample $\{y^{(1)}, ..., y^{(m)}\}$ from $p_{data}(y)$

20   Sample $\{\epsilon^{(1)}, ..., \epsilon^{(m)}\}$ from $\mathcal{N}(0, \mathbf{I})$

21   Compute ψ-gradient for student (eq. 3.18):

22         $g_\psi \leftarrow \frac{1}{m} \sum_{k=1}^{k=m} \nabla_\psi [D_{KL}(p_\theta(y|G_\phi(y^{(k)}, \epsilon^{(k)})) \parallel p_\psi(y|G_\phi(y^{(k)}, \epsilon^{(k)}))))]$

23   Update parameters of student:

24         $\psi \leftarrow \psi - \eta \times g_\psi$

25   **end**

26 **end**

Tiny-ImageNet. The Tiny-ImageNet dataset is a modified subset of the original ImageNet dataset. Here, there are 200 different classes instead of 1000 classes of ImageNet, with 100K training examples and 10K validation examples. The resolution of the images is resized to 64×64 pixels, which is different from the ImageNet. Since the Tiny-ImageNet also contains 10K testing images without labels, we can only report the test accuracies on the validation images. We explore two target resolutions: 32×32 matching that of CIFAR10 and CIFAR100, and full resolution 64×64. For 32×32 image size we therefore choose training sets of CIFAR10 and CIFAR100 as the *prior data* respectively. For resolution of 64×64, we take the Caltech101[1] and Caltech256[2] as the *prior data*, respectively.

---

[1] http://www.vision.caltech.edu/Image_Datasets/Caltech101/
[2] http://www.vision.caltech.edu/Image_Datasets/Caltech256/

4.2   Implementation Details

To verify the robustness of our method, we conduct all experiments with same hyperparameters. Note that the $p_{data}(y)$ is set to discrete uniform distribution since we suppose every dataset is of category balance. We train our proposed method with 100K iterations and batch size of 256 for all experiments, and we update the student network with 5 times at each iteration so that it can learn more sufficiently from the current generative model. To make a fair comparison, we follow the setting used in the previous literature [4,6] with a pre-trained ResNet34 as the teacher network and ResNet18 as the student. The generator architecture is modified from the one used in [4,6] and the discriminator is constructed with three convolutional layers. We optimize the generator network with Adam [10] with an initial learning rate of 10^{-3} that is divided by 10 at the 20K-th and 40K-th iteration respectively. The student and discriminator are trained by the Nesterov Accelerated Gradient (NAG) optimizer with momentum 0.9 and weight decay 5×10^{-4}. The discriminator is trained with constant learning rate of 2×10^{-4}. The initial learning rate of the student is 0.1 and decayed by 0.985 every 200 iterations. For each experiment we run it three times and report the mean accuracy.

4.3   Results

CIFAR10. Table 1 summarized test accuracies of student models trained by different methods on CIFAR10 dataset. Trained in fully supervised setting, the teacher (ResNet34) and the student networks (ResNet18) achieve accuracies of 95.53% and 93.92%, respectively. The student network trained with knowledge distillation [8] using the original training data (CIFAR10) achieves a +0.38% improvement over the one trained from scratch. In the data-free setting, using Gaussian noise as inputs results in poor performance which is only slightly better than a random guess (around 10%). For CIFAR10, we employ CIFAR90, CIFAR100 and TinyImageNet 32×32 as the *prior data*, respectively. Training with CIFAR100 achieves the highest accuracy of **93.50%** since CIFAR100 is more diverse than CIFAR90 and more relevant to CIFAR10 than TinyImageNet.

We also compare our methods with DAFL [4] and DFAD [6] using their released codes with batch size of 256. Note that our method is only slightly better than other data-free algorithms, as one reason is that the 10-category classification task with resolution 32×32 is too simple to differentiate these methods.

CIFAR100. Results on CIFAR100 obtained by different methods are also listed in Table 1. It can be found that our proposed method outperforms others with considerable improvements better than the case in CIFAR10 experiments. Specifically, while training with CIFAR10 as *prior data*, our method exceeds the DAFL [4], DFAD [6] and DeGAN [1] with **10.53%**, **4.18%** and **6.63%**, respectively. While training with TinyImagenet 32×32, our method also outperforms other state-of-the-art methods with considerable improvements. Note that the

Table 1. Test accuracies on CIFAR10 and CIFAR100. In our experiments, we employ the ResNet34 as the teacher and ResNet18 as the student model, respectively.

Model	Method	CIFAR10		CIFAR100	
		Prior data	Accuracy	Prior data	Accuracy
ResNet34	Supervised training	N/A	95.53%	N/A	77.58%
ResNet18	Supervised training	N/A	93.92%	N/A	76.51%
ResNet18	KD [8]	N/A	94.30%	N/A	76.89%
ResNet18	Gaussian noise	N/A	11.43%	N/A	1.23%
ResNet18	DAFL [4]	N/A	88.41%	N/A	61.35%
ResNet18	DFAD [6]	N/A	93.30%	N/A	67.70%
ResNet18	DeGAN [1]	N/A	N/A	CIFAR90	65.25%
ResNet18	Ours	CIFAR90	**93.41%**	CIFAR10	**71.88%**
		CIFAR100	**93.50%**	TinyImageNet	**70.26%**
		TinyImageNet	93.02%	N/A	N/A

DeGAN also takes CIFAR90 as an alternative of the original training data but achieves lower test accuracy than ours.

Tiny-ImageNet. For Tiny-ImageNet classification task, we conduct experiments on two target resolutions of 32×32 and 64×64. In order to compare our method with DAFL [4] and DFAD [6], we modified their released codes to run it on Tiny-ImageNet with the two different resolutions and all hyperparameters remain unchanged. Note that we don't report the results of DeGAN [1] since the authors didn't release their codes.

The results of Tiny-ImageNet 32×32 can be found in Table 2. Our method achieves accuracies of **46.96%** and **50.22%** with CIFAR10 and CIFAR100 as the *prior data* respectively, outperforming all other data-free approaches by a large margin. We can also observe that the proposed method trained with more diverse dataset (i.e. CIFAR100) gains higher accuracy than CIFAR10 with improvement of **+3.26%** that is considerable for a 200-category classification task.

For results of Tiny-ImageNet 64×64, as shown in Table 2, our proposed method exceeds DFAD [6] with better improvements than the case of 32×32 resolution.

Visualization Results. We plot the reconstructed images of CIFAR10 by our proposed AVKD trained with TinyImagenet in Fig. 2. Images of same category are plotted in one row, where images on the left side are sampled from the true dataset while on another side are the generated images. It can be found that the generative model in the proposed AVKD can learn the key features of different categories from the pretrained teacher and the *prior data*, hence these synthesized samples can transfer relevant knowledge about the original training data. These results, therefore, testify the effectiveness our proposed method from another perspective.

Table 2. Test accuracies on TinyImageNet of two resolutions. We employ ResNet34 as the teacher and ResNet18 as the student model, respectively.

Model	Method	TinyImageNet32 × 32		TinyImageNet64 × 64	
		Prior data	Accuracy	Prior data	Accuracy
ResNet34	Supervised training	N/A	57.68%	N/A	61.49%
ResNet18	Supervised training	N/A	54.30%	N/A	58.30%
ResNet18	KD [8]	N/A	55.06%	N/A	58.98%
ResNet18	Random noise	N/A	0.57%	N/A	0.54%
ResNet18	DAFL [4]	N/A	26.32%	N/A	13.24%
ResNet18	DFAD [6]	N/A	29.52%	N/A	15.92%
ResNet18	Ours	CIFAR10	**46.96%**	Caltech101	**46.11%**
		CIFAR100	**50.22%**	Caltech256	**46.25%**

Fig. 2. Visualization of generated images. Images on the left side are sampled from the CIFAR10 dataset while on the right side are generated by our proposed AVKD.

5   Conclusion

In this work, we introduce the Adversarial Variational Knowledge Distillation (AVKD), a framework that can distil a well-trained large-capacity teacher model into a compact student model in the absence of original training data on which the teacher are trained. Since the original training data is unavailable, we treat the data (i.e. images in this work) as latent variables and learn the generative model $q_\phi(x|y)$ to model the original training data. By employing the unlabeld prior data, experiments have shown that our method outperforms other data-free KD algorithms on various images classification tasks. Furthermore, we found that our method can exceed other methods with larger margin for more difficult tasks, indicating the effectiveness of the proposed method.

References

1. Addepalli, S., Nayak, G.K., Chakraborty, A., Babu, R.V.: DeGAN: data-enriching GAN for retrieving representative samples from a trained classifier (2019)
2. Ba, J., Caruana, R.: Do deep nets really need to be deep? In: NeurIPS (2014)
3. Buciluǎ, C., Caruana, R., Niculescu-Mizil, A.: Model compression. In: SIGKDD (2006)
4. Chen, H., et al.: Data-free learning of student networks. In: ICCV (2019)
5. Choi, Y., Choi, J., El-Khamy, M., Lee, J.: Data-free network quantization with adversarial knowledge distillation. arXiv preprint arXiv:2005.04136 (2020)
6. Fang, G., Song, J., Shen, C., Wang, X., Chen, D., Song, M.: Data-free adversarial distillation. arXiv preprint arXiv:1912.11006 (2019)
7. Haroush, M., Hubara, I., Hoffer, E., Soudry, D.: The knowledge within: methods for data-free model compression. In: CVPR (2020)
8. Hinton, G., Vinyals, O., Dean, J.: Distilling the knowledge in a neural network. arXiv preprint arXiv:1503.02531 (2015)
9. Ioffe, S., Szegedy, C.: Batch normalization: accelerating deep network training by reducing internal covariate shift. arXiv preprint arXiv:1502.03167 (2015)
10. Kingma, D.P., Ba, J.: Adam: a method for stochastic optimization. arXiv preprint arXiv:1412.6980 (2014)
11. Kingma, D.P., Welling, M.: Auto-encoding variational Bayes. arXiv preprint arXiv:1312.6114 (2014)
12. Krizhevsky, A., Sutskever, I., Hinton, G.E.: ImageNet classification with deep convolutional neural networks. In: NeurIPS (2012)
13. Lopes, R.G., Fenu, S., Starner, T.: Data-free knowledge distillation for deep neural networks. arXiv preprint arXiv:1710.07535 (2017)
14. Luo, L., Sandler, M., Lin, Z., Zhmoginov, A., Howard, A.: Large-scale generative data-free distillation. arXiv preprint arXiv:2012.05578 (2020)
15. Mescheder, L., Nowozin, S., Geiger, A.: Adversarial variational Bayes: unifying variational autoencoders and generative adversarial networks. arXiv preprint arXiv:1701.04722 (2018)
16. Micaelli, P., Storkey, A.J.: Zero-shot knowledge transfer via adversarial belief matching. In: NeurIPS (2019)
17. Nayak, G.K., Mopuri, K.R., Shaj, V., Babu, R.V., Chakraborty, A.: Zero-shot knowledge distillation in deep networks. arXiv preprint arXiv:1905.08114 (2019)
18. Rezende, D.J., Mohamed, S., Wierstra, D.: Stochastic backpropagation and approximate inference in deep generative models. arXiv preprint arXiv:1401.4082 (2014)
19. Sanh, V., Debut, L., Chaumond, J., Wolf, T.: DistilBERT, a distilled version of BERT: smaller, faster, cheaper and lighter. arXiv preprint arXiv:1910.01108 (2019)
20. Wang, T., Yuan, L., Zhang, X., Feng, J.: Distilling object detectors with fine-grained feature imitation. In: CVPR (2019)
21. Wang, X., Zhang, R., Sun, Y., Qi, J.: KDGAN: knowledge distillation with generative adversarial networks. In: NeurIPS (2018)
22. Yin, H., et al.: Dreaming to distill: data-free knowledge transfer via DeepInversion. arXiv preprint arXiv:1912.08795 (2020)
23. Zagoruyko, S., Komodakis, N.: Paying more attention to attention: improving the performance of convolutional neural networks via attention transfer. In: ICLR (2017)

Extract then Distill: Efficient and Effective Task-Agnostic BERT Distillation

Cheng Chen[1], Yichun Yin[2], Lifeng Shang[2], Zhi Wang[3,4(✉)], Xin Jiang[2], Xiao Chen[2], and Qun Liu[2]

[1] Department of Computer Science and Technology, Tsinghua University, Beijing, China
c-chen19@mails.tsinghua.edu.cn
[2] Huawei Noah's Ark Lab, Shenzhen, China
{yinyichun,shang.lifeng,jiang.xin,chen.xiao2,qun.liu}@huawei.com
[3] Tsinghua Shenzhen International Graduate School, Tsinghua University, Shenzhen, China
wangzhi@sz.tsinghua.edu.cn
[4] Peng Cheng Laboratory, Shenzhen, China

Abstract. Task-agnostic knowledge distillation, a teacher-student framework, has been proved effective for BERT compression. Although achieving promising results on NLP tasks, it requires enormous computational resources. In this paper, we propose *Extract Then Distill* (ETD), a generic and flexible strategy to reuse the teacher's parameters for efficient and effective task-agnostic distillation, which can be applied to students of any size. Specifically, we introduce two variants of ETD, ETD-Rand and ETD-Impt, which extract the teacher's parameters in a random manner and by following an importance metric, respectively. In this way, the student has already acquired some knowledge at the beginning of the distillation process, which makes the distillation process converge faster. We demonstrate the effectiveness of ETD on the GLUE benchmark and SQuAD. The experimental results show that: (1) compared with the baseline without an ETD strategy, ETD can save 70% of computation cost. Moreover, it achieves better results than the baseline when using the same computing resource. (2) ETD is generic and has been proven effective for different distillation methods (e.g., TinyBERT and MiniLM) and students of different sizes. Code is available at https://github.com/huawei-noah/Pretrained-Language-Model.

Keywords: BERT · Knowledge distillation · Structured pruning

1 Introduction

With the booming of deep learning in the natural language processing (NLP) field, many pre-trained language models (PLMs) are proposed, such as BERT [2], XLNet [27], RoBERTa [13], ALBERT [12], T5 [16], ELECTRA [1] and so on, achieving state-of-the-art (SOTA) performance on various tasks. However, these

© Springer Nature Switzerland AG 2021
I. Farkaš et al. (Eds.): ICANN 2021, LNCS 12893, pp. 570–581, 2021.
https://doi.org/10.1007/978-3-030-86365-4_46

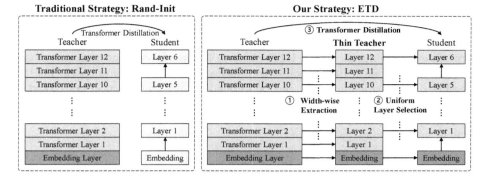

Fig. 1. Comparison between the traditional strategy (Rand-Init) and our ETD strategy. The Gray indicates that the student model in Rand-Init is initialized randomly.

large PLMs are computationally expensive and require a large memory footprint, which makes it difficult to execute them on resource-restricted devices such as mobile phones.

To tackle this problem, many works propose task-agnostic BERT distillation [11,19,25] to obtain a general small BERT model that can be fine-tuned directly as the teacher model (e.g., BERT-Base) does. However, the process of task-agnostic BERT distillation is also computationally expensive [14]. Because the corpus used in the distillation is large-scale, and each training step is computationally consuming that a forward process of teacher model and a forward-backward process of student model need to be performed.

Reusing the parameters of the teacher model to initialize the student model has been proved effective to improve the efficiency of BERT distillation (e.g., BERT-PKD [20] and DistilBERT [19]). However, these works only do the *depth-wise* extraction that simply copies some Transformer layers [22] from the teacher model, which requires the student to keep the same setting of *width dimensions* including hidden/head/FFN dimension, as the teacher. Actually, in many industrial scenarios, we need to build the student models with different widths and depths to meet various latency and memory requirements, which indicates that we need a more flexible strategy to reuse the teacher's parameters. What's more, it also shows the necessity of improving distillation efficiency, because we need to re-run a complete distillation process for each student architecture.

In this paper, we propose *Extract Then Distill* (ETD) as shown in Fig. 1, a flexible and effective method to reuse the teacher's parameters to initialize the student, which firstly allows the student to have a narrower width than the teacher. Specifically, we propose two methods: ETD-Rand and ETD-Impt, which width-wise extract the teacher's parameters randomly and depending on the importance scores, respectively. Then we adopt the strategy of uniform layer selection for depth-wise extraction. Finally, we initialize the student with the extracted parameters, then perform the task-agnostic distillation.

Our contributions are two-fold: (1) we propose an effective method ETD, which improves the efficiency of task-agnostic BERT distillation by reusing the teacher parameters to initialize the student model. The proposed ETD method is flexible and applicable to student models of any size. (2) We demonstrate the effectiveness of ETD on the GLUE benchmark and SQuAD. The extensive experimental results show that ETD can save 70% of the computation cost of the baseline, and when using the same computing resources, ETD outperforms the baselines. ETD is general and can be applied to different existing state-of-the-art distillation methods, such as TinyBERT and MiniLM, to further boost their performance. Moreover, the extraction process of ETD is efficient and brings almost no additional calculations.

2   Preliminary

2.1   Architecture of BERT

Embedding Layer. Through the embedding layer, all tokens in a sentence are mapped to vectors of the *hidden size* $\{\boldsymbol{x}_i\}_{i=1}^{|x|}$, where $|x|$ means the number of tokens in this sentence. A special token [CLS] is added at the beginning of the sentence for obtaining the representation of the entire sentence.

Stacked Transformer Layers. The Transformer layer dynamically encodes context information into the representation vector of each token through the self-attention mechanism, which tackles the problem of semantic ambiguity to a great extent. We denote the output of embedding layer $[\boldsymbol{x}_1; ...; \boldsymbol{x}_{|x|}]$ as *hidden states* $\boldsymbol{H}^0$. The stacked Transformer layers compute the contextual vectors as:

$$\boldsymbol{H}^l = \text{Transformer}_l(\boldsymbol{H}^{l-1}), l \in [1, L], \tag{1}$$

where L means the number of Transformer layers.

2.2   Architecture of Transformer

Each Transformer layer consists of two sub-modules: the multi-head attention (MHA) and the fully connected feed-forward network (FFN). *Residual connection* and *layer normalization* are employed on top of each sub-module.

MHA. In each layer, Transformer uses multiple self-attention heads to aggregate the output vectors of the previous layer. For the $(l + 1)$-th Transformer layer, the output of MHA is computed via:

$$\boldsymbol{Q}_i = \boldsymbol{H}^l \boldsymbol{W}_i^Q, \boldsymbol{K}_i = \boldsymbol{H}^l \boldsymbol{W}_i^K, \boldsymbol{V}_i = \boldsymbol{H}^l \boldsymbol{W}_i^V,$$
$$\boldsymbol{A}_i = \frac{\boldsymbol{Q}_i \boldsymbol{K}_i^T}{\sqrt{d_k}},$$
$$\text{head}_i = \text{softmax}(\boldsymbol{A}_i)\boldsymbol{V}_i, \tag{2}$$
$$\text{MHA}(\boldsymbol{H}^l) = \text{Concat}(\text{head}_1, ..., \text{head}_a)\boldsymbol{W}^O,$$
$$\boldsymbol{H}^{\text{MHA}} = \text{LayerNorm}(\boldsymbol{H}^l + \text{MHA}(\boldsymbol{H}^l)).$$

The previous layer's output $\boldsymbol{H}^l$ is linearly projected to queries, keys, and values using parameter matrices $\boldsymbol{W}^Q, \boldsymbol{W}^K, \boldsymbol{W}^V$, respectively. head_i indicates the context-aware vector which is obtained by the scaled dot-product of queries and keys in the i-th attention head. a represents the number of self-attention heads. d_k is the dimension of each attention head acting as the scaling factor, named as head dimension. $d_k \times a$ is equal to the hidden dimension d_h. $\boldsymbol{H}^{\mathrm{MHA}}$ will be the input of the next sub-module FFN.

FFN. It consists of two linear layers and a GeLU [7] function between them:

$$
\begin{aligned}
\mathrm{FFN}(\boldsymbol{H}^{\mathrm{MHA}}) &= \mathrm{GeLU}(\boldsymbol{H}^{\mathrm{MHA}}\boldsymbol{W}_1 + \boldsymbol{b}_1)\boldsymbol{W}_2 + \boldsymbol{b}_2, \\
\boldsymbol{H}^{l+1} &= \mathrm{LayerNorm}(\boldsymbol{H}^{\mathrm{MHA}} + \mathrm{FFN}(\boldsymbol{H}^{\mathrm{MHA}})).
\end{aligned}
\tag{3}
$$

2.3 Overview of BERT Distillation

There are two widely-used distillation layer mapping strategies, *uniform* and *last-layer*, adopted by TinyBERT [11] and MiniLM [25], respectively. We adopt the last-layer strategy and follow other settings of TinyBERT because we empirically find that the last-layer strategy performs better. The last-layer strategy aims to minimize the mean squared errors between the attention patterns $\boldsymbol{A}^S$, output hidden states $\boldsymbol{H}^S$ of the student's last Transformer layer and the counterpart $\boldsymbol{A}^T, \boldsymbol{H}^T$ of the teacher's last Transformer layer. The overall objective of the last-layer distillation $\mathcal{L}_{\mathrm{KD}}$ is formulated as:

$$
\mathcal{L}_{\mathrm{KD}} = \frac{1}{a}\sum_{i=1}^{a}\mathrm{MSE}(\boldsymbol{A}_i^S, \boldsymbol{A}_i^T) + \mathrm{MSE}(\boldsymbol{H}^S\boldsymbol{W}, \boldsymbol{H}^T),
\tag{4}
$$

where $\boldsymbol{A}_i^S$ and $\boldsymbol{A}_i^T$ mean the attention matrix corresponding to the i-th head in the last layer of student and teacher, respectively. The learnable matrix $\boldsymbol{W}$ is introduced to solve the problem of mismatched hidden size between the student model and the teacher model.

3   Methodology

Our proposed ETD strategy is general and can be applied to students of any size. It consists of three steps as shown in Fig. 1: (i) **Width-wise Extraction** that extracts parameters from the teacher to the *thin teacher* by following the principle of *hidden consistency* that will be introduced later. (ii) **Uniform Layer Selection** that selects layers of the thin teacher with the uniform strategy, and uses these parameters to initialize the student. (iii) **Transformer Distillation** that performs the last-layer distillation introduced before.

Width-Wise Extraction. The width-wise extraction includes the extraction of FFN neurons, head neurons, and hidden neurons, which is illustrated in Fig. 2. Specifically, we refer to the activation units in the intermediate layer of FFN as FFN neurons, which are represented by the gray circles in the figure, and call the activation units in each attention head of MHA as head neurons, which are

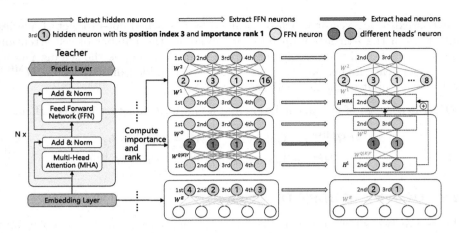

Fig. 2. Overview of width-wise extraction that includes the extraction of FFN neurons in the intermediate layer of FFN, head neurons in each attention head of MHA, and the hidden neurons.

represented by the green and blue circles in the figure. The hidden neurons, represented by the light blue circles in the figure, refer to the input and output activations of MHA and FFN, and the output of the embedding layer.

Because there are residual connections in the MHA and FFN modules, we argue that the extraction of hidden neurons should follow the principle of *hidden consistency* which means that the extracted hidden neurons of different modules/layers should have the same position indexes. For example, as illustrated in Fig. 2, the hidden neurons with some position indexes of 2 and 3 in different modules are extracted to meet the principle of hidden consistency. If the hidden consistency is not followed, the residual connection relationship will be destroyed, and the knowledge of reused teacher parameters will become chaotic. Experimental results in Table 1 confirm that if the hidden consistency principle is violated, reusing parameters of the teacher model will even bring negative effects to the student model. In addition, we call the group of hidden neurons whose position index is i in all sub-modules as the i-th hidden dimension. Extracting hidden neurons in our ETD strategy can be seen as selecting d_h' hidden dimensions from d_h ones, where d_h' and d_h refer to the hidden size of the student and the teacher, respectively.

Following this principle, we propose two different approaches to extract the teacher's parameters. (i) **ETD-Rand**: We randomly extract neurons and assign the corresponding weight parameters to the student model. (ii) **ETD-Impt**: We introduce the score-based pruning method in reference [15] to extract the relatively important weights from the teacher model. Specifically, in ETD-Impt, we calculate the importance of a neuron by the impact on the pre-training loss $\mathcal{L}$ if we remove it. Formally, we denote the i-th FFN neuron's value in the intermediate layer of FFN as $\boldsymbol{f}_i$. Using the first-order Taylor expansion, its importance I_{f_i} can be calculated as:

$$I_{f_i} = \left| \mathcal{L} - \mathcal{L}_{f_i=0} \right|,$$
$$= \left| \mathcal{L} - (\mathcal{L} + \frac{\partial \mathcal{L}}{\partial \boldsymbol{f}_i}(0 - \boldsymbol{f}_i) + R_1(\boldsymbol{f}_i)) \right|, \qquad (5)$$
$$\approx \left| \frac{\partial \mathcal{L}}{\partial \boldsymbol{f}_i} \boldsymbol{f}_i \right|.$$

The item $R_1(\boldsymbol{f}_i)$ is the remainder of the first-order Taylor expansion so we can ignore it. Similarly, we denote the i-th head neuron's value in a head as $\boldsymbol{h}_i$, whose importance I_{h_i} can be calculated by:

$$I_{h_i} = \left| \frac{\partial \mathcal{L}}{\partial \boldsymbol{h}_i} \boldsymbol{h}_i \right|. \qquad (6)$$

As shown in Fig. 2, we extract the neurons in each head while keeping the number of attention heads. Because attention-based distillation has the constraint that the head number of the student should be the same as the teacher. Then, we denote the i-th input hidden neuron of the MHA module in the l-th Transformer layer as n_i^l and the j-th hidden dimension as d_j. Their importance is denoted as $I_{n_i^l}$ and I_{d_j}, respectively, which can be calculated by:

$$I_{n_i^l} = \left| \frac{\partial \mathcal{L}}{\partial \boldsymbol{n}_i^l} \boldsymbol{n}_i^l \right|, \qquad (7)$$

$$I_{d_j} = \sum_{l=0}^{N} I_{n_j^l}, \qquad (8)$$

where $\boldsymbol{n}_i^l$ means the value of the hidden neuron, N means the number of the teacher's transformer layers. Our preliminary experiments found that summing the neurons' importance of all Transformer layers in the same hidden dimension is a better choice to obtain I_{d_j}. Finally, after calculating the importance scores of all types of neurons, we extract neurons with the highest scores.

According to [15], we choose the first 10 thousand sentences in training data to calculate the importance of neurons.[1]

Uniform Layer Selection. After width-wise extraction, we get a thin teacher model, which has the same width as the student. Assuming that the thin teacher and the student have N and M Transformer layers respectively, we choose M layers from the thin teacher model to initialize the student model, and use the set S to represent the chosen layers. It's necessary to include 0 in S because the index 0 refers to the embedding layer. Formally, the strategy of layer selection

---

[1] The FLOPs (floating-point operations) of calculating the importance score by 10 thousand sentences in training data is 2.5e15, we ignore this computational cost in Table 1 because of the large difference of magnitude.

we apply is uniform-strategy ($S = \left\{0, \lfloor \frac{N}{M} \rfloor, \lfloor \frac{2N}{M} \rfloor, ..., N\right\}$). The other two typical strategies include top-strategy ($S = \{0, N-M+1, N-M+2, ..., N\}$) and bottom-strategy ($S = \{0, 1, 2, ..., M\}$). Our experiments show that the uniform-strategy achieves better results than the other strategies.

Transformer Distillation. We empirically found that the last-layer distillation strategy performs better than the uniform one. Thus, we adopt the last-layer distillation strategy in ETD. As for the performance gap between these two strategies, we can see the experimental results shown in Table 1 as "ETD-TinyBERT" (uniform) and "ETD-Impt" (last-layer).

4   Experiments

4.1   Experimental Setup

Datasets. We use English Wikipedia and Toronto Book Corpus [30] for the distillation data. The maximum sequence length is 512. For evaluation, we use tasks from GLUE benchmark [24] and SQuADv1.1 [17]. We report F1 for SQuADv1.1, Matthews correlation (Mcc) for CoLA, and accuracy (Acc) for other tasks.

Implementation Details. We use BERT-Base as our teacher. BERT-Base is a 12-layer Transformer with 768 hidden size. Our ETD method is generic and can be applied to students with varied architectures. To prove it, we instantiate two student models, which are 6-layer and 4-layer models with 384 hidden size, respectively. They have different widths than the teacher.

We perform the last-layer distillation based on the released TinyBERT code[2] and follow the training setting: the batch size and the peak learning rate is set to 128 and 1e-4, respectively, the warm-up proportion is set to 10%. The number of training epochs for task-agnostic distillation is set to 5 by following references [9,10].[3] For GLUE fine-tuning, we set the batch size to 32, choose the learning rate from {5e-6, 1e-5, 2e-5, 3e-5} and epochs from {4, 5, 10}. For SQuADv1.1 fine-tuning, we set the batch size to 16, the learning rate to 3e-5, and the number of training epochs to 4.

Baselines. As shown in Table 1, "BERT-Base (Teacher)" is the teacher model of our distillation process. Additionally, we also report the results of Distil-BERT [19] as a baseline although it's not a fair comparison because of the different model parameter amounts (DistilBERT is a 6-layer model whose width remains the same as the teacher model). "Rand-Init" is our proposed baseline method which initializes the student randomly with the last-layer distillation strategy. The only difference with ETD is that Rand-Init does not reuse the

---

[2] The released code of TinyBERT: https://github.com/huawei-noah/Pretrained-Language-Model/tree/master/TinyBERT.

[3] The training time that we distill a 6-layer student with 384 hidden size for 5 epochs is (80 h * 8 V100 cards).

Table 1. Comparison between the performance of student models with different initialization strategies. The fine-tuning results are all averaged over 3 runs on the dev set. ‡ denotes that the results are taken from [21] and † means the models trained using the released code or the re-implemented code. We report the average score (Avg.) excluding the EM metric of SQuAD.

Strategy	#Params	#FLOPs (Training)	SST-2 (Acc)	MNLI (Acc)	MRPC (Acc)	CoLA (Mcc)	QNLI (Acc)	QQP (Acc)	STS-B (Acc)	SQuADv1.1 (F1/EM)	Avg.
BERT-Base(Teacher)	109M	6.43e19	93.6	84.7	87.9	59.6	91.6	91.4	89.6	88.4/81.0	85.85
DistilBERT‡ [19]	66M	–	91.3	82.2	87.5	51.3	89.2	88.5	86.9	85.8/77.7	82.84
Main results: distill the 6-layer student model with 384 hidden size											
Rand-Init	22M	1.55e19	90.9	81.6	86.0	36.5	89.0	89.3	88.3	85.0/76.6	80.83
ETD-Rand	22M	1.55e19	91.6	81.7	**87.2**	37.7	89.2	89.2	88.1	85.2/76.8	81.26
43% trained	22M	6.64e18	91.0	81.6	87.0	35.9	89.3	**89.4**	88.2	84.7/76.0	80.88
ETD-Impt	22M	1.55e19	91.3	**82.0**	87.1	**40.1**	**89.8**	89.2	**88.5**	**85.6/77.4**	**81.70**
28% trained	22M	4.43e18	**91.9**	81.4	87.1	37.2	89.5	89.2	88.4	84.7/76.1	81.17
ETD-wo-hidn-con	22M	1.55e19	90.6	81.0	86.0	36.1	89.1	88.9	88.2	84.9/76.1	80.60
Generality: combine with existing BERT distillation methods											
TinyBERT† [11]	22M	1.55e19	90.6	80.9	86.3	34.9	87.9	88.6	87.2	83.9/75.2	80.03
ETD-TinyBERT	22M	1.55e19	91.1	81.1	86.0	38.1	88.3	88.6	87.6	84.3/75.8	80.64
MiniLM† [25]	22M	1.55e19	90.3	81.4	84.2	35.7	88.8	89.1	88.5	84.5/75.7	80.30
ETD-MiniLM	22M	1.55e19	91.1	82.3	86.5	37.5	89.4	89.2	88.4	84.7/76.1	81.14
Generality: distill the 4-layer student model with 384 hidden size											
4L-Rand-Init	19M	1.47e19	89.2	79.2	85.0	25.4	87.9	**88.5**	87.8	81.7/72.2	78.07
4L-ETD-Impt	19M	1.47e19	**89.6**	**79.4**	84.5	**31.1**	**88.1**	88.3	**88.0**	**81.9/72.4**	**78.86**
35% trained	19M	5.25e18	89.4	78.9	**85.2**	27.4	87.5	88.2	87.8	81.1/71.5	78.18

teacher's parameters. "ETD-wo-hidn-con" is short for "ETD-without-hidden-consistency", which denotes that it violates the principle of hidden consistency. Specifically, we calculate the importance of the hidden neurons in each layer as shown in Eq. (7) and extract the most important ones inside each layer directly. Note that it does not guarantee that the position indexes of the extracted hidden neurons in each layer are the same, so it violates the principle. Moreover, in order to verify the generality of our ETD method, we apply ETD-Impt to different typical distillation methods (e.g., TinyBERT and MiniLM). "TinyBERT" refers to TinyBERT which only does task-agnostic distillation in our paper, and "ETD-TinyBERT/MiniLM" means that we use the ETD-Impt strategy to initialize the student model. We reproduced MiniLM ourselves because MiniLM doesn't share the model of this architecture setting.[4] For a fair comparison, we train them with the same hyper-parameters.

4.2   Main Results

The experimental results in Table 1 show that: 1) ETD-Rand/Impt strategies achieve comparable results to Rand-Init, while using only 43% and 28% computation cost (FLOPs), respectively. Compared with the baselines of TinyBERT

---

[4] The results differ from the original paper, possibly because we train with different hyper-parameters.

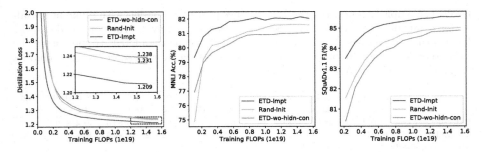

Fig. 3. The distillation loss curves and the score curves of MNLI and SQuADv1.1.

and MiniLM, ETD-Impt can achieve similar results with even less than 28% computation cost. 2) ETD-Impt is better than ETD-Rand which indicates that the fine-grained extraction is needed to achieve better results. 3) Reusing the teacher's parameters is beneficial for most tasks, especially for the tasks of CoLA and MRPC. 4) ETD is generic and can be combined with other distillation methods, such as TinyBERT or MiniLM, to improve their performance. Moreover, ETD works for the 4-layer architecture. Compared with the 6-layer architecture, the 4-layer architecture discards more knowledge in the uniform layer selection stage, which leads to more inadequate and discontinuous knowledge after it is initialized. However, it still achieves comparable results to 4L-Rand-Init with only 35% of the training time. 5) We also find that ETD-Impt can perform comparably to DistilBERT in 7 out of 8 tasks and is 3× smaller in size. 6) We demonstrate the effectiveness and necessity of following hidden consistency in Table 1 and Fig. 3. "ETD-wo-hidn-con" poses a negative effect on the performance and performs even worse than the "Rand-Init".

From the distillation loss shown in Fig. 3, we can get the same conclusion that the ETD method benefits the distillation efficiency. Moreover, the score curves of the two representative and complex tasks (MNLI and SQuADv1.1) are shown in Fig. 3. We find that lower loss during distillation largely indicates better performance at downstream tasks.

5   Ablation Study

In this section, we conduct ablation experiments to analyze the effects of different proposed techniques on the performance, such as width-wise extraction and the strategy of layer selection. Note that all student models are 6-layer with 384 hidden size in this section.

5.1   The Effect of Each Module

To understand each type of neuron's contribution, we also conduct the ablation experiments about the effect of FFN/head/hidden neurons in ETD-Impt.

Table 2. Ablation experiments to analyze the effects of different proposed techniques on the performance. The results are validated on the dev set and averaged over 3 runs. Distillation Loss refers to the final loss reached by the model at the end of training. Score refers to the average score of the GLUE tasks. We report the average score (Avg.) excluding the EM metric of SQuAD.

Setting	Distillation loss (Convergence)	Score	SQuADv1.1 (F1/EM)	Avg.
Rand-Init	1.231	80.24	85.0/76.6	80.83
ETD-Impt	**1.209**	**81.14**	**85.6/77.4**	**81.70**
ETD-Impt-rev-ffn	1.216	80.74	85.1/75.5	81.29
ETD-Impt-rev-head	1.218	80.50	85.4/76.7	81.12
ETD-Impt-rev-hidden	1.219	80.66	85.0/76.6	81.20
ETD-Impt-rev-all	1.227	80.38	84.9/76.3	80.95
ETD-Impt-top	1.215	80.55	85.3/76.8	81.14
ETD-Impt-bottom	1.217	80.64	85.2/76.7	81.21

As shown in Table 2, "ETD-Impt-rev-ffn" means that we extract the FFN neurons with the lowest importance scores instead of the highest ones. It can test the contribution of FFN neurons and the effectiveness of the importance score based method. It's the same with "ETD-Impt-rev-head" and "ETD-Impt-rev-hidden". Specially, "ETD-Impt-rev-all" means we reverse the importance ranks of all types of neurons. The results in Table 2 shown that: 1) Extracting the least important neurons hurts the performance, which means that all three types of neurons have positive effects on the distillation process and the model's performance in GLUE tasks and SQuAD. It also proves the effectiveness of our extracting method for these three types of neurons. Besides, we can know that among these three types of neurons, the FFN neuron's contribution is the smallest because the gap of distillation loss during convergence between "ETD-Impt" and "ETD-Impt-rev-ffn" is the closest. 2) The ETD method is always better than "Rand-Init", even if it reuses the least important parameters as shown in the comparison between "ETD-Impt-rev-all" and "Rand-Init", which further proves the effectiveness and necessity of reusing the teacher's parameters.

5.2 The Strategy of Layer Selection

We compare the proposed uniform-strategy with the other two strategies: top-strategy (ETD-Impt-top) and bottom-strategy (ETD-Impt-bottom). According to the comparison results, as shown in Table 2, we can find that: 1) The difference between bottom-strategy and top-strategy is not obvious. 2) The uniform strategy is the best performing strategy among them with obvious advantages. The results of the experiment indicate that uniform layer selection is a good strategy because it ensures that the student model can obtain the knowledge from the bottom to the top of the BERT model.

6   Related Work

Knowledge Distillation for BERT. Knowledge distillation [8] for BERT
compression can be categorized into task-agnostic BERT distillation [19,21,25]
and task-specific BERT distillation [9,20,22]. Task-agnostic distillation derives a
small general BERT with pre-trained BERT as the teacher and large-scale unsupervised corpus as the training dataset. Task-specific BERT distillation learns a
small fine-tuned BERT for a specific task with fine-tuned BERT as the teacher
and task dataset as the input. TinyBERT [11] proposes a two-stage distillation framework, including task-agnostic/specific distillation. Our work focuses
on task-agnostic distillation and aims to improve its efficiency.

Pruning. Model extraction is essentially a pruning method. Han [6] proposes
an iterative pruning method based on weight magnitude. Similarly, the lottery
tickets [4] use an iterative method to find the winning lottery ticket. However,
these works both require specialized hardware optimizations for acceleration due
to the irregular weight sparsity. There are some works of pruning-based Transformer compression [3,5,15,18,23,26,29]. In this paper, we propose the ETD
strategy that adopts pruning techniques to extract FFN/head/hidden neurons
of the teacher for finding a better initialization for the student.

7   Conclusion and Future Work

In this paper, we proposed a flexible strategy of reusing teacher's parameters
named ETD for efficient task-agnostic distillation. The experimental results show
that our method significantly improves the efficiency of task-agnostic distillation
and the fine-grained method ETD-Impt performs better than the random extraction ETD-Rand. In the future, we will optimize the strategy of layer selection
and study more advanced pruning methods for ETD, such as L0 penalty [23]
and group lasso [28].

Acknowledgements. This work is supported in part by NSFC (Grant No. 61872215),
Shenzhen Science and Technology Program (Grant No. RCYX20200714114523079),
and Shenzhen Nanshan District Ling-Hang Team Project (Grant No. LHTD20170005).

References

1. Clark, K., Luong, M.T., Le, Q.V., Manning, C.D.: ELECTRA: pre-training text
   encoders as discriminators rather than generators. In: ICLR 2019
2. Devlin, J., Chang, M.W., Lee, K., et al.: BERT: pre-training of deep bidirectional
   transformers for language understanding. In: NAACL 2019
3. Fan, A., Grave, E., Joulin, A.: Reducing transformer depth on demand with structured dropout. In: ICLR (2019)
4. Frankle, J., Carbin, M.: The lottery ticket hypothesis: finding sparse, trainable
   neural networks. In: ICLR (2018)
5. Gordon, M.A., Duh, K., Andrews, N.: Compressing BERT: studying the effects of
   weight pruning on transfer learning. In: ACL (2020)

6. Han, S., Pool, J., Tran, J., Dally, W.J.: Learning both weights and connections for efficient neural networks. In: NIPS (2015)
7. Hendrycks, D., Gimpel, K.: Gaussian error linear units (GELUs). arXiv preprint arXiv:1606.08415 (2016)
8. Hinton, G., Vinyals, O., Dean, J.: Distilling the knowledge in a neural network. arXiv preprint arXiv:1503.02531 (2015)
9. Hou, L., Huang, Z., Shang, L., Jiang, X., Chen, X., Liu, Q.: DynaBERT: dynamic BERT with adaptive width and depth. In: NIPS (2020)
10. Jiao, X., Chang, H., Yin, Y., et al.: Improving task-agnostic BERT distillation with layer mapping search. arXiv preprint arXiv:2012.06153 (2020)
11. Jiao, X., Yin, Y., Shang, L., et al.: TinyBERT: distilling BERT for natural language understanding. In: EMNLP 2020: Findings (2020)
12. Lan, Z., Chen, M., Goodman, S., Gimpel, K., et al.: ALBERT: a lite BERT for self-supervised learning of language representations. In: ICLR (2019)
13. Liu, Y., Ott, M., Goyal, N., Du, J., et al.: RoBERTa: a robustly optimized BERT pretraining approach. CoRR (2019)
14. McCarley, J., Chakravarti, R., Sil, A.: Structured pruning of a BERT-based question answering model. arXiv preprint arXiv:1910.06360 (2019)
15. Michel, P., Levy, O., Neubig, G.: Are sixteen heads really better than one? In: NIPS (2019)
16. Raffel, C., Shazeer, N., Roberts, A., Lee, K., Narang, S., et al.: Exploring the limits of transfer learning with a unified text-to-text transformer. In: JMLR (2020)
17. Rajpurkar, P., Zhang, J., Lopyrev, K., Liang, P.: Squad: 100,000+ questions for machine comprehension of text. In: EMNLP (2016)
18. Sajjad, H., Dalvi, F., Durrani, N., Nakov, P.: Poor man's BERT: smaller and faster transformer models. arXiv preprint arXiv:2004.03844 (2020)
19. Sanh, V., Debut, L., Chaumond, J., Wolf, T.: DistilBERT, a distilled version of BERT: smaller, faster, cheaper and lighter. arXiv preprint arXiv:1910.01108 (2019)
20. Sun, S., Cheng, Y., Gan, Z., Liu, J.: Patient knowledge distillation for BERT model compression. In: EMNLP-IJCNLP (2019)
21. Sun, Z., Yu, H., Song, X., Liu, R., Yang, Y., Zhou, D.: MobileBERT: a compact task-agnostic BERT for resource-limited devices. In: ACL (2020)
22. Tang, R., Lu, Y., Liu, L., Mou, L., et al.: Distilling task-specific knowledge from BERT into simple neural networks. arXiv preprint arXiv:1903.12136 (2019)
23. Voita, E., Talbot, D., Moiseev, F., et al.: Analyzing multi-head self-attention: specialized heads do the heavy lifting, the rest can be pruned. In: ACL (2019)
24. Wang, A., Singh, A., Michael, J., et al.: GLUE: a multi-task benchmark and analysis platform for natural language understanding. In: EMNLP (2018)
25. Wang, W., Wei, F., Dong, L., Bao, H., et al.: MiniLM: deep self-attention distillation for task-agnostic compression of pre-trained transformers. In: NIPS (2020)
26. de Wynter, A., Perry, D.J.: Optimal subarchitecture extraction for BERT. arXiv preprint arXiv:2010.10499 (2020)
27. Yang, Z., Dai, Z., Yang, Y., Carbonell, J., Salakhutdinov, R.R., Le, Q.V.: XLNet: generalized autoregressive pretraining for language understanding. In: NIPS (2019)
28. Yuan, M., Lin, Y.: Model selection and estimation in regression with grouped variables. J. R. Stat. Soc. Ser. B **68**(1), 49–67 (2006)
29. Zhang, Z., Qi, F., Liu, Z., Liu, Q., Sun, M.: Know what you don't need: single-shot meta-pruning for attention heads. arXiv preprint arXiv:2011.03770 (2020)
30. Zhu, Y., Kiros, R., Zemel, R., et al.: Aligning books and movies: towards story-like visual explanations by watching movies and reading books. In: ICCV (2015)

Medical Image Processing

Semi-supervised Learning Based Right Ventricle Segmentation Using Deep Convolutional Boltzmann Machine Shape Model

Kaimin Liao, Ziyu Gan, and Xuan Yang[✉]

Shenzhen University, Shenzhen, China
yangxuan@szu.edu.cn

Abstract. Automated Right Ventricle (RV) segmentation is a challenge due to the RV's variable shape and the lack of labelled data. This paper proposes a semi-supervised learning method based on a convolutional deep Boltzmann machine (CDBM). A CDBM is constructed to learn the complex shape of RV using the short-run MCMC. Next, a semi-supervised learning network composing of a CDBM and two CNNs is proposed. The CNNs and the CDBM have trained alternatively; labelled data are used to train the CNNs, and CDBM reconstructs the predicted results of unlabelled data using the CNNs to guide the training of CNNs further. During this procedure, the CDBM is trained at the same time. Our approach's main idea is to extract the shape information of RV and use the shape information to improve CNN's performance. Our approach takes advantage of avoiding overfitting and requiring less labelled data. Besides, our approach does not increase any extra computational cost and parameters during inference. The experiment results show that our approach can improve segmentation accuracy when the labelled training data is small.

Keywords: Deep Boltzmann Machine · Right ventricle segmentation · Semi-supervised learning · Convolutional Neural Network

1 Introduction

Evaluation of RV structure and function has got more and more attention due to its importance in most cardiac disorders. Automatic RV segmentation is a difficult task due to the fuzziness of the cavity borders and the complex crescent shapes [13]. In recent years, many RV segmentation methods based on convolutional neural networks (CNNs) are proposed with the development of deep learning. Compared with the traditional methods, such as the level set and atlas-based methods, CNN-based methods significantly improve RV segmentation accuracy.

Two commonly used network architectures to perform RV segmentation include the fully convolutional network (FCN) and the U-Net. However, the

This work was supported by the National Natural Science Foundation of China (61871269).

I. Farkaš et al. (Eds.): ICANN 2021, LNCS 12893, pp. 585–597, 2021.
https://doi.org/10.1007/978-3-030-86365-4_47

low-level features are not directly taken part in the decoder in FCN. The U-Net [15] overcame this issue by employing a series of encoders and decoders with different levels. Because of the excellent architecture and excellent performance in medical image segmentation, U-Nets have become one of the most popular models in pixel-wise segmentation. Many methods based on U-Nets are proposed to perform RV segmentation. To reduce the network model parameters, [6] use the E-Net [12], which made efficient use of scarce resources available on embedded platforms for RV segmentation and achieve high performance. Yang et al. [20] proposed a dense connected U-Net and improved the accuracy of RV segmentation by introducing dense connections in U-Net and shape constraints. To make the U-Net light, Liu et al. [7] proposed a squeeze expand attention (SEA) module, which combined squeezing, expanding, and adaptive weighting of features to generate feature maps to replace the convolution blocks in the U-Net. To improve the segmentation accuracy further, more complex and larger CNNs, such as U-Net++ [21], Attention u-net [11] and r2u-net [1], are proposed.

However, there are still issues with existed methods. The first one is lacking sufficient shape constraints in RV segmentation. Although [20] and [7] both constrained the RV shape by contour distance between the ground truth and the predicted shape, the restriction is not strong enough to lead to reasonable RV shapes. The second issue in RV segmentation is lacking enough annotation data. So far, there is a large gap between the training accuracy and testing accuracy in most CNN-based methods.

This paper focuses on tackling these limitations by employing a deep Boltzmann machine (DBM) to learn the RV shape and generate reasonable RV shapes. DBM is a network of symmetrically coupled stochastic binary units, which can be used to discover implied representations of input data. An attractive advantage of DBM is the unsupervised learning on unlabelled data and can be fine-tuned for a specific task using labelled data. Furthermore, the approximate inference procedure for DBMs incorporates top-down feedback in addition to the usual bottom-up pass, allowing DBM to incorporate uncertainty about missing or noisy inputs [17]. DBM can be used to generate shape models. Eslami et al. [2] constructed a robust model of binary shape using DBM, which can be trained on a relatively small dataset to generate realistic samples. Wu et al. [19] embedded the DBM shape into a distance regularized level set-based segmentation method for heart shape tracking. They also pointed out that the trained shape model can generate realistic samples even if trained with a relatively small-sized training dataset.

Eslami et al. [2] pointed out that the DBM has an excellent ability in inpainting corrupted images. Inspired by [2], we employ a convolutional deep Boltzmann machine (CDBM) with short-run MCMC [10] to learn the shape of RV. Moreover, a semi-supervised learning network is proposed to segment RV. Our proposed network composes of two CNNs and a CDBM. Two CNNs are with the same architecture used to predict endocardium and epicardium, respectively. The CDBM is trained to reconstruct the shape prior information of RV from unlabelled data. Two CNNs and the CDBM are trained alternatively, where two CNNs are trained using labelled data and the reconstructed shape obtained by CDBM from unlabelled data. On the other hand, two CNNs provide prediction results of unlabelled data to be the Gibbs chain's initial data to train the CDBM. Our proposed network is trained in an unsupervised learning way by combining labelled data and unlabelled data in the loss function.

To our knowledge, it is the first work to combine a DBM and CNNs to perform RV segmentation. Contributions of our work include:

– A convolutional deep Boltzmann machine is constructed and trained to learn the complex RV shapes. The short-run MCMC is used to train our CDBM and makes the training easy and robust.
– A semi-supervised learning network is proposed to perform RV segmentation. Using labelled data and unlabelled data alternatively, CNNs and our CDBM are trained alternatively. The reconstructed shape obtained by CDBM from unlabelled data introduces shape constraint into the training of CNNs, which is beneficial to improve the segmentation accuracy of CNNs.
– For a small-sized training dataset, CNN's predictive accuracy can be improved obviously by employing semi-supervised learning. More importantly, less annotation training data is required to train the network to achieve the conventional training method's accuracy using a large amount of labelled data.

2   Convolutional Deep Boltzmann Machine

2.1   Architecture of CDBM

The CDBM is evolved from the deep Boltzmann machine (DBM) by replacing the original dense layer with a convolutional layer to overcome the parameter increase problem when dealing with the high-resolution images. Compared with DBM, CDBM has a better translation invariance and fewer parameters. The architecture of our CDBM is with one visual layer and four hidden layers, as illustrated in Fig. 1. It is needed to explain that the number of hidden layers is related to the reconstruction results. When the number of hidden layers is small, for example, using three layers, the contour of reconstruction shape is not clear, or even the training procedure cannot guarantee convergence. When there are too many hidden layers, for example, more than five layers, the reconstruction shape does not improve obviously, but the network training time has increased significantly.

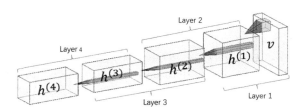

Fig. 1. The architecture of our CDBM. v is the visible layer. $h^{(l)}$ is the lth hidden layer, and $f^{(l)}$ is its corresponding convolution kernels.

The endocardium and epicardium masks are input to the CDBM as v aiming to constrain the endocardium shape and epicardium shape to each other. Indeed, based on our experiments, both endocardium and epicardium masks as input outperform only endocardium masks or only epicardium masks as input for CDBM. When only endocardium masks are provided, this mutual restraint is not required due to one input channel of v.

The energy of CDBM is defined as:

$$E(v, h; \theta) = -\sum_{i,j,k} b_k v_{ijk} - \sum_{l=1}^{4}\sum_{ijk} c_k^{(l)} h_{ijk}^{(l)} - \sum_{ijk}\left(v \otimes f^{(1)}\right)_{ijk} h_{ijk}^{(1)} - \sum_{l=2}^{4}\sum_{ijk}\left(h^{(l-1)} \otimes f^{(l)}\right)_{ijk} h_{ijk}^{(l)},$$

(1)

where $\otimes$ represents the convoltional operator; $\theta = \{b, c^{(l)}, f^{(l)}\}_{l=1,2,3,4}$ is the parameters of CDBM; $h^{(l)}, l = 1, 2, 3, 4$ is the units in the lth hidden layer; $f^{(l)}$ and $c^{(l)}$ are the convolution kernels and the bias of the lth hidden layer, respectively; b is the bias of the visible layer. i, j, k represent the index of input and the index of channel, respectively. The probability that the model assigns to visible units v is $P(v; \theta) = \frac{\sum_h e^{-E(v,h;\theta)}}{Z(\theta)}$, where $Z(\theta) = \sum_v \sum_h e^{-E(v,h;\theta)}$.

2.2   Training

Training the CDBM is to maximize the log-likelihood of $P(v_d; \theta)$, where v_d is the training data. The gradient of $P(v_d; \theta)$ with respect to θ can be derived as:

$$\frac{\partial ln P(v_d; \theta)}{\partial \theta} = -\mathbb{E}_{P(h|v_d)}\frac{\partial E(v_d, h; \theta)}{\partial \theta} + \mathbb{E}_{P(v,h)}\frac{\partial E(v, h; \theta)}{\partial \theta},$$

(2)

where $\mathbb{E}_{P(h|v_{data})}$ is the data-dependent expectation and $\mathbb{E}_{P(v,h)}$ is the model expectation. Due to intractable computation of $\mathbb{E}_{P(h|v_d)}$ and $\mathbb{E}_{P(v,h)}$, approximation computation is needed. $\mathbb{E}_{P(v,h)}$ can be approximated by Gibbs sampling [5], and the data-dependent expectation $\mathbb{E}_{P(h|v_d)}$ can be approximated using mean-field inference [9]. In mean-field inference, the true distribution $P(h^{(1)}, h^{(2)}, h^{(3)}, h^{(4)}|v)$, denoted as $P(h|v)$, is approximated by distribution $Q(h^{(1)}, h^{(2)}, h^{(3)}, h^{(4)}|v)$, denoted as $Q(h|v)$, as

$$Q(h^{(1)}, h^{(2)}, h^{(3)}, h^{(4)}|v) = \prod_{l=1}^{4}\prod_{i,j,k} Q(h_{i,j,k}^{(l)}|v).$$

(3)

To derive the expression of $Q(h^{(l)} = 1|v)$, the evidence lower bound $ELBO = ln P(v) - D_{KL}(Q(h|v)||P(h|v))$ is maximized, aiming to maiximize the log-likelihood of the training data and minmize the Kullback-Leibler divergences D_{KL} between the approximating distribution $Q(h|v)$ and true distribution $P(h|v)$. Denote $Q(h^{(l)} = 1|v)$ as $\hat{h}^{(l)}$, the $ELBO$ can be maximized by updating $\hat{h}_i^{(l)}$ iteratively with the fixed θ:

$$\hat{h}^{(1)} = \sigma\left(v \otimes f^{(1)} + \hat{h}^{(2)} \otimes^T f^{(2)} + c^{(1)}\right)$$

(4a)

$$\hat{h}^{(2)} = \sigma \left(\hat{h}^{(1)} \otimes f^{(2)} + \hat{h}^{(3)} \otimes^T f^{(3)} + c^{(2)} \right) \tag{4b}$$

$$\hat{h}^{(3)} = \sigma \left(\hat{h}^{(2)} \otimes f^{(3)} + \hat{h}^{(4)} \otimes^T f^{(4)} + c^{(3)} \right) \tag{4c}$$

$$\hat{h}^{(4)} = \sigma \left(\hat{h}^{(3)} \otimes f^{(4)} + c^{(4)} \right) \tag{4d}$$

The mean-field inference is performed by updating $\hat{h}^{(1)}, \hat{h}^{(2)}, \hat{h}^{(3)}$ and $\hat{h}^{(4)}$ alternatively using Eqs. (4a), (4b), (4c), (4d) until convergence. Correspondingly, $P(h|v)$ can be approximated and the gradient in (2) can be approximated efficiently.

Denote v_m and h_m as the units sampled by the Gibbs sampling algorithm, the computation details of gradients in (2) are described as follow:

$$\frac{\partial lnP(v_d; \theta)}{\partial f_k^{(1)}} = \frac{\sum_{i,j} (\hat{h}^{(1)}_{i,j,k} v_{d(i,j)} - h_m^{(1)}{}_{i,j,k} v_{m(i,j)})}{N_1 \times N_1} \tag{5a}$$

$$\frac{\partial lnP(v_d; \theta)}{\partial f_k^{(l)}} = \frac{\sum_{i,j} (\hat{h}^{(l)}_{i,j,k} \hat{h}^{(l-1)}_{(i,j)} - h_m^{(l)}{}_{i,j,k} h_m^{(l-1)}{}_{(i,j)})}{N_l \times N_l} \tag{5b}$$

$$\frac{\partial lnP(v_d; \theta)}{\partial b} = \frac{\sum_{i,j} (v_{di,j} - v_{mi,j})}{N_v \times N_v} \tag{5c}$$

$$\frac{\partial lnP(v_d; \theta)}{\partial c^{(l)}} = \frac{\sum_{i,j} (\hat{h}^{(l)}_{i,j} - h_m^{(l)}{}_{i,j})}{N_l \times N_l}, l = 1, 2, 3 \tag{5d}$$

where $\hat{h}^{(l)}_{i,j,k}$ and $h_m^{(l)}{}_{i,j,k}$ are the mean-field inference value and Gibbs sampling value of $h^{(l)}$ at (i,j,k), respectively; N_l and N_v are the width and height of $h^{(l)}$ and v, respectively; $f_k^{(l)}$ is the kth kernel in the l layer. $v_{(i,j)}$ denotes an $N \times N$ sub-window of v with the top-left corner at pixel $(i \times s, j \times s)$, where N is the size of the convolutional kernel in the first layer, and s is the stride of convolution in the first layer. Similarly, $h^{(k)}_{(i,j)}$ represents the sub-window of $h^{(k)}$.

CD and persistent CD (PCD) are commonly used algorithms to speed up the above iteration to "close" to its steady state. However, the CD is poor at obtaining an optimal approximation of the joint-density model [4]. PCD is faster than CD in convergence; when the learning rate is lower than the Markov chain mixing rate, PCD achieves close to the steady-state rapidly [16]. However, once the learning rate or decay schedule is not proper, the samples from Gibbs sampling will be far from the true model's expectation for PCD. These problems become severe when learning deeper DBM with variable training data.

To overcome these problems, we use the short-run MCMC [10] to train our CDBM. The difference between CD and short-run MCMC is that the short-run MCMC is initialized from noise, while CD initializes from observed images. The conventional MCMC tries to maintain the chain initialized by any distribution and iterating any number of steps. In contrast, the short-run MCMC only maintains the fixed initial distribution and a fixed number of steps so that the short-run MCMC will be easier to train. The theoretical understanding of short-run MCMC is based on a generalized moment matching estimator. In the sampling procedure of short-run MCMC, the Markov chain is initialized by a fixed distribution of p_0, such as the uniform noise distribution, and ran a fixed number, e.g., K steps. Let M_θ be the K-steps short-run MCMC transition kernel, define $q_\theta(v, h)$ as

$$q_\theta(v, h) = (M_\theta p_0)(z) = \int M_\theta(v, h) p_0(z) dz, \qquad (6)$$

which is the distribution of the CDBM units after running K-step MCMC from p_0. The data sampled by Gibbs sampling is called negative data, and the training data is called positive data. One training iteration of training our CDBM using short-run MCMC is presented in Algorithm 1.

Algorithm 1: One training iteration for CDBM with short-run MCMC
___
Input: a batch of positive data v_d, a batch of negative data v sampled from the uniform
    distribution p_0, short-run steps K, the parameters of CDBM θ
Output: θ
  1: Run K-steps Gibbs Sample initialized by v to obtain $h_m^{(l)}$ and v_m;
  2: Run mean-field updates with v_d using (4a), (4b), (4c), (4d) to obtain $\hat{h}^{(l)}$;
  3: Calculate the gradient using (5a), (5b), (5c) and (5d);
  4: update θ.

Moreover, the layer-wise pre-training algorithm proposed by [16] is employed to find the proper initial parameters of our CDBM. Here, the CDBM is treated as the stack of convolutional RBMs, and these RBMs are trained from bottom to top.

3   Semi-supervised Learning Network

To segment RV, a semi-supervised learning network is proposed, composed of two convolutional neural networks(CNNs) and a CDBM. In our proposed network, the U-Net is employed as the CNN due to their outstanding pixel-wise segmentation performance. A U-Net has four downsampling operations and four upsampling operations implemented by the 2×2 max-pooling and the 2×2 transpose convolution with 2×2 strides. The size of the convolution kernels is 3×3. All the activation functions are the Relu except for the last layer. The activation function of the final layer is the logistic function. Zero paddings are used to keep the size of the feature map the same.

For our CDBM, the training data is the mask of endocardium and epicardium, so v has two channels. The size of v is $58 \times 58 \times 2$. In the first layer of CDBM, 32 16×16 convolution kernels with strides 2 are used, so the size of $h^{(1)}$ is $22 \times 22 \times 32$. 128 convolution kernels in the second layer are 8×8 in size with strides 2, which leads to $h^{(2)}$ $8 \times 8 \times 512$ in size. 256 convolution kernels in the third layer are 4×4 in size with strides 2, and $h^{(3)}$ is $3 \times 3 \times 256$. A full connection is between $h^{(3)}$ and $h^{(4)}$, and the number of units in $h^{(4)}$ is 512.

3.1 Network Training

In the network training, the U-Nets and the CDBM are trained alternatively. The entire training procedure of our network is shown in Fig. 2. At first, the labelled images are input to two U-nets to predict endocardium and epicardium, respectively. Part of the loss function $L_{labelled}$ is the cross-entropy loss between the prediction results p and the ground truth g. Next, the unlabelled images are input to the U-nets to predict endocardium and epicardium, and these prediction results v are input to the CDBM to reconstruct the RV shapes r by inference procedure. Correspondingly, $L_{unlabelled}$ is computed as the cross-entropy loss between the prediction results v and the reconstruction shape r. When prediction results are close to the prior distribution of shape, v are similar to r; otherwise, there is a significant difference. The total loss function is defined as,

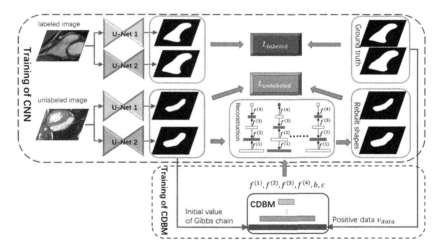

Fig. 2. The architecture and semi-supervised learning procedure of our network. The blue lines and green lines illustrate the training flow of labelled data and unlabelled data, respectively. (Color figure online)

$$L = L_{labelled} + \alpha L_{unlabelled}, \tag{7}$$

where $L_{labelled}$ and $L_{unlabelled}$ are a partial loss for labelled data and unlabelled data, respectively, which can be the soft dice loss or the cross-entropy loss; α is the weight for unlabelled loss term.

Based on Algorithm 1, the positive data v_d and the data v sampled from p_0 are needed for training CDBM. Here, the prediction results p of two U-Nets are the positive data v_d. It is required the explain that we do not take the random distribution as the initial distribution p_0 in short-run MCMC because we want to reconstruct the RV mask close to the exact RV shape. However, the random initial distribution of p_0 will generate RV shapes variously. This diversity might result in RV shapes far away from our expectations. The most intuitive idea is taking U-Net's output as p_0 so that the samples from p_0 are close to our expectations. Correspondingly, our CDBM will learn the detailed difference between the RV shape and the prediction result.

Another issue that should be explained during the reconstruction procedure is the partial reconstruction in CDBM. The Gibbs chain starts with the predictive results of two U-Nets and runs a few steps. The visible units are updated using the hidden layer information and are enforced close to the shape prior in the inference procedure. Finally, the visible units are the reconstructed RV shape. It is known that one of the advantages of Boltzmann machine is its ability to estimate $P(v - v_f | v_f)$ where v_f is part of the visual units v, $v_f \subseteq v$. That means partial reconstruction can be achieved using our CDBM, where $v - v_f$ is updated instead of the entire v in Gibbs sampling. Compared with reconstructing the entire mask, partial reconstruction will be more stable when the v_f is the main part of objects. We select v_f as the determined prediction results instead of the ambiguous prediction results in our experiments. The referenced result v_i will be part of v, and v_f is a fixed part of v during the inference procedure. Figure 3 demonstrates several reconstruction results using our CDBM.

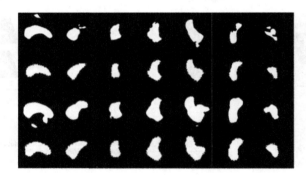

Fig. 3. Demonstration of reconstruction results. The first and third rows show the prediction results of the endocardium and epicardium using two U-Nets. The second and the fourth rows illustrate corresponding reconstruction results using our CDBM, respectively.

4   Experiments and Results

To evaluate the performance of our network, two public datasets are used. One is the MICCAI 2012 Right Ventricle Segmentation Challenge (RVSC) dataset, which consists of MR images from 48 patients. Endocardial and epicardial contours at both ED and ES phases are delineated by experts manually. The RVSC dataset includes one training set and two test sets. The training set is taken as the labelled data, and the data of the last three patients in the training set are separated as the validation set. For RVSC, all images are cropped to 176×176. The other dataset is the automatic cardiac segmentation challenge (ACDC) dataset, which consists of cardiac MRI from 150 patients divided into five evenly distributed subgroups, four pathological plus one healthy subject group. The training set contains 100 patients, and the testing set is composed of the remaining 50 patients. All images from ACDC are rescaled to 1.25 mm/pixel and cropped to 256×256. Besides, all the images that do not include the RV are deleted. Performance of RV segmentation is evaluated by dice metric (DM) and Hausdorff distance (HD).

Due to the difference in two datasets in spatial resolution, some implement detail in our experiments is different: 1) The ACDC dataset only labels the endocardium so that the segmentation network will be only one U-Net. 2) We use a 5-layer CDBM with a smaller convolution kernel size for the RVSC dataset, while a 3-layer CDBM with a larger convolution kernel size is used for the ACDC dataset. 3) The soft dice loss is used for the RVSC dataset, and the cross-entropy loss is used for the ACDC dataset because the existing researches show that the soft dice loss is more suitable for the RVSC dataset.

To compare our network's performance with the traditional U-Net, a traditional U-Net is trained to perform RV segmentation as the baseline. For the RVSC dataset, three experiments are performed to evaluate our approach; experiments 1 and 2 take test set1 and test set2 in RVSC, respectively, as the unlabelled data for training and use the other test set to evaluate the performance. Moreover, the 1092 images from the ACDC dataset are used as the unlabelled data in Experiment 3 to evaluate our network's performance on two test sets of RVSC as a whole.

Comparison results of RVSC are listed in Table 1 and Table 2. In experiments 1 and 2, about 250 unlabelled images are used, which increases the Dice by about 0.1 for the endocardium. In experiment 3, Dice increases by about 0.2 for endocardium and about 0.1 for epicardium due to more unlabelled data. We are noted that our approach outperforms the baseline greatly regarding the Dice and the HD metrics. Besides, Fig. 4 illustrates the segmentation results of Experiment 3 and baseline, respectively. It is observed that the predictive results obtained by our network are more consistent with the ground-truth in RV shapes.

Table 1. Comparison of evaluation metrics Dice and HD using the baseline and our network.

	Testset1				Testset2			
	Endocardium		Epicardium		Endocardium		Epicardium	
	Dice	HD	Dice	HD	Dice	HD	Dice	HD
Baseline	0.846	8.70	0.883	8.79	0.867	5.41	0.891	6.25
Experiment 1	–	–	–	–	0.877	5.12	0.896	5.83
Experiment 2	0.861	7.72	0.885	8.11	–	–	–	–
Experiment 3	**0.880**	**6.90**	**0.898**	**6.46**	**0.886**	**5.07**	**0.904**	**5.44**

Furthermore, the comparison of our network and the state-of-art works are provided in Table 2. It can be seen that our network outperformed these works, whether for endocardium or epicardium segmentation and whether for Dice and HD metrics. This experiment implies that by employing more unlabelled data, more accurate results can be achieved. This conclusion supports our approach's basic idea in this paper, that is, through semi-supervised learning, better results can be obtained on small annotation training samples.

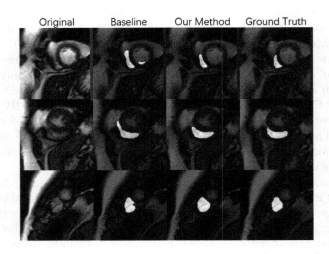

Fig. 4. Illustration of segmentation results of our approach and baseline.

Additionally, several experiments are performed using the ACDC dataset to compare our semi-supervised learning network's performance and that of the supervised learning network. Since the ACDC provides thousands of training images, which are enough to train the conventional CNN, we only take part in training data to compare our semi-supervised learning network and the supervised-learning network the U-Net. In this experiment, 10 patients, 20 patients, 40 patients, and 80 patients are used as the labelled data, respectively, and the rest patients are the unlabelled data. Five patients are selected to be the validation set, and there are 105 images. The other 15 patients, 235 test images, are selected to be the test set, which does not coincide with the training data. The numbers of labelled and unlabelled images are listed in Table 3.

Table 2. Comparison of evaluation metrics with the state-of-art researches using the RVSC dataset.

	Overall				Testset1				Testset2			
	Endocardium		Epicardium		Endocardium		Epicardium		Endocardium		Epicardium	
	Dice	HD	Dice	HD	Dice	HD	Dice	HD	Dice	HD	Dice	HD
Our approach	**0.883**	**5.985**	**0.901**	**5.95**	**0.880**	**6.90**	**0.898**	**6.46**	**0.886**	**5.07**	**0.904**	**5.44**
Guo et al. [3]	0.86	7.78	–	–	0.85	8.63	–	–	0.87	6.93	–	–
Luo et al. [8]	0.86	6.9	0.84	8.9	–	–	–	–	–	–	–	–
Tran V [18]	0.84	8.86	0.86	9.33	–	–	–	–	–	–	–	–
Ringenberg et al. [14]	0.83	8.89	0.86	9.30	0.83	9.05	0.86	9.60	0.83	8.73	0.86	9.00
Yang et al. [20]	0.865	6.43	0.892	6.62	–	–	–	–	–	–	–	–
Liu et al. [20]	0.86	7.32	0.88	8.52	–	–	–	–	–	–	–	–

Comparison of Dice and HD metrics between the supervised-learning-based network and our network is listed in Table 3. It can be seen that when the labelled data is small, such as experiment a, our network outperformed the supervised-learning-based network significantly. It shows that by introducing unlabelled data in training, the network's predicted performance can be improved. Moreover, it also implies that our CDBM can infer the RV shape constraint correctly. It is needed to emphasize that the dice achieved by the supervised-learning network is 0.917 when all training datasets are used, while our network can achieve the comparable segmentation accuracy only using half of the training data. It further validates the advantages of our network in the absence of training data.

Figure 5 provides a comparison of the Dice curve with iterations during the U-Net training procedure and our network in Experiment a. 141 labelled training images, and 1077 additional unlabelled images are used in our network. It can be seen that our network consistently outperforms U-Net when small labelled training data provided. It implies that our network can provide reasonable RV shapes even the CNN cannot predict RV accurately in the initial stage of network training. Moreover, the more unlabelled data used, the more pronounced the performance improvement. Furthermore, it implies that the advantage of our approach for training speed as well.

Table 3. Segmentation accuracy on the 2017 MICCIA ACDC dataset.

Exp	Labelled data	Unlabelled data	Our method		Fully supervised	
			Dice	HD	Dice	HD
a	10 patients (141 images)	70 patients (1077 images)	0.845	15.42	0.73	20.78
b	20 patients (308 images)	60 patients (910 images)	0.895	9.80	0.882	12.32
c	40 patients (608 images)	40 patients (610 images)	**0.917**	**7.42**	0.905	8.25

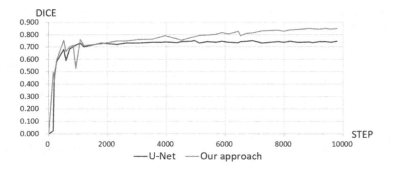

Fig. 5. The comparison of the Dice curve for Experiment a. The blue curve is the dice using fully-supervised U-Net, and the orange curve is that using our network. (Color figure online)

5   Conclusion

A semi-supervised learning network composed of CNNs and a CDBM is proposed to segment RV in this paper. A CDBM is constructed and trained using the short-run MCMC algorithm, which can learn RV shape distribution and generate new RV shapes. By combing the predictive results of CNNs and reconstructed shapes generated by CDBM, traditional CNNs are trained in a semi-supervised learning way. At the same time, the CDBM is trained using unlabelled data and output of CNNs. Guided by the reconstructed shapes, CNN's predictive results can be enforced to be consistent with the RV shapes. Experimental results show that the performance improvement in RV segmentation benefits from the reconstructed mask of unlabelled data. Moreover, through semi-supervised learning, better results can be obtained when only a small number of annotation data provided, which shows the advantages of our network in the absence of training data and our network prospects in applications.

References

1. Alom, M.Z., Hasan, M., Yakopcic, C., Taha, T.M., Asari, V.K.: Recurrent residual convolutional neural network based on U-Net (R2U-Net) for medical image segmentation. arXiv preprint arXiv:1802.06955 (2018)
2. Eslami, S.A., Heess, N., Williams, C.K., Winn, J.: The shape Boltzmann machine: a strong model of object shape. Int. J. Comput. Vision **107**(2), 155–176 (2014)
3. Guo, Z., Tan, W., et al.: Local motion intensity clustering (LMIC) model for segmentation of right ventricle in cardiac MRI images. IEEE J. Biomed. Health Inform. **23**(2), 723–730 (2018)
4. Hinton, G.E.: A practical guide to training restricted Boltzmann machines. In: Montavon, G., Orr, G.B., Müller, K.-R. (eds.) Neural Networks: Tricks of the Trade. LNCS, vol. 7700, pp. 599–619. Springer, Heidelberg (2012). https://doi.org/10.1007/978-3-642-35289-8_32

5. Hinton, G.E., Sejnowski, T.J.: Optimal perceptual inference. In: Proceedings of the IEEE Conference on Computer Vision and Pattern Recognition, vol. 448. Citeseer (1983)
6. Lieman-Sifry, J., Le, M., Lau, F., Sall, S., Golden, D.: FastVentricle: cardiac segmentation with ENet. In: Pop, M., Wright, G.A. (eds.) FIMH 2017. LNCS, vol. 10263, pp. 127–138. Springer, Cham (2017). https://doi.org/10.1007/978-3-319-59448-4_13
7. Liu, Z., Yang, X.: A squeeze convolutional network for MRI right ventricle segmentation. In: 2019 IEEE International Conference on Bioinformatics and Biomedicine (BIBM), pp. 697–700. IEEE (2019)
8. Luo, G., An, R., Wang, K., Dong, S., Zhang, H.: A deep learning network for right ventricle segmentation in short-axis MRI. In: 2016 Computing in Cardiology Conference (CinC), pp. 485–488. IEEE (2016)
9. Neal, R.M., Hinton, G.E.: A view of the EM algorithm that justifies incremental, sparse, and other variants. In: Jordan, M.I. (ed.) Learning in Graphical Models, pp. 355–368. Springer, Dordrecht (1998). https://doi.org/10.1007/978-94-011-5014-9_12
10. Nijkamp, E., Hill, M., et al.: Learning non-convergent non-persistent short-run MCMC toward energy-based model. In: Advances in Neural Information Processing Systems, pp. 5232–5242 (2019)
11. Oktay, O., et al.: Attention U-Net: learning where to look for the pancreas. arXiv preprint arXiv:1804.03999 (2018)
12. Paszke, A., Chaurasia, A., Kim, S., Culurciello, E.: ENet: a deep neural network architecture for real-time semantic segmentation. arXiv preprint arXiv:1606.02147 (2016)
13. Petitjean, C., et al.: Right ventricle segmentation from cardiac MRI: a collation study. Med. Image Anal. $19(1)$, 187–202 (2015)
14. Ringenberg, J., Deo, M., et al.: Fast, accurate, and fully automatic segmentation of the right ventricle in short-axis cardiac MRI. Comput. Med. Imaging Graph. $\mathbf{38}(3)$, 190–201 (2014)
15. Ronneberger, O., Fischer, P., Brox, T.: U-Net: convolutional networks for biomedical image segmentation. In: Navab, N., Hornegger, J., Wells, W.M., Frangi, A.F. (eds.) MICCAI 2015. LNCS, vol. 9351, pp. 234–241. Springer, Cham (2015). https://doi.org/10.1007/978-3-319-24574-4_28
16. Salakhutdinov, R., Hinton, G.: Deep Boltzmann machines. In: Artificial Intelligence and Statistics, pp. 448–455 (2009)
17. Srivastava, N., et al.: Multimodal learning with deep Boltzmann machines. J. Mach. Learn. Res. $15(1)$, 2949–2980 (2014)
18. Tran, P.V.: A fully convolutional neural network for cardiac segmentation in short-axis MRI. arXiv preprint arXiv:1604.00494 (2016)
19. Wu, J., Mazur, T.R., et al.: A deep Boltzmann machine-driven level set method for heart motion tracking using cine MRI images. Med. Image Anal. $\mathbf{47}$, 68–80 (2018)
20. Yang, H., Liu, Z., Yang, X.: Right ventricle segmentation in short-axis MRI using a shape constrained dense connected U-Net. In: Shen, D., et al. (eds.) MICCAI 2019. LNCS, vol. 11765, pp. 532–540. Springer, Cham (2019). https://doi.org/10.1007/978-3-030-32245-8_59
21. Zhou, Z., Rahman Siddiquee, M.M., Tajbakhsh, N., Liang, J.: UNet++: a nested U-Net architecture for medical image segmentation. In: Stoyanov, D., et al. (eds.) DLMIA/ML-CDS -2018. LNCS, vol. 11045, pp. 3–11. Springer, Cham (2018). https://doi.org/10.1007/978-3-030-00889-5_1

Improved U-Net for Plaque Segmentation of Intracoronary Optical Coherence Tomography Images

Xinyu Cao[1], Jiawei Zheng[2], Zhe Liu[1], Peilin Jiang[1(✉)], Dengfeng Gao[2], and Rong Ma[3]

[1] School of Software, Xi'an Jiaotong University, Xi'an, China
`pljiang@xjtu.edu.cn`
[2] Department of Cardiovascular Medicine, Second Affiliated Hospital of Xi'an Jiaotong University, Xi'an, China
[3] School of Mathematics and Statistics, Northwestern Polytechnical University, Xi'an, China

Abstract. Optical coherence tomography (OCT) has been widely used in the assessment of coronary atherosclerotic plaques. Traditional machine learning methods are mainly based on the image texture features for the plaque segmentation. However, the texture features only represent the information of the local area, which may lead to unsatisfactory results. U-Net and its improved versions use continuous convolution and pooling to extract more advanced features, resulting in the loss of image spatial information and low plaque segmentation accuracy. This paper introduces a spatial pyramid pooling module and a multi-scale dilated convolution module into the U-Net to capture more advanced features while retaining sufficient spatial information. Based on our method, the F1 Score of the segmentation results of the four types of plaques including fibrosis, calcification, lipid and background are 0.85, 0.81, 0.80, 0.99, and the mIOU is 0.7663. Compared to other state-of-the-art methods, our method achieves better plaque segmentation accuracy.

Keywords: Plaque segmentation · U-Net · Dilated convolution · SPP layer · Optical coherence tomography

1 Introduction

Coronary atherosclerosis can lead to stenosis or even blockage of the vascular lumen, causing myocardial ischemia, hypoxia and even necrosis, which in turn leads to the occurrence of coronary heart disease. OCT is a non-contact, high-resolution tomography and biological microscope imaging device which can provide precise details of coronary plaque morphology, and has been widely used in the evaluation of coronary atherosclerotic plaque. Atherosclerotic plaques are generally divided into three categories: fibrosis plaque, lipid plaque and calcified plaque [1]. At present, the analysis of plaque based on OCT images is done

© Springer Nature Switzerland AG 2021
I. Farkaš et al. (Eds.): ICANN 2021, LNCS 12893, pp. 598–609, 2021.
https://doi.org/10.1007/978-3-030-86365-4_48

by doctors manually, which is time-consuming and prone to human bias [2]. Therefore, achieving automatic and accurate plaque segmentation is of great significance to assist in the diagnosis and treatment of cardiovascular diseases.

In recent years, a series of plaque segmentation methods have been proposed. In the field of machine learning, Prakash [3] proposed one method based on image texture features; Celi [4] proposed the best global threshold segmentation method; Athanasiou [5] proposed a method based on texture features and random forest classifier; Shalev [6] and Guo [7] proposed a method based on texture features and support vector machine classifier; Rico Jimenez [8] extracted 11 morphological features and used a linear discriminant analysis algorithm. In the field of deep learning, Abdolmanafi [9] used CNN as feature extractor, combined with classification methods to achieve automatic plaque segmentation; He [10] combined texture features with CNN classifier; Zhang [11] used U-Net [12] and FC-DenseNet [13] separately to achieve automatic plaque segmentation.

In the more general field of image segmentation, lots of U-Net variants are applied in different medical image segmentation tasks, including optic disc segmentation, retinal blood vessel detection and cell contour segmentation. Zhou [14] proposed the Nested U-Net where the original skip connection structure was redesigned—nested and dense skip connections were proposed to integrate the shallow and deep features flexibly to reduce the semantic gap. However, this only recombined features at different levels, but failed to extract enough multi-scale information. Attention U-Net proposed by Oktay [15] introduced an attention gating model into decoder and used the self-attention mechanism to inhibit the activation of irrelevant area features. MultiResUNet proposed by Ibtehaz [16] added MutiRes module to the encoder to extract multi-scale features. But continuous convolution operation in the MutiRes module might lead to spatial information loss, resulting in accuracy decrease.

Based on U-Net, we add the spatial pyramid pooling (SPP) module [17] at the end of the encoder. In the module, multi-scale features are extracted by adopting multi-scale pooling. In addition, we introduce the multi-scale dilated convolution (MDC) module before the feature concatenation of the encoders and decoders at each layer. The features of the encoder at each layer are further processed and then combined with the features of the decoder. Inspired by the Inception structure [18], we designed MDC module. This module contains four parallel paths with dilated convolution [19] to achieve multi-scale semantic aggregation while preserving spatial information. In general, the main contributions of this paper include:

1) Multi-scale advanced features are captured by adding the SPP module at the end of the encoder.
2) The introduction of MDC module helps extract multi-scale features of the encoding results at each layer while retaining more spatial information.
3) The method proposed in this paper performs better than the most advanced existing methods on the task of plaque segmentation of intracoronary OCT images.

2   Data and Method

2.1   Data Acquisition and Processing

The OCT images are collected by ILUMIEN OPTIS System. The acquired OCT sequences contain all kinds of typical atherosclerotic lesions. The experts labeled the plaque by ITK-Snap [20] software. The labeling example is shown in Fig. 1. Three different colors are used to label the three kinds of plaque: calcification (calc), lipid and fibrosis.

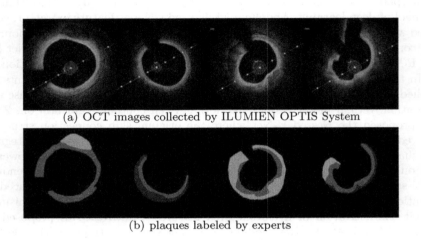

(a) OCT images collected by ILUMIEN OPTIS System

(b) plaques labeled by experts

Fig. 1. a) shows four OCT image samples of coronary artery; b) shows the corresponding annotated results: red represents fibrosis, green represents calc, blue represents lipid and black represents background (bg). (Color figure online)

We cut the original image to the size of 415 × 415 to remove redundant information. 576 OCT images are provided by the Department of Cardiovascular Medicine of the Second Affiliated Hospital of Xi'an Jiaotong University as experimental data, of which 173 images are used as the test set, and the remaining 403 images were augmented to 4836 images as the training set. The augmentation methods include: 90°, 180° and 270° rotation; horizontal and vertical flip.

2.2   Plaque Segmentation Method

Based on U-Net, our method introduces SPP module and MDC module to extract multi-scale features while retaining enough spatial information. The overall network architecture is shown in Fig. 2.

Network Architecture. We use U-Net as the backbone, and attach SPP module at the end of the whole encoder to further encode the feature map and capture new multi-scale features. MDC module is introduced into the skip connection between the encoder and decoder at each layer where the results of the encoder are processed to generate multi-scale features while retaining abundant spatial information.

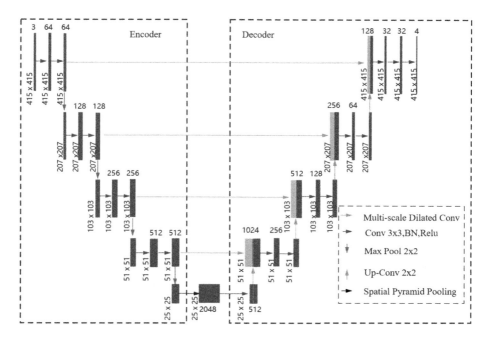

Fig. 2. The network includes two parts: Encoder and Decoder. First, the image ($415 \times 415 \times 3$) is input to the encoder and encoded for four times. Later the encoded result ($25 \times 25 \times 512$) is input to SPP module (black arrow), and then input to the decoder. Meanwhile, MDC module (orange arrow) is applied to the end of encoder at each layer. After four rounds of decoding, we get the predicted results ($415 \times 415 \times 4$). (Color figure online)

Spatial Pyramid Pooling (SPP). To extract multi-scale features and enhance the network's robustness to spatial layout and resolution difference, we apply SPP module (Fig. 3) at the end of the whole encoder. Multi-scale sliding windows are applied to max-pool the input feature map. After up-sampling process, the feature maps are concatenated and passed to the next convolutional layer.

Multi-scale Dilated Conv (MDC). Compared to the standard convolution, Dilated Conv introduced one hyper parameter—dilation rate. In the network with the same number of parameters, the Dilated Conv has a larger receptive field without reducing the spatial resolution. By setting different dilation rate, it is possible to capture multi-scale context information while retaining enough spatial information.

In Fig. 4, the MDC module has four parallel branches, including three Dilated Conv branches with dilation rates of 1, 3, and 5 and one branch with max-pooling of 3 × 3. Besides, we add the original features using shortcut connection. The receptive field of each branch changes with the dilation rate. Generally, the small receptive field is better suited to the extraction of small targets and shallow features, while the large receptive field is more conducive to the extraction and generation of large targets and abstract features. By combining the Dilated Conv with different dilation rates, MDC module realizes the extractation of multi-scale features.

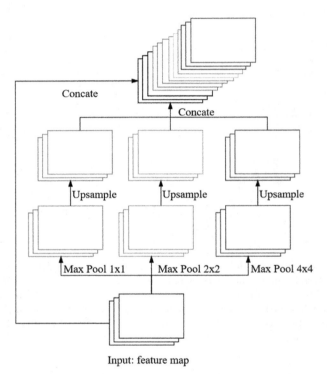

Fig. 3. Take the feature map of the encoder as the input, max-pooling with the window of 1 × 1, 2 × 2, 4 × 4, up-sampling, and concatenate new feature maps with the input.

Loss Function. In one OCT sequence, the atherosclerotic plaque areas are usually continuous which means there may be multiple consecutive frames with or without atherosclerotic plaque. The distribution of plaques is not regular, and the number of various types of plaques is also uneven. Therefore, we choose Focal Loss [21] as the loss function to overcome the imbalance of positive and negative sample ratio. Though the definition of Focal Loss in the paper is for binary classification, we manage to apply it in multi-class classification by replacing the binary cross-entropy loss function with the multi-class one. The related definition is shown in the following Eq. (1) (2) (3).

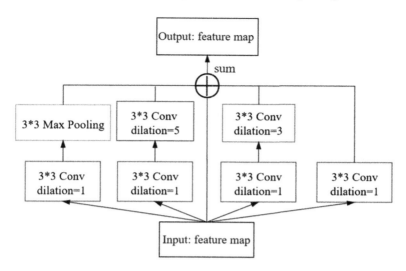

Fig. 4. The DMC module has four parallel Dilated Conv branches. Each branch has different receptive fields and can extract features of different scales. Meanwhile, we use shortcut connections to add original feature map. Finally, feature maps of each branch are added to obtain a multi-scale feature map.

$$CE(x) = -\sum_{i=1}^{C} (y_i \cdot \log f_i(x)) \tag{1}$$

$$pt = e^{-CE(x)} \tag{2}$$

$$FocalLoss = -(1 - pt)^{\gamma} \cdot \alpha \cdot \log pt \tag{3}$$

y_i represents the real label corresponding to the i-th class, $f_i(x)$ is the prediction result after softmax, C is the total number of classes, α is the class weight, and γ is the adjustment factor of sample learning difficulty.

The number of samples (number of pixels) of four classes are 775138467 (bg), 27216489 (fibrosis), 13131162 (calc), and 17393982 (lipid). The number of samples of bg class is more than an order of magnitude larger than all other classes combined. Although the Focal Loss can alleviate the problem of sample imbalance to some extent, due to the large quantity gap between the number of lesion samples (fibrosis, calc and lipid) and the number of bg samples, the problem of sample imbalance may seriously affect model training. So we decide to add weight parameters into the cross-entropy loss function of the Focal Loss to further balance the sample distribution. Eq. (4) is the new definition of cross-entropy, where w_i is the weight of each class.

$$CE(x) = -\sum_{i=1}^{C} (w_i \cdot y_i \cdot \log f_i(x)) \tag{4}$$

3   Experimental Results and Discussion

To validate the individual contribution of different components to the segementation performance, we perform an ablation experiment under different settings. Table 1 reports the results of the different modules. Compared to U-Net, we observe that by integrating either a SPP or MDC module in the U-Net the performance improves about 1% in terms of F1 Score and mIOU. And the integration of these two modules together brings further improvements.

Table 1. Ablation experiment

Model/Index	Average F1 score	mIOU
UNet	0.8450	0.7387
UNet+SSP	0.8503	0.7508
UNet+MDC	0.8488	0.7499
Ours	0.8550	0.7571

To test the effectiveness of our model, we conduct comparative experiments on U-Net, Nested U-Net, Att-UNet, and MultiResUNet. Use the trained model to classify the images of the test set at the pixel level, and compare the segmentation results with the annotation of the experts. The related evaluation indexs include sensitivity (Sen), precision (Pre), F1 Score and mIOU.

First, the original Focal Loss (non-weighted) is used to train the model. Fig. 5 below shows examples of experts' annotation results and segmentation results of various models. We can see the segmentation results of our method are more accurate, with fewer misjudgments and omissions, and the results are continuous, which is more in line with the developing trend of diseased plaques under real conditions.

Table 2 is the evaluation results of our model and other models on the test set. The F1 Score of our model is 0.99 (bg), 0.84 (fibrosis), 0.79 (calc) and 0.80 (lipid). For the classification of bg and fibrosis, the F1 Score of our model is the same as that of other models, but for the classification of calc and lipid, our model performs better than other models. For calc class, the best F1 Score of the other models is 0.78, and the worst is 0.75. The relevant index of our model is 0.79, which is better than other models. For lipid class, the best F1 Score of the other models is 0.77, and the worst is 0.74. The relevant index of our model is 0.80. The calc and lipid are the two classes with less samples, and their classification results are worse than bg and fibrosis in all models. By extracting multi-scale features while retaining sufficient spatial information, our model manages to improve the segmentation performance of these two classes.

In summary, the overall evaluation index mIOU of our model has reached 0.7571, and the mIOU of the other four models are 0.7387, 0.7195, 0.7274 and 0.7288. The segmentation result of our model is better than that of the other four models and improves significantly.

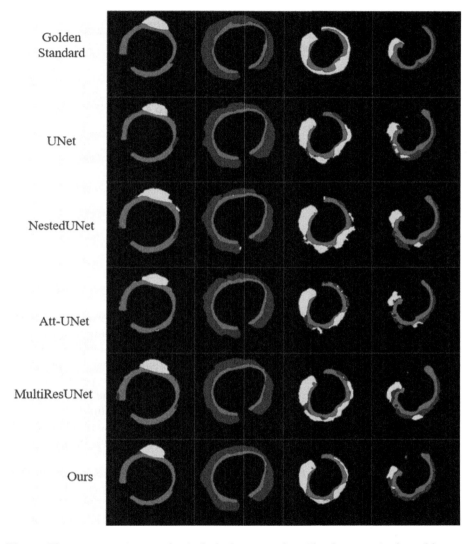

Fig. 5. The segmentation results include four samples. The first row is the gold standard marked by the expert (red is fibrosis, green is calc, blue is lipid, black is bg). The second to fourth rows are plaque segmentation results of U-Net, Nested U-Net, Att-UNet and MultiResUNet. The last row is the segmentation result of our model. (Color figure online)

Table 2. Evaluation of segmentation results on different models

Model/Index		Sensitivity	Precision	F1 score	mIOU
U-Net	bg	0.99	0.99	**0.99**	0.7387
	fibrosis	0.83	0.85	**0.84**	
	calc	0.75	0.80	0.78	
	lipid	0.82	0.72	0.77	
Nested U-Net	bg	0.99	0.99	**0.99**	0.7195
	fibrosis	0.84	0.84	**0.84**	
	calc	0.71	0.79	0.75	
	lipid	0.75	0.73	0.74	
Att-UNet	bg	0.99	0.99	**0.99**	0.7274
	fibrosis	0.84	0.84	**0.84**	
	calc	0.71	0.80	0.75	
	lipid	0.76	0.75	0.76	
MultiResUNet	bg	0.99	0.99	**0.99**	0.7288
	fibrosis	0.82	0.85	0.83	
	calc	0.73	0.80	0.76	
	lipid	0.81	0.71	0.76	
Ours	bg	0.99	0.99	**0.99**	**0.7571**
	fibrosis	0.83	0.86	**0.84**	
	calc	0.81	0.78	**0.79**	
	lipid	0.82	0.78	**0.80**	

Then we train the model with weighted Focal Loss. As there is a large gap between the number of bg samples and the number of other samples, the class weight should not simply be determined by the number of samples per class which may lead to pretty high sensitivity but unfortunately very low precision.

First, since bg is normal plaque, and the remaining three types belong to a large category of lesion plaque; Then, assume the weight of the normal sample (bg) is w, the weight of the lesion sample (fibrosis, calc and lipid) is $(1 - w)$; Last, determine the weight of fibrosis, calc and lipid based on the number of their samples—the weight of fibrosis, calc and lipid is $0.21 * (1 - w)$, $0.44 * (1 - w)$ and $0.35 * (1 - w)$.

U-Net model is used as the experimental network, the searching range of w is $[0.01, 0.25]$, the interval step is 0.01, and the mIOU and Average F1 Score are calculated to determine the best w.

Figure 6 is a statistical chart of the mIOU and Average F1 Score of the model prediction result as w changes. With the change of the weight w, the two indicators basically show a trend of rising first and then falling. We finally set the weights of the four class as 0.145, 0.1796, 0.3762 and 0.2992.

In Table 3, the left two columns are the results training with non-weighted Focal Loss, and the right two columns are the results training with weighted Focal Loss. The F1 Score and mIOU of the segmentation results of each network

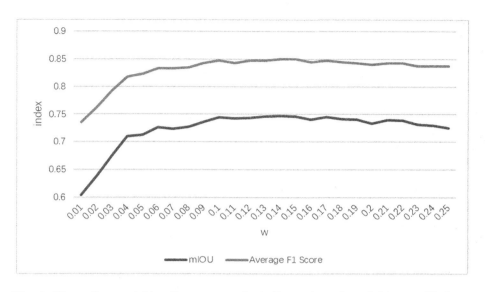

Fig. 6. The yellow and blue lines separately indicate the value of Average F1 Score and mIOU with the change of w. (Color figure online)

Table 3. Evaluation of segmentation results on different models

Model/Index		F1 Score	mIOU	F1 Score	mIOU
U-Net	bg	0.99	0.7387	0.99	0.7441
	fibrosis	0.84		0.84	
	calc	0.78		0.79	
	lipid	0.77		0.77	
Nested U-Net	bg	0.99	0.7195	0.99	0.7344
	fibrosis	0.84		0.84	
	calc	0.75		0.78	
	lipid	0.74		0.75	
Att-UNet	bg	0.99	0.7274	0.99	0.7421
	fibrosis	0.84		0.83	
	calc	0.75		0.78	
	lipid	0.76		0.77	
MultiResUNet	bg	0.99	0.7288	0.99	0.7326
	fibrosis	0.83		0.82	
	calc	0.76		0.79	
	lipid	0.76		0.76	
Ours	bg	0.99	**0.7571**	0.99	**0.7663**
	fibrosis	0.84		0.85	
	calc	0.79		0.81	
	lipid	0.80		0.80	

have improved with weighted Focal Loss. In our model, the F1 Score of the fibrosis and calc rise from 0.84 and 0.79 to 0.85 and 0.81, the F1 Score of bg and lipid remain the same, and the overall mIOU rises from 0.7571 to 0.7663. In general, the weighted Focal Loss further alleviates the problem of uneven sample distribution and improves the performance of plaque segmentation.

4   Conclusion

Based on the U-Net, we add a spatial pyramid pooling (SPP) module at the end of the whole encoder to achieve multi-scale feature extraction. At the same time, the multi-scale dilated convolution (MDC) module is introduced before concatenating the features of encoder and decoder at each layer. By further encoding the features of encoder at each layer using MDC Module, we realize multi-scale semantic feature aggregation while preserving sufficient spatial information.

The experimental results prove that our model performs better than the U-Net and its variants. Meanwhile, we introduce the weighted Focal Loss to further alleviate the imbalance problem of sample distribution and manage to improve the plaque segmentation performance of our model.

References

1. Prati, F., Guagliumi, G., Mintz, G.: Expert review document part 2: methodology, terminology and clinical applications of optical coherence tomography for the assessment of interventional procedures. Eur. Heart J. **33**(20), 2513–2520 (2012). https://doi.org/10.1093/eurheartj/ehs095
2. Finet, G., Ohayon, J., Rioufol, G.: Biomechanical interaction between cap thickness, lipid core composition and blood pressure in vulnerable coronary plaque: impact on stability or instability. Coron. Artery Dis. **15**(1), 13–20 (2004)
3. Prakash, A., Hewko, M., Sowa, M.: Texture based segmentation method to detect atherosclerotic plaque from optical tomography images. In: Bouma, R., Leitgeb, B. (eds.) Optical Coherence Tomography and Coherence Techniques VI. SPIE Proceedings, vol. 8802, p. 88020S. Optical Society of America, Munich (2013)
4. Celi, S., Berti, S.: In-vivo segmentation and quantification of coronary lesions by optical coherence tomography images for a lesion type definition and stenosis grading. Med. Image Anal. **18**(7), 1157–1168 (2014). https://doi.org/10.1016/j.media.2014.06.011
5. Athanasiou, L.S., Bourantas, C.V., Rigas, G.: Methodology for fully automated segmentation and plaque characterization in intracoronary optical coherence tomography images. J. Biomed. Opt. **19**(2), 1–14 (2014). https://doi.org/10.1117/1.JBO.19.2.026009
6. Shalev, R., Prabhu, D., Tanaka, K.: Intravascular optical coherence tomography image analysis method. In: 2015 41st Annual Northeast Biomedical Engineering Conference (NEBEC), pp. 1–2 (2015). https://doi.org/10.1109/NEBEC.2015.7117058
7. Guo, X., Tang, D., Molony, D.: A machine learning-based method for intracoronary oct segmentation and vulnerable coronary plaque cap thickness quantification. Int. J. Comput. Methods **16**(03), 1842008 (2018). https://doi.org/10.1142/S0219876218420082

8. Rico-Jimenez, J.J., Campos-Delgado, D.U., Villiger, M.: Automatic classification of atherosclerotic plaques imaged with intravascular OCT. Biomed. Opt. Express **7**(10), 4069–4085 (2016). https://doi.org/10.1364/BOE.7.004069

9. Abdolmanafi, A., Duong, L., Dahdah, N.: Characterization of coronary artery pathological formations from OCT imaging using deep learning. Biomed. Opt. Express **9**(10), 4936–4960 (2018). https://doi.org/10.1364/BOE.9.004936

10. He, S., Zheng, J., Maehara, A.: Convolutional neural network based automatic plaque characterization for intracoronary optical coherence tomography images. In: Proceedings of SPIE, vol. 10574, March 2018. https://doi.org/10.1117/12.2293957

11. Zhang, C., Guo, X., Guo, X.: Machine Learning Model Comparison for Automatic Segmentation of Intracoronary Optical Coherence Tomography and Plaque Cap Thickness Quantification (2020). https://doi.org/10.32604/cmes.2020.09718

12. Ronneberger, O., Fischer, P., Brox, T.: U-Net: convolutional networks for biomedical image segmentation. In: Navab, N., Hornegger, J., Wells, W.M., Frangi, A.F. (eds.) MICCAI 2015. LNCS, vol. 9351, pp. 234–241. Springer, Cham (2015). https://doi.org/10.1007/978-3-319-24574-4_28

13. Jegou, S., Drozdzal, M., Vazquez, D.: The one hundred layers tiramisu: fully convolutional densenets for semantic segmentation. In: Proceedings of the IEEE Conference on Computer Vision and Pattern Recognition (CVPR) Workshops, July 2017

14. Zhou, Z., Rahman Siddiquee, M.M., Tajbakhsh, N., Liang, J.: UNet++: a nested U-net architecture for medical image segmentation. In: Stoyanov, D., et al. (eds.) DLMIA/ML-CDS -2018. LNCS, vol. 11045, pp. 3–11. Springer, Cham (2018). https://doi.org/10.1007/978-3-030-00889-5_1

15. Oktay, O., Schlemper, J., Folgoc, L.: Attention U-Net: Learning Where to Look for the Pancreas (2018)

16. Ibtehaz, N., Rahman, M.S.: MultiResUNet: rethinking the U-Net architecture for multimodal biomedical image segmentation. Neural Netw. **121**, 74–87 (2020). https://doi.org/10.1016/j.neunet.2019.08.025

17. He, K., Zhang, X., Ren, S.: Spatial pyramid pooling in deep convolutional networks for visual recognition. IEEE Trans. Pattern Anal. Mach. Intell. **37**(9), 1904–1916 (2015). https://doi.org/10.1109/TPAMI.2015.2389824

18. Szegedy, C., Liu, W., Jia, Y.: Going deeper with convolutions. In: Proceedings of the IEEE Conference on Computer Vision and Pattern Recognition (CVPR), June 2015

19. Yu, F., Koltun, V.: Multi-Scale Context Aggregation by Dilated Convolutions, November 2016

20. Yushkevich, P.A., Piven, J., Hazlett, H.C.: User-guided 3D active contour segmentation of anatomical structures: significantly improved efficiency and reliability. Neuroimage **31**(3), 1116–1128 (2006). https://doi.org/10.1016/j.neuroimage.2006.01.015

21. Lin, T.Y., Goyal, P., Girshick, R.: Focal loss for dense object detection. In: Proceedings of the IEEE International Conference on Computer Vision (ICCV), October 2017

Approximated Masked Global Context Network for Skin Lesion Segmentation

Chunguang Jiang[1], Yueling Zhang[1,2][(✉)], Jiangtao Wang[1,3][(✉)], and Weiting Chen[1]

[1] East China Normal University, Shanghai, China
51194501049@stu.ecnu.edu.cn, {ylzhang,jtwang,
wtchen}@sei.ecnu.edu.cn
[2] Singapore Management University, Singapore, Singapore
[3] National Trusted Embedded Software Engineering Technology Research Center,
Shanghai, China

Abstract. The number of skin cancer cases worldwide is increasing by millions every year. A large number of patients bring great pressure to the diagnosis and treatment of skin cancer, it is urgent to apply automatic segmentation techniques to skin lesions to help the diagnosis of skin lesions and the evaluation of recovery. At present, there are still challenges in automatic skin lesion segmentation, including blurring irregular lesion boundaries, low contrast between the lesion and surrounding skin, and all kinds of interference with bubbles, lights, and hairs. We found that modeling the context relationship by using the strongest consistent masked global context can focus only on the lesion region with a high degree. Based on the observation, we propose an approximated masked global context network (AMGC-Net), which firstly approximates the masked global context by constructing the approximated masked global context, and calculates the similarity between each pixel and the approximated masked global information at the spatial level to form a global context requirements gating coefficient matrix, and then captures the dependencies between channels at the channel level to improve segmentation performance. The AMGC-Net is assessed on three public skin challenge datasets: PH2, ISBI2016, and ISIC2018. It achieves state-of-the-art results when compared to some new methods in terms of sensitivity.

Keywords: Strong consistency · Approximated masked global context · Context modeling · Spatial level and channel level · Skin lesion segmentation

1 Introduction

Skin cancer has become a serious public health problem due to its increasing morbidity and mortality. According to relevant statistics, there are 5.4 million new skin cancer cases every year [14]. To reduce the incidence and mortality of skin diseases, safe and effective dermoscopy is commonly used to diagnose skin diseases in medicine. However, based on dermoscopic images, experts often spend a lot of time to accurately determine the location of skin lesions, and there will be subjective differences in this method. Therefore, the novel method of using computer-aided diagnosis for automatic segmentation of skin

© Springer Nature Switzerland AG 2021
I. Farkaš et al. (Eds.): ICANN 2021, LNCS 12893, pp. 610–622, 2021.
https://doi.org/10.1007/978-3-030-86365-4_49

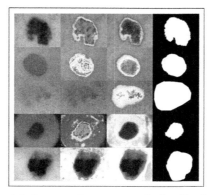

Fig. 1. Comparison of the global context feature maps obtained by the global context module of the ACNet [4] and the masked global context feature maps on ISIC2018.

lesions is highly sought after. But due to the large differences in the location, shape, and color of skin lesions, the low contrast between the lesion and its surrounding normal skin, and other interfering factors (such as bubbles, lights, and hair), skin lesion segmentation is still a challenging task.

Recently, with the development of deep learning, especially the fully convolutional neural networks (FCNs) [11], a lot of great works utilizing context information such as [4, 16, 21, 23, 24] have obtained promising results in terms of semantic segmentation. However, these methods utilize the inherent multi-scale context of the different stages or the global context from the feature map at the current stage, which may be misleading due to its noise, and the context information is not strongly consistent.

As shown in Fig. 1, the context feature maps (the third column) with the strongest consistent mask global information pay more attention to the lesion regions, while the normal global context feature maps (the second column) will also focus on some irrelevant regions, and the degree of attention to lesion regions is not high enough.

Based on the observation, we generate the approximated mask global information by approximating the real masked global context to obtain strong consistent global information and make reasonable use of it both at the spatial level and channel level.

Therefore, we design an approximated masked global context module (AMGCM). Specifically, we perform semantic aggregation and prediction on the current feature map to get the binary classification results, thereby generating the approximated masked global context. To enhance the consistency of the approximated masked global context, we perform supervised learning on the binary classification results and the approximated masked global context. At the same time, considering that different pixels have different requirements for the global context, we design a context modeling module (CMM), which generates a global requirement gating coefficient matrix by calculating the Euclidean distance between each pixel and the acquired global features to obtain the requirement for global features of each pixel. The greater the demand, the greater the probability that the pixel is predicted to be the correct category. Besides, inspired by SENet [6], the importance of different channels may be different. We design a channel attention module (CAM) to obtain the dependencies of channels, which combines the aggregated feature and the context feature in the CMM to obtain more accurate channel weight parameters and refine segmentation performance.

To demonstrate the effectiveness of the proposed approximated masked global context module, we cascade two such modules to construct an approximated masked global context network (AMGC-Net) based on the encoder-decoder network, and the main contributions of this paper can be summarized as follows:

- We find the strongest consistent mask global information is helpful to focus on useful semantic areas and reduce the impact of useless information and we explore to get the approximated mask global information.
- We design a context modeling module and a channel attention module to make reasonable use of the obtained strong consistent context information.
- The proposed AMGC-Net shows state-of-the-art performance on three skin lesion datasets. In particular, only with a simple resizing and rotating of the input images, the scores of the sensitivity (SEN) of our method on the PH2, ISBI2016, and ISIC2018 three datasets are 96.98%, 95.06%, and 91.05%, respectively.

2 Related Work

Context Information. In image segmentation tasks, context information is essentially important. BiseNet [22] designs a context path and uses the global average pooling to capture the global context. EncNet [23] uses a context encoding module in the encoding layer to capture global context information and highlight category information associated with the scene. PFAN [24] designs a context-aware pyramid feature extraction (CPEE) module for multi-scale high-level feature mapping to obtain rich context features. Nonlocal U-Net [20] designs a global aggregation block to view the global information during up-sampling and down-sampling to obtain a more accurate segmentation map.

Attention and Gating Mechanisms. Attention mechanisms are used to improve the performance of segmentation tasks. SENet [6] explores channel information and obtains excellent performance through the attention of learning channels. GFF [8] proposes gated fully fusion (GFF) to generate high-resolution and high-level feature maps from multi-level feature maps and uses a gate mechanism to selectively fuse features from multiple levels, thereby reducing noise interference. FCA-Net [15] proposes a factorized channel attention (FCA) block integrating channel attention and residual one-dimensional factorized convolutions to enhance the distinguishing ability between skin lesions and non-lesion pixels.

Different from these works, we introduce a new gating mechanism to capture and utilize strong consistent context information both at the spatial level and channel level.

3 Methodology

Context information is effective for image segmentation, but the context information of current methods lacks strong consistency. In this work, we propose an AMGC-Net to obtain and utilize the strong consistent context information.

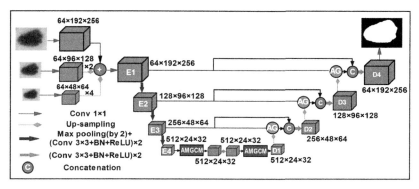

Fig. 2. The architecture of the proposed AMGC-Net.

The entire architecture of the proposed AMGC-Net is shown in Fig. 2. It adopts Attention U-Net [13] as the backbone network, and the AG module is the attention gate module proposed by Attention U-Net [13]. In the backbone network, we adopt a multi-scale input strategy, that is, besides the original scale, we also add the ratios of 1/2, 1/4 of the original scale as input. Between E4 and D1 in Fig. 2, two approximated masked global context modules are employed, where the features have relatively high semantic consistency than the features of other stages.

3.1 Approximated Masked Global Context

Global context can usually guide large objects in terms of semantics, thus rectifying misclassification and inconsistent parsing results. Many methods, such as [3, 4, 16], obtain global context by performing global average pooling on the current feature map to understand comprehensive information. However, if the feature map does not learn the lesion information well and contains interference information, the global feature would deviate from the real global feature, which would lead to large errors in subsequent calculations that rely on it. Encouraged by the strongest consistent masked global feature, we consider constructing an approximated masked global context with stronger consistency than the global feature of the current methods.

As shown in Fig. 3, we first propose an aggregation module, which uses two groups of asymmetric convolutions (to keep the equal size of receptive filed and decrease computation) to aggregates spatial information. Then a global average pooling (GAP) and a sigmoid function are used to capture the channel-wise weighted vector. Since skin lesion segmentation is a pixel binary classification problem, the binary result has no other interference information, and it can be supervised by ground truth, we perform the prediction operation on the enhanced feature map and use the prediction result to obtain the appropriated masked global context g_1, which is defined as:

$$g_1 = F_{sq}(F_{pred}(F_{Agg}(Input)))$$ (1)

Where the $F_{Agg}(\cdot)$ is the Aggregation module, $F_{pred}(\cdot)$ is a 3×3 convolution with 2 out channels and the argmax function, and the $F_{sq}(\cdot)$ is global average pooling.

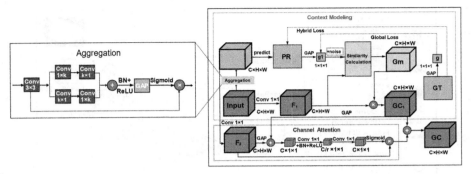

Fig. 3. An illustration of the proposed approximated masked global context module including (1) Aggregation module, (2) Context modeling module, and (3) Channel attention module. The k (set 9 in the experiment) in (1) denotes the filter size of the fully separable convolution, BN denotes batch normalization, and GAP denotes global average pooling.

Considering that there be a gap between the g_1 and the real masked global context g, we have formulated two safeguards: 1) Only in the training phase, we add random noise (20% upper and lower bounds of g_1) to enhance the robustness of the model to global information. 2) Besides the hybrid loss (HL) in Eq. (9), we add a loss function called global loss (GL) for the preliminary prediction, which is defined as:

$$GL = |g_1 - g|/g + |g_1 - g|/(1 + \varepsilon - g) + |g_1 - g|/(g_1 + \varepsilon) \tag{2}$$

Where g is the real masked global information, ε is a small number (set to 0.0001 in the experiment) to prevent the denominator from being 0.

3.2 Context Modeling Module

The contribution of each pixel to the object area is inconsistent, the global context requirements for each pixel should be treated differently. We design a context modeling module (CMM), as shown in Fig. 3 (2), to make reasonable use of the approximated masked global context, which calculates the global requirements for each pixel. Firstly, we add a 1×1 convolution for the input to obtain a new feature map F_1 and then use the g_1 to calculate the similarity distance matrix S. For each pixel p_1 in normalized F_1, the similarity distance $d_i \in S$ is defined as follows:

$$d_i = (p_i - g_1)^2 \tag{3}$$

Then we acquire the global context requirements gating coefficient matrix $G_m \in (0, 1]$ through a smooth exponential function, which is defined as:

$$G_m = exp((min(d_i) - d_i)/\mu) \tag{4}$$

Where μ is to balance the difference between high response and low response.

Finally, we multiply the feature map F_1 by the gating coefficient G_m to get the initial masked global context information GC_1, which is defined as:

$$GC_1 = (F_1 \times G_m) \tag{5}$$

3.3 Channel Attention Module

Different feature channels in CNN have diverse responses to different semantic information, so it is necessary to capture the dependencies between channels. Most of the existing channel attention methods are derived from the work [6], which firstly squeeze the spatial information of the current feature map through global average pooling and obtain the global receptive field, and then use the exciting operation to generate weights for each feature channel. It can be seen that the method relies on the squeeze operation, so we consider using the preliminary global context of the above-mentioned CMM to construct a new channel attention module (CAM) that attempts to capture more accurate channel weight parameters.

The channel attention module is shown in Fig. 3 (3), which squeezes the aggregated feature map F_2 and the GC_1 in the CMM to obtain a more comprehensive and effective global receptive field. And the results of the squeeze experiment are shown in Table 2. Formally, the squeeze operation is generated by shrinking the target feature map on the spatial size $H \times W$, so the output z after squeeze here is as follows:

$$z = \frac{1}{H \times W} \sum\nolimits_{i=1}^{H} \sum\nolimits_{j=1}^{W} (F_2(i,j)) + \frac{1}{H \times W} \sum\nolimits_{i=1}^{H} \sum\nolimits_{j=1}^{W} (GC_1(i,j)) \qquad (6)$$

Then two convolution activation operations (called F_{ex}) to activate the global features of the squeeze operation, thus generating the nonlinear relationship between channels. The first convolution activation is mainly for dimensionality reduction, which is achieved by setting the channel scaling factor r (shown in Table 2). The second convolution activation is to restore the original dimension and obtain the nonlinear relationship of the channels. The output X of the module is defined as follows:

$$X = F_{ex}(z) \times F_2 \qquad (7)$$

Finally, by integrating the GC_1 and the X, we can obtain the final approximated masked global context GC, which is defined as follows:

$$GC = GC_1 + X \qquad (8)$$

3.4 Hybrid Loss Function

To optimize the proposed model, we adopt a hybrid loss function: focal loss function [9] L_{FL}, Jaccard distance loss function L_{JAC}, and End point Error [18] loss function L_{EPE}. Therefore, the hybrid loss function HL is as follows:

$$HL = \beta L_{FL} + L_{JAC} + \theta L_{EPE} \qquad (9)$$

Where β and θ are the balance weight parameters specified by the user.

The focal loss function is used to balance the ratio of the foreground target of interest to the image background, which is defined as follows:

$$L_{FL} = -\alpha (1 - p)^{\gamma} log(p) \qquad (10)$$

The variables $\alpha \in [0, 1]$ and $\gamma \geq 0$ are the tunable focusing parameters. Besides, $p \in [0, 1]$ is the predicted probability of the model for the positive class.

Jaccard distance loss function compares the similarity between the predicted result and the ground truth distribution. is defined as follows:

$$L_{JAC} = 1 - \frac{\sum_{i=1}^{N} p_i \times g_i}{\sum_{i=1}^{N} p_i + \sum_{i=1}^{N} g_i - \sum_{i=1}^{N} p_i \times g_i} \tag{11}$$

Where p and g are prediction probability and ground truth respectively, and N is the total number of pixels of the prediction image.

The EPE loss function compares the boundary of the prediction result with the boundary of the ground truth in size and direction, which is defined as follows:

$$L_{EPE} = \sqrt{(p_x - g_x)^2 + (p_y - g_y)^2} \tag{12}$$

Where (p_x, p_y) and (g_x, g_y) are the first derivatives of the prediction result and ground truth in the x-direction and the y-direction respectively.

4   Experiments

4.1   Datasets

To evaluate the performance of our proposed method, we conduct extensive experiments on three publicly available skin lesion datasets, which are named PH2[1], ISBI2016[2], and ISIC2018[3]. In the PH2 dataset, there are a total of 200 annotated datasets, and the image size ranges from 553×763 to 577×769. In the ISBI2016 dataset, there are 900 annotated training images and 397 annotated images, ranging from 542×718 to 2848×4288. In the ISIC2018 dataset, there are a total of 2594 annotated RGB lesion images with a resolution ranging from 540×722 to 4499×6748.

4.2   Implementation Details

Each image is resized to192×256. And we use Adam as an optimizer to train our model and set β_1, β_2, and weight_decay to 0.9, 0.999, and 0.0001 respectively. During the training process, we employ a multivariate learning rate strategy, where the initial learning rate is set to 0.0003, then the learning rate is halved every 50 epochs. A total of 4 halving treatments are performed. The parameters μ, β, θ, α, and γ in Eq. (4), Eq. (9), Eq. (9), Eq. (10), and Eq. (10) are set to 0.2, 50, 0.05, 0.25, and 2 respectively. Our experiments are all conducted on NVIDIA GeForce RTX 3090 GPU.

---

[1] https://www.fc.up.pt/addi/.

[2] http://challenge2016.isic-archive.com/.

[3] http://challenge2018.isic-archive.com/.

4.3   Ablation Studies of Different Modules

To verify the performance of the proposed modules, we design a series of ablation experiments. We firstly train the baseline (BL) model, which is based on Attention U-Net [13], we cancel the last layer of the encoder in Attention U-Net [13], then directly connect the penultimate layer of the encoder with the first layer of the decoder.

Ablation Study on Context Modeling Module: To evaluate the effectiveness of the proposed context modeling module (CMM), we conducted a set of experiments on the PH2 dataset. We embed GCB [3], GCM [4], and the proposed CMM into the last layer of the baseline encoder as the CMM ablation experiment. Since the CMM also contains the process of obtaining approximated masked global context, we also conducted experiments on it. As shown in Table 1, even for the model BL+CMM (w/o Agg+w/o noise+HL), its scores are still higher than the model BL, the model BL+GCB [3], and the model BL+GCM [4]. And the score of the model BL+CMM (Agg+noise2+HL+GL) is very high, achieves 95.61%, 92.89%, 94.77%, and 96.28% on ACC (accuracy), DC (Dice Coefficient), SEN (sensitivity), and SPE (specificity) respectively.

Table 1.   Ablation experiments of context modeling module (CMM) on the PH2 dataset. Where w/o means without, Agg means the aggregation module (When without Agg, we use raw input instead of the aggregated feature), noise ($noise1 \in [-0.1 \times g_1, 0.1 \times g_1], noise2 \in [-0.2 \times g_1, 0.2 \times g_1]$) is random noise added to the g_1 (approximated masked global context), GL is the global loss, and HL is the hybrid loss. And the best results are marked in bold.

Methods	ACC	DC	SEN	SPE
BL	93.56	90.67	90.39	95.41
BL+GCB [3]	94.26	90.53	89.18	96.56
BL+GCM [4]	94.74	91.29	89.34	**97.29**
BL+CMM (w/o Agg+w/o noise+HL)	94.13	91.97	94.11	95.44
BL+CMM (Agg+w/o noise+HL)	95.05	92.17	94.44	95.80
BL+CMM (Agg+noise1+HL)	95.12	92.20	94.58	96.32
BL+CMM (Agg+noise2+HL)	95.30	92.44	94.61	96.22
BL+CMM(Agg+noise2+HL+GL)	**95.61**	**92.89**	**94.77**	96.28

Ablation Study on Channel Attention Module: The channel attention module helps to assign weights according to the channel's response to the target object. More accurate channel weight parameters can be obtained by squeeze the GC_1 in CMM and the aggregated feature map F_2. We embed the channel attention module (CAM) into the last layer of the baseline encoder as the ablation experiment. As shown in Table 2, we compare the SEBlock [6], CAM1 that only performs squeeze operation on the F_2, CAM2 that only performs squeeze operation on the obtained context information GC_1 in the CMM. It can be found that no matter what kinds of channel attention modules, their performance

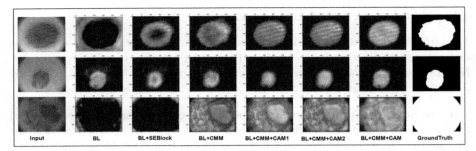

Fig. 4. Visualization results of CAM ablation experiments on the ISIC2018 dataset.

is better than the unadded ones. Moreover, the proposed CAM performs best, with the highest scores when $r = 2$, and the ACC and SEN are 95.47% and 95.96%, respectively. And the visualization results in Fig. 4. Therefore, the following conclusions can be drawn: 1) The channel attention module can capture the dependence between channels and improve the performance of image segmentation. 2) The channel attention module that performs squeeze operations on the F_2 and GC_1 in the CMM can capture more accurate channel dependence and learn more accurate channel weight parameters, which can further improve performance.

Table 2. Ablation experiments of context modeling module (CMM) on the PH2 dataset.

Methods	ACC	DC	SEN	SPE
BL	93.56	90.67	90.39	95.41
BL+SEBlock [6]	94.85	92.09	91.04	96.53
BL+CMM+CAM1 ($r = 2$)	94.98	92.12	93.74	96.02
BL+CMM+CAM2 ($r = 2$)	95.12	92.53	95.43	95.68
BL+CMM+CAM ($r = 2$)	**95.47**	**92.99**	**95.96**	96.21
BL+CMM+CAM ($r = 4$)	95.35	92.72	95.07	**96.59**
BL+CMM+CAM ($r = 8$)	95.23	92.89	94.88	96.38

Ablation Study on Approximated Masked Global Context Module: We integrate CMM and CAM, and further propose an approximated masked global context module (AMGCM) to optimize our model, and design a series of ablation experiments on the ISIC2018 dataset. As shown in Table 3, when we cascade two AMGCMs, the ACC score increases to 95.23%, and the SEN score increases to 90.41%. Besides, we also test the performance of adding multi-scale input (MSI) and hybrid loss (HL) function, and the final best ACC score and SEN score are 95.83% and 91.05%, respectively. The final segmentation result is visualized as shown in Fig. 5.

Table 3. Ablation experiments of the AMGCM on the ISIC2018 dataset.

Methods	ACC	DC	SEN	SPE
BL	93.60	85.74	84.15	95.26
BL+ACB [4]	94.04	86.29	84.67	95.42
BL+AMGCM×1	94.86	88.92	89.82	95.68
BL+AMGCM×2	95.23	89.68	90.41	96.02
BL+AMGCM×2+MSI	95.57	90.25	90.82	96.47
BL+AMGCM×2+MSI+HL	**95.83**	**90.87**	**91.05**	**96.88**

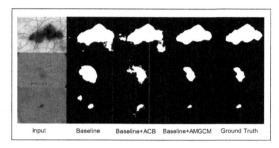

Fig. 5. Visualization results of LCM ablation experiments on the ISIC2018 dataset.

4.4 Comparison to State-of-the-Art

To further verify the effectiveness of the proposed AMGC-Net, we compare it with other state-of-the-art methods and conduct extensive experiments to prove it.

Table 4 shows the performance results of the AMGC-Net and several other state-of-the-art segmentation methods on the PH2 dataset. It can be seen that the SPE score of the AMGC-Net is lower than the work [7], and the same for most of the other tables.

That is because our theme and method focus more on positive samples, the SPE score dominated by negative samples will be weaker. But our method achieves the best value on the other three metrics, the ACC score, DC score, and SEN score are 96.37%, 94.13%, and 96.98% respectively.

Table 5 shows the scores of several methods on the ISBI2016 test dataset. The best ACC score of [21] is 0.12% higher than our method, but our method achieves the highest SEN score. Also, [15] obtains a slightly higher DC score and SPE score than our model but its other scores are lower than our model, especially the SEN score.

Table 4. Comparison with other methods on the PH2 dataset.

Methods	ACC	DC	SEN	SPE
SENet [6]	94.48	91.46	93.46	95.78
FrCN [1]	95.08	91.77	93.72	95.65
DCL-PSI [2]	95.30	92.10	96.23	95.30
GCNet [3]	95.11	92.41	94.26	95.96
ACNet [4]	95.18	91.29	92.94	95.02
DSNet [5]	–	–	92.90	96.90
GFF-Net [8]	95.27	92.30	94.41	97.12
CSARM-CNN [7]	95.23	88.32	93.72	**99.45**
iMSCGnet [16]	95.71	93.36	–	–
DoNet [19]	94.60	93.10	–	–
Ours (AMGC-Net)	**96.37**	**94.13**	**96.98**	96.15

Table 5. Comparison with other methods on the ISBI2016 dataset.

Methods	ACC	DC	SEN	SPE
Attention-Net [13]	94.51	86.81	88.94	96.16
RefineNet [10]	93.03	83.97	86.08	95.71
SENet [6]	94.95	90.38	91.87	95.12
DCL-PSI [2]	95.78	91.77	93.11	96.05
GCNet [3]	94.56	90.01	91.02	95.62
ACNet [4]	94.43	89.54	90.17	95.06
FCA-Net [15]	95.93	**92.80**	91.63	**97.07**
GFF-Net [8]	93.86	88.73	89.76	94.43
iMSCGnet [16]	96.08	91.91	–	–
Wang et al. [21]	**96.10**	92.60	94.60	96.00
Ours (AMGC-Net)	95.98	91.96	**95.06**	96.22

In Table 6, the proposed model is compared with several state-of-the-art methods on the ISIC2018 dataset. As shown in the table, AMGC-Net achieves the best performance on the ACC, DC, and SEN sores, 95.83%, 90.87%, and 91.05%, respectively.

Table 6. Comparison with other methods on the ISIC2018 dataset.

Methods	ACC	DC	SEN
Attention U-Net [13]	93.12	86.14	84.59
SENet [6]	93.27	86.27	86.02
BiSeNet [22]	93.32	86.13	85.97
GCNet [3]	93.31	85.50	84.86
ACNet [4]	92.67	84.35	84.16
Mask-RCNN [12]	94.20	89.80	90.60
GFF-Net [8]	94.36	88.03	85.72
DONet [19]	95.00	88.10	–
TMD-Unet [17]	–	87.27	–
Ours (AMGC-Net)	**95.83**	**90.87**	**91.05**

5   Conclusion

In this paper, we propose a new concept of the masked global context and find its strong consistency. Motivated by it, we utilize the generated approximated masked global context to design an AMGCM with strong consistency, which includes a context modeling module (CMM) and channel attention module (CAM) to guide each pixel to obtain high confidence in the correct category and more accurate channel dependencies. Besides, we use two AMGCMs to construct an approximated masked context network (AMGC-Net) for skin lesion segmentation. Extensive experiments demonstrate the outstanding performance of AMGC-Net compared to other state-of-the-art methods.

References

1. APAAl-Masni, M.A., Al-Antari, M.A., Choi, M.T., Han, S.M., Kim, T.S.: Skin lesion segmentation in dermoscopy images via deep full resolution convolutional networks. Comput. Methods Prog. Biomed. **162**, 221–231 (2018)
2. Bi, L., Kim, J., Ahn, E., Kumar, A., Feng, D., Fulham, M.: Step-wise integration of deep class-specific learning for dermoscopic image segmentation. Pattern Recogn. **85**, 78–89 (2019)
3. Cao, Y., Xu, J., Lin, S., Wei, F., Hu, H.: Gcnet: non-local networks meet squeeze-excitation networks and beyond. In: ICCVW (2019)
4. Fu, J., et al.: Adaptive context network for scene parsing. In: ICCV, pp. 6748–6757 (2019)
5. Hasan, M.K., Dahal, L., Samarakoon, P.N., Tushar, F.I., Martí, R.: DSNet: automatic dermoscopic skin lesion segmentation. Comput. Biol. Med. **120**, 103738 (2020)
6. Hu, J., Shen, L., Sun, G.: Squeeze-and-excitation networks. In: CVPR, pp. 7132–7141 (2018)
7. Jiang, Y., Cao, S., Tao, S., Zhang, H.: Skin lesion segmentation based on multi-scale attention convolutional neural network. IEEE Access **8**, 122811–122825 (2020)
8. Li, X., Zhao, H., Han, L., Tong, Y., Tan, S., Yang, K.: Gated fully fusion for semantic segmentation. AAAI **34**(7), 11418–11425 (2020)
9. Lin, T.Y., Goyal, P., Girshick, R., He, K., Dollár, P.: Focal loss for dense object detection. In: ICCV, pp. 2980–2988 (2017)

10. Lin, G., Milan, A., Shen, C., Reid, I.: Refinenet: multi-path refinement networks for high-resolution semantic segmentation. In: CVPR, pp. 1925–1934 (2017)
11. Long, J., Shelhamer, E., Darrell, T.: Fully convolutional networks for semantic segmentation. In: CVPR, pp. 3431–3440 (2015)
12. Mishra, R., Daescu, O.: AlgoDerm: an end-to-end mobile application for skin lesion analysis and tracking. In: Proceedings of the International Conference on Medical and Health Informatics System, pp. 3–9 (2019)
13. Oktay, O., et al.: Attention u-net: learning where to look for the pancreas (2018). https://arxiv.org/abs/1804.03999
14. Rogers, H.W., Weinstock, M.A., Feldman, S.R., Coldiron, B.M.: Incidence estimate of nonmelanoma skin cancer (keratinocyte carcinomas) in the US population (2012. JAMA Dermatol. **151**(10), 1081–1086 (2015)
15. Singh, V.K., et al.: FCA-Net: adversarial learning for skin lesion segmentation based on multi-scale features and factorized channel attention. IEEE Access **7**, 130552–130565 (2019)
16. Tang, Y., Fang, Z., Yuan, S., Xing, Y., Zhou, J.T., Yang, F.: iMSCGnet: iterative multi-scale context-guided segmentation of skin lesion in dermoscopic images. IEEE Access **8**, 39700–39712 (2020)
17. Tran, S.T., Cheng, C.H., Nguyen, T.T., Le, M.H., Liu, D.G.: TMD-Unet: triple-unet with multi-scale input features and dense skip connection for medical image segmentation. Healthc. Multidiscip. Digital Publ. Inst. **9**(1), 54 (2021)
18. Tu, W., et al.: Segmentation of lesion in dermoscopy images using dense-residual network with adversarial learning. In: ICIP, pp. 1430–1434 (2019)
19. Wang, Y., Wei, Y., Qian, X., Zhu, L., Yang, Y.: DONet: dual objective networks for skin lesion segmentation (2020). https://arxiv.org/abs/2008.08278
20. Wang, Z., Zou, N., Shen, D., Ji, S.: Non-local U-nets for biomedical image segmentation. In: AAAI, pp. 6315–6322 (2020)
21. Wang, R., Chen, S., Fan, J., Li, Y.: Cascaded context enhancement for automated skin lesion segmentation (2020). https://arxiv.org/abs/2004.08107
22. Yu, C., Wang, J., Peng, C., Gao, C., Yu, G., Sang, N.: BiSeNet: bilateral segmentation network for real-time semantic segmentation. In: Ferrari, V., Hebert, M., Sminchisescu, C., Weiss, Y. (eds.) ECCV 2018. LNCS, vol. 11217, pp. 334–349. Springer, Cham (2018). https://doi.org/10.1007/978-3-030-01261-8_20
23. Zhang, H., et al.: Context encoding for semantic segmentation. In: CVPR, pp. 7151–7160 (2018)
24. Zhao, T., Wu, X.: Pyramid feature attention network for saliency detection. In: CVPR, pp. 3085–3094 (2019)

DSNet: Dynamic Selection Network for Biomedical Image Segmentation

Xiaofei Qin[1,2,3], Yan Liu[1], Liang Tang[1], Shuhui Zhao[4], Xingchen Zhou[4], Xuedian Zhang[1,2,3], and Dengbin Wang[4(✉)]

[1] School of Optical-Electrical and Computer Engineering, University of Shanghai for Science and Technology, Shanghai, China
xiaofei.qin@usst.edu.cn
[2] Shanghai Key Laboratory of Contemporary Optics System, Shanghai, China
[3] Key Laboratory of Biomedical Optical Technology and Devices of Ministry of Education, Shanghai, China
[4] Department of Radiology, Xinhua Hospital Affiliated to Shanghai Jiao Tong University School of medicine, Shanghai, China
wangdengbin@xinhuamed.com.cn

Abstract. This paper focuses on uterine segmentation, an important clue for understanding MRI images and medical analysis of expectant mothers, which has long been underestimated. Related works have proven that the receptive field is crucial in computer vision. However, current methods usually use pooling operations to continuously enlarge the receptive field, which leads to some inevitable information loss. In this paper, we design the Dynamic Selection Module (DSM) to effectively capture the spatial perception of medical images. Specifically, DSM adopts dynamic convolution kernel to adaptively adjust the receptive field in the horizontal and vertical directions. We then combine DSM and residual block to construct a Dynamic Residual Unit (DRU) which further learns feature representation. Then DRU is embedded in the standard U-Net termed Dynamic Selection Network (DSNet). We evaluate our method on the Uterus dataset we acquired. To validate the generalization of this method, we also do the same experiment on the Gland Segmentation dataset and Lung dataset. The results demonstrate that DSNet can significantly boost the performance of medical image segmentation than other related encoder-decoder architectures.

Keywords: Medical image segmentation · Adaptive receptive field · Encoder-decoder

1 Introduction

Placenta previa is a hazardous situation during pregnancy that can easily lead to bleeding in late pregnancy. But in recent years, a new kind of pernicious placenta previa has been found [1]. Pernicious placenta previa is attached to the scar incision of previous cesarean section, which is prone to placental accretion and placental adhesion [2]. It is so difficult for placental detachment during

© Springer Nature Switzerland AG 2021
I. Farkaš et al. (Eds.): ICANN 2021, LNCS 12893, pp. 623–634, 2021.
https://doi.org/10.1007/978-3-030-86365-4_50

cesarean section, which is one of the main causes of prenatal, intrapartum and postpartum hemorrhage [3]. If it is not detected and handled in time, it will pose a threat to maternal and fetal health. Therefore, the accurate location of the expectant woman's uterus plays an important role in clinical quantitative analysis.

However, medical images have the characteristics of less data, blurred boundaries, lack of objective segmentation standard, a large image difference among patient extent, and multiple types of noise. In recent years, automatic recognition and segmentation have been introduced to medical image processing [18]. As far as we know, the existing methods have achieved good performance. In the encoder-decoder network, with iterative convolution and pooling layers, the receptive field size of kernels will expand continuously. But a too large receptive field still cannot capture context information effectively. In this paper, we present the Dynamic Selection Module (DSM), which uses horizontal and vertical convolution to capture global correlations in the H and W dimension, respectively.

Several studies [16] have documented that not all pixels in the receptive field contribute equally to the output. The expansion of receptive field size can help the neural network to learn the features of the specific scale objects more efficiently. The larger the receptive field, the more obvious the context information of the perceived object. But too large a receptive field will ignore detailed information. Eventually, the model will be unable to capture the effective regions. For example, if the receptive field is too large in medical images, the segmented object will be relatively small compared to it. But if the receptive field is too small, the segmented object will not be covered by the receptive field. As a result, based on the previous step, we further introduce the dynamic receptive field and enhance the perceptual capability by effectively selecting the convolution kernel.

Based on the above design, we then introduce a novel residual block to improve long-range dependencies, called Dynamic Residual Unit. Finally, we propose Dynamic Selection Network (DSNet) based on the U-Net framework and DRU, which has powerful spatial perception capability for medical image segmentation. Thus, it can greatly improve the segmentation performance of the network. To summarize, efficient and effective segmentation of raw medical images with deep learning plays a better reference role in determining the clinical diagnosis.

Our main contributions of this work can be summarized as follows:

- We design a specific module, Dynamic Selection Module (DSM), which can exploit dynamic receptive fields for medical image segmentation. Specifically, we dynamically adjust the size of the receptive field in both horizontal and vertical directions.
- Combined with the residual connection, we propose the Dynamic Residual Unit (DRU) to further change the internal perception capability of the network.
- We embed the DRU into standard U-Net and conduct extensive experiments on three medical datasets, including Uterus, Gland, and Lung datasets. Furthermore, we achieve superior results than other related encoder-decoder architectures.

2 Related Work

2.1 Model Architectures for Medical Image Segmentation

FCN [4] was proposed as a pioneer and representative framework in the deep learning field. It first proposed an end-to-end image processing method for pixelwise segmentation. Ronneberger et al. [7] proposed U-Net, which introduced skip connection and combined features from the previous layer with features from the contracting path to get the output. It has also achieved a good breakthrough in biomedical image segmentation [5,6]. Since then, a series of U-Net-based frameworks have been proposed. Zhou et al. [8] proposed UNet++, which filled U-Net with more skip structure but increased the parameters. It adopted the summation of dice loss and cross-entropy loss as the loss of the network, and finally got good results on a series of biomedical tasks. Inspired by the attention mechanism and U-Net, Oktay et al. [19] proposed Attention U-Net, which adjusted the output features before combining the features of the contracting path and the expanding path to guide the network segmentation. SENet [9] can selectively focus on effective information by imposing weights on each channel and adaptively recalibrate channel-wise feature responses. Zhang et al. [22] designed ET-Net, which highlighted the valuable features of high-level layers and embedded edge supervision based on the encoder-decoder structure to guide the final segmentation result.

2.2 Receptive Field

The receptive field size has played an important role in the neural network, especially for medical image segmentation. Pyramid Scene Parsing Network [12] adopted multi-scale pooling to obtain the features of different receptive fields so that the network can obtain multi-scale perception [14]. DeepLab [13] modified the ASPP by using 1×1 convolution instead of 3×3 convolution layers with a dilation rate of 24 to make the convolution weight more compact. Deformable Convolutional Networks [20] augmented the spatial sampling locations with additional offsets. It enabled the convolution kernel to be deformed arbitrarily and improved the adaptability of the convolution kernel. Res2Net [21] embedded more residual connection structures in each residual unit to capture details and global features, but it also added additional computational complexity. Recently, [15] introduced the dynamic receptive field to selectively obtain effective regions, which can significantly reduce computational costs. [10] proposed an efficient plug-and-play module for long but narrow objects, which enabled the network to efficiently capture long-range dependencies.

3 Methods

3.1 Dynamic Selection Module

To the best of our knowledge, previous work has proved that the expansion of the receptive field plays a vital role in the perceptual capability of neural networks.

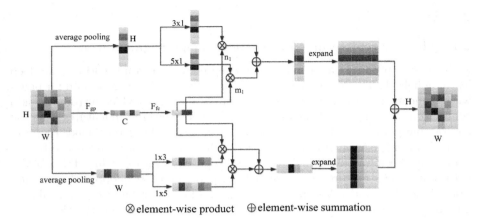

⊗ element-wise product   ⊕ element-wise summation

Fig. 1. Illustration of the Dynamic Selection Module. There are three steps: horizontal and vertical pooling, computing the attentional feature map, and fusing features of each branch. $(k \times 1)$ and $(1 \times k)$ denote the kernel size of 1D convolution. Only two parallel convolution layers for the horizontal or vertical branch are shown and it can be easily extended to more cases.

However, different objects need different perception ranges. We leverage horizontal and vertical directions to capture object features and improve efficiency. In this section, we elaborately describe the Dynamic Selection Module (DSM), as shown in Fig. 1. Given a 3D input tensor $\mathbf{X} \in \mathbb{R}^{C \times H \times W}$, where $H \times W$ is the spatial resolution of the input image and C is the number of channels. Then follow a series of steps: horizontal and vertical pooling, computing the attentional feature map, and fusing features of each branch.

First, $\mathbf{X}$ is fed into two parallel branches, each of which contains a horizontal or vertical pooling layer and dynamic adjustment of the receptive field. $\mathbf{G}_h \in \mathbb{R}^{H \times 1}$ is obtained after horizontal pooling can be written as:

$$\mathbf{G}_h = \frac{1}{W} \sum_{j=1}^{W} \mathbf{X}(i, j) \tag{1}$$

In order to adjust the size of the receptive field dynamically, we follow convolution layers with kernel sizes of 3 and 5 in each branch respectively, which results in the features $\overline{\mathbf{G}}_h$ and $\widetilde{\mathbf{G}}_h$. We can obtain more global priors by using the global average pooling on the input feature map, and transform it into $\mathbf{X}' \in \mathbb{R}^{C \times 1}$.

$$\mathbf{X}' = F_{gp}(\mathbf{X}) = \frac{1}{H \times W} \sum_{i=1}^{H} \sum_{j=1}^{W} \mathbf{X}(i, j) \tag{2}$$

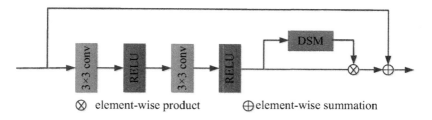

$\otimes$ element-wise product $\oplus$ element-wise summation

Fig. 2. Illustration of the dynamic residual unit. The green box (dynamic selection module) is shown in Fig. 1. (Color figure online)

Then, we adopt fully-connected operation to reduce dimension, which can produce weights m, n. It can significantly reduce computational costs.

$$(m, n) = F_{fc}(\mathbf{X}') = \sigma(\delta(\mathbf{W}\mathbf{X}')) \tag{3}$$

where δ is a *RELU* [17] function and σ is a fully-connected function. In the horizontal pooling direction, $\mathbf{G}'_h$ is obtained by fusing weight information of each convolution kernel.

$$\mathbf{G}'_h = m_1 \cdot \overline{\mathbf{G}}_h + n_1 \cdot \widetilde{\mathbf{G}}_h \tag{4}$$

Similarly, $\mathbf{G}'_v$ is obtained after the vertical pooling branch.

$$\mathbf{G}'_v = m_2 \cdot \overline{\mathbf{G}}_v + n_2 \cdot \widetilde{\mathbf{G}}_v \tag{5}$$

After that, the output feature maps of the two branches are expanded to the same size as the input. Finally, the feature maps of different branches are fused to produce the weight matrix $\mathbf{Y} \in \mathbb{R}^{C \times H \times W}$.

$$\mathbf{Y} = expand(\mathbf{G}'_h) + expand(\mathbf{G}'_v) \tag{6}$$

where *expand* refers to expand the feature map to the same size as the input size. It is worth noting that we only show two parallel convolutions for horizontal or vertical branch, which can be easily extended to more convolutions.

3.2   Overall Architecture

As described in Fig. 2, each Dynamic Residual Unit (DRU) consists of two 3×3 convolution layers, a DSM, a residual connection. In general, the introduction of DRU can enhance the spatial perception capability of the network. For different objects, DRU can dynamically adjust the internal perception of the network and improve the feature representation. Note that it can directly replace any convolution layer in the neural network and improve the performance of the network by selectively capturing long-range dependencies.

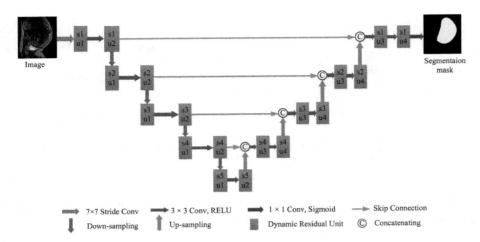

Fig. 3. An overview of our proposed DSNet architecture. Each blue box represents a DRU (is shown by Fig. 2). si and uj refer to i^{th} stage and j^{th} unit, respectively. (Color figure online)

As described in Fig. 3, we replace the convolution layer in the standard U-Net with this novel DRU, formed Dynamic Selection Network (DSNet), because U-Net [7] is one of the most advanced medical image segmentation frameworks. Experimental results demonstrate our proposed DSNet can improve the accuracy by about 3% compared to the standard U-Net.

3.3   Loss Function

In this paper, we propose to use Dice coefficient loss instead of the common cross-entropy loss. Dice coefficient loss can solve the imbalance problem of different samples because the object in the medical image (such as the cup and the optic disc) is a very small region in the image. The Dice coefficient loss is defined as follows:

$$L_{dice} = 1 - \sum_{k=0}^{K} \frac{2w_k \sum_i^N y_{gt} y_{pre}}{\sum_i^N y_{gt}^2 + \sum_i^N y_{pre}^2} \qquad (7)$$

where N and K are the pixel number and the class number. w_k represents the weight for class k. $y_{gt} \in 0,1$ and $y_{pre} \in [0,1]$ denote the ground truth label and the prediction probability for class k, respectively.

The final loss is

$$L_{loss} = L_{dice} + L_{reg} \qquad (8)$$

where L_{reg} denotes the regularization loss [23] to avoid overfitting.

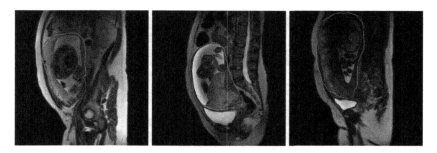

Fig. 4. Visualization of uterine segmentation. The red curve represents manual segmentation, and the yellow curve represents automatic segmentation using our method.

4   Experiments

4.1   Datasets

In this study, we use three medical datasets for evaluating our method, i.e. Uterus dataset, Gland Segmentation dataset and Lung dataset. The Gland Segmentation dataset and the Lung dataset are public medical image datasets. The Uterus dataset is a private dataset. It was collected from hospital, including 40 3D uterine MRIs from 40 pregnant women. Each case had 30 to 45 two-dimensional transverse slices, and we selected the 25 most representative slices in each case. A total of 1000 images were used as the initial segmented dataset to evaluate the proposed model. In order to expand the number of images and the effectiveness of segmentation, the selected MRI slices were seen as independent images and adopted data augmentation techniques. Then all MRI slices were stored in PNG format with an image size of 512×512 pixels.

4.2   Implementation Details

Our method is implemented in PyTorch. The number of medical samples is very small, so we apply data augmentation on the obtained dataset during training, which mainly includes horizontal and vertical flips, $\pm 20\%$ rotation, and random scaling. We randomly used 80% of the dataset as the 5-fold cross-validation and the remaining 20% as the test data. We repeated the experiment 4 times to obtain 20 sets of experimental results and employed the mean value as the final score.

We employ Adam optimizer with momentum 0.9, weight decay 0.00001 and batch size 16. We train our models for 400 epochs with an initial learning rate of 0.01. During training, if the loss is not decreased for 10 consecutive iterations, the learning rate will be reduced to half until the learning rate drops to 5e-7, and then training will be stopped. If the loss is not decreased for 20 consecutive iterations during training, training will be stopped.

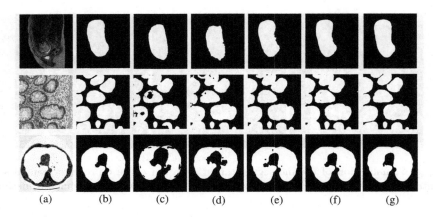

(a)   (b)   (c)   (d)   (e)   (f)   (g)

Fig. 5. Results of different representations of uterus, gland and lung segmentation. (a) Input image (b) Ground truth (c) U-Net [7] (d) UNet++ [8] (e) SENet [9] (f) SPNet [10] (g) DSN (ours).

4.3   Uterus Segmentation

For quantitative analysis, we use Dice Accuarcy and Jccard Index to evaluate our proposed method. They are commonly used evaluation metrics in medical image segmentation. As shown in Table 1, we summarize the common medical image segmentation models and recent outstanding networks such as FCN [4], U-Net [7], UNet++ [8], PSPNet [19], SENet [9] and SPNet [10]. Specifically, in terms of Dice accuracy, our proposed method achieves the performance of 85.67% on the Uterus dataset which is already better than other advanced methods in performance. Compared to the U-Net baseline, our method obtains an absolute gain of 2.76% in Dice accuracy. Similarly, our proposed method achieves an improvement of 1.12% with respect to state-of-the-art methods. It is evident that selecting the appropriate receptive field is very helpful to the improvement of segmentation performance. Moreover, in the first row of Fig. 5, we visualize the predictions of uterus segmentation using different methods. In Fig. 4, we can see that three abdominal MRI images, where the red curve represents the result of manual uterine segmentation, and the yellow curve represents the result of uterine segmentation using our proposed method. The results of these two methods are basically similar.

4.4   Gland Segmentation and Lung Segmentation

To validate the generalization of this method, we also do the same experiment on the Gland Segmentation dataset [11] and Lung dataset. The quantitative results with other methods are shown in Table 2. It is obvious that our proposed DSNet performs much better than other methods, achieving the performance of 83.57% and 99.12% on these two pubic datasets. In Fig. 5, the second row is gland segmentation using different methods, and the third row is lung segmentation using different methods. We can observe that the boundary segmentation mask is not

Table 1. Quantitative results on the Uterus dataset (mean ± standard deviation).

Model	Dice (%)	Jaccard index (%)
FCN [4]	81.37 ± 0.31	74.79 ± 0.42
U-Net [7]	82.91 ± 0.28	75.24 ± 0.20
UNet++ [8]	82.64 ± 0.26	74.82 ± 0.56
PSPNet [12]	83.55 ± 0.17	75.85 ± 0.74
SENet [9]	84.06 ± 0.08	76.13 ± 0.26
SPNet [10]	84.55 ± 0.03	76.52 ± 0.16
DSNet (ours)	**85.67 ± 0.01**	**77.83 ± 0.04**

Table 2. Quantitative results on the Gland Segmentation dataset and Lung dataset.

Method	Gland dataset		Lung dataset	
	Dice acc (%)	Jaccard index (%)	Dice acc (%)	Jaccard index (%)
FCN [4]	78.77	66.69	94.88	90.68
U-Net [7]	79.76	67.63	96.64	92.64
UNet++ [8]	80.53	68.19	95.38	91.28
PSPNet [12]	81.69	69.39	95.90	91.73
SENet [9]	81.72	70.03	96.15	92.96
SPNet [10]	82.16	71.823	98.20	93.81
DSNet (ours)	**83.57**	**72.36**	**99.12**	**94.76**

completely detected in other methods. We conclude that DSN can encode long-range dependence by learning feature representations in different directions. In addition, regardless of the size and location of the object, our method outperforms other previous methods. This indicates that the appropriate adjustment of the size of the receptive field plays a key role in our experiment.

4.5 Ablation Studies

We explore the effect of different branches on the Uterus dataset in Table 3. We take U-Net [7] as our baseline for medical image segmentation. It can be seen that only learn features from the height direction, and the dice accuracy increases from 82.91% to 84.07%, achieving an improvement of 1.16%. However, only 0.7% performance improvement from the width direction. This may be due to the location of the medical dataset. If the target objects are long-range discretely distributed, we may achieve better performance using only the width direction. Table 4 shows the effect of different convolution kernel combinations. We can observe that the combination of 3×1 and 5×1 convolution is the best. The result of the combination 3×1, 5×1 with 7×1 is worst, but it still obtains a 0.9% gain than U-Net. It is highly likely that the location of the uterus is

632   X. Qin et al.

Table 3. The effect of different branches. 'HDSM' and 'WDSM' denote only learning features from the height and width directions, respectively.

Model	Dice (%)	Jaccard index (%)
U-Net	82.91	75.24
U-Net + HDSM	84.07	76.18
U-Net + WDSM	83.61	75.86
U-Net + HDSM + WDSM	84.77	75.76

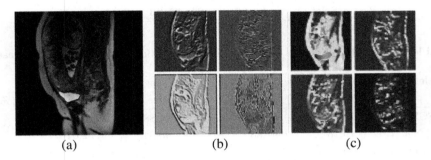

(a)   (b)   (c)

Fig. 6. Visualization of feature maps. (a) Input image. (b) Feature maps before DSM in stage 1 unit 4. (c) Feature maps after DSM in stage 1 unit 4.

relatively fixed, and too large a receptive field may reduce its performance. As a result, we often set two convolution layers for each branch.

Table 5 shows the comparison of the results after each module. Although without dynamic convolution, it still has an improvement of a 1.86% than U-Net on the Uterus dataset, which indicates that capturing features from two directions is useful. Then, the introduction of DRU enables the model to learn more global priors, which further improves the performance by almost 0.9%. Additionally, we visualize the feature map before and after this module (see Fig. 6). Due to the high-resolution feature map with rich semantic information, we choose the feature map from stage 1 unit 4. We choose quarter channels for demonstration. The results show that the network has a better perception of medical images after adding DSM.

Table 4. Performance comparison of different convolution kernel combinations.

3×1	5×1	7×1	Dice (%)	Jaccard index (%)
×	✓	✓	84.28	77.30
✓	×	✓	84.85	77.79
✓	✓	×	**85.67**	**77.83**
✓	✓	✓	83.81	77.27

Table 5. Performance comparison with each component of DSNet.

Method	Uterus dataset		Gland dataset	
	Dice (%)	Jaccard index (%)	Dice (%)	Jaccard index (%)
U-Net	82.91	75.24	79.76	67.63
UNet+DSM	84.77	76.07	81.21	69.13
UNet+DSM+DRU	85.67	77.83	83.57	72.36

5 Conclusion

In this paper, we present a novel design to dynamically adjust the size of the receptive field, Dynamic Selection Module (DSM). It captures context information from horizontal and vertical directions. Specifically, in each branch, we adopt different convolution kernel sizes to improve the modulation capability of the receptive field. Based on DSM and residual connection, we design a new Dynamic Residual Unit (DRU) and insert it into the U-structure. It can further improve the spatial perception of medical image segmentation. Extensive experiments on three datasets demonstrate that our method can improve the performance of medical segmentation. For future work, it will be interesting to apply our method to 3D data.

Acknowledgements. This work was supported by the Artificial Intelligence Program of Shanghai under Grant 2019-RGZN-01077.

References

1. Zhao, B., Lv, M., Dong, T., et al.: Transverse parallel compression suture: a new suturing method for successful treating pernicious placenta previa during cesarean section. Arch. Gynecol. Obstet. **301**, 465–472 (2020)
2. Fox, K., et al.: Conservative management of morbidly adherent placenta: expert review. Am. J. Obstet. Gynecol. **213**(6), 755–760 (2015)
3. Zhang, S., et al.: Attention guided network for retinal image segmentation. In: Shen, D., et al. (eds.) MICCAI 2019. LNCS, vol. 11764, pp. 797–805. Springer, Cham (2019). https://doi.org/10.1007/978-3-030-32239-7_88
4. Long, J., Shelhamer, E., Darrell, T.: Fully convolutional networks for semantic segmentation. In: CVPR, pp. 3431–3440 (2015)
5. Çiçek, Ö., Abdulkadir, A., Lienkamp, S.S., Brox, T., Ronneberger, O.: 3D U-Net: learning dense volumetric segmentation from sparse annotation. In: Ourselin, S., Joskowicz, L., Sabuncu, M.R., Unal, G., Wells, W. (eds.) MICCAI 2016. LNCS, vol. 9901, pp. 424–432. Springer, Cham (2016). https://doi.org/10.1007/978-3-319-46723-8_49
6. Zhao, N., Tong, N., Ruan, D., Sheng, K.: Fully automated pancreas segmentation with two-stage 3D convolutional neural networks. In: Shen, D., et al. (eds.) MICCAI 2019. LNCS, vol. 11765, pp. 201–209. Springer, Cham (2019). https://doi.org/10.1007/978-3-030-32245-8_23

7. Ronneberger, O., Fischer, P., Brox, T.: U-Net: convolutional networks for biomedical image segmentation. In: Navab, N., Hornegger, J., Wells, W.M., Frangi, A.F. (eds.) MICCAI 2015. LNCS, vol. 9351, pp. 234–241. Springer, Cham (2015). https://doi.org/10.1007/978-3-319-24574-4_28

8. Zhou, Z., Rahman Siddiquee, M.M., Tajbakhsh, N., Liang, J.: UNet++: a nested U-net architecture for medical image segmentation. In: Stoyanov, D., et al. (eds.) DLMIA/ML-CDS -2018. LNCS, vol. 11045, pp. 3–11. Springer, Cham (2018). https://doi.org/10.1007/978-3-030-00889-5_1

9. Hu, J., Shen, L., Sun, G.: Squeeze-and-excitation networks. In: CVPR, pp. 7132–7141 (2018)

10. Hou, Q., Zhang, L., Cheng, M., Feng, J.: Strip pooling: rethinking spatial pooling for scene parsing. In: CVPR, pp. 4003–4012 (2020)

11. Sirinukunwattana, K., et al.: Gland segmentation in colon histology images: the GlaS challenge contest. Med. Image Anal. **35**, 489–502 (2017)

12. Zhao, H., Shi, J., Qi, X., Wang, X., Jia, J.: Pyramid scene parsing network. In: CVPR, pp. 2881–2890 (2017)

13. Chen, L., Papandreou, G., Iasonas, K., Murphy, K., Yuille, A.: DeepLab: semantic image segmentation with deep convolutional nets, atrous convolution, and fully connected CRFs. IEEE Trans. Pattern Anal. Mach. Intell. **40**(4), 834–848 (2017)

14. Lin, D., Ji, Y., Lischinski, D., Cohen-Or, D., Huang, H.: Multi-scale context intertwining for semantic segmentation. In: Ferrari, V., Hebert, M., Sminchisescu, C., Weiss, Y. (eds.) ECCV 2018. LNCS, vol. 11207, pp. 622–638. Springer, Cham (2018). https://doi.org/10.1007/978-3-030-01219-9_37

15. Li, X., Wang, W., Hu, X., Yang, J.: Selective kernel networks. In: CVPR, pp. 510–519 (2019)

16. Valanarasu, J.M.J., Sindagi, V.A., Hacihaliloglu, I., Patel, V.M.: KiU-Net: towards accurate segmentation of biomedical images using over-complete representations. In: Martel, A.L., et al. (eds.) MICCAI 2020. LNCS, vol. 12264, pp. 363–373. Springer, Cham (2020). https://doi.org/10.1007/978-3-030-59719-1_36

17. Nair, V., Hinton, G.E.: Rectified linear units improve restricted Boltzmann machines. In: CLML (2010)

18. Litjens, G., et al.: A survey on deep learning in medical image analysis. Med. Image Anal. **42**, 60–88 (2017)

19. Oktay, O., Schlemper, J., Folgoc, L.L., Lee, M.: Attention u-net: learning where to look for the pancreas. arXiv preprint arXiv:1804.03999 (2018)

20. Dai, J., et al.: Deformable convolutional networks. In: ICCV, pp. 764–773 (2017)

21. Gao, S., et al.: Res2net: a new multi-scale backbone architecture. IEEE Trans. Pattern Anal. Mach. Intell. (2019)

22. Zhang, Z., Fu, H., Dai, H., Shen, J., Pang, Y., Shao, L.: ET-Net: a generic edge-attention guidance network for medical image segmentation. In: Shen, D., et al. (eds.) MICCAI 2019. LNCS, vol. 11764, pp. 442–450. Springer, Cham (2019). https://doi.org/10.1007/978-3-030-32239-7_49

23. Hoerl, A.E., Kennard, R.W.: Ridge regression: biased estimation for nonorthogonal problems. Technometrics **42**(2000), 80–86 (1970)

Computational Approach to Identifying Contrast-Driven Retinal Ganglion Cells

Richard Gault[1]([envelope]) [ORCID], Philip Vance[2] [ORCID], T. Martin McGinnity[2,3] [ORCID],
Sonya Coleman[2] [ORCID], and Dermot Kerr[2] [ORCID]

[1] School of Electronics, Electrical Engineering and Computer Science,
Queen's University, Belfast, Northern Ireland, UK
`richard.gault@qub.ac.uk`
[2] Intelligent Systems Research Centre, Ulster University,
Derry/Londonderry, Northern Ireland, UK
{`p.vance,tm.mcginnity,sa.coleman,d.kerr`}`@ulster.ac.uk`
[3] Department of Computer Science, Nottingham Trent University, Nottingham, UK
`martin.mcginnity@ntu.ac.uk`

Abstract. The retina acts as the primary stage for the encoding of visual stimuli in the central nervous system. It is comprised of numerous functionally distinct cells tuned to particular types of visual stimuli. This work presents an analytical approach to identifying contrast-driven retinal cells. Machine learning approaches as well as traditional regression models are used to represent the input-output behaviour of retinal ganglion cells. The findings of this work demonstrate that it is possible to separate the cells based on how they respond to changes in mean contrast upon presentation of single images. The separation allows us to identify retinal ganglion cells that are likely to have good model performance in a computationally inexpensive way.

Keywords: Retinal modelling · Encoding natural images · Identifying cell behaviour · Visual modelling

1 Introduction

Visual perception begins with the encoding of visual stimuli into neuronal spikes by the retina. The retina receives few afferent signals from the central nervous system allowing the function of the retina to be studied as a black box with an input, i.e. light stimulus, and output, i.e. spiking activity of retinal ganglion cells (RGCs). Recent studies have tried to gain insight in to the internal operations using deep learning [1]. The majority of RGCs can be classified as being either ON- and/or OFF-cells that are described as being transient or sustained [2]. ON-cells respond to an increase in light intensity while conversely OFF-cells respond

The authors would like to thank Jian Liu, Tim Gollisch and the "Sensory Processing in the Retina" research group at the Department of Ophthalmology, University of Göttingen who supplied the experimental data as part of the "VISUALISE" project funded under the European Union Seventh Framework Programme (FP7-ICT-2011.9.11); grant number [600954] ("VISUALISE").

I. Farkaš et al. (Eds.): ICANN 2021, LNCS 12893, pp. 635–646, 2021.
https://doi.org/10.1007/978-3-030-86365-4_51

to a decrease in light intensity. A subdivision of each class can be made into transient and sustained responses. RGCs described as sustained produce continual firing in response to stimulus while transient cells respond only momentarily to temporal changes. For the investigation of how the retina encodes single images it is likely that sustained RGCs are of greatest interest to model the encoding using the corresponding spiking responses [2]. Many types of RGC have been documented for their selective response to particular types of stimuli, for example, direction specific motion, orientation or global environmental changes [2]. It is unlikely that cells with such diverse functionality are as important for single image processing as those with a sustained response.

The stimuli directly responsible for a RGC's activity are solely contained within the receptive field (RF) of the cell. Environmental changes or saccades of the eye mean that the stimuli that falls on the receptive field is constantly changing. It is therefore not surprising a significant proportion of RGC behaviour is directly coupled with temporal changes in environment. RGCs with transient responses are sensitive to subtle temporal changes in the RF but not stationary patterns [3]. In order to model the retinal encoding of single images it is important to identify RGCs whose behaviour is sustained over longer temporal periods. The ability to identify RGCs with sustained (or transient) responses to single images during the analysis stage would remove the need to use artificial stimuli which is known to not comprehensively probe the cell's functionality.

RGCs receive inputs from various networks of cells in the preceding layers of the retina which all contribute to forming the RF. Identification of the stimulus values that contribute to a cell eliciting a response is an essential stage in identifying the cells receptive field. Factorisation techniques have been used to infer potential sub-receptive fields (SRFs) that contribute to the overall RFs. Accurate identification of these sub-receptive fields and the underlying bipolar cells is essential in order to develop an accurate retinal model [4]. Models that consider the SRFs of the RGCs have been shown to provide improved accuracy when compared with approaches that consider the information contained in the entire RF as one single input [4]. SRFs allow detailed spatial information to be efficiently combined in a non-linear manner within RGCs when compared with single RF modelling approaches.

The aim of this work is to present an approach that can efficiently identify RGCs suitable for single image retinal models. Section 2 will outline the methodology used; this includes Sects. 2.2 and 2.3 that outline the investigation of cell identification and the modelling approaches used for single image processing. The results are first presented in Sect. 3 before being discussed in detail in Sect. 4. Section 5 provides a discussion of the findings of this work and an outline of directions for future work.

2   Methods

Multi-electrode array recordings from isolated Tiger Salamander retinas were prepared and conducted at the Gollisch Lab, University Medical Center Göttingen as outlined and described in [4–6]. The stimulus set comprised of a wide range of three hundred grayscale natural images from the "McGill Calibrated Colour Image Database" (http://tabby.vision.mcgill.ca/html/browsedownload. html) which were presented to the isolated retinas at a resolution of 256×256 pixels. Images were presented in a pseudo-random order for 200 ms with an inter-stimulus interval of 800 ms allowing sufficient time for no overlap in the cells response to different images. Spikes occurring within 300 ms of stimulus onset were considered to be evoked by the stimulus whilst later activity was considered to be evoked by the removal of the stimulus and are ignored in this study.

The overall data analyses pipeline for the present study is comprised of identifying the RF of each cell and subsequently modelling and optimising SRFs for each cell. The input-output relationship that maps the information contained in the stimulus image to the resulting spiking activity is determined and modelled using the RF and SRFs. These components are described in detail through the remainder of Sect. 2.

The initial RF estimate was determined using a reverse correlation approach. Each retina was stimulated with spatio-temporal checker stimuli and the resultant spike-triggered average (STA) calculated. Singular Value Decomposition (SVD) is used to extract the spatial element of the STA over time [7]. The size, location and shape of a RGC's RF is approximated by fitting a 2D Gaussian distribution to the extracted data. Artificial stimuli are known to not capture the complexity of natural images and it has been shown that RGCs produce a different RF response when stimulated with natural images [8,9]. Therefore in this study the RF is refined using a subset of natural images based on the approach outlined in [10].

We then apply a number of machine learning methods to derive input-output models of the RGC using RFs that are comprised of different numbers of SRFs, and then compare the models' responses against the actual real RGC neuron's response. Results gathered from experiments involving several RGCs provide quantitative evidence on the benefits of considering SRFs of RGCs when deriving computational models rather than considering the complete RF as a summation of all its parts.

2.1 Modelling Sub-receptive Fields

Considering the stimulus values contained within the RF as a singular value, such as the mean contrast, results in the loss of much of the spatial information contained within this RF [11]. A better approach is to consider the RF as composed of a number of SRFs and corresponding singular values from each of these SRF regions. Here, the SRFs are characterised using two separate approaches. The first approach is a straightforward geometric approximation of the RF into several equal sectors. While analytically simple, this approach is in no way biologically plausible. Each SRF is obtained by segmenting the elliptical RF along its circumference and intersecting these points in the centre of the RF. Each of the resulting sectors that the elliptical RF is now composed is considered to be a SRF in such a way that there is approximately equal pixel coverage across each of the SRFs. An illustration of this approach is shown in Fig. 1 No emphasis

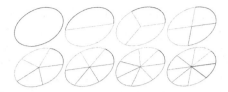

Fig. 1. Illustration of a geometric segmentation of a RF in to 2,...,8 SRFs

is placed on the particular arrangement or orientation of each SRF as no prior knowledge of the underlying biological SRF is known.

The second approach to identify SRFs is aimed at approximating the receptive fields of the bipolar cells in a more biologically plausible way using non-negative matrix factorisation (NNMF) [4]. The pixels of 300 natural images (each image being 256×256) are restructured into a matrix, X, of dimension $256^2 \times 300$. The NNMF methodology allows for the dimension of the original problem to be reduced by approximating X as follows

$$X \approx FY \tag{1}$$

where F is a $256^2 \times n$ non-negative dictionary matrix of n factors and Y is the $n \times 300$ expansion matrix of weights. This technique is naturally suited for decomposing grayscale images as the original images and the corresponding factors contain only non-negative values. Each column vector of F can be restructured in to a 256×256 pixels image by reversing the process used to originally restructure the natural images into column vectors. The NNMF was carried out using the MAT-LAB function `nnmf` with alternating least-squares approach. The number of non-negative factors, n, equated to the number of SRFs being modelled.

Given the factors of each cell, now restructured to a resolution of 256×256 pixels, the SRFs are identified by fitting 2D-Gaussian distributions to each factor in a similar way to the original RF approximation. In the case of the geometric approach, 100% of the receptive field is covered by SRFs while the NNMF approach cannot guarantee such coverage. A Genetic Algorithm (GA) is used to optimise the size of the NNMF generated SRFs to maximise their coverage within the RF. The sizes of the SRFs are constrained such that at least 60% of the SRF must be located within the original RF and no two SRFs may overlap by more than 30% of their individual size. An example of these optimised SRFs (where the number being modelled is 1–8 SRFs) is shown in Fig. 2 for one particular RGC.

2.2   Assessing Input-Output Relationship

Information present in grayscale images can be represented in many different ways. In this study the mean contrast of each SRF contained within the RF is considered in line with previous studies [10,12,14]. The mean contrast is defined as

$$C_{RF} = \frac{M_{RF} - M_{gray}}{M_{gray}} \tag{2}$$

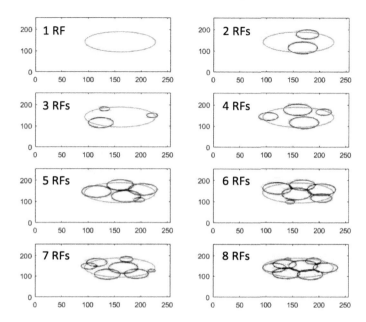

Fig. 2. Example of a cell's optimised SRFs (red) of the full RF (green) for 1–8 SRFs displayed relative to the 256×256 pixel stimuli size (Color figure online)

where M_{RF} is the mean intensity of the RF and M_{gray} is the mean intensity of the entire image. The output is considered to be the average spike count of each cell in response to each image. To assess the significance of the input-output relationships for each cell, the input-output pairs are fitted with a linear regression model. This provides an efficient approach to describe the significance of the input-output relationships. The gradient of the linear least-squares fit quantifies the rate of change in output with respect to change in the input quantity. Therefore, a large gradient (either positive or negative) indicates there is a significant change in the output behaviour relative to the input feature. Conversely, little or no gradient indicates that similar outputs are found for varying input values. An illustration of a large gradient is shown in the fitted data of Fig. 3a whilst an example where there is a weak input-output gradient is shown in Fig. 3b. It is clear from the example in Fig. 3b that if varying input values create the same output that the input feature of the image does not represent the driving force behind the cell's behaviour.

2.3   Modelling Retinal Behaviour

Inspired by previous modelling approaches for natural image processing [12,13, 15] a number of different machine learning techniques are considered in this study; namely a Multi-Layer Perceptron (MLP) [16], Bayesian Regularised Neural Networks (BRNN) [17], Support Vector Regression (SVR) [18] and k-Nearest

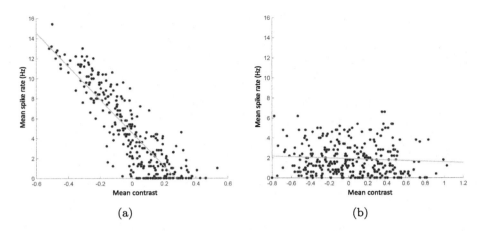

(a)   (b)

Fig. 3. Illustration of the linear least-squares fit (gray) to an example of a strong input-output relationship (a) and a weak input-output relationship (b) for two different cells across all input images; in these cases the input property is the mean contrast of each image.

Neighbours (k-NN) [19]. Methodological details of each model can be found in the associated literature [20]. The data are randomly separated into training (80%) and testing (20%) sets which remained constant across all modelling approaches. Each cell is modelled individually with 80% of the images used for training and 20% of the images used for testing. The same training and testing images are used for each cell. Each cell model is subject to 5 fold cross-validation and evaluated on the test data in each fold. In a practical sense the MLP is implemented in MATLAB by first constructing a network with 10 neurons in the hidden layer (using `fitnet`) before training the network using the training function `trainlm`. The trained network is then evaluated using the unseen testing data. The BRNN model is implemented in a similar way to the MLP case with the exception that the training function used is `trainbr`. The number of neurons found in the hidden layers of the MLP and BRNN (i.e. 10) is chosen arbitrarily for this preliminary investigation. Future work could include the optimisation of the network architecture. The SVR model is fitted to the training data using the function `fitrsvm` with a radial basis kernel function. The k-NN model is implemented using the `knnsearch` function with the distance metric being the Euclidean distance. The optimum value for k was determined through an exhaustive search of possible values for k between 1 and 100 with k chosen to minimise the model's error.

Additionally, more classical modelling approaches are used as computationally efficient alternatives to the machine learning approaches outlined above; namely linear regression and non-linear (quadratic) modelling. The linear model is fitted using an ordinary least-squares approach utilising the `fitlm` function in MATLAB. The quadratic model is fitted using the MATLAB function `fitnlm` using a unitary initial guess and a constant error based variance model.

3   Performance Evaluation

To evaluate the effectiveness of each model in representing the behaviour of the RGCs in response to natural images, the coefficient of determination, or R^2 measure, is used. Given the model's predictions, p, compared with the true RGC output, t, over the 300 images the R^2 measure defined as

$$R^2 = 1 - \frac{\sum(t-p)^2}{\sum(t-\bar{t})^2} \qquad (3)$$

where $\bar{t}$ denotes the mean of the true spike rates t over all images. The model is considered to perfectly match the real world behaviour when $R^2 = 1$ and the R^2 metric is bounded below by 0.

Figure 4 shows the average performance across all cell models when a threshold is placed on the absolute value of the input-output least-squares gradient (described in Section II-B). The input is considered to be the mean contrast for the entire receptive field of each cell. The y-axis indicates the average model performance across all cells with an absolute input-output least-squares gradient of at least the threshold indicated on the x-axis.

Figure 4 illustrates that when using the mean contrast as model input we can observe a positive relationship between the gradient of the least-squares fit and the average R^2 across all the models. A gradient threshold may be used to divide the cells into two groups for further analysis. This removes the need for individual analysis of each cell to consider those where spiking response is unlikely to be correlated to differing mean contrasts within the RF. The threshold is chosen to be indicative of a significant input-output gradient. Therefore, for the remainder of this analysis the upper-quartile of the input-output gradients is selected as the threshold (this represents the median value of the upper portion of the gradients).

The second stage of the analysis is concerned with modelling performance when considering additional spatial information through the use of SRFs. The 138 cells are now separated into two groups. Firstly the absolute input-output gradient of all cells is considered. The upper-quartile of these data is taken to be the differentiation point. Group 1 consists of those cells with a minimum absolute input-output gradient of the upper-quartile (3.61) and Group 2 consists of cells with an absolute input-output gradient below this threshold. When considering cells from Group 1 (35 cells) all models perform significantly better (at least $R^2 = 0.4$) compared with the inclusion of all cells (at most $R^2 = 0.28$) as seen in Figs. 5 and 4 respectively. Conversely, when the cells in Group 2 (103) are considered in isolation (Fig. 6) the cell model performance is greatly reduced ($R^2 \in [0.1, 0.3]$) compared with the performance observed when modelling Group 1 cells ($R^2 \in [0.4, 0.72]$). This is true irrespective of the modelling technique or the number of SRFs considered. Thus, it has been possible to identify RGCs suitable for the processing contrast-driven natural images through the division of the entire cell dataset into two groups prior to modelling.

As the geometric approach to SRF modelling does not yield biologically realistic SRF of the cells, the NNMF approach to modelling SRF is considered on

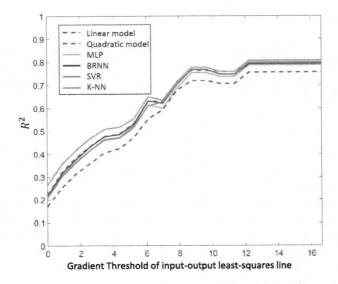

Fig. 4. Average performance for each model given cells with a minimum input-output gradient listed along the x-axis.

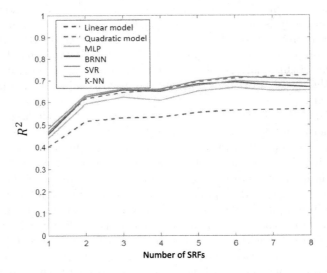

Fig. 5. The average model performance across all Group 1 cells for varying numbers of geometrically defined SRFs with an absolute input-output gradient of at least 3.61.

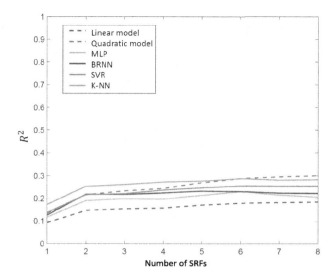

Fig. 6. The average model performance across all Group 2 cells for varying numbers of geometrically defined SRFs with an input-output gradient of less than 3.61.

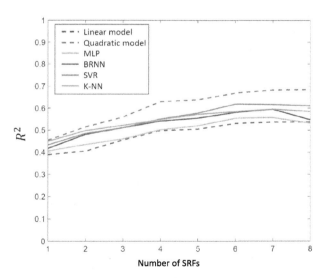

Fig. 7. The average model performance across all cells for varying numbers of NNMF defined SRFs with an absolute input-output gradient of at least 3.61.

those cells in Group 1. The results are illustrated in Fig. 7. The results show again that including SRF models improves modelling performance compared with modelling only a single RF irrespective of the modelling approach used. However, comparing each model in turn leads in general to the unexpected finding that NNMF defined SRFs (results shown in Fig. 7) did not provide better performance than the geometrically defined counterparts (results shown in Fig. 5). One possible explanation could be that SRFs derived through NNMF did not cover all of the RF and thus may omit some spatial information in contrast to the geometric approach to SRF modelling.

4 Discussion

The primary aim of this work was to investigate whether it is possible to identify relevant RGCs for processing natural images i.e. cells that predominantly respond to variations in mean contrast. Analysis indicated that model performance was improved with an increase in the absolute gradient of the input-output least-squares fit (Fig. 4). The simple process of fitting a linear least-squares line to the input-output data provided the basis for data to be segmented into two groups. It was determined that cells with a large absolute gradient were most likely to provide the best model performance. It is appropriate to separate RGCs by functionality as different cell types are known to have disjoint pathways. We postulate that the proposed approach is a step towards an analytical approach for classifying cell functionality.

It is well known that modelling a RGC Receptive Field using a singular value results in a loss of spatial information. Vance et al. [11] have shown that using finer grained spatial information led to improved model performance compared with single RF models (Figs. 5, 6 and 7). The NNMF constructed SRFs provide improved modelling performance over single RFs models (Fig. 7); however, surprisingly the results from of the NNMF approach did not, in general, improve upon the results from the geometrically defined SRFs (Fig. 5). Comparing the geometric and NNMF approaches, it can be deduced that it is possible to produce models with at least the accuracy of the bio-inspired NNMF SRF methodology with a relatively efficient and simple geometric approach. Further work is required to ascertain the reason why the geometric approach produced the best results for SRF modelling despite having no immediately apparent biological connection to the SRFs of the RGCs.

A number of machine learning and regression modelling approaches were considered in this work. Figures 5, 6 and 7 show the regression approaches (illustrated with dotted lines) performed similar to the machine learning approaches. The quadratic model performed better than the linear model irrespective of the number of SRFs taken into account. This is unsurprising as the RGCs are known to respond in a non-linear way to stimuli [21]. In the case of NNMF derived SRF models (Fig. 7) the quadratic model outperformed all other modelling approaches irrespective of the number of RFs modelled. Using the geometrically derived SRFs the quadratic model provided the overall best performance (0.72, Fig. 5) compared with all other models with the maximum number of SRFs. Amongst the machine learning approaches SVR performed, in general, the strongest across different numbers of SRFs whilst MLP consistently performed poorly. It should be noted that all modelling approaches, with the possible exception of the linear model, performed similarly and showed that an accurate model of single image processing can be achieved once appropriate cells are identified and at least 6 SRFs are considered (Figs. 5 and 7).

5   Conclusion

The encoding of visual information is carried out by a variety of functionally diverse cells whose response is driven by a particular characteristic of the stimuli. To create bio-inspired models of retinal processing of visual information this work aimed to identify a method for generating a subset of functionally similar retinal cells appropriate for single image processing. A computationally efficient linear fit of the input-output relationship of a stimulus attribute, such as mean contrast, and the RGC response, namely the mean firing rate, was used to identify cells whose behaviour is proportional to the stimulus attribute. It was possible to divide the cells into two groups using this information prior to modelling the RGC behaviour. Separating cells in this way allows us to identify those cells that could be modelled accurately. Therefore, it is postulated that the identified cells are appropriate for single image processing. Increasing the number of SRFs modelled in general led to increased model performance irrespective of the modelling approach used. The machine learning models performed comparably with the more computationally efficient quadratic model.

Future work is required to identify additional attributes of input stimuli that can be used to construct functionally homogeneous subgroups of RGCs such as those that respond to transient stimuli rather than stationary stimuli. Accurate modelling of RGC behaviour with distinct functionality could provide the building blocks to construct a complete representation of the encoding of visual information by the retina. Future work will also need to consider a greater repertoire of cell functionality including modelling the temporal encoding by RGCs compared with the firing rate models considered in the present work.

References

1. Zhang, Y., et al.: Reconstruction of natural visual scenes from neural spikes with deep neural networks. Neural Netw. **125**, 19–30 (2020)
2. Dhande, O.S., Stafford, B.K., Lim, J.-H.A., Huberman, A.D.: Contributions of retinal ganglion cells to subcortical visual processing and behaviors. Ann. Rev. Vis. Sci. **1**, 291–328 (2015)
3. Gollisch, T., Meister, M.: Eye smarter than scientists believed: neural computations in circuits of the retina. Neuron **65**(2), 150–164 (2010)
4. Liu, J.K., et al.: Inference of neuronal functional circuitry with spike-triggered non-negative matrix factorization. Nature Commun. **8**(1), 149 (2017)

646   R. Gault et al.

5. Liu, J.K., Gollisch, T.: Spike-triggered covariance analysis reveals phenomenological diversity of contrast adaptation in the retina. PLoS Comput. Biol. **11**(7), e1004435 (2015)
6. Onken, A., et al.: Using matrix and tensor factorizations for the single-trial analysis of population spike trains. PLoS Comput. Biol. **12**(11), e1005189 (2016)
7. Gauthier, J.L., et al.: Receptive fields in primate retina are coordinated to sample visual space more uniformly. PLoS Biol. **7**(4), e1000063 (2009)
8. Rapela, J., Mendel, J.M., Grzywacz, N.M.: Estimating nonlinear receptive fields from natural images. J. Vis. **6**(4), 11 (2006)
9. Touryan, J., Felsen, G., Dan, Y.: Spatial structure of complex cell receptive fields measured with natural images. Neuron **45**(5), 781–791 (2005)
10. Vance, P.J., Das, G.P., Kerr, D., Coleman, S.A., McGinnity, T.M.: Refining receptive field estimates using natural images for retinal ganglion cells. Iaria, Cognitive, pp. 77–82 (2016)
11. Vance, P.J., et al.: Bioinspired approach to modeling retinal ganglion cells using system identification techniques. IEEE Trans. Neural Netw. Learn. Syst. **29**(5), 1796–1808 (2017)
12. Vance, P.J., Das, G.P., Coleman, S.A., Kerr, D., Kerr, E.P., McGinnity, T.M.: Investigation into sub-receptive fields of retinal ganglion cells with natural images. In: 2018 International Joint Conference on Neural Networks (IJCNN), pp. 1–8 (2018)
13. Kerr, D., Coleman, S.A., McGinnity, T.M.: Modelling and analysis of retinal ganglion cells with neural networks. In: Irish Machine Vision and Image Processing, pp. 95–100 (2014)
14. Das, G.P., et al.: Computational modelling of salamander retinal ganglion cells using machine learning approaches. Neurocomputing **325**, 101–112 (2019)
15. Das, G., Vance, P., Kerr, D., Coleman, S.A., McGinnity, T.M.: Modelling retinal ganglion cells stimulated with static natural images. In: COGNITIVE 2016: The Eighth International Conference on Advanced Cognitive Technologies and Applications, Rome, Italy. IARIA (2016)
16. Haykin, S., Network, N.: A comprehensive foundation. Neural Netw. **2**(2004), 41 (2004)
17. MacKay, D.J.C.: A practical Bayesian framework for backpropagation networks. Neural Comput. **4**(3), 448–472 (1992)
18. Cortes, C., Vapnik, V.: Support-vector networks. Mach. Learn. **20**(3), 273–297 (1995)
19. Altman, N.S.: An introduction to kernel and nearest-neighbor nonparametric regression. Am. Stat. **46**(3), 175–185 (1992)
20. Hastie, T., Tibshirani, R., Friedman, J.: The Elements of Statistical Learning: Data Mining, Inference, and Prediction. Springer Series in Statistics, Springer, New York (2013). https://doi.org/10.1007/978-0-387-84858-7
21. Pillow, J.W., Paninski, L., Uzzell, V.J., Simoncelli, E.P., Chichilnisky, E.J.: Prediction and decoding of retinal ganglion cell responses with a probabilistic spiking model. J. Neurosci. **25**(47), 11003–11013 (2005)

Radiological Identification of Hip Joint Centers from X-ray Images Using Fast Deep Stacked Network and Dynamic Registration Graph

Fuchang Han[1], Shenghui Liao[1(✉)], Renzhong Wu[1], Shu Liu[1], Yuqian Zhao[2], and Xiantao Shen[3]

[1] School of Computer Science and Engineering, Central South University, Changsha, China
lsh@csu.edu.cn
[2] School of Automation, Central South University, Changsha, China
[3] Tongji Medical College, Huazhong University of Science and Technology, Wuhan, China

Abstract. Locating the hip joint center (HJC) from X-ray images is frequently required for the evaluation of hip dysplasia. Existing state-of-the-art methods focus on developing functional methods or regression equations with some radiographic landmarks. Such developments employ shallow networks or single equations to locate the HJC, and little attention has been given to deep stacked networks. In addition, existing methods ignore the connections between static and dynamic landmarks, and their prediction capacity is limited. This paper proposes an innovative hybrid framework for HJC identification. The proposed method is based on fast deep stacked network (FDSN) and dynamic registration graph with four improvements: (1) an anatomical landmark extraction module obtains comprehensive prominent bony landmarks from multipose X-ray images; (2) an attribute optimization module based on grey relational analysis (GRA) guides the network to focus on useful external anatomical landmarks; (3) a multiverse optimizer (MVO) module appended to the framework automatically and efficiently determines the optimal model parameters; and (4) the dynamic fitting and two-step registration approach are integrated into the model to further improve the accuracy of HJC localization. By integrating the above improvements in series, the models' performances are gradually enhanced. Experimental results show that our model achieves superior results to existing HJC prediction approaches.

Keywords: Hip joint center · Fast deep stacked network · Dynamic registration graph · Anatomical landmarks · Multiverse optimizer

1 Introduction

The hip joint center (HJC) is an important reference point for decisions regarding the treatment of hip dysplasia. Unlike prominent bony landmarks, the HJC cannot be palpated, and thus, its determination must be calculated [1]. In the clinic, the HJC location is manually estimated by expert orthopedists, which is time consuming and labor intensive. It has become increasingly important to automatically and efficiently determine the HJC coordinates.

© Springer Nature Switzerland AG 2021
I. Farkaš et al. (Eds.): ICANN 2021, LNCS 12893, pp. 647–659, 2021.
https://doi.org/10.1007/978-3-030-86365-4_52

Current state-of-the-art methods for HJC determination can be categorized into three classes: Mose circle methods, functional methods and regression methods. (1) The Mose circle method is a quantitative approach used to estimate the HJC by using a template of concentric circles [2], and some modified Mose circle techniques have been proven to provide a more accurate approximation of the HJC than manual prediction [3]. However, when the ossification of the femoral skull epiphysis is insufficient, the HJC position determined by this method may be eccentric. (2) Functional methods calculate the trajectories of markers attached to the thigh and then locate the HJC by estimating the relative motion of the thigh and pelvis [4]. Many optimization approaches have been proposed to improve the accuracy and calculation time [5], such as the quadratic best sphere fitting [6], bias-compensated quartic best fitted sphere [7], and Reuleaux [8] methods. However, the estimation of the HJC relies heavily on the quality and range of movement during calibration trials. Due to soft tissue artifacts and limited circumduction movement, it is difficult to establish a reliable local coordinate system (LCS) of the femur or pelvis. A functional method would result in HJC location errors of 26 mm when performing substantially limited hip circumduction movement [4]. Functional calibration is challenging for those with impaired movement control or reduced range of motion, and recent studies suggest that it may be less accurate in clinical populations [9–11]. (3) Regression methods use empirical regression equations between palpable bone landmarks and the HJC as an anthropometric quantity function, and regression parameters are obtained by pelvis samples isolated in vivo and via medical imaging. However, these equations are not applicable universally since HJC-related measurements are quite variable between races or even communities [12]. The mean error is estimated in the range of 15–30 mm when using available regression equations [5, 10, 11, 13, 14]. Thus, more accurate and adaptive prediction approaches are desired.

However, within the context of HJC determination, the challenges stem from three aspects. (1) The first aspect is large-scale cartilage. Due to insufficient ossification of the femoral head, the acetabular curvature displayed on the orthographic image of the hip joint is far smaller than the actual curvature. This property brings a new challenge to general regression methods. (2) The second aspect is intraclass variations. There are obvious differences between study subjects, such as the width and height of the pelvis, the ossification degree of the acetabulum and femur, inconsistent abduction/adduction performance, and an unexpectedly tilted or rotated pelvis when examinations are performed. These differences often fail to yield effective results. (3) The third aspect is adaptive HJC prediction. Different empirical regression equations have been proposed in the past to identify the HJC, but these methods are suitable only for certain groups of people [15]. How to adaptively predict HJC using intelligent learning models remains unsolved. Note that the deep learning approaches have been widely used in the field of medical images [16–18], but there are few studies to explore the deep learning approaches for the HJC prediction.

To accurately identify the HJC, this paper advocates the idea that static to dynamic prominent bony landmarks contribute to object localization. This idea is motivated by the following intuitive concepts: pelvis bone landmarks remain unchanged regardless of what movement the legs perform, and bone landmarks from the hip joint are dynamic when the legs perform large abduction/adduction and flexion/extension movements. Thus, it is desirable to investigate static to dynamic landmarks to achieve better predictions.

To this end, we propose an innovative hybrid framework for HJC identification. It is equipped with a fast deep stacked network (FDSN)-based fast prediction module and a dynamic registration graph-based accurate positioning module with the following four aspects.

(1) Comprehensive prominent bony landmarks are extracted. Our method is based on X-ray images, and the extraction of the most comprehensive bone anatomical landmarks is desired. The coordinate system is built on multipose X-ray images (including abduction images and adduction images), and eight anatomical landmarks on each hip are annotated by expert orthopedists.

(2) We introduce a new attribute optimization module, guiding the network to focus on useful anatomical landmarks. By ranking the correlation coefficients between the prominent bony landmarks and the HJC using the grey relational analysis (GRA) method, we select the high-importance attributes to train our model since some landmarks may be damaged.

(3) The proposed FDSN method considers adaptive HJC prediction to tackle the problem of automated model optimization. Specifically, a regularized extreme learning machine (RELM) is employed to train the modules, and random feature mapping is shared among the modules to speed up the FDSN training. We initialized the model with optimal parameters obtained by the multiverse optimizer (MVO) method [19]. This MVO can be easily added to model architectures, increasing prediction accuracy.

(4) The proposed dynamic registration graph-based positioning method is based on multipose X-ray images. A two-step registration approach is used to align two pelvis images, and we fit the circle center in a dynamic abduction/adduction manner for accurate HJC positioning. The proposed innovative hybrid framework features better accuracy and reliability than previously developed approaches.

2 The Proposed Method

2.1 Method Architecture

Our goal is to automatically and efficiently determine the position coordinates of the HJC. This goal requires that both static and dynamic anatomical landmarks be investigated for the best prediction of the HJC. To this end, we propose an innovative hybrid prediction framework, as shown in Fig. 1. It involves one landmark extraction module for the comprehensive prominent bony landmarks, one GRA optimization module for the importance measure of landmarks, one FDSN module that achieves fast HJC prediction in static cases and one dynamic registration strategy to fit the HJC in dynamic cases. Next, we will detail these modules.

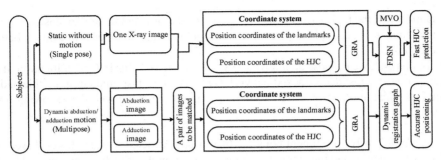

Fig. 1. The overall flowchart of our proposed method.

2.2 Landmark Extraction

Comprehensive prominent bony landmarks should be extracted from multipose X-ray images of hip joints. Considering that there were obvious differences between the study subjects, such as the width and height of the pelvis, the ossification degree of the acetabulum and femur, and inconsistent abduction/adduction performance, we built a coordinate system on each image according to the posterior inferior iliac spine on both sides, as shown in Fig. 2(a). Specifically, the subjects were asked to perform dynamic abduction/adduction movements. Sixteen prominent bony landmarks were annotated by orthopedists, as displayed in Fig. 2(b) and Table 1, and the HJC was determined by Mose circles with a template of concentric circles, as displayed in Fig. 2(c) and (d).

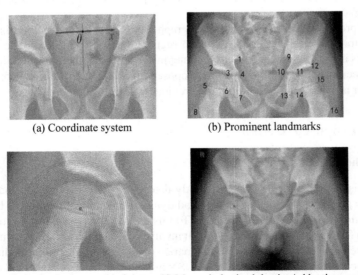

(a) Coordinate system   (b) Prominent landmarks

(c) Mose circles in single-pose hip joints   (d) Mose circles in abduction/adduction movements

Fig. 2. Image processing.

Table 1. Annotated anatomical landmarks.

Landmarks	Definition	Position	Status
1, 9	Posterior inferior iliac spine	Pelvis	Static
2, 12	Outer margin of acetabulum	Pelvis	Static
3, 11	Inner margin of acetabulum	Pelvis	Static
4, 10	Apex of Y-shaped cartilage	Pelvis	Static
5, 15	Outer margin of epiphyseal plate	Hip joint	Dynamic
6, 14	Inner margin of epiphyseal plate	Hip joint	Dynamic
7, 13	Inferior margin of teardrop	Pelvis	Static
8, 16	Tip of greater trochanters	Hip joint	Dynamic
R	HJC	Hip joint	Static

2.3 Grey Relational Analysis

GRA is a quantitative analysis and development trend comparison method, and it is used to analyze the relevance between input attributes and output predictions. The basic idea of the GRA method is to judge the closeness degree based on the geometric similarity between the reference sequence and the multiple comparison sequences [20]. In our study, the input attributes are the coordinates of prominent landmarks (also called the comparison sequence), and the output predictions are the coordinates of the HJC determined by Mose circles (also called the reference sequence). Note that our model takes the most prominent bone anatomical landmarks as the predictors, and the GRA optimization module can exclude some incorrect landmarks, such as damaged or broken landmarks.

The core ideas of GRA are as follows: the reference sequence is described as $x_0 = \{x_0(1), x_0(2), \ldots x_0(n)\}$, and the comparison sequence is represented by $x_i = \{x_i(1), x_i(2), \ldots x_i(n)\}$, where n represents the number of the samples and i represents the i-th input attribute. We normalize the original sequence and can obtain the initialized reference sequence and the comparison sequences, $y_0 = \{y_0(1), y_0(2), \ldots y(n)\}$ and $y_i = \{y_i(1), y_i(2), \ldots y_i(n)\}$, respectively. After the nondimensional transformation, the correlation coefficient between $y_0(t)$ and $y_i(t)$ at time k can be calculated:

$$\xi_i(k) = \frac{\min_i(\Delta_i(min)) + \beta \max_i(\Delta_i(max))}{|y_0(k) - y_i(k)| + \beta \max_i(\Delta_i(max))} \tag{1}$$

where $\Delta_i(min) = min_k(|y_0(k) - y_i(k)|)$, $\Delta_i(max) = max_k(|y_0(k) - y_i(k)|)$, and β represent the distinguishing coefficients. The grey correlation grade γ_i between the reference sequence and the multiple comparison sequences is the average value of all the correlation coefficients.

If the coordinates of a prominent landmark obtain the highest grey correlation grade with the coordinates of the HJC, this landmark is most relevant to the HJC. Therefore, we introduce a new attribute selection module, guiding the network to focus on meaningful landmarks at input variables. The correlation coefficient is estimated to determine whether prominent landmarks should be added to train the models. By ranking the correlation coefficients between the prominent landmark and the HJC using the GRA method, we select the high-importance landmarks to train the model.

2.4 Fast HJC Prediction Module

The proposed FDSN method is shown in Fig. 3, which takes the prominent landmark coordinates as model inputs and achieves fast HJC prediction. Specifically, a regularized extreme learning machine (RELM) is employed to train the modules of the FDSN. This idea is motivated by the following intuitive concepts: (1) As an efficient approach to train neural networks, ELMs have low computational cost and good generalization performance [21]. (2) ELM-based random feature mapping is shared among the modules in the FDSN to speed up the training process. In the FDSN, the first module is trained using the RELM-based approach with additive nodes: random weights W_1 and biases v_1. Matrix H_1 is calculated as shown in Eq. (2).

$$\begin{cases} H_1 = G(\eta_1) \\ \eta_1 = X_1 W_1 + N_1 \end{cases} \tag{2}$$

where G is an operator, X_1 is the input, and N_1 is the v_1 vector in each row. As the weight matrix connecting the output and hidden layers, B_1 is calculated using H_1 and the chosen RELM-based algorithm. The first module output is described by $\overline{T}_1 = H_1 B_1$.

Note that the modules of the FDSN are stacked on top of each other, and the input and the output of a module make up the input of the following module [22]. The FDSN can suffer from a badly chosen initial weight since some weights and calculations are reused when accelerating the training of the DSN and reducing memory usage. The FDSN algorithm has three extremely important parameters (including the number of hidden neurons (N), regularization parameter (r), and maximal number of modules (s)), and the manual tuning of these parameters can be a time-consuming and tedious process. To automatically and efficiently determine the optimal FDSN model parameters, we added an MVO global optimization module to the framework. The main inspirations of this MVO algorithm are based on three concepts in cosmology: white holes, black holes, and wormholes. A universe with a high expansion rate is considered to have white holes, and a universe with a low expansion rate is considered to have black holes. Each universe has wormholes to transport its objects through space randomly, and the objects are transferred from the black hole in the source universe to the black hole in the target universe. Mathematical models of these three concepts are developed to perform exploration, exploitation, and a local search.

In the MVO algorithm, a set of random universes is created to start the optimization process. During each iteration, objects in the universes with high inflation rates tend to move to the universes with low inflation rates via white/black holes. Note that every single universe performs random teleportation in its objects through wormholes towards the best universe [19]. The computational complexity of the MVO algorithms mainly depends on four factors (including the number of iterations, number of universes, roulette wheel mechanism, and universe sorting mechanism). Note that universes are sorted in every iteration, and the Quicksort algorithm is employed in this study, which has the complexity of $O(n\log n)$ and $O(n^2)$ in the best and worst cases, respectively. We conduct roulette wheel selection in every universe over the iterations and can obtain the complexity $O(n)$ or $O(\log n)$ based on implementation. Finally, the overall computational complexity can be obtained:

$$\begin{cases} O(MVO) = O(l(O(\text{Quick sort}) + n \times d \times (O(\text{roulette wheel})))) \\ O(\text{MVO}) = O(l(n^2 + n \times d \times \log n)) \end{cases} \quad (3)$$

where n represents the number of universes, l represents the maximum number of iterations, and d represents the number of objects. This MVO module can be easily added to model architectures for the optimal model parameters and increasing prediction accuracy.

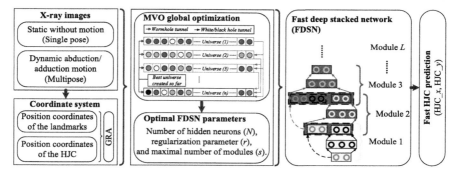

Fig. 3. Fast HJC prediction module based on the FDSN.

2.5 Accurate HJC Positioning Module

Calculating the trajectories of annotated bone landmarks under dynamic behaviors is desired. However, this calculation also introduces two issues. One issue is that bone landmarks are manually annotated by orthopedists. The manual tuning of landmark coordinates can be a time-consuming and tedious process. Moreover, it is difficult to obtain optimal fixed points for accurate registration. The other issue is that two pairs of dynamic points (dynamic landmarks in hip joints in abduction images and adduction images, as shown in Table 1) are too weak to identify the HJC, leading to an amplified distance error after fitting circles. Thus, it is necessary to further tune the control point locations (static landmarks in the pelvis in Table 1) and select enough dynamic landmarks (dynamic landmarks in hip joints in Table 1) as informative spatial locations for HJC localization.

To align two pelvis images (abduction images and adduction images), a two-step registration approach is used in this study. First, we tune the control point locations (static landmarks in the pelvis in Table 1) using the cross-correlation method, and the adjusted coordinates are accurate up to one-tenth of a pixel, which more closely matches the positions of the fixed landmarks than previous methods can achieve [23]. Note that the cross-correlation method is used to obtain subpixel accuracy from the image content and coarse control point selection. Second, we fit a geometric transformation to the adjusted control point pairs (adjusted static landmarks in the pelvis in abduction images and adduction images). Finally, every two pairs of dynamic landmarks (landmarks 5, 6 and 8 in abduction images and adduction images) are fitted to a circle center, and the average value of all the centers is taken as the final HJC, as shown in Fig. 4.

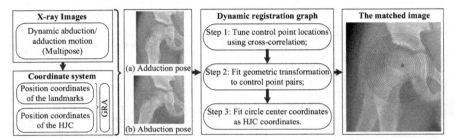

Fig. 4. HJC positioning module based on the dynamic registration graph.

3   Experimental Results

3.1 Data Processing and Analysis

To show the effectiveness of our proposed HJC prediction method, we validated it on a dataset from the Wuhan Women and Children's Health Care Center in China. In 100 subjects' X-ray images and a total of 200 hips, a coordinate system was established on each X-ray image according to the posterior inferior iliac spine on both sides. Sixteen prominent bony landmarks were annotated by orthopedists. Taking the left hip joint as an example, the correlation between the coordinates of each landmark and the HJC was analyzed using the GRA method, as shown in Fig. 5. A relational grade value closer to 1 indicates a better corresponding landmark. Those landmarks with strong correlation (comprehensive relational grade value > 0.7) were retained as the input variables of the model.

3.2 Experimental Settings

Our static prediction module is based on the implementation of the FDSN. By considering the number of landmarks and the HJC, the end-to-end parameters of our model include the number of input neurons (16) and the number of output neurons (2). Note that 70% of

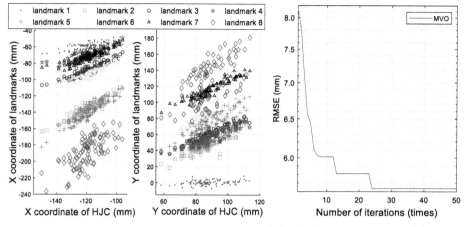

Fig. 5. Grey relational analysis results.

Fig. 6. Convergence curve of the MVO.

the samples are used to train the model, and the remaining 30% of the samples are used for testing. Our optimization objective function is the average root mean square error (RMSE) from ten 10-fold validation processes performed on the training data using the FDSN method. Figure 6 shows the convergence curve of the global optimization obtained with the MVO. The optimal parameters obtained by the MVO include the number of hidden neurons (443), regularization parameter (1) and maximum number of modules (10). Our dynamic positioning module takes the average value of three fitted circle centers as the final HJC. All experiments are performed on the same computer with an Intel Core i7-8700 3.20 GHz CPU and 16 GB memory.

3.3 Comparison with State-of-the-Art Methods

The experimental results of our proposed FDSN method are shown in Fig. 7. We compared the proposed FDSN model with the Elman [24], radial basis function (RBF) [25], ELM [21], RELM [26], stacked ELM (SELM) [27], SELM-based autoencoder (AE-SELM) [27], and DSNELM [28] models. All experiments are performed with optimal parameters obtained by the MVO algorithm. We used the RMSE, mean absolute percentage error (MAPE), and R-squared (R^2) value as evaluation metrics. We used the mean and standard deviation (SD) to analyze the results. We ran the experiment 1000 times (independently), and the average results for the testing sets are shown in Table 2. Obviously, (1) our FDSN method outperformed the seven state-of-the-art methods. Our method achieved the smallest RMSE, the smallest MAPE, and the largest R^2 value. In addition, our algorithm achieved the smallest standard deviation among the three indicators. These results imply the effectiveness and robustness of our algorithm. (2) The ELM model achieved inferior performances. The reason for this is that the ELM is a single-layer feedforward network (SLFN) and is prone to underfitting or overfitting.

In addition, we compared the proposed dynamic registration approach with traditional functional and regression methods. The proposed dynamic registration graph

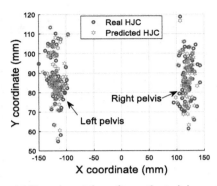 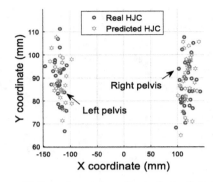

(a) Experimental results on the training set   (b) Experimental results on the testing set

Fig. 7. Experimental results of our proposed method.

Table 2. Average results of the 1000 independent runs for the testing set.

Models	RMSE (mm)		MAPE		R^2	
	Mean	SD	Mean	SD	Mean	SD
Elman [24]	10.5210	1.6829	8.4706	1.6935	0.9895	0.0034
RBF [25]	14.6769	4.0218	12.2432	3.9119	0.9786	0.0123
ELM [21]	5.2951e + 3	1.6901e + 4	1.8938e + 3	6.2453e + 3	0.4431	0.4644
RELM [26]	9.0559	1.8917	7.1431	1.6010	0.9921	0.0033
SELM [27]	8.3223	1.7025	6.5612	1.4829	0.9933	0.0027
AESELM [27]	8.4867	1.6463	6.7554	1.4576	0.9931	0.0026
DSNELM [28]	6.9904	1.5047	5.5590	1.2870	0.9952	0.0021
Our method	**6.9656**	**1.4984**	**5.5235**	**1.2612**	**0.9953**	**0.0020**

method does not participate in the training process and achieves the following results: RMSE = 0.4139 mm, MAPE = 1.4660, and R^2 = 0.9962. The traditional functional method results in unsatisfactory location errors of up to 26 mm [4], the mean error of the traditional regression method is in the range of 15–30 mm [5, 10, 11, 13, 14], and the modified Ranawat method and pelvic height ratio method have estimation errors <5 mm [29]. We can clearly observe that the proposed static FDSN model and dynamic registration approach have better accuracy than traditional functional methods and traditional regression methods; in particular, the proposed dynamic registration graph features superior accuracy (RMSE = 0.4139 mm, MAPE = 1.4660, and R^2 = 0.9962). These findings show that our framework obtains coordinates much closer to the real HJC than the previously developed approaches.

3.4 Ablation Analysis

To better demonstrate the effectiveness of the proposed FDSN method, we performed ablation experiments on our model, as shown in Table 3. The results indicate that (1) the model performance is evidently improved by combining the static landmarks in the pelvis and dynamic landmarks in the hip joint. Clearly, both the static landmarks and dynamic landmarks can help identify the HJC, and our fusion strategy can provide richer feature representations than single static/dynamic landmarks. (2) Applying an MVO global optimization module further optimizes the prediction of the proposed FDSN method (complexity analysis: 9.2598e−04 s with the MVO module and 2.8210e−04 s without the MVO module). Obviously, our proposed FDSN method greatly enhances the effectiveness and robustness in HJC identification.

Table 3. Average ablation results obtained with our proposed method.

Models	RMSE (mm)		MAPE		R^2	
	Mean	SD	Mean	SD	Mean	SD
Static + FDSN	7.4743	1.6296	5.9458	1.3787	0.9946	0.0024
Dynamic + FDSN	7.6815	1.5249	6.1926	1.3888	0.9944	0.0022
Static + Dynamic + FDSN	7.3728	1.5592	5.9215	1.3692	0.9948	0.0023
Static + Dynamic + MVO + FDSN (**Our method**)	**6.9656**	**1.5047**	**5.5235**	**1.2870**	**0.9953**	**0.0020**

4 Conclusion

This paper proposes a novel framework to address the problem of HJC determination. First, comprehensive prominent landmarks from multipose X-ray images are extracted, and grey relational analysis (GRA) is used to guide the network to focus on useful variables. Then, a fast deep stacked network (FDSN) with a multiverse optimizer (MVO) is designed to achieve fast HJC prediction, and it considers adaptive HJC prediction to tackle the problem of automated model optimization. Finally, using a dynamic registration graph, the HJC localization ability of the whole framework is enhanced. Validation on a dataset from the China Wuhan Women and Children's Health Care Center demonstrates the effectiveness of our hip joint center (HJC) determination method on X-ray images.

Acknowledgments. This work was supported by the National Natural Science Foundation of China (No.61772556), National Key R&D Program of China (No.2018YFB1107100, No.2016 YFC1100600), Postgraduate Research and Innovation Project of Hunan (No.CX20200321) and Fundamental Research Funds for the Central Universities of Central South University (2020zzts140).

References

1. Harrington, M.E., Zavatsky, A.B., Lawson, S.E.M., Yuan, Z., Theologis, T.N.: Prediction of the hip joint centre in adults, children, and patients with cerebral palsy based on magnetic resonance imaging. J. Biomech. **40**(3), 595–602 (2007)
2. Mose, K.: Methods of measuring in Legg-Calvé-Perthes disease with special regard to the prognosis. Clin. Orthop. Relat. Res. **150**, 103–109 (1980)
3. Cuomo, A.V., Moseley, C.F., Fedorak, G.T.: A practical approach to determining the center of the femoral head in subluxated and dislocated hips. J. Pediatr. Orthop. **35**(6), 556–560 (2015)
4. Piazza, S.J., Erdemir, A., Okita, N., Cavanagh, P.R.: Assessment of the functional method of hip joint center location subject to reduced range of hip motion. J. Biomech. **37**(3), 349–356 (2004)
5. Camomilla, V., Cereatti, A., Vannozzi, G., Cappozzo, A.: An optimized protocol for hip joint centre determination using the functional method. J. Biomech. **39**(6), 1096–1106 (2006)
6. Silaghi, M.-C., Plänkers, R., Boulic, R., Fua, P., Thalmann, D.: Local and global skeleton fitting techniques for optical motion capture. In: Magnenat-Thalmann, N., Thalmann, D. (eds.) CAPTECH 1998. LNCS (LNAI), vol. 1537, pp. 26–40. Springer, Heidelberg (1998). https://doi.org/10.1007/3-540-49384-0_3
7. Gamage, S.S.H.U., Lasenby, J.: New least squares solutions for estimating the average centre of rotation and the axis of rotation. J. Biomech. **35**(1), 87–93 (2002)
8. Halvorsen, K., Lesser, M., Lundberg, A.: A new method for estimating the axis of rotation and the center of rotation. J. Biomech. **32**(11), 1221–1227 (1999)
9. Assi, A., et al.: Validation of hip joint center localization methods during gait analysis using 3D EOS imaging in typically developing and cerebral palsy children. Gait Posture **48**, 30–35 (2016)
10. Sangeux, M., Pillet, H., Skalli, W.: Which method of hip joint centre localisation should be used in gait analysis? Gait Posture **40**(1), 20–25 (2014)
11. Peters, A., Baker, R., Morris, M.E., Sangeux, M.: A comparison of hip joint centre localisation techniques with 3-DUS for clinical gait analysis in children with cerebral palsy. Gait Posture **36**(2), 282–286 (2012)
12. Miller, E.J., Kaufman, K.R.: Verification of an improved hip joint center prediction method. Gait Posture **59**, 174–176 (2018)
13. Sangeux, M.: On the implementation of predictive methods to locate the hip joint centres. Gait Posture **42**(3), 402–405 (2015)
14. Sangeux, M., Peters, A., Baker, R.: Hip joint centre localization: evaluation on normal subjects in the context of gait analysis. Gait Posture **34**(3), 324–328 (2011)
15. Bombaci, H., Simsek, B., Soyarslan, M., Murat Yildirim, M.: Determination of the hip rotation centre from landmarks in pelvic radiograph. Acta Orthop. Traumatol. Turc. **51**(6), 470–473 (2017)
16. Wang, X., et al.: Obstructive sleep apnea detection using ecg-sensor with convolutional neural networks. Multimedia Tools Appl. **79**(23), 15813–15827 (2020)
17. Shi, W., Liu, S., Jiang, F., Zhao, D., Tian, Z.: Anchored neighborhood deep network for single-image super-resolution. EURASIP J. Image Video Process. **2018**(1), 34 (2018)
18. Jiang, F., et al.: Medical image semantic segmentation based on deep learning. Neural Comput. Appl. **29**(5), 1257–1265 (2018)
19. Mirjalili, S., Mirjalili, S.M., Hatamlou, A.: Multi-verse optimizer: a nature-inspired algorithm for global optimization. Neural Comput. Appl. **27**(2), 495–513 (2015). https://doi.org/10.1007/s00521-015-1870-7
20. Sun, G., Xin, G., Xiao, Y., Zheng, Z.: Grey relational analysis between hesitant fuzzy sets with applications to pattern recognition. Exp. Syst. Appl. **92**(9), 521–532 (2018)

21. Huang, G., Zhou, H., Ding, X., Zhang, R.: Extreme learning machine for regression and multiclass classification. IEEE Trans. Syst. Man Cybernet. Part B (Cybernet.) **42**(2), 513–529 (2012)
22. da Silva, B.L.S., Inaba, F.K., Salles, E.O.T., Ciarelli, P.M.: Fast deep stacked networks based on extreme learning machine applied to regression problems. Neural Netw. **131**, 14–28 (2020)
23. Goshtasby, A.: Image registration by local approximation methods. Image Vis. Comput. **6**(4), 255–261 (1988)
24. Yuan-Chu, C., Wei-Min, Q., Wei-You, C.: Dynamic properties of Elman and modified Elman neural network. In: Proceedings of the International Conference on Machine Learning and Cybernetics, pp. 637–640 (2002)
25. Park, J., Sandberg, I.W.: Universal approximation using radial-basis-function networks. Neural Comput. **3**(2), 246–257 (1991)
26. Deng, W., Zheng, Q., Chen, L.: Regularized extreme learning machine. In: 2009 IEEE Symposium on Computational Intelligence and Data Mining, pp. 389–395 (2009)
27. Zhou, H., Huang, G., Lin, Z., Wang, H., Soh, Y.C.: Stacked extreme learning machines. IEEE Trans. Cybernet. **45**(9), 2013–2025 (2015)
28. Li, D.: A tutorial survey of architectures, algorithms, and applications for deep learning. Apsipa Trans. Signal Inf. Process. **3**, e2 (2014)
29. Fujii, M., Nakamura, T., Hara, T., Nakashima, Y.: Is Ranawat triangle method accurate in estimating hip joint center in Japanese population? J. Orthop. Sci. **26**(2), 219–224 (2021)

A Two-Branch Neural Network for Non-Small-Cell Lung Cancer Classification and Segmentation

Borui Gao[1], Guangtai Ding[1(✉)], Kun Fang[1], and Peilin Chen[2]

[1] School of Computer Engineering and Science, Shanghai University,
Shanghai, China
gtding@shu.edu.cn
[2] Department of Data System, 3D Medicines Inc., Shanghai, China

Abstract. Immunotherapy has great potential in the treatment of Non-Small-Cell Lung Cancer (NSCLC). The treatment decision for patients is based on the pathologist's analysis of NSCLC biopsy images. Using deep learning (DL) methods to automatically segment and classify tissues enable quantitative analysis of biopsy images. However, distinguishing between positive tumor tissues and immune tissues remains challenging due to the similarity between these two types of tissues. In this paper, we present a two-branch convolutional neural network (TBNet) combining segmentation network and patch-based classification network. The segmentation branch feeds additional information to the classification branch to improve the performance of patch classification. Then the classification results are fed back to the segmentation branch to obtain segmented tissue regions classified as positive tumor or immune. The experimental results show that the proposed method improves the classification accuracy by an average of 4.3% over a single classification model and achieves 0.864 and 0.907 dice coefficient of positive tumor tissue region and immune tissue region in segmentation task.

Keywords: Pathological image analysis · Deep learning · Semantic segmentation · Image classification

1 Introduction

Lung cancer is one of the most widespread cancer diseases, and about 80% to 85% of lung cancer cases are Non-Small-Cell Lung Cancer (NSCLC) [1]. In recent years, immunotherapy has become the focus of NSCLC therapy. The level of PD-L1 expression is a key biomarker for the sensitivity of tumors to immunotherapy, which is used to predict the efficacy of the treatment [24]. In clinical practice, pathologists inspect the NSCLC biopsy slide for the relevant tissue regions, known as regions-of-interest (RoI), and then quantify the percentage of tumor cells exhibiting positive membrane staining to evaluate the PD-L1 expression. Due to the similarity between positive tumor cells and immune cells,

© Springer Nature Switzerland AG 2021
I. Farkaš et al. (Eds.): ICANN 2021, LNCS 12893, pp. 660–670, 2021.
https://doi.org/10.1007/978-3-030-86365-4_53

this process often poses challenges for a pathologist to have an accurate esti-mation. Recent research has shown that deep learning (DL) can improve the accuracy and automation of pathological image analysis [14].

DL methods have achieved promising performance in pathological semantic segmentation [11,17]. The pixel-level segmentation, which can predict the pre-cise delineation of tissue regions, is a straightforward method to quantify the proportion of each tissue. However, applying semantic segmentation methods to NSCLC biopsy images is faced with the following challenges: (1) The complex-ity of tissues makes it hard to distinguish some tissues. (2) Obtaining sufficient pixel-wise annotations for training is an expensive and time-consuming task, because precise labeling of boundaries for each relevant tissue region requires professional experience. (3) The unmanageable class imbalance in pathological images also increases the difficulty of model training.

Compared with pixel-level annotation, the cost of image-level annotation for classification task is much lower. There are many achievements using convo-lutional neural networks (CNNs) for the automatic classification of pathologi-cal images [2,4]. These achievements show the efficiency of DL-based classifi-cation algorithms in complex tissue samples. Considering that the pathological images are large and tissues are spatially mixed in an individual image, most studies divided a large image into small patches and trained models with these patches. However, the patch contains less information than the original image. The patch-based method only considers individual patches and ignores the cor-relation between the patch and its neighbors, resulting in biased prediction [23].

In this paper, we propose a two-branch convolutional neural network (TBNet) that combines segmentation and classification network. The segmentation branch extracts each individual relevant tissue region (positive tumor and immune tis-sues) without recognizing the type of these tissues, and the classification branch focuses on classifying the obtained tissue regions as positive tumor or immune. The main contributions of our approach are: (1) The classification branch sim-plifies the task of segmentation and thus reduces the dependency on pixel-level annotation datasets. (2) In the classification branch, a module is designed for revising the classification prediction using additional information provided by the segmentation branch. (3) In the segmentation branch, we adopt focal loss [13] as the loss function to address the imbalance between relevant tissue and background class during training.

2   Related Work

2.1   Semantic Segmentation

Semantic segmentation is a pixel-wise classification problem, which aims to clas-sify each pixel into several semantic groups [16]. There are many published DL methods for semantic segmentation. FCN [15] is one of the first DL methods using CNN for semantic segmentation. It replaces fully-connected layers with convolutional layers and adds deconvolutional layers to upsample feature maps to the same size as the input image. As a result, FCN takes an image of any size as input and outputs a segmentation map of the same size. Furthermore, skip connections are used to concatenate high-level features and low-level features in order to produce an accurate segmentation map. SegNet [3] and U-Net [18] are based on convolutional encoder-decoder architecture. SegNet records the pooling index in the encoder and uses the max-pooling indices to upsample feature maps to retain position information. U-Net is initially proposed for biomedical image segmentation, which is the most common pathological image segmentation method. It is composed of a symmetrical down-sampling part and up-sampling part. Inspired by FCNs, U-Net also adopts skip connections. Feature maps from each stage of down-sampling layers are copied to the up-sampling layers to fuse high-level and low-level features.

In pathological semantic segmentation, sufficient pixel-level annotation data are expensive to be obtained. Some recent works have proposed methods to reduce the labeling cost. For example, Lerousseau et al. [10] proposed a weakly-supervised framework for whole slide image (WSI) segmentation, which uses a multiple instance learning scheme to train models. The model training uses only binary annotations over the entire WSIs. Shen et al. [19] presented a deep active learning scheme for breast cancer segmentation, which significantly decreases the burden of manual annotation by selecting the most informative subset for labeling. Kapil et al. [8] explored a semi-supervised learning solution to score the PD-L1 expression in the large NSCLC biopsy images automatically. This method uses raw unlabeled data to lower the amount of needed labeled data.

2.2   Pathological Classfication

In addition to pixel-level segmentation, image-level classification also plays an essential role in pathological image analysis tasks. In recent years, DL-based classification methods have been successfully used for pathological image analysis such as breast cancer diagnosis [2], lung cancer mutation prediction [4], colon tumor analysis [21], and lung adenocarcinoma growth patterns distinguish [6]. These methods have excellent performance in cancer recognition and show the capability of DL to distinguish tissues with similar appearance from pathological images. However, most works use patch-based classification models that only consider local information in the patch. In order to take advantage of contextual information, Gertych et al. [6] use a contextual classification to revise the patch prediction. The final decision of each patch prediction is made by leveraging prediction scores of the neighboring patches. But this method does not include the interpretation of the relationship between patches.

3   Method

In this section, we explain the proposed TBNet. The main structure of our model is shown in Fig. 1. (A) is the segmentation branch. A original image is passed to the segmentation branch to obtain a pixel-level prediction with relevant tissues segmented, and the result is fed to the classification branch (B). In the meantime, patches are extracted from the original image in an overlapping way. After filtering out background patches, these patches are sent to the classification branch to predict class labels. The classification branch is composed of two stages, a binary-classification network for prediction and then an adjustment module for correcting the predicted results. As the output of the classification network, patches' prediction scores are aggregated to obtain image-level probability score map. Then, the adjustment module adjusts the probability map with additional information to determine the final prediction of each patch, which is explained in detail in Sect. 3.2. Finally, the revised patch-level predictions are applied to pixel-level prediction to classify separated tissues into two classes, namely, positive tumor and immune.

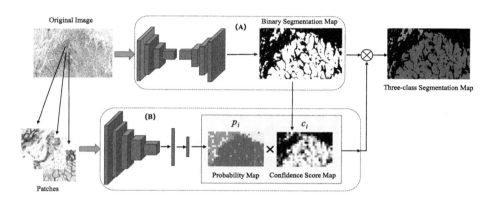

Fig. 1. Overview of the proposed TBNet. First, original image and patches extracted from the image are input into segmentation branch (A) and classification branch (B), respectively. Next, confidence scores of patches are generated by the binary segmentation map (white: relevant tissues). Then, the probability map and the confidence score map are combined in the adjustment module to obtain class label of each patch (Fig. 2). Finally, the three-class segmentation map (red: positive tumor tissues, green: immune tissues) is obtained by applying patch labels on the binary segmentation map. (Color figure online)

3.1 Segmentation Branch

In view of the promising performance of U-Net in biomedical image segmentation task, we adopt U-Net as the backbone of the segmentation branch in our method.

Focal Loss. Since the proportion of relevant tissue regions in training images is much lower than background, the segmentation model faces a large class imbalance during training. A large number of negative and easy examples will dominate the gradient descent and lead to the degeneration of the model. To address this problem, focal loss [13] is obtained as the loss function during the training process, which is defined as:

$$L(y, p_t) = -\sum_t \alpha_t (1 - p_t)^\gamma \log(p_t) \tag{1}$$

y and p_t denote the one-hot-encoded label and the prediction probability of pixels respectively. Balance variant α_t is used to resolve the imbalance problem between different categories. In this paper, we set the value of α_t dynamically according to the ratio of pixels of each class. γ is the focusing parameter to reduce the loss contribution from easy examples, which is set as 2 in our method.

3.2   Classification Branch

Classification Network. We use a CNN architecture to predict class label for a given patch. In order to select the best binary-classification CNN in our method, we use ResNet50 [7], Inception [22], and VGG-16 [20] as a backbone respectively. For each model: (1) global average pooling layer, which can reduce overfitting [12], is added before fully-connected layers, (2) the softmax layer is replaced by a sigmoid layer to output a binary-label prediction, (3) dropout is used between fully-connected layer and sigmoid layer, (4) the input patch size is set to 128 × 128 pixels in order to improve the efficiency and reduce the negative effects caused by the mixing of multiple tissues in a patch, (5) the model is pre-trained on ImageNet [5] database.

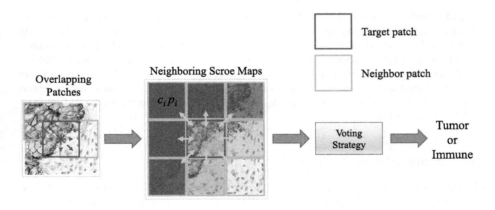

Fig. 2. The operation process of the adjustment module.

Adjustment Module. To avoid unsatisfied classification performance caused by the limited information in a patch, we propose an adjustment module to add contextual information into consideration. The prediction result of segmentation branch can provide RoI information of a patch and its neighbors. RoI is associated with the reliability of a patch's prediction result, and RoI in the overlapping area reveals the relationship between target patch and its neighboring patch. First, the confidence score of a patch is set by the value of the RoI in the target patch and the overlapping area with its neighboring patches. Then, as Fig. 2 shows, the prediction score and the confidence score of patches are combined by a soft voting approach to render a final decision of the target patch, which can be formulated as:

$$y_{patch} = \arg\max_{j} \sum_{i} c_i p_{ij} \tag{2}$$

p_{ij} is the prediction score of i-th patch belonging to class $j \in (tumor, immune)$, and c_i is the confidence score.

4   Experiments

4.1   Dataset

We evaluate our proposed model on NSCLC biopsy dataset, which contains pixel-level annotated images and image-level annotated images. The pixel-level annotation dataset consists of 273 images with a size of 512 × 512 and 75 images with a size of 1024 × 1024, and the image-level annotation dataset contains 11335 images with a size of 128 × 128. These images are labeled under the guidance of a pathologist.

Preprocessing. The images with pixel-level annotation are randomly divided into training set and test set by 4:1, and all images with image-level annotation are taken as the training set for classification. Furthermore, we cut out patches of 128 × 128 pixels from the pixel-level training set and filter out patches with no-annotated pixels. Then, we label these patches as tumor or immune based on the pixel annotation. These labeled patches are used as a supplement to the classification training set. In order to improve the generalization ability of the binary-classification model and to avoid the imbalance between two classes, we augment the classification training set to 10k patches for each class by random flipping and rotation. Both segmentation and classification training set are divided: 90% for training and 10% for validation.

4.2   Implementation Detail

In our method, we train the binary-classification network and the segmentation network separately. Experiments are conducted in TensorFlow 2.0.1 with an NVIDIA GTX 2080Ti GPU of 11 GB memory. We train the binary-classification model with stochastic gradient descent, and the learning rate and momentum are set to 0.0001 and 0.9, respectively. Model is trained 80 epochs with a batch size of 64. We use Adam optimization [9] method for the segmentation model, and the learning rate is set to 0.0001. The model is trained 100 epochs with a batch size of 32.

4.3   Results and Analysis

Performance in segmentation and classification are evaluated separately. For classification, we use VGG16, ResNet50, and Inception to implement the classification branch of our model respectively, and then compare the classification accuracy of TBNet with the corresponding classification-only models. Predictions are performed on testing images in a sliding window manner with a fixed stride of 64. The ground-truth of each patch is based on the pixel annotation.

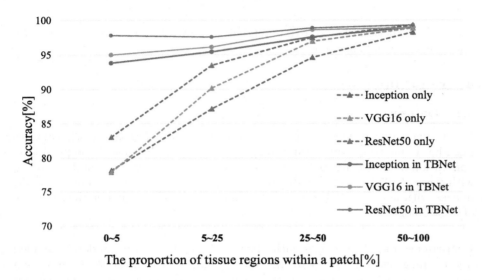

Fig. 3. Classification accuracy of patches.

As Table 1 shows, the classification accuracy of TBNet improves by an average of 4.3% compared with classification-only models. In Fig. 3, we present the classification accuracy of patches which are grouped according to the proportion of relevant tissue regions within a patch. Compared with the classification-only model, the classification performance of TBNet on each group of patches is improved, especially on patches with less than 25% of relevant tissues. Classification-only methods use only patch-scale local information, hence it has a poor performance on low-tissue-content patches which contain less available information. The improvements in classification performance of our method derive from that we take the relationship of neighboring patches into consideration.

Table 1. Comparison of classification accuracy between TBNet and classification-only models.

Backbone	Accuracy(%)		
	Classification only	TBNet	Increment
VGG16	92.8	97.5	+4.7
Inception	91.9	96.9	+5.0
ResNet50	95.3	**98.4**	+3.1
Mean	93.3	97.6	+4.3

For segmentation, FCN, SegNet, U-Net, and our method are compared. The ResNet50, which has the best performance in the classification task, is adopted to the classification network of our method. We utilize Dice coefficient, Intersection-over-Union (IoU) and sensitivity (SE) as evaluation metrics to measure the performance of segmentation, which are calculated as follows:

$$SE = \frac{TP}{TP + TN}$$

$$IoU = \frac{|A \cap B|}{|A \cup B|}$$

$$Dice = \frac{2|A \cap B|}{|A| + |B|}$$

Where TP and TN represent the number of true positives and true negatives, A and B denote the ground truth and the predicted segmentation maps, respectively.

Table 2. Segmentation results on the NSCLC biopsy dataset.

Method	Dice		IoU		SE	
	Tumor	Immune	Tumor	Immune	Tumor	Immune
FCN	0.839	0.776	0.728	0.635	0.806	0.879
SegNet	0.825	0.786	0.702	0.648	0.767	0.872
U-Net	0.846	0.802	0.739	0.670	0.824	0.948
TBNet (ours)	**0.864**	**0.907**	**0.760**	**0.829**	**0.856**	**0.958**

The comparison results are presented in Table 2. We can observe that TBNet achieves the highest score in SE, IoU, and dice coefficient. Furthermore, Fig. 4 shows a visual comparison of segmentation results between the TBNet and the U-Net model. The results show that the segmentation model trained separately on the existing pixel-level annotation data has a high misjudgment in positive tumor tissues and immune tissues. In our method, the classification branch is added to reduce the dependence of the segmentation model on pixel-level annotation datasets.

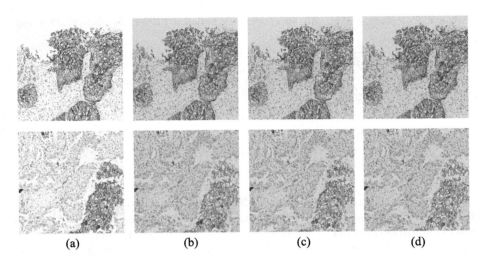

                (a)   (b)   (c)   (d)

Fig. 4. Examples of segmentation results on the NSCLC biopsy dataset. Red: positive tumor region, Green: immune region. (a): original image, (b): ground truth, (c): U-Net, (d): TBNet. (Color figure online)

5 Conclusion

In this paper, we present TBNet for NSCLC tissue classification and segmentation. TBNet uses two-branch architecture to fuse the advantages of DL classification and segmentation algorithms, and improves performance by passing more information between branches. The experiments conducted on the NSCLC biopsy dataset show that our method achieves state-of-the-art performance on both classification and segmentation tasks. In future researches, we will apply TBNet to other datasets and explore an end-to-end learning optimization method of TBNet.

References

1. American Cancer Society. https://www.cancer.org/cancer/lung-cancer.html
2. Alom, M.Z., Yakopcic, C., Shamima, M.: Histopathological images with inception recurrent residual convolutional neural network. J. Digit. Imaging **32**(4), 605–617 (2019). https://doi.org/10.1007/s10278-019-00182-7
3. Badrinarayanan, V., Kendall, A., Cipolla, R.: SegNet: a deep convolutional encoder-decoder architecture for image segmentation. IEEE Trans. Pattern Anal. Mach. Intell. **39**(12), 2481–2495 (2017). https://doi.org/10.1109/TPAMI.2016.2644615
4. Coudray, N., Ocampo, P.S., Sakellaropoulos, T., Narula, N., Snuderl, M.: Classification and mutation prediction from non-small cell lung cancer histopathology images using deep learning. Nat. Med. **24**(10), 1559–1567 (2018). https://doi.org/10.1038/s41591-018-0177-5

5. Deng, J., Dong, W., Socher, R., Li, L., Li, K., Fei-Fei, L.: ImageNet: a large-scale hierarchical image database. In: 2009 IEEE Conference on Computer Vision and Pattern Recognition (CVPR), pp. 248–255 (2009). https://doi.org/10.1109/CVPR.2009.5206848

6. Gertych, A., et al.: Convolutional neural networks can accurately distinguish four histologic growth patterns of lung adenocarcinoma in digital slides. Sci. Rep. **9**(1), 1483 (2019). https://doi.org/10.1038/s41598-018-37638-9

7. He, K., Zhang, X., Ren, S., Sun, J.: Deep residual learning for image recognition. In: 2016 IEEE Conference on Computer Vision and Pattern Recognition (CVPR), pp. 770–778 (2016). https://doi.org/10.1109/CVPR.2016.90

8. Kapil, A., et al.: Deep semi supervised generative learning for automated tumor proportion scoring on NSCLC tissue needle biopsies. Sci. Rep. **8**(1), 17343 (2018). https://doi.org/10.1038/s41598-018-35501-5

9. Kingma, D.P., Ba, J.: Adam: a method for stochastic optimization (2017)

10. Lerousseau, M., et al.: Weakly supervised multiple instance learning histopathological tumor segmentation. In: Martel, A.L., et al. (eds.) MICCAI 2020, Part V. LNCS, vol. 12265, pp. 470–479. Springer, Cham (2020). https://doi.org/10.1007/978-3-030-59722-1_45

11. Li, W., Manivannan, S., Akbar, S., Zhang, J., Trucco, E., McKenna, S.J.: Gland segmentation in colon histology images using hand-crafted features and convolutional neural networks. In: 2016 IEEE 13th International Symposium on Biomedical Imaging (ISBI), pp. 1405–1408 (2016). https://doi.org/10.1109/ISBI.2016.7493530

12. Lin, M., Chen, Q., Yan, S.: Network in network (2014)

13. Lin, T., Goyal, P., Girshick, R., He, K., Dollár, P.: Focal loss for dense object detection. IEEE Trans. Pattern Anal. Mach. Intell. **42**(2), 318–327 (2020). https://doi.org/10.1109/TPAMI.2018.2858826

14. Litjens, G., Sánchez, C., Timofeeva, N., Hermsen, M.: Nagtegaal: deep learning as a tool for increased accuracy and efficiency of histopathological diagnosis. Sci. Rep. **6**(1), 26286 (2016)

15. Long, J., Shelhamer, E., Darrell, T.: Fully convolutional networks for semantic segmentation. In: 2015 IEEE Conference on Computer Vision and Pattern Recognition (CVPR), pp. 3431–3440 (2015). https://doi.org/10.1109/CVPR.2015.7298965

16. Minaee, S., Boykov, Y., Porikli, F., Plaza, A., Kehtarnavaz, N., Terzopoulos, D.: Image segmentation using deep learning: a survey (2020)

17. Qaiser, T., Tsang, Y.-W., Epstein, D., Rajpoot, N.: Tumor segmentation in whole slide images using persistent homology and deep convolutional features. In: Valdés Hernández, M., González-Castro, V. (eds.) MIUA 2017. CCIS, vol. 723, pp. 320–329. Springer, Cham (2017). https://doi.org/10.1007/978-3-319-60964-5_28

18. Ronneberger, O., Fischer, P., Brox, T.: U-Net: convolutional networks for biomedical image segmentation. In: Navab, N., Hornegger, J., Wells, W.M., Frangi, A.F. (eds.) MICCAI 2015, Part III. LNCS, vol. 9351, pp. 234–241. Springer, Cham (2015). https://doi.org/10.1007/978-3-319-24574-4_28

19. Shen, H., et al.: Deep active learning for breast cancer segmentation on immunohistochemistry images. In: Martel, A.L., et al. (eds.) MICCAI 2020, Part V. LNCS, vol. 12265, pp. 509–518. Springer, Cham (2020). https://doi.org/10.1007/978-3-030-59722-1_49

20. Simonyan, K., Zisserman, A.: Very deep convolutional networks for large-scale image recognition (2015)

21. Sirinukunwattana, K., Raza, S.E.A., Tsang, Y., Snead, D.R.J., Cree, I.A., Rajpoot, N.M.: Locality sensitive deep learning for detection and classification of nuclei in routine colon cancer histology images. IEEE Trans. Med. Imaging **35**(5), 1196–1206 (2016). https://doi.org/10.1109/TMI.2016.2525803
22. Szegedy, C., et al.: Going deeper with convolutions. In: 2015 IEEE Conference on Computer Vision and Pattern Recognition (CVPR), pp. 1–9 (2015). https://doi.org/10.1109/CVPR.2015.7298594
23. Takahama, S., et al.: Multi-stage pathological image classification using semantic segmentation. In: 2019 IEEE/CVF International Conference on Computer Vision (ICCV), pp. 10701–10710 (2019). https://doi.org/10.1109/ICCV.2019.01080
24. Udall, M., et al.: PD-L1 diagnostic tests: a systematic literature review of scoring algorithms and test-validation metrics. Diagn. Pathol. **13**(1), 12 (2018)

Uncertainty Quantification and Estimation in Medical Image Classification

Sidi Yang$^{(\boxtimes)}$ⓘ and Thomas Fevensⓘ

Concordia University, Montréal, QC, Canada
y_sidi@live.concordia.ca, thomas.fevens@concordia.ca

Abstract. Deep Neural Networks (DNNs) have shown tremendous success in numerous AI-related fields. However, despite DNNs exhibiting remarkable performance, they still can make mistakes. Therefore, estimation and quantification of uncertainty have become an essential parameter in Deep Learning practical applications, especially in medical imaging. Measuring uncertainty can help with better decision making, early diagnosis, and a variety of tasks. In this paper, we explore uncertainty quantification (UQ) approaches and propose an uncertainty quantification (UQ) system for general medical imaging classification tasks. For its practical use, we adapt our UQ system for the problem of medical pre-screening, where patients are referred to a medical specialist if the DNN model classification or diagnosis is too uncertain. In experiments, we apply the UQ system to two medical imaging databases, a SARS-CoV2 CT dataset and the BreaKHis dataset. We show how to capture the most uncertain samples and predict the most uncertain category. For the application of medical pre-screening, we demonstrate that we can obtain more accurate results than initial modeling results by removing a percentage of the most uncertain input data.

Keywords: Uncertainty quantification · Bayesian deep neural networks · Medical imaging classification

1 Introduction

Recent Deep Learning (DL) methods have resulted in a revolution in many fields over the past decades, including bioinformatics [20], natural language processing [22], and autonomous driving [21]. Despite their success, DL methods still have restrictions due to possible inadequate predictions on some tasks, such as overconfidence on out-of-distribution data. For example, a classifier trained on cats and dogs' images may be overconfident in its prediction for a bird image.

Therefore, the reliability and safety of DL models have become a crucial issue lately. Overconfidence can sometimes cause unintended and harmful behaviours [2]. Our goal is to improve and optimize existing systems by estimating and quantifying uncertainty inside the dataset and its related modeling. Accordingly, we combined Transfer Learning methods and Uncertainty Quantification

© Springer Nature Switzerland AG 2021
I. Farkaš et al. (Eds.): ICANN 2021, LNCS 12893, pp. 671–683, 2021.
https://doi.org/10.1007/978-3-030-86365-4_54

approaches to improve DL model performance on medical classification tasks. This research explores uncertainty on classification tasks for medical imaging to reduce errors in automatic medical diagnosis systems.

2   Background and Related Work

Uncertainty Quantification (UQ) is the science of quantitative depiction and uncertainty reduction in computational and practical applications. Generally speaking, we know there exist unknown factors a model does not know and does not learn from training. We seek to learn what exactly a model does not know. UQ plays a vital role in numerous tasks, especially those with high safety requirements. In particular, various UQ applications include decision making and object detection in medical diagnosis [4], removal of noisy and limited data based on an uncertainty distribution [2], and automating mechanical technology security concerns [13].

2.1   Bayesian Probabilistic Modeling

Deep Learning methods (e.g., DNNs) have become powerful tools for researchers and engineers in recent years. However, neural networks (NNs) are overconfident with their predictions occasionally. Thus, our motivation is to explore uncertainty distribution science within NNs. Besides, we often need probabilistic predictions to reflect uncertainty or model confidence in classification tasks. Bayesian Neural Networks (BNNs) fit into this role as a standard methodology of quantifying uncertainty.

A BNN consists of a probabilistic model and NNs. In some deep NNs, we already use probability distributions. For instance, the *Dropout* layer in NNs is used for stochastic computations or generative modeling with a distribution over x. The objective of BNNs implementation is to combine the strengths of stochastic modeling and neural networks.

Bayesian probabilistic modeling estimates the posterior distribution over weights to capture uncertainty:

$$p(w|D) = \frac{p(D|w)p(w)}{p(D)} = \frac{p(D|w)p(w)}{\int p(D|w)p(w)dw}$$

where w is the weight, D as data, $P(w)$ as the prior probability based on w, and $p(D|w)$ as the likelihood of the observations. $p(w|D)$ is the posterior probability which can be used for uncertainty estimation.

2.2   Monte-Carlo Dropout as a Bayesian Approximation in Neural Networks

The standard DL techniques in medical imaging tasks do not capture uncertainty. It is expected to estimate and quantify uncertainty in DL models. To achieve this, Gal and Ghahramani [8] proposed the Monte-Carlo dropout (MC dropout) method for estimating uncertainty.

In statistics, Monte-Carlo (MC) methods refer to a broad class of computational algorithms depending on repeated random sampling technique and Variational Inference to receive numerical results. The MC dropout approach's core idea is to propose how to interpret a regular dropout before every weight layer to be used as a Bayesian approximation of the Gaussian process, which refers to a probabilistic model. We can consider this probabilistic model as a BNN with the probabilities distributions as the output. This model's key component to implementing the MC dropout approach is the *dropout* layer. The key concept of the *dropout* [19] function is to randomly drop units and their connections from the NNs during training.

To be specific in our classification tasks, we receive each image's probability results to decide its category by the *Softmax* layer. Due to the random characterization of BNN modeling, we can obtain multiple different predictions for each image in multiple MC sampling procedures. Eventually, we collect the prediction results and apply computation measures to receive each image's uncertainty values.

2.3 Deep Ensemble Approach

Unfortunately, the convenient MC dropout approach, which is positively related to BNNs, occasionally comes with a high cost. As an alternative method to quantify uncertainty, the deep ensembles method was proposed by Google Deep Mind in 2017 [11]. The deep ensembles method also yields remarkable predictive uncertainty estimations on experiments. The three steps in the deep ensembles method include choosing proper scoring rules, adversarial training to smooth the predictive distributions, and training an ensemble.

2.4 Ensemble MC Dropout Approach

After exploring the above two UQ techniques, we settled on the MC dropout technique applied to one BNN and the deep ensembles technique on five normal NNs. Both showed outstanding performance in our classification experiments. To discover if combining these two methods would reach another state-of-art performance, we look into the ensemble MC dropout approach [15]. But instead of using normal NNs in the deep ensembles, we replaced them with Bayesian NNs and applied the MC dropout technique. Hence, with each model's probability results in the ensembles, we will receive probabilistic predictions of Bayesian NNs with five models.

2.5   Medical Pre-screening

In most research work, we often apply models to evaluate all the images in the database. However, in practice, we usually have other choices, e.g., to ask experts if we are uncertain. Figure 1 illustrates an example of an automatic diagnosis system in real-world medical applications. A probabilistic model accepts the test data X^{test}. Then it returns the uncertainty results (e.g. σ_{pred}, H_{pred}). There is an uncertainty threshold of T. The predictions of uncertainty below T will be sent to the model and classified to return the output y_{pred}^{test}. Otherwise, it will be transferred to a medical expert.

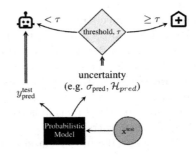

Fig. 1. Automatic diagnosis system [7]

A benchmark of Diabetic Retinopathy Tasks has been proposed in 2019, which guides a systemic way to present Bayesian Deep Learning (BDL) in medical diagnostics [7]. They detected diabetic retinopathy and selected the most uncertain samples to an expert for further analysis. Inspired by their work, we compare accuracy with uncertainty results by setting up different thresholds T to better describe how UQ can optimize real-world medical applications by incorporating medical pre-screening.

3   Datasets

The two databases we explored in our experiments are the SARS-CoV2 CT-scan database [16] and the BreaKHis database [17].

Recent research has discovered imaging patterns in the Computed Tomography (CT) images of patients with coronavirus disease [12]. Accordingly, CT-scan imaging represents an essential role in COVID-19 diagnosis. The SARS-CoV-2 CT-scan database [16] has been collected CT-scan images from patients from hospitals in Sao Paulo, Brazil. SARS-CoV-2 CT-scan dataset contains 2,482 CT-scan images with two categories: 1252 images for patients infected by SARS-CoV-2 and 1230 CT scans for non-infected by SARS-CoV-2 patients but who presented other pulmonary diseases. Each category was composed of 60 patients with balanced gender distributions.

The Breast Cancer Histopathological Image Classification (BreaKHis) database was published by the Federal University of Parana and LITIS Lab, the University of Rouen in 2016 [17]. The BreaKHis database contains two main categories: Benign and Malignant. Each main category contains four distinct histological sub-types at four different magnifying factors (40X, 100X, 200X, and 400X). In total, there are eight types of images in the BreaKHis database. All the 7,908 images are 700X460 pixels, 3-channel RGB (8-bit depth in each channel) in the PNG format. Our experiments focus on classification and uncertainty quantification tasks between the eight sub-type images as an exploration of uncertainty in a multi-classification task.

4 Experiments and Results

4.1 Data Preprocessing

Before feeding data to the models, we apply some common image pre-processing procedures, including re-scaling, shearing intensity, and brightness normalization. Besides these, we also apply data argumentation techniques such as height and weight shift, horizontal and vertical flips. We notice the imbalance of the data distribution of BreaKHis. Therefore, we apply data augmentation on the training and validation sets and keep the test set inits original size. We split the train/validation/test sets with a ratio of $7:2:1$.

The configuration of UQ estimation methods used for all the following experiments is as follows. At the classification task stage, we use pre-trained models (ResNet152V2, Inception-V3, and Inception-ResNet-V2). One activated *dropout* layer is added before the last *softmax* layer at both the training and test time for MC dropout and ensemble MC dropout approaches. We use five as the number of NNs in the deep ensembles and the ensemble MC dropout methods due to computation time limitation, and it can yield uncertainty quality improvement with reasonable computational cost [11]. The size of the MC samples is 100. The numerical uncertainty value on each image is computed using predictive entropy.

4.2 Uncertainty Quantification on SARS-CoV2

This section explores the uncertainty distribution in the SARS-CoV2 database and studies the association of uncertainty between accuracy and related model optimization measures via UQ methods.

4.2.1 Finding the Most Uncertain Images in SARS-CoV2

To detect how uncertainty is related to the accuracy, we develop how the accuracy will be affected by removing the most uncertain images from the database. If the accuracy improves when we move a few images with the highest uncertainties from the whole database, we can say that uncertainty and accuracy are positively related. As an example, we use the experimental setup of ResNet as a pre-trained model and MC dropout as the UQ method on the test set here.

After applying ResNet to train data to receive a Bayesian model, feeding test data to the model with five ensembles and 100 times MC sampling to obtain the uncertainties, and evaluating outputs, we obtain the uncertainty results and a Bayesian model. The accuracy of this model on the test set is 0.9635.

Then, we remove the most uncertain samples by using entropy as the computation metrics to capture uncertainty in this experiment. Therefore, the most uncertain samples are the ones with the highest entropy value. We pick the ten most uncertain samples out of 248 images in the test set. The mean uncertainty value of the test set is 0.0441, with a standard deviation of 0.1304. Table 1 displays the index and uncertainty values of the ten most uncertain samples. After removing these ten most uncertain samples, the **accuracy** of the remaining test images has improved from **0.9635** to **0.9749**. In contrast, the accuracy of these removed samples is only 0.5. Furthermore, the **sensitivity** of class infected has increased from **0.95** to **0.97**, and the **specificity** has increased from **0.98** to **0.99**. These suggest the model's ability to analyze both infected by SARS-CoV2 and non-infected has improved after removing the ten most uncertain images.

To summarize this experiment, we discover five wrongly predicted images by removing the ten most uncertain images. The accuracy, sensitivity, and specificity are all improved. We can find that using UQ approaches can make our modeling more efficient and accurate. It can also lead the model to extract more specific features. In the next section, we will describe how modeling can be optimized systemically and practically.

4.2.2   Uncertainty Distribution Quantification on Data Retention

In this subsection, we compare accuracy with uncertainty results by setting up different thresholds T to better describe how UQ can improve the accuracy of real-world medical applications by incorporating **medical pre-screening**.

Instead of removing the most uncertain ten images as in the last experiment, we remove uncertain samples by data proportion in this experiment. We need to set up a threshold T. Let us assume T as 80%. We want to send the most certain 80% data to the model for analyzing and refer the uncertain rest data to medical experts. It means we need to remove 20% uncertain data from modeling work. We consider the rest of 80% data as uncertain and safe as *retained data* for further Deep Learning modeling work. To apply this system to the SARS-CoV2 database, we compare three UQ methodologies with three models for both validation and test sets separately. Figure 2 displays how accuracy (y-axis) behaves based on how much the retained data (x-axis) holds.

From Fig. 2, we discover that the start points of accuracy on validation sets are higher than test sets. Meanwhile, we notice that the ensemble MC dropout usually achieves better accuracy with the same retained proportion than deep ensembles and MC dropout on the SARS-CoV2 database; Inception-ResNet has a higher accuracy start point than the other two models for both validation and test sets. We can say Inception-ResNet could be a better classifier among these three models on the SARS-CoV2 database.

There are other observations we can make. The most significant discovery in these experiments is that accuracy keeps improving, as may be expected, as more uncertain samples are removed. We can notice that after removing $40-50\%$ data, most methods can reach 100% accuracy. Generally, in DL modeling work, we usually use methods, for example, such as data argumentation and adding layers to make a model deeper to improve accuracy. For example, this experiment offers a new method by uncertainty measurement to better extract primary features and make DL models more efficient. It is also convenient and useful for further work, e.g., generalization, comparing different models' stability.

In reality, it may not be possible to send around half of the uncertain data to medical experts due to the effectiveness. However, it is still significantly considerable to send the most uncertain samples with a reasonable threshold T to promise the safety and accurateness of a DL modeling work.

Table 1. The indexes (row 1) and uncertainty (row 2) values of ten most uncertain samples in the SARS-CoV2 database. The samples in **bold** are wrong predicted found by the model. The prediction outcomes (row 3) and right labels (row 4) are shown as a comparison.

Index	124	**189**	**183**	220	122	**125**	**179**	**123**	24	**222**
Unc	0.425	0.521	0.589	0.622	0.638	0.648	0.656	0.656	0.678	0.687
Pred	0	**0**	**0**	1	0	**1**	**0**	**1**	0	**1**
True	0	**1**	**1**	1	0	**0**	**1**	**0**	0	**1**

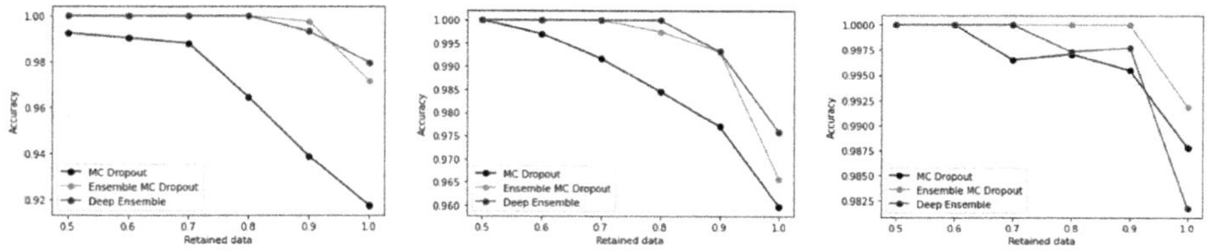

(a) ResNet, Valid. (b) Inception-V3, Valid. (c) Inception-ResNet,Valid.

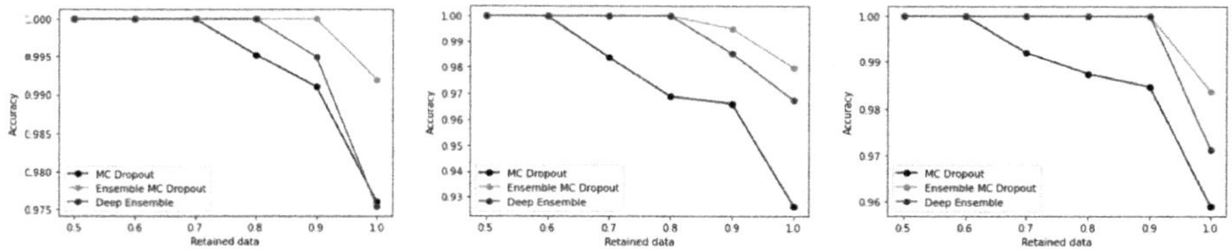

(d) ResNet, Test (e) Inception-V3, Test (f) Inception-ResNet, Test

Fig. 2. Accuracy vs retained data distribution of three models via three UQ approaches on validation/test sets for the SARS-CoV2 database. The caption of each plot is named as {*model, dataset*}.

4.3 Uncertainty Quantification on BreaKHis

The multi-classification task on breast cancer images mainly refers to the identification of one of eight subordinate categories. In this section, our experiment is separated into three phases that appear in the following three subsections: the main classification problem, UQ exploration at the four magnifications of the images in the data set, and the determination of the most uncertain category.

4.3.1 Classification of Eight Categories on BreaKHis

We first explore different DNN models with a small amount of data from BreaKHis and review some baselines on BreaKHis multi-classification research [1,14] to decide the valid pre-trained models for this experiment. We skip the experimental details due to space constraints, but this preliminary work shows that Inception-V3 and Inception-ResNet-V2 models return good classification

Table 2. Accuracy on validation/test sets by MC dropout (*MCD*), Deep ensembles (*Deep Ens*) and Ensemble MC dropout (*Ensemble MCD*) UQ approaches with Inception-V3 (*IncepV3*) and Inception-ResNet-V2 (*IncepRes*) models at four magnifications)

Magnification		40X		100X		200X		400X	
Dataset		vali	test	vali	test	vali	test	vali	test
IncepV3	MCD	0.869	0.843	0.916	0.858	0.874	0.786	0.831	0.769
	Deep Ens	0.906	0.899	0.923	0.849	**0.913**	**0.885**	0.865	0.785
	Ens MCD	0.894	0.883	0.934	0.861	0.912	0.819	0.864	0.781
IncepRes	MCD	0.880	0.847	0.936	0.841	0.894	0.795	0.836	0.794
	Deep Ens	0.938	0.882	**0.939**	**0.882**	0.905	0.830	0.884	0.794
	Ens MCD	**0.897**	**0.907**	0.937	0.864	0.912	0.861	**0.896**	**0.825**

results and have an acceptable computation cost. Hence, we choose these two pre-trained DNN models as the start point of the classification task.

Table 2 displays the accuracy of validation and test sets using three UQ approaches with two base DNN models at four magnifications (40X, 100X, 200X, and 400X), separately. The best accuracy was found using Inception-ResNet-V2, except for 200X, using Deep ensembles and Ensemble MC dropout. For 200X, Inception-V3 with Deep ensembles had the best performance.

4.3.2   Uncertainty Exploration at Four Magnifications

Figure 3 shows the accuracy performance as a function of the amount of retained data (T) at four magnifications on validation and test sets, separately. Each graph contains six plots with a combination of three UQ measures and two models. From the validation set results, we find that by removing more uncertain samples by decreasing the threshold T, the accuracy increases.

We notice that Inception-ResNet-V2, for the most part, performs better than Inception-V3 on validation sets. However, Inception-V3 can achieve better performance occasionally. Specifically, when we conclude the best performed combination of {*model, UQ measure*}, we find at 200X {*Inception-V3, Ensemble MC Dropout*} model (orange line in Fig. 3 (c)) is the best functioning combination. It also performs as one of the best combinations at 40X. At 100X and 400X, {*Inception-ResNet-V3, Ensemble MC Dropout*} achieves better performance than others (purple lines in Fig. 3 (b) and (d)).

In terms of UQ approaches, we see that **Deep ensembles** can achieve the best performance on validation sets. However, when considering the test sets, Deep ensembles results are not as stable as the other two methods, which is not a good sign for generalization. Although the accurateness by **MC dropout** is not as good as the other two methods, it performs more stably on the test set than Deep ensembles. It can detect uncertainty and improve modeling as expected. Another advantage of MC dropout is that it can save more computation cost since it only needs one model and MC sampling for implementation compared

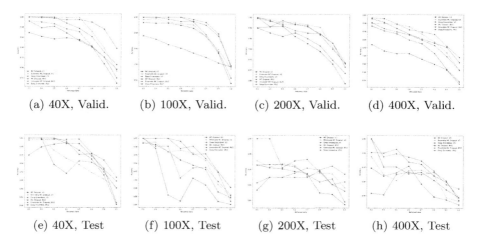

(a) 40X, Valid.   (b) 100X, Valid.   (c) 200X, Valid.   (d) 400X, Valid.

(e) 40X, Test   (f) 100X, Test   (g) 200X, Test   (h) 400X, Test

Fig. 3. Accuracy vs retained data distribution on **validation** and **test** sets at four magnifications. The captions are named in the form of {*Magnification, Dataset*}. Each graph contains six plots presenting the combination of three UQ approaches and two models by different colors. Each plot is named by the way of {*UQ Approach, Model*}, which can be found at the corner of each graph. (Color figure online)

with Deep ensembles and Ensemble MC dropout, which are built upon multiple models. **Ensemble MC dropout** performs relevantly stable compared with the other two UQ measures. We can also find that both inception models' accuracy is higher than the other two UQ measures on test sets. Therefore, for accurateness improvement and potential generalization in the future, we find ensemble MC dropout would be a suitable choice for detecting uncertainty in the eight-class classification task on BreaKHis under the condition of reasonable computational cost.

To experiment with the idea of **medical pre-screening**, we set the threshold T as 80% to keep a balance between modeling and sending uncertain images to medical professionals under the automatic diagnosis system. Then we compare our results while 80% data retained with currently published approaches of multi-classification tasks of BreaKHis, as shown in Table 3. The results in this table are only a partial comparison since the accuracy of the medical professional is unknown, but, at least for 40X {*Inception-ResNet-V3, Deep Ensemble*} and 100X {*Inception-ResNet-V3, Ensemble MC Dropout*} images, medical pre-screening will lead to more reliable diagnosis compared to the state-of-the-art.

4.3.3 Finding the Most Uncertain Category

This section proposes another UQ application to find the most uncertain category in a multi-classification task. This analysis is accomplished using the comparison results of accuracy and retained data from the last section. We set the threshold T to 70% and compute the *removing percentage* as the ratio of the

Table 3. Comparison of the accuracy performance of the eight-class classification on BreaKHis with the previous work. For the first six references, 100% of testing data was used.

References	Methods	Accuracy at four magnifications			
		40X	100X	200X	400X
F. Spanhol et al.(2016) [18]	CNN + patches	85.6	83.5	83.1	80.8
Z. Han et al. (2017) [9]	AlexNet + aug	70.1	75.8	73.6	84.6
	CSDCNN + aug	92.8	93.9	**93.7**	**92.9**
D. Bardou et al. (2018) [3]	CNN + aug	83.97	84.48	80.83	81.03
	Ensemble CNN model	88.23	84.64	83.31	83.98
H. Erfankhah et al. (2019) [6]	LBP	88.3	88.3	87.1	83.4
Y. Jiang et al. (2019) [10]	BHCNet-6 + ERF	94.43	94.45	92.27	91.15
S. Boumaraf et al. (2020) [5]	BW fine-tuned ResNet-18	94.49	93.27	91.29	89.56
Present work (80% retained)	IncepV3 + MCD	95.06	92.54	82.40	79.68
	IncepV3 + DE	91.66	95.16	89.82	88.24
	IncepV3 + Ens MCD	91.84	94.70	90.75	87.38
	IncepRes + MCD	95.80	88.78	86.00	85.50
	IncepRes + DE	96.28	**96.28**	89.57	87.01
	IncepRes + Ens MCD	**96.45**	93.02	89.16	88.73

number of removed images divided by the total number of images, which assists us in finding the most uncertain category.

Removing percentage refers to the proportion of the removed samples from the total number of samples of one category. Then, we compute the uncertainty values directly on the test sets. We rank the values from the maximum (most uncertain) to the minimum (most certain) and compare these results with the ranking of the removing percentage values. If they point to the same most uncertain category, this means *removing percentage* can be used to predict the most uncertain type as we expected.

Figure 4 present our experiments on test sets with {*Inception-ResNet-V2, Ensemble MC Dropout*} at four magnifications. The blue plots are our predicted removing percentage, and the most uncertain categories are highlighted. The green plots are the uncertainty values of true labels.

We find that by computing *removing percentage* values of each category, we find the most uncertain types as expected. During the experiments, one constraint is that although the most uncertain category features are apparent and can be predicted precisely with a reasonable threshold, the differences between certain categories are not as noticeable as the uncertain ones. Hence, future work would be to optimize the computation and evaluation of the most uncertain category in a multi-classification problem.

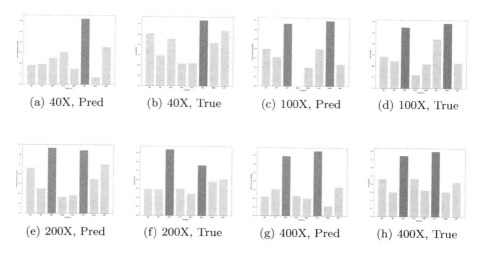

(a) 40X, Pred   (b) 40X, True   (c) 100X, Pred   (d) 100X, True

(e) 200X, Pred   (f) 200X, True   (g) 400X, Pred   (h) 400X, True

Fig. 4. Removing percentage based on uncertainty predictions (Pred) vs. uncertainty of true labels (True) at different magnifications (40X, 100X, 200X, 400X) (Color figure online)

5   Conclusion and Future Work

This paper studies what uncertainty is, where it comes from, and explores the uncertainty quantification (UQ) approaches in binary and multi-classification problems. Meanwhile, we also contribute to exploring how accuracy is related to uncertainty and building up some UQ applications, such as finding the most uncertain samples, applying UQ to medical pre-screening, or determining the most uncertain category in a multi-class project.

Our research's potential future work directions include evaluating uncertainty in object detection tasks, computing aleatoric and epistemic uncertainty separately in multi-classification tasks, and summarizing a generalization approach of UQ applications.

References

1. Alom, M.Z., Yakopcic, C., Taha, T.M., Asari, V.K.: Breast cancer classification from histopathological images with inception recurrent residual convolutional neural network. arXiv preprint arXiv: 1811.04241 (2018)
2. Amodei, D., Olah, C., Steinhardt, J., Christiano, P.F., Schulman, J., Mané, D.: Concrete problems in AI safety. arXiv preprint arXiv: 1606.06565 (2016)
3. Bardou, D., Zhang, K., Ahmad, S.M.: Classification of breast cancer based on histology images using convolutional neural networks. IEEE Access 6, 24680–24693 (2018). https://doi.org/10.1109/ACCESS.2018.2831280
4. Begoli, E., Bhattacharya, T., Kusnezov, D.F.: The need for uncertainty quantification in machine-assisted medical decision making. Nat. Mach. Intell. 1(1), 20–23 (2019). https://doi.org/10.1038/s42256-018-0004-1

5. Boumaraf, S., Liu, X., Zheng, Z., Ma, X., Ferkous, C.: A new transfer learning based approach to magnification dependent and independent classification of breast cancer in histopathological images. Biomed. Signal Process. Control **63**, 102192 (2021). https://doi.org/10.1016/j.bspc.2020.102192

6. Erfankhah, H., Yazdi, M., Babaie, M., Tizhoosh, H.R.: Heterogeneity-aware local binary patterns for retrieval of histopathology images. IEEE Access **7**, 18354–18367 (2019). https://doi.org/10.1109/ACCESS.2019.2897281

7. Filos, A., et al.: A systematic comparison of Bayesian deep learning robustness in diabetic retinopathy tasks. arXiv preprint arXiv:1912.10481 (2019)

8. Gal, Y., Ghahramani, Z.: Dropout as a Bayesian approximation: representing model uncertainty in deep learning. In: Proceedings of the 33rd International Conference on International Conference on Machine Learning, ICML 2016, vol. 48, pp. 1050–1059. JMLR.org (2016)

9. Han, Z., Wei, B., Zheng, Y., Yin, Y., Li, K., Li, S.: Breast cancer multi-classification from histopathological images with structured deep learning model. Sci. Rep. **7**, 1–10 (2017). https://doi.org/10.1038/s41598-017-04075-z

10. Jiang, Y., Chen, L., Zhang, H., Xiao, X.: Breast cancer histopathological image classification using convolutional neural networks with small SE-ResNet module. PLOS ONE **14**(3), 1–21 (2019). https://doi.org/10.1371/journal.pone.0214587

11. Lakshminarayanan, B., Pritzel, A., Blundell, C.: Simple and scalable predictive uncertainty estimation using deep ensembles (2017)

12. Mayo Clinic Staff: Coronavirus disease 2019 (covid-19) (September 2020). https://www.mayoclinic.org/diseases-conditions/coronavirus/symptoms-causes/syc-20479963. Accessed 25 Oct 2020

13. Nokelainen, P., Nevalainen, T., Niemi, K.: Mind or machine? Opportunities and limits of automation. In: Harteis, C. (ed.) The Impact of Digitalization in the Workplace. PPL, vol. 21, pp. 13–24. Springer, Cham (2018). https://doi.org/10.1007/978-3-319-63257-5_2

14. Satpute, A.: BreakHist-dataset-image-classification. GitHub repository (2020). https://github.com/Anki0909/BreakHist-Dataset-Image-Classification. Accessed 15 Sep 2020

15. Smith, L., Gal, Y.: Understanding measures of uncertainty for adversarial example detection. arXiv preprint arXiv: 1803.08533 (2018)

16. Soares, E., Angelov, P., Biaso, S., Higa Froes, M., Kanda Abe, D.: SARS-CoV-2 CT-scan dataset: a large dataset of real patients CT scans for SARS-CoV-2 identification. medRxiv (2020). https://doi.org/10.1101/2020.04.24.20078584

17. Spanhol, F.A., Oliveira, L.S., Petitjean, C., Heutte, L.: A dataset for breast cancer histopathological image classification. IEEE Trans. Biomed. Eng. (TBME) **63**(7), 1455–1462 (2016)

18. Spanhol, F.A., Oliveira, L.S., Petitjean, C., Heutte, L.: Breast cancer histopathological image classification using convolutional neural networks. In: 2016 International Joint Conference on Neural Networks (IJCNN), pp. 2560–2567 (2016). https://doi.org/10.1109/IJCNN.2016.7727519

19. Srivastava, N., Hinton, G., Krizhevsky, A., Sutskever, I., Salakhutdinov, R.: Dropout: a simple way to prevent neural networks from overfitting. J. Mach. Learn. Res. **15**(56), 1929–1958 (2014)

20. Tang, B., Pan, Z., Yin, K., Khateeb, A.: Recent advances of deep learning in bioinformatics and computational biology. Front. Genet. **10**, 214 (2019). https://doi.org/10.3389/fgene.2019.00214

21. Uçar, A., Demir, Y., Güzeliş, C.: Object recognition and detection with deep learning for autonomous driving applications. SIMULATION **93**(9), 759–769 (2017). https://doi.org/10.1177/0037549717709932
22. Young, T., Hazarika, D., Poria, S., Cambria, E.: Recent trends in deep learning based natural language processing. IEEE Comput. Intell. Mag. **13**(3), 55–75 (2018). https://doi.org/10.1109/MCI.2018.2840738

Labeling Chest X-Ray Reports Using Deep Learning

Maram Mahmoud A. Monshi[1,2]([✉])[iD], Josiah Poon[1][iD], Vera Chung[1][iD],
and Fahad Mahmoud Monshi[3][iD]

[1] School of Computer Science, The University of Sydney, Camperdown, NSW 2006,
Australia
mmon4544@uni.sydney.edu.au, {josiah.poon,vera.chung}@sydney.edu.au
[2] Department of Information Technology, Taif University, Taif 26571, Saudi Arabia
[3] Radiology and Medical Imaging Department, King Saud University Medical City,
Riyadh 12746, Saudi Arabia
Fmonshi@ksu.edu.sa

Abstract. One of the primary challenges in the development of Chest
X-Ray (CXR) interpretation models has been the lack of large datasets
with multilabel image annotations extracted from radiology reports. This
paper proposes a CXR labeler that can simultaneously extracts fourteen observations from free-text radiology reports as positive or negative,
abbreviated as CXRlabeler. It fine-tunes a pre-trained language model,
AWD-LSTM, to the corpus of CXR radiology impressions and then uses
it as the base of the multilabel classifier. Experimentation demonstrates
that a language model fine-tuning increases the classifier F1 score by
12.53%. Overall, CXRlabeler achieves a 96.17% F1 score on the MIMIC-
CXR dataset. To further test the generalization of the CXRlabeler model,
it is tested on the PadChest dataset. This testing shows that the CXR-
labeler approach is helpful in a different language environment, and the
model (available at https://github.com/MaramMonshi/CXRlabeler) can
assist researchers in labeling CXR datasets with fourteen observations.

Keywords: Chest X-Ray report · Natural Language Processing ·
Recurrent neural network

1 Introduction

There is an urgent need to automatically label large Chest X-Ray (CXR) datasets
using radiology reports to facilitate the training of deep neural networks. However, this task creates a significant bottleneck as it requires considerable medical
skills and time to output high-quality information. Fortunately, Natural Language Processing (NLP) methods offer the ability to annotate free-text reports

This material is based upon work supported by Google Cloud Research credit program.

© Springer Nature Switzerland AG 2021
I. Farkaš et al. (Eds.): ICANN 2021, LNCS 12893, pp. 684–694, 2021.
https://doi.org/10.1007/978-3-030-86365-4_55

automatically. Researchers have implemented several rule-based and expert-defined labeling systems [1,2] to extract labels from CXR reports by running these reports through a rule-based NLP model. Even though these systems have been valuable to the research community, they suffer from several issues, including low accuracy and run-time speed [3].

Currently, there are three public CXR datasets that release complete radiology reports, which are Open-I [4], Pathology Detection in Chest Radiology (PadChest) [5], and Medical Information Mart for Intensive Care Chest X-ray (MIMIC-CXR) [6], as shown in Table 1. Figure 1 shows an example of a labeled report from the MIMIC-CXR dataset. Each label contains one of four values: 1.0, -1.0, 0.0, or NaN, which indicate positive, negative, uncertain, or missing observations, respectively.

For multilabel classification in the radiology domain, the task is to predict the probability of multiple target medical observations linked to a report. This type of classification is a common task in many real-life domains, such as extracting probable diseases based on observed clinical symptoms and automatic tagging of documents [7]. CXR radiology reports are typically semi-structured, where the impression section summarizes the most relevant findings, describing multiple observations and important features of the CXR [8].

This paper proposes a simple approach for gaining the benefits of both language model (LM) fine-tuning and classifier fine-tuning to achieve highly accurate automated CXR report labeling. The method begins with a pre-trained AWD-LSTM model [9] and conducts further fine-tuning on a large corpus of radiology text. The LM learning is transferred to the multilabel classification task of CXR report labeling, with the resulting model called CXRlabeler.

Table 1. Public CXR datasets with radiology reports

Dataset	Images	Reports		Labels
Open-I [4]	8,121	3,996	English	–
PadChest [5]	160,868	206,222	Spanish	193
MIMIC-CXR [6]	473,057	206,563	English	14

2   Related Work

Several NLP systems have been proposed for extracting medical labels from CXR reports. These are based on feature engineering, such as NegBio [1] and CheXpert [2], or deep learning algorithms, like RNN-ATT [5], CheXpert++ [3] and CheXbert [10]. Table 2 summarizes theses existing labelers.

Feature engineering-based methods are rule-based systems that rely on medical terms and grammatical rules to extract structured labels from CXR reports. For example, NegBio employs universal dependency and subgraph matching for

Report

PORTABLE AP CHEST FILM, ___ AT 11:18

CLINICAL INDICATION: ___-year-old status post CABG, status post chest tube removal, question pneumothorax.

Comparison to prior study of ___ at 7:26.

A portable AP upright chest film, ___ at 11:18 is submitted.

IMPRESSION: 1. Interval removal of the left chest tube. No evidence of pneumothorax. Right internal jugular central line has its tip in the distal SVC near the cavoatrial junction, unchanged. Status post median sternotomy for CABG with stable postoperative cardiac and mediastinal contours. There is elevation of the left hemidiaphragm with some adjacent streaky opacities, suggestive of atelectasis. Blunting of the left costophrenic angle likely reflects a small effusion. There is also possibly a tiny right pleural effusion. No evidence of pulmonary edema.

Labels

Atelectasis	**1.0**
Cardiomegaly	**NaN**
Consolidation	**NaN**
Edema	**-0**
Enlarged Cardiom.	**-1.0**
Fracture	**NaN**
Lung Lesion	**NaN**
Lung Opacity	**1.0**
Pleural Effusion	**1.0**
Pleural Other	**NaN**
Pneumonia	**NaN**
Pneumothorax	**0.0**
Support Devices	**1.0**
No Finding	**NaN**

Fig. 1. Example of a labeled report from the MIMIC-CXR dataset. Each label contains one of four values: 1.0, −1.0, 0.0, or NaN, which indicate positive, negative, uncertain, or missing observations, respectively

pattern definition and graph traversal search, respectively. However, it extracts mentioned observations from the reports automatically using MetaMap [11] and DNorm which may result in weak extraction. To overcome this limitation, CheXpert avoids automatic mention extractors and captures the variation of negation and uncertainty. Although CheXpert is very useful in extracting thoracic labels, McDermott et al. [3] demonstrate three significant issues associated with its performance: the slow run-time speed, lack of differentiability, and lack of availability of continuous probabilistic output as it produces binary labels.

NegBio and CheXpert have been employed to generate labels for the most extensive publicly available CXR datasets, including ChestXray14 [12], CheXpert, and MIMIC-CXR [6], despite their known limitations relating to label quality. For example, Oakden-Rayner et al. [13] estimated that the positive predictive values of ChestXray14 [12] labels are 10–30% lower than the values noted in the clinical records.

In contrast to the feature engineering-based approach to labelling radiology reports, deep learning-based methods are capable of capturing the complexity, ambiguity, and subtlety in the text. Therefore, the recently introduced CheXpert++ and CheXbert are based on a Bidirectional Encoder Representation from Transformers (BERT) [14]. The CheXpert++ model is initialized from the clinical BERT [15] with a multitask classification head. It is a suitable drop-in replacement for the rule-based system, CheXpert, because it runs 1.8 times faster, generates better labels, and can be integrated with neural pipelines and active learning systems. Furthermore, CheXbert performs a more detailed annotation study using two board-certified radiologists and error resolution policies, improving the labeling performance. However, CheXbert was fine-tuned with a small set of manual annotations augmented with automatic back-translation that introduced noise into the reports. To learn diverse text representations for each label, Bustos et al. [5] combined a bi-directional LSTM and a per-label attention mechanism [16] in a Recurrent Neural Network (RNN-ATT). This model achieved a 0.93 MicroF1 score and was used to label 73% of the PadChest dataset. One downside is that the generated labeles are not reliable when considering equal weights to each class because the Macro F1 score is low (60.1%).

This research is related to deep learning approaches because rule-based methods cannot handle the extensive linguistic ambiguity in radiology reports, including misspellings and broken grammar. Even in the absence of trustworthy training labels, deep learning models have been shown to be beneficial in the training of high-quality models [17]. This paper proposes CXRlabeler, a deep learning labeler that inputs raw radiology text and extracts 14 positive/negative CXR observations as its output. For labeling these reports, it utilizes the encoder learned from fine-tuning an LM on radiology reports.

Table 2. Labelers for CXR radiology reports

Labeler	Approach	Labelled dataset
NegBio [1]	Feature engineering	ChestX-ray14
CheXpert [2]	Feature engineering	CheXpert & MIMIC-CXR
CheXpert++ [3]	Deep learning	–
CheXbert [10]	Deep learning	–
RNN-ATT [5]	Deep learning	PadChest

3   Dataset and Method

As an input, CXRlabeler takes a radiology text with 14 pre-tagged mentions of CXR observations and checks whether a particular observation is positive or negative. The study used the pre-trained LM Averaged stochastic gradient descent Weight-Dropped Long Short-Term Memory networks (AWD-LSTM) [9]. Figure 2 represents the overall pipeline of the CXRlabeler. The detailed steps are explained in the following subsections.

3.1   Dataset

MIMIC-CXR [6] consists of 227,827 CXR radiology reports, 377,110 radiographers and 14 labels. These labels include 12 pathologies (atelectasis, cardiomegaly, consolidation, edema, enlarged cardiomediastinum, fracture, lung lesion, lung opacity, pleural effusion, pleural other, pneumonia, and pneumothorax) as well as "support devices" and "no finding", which indicates the absence of all pathologies. Each label was extracted from the associated report by the CheXpert automatic labeling tool [2] and had four classes (positive, negative,

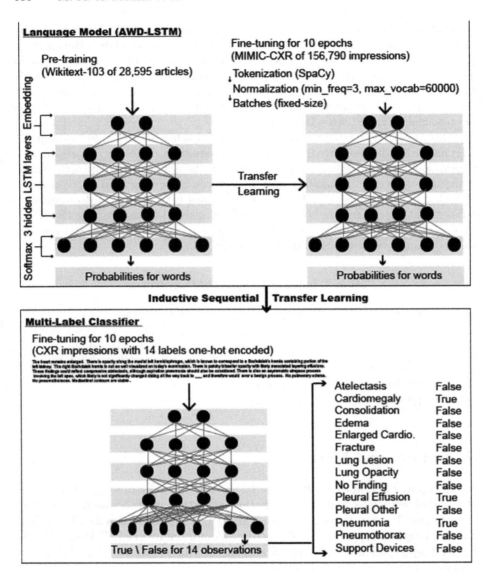

Fig. 2. CXRlabeler structure

uncertain, or missing). The study extracted 152,855 unique impressions for training and 3,935 for testing (merging the official validation and test split). A binary mapping approach was followed, called the U-Zeros model [2], where uncertain and missing values are mapped to negative instances. Table 3 records the frequency of the 14 labels in the preprocessed MIMIC-CXR dataset.

Table 3. Frequency of 14 labels in the preprocessed MIMIC-CXR dataset. The study extracted 156,790 unique impressions, of which 152,855 were used for training and 3,935 for testing. It reported the number of positive and negative cases for each label, with missing and uncertain labels considered negative labels.

Label	Positive			Negative		
	Train	Test	%	Train	Test	%
Atelectasis	42,052	1,038	27	110,803	2,897	73
Cardiomegaly	40,970	1,160	27	111,885	2,775	73
Consolidation	9,962	293	7	142,893	3,642	93
Edema	24,035	842	16	128,820	3,093	84
Enlarged cardio.	6,589	199	4	146,266	3,736	96
Fracture	4,040	99	3	148,815	3,836	97
Lung lesion	5,843	183	4	147,012	3,752	96
Lung opacity	47,757	1,368	31	105,098	2,567	69
No finding	24,487	472	16	128,368	3,463	84
Pleural effusion	50,035	1,497	33	102,820	2,438	67
Pleural other	1,851	71	1	151,004	3,864	99
Pneumonia	14,665	433	10	138,190	3,502	90
Pneumothorax	9,644	178	6	143,211	3,757	94
Support devices	61,768	1,634	40	91,087	2,301	60

PadChest [5] contains 109,931 Spanish reports, 160,868 CXRs, and 193 English labels. These labels can be used regardless of the language because they were mapped onto the standard Unified Medical Language System (UMLS) [18]. They consist of 19 diagnoses, 104 anatomic locations, and 174 findings. Nine labels were extracted that matched those of the MIMIC-CXR dataset (atelectasis, cardiomegaly, consolidation, edema, fracture, pleural effusion, pneumonia, and pneumothorax). As a result, the study ended up with 121,808 unique Spanish reports for training and 39,053 for testing, drawn from the PadChest reports manually labeled by qualified radiologists. Table 4 reports the frequency of the nine labels in the preprocessed PadChest dataset.

3.2   Language Model

Before building a multilabel classifier, the LM was pre-trained on Wikitext-103 [19], containing 28,595 preprocessed Wikipedia articles, and 103 million words. Then, the LM was fine-tuned to the radiology corpus to introduce the LM to the medical language, medical terms and informative sentence structures. This approach of fine-tuning has been introduced and found to enhance the classifier prediction significantly [20]. For the PadChest dataset, the LM was pre-trained on Spanish Wikipedia with a 15,000-word vocabulary.

Table 4. Frequency of 9 English labels in the preprocessed PadChest dataset. The study extracted 29,365 unique Spanish reports, of which 22,275 were for training and 7,090 for testing. The testing split was manually labeled by PadChest paper

Label	Positive			Negative		
	Train	Test	%	Train	Test	%
Atelectasis	4,401	1,471	20	17,874	5,619	80
Cardiomegaly	5,898	2,300	28	16,377	4,790	72
Consolidation	1,370	232	5	20,905	6,858	95
Edema	1,169	71	4	21,106	7,019	96
Fracture	2,101	751	10	20,174	6,339	90
No finding	3,042	1,303	15	19,233	5,787	85
Pleural effusion	5,520	1,193	23	16,755	5,897	77
Pneumonia	3,854	1,084	17	18,421	6,006	83
Pneumothorax	275	67	1	22,000	7,023	99

The LM was fine-tuned on the entire CXR radiology corpus regardless of the data split, following the transfer learning and freezing/unfreezing layer protocol [20]. For this self-supervised learning, all impression sections in the MIMIC-CXR dataset were fed to the LM without labels as it is able to get labels from the data automatically. The resulting LM could predict the next word in a radiology report based on previous words with an accuracy of 62.92% for MIMIC-CXR and 49.99% for PadChest.

3.3 Multi-label Classifier

In multilabel classification, the task is to learn a function, $h : X \rightarrow 2^Y$, which assigns a subset of related medical observations from a finite set of Q predefined labels, $Y = \{y_1, y_2, ..., y_Q\}$, to each report from an instance space, $X = \{x_1, ..., x_N\}$, $X \subseteq R^n$. First, the learned encoder was loaded from the LM, which was then used for vocabulary and text. Second, all the pretrained layers were frozen, and the last layer was trained for one epoch. Finally, all layers were unfrozen and trained for ten epochs while adjusting the learning rates using the discriminative learning rates protocol [20].

This approach is based on the inductive sequential transfer learning, where the source and the target task are not the same, and the source data's general knowledge is transferred to a single task [21]. Becker [22] concludes that this method of transfer learning has led to the most significant improvements in text classification by decreasing errors by an incredible 18–24%.

4   Experiment

For deep learning training, the study used PyTorch software [23], the Fastai v2 library [24], and an n1-highmem-8 (8 vCPUs, 52 GB memory) machine with a single NVIDIA Tesla V100 GPU. Fastai outperforms existing deep learning libraries in handling the multilabel text classification task [25]. To avoid over-fitting, training was continued while validation losses is lower than the training loss. From the Learning Rate (LR) Finder graph, the study selected the middle point of the most significant downward slope as the LR.

5   Evaluation

5.1   Result

Accuracy, the macro area under a receiver operating characteristic curve (AUC), macro precision, macro recall, and macro F1 score were used to evaluate the CXRlabeler. Each matrix gives valuable insight into the CXRlabeler's performance. However, the accuracy and AUC metrics are not adequate for a highly imbalanced dataset, as shown in Table 3 and 4. Therefore, the thresholds for accuracy were set to above 0.8 to build a robust model. The F1 score, on the other hand, combined the strengths of recall (i.e., the ratio of true positive predictions to positive samples) and precision (i.e., the ratio of true positive predictions to the sum of all positive predictions, true and false). Hence, the F1 score could fairly compare CXRlabeler with the benchmarks regardless of CXR dataset imbalance, where most cases are negative (i.e., healthy patients).

Table 5 compares the CXRlabeler with other models on the multilabel classification task. Existing labelers use input sentences from a CXR report, and the output for each finding is one of the following classes: positive, negative, uncertain, or blank. For the CXRlabeler, the outputs are one of the two following classes: positive or negative. CXRlabeler achieved an F1 of 96.17%, significantly higher than the baseline performance with RNN-ATT (60.10%), CheXpert++ (79.10%), CheXbert (79.80%), NegBio (94.40%), and CheXpert (94.80%). Transfer learning a fine-tuned LM increased the classifier F1 score by 12.53%.

Table 6 illustrates some examples of the labels extracted from radiology reports using the automated labeling system, CXRlabeler. In most cases, the labeler extracted all observations correctly. Benchmark NLP labelers such as NegBio and CheXpert were built and validated using ChestX-ray14 and CheXpert datasets, respectively. These datasets released images and associated labels without the associated radiology reports. Since the study did not have access to these reports, the model was evaluated using the MIMIC-CXR, and the PadChest datasets.

5.2   Discussion and Future Work

Advance CXR report labelers lead to higher-performing models that interpret CXR images. Jain et al. [26] demonstrate how robust CXR labelers (in particular, VisualCheXbert [27]) can assist in further increasing the accuracy of CXR classification models. In the future, deep learning models will be trained on labels generated by the CXRlabeler models and recent automatic CXR reports labelers.

This study follows the binary assignment of 0s (negative) and 1s (positive), where the uncertainty label does not add information to the classifier and hence may degrade the decision-making performance. Irvin et al. [2] suggest treating the uncertain label u as a separate class to better disambiguate the uncertain cases, where the probability output of the three classes is $p_0, p_1, p_u \in [0,1]$, $p_0 + p_1 + p_u = 1$. In the future, the scope of this method will be extended to detect uncertainty, which can be critical knowledge in the medical domain.

Table 5. Comparing the CXRlabeler with benchmarks in labeling CXR reports. The CXRlabeler model classifies each label as positive or negative.

Model	Dataset	Accuracy	AUC	Precision	Recall	F1
NegBio [1]	OpenI	–	–	89.80	85.70	87.30
NegBio [1]	ChestX-ray14	–	–	94.40	95.70	94.40
CheXpert [2]	CheXpert	–	–	–	–	94.80
CheXpert++ [3]	CheXpert++	–	–	–	–	79.10
RNN-ATT [5]	PadChest	86.40	–	–	–	60.10
CXRlabeler (without LM)	PadChest	95.26	92.94	65.53	58.80	60.06
CXRlabeler (with LM)	PadChest	99.16	98.95	96.55	89.01	92.08
CheXbert [10]	MIMIC-CXR	–	–	–	–	79.80
CheXpert [2]	MIMIC-CXR	–	–	79.30	91.16	82.54
CXRlabeler (without LM)	MIMIC-CXR	97.58	98.10	87.62	81.24	83.64
CXRlabeler (with LM)	**MIMIC-CXR**	**99.23**	**99.80**	**95.92**	**96.45**	**96.17**

Table 6. Examples of the predicted labels by the CXRlabeler model and the target labels

Ex.	Input	Target	Predicted	Result
1	Large right and moderate left pleural effusions and severe bibasilar\n atelectasis are unchanged. Cardiac silhouette is obscured. No pneumothorax. \n Pulmonary edema is mild.	Atelectasis, Edema, Pleural Effusion	Atelectasis, Edema, Pleural Effusion	Correct
2	1. Slowly growing peripheral right upper lobe lung nodule is concerning for primary lung adenocarcinoma. 2. Low lung volumes limit assessment of the lung bases for pneumonia.	Lung Lesion, Pneumonia	Lung Lesion, Pneumonia	Correct
3	xxmaj the pre-existing very diffuse bilateral interstitial opacities , likely reflecting interstitial lung edema, are unchanged. xxmaj this is supported by the presence of pleural effusion, evident on the lateral image . xxmaj however , in the right lung , subtle calcified granulomas are present . xxmaj the patient also shows several calcified mediastinal lymph nodes.	Cardiomegaly, Edema, Lung Opacity, Pleural Effusion, Pneumonia, Support Devices	Cardiomegaly, Edema, Lung Opacity, Pleural Effusion, Pneumonia	Wrong (missed support devices)

5.3   Conclusion

This paper proposes CXRlabeler, a labeler that extracts 14 observations from CXR radiology reports. It fine-tuned a pre-trained LM to the corpus of radiology impressions and then used the LM encoder with a new head to classify radiology reports.

References

1. Peng, Y., Wang, X., Lu, L., Bagheri, M., Summers, R., Lu, Z.: NegBio: a high-performance tool for negation and uncertainty detection in radiology reports. AMIA Summits Trans. Sci. Proc. **2018**, 188 (2018)
2. Irvin, J., et al.: CheXpert: a large chest radiograph dataset with uncertainty labels and expert comparison. In: Proceedings of the AAAI Conference on Artificial Intelligence, vol. 33, pp. 590–597 (2019)
3. McDermott, M.B.A., Hsu, T.M.H., Weng, W.-H.,M. Ghassemi, Szolovits, P.: CheXpert++: approximating the CheXpert labeler for speed, differentiability, and probabilistic output. In: Machine Learning for Healthcare Conference, pp. 913–927. PMLR (2020)
4. Demner-Fushman, D., et al.: Preparing a collection of radiology examinations for distribution and retrieval. J. Am. Med. Inf. Assoc. **23**(2), 304–310 (2016)
5. Bustos, A., Pertusa, A., Salinas, J.-M., de la Iglesia-Vayá, M.: PadChest: a large chest x-ray image dataset with multi-label annotated reports. Med. Image Anal. **66**, 101797 (2020)
6. Johnson, A.E.W., et al.: MIMIC-CXR, a de-identified publicly available database of chest radiographs with free-text reports. Sci. Data **6**, 1–8 (2019)
7. Mańdziuk, J., Żychowski, A.: Dimensionality reduction in multilabel classification with neural networks. In: 2019 International Joint Conference on Neural Networks (IJCNN), pp. 1–8. IEEE (2019)
8. Monshi, M.M.A., Poon, J., Chung, V.: Deep learning in generating radiology reports: a survey. Artif. Intell. Med. **106**, 101878 (2020)
9. Merity, S., Keskar, N.S., Socher, R.: Regularizing and optimizing LSTM language models. arXiv preprint arXiv:1708.02182 (2017)
10. Smit, A., Jain, S., Rajpurkar, P., Pareek, A., Ng, A.Y., Lungren, M.P.: CheXbert: combining automatic labelers and expert annotations for accurate radiology report labeling using BERT. arXiv preprint arXiv:2004.09167 (2020)
11. Aronson, A.R., Lang, F.-M.: An overview of MetaMap: historical perspective and recent advances. J. Am. Med. Inform. Assoc. **17**(3), 229–236 (2010)
12. Wang, X., Peng, Y., Lu, L., Lu, Z., Bagheri, M., Summers, R.M.: ChestX-ray8: hospital-scale chest x-ray database and benchmarks on weakly-supervised classification and localization of common thorax diseases. In: Proceedings of the IEEE Conference on Computer Vision and Pattern Recognition, pp. 2097–2106 (2017)
13. Oakden-Rayner, L.: Exploring large-scale public medical image datasets. Acad. Radiol. **27**(1), 106–112 (2020)
14. Devlin, J., Chang, M.-W., Lee, K., Toutanova, K.: BERT: pre-training of deep bidirectional transformers for language understanding. arXiv preprint arXiv:1810.04805 (2018)
15. Alsentzer, E., et al.: Publicly available clinical BERT embeddings. arXiv preprint arXiv:1904.03323 (2019)

16. Mullenbach, J., Wiegreffe, S., Duke, J., Sun, J., Eisenstein, J.: Explainable prediction of medical codes from clinical text. In: NAACL-HLT (2018)
17. Liventsev, V., Fedulova, I., Dylov, D.: Deep text prior: weakly supervised learning for assertion classification. In: Tetko, I.V., Kůrková, V., Karpov, P., Theis, F. (eds.) ICANN 2019. LNCS, vol. 11731, pp. 243–257. Springer, Cham (2019). https://doi. org/10.1007/978-3-030-30493-5_26
18. Bodenreider, O.: The unified medical language system (UMLS) integrating biomedical terminology. Nucleic Acids Res. 32(suppl_1), D267–D270 (2004)
19. Merity, S., Xiong, C., Bradbury, J., Socher, R.: Pointer sentinel mixture models. arXiv preprint arXiv:1609.07843 (2016)
20. Howard, J., Ruder, S.: Universal language model fine-tuning for text classification. arXiv preprint arXiv:1801.06146 (2018)
21. Ruder. S.: Neural transfer learning for natural language processing (2019)
22. Becker, C.: Chapter 7 transfer learning for NLP I — modern approaches in natural language processing (2020). https://compstat-lmu.github.io/seminar_nlp_ss20/ transfer-learning-for-nlp-i.html#sequential-inductive-transfer-learning
23. Ketkar, N.: Introduction to PyTorch. In: Deep Learning with Python, pp. 195–208. Apress, Berkeley (2017). https://doi.org/10.1007/978-1-4842-2766-4_12
24. Howard, J., Gugger, S.: fastai: a layered API for deep learning. Information 11(2), 108 (2020)
25. Harsha Kadam, S., Paniskaki, K.: Text analysis for email multi label classification. Open Digital Repository (2020)
26. Jain, S., Smit, A., Ng, A.Y., Rajpurkar, P.: Effect of radiology report labeler quality on deep learning models for chest X-ray interpretation. arXiv preprint arXiv:2104.00793 (2021)
27. Jain, S., et al.: VisualCheXbert: addressing the discrepancy between radiology report labels and image labels. arXiv preprint arXiv:2102.11467 (2021)

Author Index

Printed in the United States
by Baker & Taylor Publisher Services